USED BOOK

AUG 2 7 2003

Sold to Aztec Shops, Ltd.

www.wadsworth.com

wadsworth.com is the World Wide Web site for Wadsworth and is your direct source to dozens of online resources.

At *wadsworth.com* you can find out about supplements, demonstration software, and student resources. You can also send email to many of our authors and preview new publications and exciting new technologies.

wadsworth.com
Changing the way the world learns®

Classic Readings in Organizational Behavior

USED BOOK
DEC 1 0 2003
Sold to Aztec Shops
At Sundial

Classic Readings in Organizational Behavior
Third Edition

J. Steven Ott
Sandra J. Parkes
Richard B. Simpson

University of Utah

Australia • Canada • Mexico • Singapore • Spain • United Kingdom • United States

Executive Editor: David Tatom
Development Editor: Phoebe Culp
Editorial Assistant: Dianna Long
Technology Project Manager: Melinda Newfarmer
Marketing Manager: Caroline Croley
Project Manager, Editorial Production: Belinda Krohmer
Print Buyer: Doreen Suruki
Permissions Editor: Bob Kauser
Production Service: Vicki Moran, Publishing Support Services
Copy Editor: Kay Mikel
Cover Designer: Brian Salisbury
Compositor: Thompson Type
Printer: Webcom Limited

COPYRIGHT © 2003 Wadsworth, a division of Thomson Learning, Inc. Thomson Learning™ is a trademark used herein under license.

ALL RIGHTS RESERVED. No part of this work covered by the copyright hereon may be reproduced or used in any form or by any means—graphic, electronic, or mechanical, including but not limited to photocopying, recording, taping, Web distribution, information networks, or information storage and retrieval systems—without the written permission of the publisher.

Printed in Canada
1 2 3 4 5 6 7 06 05 04 03 02

For more information about our products, contact us at:
Thomson Learning Academic Resource Center
1-800-423-0563
For permission to use material from this text, contact us by:
Phone: 1-800-730-2214
Fax: 1-800-730-2215
Web: http://www.thomsonrights.com

Library of Congress Control Number: 2002110917
ISBN 0-155-05896-7

Wadsworth/Thomson Learning
10 Davis Drive
Belmont, CA 94002-3098
USA

Asia
Thomson Learning
5 Shenton Way #01-01
UIC Building
Singapore 068808

Australia
Nelson Thomson Learning
102 Dodds Street
South Melbourne, Victoria 3205
Australia

Canada
Nelson Thomson Learning
1120 Birchmount Road
Toronto, Ontario M1K 5G4
Canada

Europe/Middle East/Africa
Thomson Learning
High Holborn House
50/51 Bedford Row
London WC1R 4LR
United Kingdom

Latin America
Thomson Learning
Seneca, 53
Colonia Polanco
11560 Mexico D.F.
Mexico

Spain
Paraninfo Thomson Learning
Calle/Magallanes, 25
28015 Madrid, Spain

Foreword to the Foreword

Apparently the innovative lives side by side with the classic, because I have been given the unusual task of writing a foreword to the foreword written by Fred Fiedler for the second edition of *Classic Readings in Organizational Behavior*. It might be said that Fred's foreword has become a classic, and well it should be—and I would say so, even if Fred weren't my mentor, colleague, co-author, and old friend.

Fred's foreword makes very clear the influences of the early theorists in our field. What they may have lacked in sophisticated methodological and analytic techniques, they made up for with broad perspectives and deep insights. Many of today's research programs have sprung from the seeds offered in the classic articles, whether acknowledged or not.

The contributions of the classics are both timeless and timely. The field of organizational behavior is as healthy as it has been in a long time. When I first became a student of organizational behavior (almost forty years ago) and in the decade that followed, our field was characterized by controversy and contradiction. More recently, we see many indicators of a more vibrant and self-confident scholarship and practice. For this reason, I applaud the authors' decision to include a few contemporary (potentially impactful?) works along with the acknowledged classic articles. I, personally, am flattered to have one of my recent chapters in that category. The inclusion of recent works recognizes the positive developments in our field.

The signs of the current renaissance in the study of organizational behavior can be seen in the development of integrative theories seeking a broader, more general understanding of organizational principles. Sophisticated analytic tools (structural equation modeling, hierarchical linear modeling, and others) point researchers toward more comprehensive models and enable us to test their predictions more easily.

The draw of organizational behavior for researchers and theorists from allied disciplines is another sign—as well as a source—of vitality. Social identity theory has brought new insights about how the relationships between groups affect the internal dynamics within a group. Procedural justice research, which began with studies of distributive justice in work organizations, has returned bearing the fruits of social psychological perspectives about the nature of interpersonal relationships surrounding authority in organizations. Gender and feminist perspectives provide new bases for understanding status accrual and dominance negotiations in groups. A rich literature in social cognition is bringing greater awareness of the role of subjective forces and social construction in organizational processes. These and other new research areas, many of which certainly were suggested in the classic writings, now hold potential for the consistent revitalization on which any scientific discipline thrives.

Being asked to write a foreword awakens the sort of egotistical posture that might tempt one to make predictions about the future, so let me try. Recent developments in organizational theory and research and ideas prevalent in the broader scope of the social sciences suggest some likely direction for our field in the new century. I believe that general, integrative theory will emerge, some of it attempting to link macro (strategic) and micro (behavioral) levels of analysis. Our recognition that our planet includes more than North America will accelerate comparative work, which both assesses the contribution of cultural differences to organizational processes and investigates the effects of globalization on the sustainability or modification of those differences. Exciting work on emotions, temperament, and even psychophysiology might become a source of new ideas about motivation, satisfaction, and related processes in organizations. Finally, as our society attempts to come to grips with the implications of amazing new technologies, we must turn to the examination of ethical considerations. From the past to the future, these are interesting and exciting prospects.

Martin M. Chemers
University of California, Santa Cruz

Foreword

Who has not come across master's theses, dissertations, or journal articles that start by telling us that nobody in the whole world has ever thought of the brilliant new hypothesis, much less seen the earth-shaking results, to be unfolded to our amazed and unbelieving eyes? All too often, as it turns out, this happens to be hyperbole. In fact, if the truth be told, the history of psychology begins for many budding organizational psychologists on the day they enroll in their first psychology course. They are amazed that Nicole Machiavelli's treatise, *The Prince*, was only one early version of the "How to lead" books, and few graduate students in I/O psychology know that they owe anything to people with such strange names as Chester Barnard, Elton Mayo, or Hugo Muensterberg, who gave industrial and organizational psychology its start.

And why, one might ask, should students be concerned with these names, which they are no longer required to know on tests? Most of us feel that we don't have the time to dig up "old," outdated, and in some cases, superseded articles. Going into the stacks to rummage among old journals is not everyone's favorite occupation, especially when passing exams, preparing for the next class, or preparing another article for publication are more pressing.

Nevertheless, we do need to remember that we are building on the work of others. To think otherwise is not only a mark of arrogance but also of folly. Moreover, there is a lot of scientific pay-dirt in "them thar hills": One good example is the sudden reemergence of Max Weber's articles on the topic of charisma. This old chestnut has suddenly sprouted into one of the most active current topics in the organizational literature. It is almost embarrassing to note how many points old Max Weber made that we are now rediscovering.

Another concept that has recently come to life again is the work on leader intelligence. The problem of how the leader's intelligence contributes to leadership status or effectiveness, interestingly enough, was the topic of the very first empirical paper in leadership. In "A Preliminary Study of the Psychology and Pedagogy of Leadership," Lewis Terman (1904) anticipated current contingency theories of leadership by pointing out that the selection of a leader depends not only on the leader's own attributes but on the needs of the group. Quite apart from the scholarly tradition of citing one's predecessors when it comes to theory building, many of the great insights about how organizations work are to be found in papers that today are considered classics. I am reminded of Mark Twain's little story about how dumb his father was when Mark Twain was growing up, how much dumber the old man got year after year, and even more surprising, how much the old man learned in the few years of his son's absence.

This thoughtfully assembled collection of classic papers makes a major contribution to our thinking. It is not only a welcome reminder that the field of organizational behavior did not begin the first year we entered college, but that these early papers became classics because their insights are still valid today. They contain wisdom that has not gone out of style, and they represent a rich source of hypotheses that are yet to be tested. This selection undoubtedly will find a useful place in the graduate school curriculum, as well as provide the researcher with a valuable and convenient collection of papers, spanning the field of organizational behavior, which are not always easily obtained from the nearest library.

Fred E. Fiedler
University of Washington

Preface

Classic Readings in Organizational Behavior has been designed to meet several purposes: (1) to be a stand-alone collection of the most important writings about organizational behavior, (2) to supplement any of several excellent college and graduate-level texts in organizational behavior and administrative practice, and (3) to mesh with and to supplement Jay Shafritz's and Steven Ott's fifth edition of *Classics of Organization Theory* (2001). Only one chapter in *Classics of Organization Theory* is devoted to organizational behavior and, as Shafritz and Ott explain in their Introduction, "organizational behavior is a very large field of study unto itself with an enormous body of literature. . . . It is impossible to do much more than provide a 'flavor' of this body of theory and research in a single chapter."

As the title *Classic Readings in Organizational Behavior* implies, this book is a collection of previously published classics. Although several important recent works are included, no attempt has been made to incorporate selections that reflect all of the recent trends and developments in the field. Current trends are not the purpose of this book. Rather, this collection presents the most enduring themes and works of organizational behavior, organized in a way that is conceptually sound, useful in practice, and that enables the reader to track the historical development of the most important topics.

The older works have not been included simply because they are interesting relics, reminders of quaint but outdated thinking. Although organizational behavior has experienced marked growth and maturation over the decades, many of the basics remain the same. In fact, this is a field in which it sometimes feels as though the more we learn about the important things, the less we truly know. The laws of physics and gravity do not change with intellectual fashions or technological advances, nor do the basic psychological, cultural, or social characteristics of people. Just as those who would build spaceships have to start by studying Newton, those who would work with people in organizations must start with 1930s writers such as Mary Parker Follett and Chester I. Barnard. The future will always build upon what is enduring from the past. That is the rationale for this book—to provide those who seek to understand and/or to advance organizational behavior with a convenient place to find the essentials, indeed the classics, of organizational behavior's past. Once-dominant ideas and perspectives on organizations may lose the center stage, but they do not die. Their thinking influences subsequent writers, even those who may reject their basic assumptions and tenets. However old some of the articles may be, they are not dated. A classic is a classic because it continues to be of value to each new generation of students and practitioners.

Inherently, organizations are part of the society and the culture in which they are situated and operate. Human behavior—and thus organizational behavior—is heavily influenced by culturally rooted beliefs, values, assumptions, and behavioral norms affecting all aspects of organizational life. For this reason, a society's ways of thinking about how people behave in organizations do not develop in a vacuum. They reflect what is going on in the contemporary world of the time. Thus, contributions to organizational behavior vary by what was happening when and where, and in different cultures and subcultures. The advent of World War II, the American POWs who defected following the Korean War, the "flower child"/antiestablishment/self-development era of the 1960s, the computer/information society of the 1970s, and the competitive scare from Japanese industry in the 1980s all substantially influenced the evolution of our thinking and research about people in organizations. To truly understand organizational behavior as it exists today, one must appreciate the historical contexts through which it developed and the cultural milieux during and in which important contributions were made to its body of knowledge. To help readers place writings in their historical contexts, "A Chronology of Organizational Behavior," which reviews the most important events and publications in the field, follows the Introduction.

CRITERIA FOR SELECTION

Several criteria were used to select these particular classics of organizational behavior for inclusion. The first was the answer to this question: "Should the serious student of organizational behavior be expected to be able to identify this author and his or her basic themes?" If the answer was "yes," then it was so because such a contribution has long been, or is increasingly being recognized as, an important theme by a significant writer. We expect to be criticized for excluding other articles and writers, but it will be more difficult to honestly criticize our inclusions. The writers and classic pieces chosen are among the most widely quoted and reprinted by students and theorists in the field of organizational behavior. We felt it was important to include a sprinkling of *potentially important* current articles as well, however, and these newer articles have not been cited as extensively as those written twenty or thirty years earlier. Thus, more subjective judgments were required about their inclusion.

The second criterion is related to the first: Each article or chapter from a book had to make a basic statement that has been consistently echoed or attacked over the years. The selection had to be acknowledged as important—significant—in the sense that it must have been (or will become) an integral part of the foundation for the subsequent building of the field of organizational behavior.

The third criterion was that articles had to be readable. Fortunately, this was a relatively easy criterion to meet. Much of the literature on organizational behavior is easily understandable and interesting. However, many of the truly great works are of a length which, in our judgment, detracts from their major themes. Consequently, articles have been shortened for this book, but the only editing has been "editing out": No sentences have been changed or added to the original.

ORGANIZATION OF THE BOOK

This book is structured around the most important topics in the field of organizational behavior. The readings within each topical chapter are organized chronologically. An author's choice of major topics and the sequence of their presentation reflects his or her conceptual framework of a field. Thus, the structure of a book, in and of itself, communicates the author's implicit perspective of the field; this collection is no exception. The readings are grouped in six chapters that reflect these pervasive themes in the literature of organizational behavior:

- Leadership
- Motivation
- Individuals in teams and groups
- Effects of the work environment on individuals
- Power and influence
- Organizational change

The development of behavioral science theory tends to be cumulative, but almost never in a straight line. Sometimes the cumulative building of theory is accomplished through adoption of prior theorists' logic and research findings; in other instances, it is by trying unsuccessfully to use prior theorists' works, rejecting them, and veering off in a new exploratory direction. The chronological sequencing of readings within topics should enable the reader to track some of the important ebbs and flows of theory development over the decades.

CHANGES FROM THE SECOND EDITION

This third edition attempts to retain the essence of the earlier editions. It has not changed in level of presentation, point of view, purpose, or emphasis. Its scope has been expanded to incorporate important developments in the field, including the ever-more sophisticated integrative models of behavior that incorporate learning theory, virtual teams and networked organizations, and psychological contracts.

The structure of the third edition has changed somewhat. After considerable soul-searching, we merged the chapters on "Teamwork and Empowerment" and "Group and Intergroup Behavior." We titled the resulting new chapter *Individuals in Teams and Groups* and changed its contents markedly. We also decided that *Leadership* provided a better start to the book than *Motivation*, which had been the first chapter in the second edition. We believe these changes make the book flow more easily and logically, and we hope that you agree.

A number of people who have used the earlier editions asked that we "update" the book's coverage to include readings that "bring the book into the new millennium." Other reviewers have disagreed, urging us to resist the temptation to venture into untested new writing that has not withstood the test of time. This third edition attempts to walk the line, retaining its *classics* focus and identity while presenting a sprinkling of newer important works. For example, Chapter III is about work teams and empowerment—two themes that have influenced the field of organizational behavior markedly in the past fifteen years. These readings tend to be more recent because there are no "older" articles about workforce diversity (in its current usage) or virtual teams.

Chapter-by-chapter, the following selections have been added and deleted from the second to the third edition:

CHAPTER I: LEADERSHIP

Deletions from the Second Edition

Warren G. Bennis, "Why Leaders Can't Lead" (1990)

Margaret J. Wheatley, "Leadership and the New Science: Searching for a Simpler Way to Lead Organizations" (1992)

New Additions in the Third Edition

Daniel Goleman, "What Makes a Leader?" (1998)

Karl E. Weick, "Leadership as the Legitimation of Doubt" (2001)

Martin M. Chemers, "Efficacy and Effectiveness: Integrating Models of Leadership and Intelligence" (2002)

CHAPTER II: MOTIVATION

Deletions from the Second Edition

Edwin A. Locke, "The Ubiquity of the Technique of Goal Setting in the Theories of and Approaches to Employee Motivation" (1978)

Richard T. Mowday, "Equity Theory Predictions of Behavior in Organizations" (1983)

New Additions in the Third Edition

Nancy H. Leonard, Laura L. Beauvais, and Richard W. Scholl, "Work Motivation: The Incorporation of Self-Concept-Based Processes" (1999)

Edwin A. Locke, "Self-Set Goals and Self-Efficacy as Mediators of Incentives and Personality" (2001)

CHAPTER III: INDIVIDUALS IN TEAMS AND GROUPS

Deletions from the Second Edition

Donald F. Roy, "'Banana Time': Job Satisfaction and Informal Interaction" (1960)

J. Richard Hackman and Greg R. Oldham, "The Design of Work for Groups and Groups for Work" (1980)

Ian I. Mitroff, "Business NOT as Usual: Building the Organization of the Future Now" (1987)

J. D. Orsburn, L. Moran, E. Musselwhite, J. H. Zenger, and C. Perrin, "Self-Directed Work Teams" (1990)

Marvin R. Weisbord, "Transforming Teamwork: Work Relationships in a Fast-Changing World" (1991)

David E. Bowen and Edward E. Lawler III, "The Empowerment of Service Workers: What, Why, How, and When?" (1992)

New Additions in the Third Edition

Ruth Wageman, "Critical Success Factors for Creating Superb Self-Managing Teams" (1997)

Jessica Lipnack and Jeffrey Stamps, "Virtual Teams: The New Way to Work" (1999)

CHAPTER IV: EFFECTS OF THE WORK ENVIRONMENT ON INDIVIDUALS

Deletions from the Second Edition

William H. Whyte Jr., "The Organization Man: Conclusion" (1956)

Nancy E. Bell and Barry M. Staw, "People as Sculptors Versus Sculpture: The Roles of Personality and Personal Control in Organizations" (1989)

New Additions in the Third Edition

Jeffrey Pfeffer, "Organization Theory and Structural Perspectives on Management" (1991)

Denise M. Rousseau, "Psychological Contracts in Organizations: Violating the Contract" (1995)

CHAPTER V: POWER AND INFLUENCE

Deletion from the Second Edition

John P. Kotter, "Power, Dependence, and Effective Management" (1977)

New Addition in the Third Edition

Jeffrey Pfeffer, "Managing with Power" (1992)

CHAPTER VI: ORGANIZATIONAL CHANGE

Deletions from the Second Edition

Rosabeth Moss Kanter, "The Architecture of Culture and Strategy Change" (1983)

Richard Beckhard and Wendy Pritchard, "Focusing the Effort: Crucial Themes That Drive Change" (1992)

New Additions in the Third Edition

Warren G. Bennis, "Change: The New Metaphysics" (2000)

Richard T. Pascale, "Laws of the Jungle and the New Laws of Business" (2001)

Lillas M. Brown and Barry Z. Posner, "Exploring the Relationship Between Learning and Leadership" (2001)

The greatest single change from the second to the third edition has been the addition of two new editor-authors, Sandra J. Parkes and Richard B. Simpson. Together we have done a much better job of organizing and compiling this volume than Ott could have done alone. These two capable new colleagues have brought fresh ideas, new insights, creativity, and lots of energy to this third edition.

ACKNOWLEDGMENTS

Many people have contributed invaluable insights and assistance that have allowed us to assemble, edit, and write this third edition. We are reluctant to list names, for any listing is certain to overlook some people who should be recognized. Also, a mere listing of names is entirely inadequate thanks. Nevertheless, some individuals simply must be acknowledged. First and foremost is Jay Shafritz, at the University of Pittsburgh, who is a part of this book in so many ways.

We are very pleased that Martin Chemers, University of California, Santa Cruz, agreed to write the "Foreword to the Foreword" for this edition and that he urged us to retain the "Foreword" that Fred Fiedler wrote for the second edition. Together, these two forewords provide a wonderful opening for the book and an insightful introduction to the field of organizational behavior. We thank John W. Seybolt at Thunderbird, the American Graduate School of International Management, for his intellectual stimulation and friendship over the years. We thank the three scholars who reviewed the second edition and provided highly useful suggestions for strengthening the contents and the structuring of this third edition: Professors Douglas Ihrke, University of Wisconsin at Milwaukee; Kato Keeton, University of West Florida; and Mario Rivera, University of New Mexico. Stephen

Nelson provided thorough, accurate, and persistent assistance with the permissions. Hasan Kosebalaban helped in finding articles and chapters. We note with deep sorrow the loss of three valued colleagues who had provided unending support, constructive suggestions and encouragement when they were most needed: F. Ted Hebert, Wendy E. Rice, and David C. Williams.

Finally, we want to put readers on notice that changed standards of language are evident in some of the readings. Many terms and phrases that are sexist and racist by today's standards were in common use twenty or thirty years ago. When it was possible to do so, offensive language was removed from articles by editing out sentences or paragraphs. A few words and phrases, however, are essential to the text and could not be deleted.

J. Steven Ott
Sandra J. Parkes
Richard B. Simpson
University of Utah

Contents

Chapter II
Motivation 132

Chapter III
Individuals in Teams and Groups 220

Chapter VI
Organizational Change 434

Introduction

DEFINING ORGANIZATIONAL BEHAVIOR

Organizational behavior seeks to understand human behavior in organizational contexts. It examines the ways people cope with the problems and opportunities of organizational life. It asks questions such as these:

- Why do people behave the way they do when they are in organizations?
- Under what circumstances will people's behavior in organizations change?
- What impacts do organizations have on the behavior of individuals, formal groups (such as departments), and informal groups (such as people from several departments who meet regularly in the company lunchroom)?
- Why do different groups in the same organization develop different behavioral norms?

Organizational behavior results from the many complex interactions that occur daily between humans, groups of humans, and the organizational environment in which they spend their workday. To understand these interactions, it is first necessary to know something about the behavior of people and groups in general, organizations and organizational environments, and the behavior of people and groups when they are in organizations.

Organizational behavior has at least two very different meanings, and these differences are important. First, organizational behavior (or "OB") is the actual behavior of individuals and groups in and around purposeful organizations. It is the application of the theories, methods, and research findings of the behavioral sciences—particularly of psychology, social psychology, sociology, cultural anthropology, and to a lesser degree of economics and political science—to understanding the behavior of humans in organizations. However, understanding is not the sole goal of organizational behavior. OB practitioners apply knowledge, understanding, and techniques from the behavioral sciences in attempts to improve the functioning of organizations and to improve the fit between organizations' and their members' needs and wants.

Although behavioral scientists are interested in human behavior in any organization setting, their primary focus always has been on behavior in the workplace—on employment-related organizational behavior. Organizational behavior is mostly about behavior in settings where there tend to be constraints on people; where there is an economic relationship between individuals and their organizations.

People are not as free to establish and terminate employment relationships as they are other types of relationships with organizations. Usually there is a structured set of roles, a hierarchy of relations, and ongoing goal-related activities (although the goals may or may not be organizationally sanctioned).

Second, organizational behavior is one of several frameworks or perspectives on what makes an organization work. A *perspective* defines the organizational variables that are important enough to warrant the attention of managers and students of organizations. A perspective identifies what a person sees when looking at an organization and, therefore, almost prescribes what *levers* to use when trying to change or stabilize an organization. But a perspective is more than a way of seeing and approaching an organization. It is also a set of bedrock beliefs and values about, for example, the basic purposes for organizations, their fundamental right to existence, the nature of their links to the surrounding environment, and—most important for organizational behavior—the whole of their relationships with the people who work in them.

Students and practitioners of management have always been interested in and concerned with the behavior of people in organizations. But fundamental assumptions about the behavior of people at work did not change dramatically from the beginnings of humankind's attempts to organize until only a few decades ago. Using the traditional "the boss knows best" mind-set (set of assumptions), Hugo Münsterberg (1863–1916), the German-born psychologist whose later work at Harvard would earn him the title of "father" of industrial or applied psychology, pioneered the application of psychological findings from laboratory experiments to practical matters. He sought to match the abilities of new hires with a company's work demands, to positively influence employee attitudes toward their work and their company, and to understand the impact of psychological conditions on employee productivity (H. Münsterberg, 1913; M. Münsterberg, 1922). Münsterberg's approach characterized how the behavioral sciences tended to be applied in organizations well into the 1950s. During and following World War II, the armed services were particularly active in conducting and sponsoring research into how the military could best "find and shape people to fit its needs." This theme or quest became known as *industrial psychology* and more recently as *industrial/organizational psychology* or *I/O psychology*.

In contrast to the Hugo Münsterberg-type perspective on organizational behavior, the "modern breed" of applied behavioral scientists have focused their attention on seeking answers to questions such as how organizations could and should allow and encourage their people to grow and develop. From this perspective, it was assumed that organizational creativity, flexibility, and prosperity would flow naturally from employee growth and development. The essence of the relationship between organization and people was redefined from dependence to codependence. People were considered to be as or more important than the organization itself. The organizational behavior methods and techniques of the 1960s and 1970s could not have been used in Münsterberg's days, because we didn't believe (assume) that codependence was the "right" relationship between an organization and its employees. All of this is what is meant by a perspective.

Although practitioners and researchers have been interested in the behavior of people inside organizations for a very long time, it has only been since about 1957—when our basic assumptions about the relationship between organizations and people truly began to change—that the *organizational behavior perspective* came into being. Those who see organizations through the lens of the organizational behavior perspective focus on people, groups, and relationships among them and the organizational environment. For example, when organizational behaviorists contemplate the introduction of a new technology, they will immediately start thinking about planning ahead:

- How to minimize fear of change by involving people at all levels in designing the introduction of the changes
- How to minimize the negative impacts of the change on groups of workers (such as older, less-skilled, or younger)
- How to coopt informal leaders, especially those who might become antagonistic
- Alternatives for employees who do not see the changes as being consistent with their personal goals

Because the organizational behavior perspective places a very high value on humans as individuals, things typically are done very openly and honestly, providing employees with maximum amounts of accurate information, so they can make informed decisions with free will about their future (Argyris, 1970).

But there are other perspectives as well, each with its own assumptions, values, and levers—ways of approaching issues such as organizational change and stabilization (Shafritz & Ott, 2001). The systems perspective focuses on things such as an organization's information systems and its decision processes (Kast & Rosenzweig, 1970; Thompson, 1967); the structural perspective emphasizes things like the structural arrangement of the organization, the organization of work within the structure, and the procedures and rules that maintain order (Blau & Scott, 1962; Burns & Stalker, 1961; Mintzberg, 1979); and the power perspective looks mostly at managing conflict, building, maintaining, and using coalitions, and the nature of real and perceived power relationships (Kotter, 1985; Pfeffer, 1981, 1992; Salancik & Pfeffer, 1977).

Thus, as a perspective of organization theory, organizational behavior is one of several ways of looking at and thinking about organizations (and people). It is defined by a set of basic assumptions about people, organizations, and the relationships, dynamics, and tensions between and among them. It is common to refer to this second use of the phrase *organizational behavior* as the *human relations* or *human resources school*, *perspective*, or *frame* of organization theory. To distinguish clearly between the two meanings and thus to avoid confusion, the phrase *organizational behavior* is used throughout this book to mean "the behavior of individuals and groups in and around purposeful organizations." To differentiate, the phrase *organizational behavior perspective*, or *human relations perspective*, refers to the school or perspective of organization theory that reflects basic managerial assumptions about employees similar to those of Theory X and Theory Y, as articulated by Douglas McGregor. (See Chapter II, *Motivation*.)

Organizational behavior is solidly grounded in theory and in empirical research. It uses applications of theory, methods, and findings about the behavior of people and groups in general, about social organizations, and about people in purposeful social organizations, adapted from long-established behavioral science disciplines. No other perspective of organizations has ever had such a wealth of research findings and methods at its disposal.

It is difficult to draw a clear distinction between what behavior is and is not *organizational*, because out-of-organizational behavior affects behavior in organizations and vice versa. In general, however, behavior is considered organizational if something associated with the organization causes or enhances the behavior, the behavior results from an organizational activity or function, or organizational meaning is attached to the behavior.

Assumptions about human behavior are crucial for understanding how managers and workers interact in organizations. Each perspective on organizations has its own fundamental tenets or assumptions, which are very different. The tenets of the "modern" structural perspective and the organizational behavior perspective (as they are articulated by Bolman and Deal, 1997)[1] are presented side by side in Table 1 to emphasize the differences and to highlight how the differences cause these two schools to differ with respect to almost everything!

Assumptions are more than beliefs or values: they are givens or truths that are held so strongly that they are no longer questioned nor even consciously thought about. They are the foundation and the justification (Sathe, 1985) for the perspective's beliefs, truths, values, and ways of doing things.

The assumptions of the Münsterberg–early I/O psychology perspective continued well into the 1950s. It was assumed that people should be fit to the organization: the organization had set needs to be filled. Thus, during the "classical era" of organization theory—from the late 1800s through the 1940s—the organizational role of the applied behavioral sciences largely consisted of helping organizations find and shape people to serve as *replacement parts* for *organizational machines*. The dominant theorists of organizations during these years were people such as Frederick Winslow Taylor (1911) and his disciples in *scientific management*, and Max Weber (1922), the brilliant theorist of *bureaucracy* (Shafritz & Ott, 2001).

Although the Münsterberg–I/O psychology theme provided important early background for organizational behavior, its more important direct genealogy lies in social psychology. The one most significant set of events that led to a conscious field of organizational behavior was the multilayer work done by the Elton Mayo team at the Hawthorne plant of the Western Electric Company beginning in 1927 (Mayo, 1933; Roethlisberger & Dixon, 1939). Three other significant threads or

TABLE 1 • TENETS OF THE "MODERN" STRUCTURAL PERSPECTIVE AND THE ORGANIZATIONAL BEHAVIOR PERSPECTIVE

"Modern" Structural School	Organizational Behavior Perspective
1. Organizations are rational institutions whose primary purpose is to accomplish established objectives; rational organizational behavior is achieved best through systems of defined rules and formal authority. Organizational control and coordination are key to maintaining organizational rationality.	1. Organizations exist to serve human needs. Humans do not exist to serve organizational needs.
2. There is a "best" structure for any organization in light of its given objectives, the environmental conditions surrounding it, the nature of its products and/or services, and the technology of the production processes.	2. Organizations and people need each other. Organizations need the ideas, energy, and talent that people provide; and people need the careers, salaries, and work opportunities that organizations provide.
3. Specialization and the division of labor increase the quality and quantity of production—particularly in highly skilled operations and professions.	3. When the fit between the individual and the organization is poor, one or both will suffer. The individual will be exploited or will seek to exploit the organization or both.
4. Most problems in an organization result from structural flaws and can be solved by changing the structure (pp. 48–49).	4. When the fit is good between the individual and the organization, both benefit. Humans are able to do meaningful and satisfying work while providing the resources the organization needs to accomplish its mission (pp. 102, 103).

Source: Adapted from Lee G. Bolman and Terrence E. Deal (1997). *Reframing Organizations*. 2nd ed. San Francisco: Jossey-Bass.

forces also accounted for a great deal of the direction of industrial social psychology research and practice into the 1950s (Haire, 1954):

1. The late 1930s contributions by Kurt Lewin in group dynamics, with important contributions by Lippitt and White (group climate and leadership) and Bavelas (leadership as a group problem)
2. Jacob Moreno's work on sociometry (the network of relations among people in a group) and sociodrama (role playing)
3. The rapid rise of industry and government willingness to ask social psychologists for help during World War II, a trend that began establishing a role for social scientist (*process*) consultants that differed substantially from *content consultants*

During these early years, industrial social psychology differed quite markedly from I/O psychology in its interests and premises. Whereas I/O psychology was busily engaged in trying to solve organizational problems (for example, selecting people to fit into positions), industrial social psychology developed an early concern for creating a psychological (rather than an institutional or technical) definition of the work setting. In this arena, the Hawthorne studies of Mayo and his collaborators were extraordinary contributions.

Once again, the difference between the I/O psychology approach and the work of Mayo, Roethlisberger, and their associates at the Hawthorne plant lay in their *assumptions*. The I/O psychologists adopted these assumptions of classical organization theory and shaped their field to fits its tenets:

1. Organizations exist to accomplish production-related and economic goals.
2. There is one best way to organize for production, and that way can be found through systematic, scientific inquiry (in this instance, systematic, scientific, *psychological inquiry*).
3. Production is maximized through specialization and division of labor.
4. People and organizations act in accordance with rational economic principles.

It is important to note that the Mayo team, like the I/O psychology groups, began its work trying to fit into the mold of classical organization theory thinking. The team phrased its questions in the language and concepts industry was accustomed to using, to see and explain problems such as productivity in relationship to such factors as the amount of light, the rate of flow of materials, and alternative wage payment plans. The Mayo team succeeded in making significant breakthroughs in understanding only after it redefined the Hawthorne problems as social psychological problems—problems conceptualized in such terms as interpersonal relations in groups, group norms, control over one's own environment, and personal recognition. It was only after the Mayo team achieved this breakthrough that it became the "grandfather"—the direct precursor—of the field of organizational behavior and of the human relations perspective of organization theory. The Hawthorne studies laid the foundation for a set of assumptions that would be fully articulated and would displace the assumptions of classical organization theory twenty years later.

Despite their later start, the industrial social psychologists were years ahead of the industrial psychologists in understanding that behavior in organizations could not be understood nor controlled by viewing behavior solely as an organizational phenomenon or solely from an organizational vantage point. The organization is not the independent variable to be manipulated in order to change behavior (as a dependent variable)—even though organizations pay employees to help them achieve organizational goals. Instead, the organization must be seen as the context in which behavior occurs. It is both an independent and a dependent variable. The organization influences human behavior just as behavior shapes the organization. The interactions shape conceptualizations of jobs, human communication, and interaction in work groups, the impacts of participation in decisions about one's own work, roles (in general), and the roles of leaders.

Between 1957 and 1960, the organizational behavior perspective literally exploded onto the organization scene. On April 9, 1957, Douglas M. McGregor delivered the Fifth Anniversary Convocation address to the School of Industrial Management at the Massachusetts Institute of Technology. He titled his address, "The Human Side of Enterprise." Three years later, McGregor expanded his talk into what has become one of the most influential books on organizational behavior and organization theory. In *The Human Side of Enterprise* (1960), McGregor articulated how managerial assumptions about employees become self-fulfilling prophesies. He labeled his two sets of contrasting assumptions *Theory* X and *Theory* Y, but they are more than just theories. McGregor had articulated the basic assumptions of the organizational behavior perspective.

The organizational behavior perspective is the most optimistic of all perspectives of organization. Building from Douglas McGregor's Theory X and Theory Y assumptions, organizational behavior has assumed that under the right circumstances people and organizations will grow and prosper together. The ultimate worth of people is an overarching value of the human relations movement—a worthy end in-and-of-itself—not simply a means or process for achieving a higher-order organizational end. Individuals and organizations are not necessarily antagonists. Managers can learn to unleash previously stifled energies and creativities. The beliefs, values, and tenets of organizational behavior are noble, uplifting, and exciting. They hold a promise for humankind, especially those who will spend their lifetime working in organizations.

As one would expect of a field that is based on a very optimistic and humanistic set of assumptions and values, the strategies of organizational behavior became strongly normative (prescriptive). For many organizational behavior practitioners of the 1960s, 1970s, and 1980s, the perspective's assumptions and methods became a cause. This volume communicates these optimistic tenets and values and articulates the logical and emotional reasons the organizational behavior perspective developed into a virtual movement. In our view, this is the true essence of "organizational behavior."

As we have progressed through the 1990s and into the twenty-first century, organizational behavior has maintained its relevance, vibrancy, and optimistic perspective. The new century will be an exciting time for those of us who follow organizational behavior research, writing, and practice. Organizational behavior will continue to include interdisciplinary contributions from an array of social and behavioral sciences, the health and biological sciences, and the professional schools including business, social work, engineering, and computer sciences. Significant work will emerge as organizational behavior feels the impact of the electronic information age, new employment relationships, positive and negative consequences of innovation, and the internationalization, or globalization, of organizations.

We are now all aware of the realities of terrorism, global instability, rapid swings in economic and market cycles, rapidly shifting demographics, and the ever-increasing rate of change. Researchers will be pressed to develop new models, theories, and practices that can affect organizational excellence—as the world changes.

Our most important collective challenge as teams, organizations, and networks of organizations will be to develop an ongoing capacity to creatively link leadership, learning, and adaptive change to the important outcomes of organizational excellence.

AN ORCHESTRA AS METAPHOR

We have chosen to use a metaphor—an orchestra—at the beginning of each chapter to illustrate and to bring to life the vibrant nature of the theories and concepts reprinted in this book. These brief vignettes highlight the richness, beauty, and complexity of the emerging field of organizational behavior. As you progress from the first through the last chapter, we hope that the "orchestra" will help you to feel the artistry uniquely complementing these classic readings and bringing to life this ongoing story. You might want to consider creating your own metaphors as you move through the chapters; it can be an enjoyable learning experience.

CHAPTER NOTE

1. Bolman and Deal (1997) use the labels "human resources frame" and "structural frame."

REFERENCES

Alderfer, C. P. (1972). *Existence, relatedness, and growth: Human needs in organizational settings*. New York: Free Press.

Allport, G. W. (1954). The historical background of modern social psychology. In G. Lindzey (Ed.), *Handbook of social psychology: Volume II: Special fields and applications* (pp. 3–56). Reading, MA: Addison-Wesley.

Argyris, C. (1970). *Intervention theory and method*. Reading, MA: Addison-Wesley.

Bell, D. (1956). *Work and its discontents*. Boston: Beacon Press.

Bennis, W. G. (1976). *The unconscious conspiracy: Why leaders can't lead*. New York: AMACOM.

Berelson, B., & Steiner, G. A. (1964). *Human behavior: An inventory of scientific findings*. New York: Harcourt, Brace & World.

Blau, P. M., & Scott, W. R. (1962). *Formal organizations: A comparative approach*. San Francisco: Chandler Publishing.

Bolman, L. G., & Deal, T. E. (1997). *Reframing organizations: Artistry, choice, and leadership* (2d ed.). San Francisco: Jossey-Bass.

Burns, T., & Stalker, G. M. (1961). *The management of innovation*. London, UK: Tavistock Publications.

Cohen, A. R., Finks, S. L., Gadon, H., & Willits, R. D. (1984). *Effective behavior in organizations* (3d ed.). Homewood, IL: Richard D. Irwin.

Dunham, R. B. (1984). *Organizational behavior*. Homewood, IL: Richard D. Irwin.

Gantt, H. L. (1908). Training workmen in habits of industry and cooperation. Paper presented to the American Society of Mechanical Engineers.

George, C. S. Jr. (1972). *The history of management thought* (2d ed.). Englewood Cliffs, NJ: Prentice-Hall.

Haire, M. (1954). Industrial social psychology. In G. Lindzey (Ed.), *Handbook of social psychology: Volume II: Special fields and applications* (pp. 1104–1123). Reading, MA: Addison-Wesley.

Hampton, D. R., Summer, C. E., & Webber, R. A. (1987). *Organizational behavior and the practice of management* (5th ed.). Glenview, IL: Scott, Foresman and Company.

Hersey, P., & Blanchard, K. H. (1982). *Management of organizational behavior: Utilizing human resources* (4th ed.). Englewood Cliffs, NJ: Prentice-Hall.

Kast, F. E., & Rosenzweig, J. E. (1970). *Organization and management: A systems approach*. New York: McGraw-Hill.

Kotter, J. P. (1985). *Power and influence: Beyond formal authority*. New York: Free Press.

Kuhn, T. S. (1970). *The structure of scientific revolutions* (2d ed., enlarged). Chicago: University of Chicago Press.

Lewin, K. (1947). Frontiers in group dynamics: Concept, method and reality in social science: Social equilibrium and social change. *Human Relations*, *1*, 5–41.

Lewin, K. (1948). *Resolving social conflicts*. New York: Harper.

Luthans, F. (1972). *Contemporary readings in organizational behavior*. New York: McGraw-Hill.

Mayo, G. E. (1933). *The human problems of an industrial civilization*. Boston: Harvard Business School, Division of Research.

McClelland, D. C. (1962). Business drive and national achievement. *Harvard Business Review*, July–August, 99–112.

McGregor, D. M. (1957, April). The human side of enterprise. Address to the Fifth Anniversary Convocation of the School of Industrial Management, Massachusetts Institute of Technology. In *Adventure in thought and action*. Cambridge, MA: M.I.T. School of Industrial Management, 1957. Reprinted in W. G. Bennis, E. H. Schein, & C. McGregor (eds.), (1966), *Leadership and motivation: Essays of Douglas McGregor* (pp. 3–20). Cambridge, MA: The M.I.T. Press.

McGregor, D. M. (1960). *The human side of enterprise*. New York: McGraw-Hill.

Mintzberg, H. (1979). *The structuring of organizations*. Englewood Cliffs, NJ: Prentice-Hall.

Münsterberg, H. (1913). *Psychology and industrial efficiency*. Boston: Houghton Mifflin.

Münsterberg, M. (1922). *Hugo Münsterberg, his life and work*. New York: D. Appleton and Company.

Organ, D. W., & Bateman, T. (1986). *Organizational behavior: An applied psychological approach* (3d ed.). Plano, TX: Business Publications.

Pfeffer, J. (1981). *Power in organizations*. Boston: Pitman Publishing.

Pfeffer, J. (1992). *Managing with power: Politics and influence in organizations*. Boston: Harvard Business School Press.

Reitz, H. J. (1987). *Behavior in organizations* (3d ed.). Homewood, IL: Richard D. Irwin.

Roethlisberger, F. J., & Dixon, W. J. (1939). *Management and the worker*. Cambridge, MA: Harvard University Press.

Salancik, G. R., & Pfeffer, J. (1977). Who gets power—and how they hold on to it: A strategic-contingency model of power. *Organizational Dynamics*, *5*, 2–21.

Sathe, V. (1985). *Culture and related corporate realities*. Homewood, IL: Richard D. Irwin.

Shafritz, J. M., & Ott, J. S. (2001). *Classics of organization theory* (5th ed.). Fort Worth, TX: Harcourt College.

Taylor, F. W. (1911). *The principles of scientific management*. New York: W. W. Norton.

Thompson, J. D. (1967). *Organizations in action*. New York: McGraw-Hill.

Weber, M. (1922). Bureaucracy. In H. Gerth & C. W. Mills (Eds.), *Max Weber: Essays in sociology*. Oxford, UK: Oxford University Press.

Wilson, J. A. (1951). *The culture of ancient Egypt*. Chicago: University of Chicago Press.

Wren, D. A. (1972). *The evolution of management thought*. New York: Ronald Press.

A CHRONOLOGY OF ORGANIZATIONAL BEHAVIOR

2100 B.C. Hammurabi, King of Babylon, establishes a written code of 282 laws that control every aspect of Babylonian life, including individual behavior, interpersonal relations, and other societal matters. This may have been the first employee policy handbook.

1750 B.C. Ancient Egyptians assign ten workers to each supervisor while building the pyramids. This may have been the earliest recorded use of the span of control concept.

1491 B.C. During the exodus from Egypt, Jethro, the father-in-law of Moses, urges Moses to delegate authority over the tribes of Israel along hierarchical lines.

525 B.C. Confucius writes that obedience to the organization (government) is the most "respectable goal of citizenship." This becomes the basic justification for authority systems.

1200 Medieval European guilds function as quality circles to ensure fine craftsmanship.

1490 John Calvin, Protestant religious reformer, promotes the merit system by promising a reward "of eternal life in His (God's) kingdom to the faithful who do God's work." The Puritan movement champions the concepts of time management, duty to work, and motivation theories; wasting time is considered the "deadliest of sins."

1527 Machiavelli's *The Prince* offers managers practical advice for developing authoritarian structures within organizations. His justification is that "all men are bad and ever ready to display their vicious nature."

1651 In his essay, *Leviathan*, Thomas Hobbes advocates strong centralized leadership as a means of bringing "order to the chaos created by man." He provides a justification for autocratic rule, thereby establishing the pattern for organizations throughout the nineteenth century.

1690 In his *Two Treatises of Government*, John Locke provides the philosophical framework for the justification of the U.S. Declaration of Independence. In effect, Locke advocates participatory management when he argues that leadership is granted by the governed.

1762 Jean Jacques Rousseau in *The Social Contract* postulates that governments work best when they are chosen and controlled by the governed. This concept furthers the idea of participatory management.

1776 Adam Smith in *The Wealth of Nations* revolutionizes economic and organizational thought by suggesting the use of centralization of labor and equipment in factories, division of specialized labor, and management of specialization in factories.

1800 In Britain, the Roebuck and Garrett Company seeks to maintain organizational harmony by putting factories only in locations where workers are perceived to be "reliable, loyal, and controllable."

1811 The Luddites, workers in English textile mills, seek to destroy new textile machinery that is displacing them. This is an early example of management's need to plan for organizational change.

1813 In his "Address to the Superintendents of Manufactures," Robert Owens encourages managers to provide their *vital machines* (employees) with as much attention as they do their *inanimate machines*.

1832 In the first managerial textbooks, *The Carding and Spinning of Masters' Assistant* and *The Cotton Spinners' Manual*, James Montgomery promotes the control function of management: Managers must be "just and impartial, firm and decisive, and always alert to prevent rather than check employee faults."

1883 Frederick W. Taylor begins experiments in Midvale and Bethlehem Steel plants that eventually lead to his concepts of *scientific management*.

1902 Vilfredo Pareto becomes the "father" of the concept of *social systems;* his societal notions would later be applied by Elton Mayo and the human relationists in an organizational context.

1903 Frederick W. Taylor's book, *Shop Management*, explains the role of management in motivating workers to avoid "natural soldiering," the natural tendency of people to "take it easy."

1909 Hugo Münsterberg, considered the "father of organizational psychology," writes, "The Market and Psychology," in which he cautions managers to be concerned with "all the questions of the mind . . . like fatigue, monotony, interest, learning, work satisfaction, and rewards." He is the first to encourage government-funded research in the area of industrial psychology.

1911 Frederick W. Taylor's book, *The Principles of Scientific Management*, investigates the influence of salary, mechanical design, and work layout on individual job performance to discover the "one best way" of accomplishing a given task.

Walter D. Scott's series of articles, "The Psychology of Business," published in *System Magazine* are some of the first to apply principles of psychology to motivation and productivity in the workplace.

1912 Edward Cadbury, using his chocolate factories as a laboratory, pioneers the field of industrial psychology with his book, *Experiments in Industrial Organization*.

1913 Hugo Münsterberg's book, *Psychology and Industrial Efficiency*, addresses personnel selection, equipment design, product packaging, and other concerns in an attempt to match the "best man" with the "best work" in order to get the "best possible effect."

Lillian M. Gilbreth's "The Psychology of Management," published in *Industrial Engineering Magazine*, becomes one of the earliest contributions to the understanding of human behavior in the industrial setting.

1924 As a joint project, the National Research Council, Massachusetts Institute of Technology, and Harvard University begin their investigations of group behavior and worker sentiments at the Hawthorne works of the Western Electric Company in Chicago.

Elton Mayo explains in "The Basis of Industrial Psychology," published by the *Bulletin of the Taylor Society*, that short work breaks improve worker motivation and decrease employee turnover rates; this notion supports the importance of *social environment* in the workplace.

1926 Mary Parker Follett's chapter, "The Giving of Orders," is one of the very first calls for the use of a participatory leadership style, in which employees and employers cooperate to assess the situation and collaboratively decide what should be done.

1933 Elton Mayo makes the first significant call for the human relations movement in his Hawthorne studies interim report titled *The Human Problems of an Industrial Civilization*.

1937 The American Association for Applied Psychology is organized to study industrial and organizational psychology.

Walter C. Langer publishes *Psychology and Human Living*, in which he provides the first significant discussion of human needs, repression, and integration of personality, and their application to the workplace.

1938 *Functions of the Executive*, by Chester I. Barnard, suggests that the purpose of a manager is to balance organizational and workers' needs. This encourages and foreshadows the postwar revolution in thinking about organizational behavior.

1939 Kurt Lewin, Ronald Lippett, and Ralph K. White's article, "Patterns of Aggressive Behavior in Experimentally Created Social Climates," published in the *Journal of Social Psychology*, is the first empirical study of the effects of the various leadership styles. Their work becomes the basis of the popularity of participative management techniques.

F. J. Roethlisberger and W. J. Dickson publish *Management and the Worker*, the definitive account of the Hawthorne studies.

1940 Robert K. Merton's *Social Forces* article, "Bureaucratic Structure and Personality," explains how bureaucratic structures exert pressures on people to conform to patterns of obligations, and eventually cause people to adhere to rules as a matter of blind conformance.

1942 Carl Rogers's *Counseling and Psychotherapy* offers human relations training as a method to overcome communication barriers and enhance interpersonal skills. These techniques lead to "control through leadership rather than force."

1943 Abraham Maslow's *needs hierarchy* first appears in his *Psychological Review* article, "A Theory of Human Motivation."

1945 Kurt Lewin forms the Research Center for Group Dynamics at MIT to perform experiments in group behavior. In 1948, Lewin's research center moves to the University of Michigan and becomes a branch of the Institute for Social Research.

1946 Rensis Likert develops the Institute for Social Research at the University of Michigan to conduct studies in the social sciences.

1947 The National Training Laboratory for Group Development, the predecessor to the National Training Laboratory Institute for Applied Behavioral Science, is established in Bethel, Maine, to conduct experimentation and training in group behavior.

1948 In their *Human Relations* article, "Overcoming Resistance to Change," Lester Coch and John R. P. French Jr. note that employees resist change less when the need for it is effectively communicated to them and when the workers are involved in planning the changes.

Kenneth D. Benne and Paul Sheats's article, "Functional Role of Group Members," published in the *Journal of Social Issues*, identifies three group role categories: *group task*, *group building and maintenance*, and *nonparticipatory*. These become the basis for future leadership research and training programs.

1949 In his *Public Administration Review* article, "Power and Administration," Norton E. Long finds that power is the lifeblood of administration, and that managers have to do more than simply apply the scientific method to problems—they have to attain, maintain, and increase their power, or risk failing in their mission.

The term *behavioral sciences* is first put into use by the Ford Foundation to describe its fundings for interdisciplinary research in the social sciences; and the term is later adopted by a group of University of Chicago scientists seeking such funding.

1950 Ralph M. Stogdill in his *Psychological Bulletin* article, "Leadership, Membership, and Organization," identifies the importance of the leader's role in influencing group efforts toward goal setting and goal achievement. His ideas become the basis for modern leadership research.

1951 Alex Bavelas and Dermot Barrett's article, "An Experimental Approach to Organizational Communication," appearing in *Personnel*, recognizes that the effectiveness of an organization is based on the availability of information and that communication is "the basic process out of which all other functions derive."

Eric L. Trist and K. W. Bamforth's pioneering sociotechnical systems study of British miners, "Some Social and Psychological Consequences of the Long-wall Method of Coal-Getting," demonstrates that the introduction of new structural and technological systems can destroy important social systems.

"Effects of Group Pressure upon the Modification and Distortion of Judgments," by Solomon Asch, describes his experiments showing that a sizable minority of subjects alter their judgment to match that of the majority, even when the facts clearly demonstrate the majority is wrong.

Kurt Lewin proposes a general model of change consisting of three phases, *unfreezing*, *change*, and *refreezing*, in his *Field Theory in Social Science*. This model becomes the conceptual frame for organization development.

1953 Dorwin Cartwright's address to the Society for the Psychological Study of Social Issues, titled "Power: A Neglected Variable in Social Psychology," identifies leadership and social roles, public opinion, rumor, propaganda, prejudice, attitude change, morale, communications, race relations, and conflicts of value, as leading social issues that cannot be understood except through the concept of power.

1954 *The Practice of Management*, by Peter F. Drucker, outlines his famous *management by objectives* (MBO) approach: a way that management might give "full scope to individual strength and responsibility, and at the same time give direction of vision and effort, establish teamwork, and harmonize the goals of the individual."

Bernard M. Bass's *Psychological Bulletin* article, "The Leadership Group Discussion," identifies a leadership training program in which a leader is not selected but rather emerges from the group's task.

In their *American Sociological Review* article, "Some Findings Relevant to the Great Man Theory of Leadership," Edgar F. Borgatta, Robert F. Bales, and Arthur S. Couch promote the concept of leader assessment centers as a way to recognize individual leadership ability.

1955 Arthur H. Brayfield and Walter H. Crockett's *Psychological Bulletin* article, "Employee Attitudes and Employee Performance," claims that there is no direct influence of job satisfaction on worker performance; in other words, a happy worker is not necessarily a better worker.

The Organization Man, by William H. Whyte Jr., describes empirical findings about individuals who accept organizational values and find harmony in conforming to all policies.

1957 Chris Argyris asserts in his first major book, *Personality and Organization*, that there is an inherent conflict between the personality of a mature adult and the needs of modern organizations.

Philip Selznick in *Leadership in Administration* anticipates many of the 1980s notions of *transformational leadership* when he asserts that the function of an institutional leader is to help shape the environment in which the institution operates and to define new institutional directions through recruitment, training, and bargaining.

The first organization development (OD) program is designed by Herbert Shepard and Robert Blake and is implemented at (Esso) Standard Oil Company.

On April 9, Douglas M. McGregor delivers the Fifth Anniversary Convocation address to the School of Industrial Management at the Massachusetts Institute of Technology. His address, "The Human Side of Enterprise," was expanded into a book by the same title in 1960.

Leon Festinger's *A Theory of Cognitive Dissonance* suggests that dissonance is a motivator of human behavior.

Alvin W. Gouldner's *Administrative Science Quarterly* study, "Cosmopolitans and Locals: Toward an Analysis of Latent Social Roles," finds that people with different role orientations differ in their degree of influenceability, level of participation in the organization, willingness to accept organizational rules, and informal relations at work.

1958 Robert Tannenbaum and Warren H. Schmidt's *Harvard Business Review* article, "How to Choose a Leadership Pattern," describes "democratic management" and devises a leadership continuum ranging from authoritarian to democratic.

Organizations, by James G. March and Herbert Simon, provides an overview of the behavioral sciences' influence in organization theory.

Leon Festinger, the father of cognitive dissonance theory, writes "The Motivating Effect of Cognitive Dissonance," which becomes the theoretical foundation for the "inequity theories of motivation."

1959 John R. P. French and Bertram Raven identify five bases of power (expert, referent, reward, legitimate, and coercive) in their article "The Bases of Social Power." They argue that managers should not rely on coercive and expert power bases because they are least effective.

Herzberg, Mausner, and Snyderman's *The Motivation to Work* puts forth the motivation-hygiene theory of worker motivation.

In *Modern Organizational Theory*, Cyert and March prepare a chapter, "A Behavioral Theory of Organizational Objectives," which postulates that power and politics have an impact on the formation of organizational goals. Their work is an early precursor of the power and politics school.

1960 Herbert Kaufman's *The Forest Ranger* describes how employee conformity can be increased through organizational and professional socialization efforts.

Donald F. Roy's *Human Organization* study, "Banana Time: Job Satisfaction and Informal Interaction," finds that workers in monotonous jobs survive psychologically through informal interaction; they keep from "going nuts" by talking and fooling around in a nonstop, highly stylized, and ritualistic manner.

Douglas M. McGregor's book, *The Human Side of Enterprise*, articulates the basic assumptions of the organizational behavior perspective and becomes perhaps the single most influential work in organizational behavior and organizational theory.

1961 Burns and Stalker's *The Management of Innovation* advocates a contingency model of leadership when it articulates the need for different types of management systems (organic and mechanistic) under differing circumstances.

Rensis Likert's *New Patterns of Management* offers an empirically based defense of participatory management and organization development techniques.

1962 In his *Administrative Science Quarterly* article, "Control in Organizations: Individual Adjustment and Organizational Performance," Arnold S. Tannenbaum explains that distributing control more broadly within the organization helps to encourage involvement and adherence to the group norms by its members.

David Mechanic's *Administrative Science Quarterly* article, "Sources of Power of Lower Participants in Complex Organizations," explores factors that account for the power of lower-level participants in organizations over those above them.

Robert L. Kahn and Daniel Katz report their findings on the supervisor's role, the closeness of supervision, the quality of supportiveness, and the amount of group cohesiveness on the productivity and level of morale of organizational groups, in "Leadership Practices in Relation to Productivity and Morale."

In "The Concept of Power and the Concept of Man," Mason Haire traces the change in the ultimate sources of organizational authority from the state to organizational ownership and forecasts an eventual shift to the authority of the work group.

Robert Prethus's work, *The Organizational Society*, presents his threefold classification of patterns of organizational accommodations: *upward-mobiles*, those who accept goals and values of the organization as their own; *indifferents*, those who reject organizational values and seek personal satisfaction off the job; and *ambivalents*, those unable to cope with organizational demands but who still desire its rewards.

Blau and Scott write *Formal Organizations: A Comparative Approach*, in which they argue that all organizations have both an informal and formal structure and that one cannot understand formal structure without first understanding the informal workings of an organization.

In his article "Business Drive and National Achievement," David McClelland develops the learned needs theory, which says that motivation is closely associated with learning concepts that are culturally and socially acquired. These needs include the need for achievement, the need for affiliation, and the need for power. When a need is strong, it will motivate an individual to behave in a way that will satisfy the need.

1964 Considered the father of Transactional Analysis (TA), Eric Berne in his book, *Games People Play: The Psychology of Human Relationships*, identifies three ego states: the *parent*, the *adult*, and the *child;* he suggests that successful managers should strive for adult-adult relationships.

Robert Blake, Herb Shepard, and Jane S. Mouton, in *Managing Intergroup Conflict in Industry*, assert that the behavior of two members of an organization in relation to each other is determined by three factors: the requirements of formal role, their backgrounds of training and experience, and the role they feel themselves to be in as representatives of particular groups in the organization.

The Management Grid: Key Orientations for Achieving Production Through People, by Robert Blake and Jane Mouton, is a diagnostic device for leadership development programs that provides a *grid* of leadership style possibilities based on managerial assumptions about people and production.

In "Work and Motivation," Victor Vroom proposes a process approach to individual motivation, known as expectancy theory. He explains motivation as a process in which individuals choose among alternative voluntary activities. Vroom argues that people have preferred outcomes, and *expectancy* is the belief in the likelihood that outcomes will occur as a result of particular behaviors.

1965 Robert L. Kahn's *Organizational Stress* is the first major study of the mental health consequences of organizational role conflict and ambiguity.

James G. March prepares *Handbook of Organizations*, a series of essays that attempt to consolidate all scientific knowledge about organizations and organizational behavior.

1966 *Think Magazine* publishes David C. McClelland's article, "That Urge to Achieve," in which he identifies two groups of people: the majority group, who aren't concerned about achieving, and the minority group, who are challenged by the opportunity to achieve. This notion becomes a premise for future motivation studies.

The Social Psychology of Organizations, by Daniel Katz and Robert L. Kahn, seeks to unify the findings of behavioral science on organizational behavior through open systems theory.

Fred Fiedler, in "The Contingency Model: A Theory of Leadership Effectiveness," argues that organizations should not try to change leaders to fit them but instead should change their situations to mesh with the style of their leaders.

In "Applying Behavioral Sciences to Planned Organizational Change," a chapter from his book, *Changing Organizations*, Warren Bennis describes planned change as a link between theory and practice and as a deliberate and collaborative process involving change agents and client-systems who are brought together to solve a problem.

1967 The *Personnel Administration* article, "Organizations of the Future," by Warren Bennis states that bureaucracy will disappear due to rapid and unexpected change, unprecedented growth in organizational size, increasing complexity in modern technology, and philosophical changes in managerial controls and behaviors.

In their *Personnel Administration* article, "Grid Organization Development," Robert A. Blake and Jane S. Mouton explain that organizational goals determine managers' actions; they offer an innovative, systematic approach to "organizational development."

Fred E. Fiedler publishes his work, *A Theory of Leadership Effectiveness*, which proposes that leadership style must fit the circumstances; there is no one best way to perform leadership tasks.

Norman Maier in his *Psychological Review* article, "Assets and Liabilities in Group Problem-Solving," explains that the benefits of group versus individual problem solving depend on the "nature of the problem, the goals to be achieved, and the skill of the discussion leader."

Anthony Downs's *Inside Bureaucracy* seeks to develop laws and propositions that would aid in predicting the behavior of bureaus and bureaucrats.

William G. Scott's *Organization Theory: A Behavioral Analysis for Management* suggests that an "individual's opportunity for self-realization at work" can be actualized by applying "industrial humanism" concepts such as reducing authoritarian tendencies in organizations, encouraging participatory decision making on all levels, and integrating individual and corporate goals.

Anthony Jay's *Management and Machiavelli* applies Machiavelli's political principles (from *The Prince*) to modern organizational management.

1968 In *Group Dynamics*, Dorwin Cartwright and Alvin Zander propose that the systematic study of group dynamics would advance knowledge of the nature of groups; how they are organized; and relationships among individuals, other groups, and larger institutions.

John P. Campbell and M. D. Dunnette's "Effectiveness of T-Group Experiences in Managerial Training and Development," appearing in *Psychological Bulletin*, provides a critical review of T-Group literature. They conclude that "an individual's positive feelings about his T-Group experiences" cannot be scientifically measured, nor should they be based entirely on "existential grounds."

Frederick Herzberg's *Harvard Business Review* article, "One More Time, How Do You Motivate Employees?" catapults *motivators* or *satisfiers* and *hygiene factors* into the forefront of organizational motivation theory.

1969 In Fred E. Fiedler's *Psychology Today* article, "Style or Circumstance: The Leadership Enigma," three elements of effective leadership are identified: power of the leader, the task at hand, and the leader–member relationships. He determines that jobs should be designed to fit individual leadership styles rather than the reverse.

Paul Hersey and Kenneth R. Blanchard's "Life Cycle Theory of Leadership," appearing in *Training and Development Journal*, asserts that the appropriate leadership style for a given situation depends on the employee's education and experience levels, achievement motivation, and willingness to accept responsibility by the subordinates.

Wendell French, in his *California Management Review* article, "Organization Development: Objectives, Assumptions, and Strategies," defines organization development as a total system of planned change.

Harold M. F. Rush's *Behavioral Science: Concepts and Management Application* challenges managers to better understand the behavioral sciences so they can more effectively motivate the "new breed of employee," who is better educated, more politically, socially, and economically astute, and more difficult to control.

Richard E. Walton and John M. Dutton's *Administrative Science Quarterly* article, "The Management of Interdepartmental Conflict: A Model and Review," provides a diagnostic model for managers to determine what needs changing to prevent or terminate interdepartmental conflicts.

1970 In his book, *Organizational Psychology*, Edgar H. Schein distinguishes between formal and informal groups within organizations and indicates that effective group work is a result of considering the "characteristics of the members and assessing the likelihood of their being able to work with one another and serve one another's needs."

In "Expectancy Theory," John P. Campbell, Marvin D. Dunnette, Edward E. Lawler III, and Karl E. Weick Jr. articulate the *expectancy theories of motiva-*

tion. People are motivated by calculating how much they want something, how much of it they think they will get, how likely it is their actions will cause them to get it, and how much others in similar circumstances have received.

Chris Argyris writes *Intervention Theory and Methods*, which becomes one of the most widely cited and enduring works on organizational consulting for change that is written from the organizational behavior/organization development perspective.

1971 Rensis Likert's *Michigan Business Review* article, "Human Organizational Measurements: Key to Financial Success," emphasizes that assessing human elements of an organization can identify organizational problems before they occur; he argues that implementing human organizational measurements can help ensure an organization's long-term success.

B. F. Skinner, in *Beyond Freedom and Dignity*, demands a change in the contemporary views of people and how they are motivated in an organization; his alternative includes using *behavior modification* strategies by applying operant conditioning principles to improve employee motivation.

In their *Journal of Applied Psychology* article, "Employee Reactions to Job Characteristics," J. Richard Hackman and Edward E. Lawler III identify four core job dimensions—variety, autonomy, task identity, and feedback—which they claim relate to job satisfaction, motivation, quality of work, and decreased absenteeism.

Irving Janis's "Groupthink," first published in *Psychology Today*, proposes that group cohesion can lead to the deterioration of effective group decision-making efforts.

1972 Clayton Alderfer, in *Existence, Relatedness, and Growth: Human Needs in Organizational Settings*, agrees with Maslow that needs are hierarchically arranged but presents a hierarchy that includes existence, relatedness, and growth as needs.

1974 Robert J. House and Terrance R. Mitchell's *Journal of Contemporary Business* article, "Path-Goal Theory of Leadership," offers path-goal theory as a useful tool for explaining the effectiveness of certain leadership styles in given situations.

Victor H. Vroom's *Organizational Dynamics* article, "A New Look at Managerial Decision-Making," develops a useful model whereby leaders can perform a diagnosis of a situation to determine which leadership style is most appropriate.

Steven Kerr's *Academy of Management Journal* article, "On the Folly of Rewarding A, While Hoping for B," substantiates that many organizational reward systems are "fouled up"—they pay off for behaviors other than those they are seeking.

1975 *Behavior in Organizations*, by Lyman Porter, Edward Lawler III, and Richard Hackman, focuses on the interaction between individuals and work organizations. It examines how individual–organizational relationships emerge and grow, including how groups can exert influence on individuals in organizations and how such social influences relate to work effectiveness.

1976 Douglas W. Bray's "The Assessment Center Method," part of the *Training and Development Handbook*, promotes the idea of observing individual behaviors in simulated job-related situations (assessment centers) for evaluative purposes.

Michael Maccoby psychoanalytically interviews 250 corporate managers and discovers *The Gamesman*, a manager whose main interest lies in "competitive activity where he can prove himself a winner."

In "Moral Stakes: Where Have All the Leaders Gone?" Warren Bennis coins the phrase *social architects* to describe what he considers to be the most important roles of organizational leaders: understanding the organizational culture, having a sense of vision, and encouraging people to be innovative.

1977 The *American Psychologist* article, "Job Satisfaction Reconsidered," by Walter R. Nord, explains that a revision of accepted economic and political ideologies is necessary if distribution of power in organizations is to be altered.

Gerald Salancik and Jeffrey Pfeffer's *Organizational Dynamics* article, "Who Gets Power—And How They Hold on to It: A Strategic-Contingency Model of Power," views the power by subunits as an important means by which organizations align themselves with their critical needs; thus, suppression of the use of power reduces organizational adaptability.

John P. Kotter's *Harvard Business Review* article, "Power, Dependence, and Effective Management," describes how successful managers build their power by creating a sense of obligation in others, creating images, fostering unconscious identification with these images, and feeding people's beliefs that they are dependent on these images.

1978 Daniel Katz and Robert L. Kahn publish *The Social Psychology of Organizations*, in which they coin the term *open system approach*. They advocate creating organizations that are open to change.

Edwin A. Locke's article, "The Ubiquity of the Technique of Goal Setting in Theories of and Approaches to Employee Motivation," argues that goals motivate. His review of the Hawthorne study data, for example, demonstrates that workers are more responsive to goals-based financial incentives than to the widely reported social influences.

William G. Ouchi and Alfred M. Jaeger popularize a third *ideal type organization* in their *Academy of Management Review* article, "Type Z Organization: Stability in the Midst of Mobility." The three types include: Type A (American); Type J (Japanese); and Type Z (one that combines the best of both types). This article becomes the first of many dealing with Japanese management strategies.

Thomas J. Peters's *Organizational Dynamics* article, "Symbols, Patterns, and Settings: An Optimistic Case for Getting Things Done," is the first major analysis of symbolic management in organizations to gain significant attention in the mainstream literature of organization theory.

Herbert C. Kelman and Donald P. Warwick examine stages in organizational interventions that are likely to cause important ethical issues to surface, in *The Ethics of Social Intervention*.

1980 J. Richard Hackman and Greg R. Oldham attempt to answer the oft-asked question, "Which is better, individuals or groups?" Some tasks should be done by individuals and some by groups. In the latter case, though, tasks should be redesigned for groups and groups for the nature of the tasks; in *Work Redesign*.

1981 *Power in Organizations*, by Jeffrey Pfeffer, proposes that intergroup conflicts are inevitable in organizations because of inherent differences between perspectives and ongoing competition for scarce organizational resources; coalitions are the means through which people muster power for political contests.

In "'Democracy' as Hierarchy and Alienation," Frederick Thayer proposes that employee alienation can be ended by eradicating hierarchy and that alienation cannot be eradicated so long as hierarchy remains.

1982 Barry Staw's chapter, "Motivation in Organizations: Toward Synthesis and Redirection," echoes wide disenchantment with the usefulness of existing theories of motivation and attempts to broaden the conceptualization of motivation by viewing individuals as actors who change the "rules" of traditional motivation theories.

1983 Henry Mintzberg, in *Power in and Around Organizations*, proposes that "everyone exhibits a lust for power" and the dynamic of the organization is based on the struggle between various *influencers* to control the organization. As a result, he molds the power and politics school of organizational theory into an integrative theory of management policy.

"In Equity Theory of Predictions of Behavior in Organizations," Richard T. Mowday argues that the presence of inequity motivates individuals to change the situation through behavioral or cognitive means to return to a condition of equity.

Daniel C. Feldman and Hugh J. Arnold's *Managing Individual and Group Behavior in Organizations* concludes that individual motivation is based on the sum of intrinsic and extrinsic motivation sources and not merely on a manager's ability to motivate.

In *The Change Masters*, Rosabeth Moss Kanter defines *change masters* as architects of organizational change; they are the right people in the right places at the right time.

1984 Thomas J. Sergiovanni's "Leadership as Cultural Expression" proposes that organizational leadership is a cultural artifact: The shape and style of leadership results from the unique mixture of organizational culture and the *density* of leadership competence.

Tichy and Ulrich's *Sloan Management Review* article, "The Leadership Challenge—A Call for the Transformational Leader," describes the functions of a transformational leader as those of a cheerleader and a belief model during radical organizational change.

Caren Siehl and Joanne Martin report the findings of the first major quantitative and qualitative empirical study of organizational culture in their "The Role of Symbolic Management: How Can Managers Effectively Transmit Organizational Culture?"

In *Goal Setting: A Motivational Technique That Works*, Edwin A. Locke and Gary P. Latham encourage managers to set goals based on their findings that an individual worker's performance increases as goal difficulty increases (assuming the person is willing and has the ability to do the work).

1985 Edgar Schein writes his comprehensive and integrative statement of the organizational culture school in *Organizational Culture and Leadership*.

In a chapter from *The Politics of Management*, Douglas Yates Jr. describes the management of political conflict as the process of managing strategic conflict between actors who possess different forms of resources, and reminds managers that using power is costly: It depletes one's reservoir of credible power.

Warren Bennis and Burt Nanus reemphasize the importance of vision, power, and context for establishing leadership in organizations, in *Leaders: The Strategies for Taking Charge*.

1986 S. G. Harris and R. I. Sutton's *Academy of Management Journal* article, "Functions of Parting Ceremonies in Dying Organizations," focuses on the particular importance of symbolic leadership during periods of organizational decline.

In *The Transformational Leader*, Noel Tichy and Mary Anne Devanna propose a Lewin-type "three-act framework" for transformational leadership—the "leadership of change, innovation, and entrepreneurship."

1987 Research findings by Edward Lawler and Susan Morhman suggest that in the long term, quality circles have difficulty coexisting with traditional management approaches. Quality circles require basic management changes or they will not be effective, and alternative strategies should be used; in the *Organizational Dynamics* piece, "Quality Circles: After the Honeymoon."

Clayton P. Alderfer's analysis, "An Intergroup Perspective on Group Dynamics," explores the influence on intergroup analysis of the persistently problematic relationship between individuals and collective social processes. He asserts that intergroup theory provides interpretations for individual, interpersonal, group, intergroup, and organizational relations.

1988 Ralph Kilmann and Teresa Joyce Covin publish the first comprehensive collection of research studies and practitioner papers targeting the implementation of transformational change, in *Corporate Transformation*.

In *The Leadership Factor,* John Kotter expands on his prior studies of power and leadership in organizations to explain why organizations often do not have adequate leadership capacity and proposes steps to rectify the problems.

1989 In "People as Sculptors versus Sculpture: The Roles of Personality and Personal Control in Organizations," Nancy E. Bell and Barry M. Staw provide evidence that people may not be as malleable or open to organizational influence as they have been depicted, particularly in the literature on organizational socialization. People may shape their work environments as much as or more than they are shaped by their environments.

1990 Warren Bennis concludes that we have never needed leaders more but held them in lower regard. Circumstances and the American people conspire against them without meaning to. *Why Leaders Can't Lead: The Unconscious Conspiracy Continues* predicts that change for the better is possible, but the outlook for leadership is not optimistic.

In "Psychological Conditions of Personal Engagement and Disengagement at Work," William Kahn concludes that the three most important psychological conditions that influence the willingness of employees to engage and disengage with work organizations are psychological meaningfulness, psychological safety, and psychological availability.

Jack Orsburn, Linda Moran, Ed Musselwhite, and John Zenger write their extensive analysis of self-directed work teams—highly trained groups of employees that are fully responsible for turning out a well-defined segment of finished work; in *Self-Directed Work Teams: The New American Challenge*.

Peter Senge's book, *The Fifth Discipline: The Art and Practice of the Learning Organization*, argues that we should—and can—build organizations where people continually expand their capacity to create, where collective aspiration is set free, and where people are continually learning how to learn together.

1991 Marvin R. Weisbord's book, *Productive Workplaces*, examines the importance of effective teamwork in a fast-changing world. Teams get much "lip service," but the term rivals "quality" as a business cliché. Managers must consciously strive to transform individuals and groups into effective teams.

Jeffrey Pfeffer's article, "Organization Theory and Structural Perspectives on Management," builds a persuasive argument that an individual's structural position in an organization affects organizational behavior. "Structural position" includes network location, physical location, and demographic relationship to others.

1992 In *Changing the Essence*, Richard Beckhard and Wendy Pritchard identify the leadership behaviors necessary for initiating and managing fundamental change in organizations. They also attempt to find ways to manage the tension between dealing with short-term pressures and addressing the long-term strategic management of organizations' identities and destinies.

In "The Empowerment of Service Workers: What, Why, How, and When," David Bowen and Edward Lawler III assess the key business characteristics that determine whether empowerment of service workers is beneficial. Managers need to be certain that there is a good fit between organizational needs and their approach before deciding to empower front-line service employees.

In the second edition of *Leadership and Organizational Culture*, Edgar H. Schein shows how leaders create, embed, develop, and sometimes deliberately attempt to change cultural assumptions during different phases of an organization's development and maturation.

Margaret J. Wheatley's book, *Leadership and the New Science*, proposes that managers need to look to the "new sciences" of quantum physics, self-ordering systems, and chaos theory to find clues about how to improve their leadership behavior in organizations.

Jeffrey Pfeffer discusses the relationship between power and influence and decision making and implementation in *Managing with Power*. Effective organizations need leaders who are not afraid to exercise power and influence. The more that managers recognize and understand the importance of power, the more likely they are to be effective in implementing decisions and achieving organizational success.

1993 "Intergroup Conflict," a chapter in *Cultural Diversity in Organizations*, by Taylor Cox Jr., examines the potential benefits and the difficulties that may accrue to an organization from cultural diversity. Cox identifies various sources of conflict among culture identity groups and how intergroup conflict is manifested in organizations. He suggests ways in which intergroup conflict can be minimized.

1995 Denise Rousseau, in "Psychological Contracts in Organizations," argues that although people in organizations often fail to live up to the terms of psychological contracts, the more important issue is whether people interpret an unkept psychological contract as a "violation." When an individual perceives that a contract violation has occurred, the aftermath may include declining loyalty to the organization and increased litigation.

1997 Ruth Wageman explains why self-managing work teams often fail to meet performance expectations, in "Critical Success Factors for Creating Superb Self-Managing Teams." Her study of self-managing work teams at Xerox Corporation concluded that how teams are set up and supported is more important for team success than the behavior of team leaders or coaches.

1998 In "The Secrets of Great Groups," Warren Bennis asserts that the important problems we face are too complex to be solved by individuals. "Great groups" of strong individual achievers provide multiple perspectives, psychic support, personal fellowship, and help generate courage. Thus, they can get things done that individuals cannot.

Daniel Goleman's article, "What Makes a Leader?" emphasizes that IQ and technical skills are important but emotional intelligence is an absolute prerequisite of leadership. This article elaborates on his 1995 best selling book, *Emotional Intelligence*. Goleman points out that emotional intelligence plays a critical role in a leader's overall effectiveness and identifies five components of emotional intelligence at work: self-awareness, self-regulation, motivation, empathy, and social skills.

1999 Jessica Lipnack and Jeffrey Stamps examine complex issues caused by the emergence of twenty-first-century organizations made up of virtual teams and networks of teams, in "Virtual Teams: The New Way to Work." Networked organizations of virtual teams pose enormous new challenges that require new kinds of management and leadership skills that reflect Robert Putnam's three essential factors for developing social capital: trust, reciprocity, and dense social networks.

Leonard, Beauvais, and Scholl seek to unify theories of work motivation into a "metatheory," which includes an understanding of how the self-concept also influences behavior within organizations, in "Work Motivation: The Incorporation of Self-Concept-Based Processes."

2000 *Bowling Alone*, by Robert Putnam, presents an extensive analysis of causes and consequences of the thirty-year decline in social capital in the United States. Using data from several major databases, Putnam describes how we have become increasingly disconnected from others in our personal and work lives, and thus how our access to social capital is shrinking.

Karl Weick discusses "Leadership and the Legitimation of Doubt." Weick suggests that the hallmarks of the twenty-first century will include unknowability and unpredictability. He develops the value of uncertainty and a path through it that uses animation, improvisation, lightness, authentication, and learning.

Warren Bennis publishes *Managing the Dream: Reflections on Leadership and Change*. In the chapter titled "The New Metaphysics," Bennis discusses avenues of change, comments on innovators and leaders, and discusses how to avoid disaster during change.

2001 Edwin Locke, in his article "Self-Set Goals and Self-Efficacy as Mediators of Incentives and Personality," proposes that "self-set or personal goals and self-efficacy are the most immediate, motivational determinants of action and that they mediate or link the effects of other motivators."

In "Laws of the Jungle and the New Laws of Business," Richard Pascale identifies two imperatives that govern organizational survival and contribute to organizational excellence: agility in the face of ambiguity and a rapidly changing external environment, and a change in culture to one where there is lively, organic competitive essence. In this type of culture, ongoing learning and change support entrepreneurial initiatives that can exploit opportunities.

Martin Chemers develops the premise that intelligence (rather than a fixed and unchanging capacity) is a set of skills and knowledge that changes and develops in interaction with the environment, in "Efficacy and Effectiveness: Integrating Models of Leadership and Intelligence." Chemers has continued this work with Roya Ayman, and the second edition of their book, *An Integrated Theory of Leadership*, is scheduled for publication in 2003.

In "Exploring the Relationship Between Learning and Leadership," Lillas Brown and Barry Posner argue that active and versatile learners are more frequently involved in leadership. More successful leaders are necessarily lifelong learners. Thus, research about leadership and learning must be integrated.

CHAPTER I

Leadership

Heading off for an exciting evening at the symphony is an experience common to many of us. As audience members, we expect to be able to "sit back and enjoy the show." Before the performance begins, we relax and talk idly with family or friends as we watch an interesting array of activities. Orchestra members mill about, talk, sit and play, or tune their instruments. These seemingly random, non-coordinated, individualistic, preparatory activities are signposts that the orchestra is "getting ready" for the performance.

As the performance nears, things change. There is a "hush" or a "quiet" moment and a sense of impending "focus" just before the conductor enters the stage. Then the "leader" walks to his or her appointed position, and all eyes converge on that place. The conductor will soon enlist the aid and support of the orchestra members to create magic for the audience.

Orchestra members know which pieces are to be played, and they have a collective agenda for the performance. In a more diffuse way, they also have a sense of the symphony's role and purpose in the community, the region, the state, and the nation. Indeed, they may also have a sense of their place within the international community of orchestras.

Sometimes the magic does occur, and the audience is swept away in the ecstasy of the performance. Other times, the audience leaves with a less enthusiastic response. Members of the orchestra also experience these different types of feelings about the performance.

What are the leadership dynamics? Clearly, the way the conductor relates to each orchestra member is an important variable. The rigor and organizational skill—command and control—of the leader affects the process. The developmental stage of the orchestra also matters. For example, how long has the conductor been playing his or her role? The same could be asked of the orchestra members and members of the instrument sections. The "fit" between the orchestra as a group and the leader's style is important. Characteristics of the group, including critical cultural issues within the orchestra such as norms, expectations, climate, and status, also must be considered. Traits of the leader, such as emotional intelligence (or other intelligences), may be important factors.

In music, as in all artistic endeavors, a certain element of uncertainty or chaos can make the difference between a superb and an average performance. Strange or unique events may enter the equation of the performance and "something" just happens—and magic is the result. Finally, incremental and transformational events combine leadership with learning and cause the orchestra to evolve into something new and different. The collective cognitive capacity, talent, and potential for change gives the orchestra the competitive edge to grow and thrive.

WHAT IS LEADERSHIP?

Over the years, the importance attributed to the position of leader has led innumerable practitioners and theorists to ask the seemingly unanswerable question, "What does it take to be an effective leader?" and almost as many behavioral scientists have offered answers. This chapter discusses some of the more important approaches that have been proposed in answer to this most basic but elusive question of leadership.

Although we need to have an understanding of what leadership is in order to discuss it, it is important to realize that there are no clear-cut, universally accepted definitions. Lombardo and McCall (1978, p. 3) describe the situation well: "'Leadership' is one of the most magnetic words in the English language. Mention it, and a perceptible aura of excitement, almost mystical in nature appears . . . [Yet] if leadership is bright orange, leadership research is slate gray." Complicating this is the fact that we also need to distinguish between *leadership* (or *leader*) and *management* (or *manager*). Although the two functions and roles overlap substantially, *manager* implies that authority has been formally granted to an individual by an organization. Management involves power (usually formal authority) bestowed on the occupant of a position by a higher organizational authority. With the power of management comes responsibility and accountability for the use of organizational resources. In contrast, *leader* implies effective use of influence that is rather independent of the authority granted to one because of position. Leadership cannot be bestowed upon a person by a higher authority. Effective managers also must be leaders, and many leaders become managers, but the two sets of rules and functions differ.

One group of authors recently began defining a successful leader as one who is able to transform an organization when situations call for such action (Bennis, 1984; Bennis & Nanus, 1985; Tichy, 1983; Tichy & Devanna, 1986). The most widely accepted current definitions view leadership as an interpersonal process through which one individual influences the attitudes, beliefs, and especially the behavior of one or more other people.

The subject of leadership raises many complex issues that have plagued behavioral scientists for generations. For example, what gives a manager or a leader legitimacy? Shafritz (1988, p. 324) describes *legitimacy* as "a characteristic of a social institution, such as a government or a family [or an organization], whereby it has both a legal and a perceived right to make binding decisions." Thus, managers presumably have legitimacy because of the legal and perceived rights that accompany their organizational positions. In contrast, the legitimacy of a leader—separate and distinct from the legitimacy of a manager—cannot be addressed without introducing the concept of *charisma*. Charisma is "leadership based on the compelling personality of the leader rather than on formal position" (Shafritz, 1988, p. 89). The concept was first articulated by the German sociologist, Max Weber, who distinguished charismatic authority from the traditional authority of a monarch and the legal authority one receives by virtue of law—such as the authority that legitimizes organizational executives.

Despite the differences and the unresolved questions, two important definitional givens are evident: First, leadership involves a relationship between people in which influence and power are unevenly distributed on a legitimate basis; and second, a leader cannot function in isolation. In order for there to be a leader, someone must follow (Fiedler & Chemers, 1974, p. 4). In his enduring chapter, "The Executive Functions" (1938, reprinted in this chapter), Chester Barnard defines three essential functions of leaders of executives: to provide a system of communication, to promote the securing of essential efforts, and to formulate and define the purposes and goals of an organization. He was decades ahead of his time in arguing that the most critical function of a chief executive is to establish and communicate a system of organizational values and among organizational members. If the value system is clear and strong, the day-to-day concerns will take care of themselves.

TRAIT THEORIES

Over the years, studies of leadership have taken different approaches based on divergent perspectives. The trait approach to leadership dominated into the 1950s. The trait theories assume that leaders possess traits that are fundamentally different from the traits of followers. A *trait* is a "personality attribute or a way of interacting with others which is independent of the situation, that is, a characteristic of the person rather than of the situation" (Fiedler & Chemers, 1974, p. 22). Advocates of trait theory believe that some individuals have characteristics and qualities that enable them to "rise above the population," to assume responsibilities not everyone can execute, and therefore to become leaders (Hampton, Summer, & Webber, 1982, p. 566). Under trait theory, the task of the behavioral sciences is to identify those traits and learn how to identify people who possess them.

It is no longer fashionable to contend that people will be effective leaders because they possess certain traits—without also considering other variables that influence leadership effectiveness. The arguments against trait theory are persuasive and come from a number of points of view. First, trait theory has largely fallen out of favor because reality never matched the theory. Instead, starting in the late 1950s, it became standard practice to view leadership as a relationship, an interaction between individuals. The interaction was called a *transaction*, so the term *transactional leadership* became the umbrella label encompassing many theories of leadership of the 1950s, 1960s, and 1970s. Second, the situation strongly influences leadership. As Stogdill (1948) stated, the situation has an active influence in determining the qualities, characteristics, and skills needed in a leader.

Probably the most damaging criticism of trait theory, however, has been its lack of ability to identify which traits make an effective leader. Even among the traits that have been most commonly cited—intelligence, energy, achievement, dependability, and socioeconomic status—there is a lack of consensus across studies. Leadership involves more than possessing certain traits. A leader may be effective in one setting and ineffective in another. It depends on the situation (Fiedler, 1969).

TRANSACTIONAL APPROACHES TO LEADERSHIP

The transactional approaches to leadership had early beginnings in the 1930s but did not emerge as the dominant view of leadership until the 1950s. Two primary forces were behind the ascendancy: (1) frustration and disappointment with trait theories, and (2) dramatic post–World War II advances in the applied behavioral sciences.

Whereas the trait approaches view leadership as something(s) inherent in a leader, the transactional approaches see leadership as a set of functions and roles that develop from an interaction between two or more people. The interaction between a person who leads and those who follow is labeled a *transaction*—much the same as in transactional analysis (Berne, 1964; Harris, 1969; James & Jongeward, 1971). Although there are vast differences in emphasis among groupings of transactional leadership theories, all of them focus on the transaction—what happens and why, and what directly and indirectly influences or shapes it. Thus, for example, the transactional theorist Fiedler (1966) emphasizes the leader—but in the context of the match between leaders and followers. In contrast, Hersey and Blanchard (1969) focus on subordinates—but in a leader–follower context.

Leadership Style Theories

The early transactional leadership theories tended to assume that people have relatively fixed styles and thus were often labeled *leadership style theories*. Many of the more recent theories also involve leadership styles, but because the earlier assumption of style inflexibility has been abandoned, they usually are called *situational* or *contingency approaches*. In both cases, however, leadership is seen as a transaction. Whereas the central question for the trait approach is "who exerts leadership?" the quest of the transactional approaches is to determine "how leadership is established and exerted."

Leadership style–oriented transactional approaches all follow in the tradition of the famous Lewin, Lippitt, and White (1939) studies of the effectiveness of leadership styles on group productivity. Lewin, Lippitt, and White studied groups of 10-year-old children engaged in hobby activities. The leader in each group was classified as authoritarian, democratic, or laissez-faire. Authoritarian leaders determined all policies, set all work assignments, and were personal in their criticisms. They were product- (or task) oriented and practiced initiating structure. Democratic-oriented leaders shared decision-making powers with subordinates, decisions about assignments were left to the group, and they participated in group activities but tried not to monopolize. They used high levels of consideration. Laissez-faire-oriented leaders allowed freedom for individual and group decision making, provided information (or supplies) only when requested, and did not participate in the group except when called upon. They functioned more as facilitators.

Groups with democratic-oriented leaders were the most satisfied and productive. The authoritarian-led groups showed the most aggressive behavior and were the least satisfied, but they were highly productive (possibly because of fear of the leader). The groups with laissez-faire-oriented leaders showed low satisfaction, low production, and were behaviorally aggressive toward group members and other groups.

The leadership style–oriented transactional approaches attempt to identify styles of leader behavior that result in effective group performance. Probably the best known groups of studies using this approach were conducted at the University of Michigan and at Ohio State University. They were widely known as the Michigan studies and the Ohio State studies.

Most of the Michigan studies analyzed two extreme leadership styles, product-oriented and employee-oriented. A *product-oriented leadership style* focuses on accomplishing the task of the organization producing the product. This style is exhibited in such activities as setting organizational or group goals, assigning work to subordinates, and constantly evaluating performance. The *employee-oriented leadership style* pays more attention to how well subordinates are doing and to their feelings and attitudes.

Typically, the Michigan studies had subordinates rate their supervisors on the degree to which "he treats people under him without considering their feelings," or "he does personal favors for the people under him" (Fleishman & Harris, 1962, p. 10). Findings from the Michigan studies have shown that high productivity may be associated with either style of leadership, but product-oriented leaders tend to be confronted more often and their employees have more job dissatisfaction, high turnover rates, and higher absenteeism rates (Fleishman & Harris, 1962, p. 53). Finally, other studies have shown that work output is correlated with the freedom supervisors give to workers, and employees produce more under loose supervision than under close supervision.

Like the University of Michigan studies, the Ohio State studies classified leader behavior as either product-oriented or employee-oriented, but they used different terminology: initiation of structure and consideration. The Ohio State studies treat the two behaviors as independent dimensions rather than as scalar opposites. In other words, a leader can rank high on consideration and either high or low on initiation of structure. Thus, leaders can be grouped into four quadrants.

Initiation of structure is "the leader's behavior in delineating the relationship between himself and members of the work group and in endeavoring to establish well-defined patterns of organization, channels of command, and methods of procedure" (Bozeman, 1979, p. 208). It is a variety of leader actions used "to get the work out." The leader plans, directs, sets standards, and controls the work of subordinates.

Consideration is "any action which the leader takes to perceive the human needs of his subordinates and to support the subordinates in their own attempts to satisfy their needs" (Hampton et al., 1982, p. 569). Or as stated by Stogdill, consideration is "any behavior indicative of friendship, mutual trust, respect, and warmth in the relationship between the leader and a member of his staff" (as cited in Bozeman, 1979, p. 208).

The Ohio State studies found the productivity of individuals and groups to be higher when leaders initiate structure than when they do not. Some studies have found consideration positively related to productivity, whereas others show a negative effect or no effect at all. As far as satisfaction, studies have shown the initiation of structure to be received differently by different people in different situations. For example, House's (1971) work illustrated that the larger the organization, the more employees need some stability, order, and direction. At the other extreme, considerate behavior has almost always been shown to increase employee satisfaction (Fleishman & Harris, 1962, p. 47).

The Ohio State studies contain interesting parallels to the Michigan studies. In their 1969 article, "Life Cycle Theory of Leadership" (included in this chapter), Hersey and Blanchard emphasize that leadership should be appropriate for a given situation. They use the maturity of the work groups as a variable influencing the effectiveness of the style used. Using initiation of structure and consideration for dimensions, they develop a matrix with four leadership styles: telling, selling, participating, and delegating. When a work group is not mature enough to assume a task, the leader should be high in initiation (task) and low in consideration (relationship) behavior to help the group understand what is required of them. On the other hand, when a group is mature, the leader should be high in consideration (relationship) and low in initiation (task) behavior, because the group is able to complete its task without much guidance. Although the model is conceptually intriguing, a major weakness is its lack of a "systematic measurement device to measure maturity" (Schein, 1980).

Situational or Contingency Approaches

Probably, the earliest situationist was the classical organizational philosopher, Mary Parker Follett. In her 1926 article, "The Giving of Orders" (reprinted in this chapter), Follett discusses how orders should be given in any organization: They should be depersonalized "to unite all concerned in a study of the situation, to discover the law of the situation and obey that." Follett thus argues for a *participatory leadership style* where employees and employers cooperate to assess the situation and decide what should be done at that moment—in that situation. Once the *law of the situation* is discovered, "the employee can issue it to the employer as well as employer to employee." This manner of giving orders facilitates better attitudes within an organization because nobody is necessarily under another person; rather, all take their cues from the situation.

The early style approach to transactional leadership assumed that leaders should be trained to act in the appropriate way as called for by their organization.

This has proven to be a major weakness. When leaders return to their organization after leadership training sessions, they seldom exhibit behavior changes. Despite training, department heads will not necessarily act considerately toward subordinates if their own supervisors do not act supportively toward them. One obvious implication is that changes must be introduced into an organization as a whole—not just to certain employees.

In practice, leaders apply different styles in different situations. Thus the "pure" leadership style emphasis has given way to the contingency approaches. Unlike the trait theory and leadership style approaches, the contingency approaches take into consideration many factors that may influence a leader's style. It recognizes that a successful leader in one type of organization may not be successful in another simply because it differs from the previous one. Its situation (or context) is different, and the choice of a style needs to be contingent upon the situation. As Stogdill (1974) notes, the contingency theories stress these factors:

1. The type, structure, size, and purpose of the organization
2. The external environment in which the organization functions
3. The orientation, values, goals, and expectations of the leader, his superiors, and subordinates
4. The expert or professional knowledge required of the position

The contingency approaches assert that different leadership styles will differ in their effects in different situations. The situation (not traits or styles themselves) determines whether a leadership style or a particular leader will be effective. Thus, contingency theorists maintain that there is no "one best way" of effective leadership.

Tannenbaum and Schmidt (1958, 1973) conducted one of the first studies that actually indicated a need for leaders to evaluate the situational factors prior to the implementation of a particular leadership style (Blunt, 1981). Tannenbaum and Schmidt grouped leader decision-making behavior into seven categories along a continuum from *boss-centered* to *subordinate-centered*. Each category is based on a single variable: the degree of participation in making decisions that is allowed to subordinates. For example:

- Category 1 assumes that the leader makes all decisions and announces them to subordinates.
- Category 7 assumes that the leader defines limits but allows the group to define the problem and to make the final decision.

Tannenbaum and Schmidt (1973) also specify three factors that influence where along their continuum a decision will be made. These factors are forces in the leader, forces of the subordinates, and forces in the situation:

> The successful manager of men can be primarily characterized neither as a strong leader nor as a permissive one. Rather, he is one who maintains a high batting average in accurately assessing the forces that determine what his most appropriate behavior at any given time should be and in actually being able to behave accordingly. (p. 180)

Whereas Tannenbaum and Schmidt focused mostly on variables involving followers, Fred Fiedler has emphasized the leader (but still from a transactional perspective). In "The Contingency Model: A Theory of Leadership Effectiveness" (included in this chapter), Fiedler (1966) discusses a study done with the Belgian Naval Forces. Some earlier leadership theorists had believed that leaders could be trained to adopt styles that are suitable for situations, but Fiedler found the opposite to be true. It is easier to change the work environment, the situation, to fit a leader's style. A person's underlying leadership style depends upon his or her personality. According to Fiedler, a leader's personality is not likely to change because of a few lectures or a few weeks of intensive training. Therefore, an organization should not choose a leader who fits a situation but should change the situation to mesh with the style of its leader (see also Cooper & Robertson, 1988, p. 84).

CULTURAL AND TRANSFORMATIVE THEORIES

A growing number of leadership theorists recently have moved past the transactional approaches to write about leadership from an organizational culture perspective or, as it is sometimes called, a symbolic management perspective (Ott, 1989; Shafritz & Ott, 2001). Without question, Edgar Schein is the best known writer about organizational culture, and his book, *Organizational Culture and Leadership*, has been the most widely cited source on the topic since publication of the first edition in 1985. "The Learning Leader as Culture Manager," a chapter from the second edition (1992), is reprinted here. In it, Schein argues "that leadership and culture are closely connected. . . . Leaders create, embed, develop, and sometimes deliberately attempt to change cultural assumptions." Different kinds of culture management are needed at different stages in an organization's development and maturation: culture creation, at organizational midlife, and in mature and potentially declining organizations. Schein examines how these stages of culture management affect organizational strategy formation and discusses the implications for the selection and development of leaders.

Like Senge (in Chapter VI), Schein concludes that leaders of the future will have to be perpetual learners. "If the leaders of today want to create organizational cultures that will themselves be more amenable to learning, they will have to set the example by becoming learners themselves and involving others in the learning process. . . . In the end, cultural understanding and cultural learning start with self-insight."

Transformational leadership or *transformative leadership* is a somewhat recent slant on leadership that is theoretically consistent with the organizational culture perspective. Whereas the transactional theories of leadership apply primarily to leadership roles, functions, and behavior *within* an existing organizational culture, transformative leadership is about leadership to *change* a culture. Transactional leadership focuses on incremental change; transformative leadership is about radical change. It is interesting to note that transformational leadership theories have many similarities with the trait theories of leadership. Transformational leadership borders on "great man" theory: Leaders are born, not made. In many ways, leadership theory is once again involved in seeking to find the basis of leadership in traits rather than in relational and cultural factors.

Noel Tichy and David Ulrich's 1984 *Sloan Management Review* article, "The Leadership Challenge—A Call for the Transformational Leader" (reprinted in this chapter), describes a transformational leader as "one who must develop and communicate a new vision and get others not only to see the vision but also to commit themselves to it." They describe transformational leaders as those rare individuals who can lead employees through their fears and uncertainties to the realization of the vision. This requires transformational leadership—leadership that successfully changes people's perceptions of the organization. Transformational change is more than a rational, technical, incremental approach to change. The leader's primary function is to lead and support through carefully conceived change stages, acting as a *cheerleader* and as a *belief model*—verbally and nonverbally communicating belief in the benefits to all that will accrue from the changes.

LEADERSHIP: WHERE FROM HERE?

During the last fifty years, leadership theory has wound its way torturously over twisting and often seemingly fruitless paths. For every gain in understanding, there have been more new questions to answer. The search for a comprehensive theory of leadership is a seemingly never-ending quest. Since the 1940s, the search has led us through trait theories, myriad transactional approaches, and transformative/cultural theories. Now we are seeing a return to "trait" thinking with the concepts of emotional intelligence (Goleman, 1998, reprinted here) and multiple intelligences (Gardner, 2000) combined with integrative theories (Chemers, 2002) creatively blending components of trait, transactional, and transformative/cultural theories. Martin Chemers recently has completed a chapter (reprinted here) titled "Efficacy and Effectiveness: Integrating Models of Leadership and Intelligence" (in Murphy, Riggio, & Pirozzlo, 2002). Chemers points out:

> contemporary approaches . . . are moving in the direction of the conceptualization of a more fluid interaction between the person and the environment with an acknowledgement of the individual's actions in construction and shaping of the environment rather than just reacting to it. Thus, rather than a fixed and unchanging capacity, intelligence (or leadership) becomes a set of skills and knowledge that change and develop in interaction with an environment that can, in turn, be shaped and modified to facilitate a good (i.e., effective) fit.

Clearly, we are entering an age where leadership is considered a multidimensional process in a world of uncertainty, chaos, and change. Leadership requires all organizational members to develop and enhance their skills, knowledge, and talents to contribute effectively to organizational excellence. Organizational learning in response to continuous and ever-increasing levels of change will continue to be a top priority (see in particular the articles by Senge and by Brown and Posner in Chapter VI).

No one truly believes the answers to the most basic questions about leadership have been found. However, it looks as though we are moving in the direction of "things coming together." When confronted with the practical realities of leading, many of us share Warren Bennis's (1990) frustration: Why can't leaders lead? Where have all the leaders gone? Further, as pointed out by Karl Weick (2001, reprinted here), leadership is in reality a "Legitimation of Doubt." Weick illustrates how excellence in leadership for the twenty-first century will necessarily be crafted and developed from creative energy drawn from both science and art in a sea of continuous uncertainty, chaos, and change.

We will return to these leadership concepts in the concluding chapter of this book, *Organizational Change*, and link them with readings by Peter Senge, Anthony Pascale, Warren Bennis, and Lillas Brown and Barry Posner—authors who have been at the forefront in addressing issues of organizational change, learning, uncertainty, and chaos as they relate to organizational excellence.

REFERENCES

Allaire, Y., & Firsirotu, M. (Spring, 1985). How to implement radical strategies in large organizations. *Sloan Management Review, 26*(3), 19–34.

Barnard, C. I. (1968). *The functions of the executive*. Cambridge, MA: Harvard University Press. (Originally published in 1938)

Beckhard, R. (1988). The executive management of transformational change. In R. H. Kilmann & T. J. Covin (Eds.), *Corporate transformation* (pp. 89–101). San Francisco: Jossey-Bass.

Bennis, W. G. (1961). Revisionist theory of leadership. *Harvard Business Review, 39*.

Bennis, W. G. (1976). Mortal stakes: Where have all the leaders gone? In W. G. Bennis, *The unconscious conspiracy: Why leaders can't lead* (pp. 143–156) New York: AMACOM.

Bennis, W. G. (1984). Transformative power and leadership. In T. J. Sergiovanni & J. E. Corbally (Eds.), *Leadership and organizational culture* (pp. 64–71). Urbana: University of Illinois Press.

Bennis, W. G. (1990). *Why leaders can't lead: The unconscious conspiracy continues*. San Francisco: Jossey-Bass.

Bennis, W. G., & Nanus, B. (1985). *Leaders: The strategies for taking charge*. New York: Harper & Row.

Bergquist, W. (1993). *The postmodern organization: Mastering the art of irreversible change*. San Francisco: Jossey-Bass.

Berne, E. (1964). *Games people play*. New York: Grove Press.

Block, P. (1991). *The empowered manager: Positive political skills at work*. San Francisco: Jossey-Bass.

Blunt, B. E. (1981). *Organizational leadership*. Ann Arbor, MI: University Microfilm International.

Bozeman, B. (1979). *Public management and policy analysis*. New York: St. Martin's Press.

Cattell, R. B. (1951). New concepts for measuring leadership in terms of group syntality. *Human Relations, 4*, 161–184.

Chemers, M. M. (2002). Efficacy and effectiveness: Integrating models of leadership and intelligence. In R. E. Riggio, S. E. Murphy, & F. J. Pirozzlo (Eds.), *Multiple intelligences and leadership* (pp. 139–159). Mahwah, NJ: Lawrence Erlbaum.

Cooper, C. L., & Robertson, I. (Eds.). (1988). *International review of industrial and organizational psychology*. New York: John Wiley.

Deal, T. E. (1985). Cultural change: Opportunity, silent killer, or metamorphosis? In R. H. Kilmann, M. J. Saxton, & R. Serpa (Eds.), *Gaining control of the corporate culture* (pp. 292–331). San Francisco: Jossey-Bass.

Dublin, R. (1951). *Human relations in administration*. Englewood Cliffs, NJ: Prentice-Hall.

Dunnette, M. D. (1976). *Handbook of industrial and organizational psychology*. Chicago: Rand McNally.

Fiedler, F. E. (1966). The contingency model: A theory of leadership effectiveness. In C. W. Backman & P. F. Secord (Eds.), *Problems in social psychology* (pp. 278–289). New York: McGraw-Hill.

Fiedler, F. E. (1967). *A theory of leadership effectiveness*. New York: McGraw-Hill.

Fiedler, F. E. (March, 1969). Style or circumstance: The leadership enigma. *Psychology Today* *2*(10), 38–43.

Fiedler, F. E., & Chemers, M. M. (1974). *Leadership style and effective management*. Glenview, IL: Scott, Foresman.

Fiedler, F. E., Chemers, M. M., & Mahar, L. (1976). *Improving leadership effectiveness: The leader match concept*. New York: John Wiley.

Fleishman, E. A., & Harris, E. F. (1962). Patterns of leadership behavior related to employee grievances and turnover. *Personnel Psychology*, *15*, 43–56.

Fleishman, E. A., & Hunt, J. G. (1973). *Current developments in the study of leadership*. Carbondale: Southern Illinois University Press.

Follett, M. P. (1926). The giving of orders. In H. C. Metcalf (Ed.), *Scientific foundations of business administration*. Baltimore, MD: Williams & Wilkins.

Gardner, H. E. (2000). *Intelligence reframed: Multiple intelligences for the 21st century*. New York: Basic Books.

Goleman, D. P. (Nov.–Dec., 1998). What makes a leader? *Harvard Business Review*, 73–102.

Hampton, D. R., Summer, C. E., & Webber, R. A. (1982). *Organizational behavior and the practice of management*. Glenview, IL: Scott, Foresman.

Harris, T. A. (1969). *I'm OK—You're OK*. New York: Harper & Row.

Hemphill, J. K. (1950). *Leader behavior description*. Columbus: Ohio State University Press.

Hersey, P., & Blanchard, K. H. (May, 1969). Life cycle theory of leadership. *Training and Development Journal*, 26–34.

House, R. J. (1971). Path-goal theory of leadership effectiveness. *Administrative Sciences Quarterly*, *16*, 321–338.

House, R. J., & Mitchell, T. M. (Autumn, 1974). Path-goal theory of leadership. *Journal of Contemporary Business*, *3*(4), 81–97.

Iacocca, L. (1984). *Iacocca, an autobiography*. Toronto: Bantam Books.

James, M., & Jongeward, D. (1971). *Born to win*. Reading, MA: Addison-Wesley.

Kahn, R. L., & Katz, D. (1962). Leadership practices in relation to productivity and morale. In D. Cartwright & A. Zander (Eds.), *Group dynamics* (2d ed., pp. 554–570). New York: Harper & Row.

Kouzes, J. M., & Posner, B. Z. (1993). *Credibility: How leaders gain and lose it, and why people demand it*. San Francisco: Jossey-Bass.

Leavitt, H. J. (June, 1962). Applied organizational change: A summary and evaluation of the power equalization approaches. Seminar in the Social Science of Organizations. Pittsburgh, PA.

Lewin, K., Lippitt, R., & White, R. K. (1939). Patterns of aggressive behavior in experimentally created social climates. *Journal of Social Psychology, 10*, 271–299.

Likert, R. (1961). *New patterns of management*. New York: McGraw-Hill.

Lombardo, M. M., & McCall, M. W. Jr. (1978). Leadership. In M. W. McCall Jr. & M. M. Lombardo (Eds.), *Leadership: Where else can we go?* (pp. 3–34). Durham, NC: Duke University Press.

Ott, J. S. (1989). *The organizational culture perspective*. Chicago: The Dorsey Press.

Riggio, R. E., Murphy, S. E., & Pirozzolo, F. J. (Eds.). (2002). *Multiple intelligences and leadership*. Mahwah, NJ: Lawrence Erlbaum.

Schein, E. H. (1980). *Organizational psychology* (3d ed.). Englewood Cliffs, NJ: Prentice-Hall.

Schein, E. H. (1992). *Organizational culture and leadership* (2d ed.). San Francisco: Jossey-Bass.

Schön, D. A. (1984). Leadership as reflection-in-action. In T. J. Sergiovanni & J. E. Corbally (Eds.), *Leadership and organizational culture* (pp. 36–63). Urbana: University of Illinois Press.

Selznick, P. (1957). *Leadership in administration: A sociological interpretation*. New York: Harper & Row.

Sergiovanni, T. J. (1984). Leadership as cultural expression. In T. J. Sergiovanni & J. E. Corbally (Eds.), *Leadership and organizational culture* (pp. 105–114). Urbana, IL: University of Illinois Press.

Shafritz, J. M. (1988). *The Dorsey dictionary of politics and government*. Chicago: The Dorsey Press.

Shafritz, J. M., & Ott, J. S. (2001). *Classics of organization theory* (5th ed.). Fort Worth, TX: Harcourt College.

Stogdill, R. M. (1948). Personal factors associated with leadership: A survey of the literature. *Journal of Psychology, 25*, 35–71.

Stogdill, R. M. (1974). *Handbook of leadership: A study of theory and research*. New York: Free Press.

Stogdill, R. M., & Coons, A. E. (Eds.). (1957). *Leader behavior: Its description and measurement*. Columbus: Ohio State University Press.

Tannenbaum, R. J., & Schmidt, W. H. (March–April, 1958). How to choose a leadership pattern. *Harvard Business Review, 36*(2), 95–101.

Tannenbaum, R. J., & Schmidt, W. H. (May–June, 1973). How to choose a leadership pattern. *Harvard Business Review, 51*(3), 1–10.

Tannenbaum, R. J., Weschler, I. R., & Massarik, F. (1961). *Leadership and organization*. New York: McGraw-Hill.

Tichy, N. M. (1983). *Managing strategic change: Technical, political and cultural dynamics*. New York: John Wiley.

Tichy, N. M., & Devanna, M. A. (1986). *The transformational leader*. New York: John Wiley.

Tichy, N. M., & Ulrich, D. O. (1984). The leadership challenge—a call for the transformational leader. *Sloan Management Review, 26*, 59–68.

Vroom, V. H. (Winter, 1976). Can leaders learn to lead? *Organizational Dynamics*.

Vroom, V. H., & Yetton, P. W. (1973). *Leadership and decision making*. Pittsburgh, PA: University of Pittsburgh Press.

Weick, K. E. (2001). Leadership and the legitimation of doubt. In W. Bennis, G. M. Spreitzer, & T. G. Cummings (Eds.), *The future of leadership* (pp. 91–103). San Francisco: Jossey-Bass.

Wheatley, M. J. (2000). *Leadership and the new science*. San Francisco: Berrett-Koehler.

Zaleznik, A. (1967). *Human dilemmas of leadership*. New York: Harper & Row.

1
The Giving of Orders

Mary Parker Follett

To some men the matter of giving orders seems a very simple affair; they expect to issue their own orders and have them obeyed without question. Yet, on the other hand, the shrewd common sense of many a business executive has shown him that the issuing of orders is surrounded by many difficulties; that to demand an unquestioning obedience to orders not approved, not perhaps even understood, is bad business policy. Moreover, psychology, as well as our own observation, shows us not only that you cannot get people to do things most satisfactorily by ordering them or exhorting them; but also that even reasoning with them, even convincing them intellectually, may not be enough. Even the "consent of the governed" will not do all the work it is supposed to do, an important consideration for those who are advocating employee representation. For all our past life, our early training, our later experience, all our emotions, beliefs, prejudices, every desire that we have, have formed certain habits of mind that the psychologists call habit-patterns, action-patterns, motor-sets.

Therefore it will do little good merely to get intellectual agreement; unless you change the habit-patterns of people, you have not really changed your people. . . .

If we analyze this matter a little further we shall see that we have to do three things. I am now going to use psychological language [to]: (1) build up certain attitudes; (2) provide for the release of these attitudes; (3) augment the released response as it is being carried out. What does this mean in the language of business? A psychologist has given us the example of the salesman. The salesman first creates in you the attitude that you want his article; then, at just the "psychological" moment, he produces his contract blank which you may sign and thus release that attitude; then if, as you are preparing to sign, someone comes in and tells you how pleased he has been with his purchase of this article, that augments the response which is being released.

If we apply this to the subject of orders and obedience, we see that people can obey an order only if previous habit-patterns are appealed to or new ones created. . . .

This is an important consideration for us, for from one point of view business success depends largely on this—namely, whether our business is so organized and administered that it tends to form certain habits, certain mental attitudes. It has been hard for many old-fashioned employers to understand that *orders will not take the place of training*. I want to italicize that. Many a time an employer has been angry because, as he

Source: From "The Giving of Orders" by Mary Parker Follett, in *Scientific Foundations of Business Administration* (Baltimore: Williams & Wilkins Co., 1926). Copyright © 1926 The Williams and Wilkins Company.

expressed it, a workman "wouldn't" do so and so, when the truth of the matter was that the workman couldn't, actually couldn't, do as ordered because he could not go contrary to life-long habits. This whole subject might be taken up under the heading of education, for there we could give many instances of the attempt to make arbitrary authority take the place of training. In history, the aftermath of all revolutions shows us the results of the lack of training.

. . . A boy may respond differently to the same suggestion when made by his teacher and when made by his schoolmate. Moreover, he may respond differently to the same suggestion made by the teacher in the schoolroom and made by the teacher when they are taking a walk together. Applying this to the giving of orders, we see that the place in which orders are given, the circumstances under which they are given, may make all the difference in the world as to the response which we get. Hand them down a long way from President or Works Manager and the effect is weakened. One might say that the strength of favorable response to an order is in inverse ratio to the distance the order travels. Production efficiency is always in danger of being affected whenever the long-distance order is substituted for the face-to-face suggestion. There is, however, another reason for that which I shall consider in a moment.

. . . I should say that the giving of orders and the receiving of orders ought to be a matter of integration through circular behavior, and that we should seek methods to bring this about.

Psychology has another important contribution to make on this subject of issuing orders or giving directions: before the integration can be made between order-giver and order-receiver, there is often an integration to be made within one or both of the individuals concerned. There are often two dissociated paths in the individual; if you are clever enough to recognize these, you can sometimes forestall a Freudian conflict, make the integration appear before there is an acute stage. . . .

Business administration has often to consider how to deal with the dissociated paths in individuals or groups, but the methods of doing this successfully have been developed much further in some departments than in others. We have as yet hardly recognized this as part of the technique of dealing with employees, yet the clever salesman knows that it is the chief part of his job. The prospective buyer wants the article and does not want it. The able salesman does not suppress the arguments in the mind of the purchaser against buying, for then the purchaser might be sorry afterwards for his purchase, and that would not be good salesmanship. Unless he can unite, integrate, in the purchaser's mind, the reasons for buying and the reasons for not buying, his future sales will be imperiled, he will not be the highest grade salesman.

Please note that this goes beyond what the psychologist whom I quoted at the beginning of this section told us. He said, "the salesman must create in you the attitude that you want his article." Yes, but only if he creates this attitude by integration, not by suppression.

Apply all this to orders. An order often leaves the individual to whom it is given with two dissociated paths; an order should seek to unite, to integrate, dissociated paths. Court decisions often settle arbitrarily which of two ways is to be followed without showing a possible integration of the two, that is, the individual is often left with an internal conflict on his hands. This is what both courts and business administration should try to prevent, the internal conflicts of individuals or groups. . . .

. . . Probably more industrial trouble has been caused by the manner in which orders are given than in any other way. In the *Report on Strikes and Lockouts*, a British government publication, the cause of a number of strikes is given as "alleged harassing conduct of the foreman," "alleged tyrannical conduct of an under-foreman," "alleged overbearing conduct of officials." The explicit statement, however, of the tyranny of superior officers as the direct cause of strikes is I should say, unusual, yet resentment smoulders and breaks out in other issues. And the demand for better treatment is often explicit enough. We find it made by the metal and woodworking trades in an aircraft factory, who declared that any treatment of men without regard to their feelings of self-respect would be answered by a stoppage of work. We find it put in certain agreements with employers that "the men must be treated with proper respect, and threats and abusive language must not be used."

What happens to man, *in* a man, when an order is given in a disagreeable manner by foreman, head of department, his immediate superior in store, bank or factory? The man addressed feels that his self-respect is attacked, that one of his most inner sanctuaries is invaded. He loses his temper or becomes sullen or is on the defensive; he begins thinking of his "rights"—a fatal attitude for any of us. In the language we have been using, the wrong behavior pattern is aroused, the wrong motor-set; that is, he is now "set" to act in a way which is not going to benefit the enterprise in which he is engaged.

There is a more subtle psychological point here, too; the more you are "bossed" the more your activity of thought will take place within the bossing-pattern, and your part in that pattern seems usually to be opposition to the bossing.

This complaint of the abusive language and the tyrannical treatment of the one just above the worker is an old story to us all, but there is an opposite extreme which is far too little considered. The immediate superior officer is often so close to the worker that he does not exercise the proper duties of his position. Far from taking on himself an aggressive authority, he has often evaded one of the chief problems of his job: how to do what is implied in the fact that he has been put in a position over others. . . .

Now what is our problem here? How can we avoid the two extremes: too great bossism in giving orders, and practically no orders given? I am going to ask how *you* are avoiding these extremes. My solution is to depersonalize the giving of orders, to unite all concerned in a study of the situation, to discover the law of the situation and obey that. Until we do this I do not think we shall have the most successful business administration. This is what does take place, what has to take place, when there is a question between two men in positions of equal authority. The head of the sales departments does not give orders to the head of the production department, or vice versa. Each studies the market and the final decision is made as the market demands. This is, ideally, what should take place between foreman and rank and file, between any head and his subordinates. One *person* should not give orders to another *person*, but both should agree to take their orders from the situation. If orders are simply part of the situation, the question of someone giving and someone receiving does not come up. Both accept the orders given by the situation. Employers accept the orders given by the situation; employees accept the orders given by the situation. This gives, does it not, a slightly different aspect to the whole of business administration through the entire plant?

We have here, I think, one of the largest contributions of scientific management: it tends to depersonalize orders. From one point of view, one might call the essence of scientific management the attempt to find the law of the situation. With scientific management the managers are as much under orders as the workers, for both obey the law of the situation. Our job is not how to get people to obey orders, but how to devise methods by which we can best *discover* the order integral to a particular situation. When that is found, the employee can issue it to the employer, as well as employer to employee. This often happens easily and naturally. My cook or my stenographer points out the law of the situation, and I, if I recognize it as such, accept it, even although it may reverse some "order" I have given.

If those in supervisory positions should depersonalize orders, then there would be no overbearing authority on the one hand, nor on the other that dangerous *laissez-aller* which comes from the fear of exercising authority. Of course we should exercise authority, but always the authority of the situation. I do not say that we have found the way to a frictionless existence, far from it, but we now understand the place which we mean to give to friction. . . .

I call it depersonalizing because there is not time to go any further into the matter. I think it really is a matter of *repersonalizing*. We, persons, have relations with each other, but we should find them in and through the whole situation. We cannot have any sound relations with each other as long as we take them out of that setting which gives them their meaning and value. This divorcing of persons and the situation does a great deal of harm. I have just said that scientific management depersonalizes; the deeper philosophy of scientific management shows us personal relations within the whole setting of that thing of which they are a part. . . .

I said above that we should substitute for the long-distance order the face-to-face suggestion. I think we can now see a more cogent reason for this than the one then given. It is not the face-to-face suggestion that we want so much as the joint study of the problem, and such joint study can be made best by the employee and his immediate superior or employee and special expert on that question.

I began this talk by emphasizing the advisability of preparing in advance the attitude necessary for the carrying out of orders, as in the previous paper we considered preparing the attitude for integration; but we have now, in our consideration of the joint study of situations, in our emphasis on obeying the law of the situation, perhaps got a little beyond that, or rather we have now to consider in what sense we wish to take the psychologist's doctrine of prepared-in-advance attitudes. . . .

We should not try to create the attitude we *want*, although that is the usual phrase, but the attitude required for cooperative study and decision. This holds good even for the salesman. We said above that when the salesman is told that he should create in the prospective buyer the attitude that he wants the article, he ought also to be told that he should do this by integration rather than by suppression. We have now a hint of *how* he is to attain this integration.

I have spoken of the importance of changing some of the language of business personnel relations. We considered whether the words "grievances," "complaints," or Ford's "trouble specialists" did not arouse the wrong behaviour-patterns. I think "order" certainly does. If that word is not to mean any longer external authority, arbitrary authority, but the law of the situation, then we need a new word for it. It is often the order that people resent as much as the thing ordered. People do not like to be ordered even to take a holiday. I have often seen instances of this. The wish to govern one's own life is, of course, one of the most fundamental feelings in every human being. To call this "the instinct of self-assertion," "the instinct of initiative," does not express it wholly. . . .

We have here something far more profound than "the egoistic impulse" or "the instinct of self-assertion." We have the very essence of the human being.

This subject of orders has led us into the heart of the whole question of authority and consent. When we conceive of authority and consent as parts of an inclusive situation, does that not throw a flood of light on this question? The point of view here presented gets rid of several dilemmas which have seemed to puzzle people in dealing with consent. The feeling of being "under" someone, of "subordination," of "servility," of being "at the will of another," comes out again and again in the shop stewards movement and in the testimony before the Coal Commission. One man said before the Coal Commission, "It is all right to work *with* anyone; what is disagreeable is to feel too distinctly that you are working *under* anyone." *With* is a pretty good preposition, not because it connotes democracy, but because it connotes functional unity, a much more profound conception than that of democracy as usually held. The study of the situation involves the *with* preposition. . . .

Twice I have had a servant applying for a place ask me if she would be treated as a menial. When the first woman asked me that, I had no idea what she meant, I thought perhaps she did not want to do the roughest work, but later I came to the conclusion that to be treated as a menial meant to be obliged to be under someone, to follow orders without using one's own judgment. If we believe that what heightens self-respect increases efficiency, we shall be on our guard here.

Very closely connected with this is the matter of pride in one's work. If an order goes against what the craftsman or the clerk thinks is the way of doing his work which will bring the best results, he is justified in not wishing to obey that order. Could not that difficulty be met by a joint study of the situation? It is said that it is characteristic of the British workman to feel, "I know my job and won't be told how." The peculiarities of the British workman might be met by a joint study of the situation, it being understood that he probably has more to contribute to that study than anyone else. . . .

There is another dilemma which has to be met by everyone who is in what is called a position of authority: how can you expect people merely to obey orders and at the same time to take that degree of responsibility which they should take? Indeed, in my experience, the people who enjoy following orders blindly, without any thought on their own part, are those who like thus to get rid of responsibility. But the taking of responsibility, each according to his capacity, each according to his function in the whole . . . , this taking of responsibility is usually the most vital matter in the life of every human being, just as the allotting of responsibility is the most important part of business administration.

A young trade unionist said to me, "How much dignity can I have as a mere employee?" He can have all the dignity in the world if he is allowed to make his fullest contribution to the plant *and to assume definitely the responsibility therefor.*

I think one of the gravest problems before us is how to make the reconciliation between receiving orders and taking responsibility. And I think the reconciliation can be made through our conception of the law of the situation. . . .

We have considered the subject of symbols. It is often very apparent that an order is a symbol. The referee in the game stands watch in hand, and says "Go." It is an order, but order only as symbol. I may say to an employee, "Do so and so," but I should say it only because we have both agreed, openly or tacitly, that that which I am ordering done is the best thing to be done. The order is then a symbol. And if it is a philosophical and psychological truth that we owe obedience only to a functional unity to which we are contributing, we should remember that a more accurate way of stating that would be to say that our obligation is to a unifying, to a process.

This brings us now to one of our most serious problems in this matter of orders. It is important, but we can touch on it only briefly; it is what we spoke of . . . as the evolving situation. I am trying to show here that the order must be integral to the situation and must be recognized as such. But we saw that the situation was always developing. If the situation is never stationary, then the order should never be stationary, so to speak; how to prevent it from being so is our problem. The situation is changing while orders are being carried out, because, by and through orders being carried out. How is the order to keep up with the situation? External orders never can, only those drawn fresh from the situation.

Moreover, if taking a *responsible* attitude toward experience involves recognizing the evolving situation, a *conscious* attitude toward experience means that we note the change which the developing situation makes in ourselves; the situation does not change without changing us. . . .

. . . When I asked a very intelligent girl what she thought would be the result of profit sharing and employee representation in the factory where she worked, she replied joyfully, "We shan't need foremen any more." While her entire ignoring of the fact that the foreman has other duties than keeping workers on their jobs was amusing, one wants to go beyond one's amusement and find out what this objection to being watched really means. . . .

I have seen similar instances cited. Many workmen feel that being watched is unbearable. What can we do about it? How can we get proper supervision without this watching which a worker resents? Supervision is necessary; supervision is resented—how are we going to make the integration there? Some say "Let the workers elect the supervisors." I do not believe in that.

There are . . . other points closely connected with the subject of this paper which I should like merely to point out. First, when and how do you point out mistakes, misconduct? One principle can surely guide us here: don't blame for the sake of blaming, make what you have to say accomplish something; say it in that form, at that time, under those circumstances, which will make it a real education to your subordinate. Secondly, since it is recognized that the one who gives the orders is not as a rule a very popular person, the management sometimes tries to offset this by allowing the person who has this onus upon him to give any pleasant news to the workers, to have the credit of any innovation which the workers very much desire. One manager told me that he always tried to do this. I suppose that this is good behaviouristic psychology, and yet I am not sure that it is a method I wholly like. It is quite different, however, in the case of a mistaken order having been given; then I think the one who made the mistake should certainly be the one to rectify it, not as a matter of strategy, but because it is better for him too. . . .

2 The Executive Functions

Chester I. Barnard

The coordination of efforts essential to a system of cooperation requires, as we have seen, an organization system of communication. Such a system of communication implies centers or points of interconnection and can only operate as these centers are occupied by persons who are called executives. It might be said, then, that the function of executives is to serve as channels of communication so far as communications must pass through central positions. But since the object of the communication system is coordination of all aspects of organization, it follows that the functions of executives relate to all the work essential to the vitality and endurance of an organization, so far, at least, as it must be accomplished through formal coordination.

The executive functions serve to maintain a system of cooperative effort. They are impersonal. The functions are not, as so frequently stated, to manage a group of persons. I do not think a correct understanding of executive work can be had if this narrower, convenient, but strictly speaking erroneous, conception obtains. It is not even quite correct to say that the executive functions are to manage the system of cooperative efforts. As a whole it is managed by itself, not by the executive organization, which is a part of it. The functions with which we are concerned are like those of the nervous system, including the brain, in relation to the rest of the body. It exists to maintain the bodily system by directing those actions which are necessary more effectively to adjust to the environment, but it can hardly be said to manage the body, a large part of whose functions are independent of it and upon which it in turn depends.

The essential executive functions, as I shall present them, correspond to the elements of organization. . . .

They are, first, to provide the system of communication; second, to promote the securing of essential efforts; and, third, to formulate and define purpose. Since the elements of organization are interrelated and interdependent, the executive functions are so likewise; nevertheless they are subject to considerable specialization and as functions are to a substantial degree separable in practice. We shall deal with them only as found in complex, though not necessarily large, organizations.

I. THE MAINTENANCE OF ORGANIZATION COMMUNICATION

We have noticed in previous chapters that, when a complex of more than one unit is in question, centers of communication and corresponding executives are necessary. The need of a definite system of communication creates the first task

Source: Reprinted by permission of the publishers from *The Functions of the Executive* by Chester I. Barnard, Cambridge, Massachusetts: Harvard University Press, Copyright © 1938, 1968 by the President and Fellows of Harvard College; © 1966 by Grace F. Noera Barnard.

of the organizer and is the immediate origin of executive organization. If the purpose of an organization is conceived initially in the mind of one person, he is likely very early to find necessary the selection of lieutenants; and if the organization is spontaneous its very first task is likely to be the selection of a leader. Since communication will be accomplished only through the agency of persons, the selection of persons for executive functions is the concrete method of establishing the *means* of communication, though it must be immediately followed by the creation of positions, that is, a *system* of communication; and, especially in established organizations, the positions will exist to be filled in the event of vacancies. . . .

Therefore, the problem of the establishment and maintenance of the system of communication, that is, the primary task of the executive organization, is perpetually that of obtaining the coalescence of the two phases, executive personnel and executive positions. Each phase in turn is the strategic factor of the executive problem—first one, then the other phase, must be adjusted. This is the central problem of the executive functions. Its solution is not in itself sufficient to accomplish the work of all these functions; but no others can be accomplished without it, and none well unless it is well done. . . .

1. The Scheme of Organization

Let us call the first phase of the function—the definition of organization positions—the "scheme of organization." This is the aspect of organization which receives relatively excessive formal attention because it can apparently be reduced to organization charts, specifications of duties, and descriptions of divisions of labor, etc. It rests upon or represents a coordination chiefly of the work to be done by the organization, that is, its purposes broken up into subsidiary purposes, specializations, tasks, etc., which will be discussed in [the third section] of this chapter; the kind and quantity of *services* of personnel that can be obtained; the kind and quantity of *persons* that must be included in the cooperative system for this purpose; the inducements that are required; and the places at which and the times when these factors can be combined, which will not be specifically discussed here.

It is evident that these are mutually dependent factors, and that they all involve other executive functions which we shall discuss later. So far as the *scheme* of organization is separately attacked, it is always on the assumption that it is then the strategic factor, the other factors of organization remaining fixed for the time being; but since the underlying purpose of any change in a scheme of organization is to affect these other factors as a whole favorably, any scheme of organization at any given time represents necessarily a result of previous successive approximations through a period of time. It has always necessarily to be attacked on the basis of the present situation.

2. Personnel

The scheme of organization is dependent not only upon the general factors of the organizations as a whole, but likewise, as we have indicated, on the availability of various kinds of services for the executive positions. This becomes in its turn the strategic factor. In general, the principles of the economy of incentives apply here as well as to other more general personnel problems. The balance of factors and the technical problems of this special class, however, are not only different from those generally to be found in other spheres of organization economy but are highly special in different types of organizations.

The most important single contribution required of the executive, certainly the most universal qualification, is loyalty, domination by the organization personality. This is the first necessity because the lines of communication cannot function at all unless the personal contributions of executives will be present at the required positions, at the times necessary, without default or ordinary personal reasons. This, as a personal qualification, is known in secular organizations as the quality of "responsibility"; in political organizations as "regularity"; in governmental organizations as "complete submission" to the faith and to the hierarchy of objective religious authority.

The contribution of personal loyalty and submission is least susceptible to tangible inducements. It cannot be bought either by material inducements or by other positive incentives, except all other things be equal. This is as true of industrial organizations, I believe, as of any others. It is rather generally understood that although money or other material inducements must usually be paid to responsible persons, responsibility itself does not arise from such inducements.

However, love of prestige is, in general, a much more important inducement in the case of executives than with the rest of the personnel. Interest in work and pride in organization are other incentives that usually must be present. These facts are much obscured as respects commercial organizations, where material inducements appear to be the effective factors partly because such inducements are more readily offered in such organizations and partly because, since the other incentives are often equal as between such organizations, material inducements are the only available differential factor. It also becomes an important secondary factor to individuals in many cases, because prestige and official responsibilities impose heavy material burdens on them. Hence neither churches nor socialistic states have been able to escape the necessity of direct or indirect material inducements for high dignitaries or officials. But this is probably incidental and superficial in all organizations. It appears to be true that in all of them adequate incentives to executive services are difficult to offer. Those most available in the present age are tangible, materialistic; but on the whole they are both insufficient and often abortive.[1]

Following loyalty, responsibility, and capacity to be dominated by organization personality, come the more specific personal abilities. They are roughly divided into two classes: relatively general abilities, involving general alertness, comprehensiveness of interest, flexibility, faculty of adjustment, poise, courage, etc.; and specialized abilities based on particular aptitudes and acquired techniques. The first kind is relatively difficult to appraise because it depends upon innate characteristics developed through general experience. It is not greatly susceptible of immediate inculcation. The second kind may be less rare because the division of labor, that is, organization itself, fosters it automatically, and because it is susceptible to development (at a

[1] After much experience, I am convinced that the most ineffective services in a continuing effort are in one sense those of volunteers, or of semi-volunteers; for example, half-pay workers. What appears to be inexpensive is in fact very expensive, because non-material incentives—such as prestige, toleration of too great personal interest in the work with its accompanying fads and "pet" projects, the yielding to exaggerated conceptions of individual importance—are causes of internal friction and many other undesirable consequences. Yet in many emergency situations, and in a large part of political, charitable, civic, educational, and religious organization work, often indispensable services cannot be obtained by material incentives.

cost) by training and education. We deliberately and more and more turn out specialists; but we do not develop general executives well by specific efforts, and we know very little about how to do it.

The higher the positions in the line of authority, the more general the abilities required. The scarcity of such abilities, together with the necessity for keeping the lines of authority as short as feasible, controls the organization of executive work. It leads to the reduction of the number of formally executive positions to the minimum, a measure made possible by creating about the executives in many cases staffs of specialists who supplement them in time, energy, and technical capacities. This is made feasible by elaborate and often delicate arrangements to correct errors resulting from the faults of over-specialization and the paucity of line executives. . . .

Thus, jointly with the development of the scheme of organization, the selection, promotion, demotion, and dismissal of men becomes the essence of maintaining the system of communication without which no organization can exist. The selection in part, but especially the promotion, demotion, and dismissal of men, depend upon the exercise of supervision or what is often called "control."

Control relates directly, and in conscious application chiefly, to the work of the organization as a whole rather than to the work of executives as such. But so heavily dependent is the success of cooperation upon the functioning of the executive organization that practically the control is over executives for the most part. If the work of an organization is not successful, if it is inefficient, if it cannot maintain the services of its personnel, the conclusion is that its "management" is wrong; that is, that the scheme of communication or the associated personnel or both, that is, the executive department directly related, are at fault. This is, sometimes at least, not true, but often it is. Moreover, for the correction of such faults the first reliance is upon executive organization. The methods by which control is exercised are, of course, numerous and largely technical to each organization, and need not be further discussed here.

3. Informal Executive Organizations

The general method of maintaining an informal executive organization is so to operate and to select and promote executives that a general condition of compatibility of personnel is maintained. Perhaps often and certainly occasionally men cannot be promoted or selected, or even must be relieved, because they cannot function, because they "do not fit," where there is no question of formal competence. This question of "fitness" involves such matters as education, experience, age, sex, personal distinctions, prestige, race, nationality, faith, politics, sectional antecedents; and such very special personal traits as manners, speech, personal appearance, etc. It goes by few if any rules, except those based at least nominally on other, formal, considerations. It represents in its best sense the political aspects of personal relationship in formal organization. I suspect it to be most highly developed in political, labor, church, and university organizations, for the very reason that the intangible types of personal services are relatively more important in them than in most other, especially industrial, organizations. But it is certainly of major importance in all organizations.

This compatibility is promoted by educational requirements (armies, navies, churches, schools); by requirement of certain background (European armies, navies, labor unions, Soviet and Fascist governments, political parties); by conferences and conventions; by specifically social activities; by class distinctions connected with privileges and "authority" (in armies, navies, churches, universities). A certain conformity is required by unwritten understanding that can sometimes be formally enforced, expressed for its negative aspect by the phrase "conduct unbecoming a gentleman and an officer." There are, however, innumerable other processes, many of which are not consciously employed for this purpose.

It must not be understood that the desired degree of compatibility is always the same or is the maximum possible. On the contrary it seems to me to be often the case that excessive compatibility or harmony is deleterious, resulting in "single track minds" and excessively crystallized attitudes and in the destruction of personal responsibility; but I know from experience in operating with new emergency organizations, in which there was no time and little immediate basis for the growth of an informal organization properly coordinated with formal organization, that it is almost impossible to secure effective and efficient cooperation without it.

The functions of informal executive organizations are the communication of intangible facts, opinions, suggestions, suspicions, that cannot pass through formal channels without raising issues calling for decisions, without dissipating dignity and objective authority, and without overloading executive positions; also to minimize excessive cliques of political types arising from too great divergence of interests and views; to promote self-discipline of the group; and to make possible the development of important personal influences in the organization. There are probably other functions.

I shall comment on only two functions of informal executive organization. The necessity for avoiding formal issues, that is, for avoiding the issuance of numerous formal orders except on routine matters and except in emergencies, is important.[2] I know of major executives who issue an order or judgement settling an important issue rather seldom, although they are functioning all the time. The obvious desire of politicians to avoid important issues (and to impose them on their opponents) is based upon a thorough sense of organization. Neither authority nor cooperative disposition (largely the same things) will stand much overt division on formal issues in the present stage of human development. Hence most laws, executive orders, decisions, etc., are in effect formal notice that all is well—there is agreement, authority is not questioned.

The question of personal influence is very subtle. Probably most good organizations have somewhere a Colonel House; and many men not only exercise beneficent influence far beyond that implied by their formal status, but most of them, at the time, would lose their influence if they had corresponding formal status. The reason may be that many men have personal qualifications of high order that will not operate under the stress of commensurate official responsibility. By analogy I may mention the golfers of first class skill who cannot "stand up" in public tournaments. . . .

II. THE SECURING OF ESSENTIAL SERVICES FROM INDIVIDUALS

The second function of the executive organization is to promote the securing

[2] When writing these lines I tried to recall an important general decision made by me on my initiative as a telephone executive within two years. I could recall none, although on reviewing the record I found several. On the other hand, I can still recall without any record many major decisions made by me "out of hand" when I was a Relief Administrator. I probably averaged at least five a day for eighteen months. In the latter case I worked with a very noble group but a very poor informal organization under emergency conditions.

of the personal services that constitute the material of organizations.

The work divides into two main divisions: (I) the bringing of persons into cooperative relationship with the organization; (II) the eliciting of the services after such persons have been brought into that relationship.

1.

The characteristic fact of the first division is that the organization is acting upon persons who are in every sense outside it. Such action is necessary not merely to secure the personnel of new organizations, or to supply the material for the growth of existing organizations, but also to replace the losses that continually take place by reason of death, resignation, "backsliding," emigration, discharge, excommunication, ostracism. These factors of growth or replacement of contributors require bringing persons by organization effort within range of the consideration of the incentives available in order to induce some of these persons to attach themselves to the organization. Accordingly the task involves two parts: (*a*) bringing persons within reach of specific effort to secure services, and (*b*) the application of that effort when they have been brought near enough. Often both parts of the task occupy the efforts of the same persons or parts of an organization; but they are clearly distinct elements and considerable specialization is found with respect to them.

(*a*) Bringing persons within reach of recruiting or proselyting influence is a task which differs in practical emphasis among organizations in respect both to scope and to method. Some religious organizations—especially the Catholic Church, several Protestant Churches, the Mormon Church, for example—have as ideal goals the attachment of all persons to their organizations, and the wide world is the field of proselyting propaganda. During many decades the United States of America invited all who could reach its shores to become American citizens. Other organizations, having limits on the volume of their activities, restrict the field of propaganda. Thus many nations in effect now restrict substantial growth to those who acquire a national status by birth; the American Legion restricts its membership to those who have acquired a status by certain type of previous service, etc. Others restrict their fields practically on the basis of proportions. Thus universities "in principle" are open to all or to all with educational and character qualifications but may restrict their appeals to geographical, racial, and class proportions so as to preserve the cosmopolitan character of their bodies, or to preserve predominance of nationals, etc. Industrial and commercial organizations are theoretically limited usually by considerations of social compatibility and additionally by the costs of propaganda. They usually attempt no appeal when the geographic remoteness makes it ineffective. . . .

(*b*) The effort to induce specific persons who by the general appeal are brought into contact with an organization actually to become identified with it constitutes the more regular and routine work of securing contributors. This involves in its general aspects the method of persuasion which has already been described, the establishment of inducements and incentives, and direct negotiation. The methods required are indefinitely large in number and of very wide variety. . . .[3]

[3] I must repeat that although the emphasis is on the employee group of contributors, so far as industrial organizations are concerned, nevertheless "customers" are equally included. The principles broadly discussed here relate to salesmanship as well as employing persons.

2.
Although the work of recruiting is important in most organizations, and especially so in those which are new or rapidly expanding or which have high "turnover," nevertheless in established and enduring organizations the eliciting of the quantity and quality of efforts from their adherents is usually more important and occupies the greater part of personnel effort. Because of the more tangible character of "membership," being an "employee," etc., recruiting is apt to receive more attention as a field of personnel work than the business of promoting the actual output of efforts and influences, which are the real material of organization.[4] Membership, nominal adherence, is merely the starting point; and the minimum contributions which can be conceived as enabling retention of such connection would generally be insufficient for the survival of active or productive organization. . . . In short, every organization to survive must deliberately attend to the maintenance and growth of its authority to do the things necessary for coordination, effectiveness, and efficiency. This, as we have seen, depends upon its appeal to persons who are already related to the organization. . . .

III. THE FORMULATION OF PURPOSE AND OBJECTIVES

The third executive function is to formulate and define the purposes, objectives, ends, of the organization. It has already been made clear that, strictly speaking, purpose is defined more nearly by the aggregate of action taken than by any formulation in words; but that the aggregate of action is a residuum of the decisions relative to purpose and the environment, resulting in closer and closer approximations to the concrete acts. It has also been emphasized that purpose is something that must be accepted by all the contributors to the system of efforts. Again, it has been stated that purpose must be broken into fragments, specific objectives, not only ordered in time so that detailed purpose and detailed action follow in the series of progressive cooperation, but also ordered contemporaneously into the specializations—geographical, social, and functional—that each unit organization implies. It is more apparent here than with other executive functions that it is an entire executive organization that formulates, redefines, breaks into details, and decides on the innumerable simultaneous and progressive actions that are the stream of syntheses constituting purpose or action. No single executive can under any conditions accomplish this function alone, but only that part of it which relates to his position in the executive organization.

Hence the critical aspect of this function is the assignment of responsibility—the delegation of objective authority. Thus in one sense this function is that of the scheme of positions, the system of communication, already discussed. That is its potential aspect. Its other aspect is the actual decisions and conduct which make the scheme a working system. Accordingly, the general executive states that "this is the purpose, this the objective, this the direction, in general terms, in which we wish to move, before next year." His department heads, or the heads of his main territorial divisions, say to their departments or suborganizations: "This means for us these things now, then others next month, then others later, to be better defined after experience." Their subdepartment

[4] As an instance, note the great attention in civil service regulations, and also in political appointments, to obtaining and retaining employment, and the relatively small attention to services.

or division heads say: "This means for us such and such operations now at these places, such others at those places, something today here, others tomorrow there." Then district or bureau chiefs in turn become more and more specific, their sub-chiefs still more so. . . .

The formulation and definition of purpose is then a widely distributed function only the more general part of which is executive. In this fact lies the most important inherent difficulty in the operation of cooperative systems—the necessity for indoctrinating those at the lower levels with general purposes, the major decisions, so that they remain cohesive and able to make the ultimate detailed decisions coherent; and the necessity, for those at the higher levels, of constantly understanding the concrete conditions and the specific decisions of the "ultimate" contributors from which and from whom executives are often insulated. Without that up-and-down-the-line coordination of purposeful decisions, general decisions and general purposes are mere intellectual processes in an organization vacuum, insulated from realities by layers of misunderstanding. The function of formulating grand purposes and providing for their redefinition is one which needs sensitive systems of communication, experience in interpretation, imagination, and delegation of responsibility.

Perhaps there are none who could consider even so extremely condensed and general a description of the executive functions as has here been presented without perceiving that these functions are merely elements in an organic whole. It is their combination in a working system that makes an organization.

This combination involves two opposite incitements to action. First, the concrete interaction and mutual adjustment of the executive functions are partly to be determined by the factors of the environment of the organization—the specific cooperative system as a whole and its environment. This involves fundamentally the logical processes of analysis and the discrimination of the strategic factors. . . .

3

Life Cycle Theory of Leadership

Paul Hersey and Kenneth H. Blanchard

The recognition of task and relationships as two important dimensions of leader behavior has pervaded the works of management theorists[1] over the years. These two dimensions have been variously labeled as "autocratic" and "democratic"; "authoritarian" and "equalitarian"; "employee-oriented" and "production-oriented"; "goal achievement" and "group maintenance"; "taskability" and "likeability"; "instrumental" and "expressive"; "efficiency" and "effectiveness." The difference between these concepts and task and relationships seems to be more semantic than real. . . .

OHIO STATE LEADERSHIP STUDIES

In more recent years, the feeling that task and relationships were either/or leadership styles has been dispelled. In particular, the leadership studies initiated in 1945 by the Bureau of Business Research at Ohio State University[2] questioned whether leader behavior could be depicted on a single continuum.

In attempting to describe *how* a leader carries out his activities, the Ohio State staff identified "Initiating Structure" (task) and "Consideration" (relationships) as the two most important dimensions of leadership. "Initiating Structure" refers to "the leader's behavior in delineating the relationship between himself and members of the work-group and in endeavoring to establish well-defined patterns of organization, channels of communication, and methods of procedure." On the other hand, "Consideration" refers to "behavior indicative of friendship, mutual trust, respect, and warmth in the relationship between the leader and the members of his staff."[3]

In the leadership studies that followed, the Ohio State staff found that leadership styles vary considerably from leader to leader. The behavior of some leaders is characterized by rigidly structuring activities of followers in terms of *task* accomplishments, while others concentrate on building and maintaining good personal *relationships* between themselves and their followers. Other leaders have styles characterized by both task and relationships behavior. There are even some individuals in leadership positions whose behavior tends to provide little structure or development of interpersonal relationships. No dominant style appears. Instead, various combinations are evident. Thus, task and relationships are not either/or leadership styles as an authoritarian-democratic continuum suggests. Instead, these patterns of leader behavior are separate and distinct dimensions which can be plotted on two separate axes, rather than a single continuum. Thus, the Ohio State studies resulted in the development of

Source: This article is reprinted as originally presented in the May 1969 issue of *Training and Development Journal*. The model has been updated several times since 1969. The current information is available from The Center for Leadership Studies, Inc., Escondido, California. Used by permission.

FIGURE 1 • THE OHIO STATE LEADERSHIP QUADRANTS

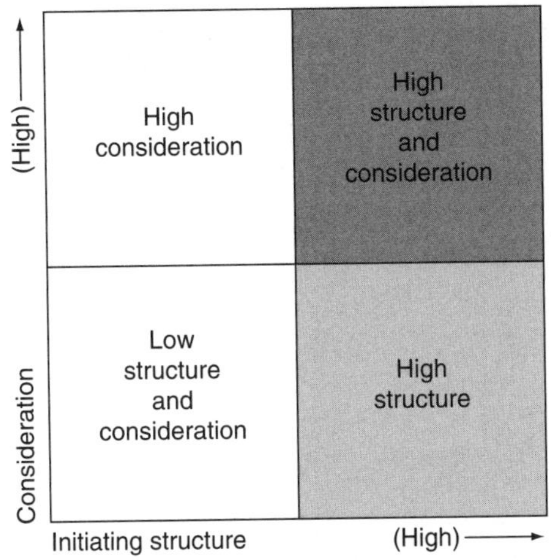

(High) ↑ Consideration		
	High consideration	High structure and consideration
	Low structure and consideration	High structure
	Initiating structure	(High) →

four quadrants to illustrate leadership styles in terms of Initiating Structure (task) and Consideration (relationships) as shown in Figure 1.

THE MANAGERIAL GRID

Robert R. Blake and Jane S. Mouton[4] in their Managerial Grid have popularized the task and relationships dimensions of leadership and have used them extensively in organization and management development programs.

In the Managerial Grid [Figure 2], five different types of leadership based on concern for production (task) and concern for people (relationships) are located in the four quadrants identified by the Ohio State studies.

Concern for *production* is illustrated on the horizontal axis. Production becomes more important to the leader as his rating advances on the horizontal scale. A leader with a rating of 9 has a maximum concern for production.

Concern for people is illustrated on the vertical axis. People become more important to the leader as his rating progresses up the vertical axis. A leader with a rating of 9 on the vertical axis has a maximum concern for people.

The Managerial Grid, in essence, has given popular terminology to five points within the four quadrants identified by the Ohio State studies.

SUGGESTING A "BEST" STYLE OF LEADERSHIP

After identifying task and relationships as two central dimensions of any leadership situation, some management writers have suggested a "best" style of leadership. Most of these writers have supported either an integrated leader behavior style (high task and high relationships) or a permissive, democratic, human relations approach (high relationships).

Andrew W. Halpin,[5] of the original Ohio State staff, in a study of school superintendents, pointed out that according to his findings "effective or desirable leadership behavior is characterized by high ratings on both Initiating Structure and Consideration. Conversely,

FIGURE 2 • THE MANAGERIAL GRID LEADERSHIP STYLES

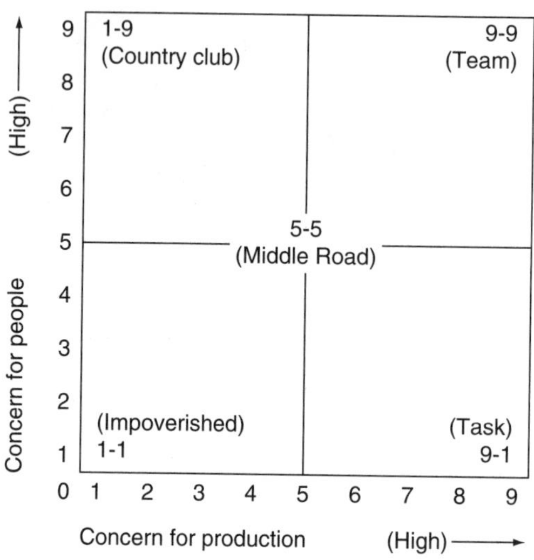

ineffective or undesirable leadership behavior is marked by low ratings on both dimensions." Thus, Halpin seemed to conclude that the high Consideration and high Initiating Structure style is theoretically the ideal or "best" leader behavior, while the style low on both dimensions is theoretically the "worst."

Blake and Mouton in their Managerial Grid also imply that the most desirable leadership style is "team management" (maximum concern for production and people) and the least desirable is "impoverished management" (minimum concern for production and people). In fact, they have developed training programs designed to change the behavior of managers toward this "team" style.[6]

LEADERSHIP STYLE SHOULD VARY WITH THE SITUATION

Some of the most convincing evidence which dispels the idea of a single "best" style of leader behavior was gathered and published by A. K. Korman[7] in 1966. Korman attempted to review all the studies which examined the relationship between the Ohio State behavior dimensions of Initiating Structure (task) and Consideration (relationships) and various measures of effectiveness, including group productivity, salary, performance under stress, administrative reputation, work group grievances, absenteeism, and turnover. . . .

Thus, Korman found the use of Consideration and Initiating Structure had no significant predictive value in terms of effectiveness as situations changed. *This suggests that since situations differ, so must leader style*.

Fred E. Fiedler,[8] in testing his contingency model of leadership in over fifty studies covering a span of fifteen years (1951–1967), concluded that both directive, task-oriented leaders and nondirective, human relations-oriented leaders are successful under some conditions. . . .

In summary, empirical studies tend to show that there is no normative (best) style of leadership; that successful leaders are those who can adapt their leader behavior to meet the needs of their followers and the particular situation. Effectiveness is dependent upon the leader, the followers, and other situational elements. In managing for effectiveness a leader must be able to diagnose his own leader behavior in light of his environment. Some of the variables other than his followers which he should examine include the organization, superiors, associates, and job demands. This list is not all inclusive, but contains interacting components which used to be important to a leader in many different organizational settings.

ADDING AN EFFECTIVENESS DIMENSION

To measure more accurately how well a leader operates within a given situation, an "effectiveness dimension" should be added to the two-dimension Ohio State model. This is illustrated in Figure 3.

By adding an effectiveness dimension to the Ohio State model, a three-dimensional model is created.[9] This Leader Effectiveness Model attempts to integrate the concepts of leader style with situational demands of a specific environment. When the leader's style is appropriate in a given environment measured by results, it is termed *effective;* when his style is inappropriate to a given environment, it is termed *ineffective*.

If a leader's effectiveness is determined by the interaction of his style and environment (followers and other situational variables), it follows that any of the four styles depicted in the Ohio State model may be effective or ineffective depending on the environment. . . .

While a high task style might be effective for a combat officer, it might not be effective in other situations even within the military. This was pointed out when the officers trained at West Point were sent to command outposts in the Dew Line, which was part of an advanced warning system. The scientific personnel involved, living in close quarters in an Arctic region, did not respond favorably to the task-oriented behavior of these combat trained officers. The level of education and maturity of these people was such that they did not need a great deal of structure in their work. In fact, they tended to resent it.

FIGURE 3 • ADDING AN EFFECTIVENESS DIMENSION

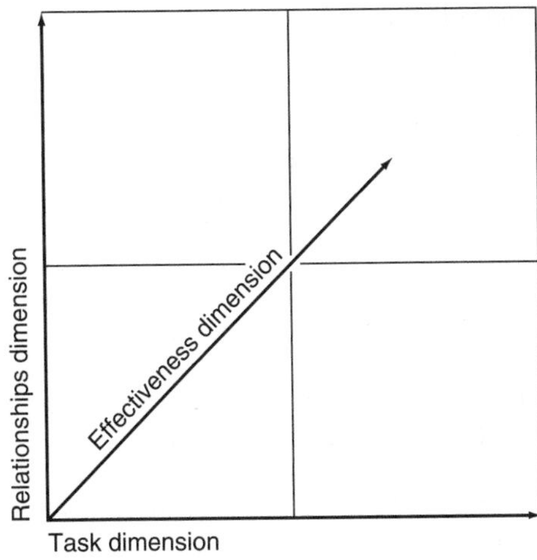

Other studies of scientific and research-oriented personnel show also that many of these people desire, or need, only a limited amount of socio-emotional support. Therefore, there are situations in which the low task and relationships style, which has been assumed by some authors to be theoretically a poor leadership style, may be an appropriate style.

In summary, an effective leader must be able to *diagnose* the demands of the environment and then either *adapt* his leader style to fit these demands, or develop the means to *change* some or all of the other variables.

ATTITUDINAL VS. BEHAVIORAL MODELS

In examining the dimensions of the Managerial Grid (*concern* for production and *concern* for people), one can see that these are attitudinal dimensions. That is, concern is a feeling or emotion toward something. On the other hand, the dimensions of the Ohio State Model (Initiating Structure and Consideration) and the Leader Effectiveness Model (task and relationships) are dimensions of *observed* behavior. Thus, the Ohio State and Leader Effectiveness Models measure *how* people behave, while the Managerial Grid measures *predisposition* toward production and people. As discussed earlier, the Leader Effectiveness Model is an outgrowth of the Ohio State Model but is distinct from it in that it adds an effectiveness dimension to the two dimensions of behavior.

Although the Managerial Grid and the Leader Effectiveness Model measure different aspects of leadership, they are not incompatible. A conflict develops, however, because behavioral assumptions have often been drawn from analysis of the attitudinal dimensions of the Managerial Grid.[10] While high *concern* for both production and people is desirable in many organizations, managers having a high concern for both people and production do not always find it appropriate in all situations to initiate a high degree of structure and provide a high degree of socio-emotional support. . . .

. . . Korman suggests the possibility of a curvilinear relationship rather than a simple linear relationship between Structure and Consideration and other variables. The Life Cycle Theory of Leadership which we have developed is based on a curvilinear relationship between task and relationships and "maturity." This theory will attempt to provide a leader with some understanding of the relationship between an effective style of leadership and the level of maturity of one's followers. The emphasis in the Life Cycle Theory of Leadership will be on the followers. As Fillmore H. Sanford has indicated, there is some justification for regarding the followers, "as the most crucial factor in any leadership event."[11] Followers in any situation are vital, not only because individually they accept or reject the leader, but as a group they actually determine whatever personal power he may have.

According to Life Cycle Theory, as the level of maturity of one's followers continues to increase, appropriate leader behavior not only requires less and less structure (task) but also less and less socio-emotional support (relationships). This cycle can be illustrated in the four quadrants of the basic styles portion of the Leader Effectiveness Model as shown in Figure 4.

Maturity is defined in Life Cycle Theory by the relative independence,[12] ability to take responsibility, and achievement-motivation[13] of an individual or group. These components of maturity are often influenced by level of education and amount of experience.

FIGURE 4 • LIFE CYCLE THEORY OF LEADERSHIP

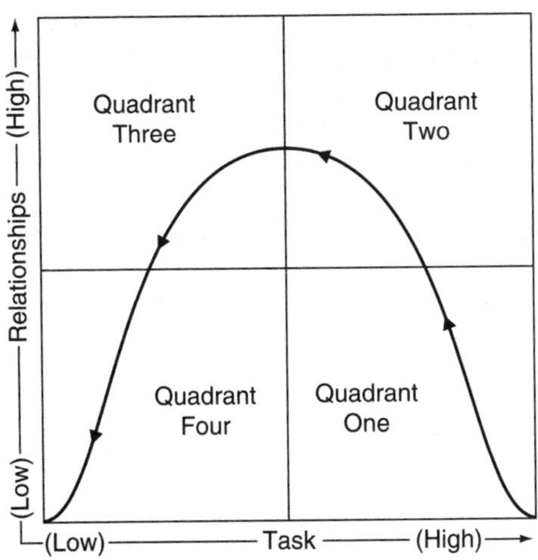

While age is a factor, it is not directly related to maturity as used in the Life Cycle. Our concern is for psychological age, not chronological age. Beginning with structured task behavior which is appropriate for working and immature people, Life Cycle Theory suggests that leader behavior should move from: (1) high task–low relationships behavior to (2) high task–high relationships and (3) high relationships–low task behavior to (4) low task–low relationships behavior, if one's followers progress from immaturity to maturity.

An illustration of this Life Cycle Theory familiar to everyone is the parent-child relationship. As a child begins to mature, it is appropriate for the parent to provide more socio-emotional support and less structure. Experience shows us that if the parent provides too much relationship behavior as rewards before a child is somewhat mature, this behavior is often misinterpreted by the child as permissiveness. Thus it is appropriate to increase one's relationships behavior as the child is able to increase his maturity or capacity to take responsibility. . . .

OTHER ASPECTS OF THE LIFE CYCLE

The parent-child relationship is only one example of the Life Cycle. This cycle is also discernible in other organizations in the interaction between superiors and subordinates. An interesting example is found in Research and Development work. In working with highly trained and educated Research and Development personnel, the most effective leader behavior style might be low task–low relationships. However, during the early stages of a particular project, the director must impose a certain amount of structure as the requirements and limitations of the project are established. Once these limitations are understood, the R&D director moves rapidly through the "*project cycle*" back to the mature low task–low relationships style.

We realize that most groups in our society do not reach the backward bending aspect of the cycle. But there is some evidence that as the level of education and experience of a group increases, appropriate movement in this direction will take place. However, the demands of the job may often be a limiting factor on the development of maturity in workers. For example, an assembly line operation in an automobile plant is so highly structured that it offers little opportunity for the maturing process to occur. With such monotonous tasks, workers are given minimal control over their environment and are often encouraged to be passive, dependent, and subordinate.

LIFE CYCLE AND SPAN OF CONTROL

For years it has been argued by many management writers that one man can *supervise* only a relatively few people; therefore, all managers should have a limited span of control. . . .

. . . Yet the Life Cycle Theory of Leadership suggests that span of control may not depend on the level of the management hierarchy but should be a function of the maturity of the individuals being supervised. The more independent, able to take responsibility, and achievement-motivated one's subordinates are, the more people a manager can supervise. It is theoretically possible to supervise an infinite number of subordinates if everyone is completely mature and able to be responsible for his own job. This does not mean there is less control, but these subordinates are self-controlled rather than externally controlled by their superior. Since people occupying higher level jobs in an organization tend to be more "mature" and therefore need less close supervision than people occupying lower level jobs, it seems reasonable to assume that top managers should be able to supervise more subordinates than their counterparts at lower levels.[14]

CONCLUSIONS

Rensis Likert[15] found in his research that supervisors with the best records of performance were employee-centered (high relationships), while job-centered (high task) supervisors were found more often to have low-producing sections. While this relationship seemed to exist, Likert raised the question of which variable was the causal factor. Is the style of the supervisor causing the level of production or is the level of production encouraging the style of the managers? As Likert suggests, it may very well be that high-producing sections allow for general supervision rather than close supervision and relationship behavior rather than task behavior. The supervisor soon learns that his subordinates are mature enough to structure their own environment, thus leaving him time for other kinds of activities. At the same time a low-producing section may leave the supervisor with no choice but to be job-centered. If he attempted to use a relationships style this may be misunderstood and interpreted as reinforcement for their low level of performance. The point is, the supervisor must change appropriately.

CHANGING STYLE

The problem with the conclusions of Likert and other behavioral scientists comes in implementation. Practitioners read that employee-centered supervisors tend to have higher-producing sections than job-centered supervisors. Wanting to implement these findings overnight, they encourage all supervisors to become more employee-oriented. Consequently, a foreman who has been operating as a task-oriented authoritarian leader for many years may be encouraged to change his style—"get in step with the times." Upon returning from a "human relations" training program, the foreman will probably try to utilize some of the new relationships techniques he has recently been taught. The problem is that his personality is not compatible with the new concepts, but he tries to use them anyway. As long as things are running smoothly, there is no difficulty. However, the minute an important issue or crisis develops he tends to revert to his old basic style and becomes inconsistent, vacillating between the new relationships style he has been taught, and his old task style which has the force of habit behind it.

This idea was supported in a study conducted by the General Electric Company at one of its turbine and generator plants. In this study, the leadership styles of about 90 foremen were analyzed and rated as "democratic," "authoritarian" or "mixed." In discussing the findings, Saul W. Gellerman[16] reported that:

> The lowest morale in the plant was found among those men whose foremen were rated *between* the democratic and authoritarian extremes. The GE research team felt that these foremen might have varied inconsistently in their tactics, permissive at one moment and hard-fisted the next, in a way that left their men frustrated and unable to anticipate how they would be treated. The naturally autocratic supervisor who is exposed to human relations training may behave in exactly such a manner . . . a pattern which will probably make him even harder to work for than he was before being "enlightened."

Thus, changing the style of managers is a difficult process, and one that takes considerable time to accomplish. Expecting miracles overnight will only lead to frustration and uneasiness for both managers and their subordinates. Yet industry invests many millions of dollars annually for training and development programs which concentrate on effecting change in the style of managers. As Fiedler[17] suggests:

> A person's leadership style . . . reflects the individual's basic motivational and need structure. At best it takes one, two, or three years of intensive psychotherapy to effect changes in personality structure. It is difficult to see how we can change in more than a few cases an equally important set of core values in a few hours of lectures and role playing or even in the course of a more intensive training program of one or two weeks.

Fiedler's point is well-taken. It is indeed difficult to effect changes in the styles of managers overnight. However, it is not completely hopeless. But, at best, it is a slow and expensive process which requires creative planning and patience. In fact, Likert[18] found that it takes from three to seven years, depending on the size and complexity of the organization, to effectively implement a new management theory.

CHANGING PERFORMANCE

Not only is it difficult to effect changes in the styles of managers overnight, but the question that we raise is whether it is even appropriate. It is questionable whether a work group whose performance has been continually low would suddenly leap to high productivity with the introduction of an employee-centered supervisor. In fact, they might take advantage of him and view him as a "soft-touch." These workers lack maturity and are not ready for more responsibility. Thus the supervisor must bring them along slowly, becoming more employee-centered and less job-centered as they mature. When an individual's performance is low, one cannot expect drastic changes overnight, regardless of changes in expectations or other incentives. The key is often reinforcing positively "*successive approximations*." By successive approximations we mean behavior which comes closer and closer to the supervisor's expectations of good performance. Similar to the child learning some new behavior, a manager should not expect high levels of performance at the outset. As a parent or teacher, we would use positive reinforcement as the child's behavior approaches the desired level of performance. Therefore, the manager must be aware of any progress of his subordinates so that he is in a position to reinforce appropriately improved performance.

Change through the cycle from quadrant 1 to quadrant 2, 3, and then 4 [Figure 4] must be gradual. This process by its very nature cannot be revolutionary but must be evolutionary—gradual developmental changes, a result of planned growth and the creation of mutual trust and respect.

REFERENCES

1. As examples see the following: Robert F. Bales, "Task Roles and Social Roles in Problem-Solving Groups," in *Readings in Social Psychology*, E. E. Maccoby, T. M. Newcomb and E. L. Hartley (eds.), Holt, Rinehart and Winston, 1958; Chester I. Barnard, *The Functions of the Executive*, Harvard University Press, 1938; Dorwin Cartwright and Alvin Zander (eds.), *Group Dynamics: Research and Theory*, second edition, Row, Peterson and Co., 1960; D. Katz, N. Maccoby, and Nancy C. Morse, *Productivity Supervision, and Morale in an Office Situation*, The Darel Press, Inc., 1950; Talcott Parsons, *The Social System*, The Free Press, 1951.
2. Roger M. Stogdill and Alvin E. Coons (eds.), *Leader Behavior: Its Description and Measurement*, Research Monograph No. 88, Bureau of Business Research, The Ohio State Univ., 1957.
3. Stogdill and Coons, *Leader Behavior . . .* See also Andrew W. Halpin. *The Leadership Behavior of School Superintendents*, Midwest Administration Center, The University of Chicago, 1959.
4. Robert R. Blake and Jane S. Mouton, *The Managerial Grid*, Gulf Publishing, 1964.
5. Halpin, *The Leadership Behavior of School Superintendents*.
6. Robert R. Blake, *et al.*, "Breakthrough in Organization Development," *Harvard Business Review*, Nov.–Dec. 1964.
7. A. K. Korman, "'Consideration,' 'Initiating Structure,' and Organizational Criteria—A Review," *Personnel Psychology: A Journal of Applied Research*, Vol. 19, No. 4 (Winter, 1966), pp. 349–361.
8. Fred E. Fiedler, *A Theory of Leadership Effectiveness*, McGraw-Hill, 1967.
9. Paul Hersey and Kenneth H. Blanchard, *Leader Behavior*, Management Education & Development, Inc., 1967; see also Hersey and Blanchard, *Management of Organizational Behavior: Utilizing Human Resources*, Prentice-Hall, Inc., and William J. Reddin, "The 3-D Management Style Theory," *Training and Development Journal*, Apr. 1967.
10. Fred E. Fiedler in his Contingency Model of Leadership Effectiveness (Fiedler, *A Theory of Leadership Effectiveness*) tends to make behavioral assumptions from data gathered from an attitudinal measure of leadership style. A leader is asked to evaluate his least preferred co-worker (LPC) on a series of Semantic Differential type scales. Leaders are classified as high or low LPC depending on the favorableness with which they rate their LPC.
11. Fillmore H. Sanford, *Authoritarianism and Leadership*, Institute for Research in Human Relations, 1950.
12. Chris Argyris, *Personality and Organization*, Harper & Row, Publishers, Inc., 1957; *Interpersonal Competence and Organizational Effectiveness*, Dorsey Press, 1962; and *Integrating the Individual and the Organization*, Wiley, 1964.
13. David C. McClelland, J. W. Atkinson, R. A. Clark, and E. L. Lowell, *The Achievement Motive*, Appleton-Century-Crofts, Inc., 1953, and *The Achieving Society*, D. Van Nostrand Co., 1961.
14. Support for this discussion is provided by Peter F. Drucker, *The Practice of Management*, Harper & Bros., 1954, pp. 139–40.
15. Rensis Likert, *New Patterns of Management*, McGraw-Hill, 1961.
16. Saul Gellerman, *Motivation and Productivity*, American Management Assn., 1963.
17. Fiedler, *A Theory of Leadership Effectiveness*.
18. Likert, *New Patterns of Management*.

4

The Contingency Model: A Theory of Leadership Effectiveness[1]

Fred E. Fiedler

Leadership, as a problem in social psychology, has dealt primarily with two questions, namely, how one becomes a leader, and how one can become a *good* leader, that is, how one develops effective group performance. Since a number of excellent reviews (e.g., Stogdill, 1948; Gibb, 1954; Mann, 1959; Bass, 1960) have already dealt with the first question we shall not be concerned with it in the present paper.

The second question, whether a given leader will be more or less effective than others in similar situations, has been a more difficult problem of research and has received correspondingly less attention in psychological literature. The theoretical status of the problem is well reflected by Browne and Cohn's (1958) statement that "... leadership literature is a mass of content without coagulating substances to bring it together or to produce coordination. . . ." McGrath (1962), in making a similar point, ascribed this situation to the tendency of investigators to select different variables and to work with idiosyncratic measures and definitions of leadership. He also pointed out, however, that most researchers in this area have gravitated toward two presumably crucial clusters of leadership attitudes and behaviors. These are the critical, directive, autocratic, task oriented versus the democratic, permissive, considerate, person-oriented type of leadership. While this categorization is admittedly oversimplified, the major controversy in this area has been between the more orthodox viewpoint, reflected in traditional supervisory training and military doctrine that the leader should be decisive and forceful, that he should do the planning and thinking for the groups, and that he should coordinate, direct and evaluate his men's actions. The other viewpoint, reflected in the newer human relations oriented training and in the philosophy behind non-directive and brainstorming technique, stresses the need for democratic, permissive, group-oriented leadership techniques. Both schools of thought have strong adherents and there is evidence supporting both points of view (Gibb, 1954; Hare, 1962).

[1] The present paper is mainly based on research conducted under Office of Naval Research Contracts 170–106, N6-ori-07135 (Fred E. Fiedler, Principal Investigator) and RN 177–472, Noor 1834(36). (Fred E. Fiedler, C. E. Osgood, L. M. Stolurow, and H. C. Triandis, Principal Investigators.) The writer is especially indebted to his colleagues, A. R. Bass, L. J. Cronbach, M. Fishbein, J. E. McGrath, W. A. T. Meuwese, C. E. Osgood, H. C. Triandis, and L. R. Tucker, who offered invaluable suggestions and criticisms at various stages of the work.

Source: From "The Contingency Model: A Theory of Leadership Effectiveness" by Fred E. Fiedler, in *Problems in Social Psychology*, edited by Carl W. Backman and Paul F. Secord, pp. 279–289. New York: McGraw-Hill Book Company, 1970. Reprinted by permission of the author.

While one can always rationalize that contradictory findings by other investigators are due to poor research design, or different tests and criteria, such problems present difficulties if they appear in one's own research. We have, during the past thirteen years, conducted a large number of studies on leadership and group performance, using the same operational definitions and essentially similar leader attitude measures. The inconsistencies which we obtained in our own research program demanded an integrative theoretical formulation which would adequately account for the seemingly confusing results.

The studies which we conducted used as the major predictor of group performance an interpersonal perception or attitude score which is derived from the leader's description of his most and of his least preferred co-workers. He is asked to think of all others with whom he has ever worked, and then to describe first the person with whom he worked best (his most preferred co-worker) and then the person with whom he could work least well (his least preferred co-worker, or *LPC*). These descriptions are obtained, wherever possible, before the leader is assigned to his team. However, even when we deal with already existing groups, these descriptions tend to be of individuals whom the subject has known in the past rather than of persons with whom he works at the time of testing.

The descriptions are typically made on 20 eight-point bi-polar adjective scales, similar to Osgood's Semantic Differential (Osgood, et al, 1957), e.g.,

Pleasant _:_:_:_:_:_:_:_ Unpleasant

Friendly _:_:_:_:_:_:_:_ Unfriendly

These items are scaled on an evaluative dimension, giving a score of 8 to the most favorable pole (i.e., Friendly, Pleasant) and a score of 1 to the least favorable pole. Two main scores have been derived from these descriptions. The first one, which was used in our earlier studies, is based on the profile similarity measure *D* (Cronbach and Gleser, 1953) between the descriptions of the most and of the least preferred co-worker. This score, called the Assumed Similarity between Opposites, or *ASo*, indicates the degree to which the individual perceives the two opposites on his co-worker continuum as similar or different. The second score is simply based on the individual's description of his least preferred co-worker, *LPC*, and indicates the degree to which the subject evaluates his *LPC* in a relatively favorable or unfavorable manner. The two measures are highly correlated (.80 to .95) and will here be treated as interchangeable.

We have had considerable difficulty in interpreting these scores since they appear to be uncorrelated with the usual personality and attitude measures. They are, however, related to the Ohio State University studies' "Initiation of structure" and "Consideration" dimensions (Stogdill and Coons, 1957). Extensive content analysis (Meuwese and Oonk, 1960; Julian and McGrath, 1963; Morris and Fiedler, 1964) and a series of studies by Hawkins (1962) as well as research by Bass, Fiedler, and Krueger (1964) have given consistent results. These indicate that the person with high *LPC* or *ASo*, who perceives his least preferred co-worker in a relatively favorable, accepting manner, tends to be more accepting, permissive, considerate, and person-oriented in his relations with group members. The person who perceives his most and least preferred co-workers as quite different, and who sees his least preferred co-worker in a very unfavorable, rejecting manner tends to be directive, task-oriented and controlling on task relevant group behaviors in his interactions. . . .

The results of these investigations clearly showed that the direction and magnitude of the correlations were contingent upon the nature of the group-task situation with which the leader had to deal. Our problem resolved itself then into (*a*) developing a meaningful system for categorizing group-task situations; (*b*) inducing the underlying theoretical model which would integrate the seemingly inconsistent results obtained in our studies, and (*c*) testing the validity of the model by adequate research.

DEVELOPMENT OF THE MODEL

Key Definitions. We shall here be concerned solely with "interacting" rather than "co-acting" task groups. By an interacting task group we mean a face-to-face team situation (such as a basketball team) in which the members work *interdependently* on a common goal. In groups of this type, the individual's contributions cannot readily be separated from total group performance. In a co-acting group, however, such as a bowling or a rifle team, the group performance is generally determined by summing the members' individual performance scores. . . .

The leader's effectiveness is here defined in terms of the group's performance on the assigned primary task. . . .

The Categorization of Group-Task Situations. Leadership is essentially a problem of wielding influence and power. When we say that different types of groups require different types of leadership we imply that they require a different relationship by which the leader wields power and influence. Since it is easier to wield power in some groups than in others, an attempt to categorize groups might well begin by asking what conditions in the group-task situation will facilitate or inhibit the leader's exercise of power. On the basis of our previous work we postulated three important aspects in the total situation which influence the leader's role.

1. *Leader-member relations*. The leader who is personally attractive to his group members, and who is respected by his group, enjoys considerable power (French, 1956). In fact, if he has the confidence and loyalty of his men he has less need of official rank. This dimension can generally be measured by means of sociometric indices or by group atmosphere scales (Cf. Fiedler, 1962) which indicate the degree to which the leader experiences the groups as pleasant and well disposed toward him.

2. *Task structure*. The task generally implies an order "from above" which incorporates the authority of the superior organization. The group member who refuses to comply must be prepared to face disciplinary action by the higher authority. For example, a squad member who fails to perform a lawful command of his sergeant may have to answer to his regimental commander. However, compliance with a task order can be enforced only if the task is relatively well structured, i.e., if it is capable of being programmed, or spelled out step by step. One cannot effectively force a group to perform well on an unstructured task such as developing a new product or writing a good play.

Thus, the leader who has a structured task can depend on the backing of his superior organizations, but if he has an unstructured task the leader must rely on his own resources to inspire and motivate his men. The unstructured task thus provides the leader with much less effective power than does the highly structured task.

We operationalized this dimension by utilizing four of the aspects which Shaw (1962) recently proposed for the classification of group task. These are, (*a*) decision *verifiability*, the degree to which the correctness of the solution can be demonstrated objectively; (*b*) *good clarity*, the degree to which the task requirements are clearly stated or known to the group; (*c*) *goal path multiplicity*, the degree to which there are many or few procedures available for performing the task (reverse scoring); and (*d*) *solution specificity*, the degree to which there is one rather than an infinite number of correct solutions (e.g., writing a story vs. solving an equation). Ratings based on these four dimensions have yielded interrater reliabilities of .80 to .90.

3. *Position power.* The third dimension is defined by the power inherent in the position of leadership irrespective of the occupant's personal relations with his members. This includes the rewards and punishments which are officially or traditionally at the leader's disposal, his authority as defined by the group's rules and by-laws, and the organizational support given to him in dealing with his men. . . .

A Three-Dimensional Group Classification. Group-task situations can now be rated on the basis of the three dimensions of leader-member relations, task structure, and position power. This locates each group in a three-dimensional space. A rough categorization can be accomplished by halving each of the dimensions so that we obtain an eight celled cube (Fig. 1). We can now determine whether the correlations between leader attitudes and group performance within each of these eight cells, or octants, are relatively similar in magnitude and direction. If they are, we can infer that the group classification has been successfully accomplished since it shows that groups falling within the same octant require similar leader attitudes.

An earlier paper has summarized 52 group-task situations which are based on our previous studies (Fiedler, 1964). These 52 group-task situations have been ordered into the eight octants. As

FIGURE 1 • A MODEL FOR THE CLASSIFICATION OF GROUP-TASK SITUATIONS

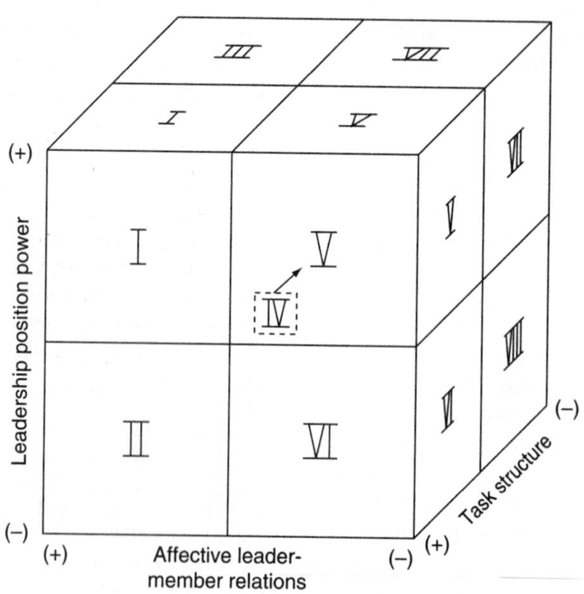

TABLE 1 • MEDIAN CORRELATION BETWEEN LEADER *LPC* AND GROUP PERFORMANCE IN VARIOUS OCTANTS

	Leader-Member Relations	Task Structure	Position Power	Median Correlation	Number of Relations Included in Median
Octant I	Good	Structured	Strong	–.52	2
Octant II	Good	Structured	Weak	–.58	3
Octant III	Good	Unstructured	Strong	–.41	4
Octant IV	Good	Unstructured	Weak	.47	10
Octant V	Mod. poor	Structured	Strong	.42	6
Octant VI	Mod. poor	Structured	Weak		0
Octant VII	Mod. poor	Unstructured	Strong	.05	10
Octant VIII	Mod. poor	Unstructured	Weak	–.43	12

can be seen from Table 1, groups falling within the same octant show correlations between the leader's *ASo* or *LPC* score and the group performance criterion which are relatively similar in magnitude and direction. We can thus infer that the group classification has been accomplished with at least reasonable success.

Consideration of Figure 1 suggests a further classification of the cells in terms of the effective power which the group-task situation places at the leader's disposal, or more precisely, the favorableness of the situation for the leader's exercise of his power and influence.

Such an ordering can be accomplished without difficulty at the extreme poles of the continuum. A liked and trusted leader with high rank and a structured task is in a more favorable position than is a disliked and powerless leader with an ambiguous task. . . . In the present instance we have postulated that the most important dimension in the system is the leader-member relationship since the highly liked and respected leader is less in need of position power or the power of the higher authority incorporated in the task structure. The second-most important dimension in most group-task situations is the task structure since a leader with a highly structured task does not require a powerful leader position. . . . This leads us here to order the group-task situations first on leader-member relations, then on task structure, and finally on position power. While admittedly not a unique solution, the resulting ordering constitutes a reasonable continuum which indicates the degree of the leader's effective power in the group.[2]

As was already apparent from Table 1, the relationship between leader attitudes and group performance is contingent upon the accurate classification of the group-task situation. A more meaningful model of this contingency

[2] Another cell should be added which contains real-life groups which reject their leader. Exercise of power would be very difficult in this situation and such a cell should be placed at the extreme negative end of the continuum. Such cases are treated in the section on validation.

FIGURE 2 • CORRELATIONS OF LEADER *LPC* AND GROUP PERFORMANCE PLOTTED AGAINST OCTANTS

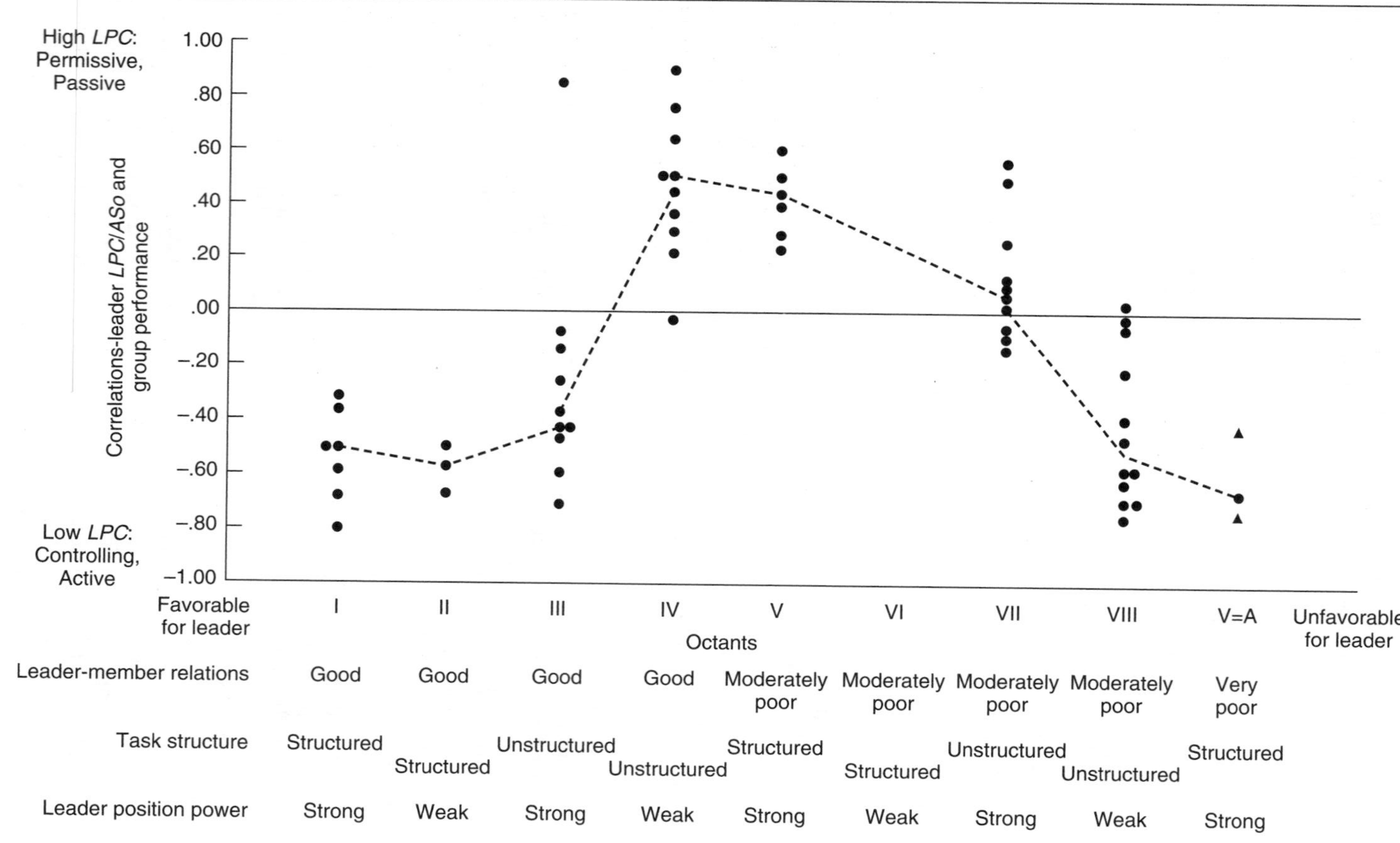

relationship emerges when we now plot the correlation between *LPC* or *ASo* and group performance on the one hand, against the octants ordered on the effective power, or favorableness-for-the-leader dimension on the other. This is shown on Figure 2, Note that each point in the plot is a *correlation* predicting leadership performance or group effectiveness. The plot therefore represents 53 *sets of groups* totaling over 800 separate groups.

As Figure 2 shows, managing, controlling, directive (low *LPC*) leaders perform most effectively either under very favorable or under very unfavorable situations. Hence we obtain negative correlations between *LPC* and group performance scores. Considerate, permissive accepting leaders obtain optimal group performance under situations intermediate in favorableness. These are situations in which (*a*) the task is structured, but the leader is disliked and must, therefore, be diplomatic; (*b*) the liked leader has an ambiguous, unstructured task and must, therefore, draw upon the creativity and cooperation of his members. Here we obtain positive correlations between *LPC* and group performance scores. Where the task is highly structured and the leader is well-liked, non-directive behavior or permissive attitudes (such as asking how the group ought to proceed with a missile count-down) is neither appropriate nor beneficial. Where the situation is quite unfavorable, e.g., where the disliked chairman of a volunteer group faces an ambiguous task, the leader might as well be autocratic and directive since a positive, non-directive leadership style under these conditions might result in complete inactivity on the part of the group. This model, thus, tends to shed some light on the apparent inconsistencies in our own data as well as in data obtained by other investigators.

EMPIRICAL TESTS EXTENSION OF THE MODEL

The basic hypothesis of the model suggests that the directive, controlling, task oriented (low *LPC*) leader will be most successful in group-task situations which are either very favorable or else very unfavorable for the leader. The permissive, considerate, human relations oriented (high *LPC*) leader will perform best under conditions which are intermediate in favorableness. . . .

Experimental Test of the Contingency Model

In cooperation with the Belgium Naval Forces we recently conducted a major study which served in part as a specific test of the model. Only aspects immediately relevant to the test are here described. The investigation was conducted in Belgium where the French and Dutch speaking (or Flemish) sectors of the country have been involved in a long-standing and frequently acrimonious dispute. This conflict centers about the use of language, but it also involves a host of other cultural factors which differentiate the 60 percent Flemish and 40 percent French speaking population groups in Wallonie and Brussels. This "linguistic problem," which is rooted in the beginning of Belgium's national history, has in recent years been the cause of continuous public controversy, frequent protest meetings, and occasional riots.

The linguistic problem is of particular interest here since a group, consisting of members whose mother tongue, culture, and attitudes differ, will clearly present a more difficult problem in leadership than a group whose members share the same language and culture. We were thus able to test the major hypothesis of the model as well as to extend the research by investigating the type of leadership which linguistically and culturally heterogeneous groups require.

Design. The experiment was conducted at the naval training center at Ste. Croix-Bruges.[3] It utilized 48 career petty officers and 240 recruits who had been selected from a pool of 546 men on the basis of a pre-test in which we obtained *LPC*, intelligence, attitude, and language comprehension scores.

The experiment was specifically designed to incorporate the three major group classification dimensions shown on Figure 1, namely, leader-member relations, position power, and task structure. It also added the additional dimension of group homogeneity vs. heterogeneity. Specifically, 48 groups had leaders with high position power (petty officers) while 48 had leaders with low position power (recruits); 48 groups began with the unstructured task, while the other 48 groups began with two structured tasks; 48 groups were homogeneous, consisting of three French or three Dutch speaking men, while the other 48 groups were heterogeneous, consisting of a French speaking leader and two Flemish members, or a Dutch speaking, Flemish leader and two French speaking members. The quality of the leader-member relations was measured as in our previous studies by means of a group atmosphere scale which the leader completed after each task session.

Group Performance Criteria. Two essentially identical structured tasks were administered. Each lasted 25 minutes and required the groups to find the shortest route for a ship which, given certain fuel capacity and required ports of call, had to make a round trip calling at respectively ten or twelve ports. The tasks were objectively scored on the basis of sea miles required for the trip. Appropriate corrections and penalties were assigned for errors.

The unstructured task required the groups to compose a letter to young men of 16 and 17 years, urging them to choose the Belgian Navy as a career. The letter was to be approximately 200 words in length and had to be completed in 35 minutes. Each of the letters, depending upon the language in which it was written, was then rated by Dutch or by French speaking judges on style and use of language, as well as interest value, originality, and persuasiveness. Estimated reliability was .92 and .86 for Dutch and French speaking judges, respectively.

It should be noted in this connection that the task of writing a letter is not as unstructured as might have been desirable for this experiment. . . . High and low task-structure is, therefore, less well differentiated in this study than it has been in previous investigations.

Results. The contingency model specifies that the controlling, managing low *LPC* leaders will be most effective either in very favorable or else in relatively unfavorable group-task situations, while the permissive, considerate, high *LPC* leaders will be more effective in situations intermediate in difficulty. . . .

[3] This investigation was conducted in collaboration with Dr. J. M. Nuttin (Jr.) and his students while the author was Ford Faculty Research Fellow at the University of Louvain, 1963–1964. The experiment, undertaken with permission of Commodore L. Petitjean, then Chief of Staff of the Belgian Naval Forces, was carried out at the Centre de Formation Navale, Ste. Croix-Bruges. The writer wishes to express his especial gratitude and appreciation to the commandant of the center, Captain V. Van Laethem, who not only made the personnel and the facilities of the center available to us, but whose active participation in the planning and the execution of the project made this study possible. We are most grateful to Dr. U. Bouvier, Director of the Center for Social Studies, Ministry of Defense, to Capt. W. Cafferata, USN, the senior U.S. Naval representative of the Military Assistance and Advisory Group, Brussels, and to Cmdr. J. Robison, U.S. Naval Attache in Brussels, who provided liaison and guidance.

The hypothesis can be tested most readily with correlations of leader *LPC* and group performance in homogeneous groups on the more reliably scorable second structured task. . . . We have here made the fairly obvious assumption that the powerful leader or the leader who feels liked and accepted faces an easier group-task situation than low ranking leaders and those who see the groups as unpleasant and tense. Each situation is represented by two cells of six groups, each. Since there were two orders of presentation—half the groups worked first on the structured task, the other half on the unstructured task, arranging the group-task situations in order of favorableness for the leader then gives us the following results:

	Order 1	**Order 2**
High group atmosphere and high position power	−.77	−.77
High group atmosphere and low position power	+.60	+.50
Low group atmosphere and high position power	+.16	+.01
Low group atmosphere and low position power	−.16	−.43

These are, of course, the trends in size and magnitude of correlations which the model predicts. Low *LPC* leaders are again most effective in favorable and unfavorable group-task situations: the more permissive, considerate high *LPC* leaders were more effective in the intermediate situations. . . .

The resulting weighting system leads to a scale from 12 to 0 points, with 12 as the most favorable pole. If we now plot the median correlation coefficients of the 48 group-task situations against the scale indicating the favorableness of the situation for the leader, we obtain the curve presented on Figure 3.

As can be seen, we again obtain a curvilinear relationship which resembles that shown on Figure 2. Heterogeneous groups with low position power and/or poor leader-member relations fall below point 6 on the scale, and thus tend to perform better with controlling, directive, low *LPC* leaders. Only under otherwise very favorable conditions do heterogeneous groups perform better with permissive, considerate high *LPC* leaders, that is, in group-task situations characterized by high group atmosphere as well as high position power, four of the six correlations (66%) are positive, while only five of eighteen (28%) are positive in the less favorable group-task situations.

It is interesting to note that the curve is rather flat and characterized by relatively low negative correlations as we go toward the very unfavorable end of the scale. This result supports Meuwese's (1964) . . . study which showed that correlations between leader *LPC* as well as between leader intelligence and group performance tend to become attenuated under conditions of relative stress. These findings suggest that the leader's ability to influence and control the group decreases beyond a certain point of stress and difficulty in the group-task situation.

DISCUSSION

The contingency model seeks to reconcile results which up to now had to be considered inconsistent and difficult to understand. . . .

The model has a number of important implications for selection and training, as well as for the placement of leaders and organizational strategy. Our research suggests, first of all, that we can utilize a very broad spectrum of individuals for positions of leadership. The

FIGURE 3 • MEDIAN CORRELATIONS BETWEEN LEADER *LPC* AND GROUP PERFORMANCE SCORES PLOTTED AGAINST FAVORABLENESS-FOR-LEADER SCALE IN THE BELGIAN NAVY STUDY

Code for two-digit numbers. Figure indicating the type of group involved.

Composition	Position Power	High Group Atmos.	Low Group Atmos.	Task	1st Pres.	2nd Pres.
Homogeneous	High	1	5	Structured I	1	2
Homogeneous	Low	2	6	Structured II	3	4
Heterogeneous	High	3	7	Unstructured	5	6
Heterogeneous	Low	4	8			

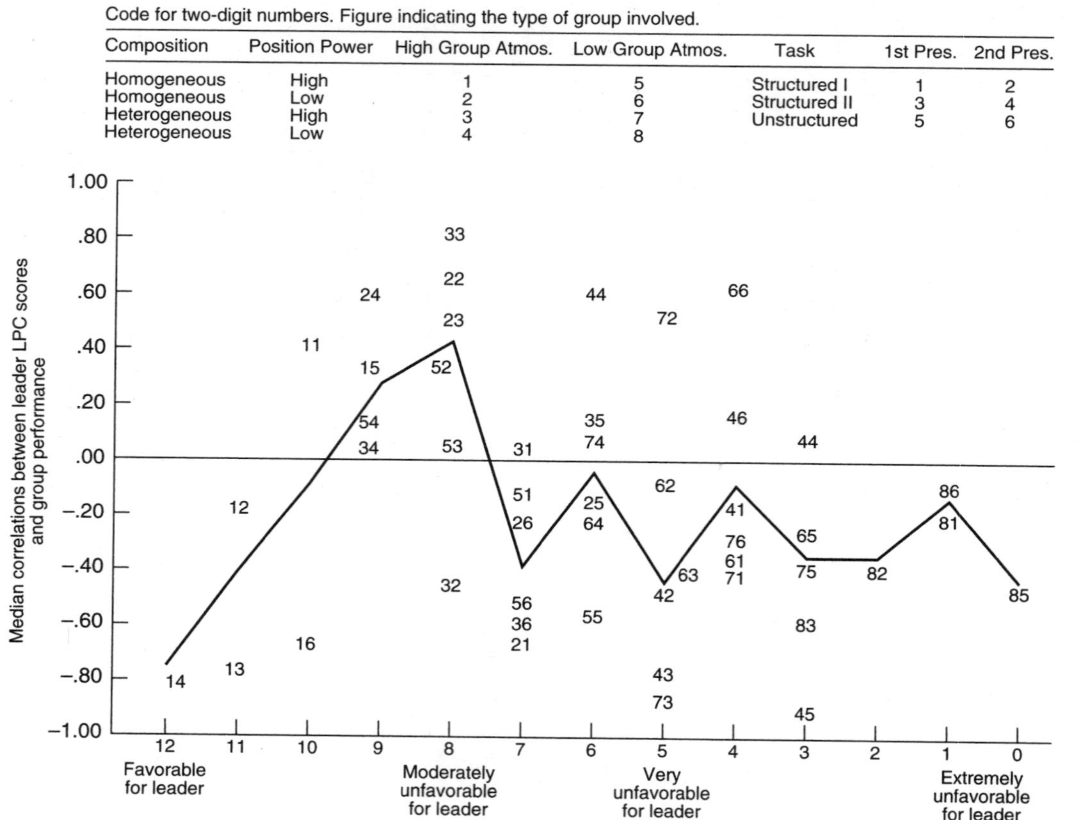

problem becomes one of placement and training rather than of selection since both the permissive, democratic, human-relations oriented, and the managing, autocratic, task-oriented leader can be effectively utilized. Leaders can be trained to recognize their own style of leadership as well as the conditions which are most compatible with their style.

The model also points to a variety of administrative and supervisory strategies which the organization can adopt to fit the group-task situation to the needs of the leader. Tasks can, after all, be structured to a greater or lesser extent by giving very specific and detailed, or vague and general instructions; the position power of the group leader can be increased or decreased and even the congeniality of a group, and its acceptance of the leader can be affected by appropriate administration action, such as for instance increasing or decreasing the group's homogeneity.

The model also throws new light on phenomena which were rather difficult to fit into our usual ideas about measurement in social psychology. Why, for example, should groups differ so markedly in their performance on nearly parallel tasks? The model—and our data—shows that the situation becomes easier for the leader as the group moves from the novel to the already known group-task situations. The leaders who excel under relatively novel and therefore more difficult conditions are not necessarily those who excel under those which are more routine, or better known and therefore more favorable. Likewise, we find that different types of task structure require different types of leader behavior. Thus, in a research project's early phases the project director tends to be democratic and permissive; everyone is urged to contribute to the plan and to criticize all aspects of the design. This situation changes radically in the more structured phase when the research design is frozen and the experiment is under way. Here the research director tends to become managing, controlling, and highly autocratic and woe betide the assistant who attempts to be creative in giving instructions to subjects, or in his timing of tests. A similar situation is often found in business organizations where the routine operation tends to be well structured and calls for a managing, directive leadership. The situation becomes suddenly unstructured when a crisis occurs. Under these conditions the number of discussions, meetings, and conferences increases sharply so as to give everyone an opportunity to express his views.

At best, this model is of course only a partial theory of leadership. The leader's intellectual and task-relevant abilities, and the members' skills and motivation, all play a role in affecting the group's performance. It is to be hoped that these other important aspects of group interaction can be incorporated into the model in the not too distant future.

REFERENCES

Bass, A. R., Fiedler, F. E., and Krueger, S. Personality correlates of assumed similarity (ASo) and related scores. Urbana, Ill.: Group Effectiveness Research Laboratory, University of Illinois, 1964.

Bass, B. M. *Leadership psychology and organizational behavior*. New York: Harper Brothers, 1960.

Browne, C. G., and Cohn, T. S. (Eds.) *The study of leadership*. Danville, Illinois. The Interstate Printers and Publishers, 1958.

Cleven, W. A., and Fiedler, F. E. Interpersonal perceptions of open hearth foremen and steel production. *J. Appl. Psychol.*, 1956. 40, 312–314.

Cronbach, J. J., and Gleser, Goldene, C. Assessing similarity between profiles. *Psychol. Bull.*, 1953, 50, 456–473.

Fiedler, F. E. Assumed similarity measures as predictors of team effectiveness. *J. Abnorm. Soc. Psychol.*, 1954, 49, 381–388.

Fiedler, F. E. Leader attitudes, group climate, and group creativity. *J. Abnorm. Soc. Psychol.*, 1962, 64, 308–318.

Fiedler, F. E. A contingency model of leadership effectiveness. In L. Berkowitz (Ed.) *Advances in Experimental Social Psychology*. New York: Academic Press, 1964, Vol. I.

Fiedler, F. E., and Meuwese, W. A. T. The leader's contribution to performance in cohesive and uncohesive groups. *J. Abnorm. Soc. Psychol.*, 1963, 67, 83–87.

Fiedler, F. E., Meuwese, W. A. T., and Oonk, Sophie. Performance of laboratory tasks requiring group creativity. *Acta Psychologica*, 1961, 18, 100–119.

French, J. R. P. Jr. A formal theory of social power. *Psychol. Rev.*, 1956, 63, 181–194.

Gibb, C. A. "Leadership" in G. Lindzey (Ed.) *Handbook of Social Psychology*, Vol. II, Cambridge, Mass.: Addison-Wesley, 1954.

Godfrey, Eleanor P., Fiedler, F. E., and Hall, D. M. *Boards, Management, and Company Success*. Danville, Illinois: Interstate Printers and Publishers, 1959.

Hare, A. P. *Handbook of Small Group Research*. New York: Free Press, 1962.

Hawkins, C. A study of factors mediating a relationship between leader rating behavior and group productivity. Unpublished Ph.D. dissertation, University of Minnesota, 1962.

Hutchins, E. B., and Fiedler, F. E. Task-oriented and quasi-therapeutic role functions of the leader in small military groups. *Sociometry*, 1960, 23, 293–406.

Julian, J. W., and McGrath, J. E. The influence of leader and member behavior on the adjustment and task effectiveness of negotiation groups. Urbana, Ill.: Group Effectiveness Research Laboratory, University of Illinois, 1963.

McGrath, J. E. A summary of small group research studies. Arlington Va.: Human Sciences Research Inc., 1962 (Litho.).

Mann, R. D. A review of the relationship between personality and performance in small groups. *Psychol. Bull.*, 1959, 56, 241–270.

Meuwese, W. A. T. The effect of the leader's ability and interpersonal attitudes on group creativity under varying conditions of stress. Unpublished doctoral dissertation, University of Amsterdam, 1964.

Meuwese, W., and Oonk, Sophie. Enkele determinanten von creativiteit, structuur en proces in kleine experimentele groepen. Unpublished Working Paper. Amsterdam: University of Amsterdam, 1960.

Morris, C. G., and Fiedler, F. E. Application of a new system of interaction analysis to relationships between leader attitudes and behavior in problem solving groups. Urbana, Ill.: Group Effectiveness Research Laboratory, University of Illinois, 1964.

Osgood C. A., Suci, G. A., and Tannenbaum, P. H. *The Measurement of Meaning*. Urbana, Ill.: University of Illinois Press, 1957.

Shaw, M. E. Annual Technical Report, 1962. Gainsville, Florida: University of Florida, 1962 (Mimeo.).

Stogdill, R. Personal factors associated with leadership: a survey of the literature. *J. of Psychol.*, 1948, 25, 35–71.

Stogdill, R. M., and Coons, A. E. Leader behavior: its description and measurement. Columbus, Ohio: Ohio State University, *Research Monograph*, No. 88, 1957.

5

The Leadership Challenge—A Call for the Transformational Leader

Noel M. Tichy and David O. Ulrich

Some optimists are heralding in the age of higher productivity, a transition to a service economy, and a brighter competitive picture for U.S. corporations in world markets. We certainly would like to believe that the future will be brighter, but our temperament is more cautious. We feel that the years it took for most U.S. companies to get "fat and flabby" are not going to be reversed by a crash diet for one or two years. Whether we continue to gradually decline as a world competitive economy will largely be determined by the quality of leadership in the top echelons of our business and government organizations. Thus, it is our belief that now is the time for organizations to *change* their corporate lifestyles.

To revitalize organizations such as General Motors, American Telephone and Telegraph, General Electric, Honeywell, Ford, Burroughs, Chase Manhattan Bank, Citibank, U.S. Steel, Union Carbide, Texas Instruments, and Control Data—just to mention a few companies currently undergoing major transformations—a new brand of leadership is necessary. Instead of managers who continue to move organizations along historical tracks, the new leaders must *transform* the organizations and head them down new tracks. What is required of this kind of leader is an ability to help the organization develop a vision of what it can be, to mobilize the organization to accept and work toward achieving the new vision, and to institutionalize the changes that must last over time. Unless the creation of this breed of leaders becomes a national agenda, we are not very optimistic about the revitalization of the U.S. economy.

We call these new leaders transformational leaders, for they must create something new out of something old: out of an old vision, they must develop and communicate a new vision and get others not only to see the vision but also to commit themselves to it. Where transactional managers make only minor adjustments in the organization's mission, structure, and human resource management, transformational leaders not only make major changes in these three areas but they also evoke fundamental changes in the basic political and cultural systems of the organization. The revamping of the political and cultural systems is what most distinguishes the transformational leader from the transactional one.

Source: Reprinted from "The Leadership Challenge—A Call for the Transformational Leader" by N. M. Tichy and D. O. Ulrich in *Sloan Management Review* (Fall 1984), pp. 59–68, by permission of the publisher. Copyright © 1984 by the Sloan Management Review Association. All rights reserved.

LEE IACOCCA: A TRANSFORMATIONAL LEADER

One of the most dramatic examples of transformational leadership and organizational revitalization in the early 1980s has been the leadership of Lee Iacocca, the chairman of Chrysler Corporation. He provided the leadership to transform a company from the brink of bankruptcy to profitability. He created a vision of success and mobilized large factions of key employees toward enacting that vision while simultaneously downsizing the workforce by 60,000 employees. As a result of Iacocca's leadership, by 1984 Chrysler had earned record profits, had attained high levels of employee morale, and had helped employees generate a sense of meaning in their work.

Until Lee Iacocca took over at Chrysler, the basic internal political structure had been unchanged for decades. It was clear who reaped what benefits from the organization, how the pie was to be divided, and who could exercise what power. Nonetheless, Mr. Iacocca knew that he needed to alter these political traditions, starting with a new definition of Chrysler's link to external stakeholders. Therefore, the government was given a great deal of control over Chrysler in return for the guaranteed loan that staved off bankruptcy. Modification of the political system required other adjustments, including the "trimming of fat" in the management ranks, limiting financial rewards for all employees, and receiving major concessions for the UAW. An indicator of a significant political shift was the inclusion of Douglas Frazer on the Chrysler Board of Directors as part of UAW concessions.

Equally dramatic was the change in the organization's cultural system. First, the company had to recognize its unique status as a recipient of a federal bailout. This bailout came with a stigma, thus Mr. Iacocca's job was to change the company's cultural values from a loser's to a winner's feeling. Still, he realized that employees were not going to be winners unless they could, in cultural norms, be more efficient and innovative than their competitors. The molding and shaping of the new culture was clearly and visibly led by Mr. Iacocca, who not only used internal communication as a vehicle to signal change but also used his own personal appearance in Chrysler ads to reinforce these changes. Quickly, the internal culture was transformed to that of a lean and hungry team looking for victory. Whether Chrysler will be able to sustain this organizational phenomenon over time remains to be seen. If it does, it will provide a solid corporate example of what Burns referred to as a transforming leader.[1]

Lee Iacocca's high visibility and notoriety may be the *important* missing elements in management today: there seems to be a paucity of transformational leader role models at all levels of the organization.

ORGANIZATIONAL DYNAMICS OF CHANGE

Assumption One: Trigger Events Indicate Change Is Needed

Organizations do not change unless there is a trigger which indicates change is needed. This trigger can be as extreme as the Chrysler impending bankruptcy or as moderate as an abstract future-oriented fear that an organization may lose its competitiveness. For example, General Electric's trigger for change is a view that by 1990 the company will not be world competitive unless major changes occur in productivity, innovation, and marketing. . . . For General Motors, economic factors of world competition, shifting consumer preferences, and technological change have driven it to change.

In a decade of increased information, international competition, and technological advances, triggers for change have become commonplace and very pressing. However, not all potential trigger events lead to organizational responses, and not all triggers lead to change. Nonetheless, the trigger must create a *felt need* in organizational leaders. Without this felt need, the "boiled frog phenomenon" is likely to occur.

The Boiled Frog. This phenomenon is based on a classic experiment in biology. A frog which is placed in a pan of cold water but which still has the freedom to jump out can be boiled if the temperature change is gradual, for it is not aware of the barely detectable changing heat threshold. In contrast, a frog dropped in a pot of boiling water will immediately jump out: it has a felt need to survive. In a similar vein, many organizations that are insensitive to gradually changing organizational thresholds are likely to become "boiled frogs"; they act in ignorant bliss of environmental triggers and eventually are doomed to failure. This failure, in part, is a result of the organization having no felt need to change.

Assumption Two: A Change Unleashes Mixed Feelings

A felt need for change unleashes a mix of forces, both a positive impetus for change as well as a strong negative individual and organizational resistance. These forces of resistance are generated in each of three interrelated systems—technical, political, cultural—which must be managed in the process of organizational transitions (see Table 1).[2] Individual and organizational resistance to change in these three systems must be overcome if an organization is to be revitalized.[3]

Managing technical systems refers to managing the coordination of technology, capital information, and people in order to produce products or services desired and used in the external marketplace. Managing political systems refers to managing the allocation of organizational reward such as money, status, power, and career opportunities and to exercising power so employees and departments perceive equity and justice. Managing cultural systems refers to managing the set of shared values and norms which guides the behavior of members of the organization.

When a needed change is perceived by the organizational leaders, the dominant group in the organization must experience a dissatisfaction with the status quo. . . .

The technical, political, and cultural resistances are most evident during early stages of an organizational transformation. At GM the early 1980s were marked by tremendous uncertainty concerning many technical issues such as marketing strategy, production strategy, organization design, factory automation, and development of international management. Politically, many powerful coalitions were threatened. The UAW was forced to make wage concessions and accept staffing reductions. The white-collar workers saw their benefits being cut and witnessed major layoffs within the managerial ranks. Culturally, the once dominant managerial style no longer fit the environmental pressures for change: the "GM way" was no longer the right way.

One must be wary of these resistances to change as they can lead to organizational stagnation rather than revitalization. In fact, some managers at GM in late 1983 were waiting for "the good old days" to return. Such resistance exemplifies a dysfunctional reaction to the felt need. As indicated in Figure 1, a key

TABLE 1 • A LIST OF TECHNICAL, POLITICAL, AND CULTURAL SYSTEM RESISTANCES

Technical System Resistances Include:

Habit and inertia. Habit and inertia cause task-related resistance to change. Individuals who have always done things one way may not be politically or culturally resistant to change, but may have trouble, for technical reasons, changing behavior patterns. Example: some office workers may have difficulty shifting from electric typewriters to word processors.

Fear of the unknown or loss of organizational predictability. Not knowing or having difficulty predicting the future creates anxiety and hence resistance in many individuals. Example: the introduction of automated office equipment has often been accompanied by such resistances.

Sunk costs. Organizations, even when realizing that there are potential payoffs from a change, are often unable to enact a change because of the sunk costs of the organizations' resources in the old way of doing things.

Political System Resistances Include:

Powerful coalitions. A common threat is found in the conflict between the old guard and the new guard. One interpretation of the exit of Archie McGill, former president of the newly formed AT&T American Bell, is that the backlash of the old-guard coalition exacted its price on the leader of the new-guard coalition.

Resource limitations. In the days when the economic pie was steadily expanding and resources were much less limited, change was easier to enact as every part could gain—such was the nature of labor management agreements in the auto industry for decades. Now that the pie is shrinking, decisions need to be made as to who shares a smaller set of resources. These zero-sum decisions are much more politically difficult. As more and more U.S. companies deal with productivity, downsizing, and divestiture, political resistance will be triggered.

Indictment quality of change. Perhaps the most significant resistance to change comes from leaders having to indict their own past decisions and behaviors to bring about a change. Example: Roger Smith, chairman and CEO of GM, must implicitly indict his own past behavior as a member of senior management when he suggests changes in GM's operations. Psychologically, it is very difficult for people to change when they were party to creating the problems they are trying to change. It is much easier for a leader from the outside, such as Lee Iacocca, who does not have to indict himself every time he says something is wrong with the organization.

Cultural System Resistances Include:

Selective perception (cultural filters). An organization's culture may highlight certain elements of the organization, making it difficult for members to conceive of other ways of doing things. An organization's culture channels that which people perceive as possible; thus, innovation may come from outsiders or deviants who are not as channeled in their perceptions.

Security based on the past. Transition requires people to give up the old ways of doing things. There is security in the past, and one of the problems is getting people to overcome the tendency to want to return to the "good old days." Example: today, there are still significant members of the white-collar workforce at GM who are waiting for the "good old days" to return.

Lack of climate for change. Organizations often vary in their conduciveness to change. Cultures that require a great deal of conformity often lack much receptivity to change. Example: GM with its years of internally developed managers must overcome a limited climate for change.

FIGURE 1 • TRANSFORMATIONAL LEADERSHIP

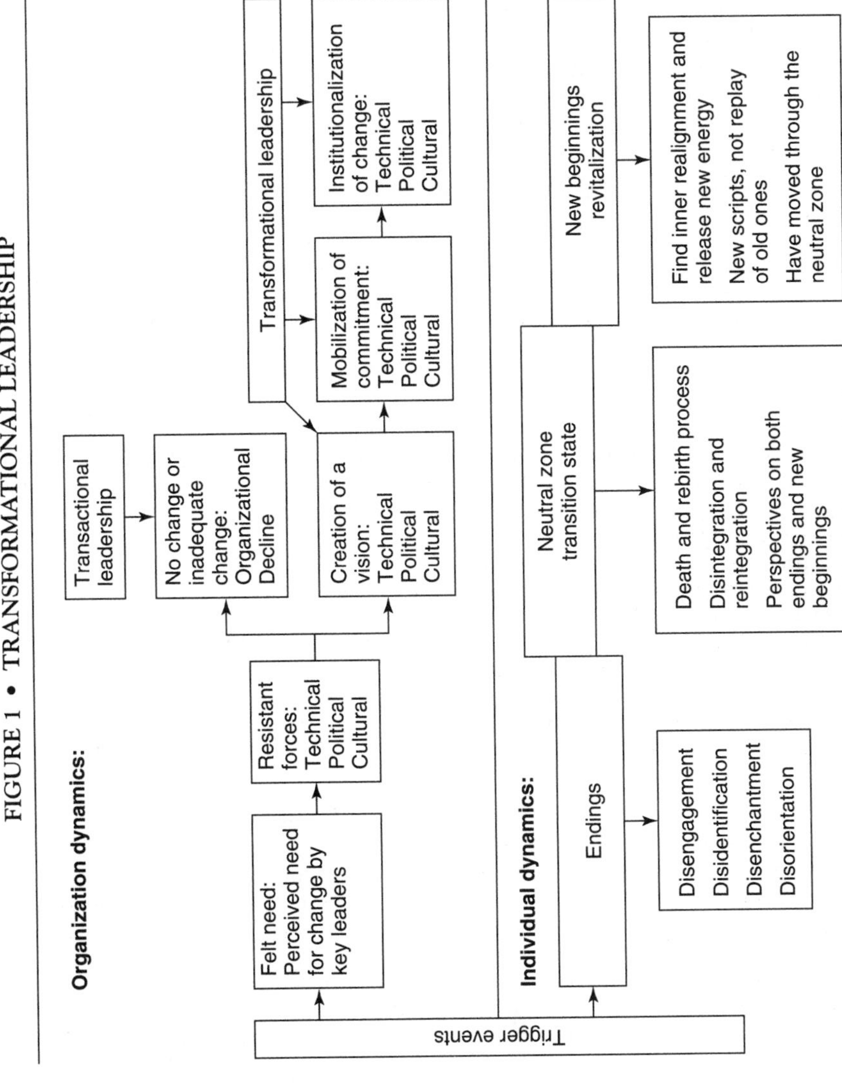

to whether resistant forces will lead to little or inadequate change and hence organizational decline or revitalization lies in an organization's leadership. Defensive, transactional leadership will not rechannel the resistant forces. . . .

Assumption Three: Quick-Fix Leadership Leads to Decline

Overcoming resistance to change requires transformational leadership, not defensive, transactional managers who are in search of the one minute quick fix. The transformational leader needs to avoid the trap of simple, quick-fix solutions to major organizational problems. Today, many versions of this quick-fix mentality abound: the book, *The One Minute Manager*, has become a best seller in companies in need of basic transformation.[4] Likewise, *In Search of Excellence* has become a cookbook for change.[5] In fact, a number of CEOs have taken the eight characteristics of the "excellent" companies and are trying to blindly impose them on their organizations without first examining their appropriateness. For example, many faltering organizations try to copy such company practices as Hewlett-Packard's (HP) statement of company values. Because they read that HP has a clearly articulated statement of company values—the HP equivalent of the ten commandments—they want to create their list of ten commandments. . . .

The problem with the ten commandments quick fix is that the CEOs tend to overlook the lesson Moses learned several thousand years ago—namely, getting the ten commandments written down and communicated is the easy part; getting them implemented is the challenge. How many thousands of years has it been since Moses received the ten commandments, and yet today there still seems to be an implementation challenge. Transformational leadership is different from defensive, transactional leadership. Lee Iacocca did not have to read about what others did to find a recipe for his company's success.

Assumption Four: Revitalization Requires Transformational Leadership

There are three identifiable programs of activity associated with transformational leadership.

1. *Creation of a Vision*. The transformational leader must provide the organization with a vision of a desired future state. While this task may be shared with other key members of the organization, the vision remains the core responsibility of the transformational leader. The leader needs to integrate analytic, creative, intuitive, and deductive thinking. Each leader must create a vision which gives direction to the organization while being congruent with the leader's and the organization's philosophy and style.

For example, in the early 1980s at GM, after several years of committee work and staff analysis, a vision of the future was drafted which included a mission statement and eight objectives for the company. The statement was the first articulation of a strategic vision for General Motors since Alfred Sloan's leadership. This new vision was developed consistently with the leadership philosophy and style of Roger Smith. Many people were involved in carefully assessing opportunities and constraints for General Motors. Meticulous staff work culminated in committee discussions to evoke agreement and commitment to the mission statement. Through this process a vision was created which paved the way for the next phases of the transformation at GM.

At Chrysler, Lee Iacocca developed a vision without committee work or heavy staff involvement. Instead, he relied more on his intuitive and directive leadership, philosophy, and style. Both GM and Chrysler ended up with a new vision because of transformational leader proactively shaping a new organization mission and vision. . . .

2. *Mobilization of Commitment*. Here, the organization, or at least a critical mass of it, accepts the new mission and vision and makes it happen. At General Motors, Roger Smith took his top 900 executives on a five-day retreat to share and discuss the vision. The event lasted five days not because it takes that long to share a one-paragraph mission statement and eight objectives, but because the process of evolving commitment and mobilizing support requires a great deal of dialogue and exchange. It should be noted that mobilization of commitment must go well beyond five-day retreats; nevertheless, it is in the phase that transformational leaders get deeper understanding of their *followers*. . . . After transformational leaders create a vision and mobilize commitment, they must determine how to institutionalize the new mission and vision.

3. *Institutionalization of Change*. Organizations will not be revitalized unless new patterns of behavior within the organization are adopted. Transformational leaders need to transmit their vision into reality, their mission into action, their philosophy into practice. New realities, action, and practices must be shared throughout the organization. Alterations in communication, decision making, and problem-solving systems are tools through which transitions are shared so that visions become a reality. At a deeper level, institutionalization of change requires shaping and reinforcement of a new culture that fits with the revitalized organization. The human resource systems of selection, development, appraisal, and reward are major levers for institutionalizing change.

INDIVIDUAL DYNAMICS OF CHANGE

The previous section outlined requisite processes for organizational revitalization. Although organizational steps are necessary, they are not sufficient in creating and implementing change. In managing transitions, a more problematic set of forces which focuses on individual psychodynamics of change must be understood and managed. Major transitions unleash powerful conflicting forces in people. The change invokes simultaneous positive and negative personal feelings of fear and hope, anxiety and relief, pressure and stimulation, leaving the old and accepting a new direction, loss of meaning and new meaning, threat to self-esteem and new sense of value. The challenge for transformational leaders is to recognize these mixed emotions, act to help people move from negative to positive emotions, and mobilize and focus energy that is necessary for individual renewal and organizational revitalization.

Figure 1 provides a set of concepts for understanding the individual dynamics of transitions. The concepts, drawn from the work by Bridges, propose a three-phase process of individual change: first come endings, followed by neutral zones, and then new beginnings.[6] During each of these phases, an identifiable set of psychological tasks can be identified which individuals need to successfully complete in order to accept change.

The Three-Phase Process

Endings. All individual transitions start with endings. Endings must be accepted and understood before transitions can begin. Employees who refuse to accept the fact that traditional behaviors have ended will be unable to adopt new behaviors. The first task is to disengage, which often accompanies a physical transaction. For example, when transferring from one job to another, individuals must learn to accept the new physical setting and disengage from the old position: when transferred employees continually return to visit former colleagues, this is a sign that they have inadequately disengaged. The second task is to disidentify. Individual self-identity is often tied to a job position in such a way that when a plant manager is transferred to corporate staff to work in the marketing department, he or she must disidentify with the plant and its people and with the self-esteem felt as a plant manager. At a deeper personal level, individual transactions require disenchantment. Disenchantment entails recognizing that the enchantment or positive feelings associated with past situations will not be possible to replicate in the future. . . . Finally, individuals need to experience and work through disorientation which reflects the loss of familiar trappings. As mature organizations become revitalized, individuals must disengage, disidentify, disenchant, and disorient with past practices and discover in new organizations a new sense of worth or value.

To help individuals cope with endings, transformational leaders need to replace past glories with future opportunities. However, leaders must also acknowledge individual resistances and senses of loss in a transitional period while encouraging employees to face and accept failures as learning opportunities. Holding on to past accomplishments and memories without coming to grips with failure and the need to change may be why companies such as W. T. Grant, International Harvester, and Braniff were unsuccessful at revitalization. There is a sense of dying in all endings, and it does not help to treat transactions as if the past can be buried without effort. Yet, one should see the past as providing new directions.

Neutral Zone. The key to individuals being able to fully change may be in the second phase which Bridges terms the neutral zone.[7] This phase can be interpreted as a seemingly unproductive "time out" when individuals feel disconnected from people and things of the past and emotionally unconnected with the present. In reality, this phase is a time of reorientation where individuals complete endings and begin new patterns of behavior. Often Western culture, especially in the U.S., avoids this experience and treats the neutral zone like a busy street, to be crossed as fast as possible and certainly not a place to contemplate and experience. However, running across the neutral zone too hurriedly does not allow the ending to occur nor the new beginning to properly start. A death and rebirth process is necessary so that organizational members can work through the disintegration and reintegration. To pass through the neutral zone requires taking the time and thought to gain perspective on both the endings—what went wrong, why it needs to be changed, and what must be overcome in both attitude and behavioral change—and the new beginning—what the new priorities are, why they are needed, and what new attitudes and behaviors will be required. It is in this phase that the most skillful transformational leadership is called upon. . . .

Failure to lead individuals through the neutral zone may result in aborted new beginnings. In 1983, International Harvester appeared to be stuck in the neutral zone. In order for International Harvester to make a new beginning, it must enable people to find a new identification with the future organization while accepting the end of the old organization. Such a transformation has successfully occurred at Chrysler Corporation where morale and esprit de corps grew with the new vision implanted by Lee Iacocca. In the end, organizational revitalization can only occur if individuals accept past failures and engage in new behaviors and attitudes.

New Beginnings. After individuals accept endings by working through neutral zones, they are able to work with new enthusiasm and commitment. New beginnings are characterized by employees learning from the past rather than reveling in it, looking for new scripts rather than acting out old ones, and being positive and excited about current and future work opportunities rather than dwelling on past successes or failures. When Mr. Iacocca implemented his vision at Chrysler, many long-term employees discovered new beginnings. They saw the new Chrysler as an opportunity to succeed, and they worked with a renewed vigor.

WHAT QUALITIES DO TRANSFORMATIONAL LEADERS POSSESS?

So what does it take to transform an organization's technical, political, and cultural systems? The transformational leader must possess a deep understanding, whether it be intuitive or learned, of organizations and their place both in society at large and in the lives of individuals. The ability to build a new institution requires the kind of political dialogue our founding fathers had when Jefferson, Hamilton, Adams, and others debated issues of justice, equity, separation of powers, checks and balances, and freedom. This language may sound foreign to corporate settings but when major organization revitalization is being undertaken, all of these concepts merit some level of examination. At Chrysler, issues of equity, justice, power, and freedom underlay many of Mr. Iacocca's decisions. Thus, as a start, transformational leaders need to understand concepts of equity, power, freedom, and the dynamics of decision making. In addition to modifying systems, transformational leaders must understand and realign cultural systems.

In addition to managing political and cultural systems, transformational leaders must make difficult decisions quickly. Leaders need to know when to push and when to back off. Finally, transformational leaders are often seen as creators of their own luck. These leaders seize opportunities and know when to act so that casual observers may perceive luck as a plausible explanation for their success; whereas, in reality it is a transformational leader who knows when to jump and when not to jump. Again, Mr. Iacocca can be viewed either as a very lucky person or as the possessor of a great ability to judge when to act and when not to act.

THE SIGNIFICANCE OF CORPORATE CULTURES

Much has been written about organizational cultures in recent years.[8] . . .

Culture plays two central roles in organizations. First, it provides organizational members with a way of understanding and making sense of events and symbols. Thus, when employees are confronted with certain complex problems, they "know" how to approach them the "right" way. Like the Eskimos who have a vocabulary that differentiates the five types of snow, organizations create vocabularies to describe how things are done in the organization. At IBM, it is very clear to all insiders how to form a task force and to solve problems since task forces and problem solving are a way of life in IBM's culture.

Second, culture provides meaning. It embodies a set of values which helps justify why certain behaviors are encouraged at the exclusion of other behaviors. Companies with strong cultures have been able to commit people to the organization and have them identify very personally and closely with the organization's success. Superficially, this is seen in the "hoopla" activities associated with an IBM sales meeting, a Tupperware party, or an Amway distributor meeting. Outsiders often ridicule such activities, yet they are part of the process by which some successful companies manage cultural meaning. On one level, corporate culture is analogous to rituals carried out in religious groups. The key point in assessing culture is to realize that in order to transform an organization the culture that provides meaning must be assessed and revamped. The transformational leader needs to articulate new values and norms and then to use multiple change levers ranging from role modeling, symbolic acts, creation of rituals, and revamping of human resource systems and management processes to support new cultural messages.

CONCLUSION

Based on the premise that the pressure for basic organizational change will intensify and not diminish, we strongly believe that transformational leadership, not transactional management, is required for revitalizing our organizations. Ultimately, it is up to our leaders to choose the right kind of leadership and corporate lifestyle.

REFERENCES

1. See J. M. Burns, *Leadership* (New York: Harper & Row, 1978).
2. See N. M. Tichy, *Managing Strategic Change: Technical, Political and Cultural Dynamics* (New York: John Wiley & Sons, 1983).
3. Ibid.
4. See K. H. Blanchard and S. Johnson, *The One Minute Manager* (New York: Berkeley Books, 1982).
5. See T. J. Peters and R. J. Waterman, Jr., *In Search of Excellence* (New York: Harper & Row, 1982).
6. See W. Bridges, *Making Sense of Life's Transitions* (New York: Addison-Wesley, 1980).
7. Ibid.
8. See: T. E. Deal and A. A. Kennedy, *Corporate Cultures* (Reading, MA: Addison-Wesley, 1982); "Corporate Culture: The Hard-to-Change Values That Spell Success or Failure," *Business Week*, 27 October 1980, pp. 148–160; W. Ulrich, "HRM and Culture: History, Rituals, and Myths," *Human Resource Management* (23/2) Summer 1984.

6
The Learning Leader as Culture Manager

Edgar H. Schein

Leadership can occur anywhere in the organization. Leadership is the attitude and motivation to examine and manage culture. Accomplishing this goal is more difficult lower down in the organization but by no means impossible in that subcultures can be managed just as can overall organizational cultures.

The issues that make the most difference to the kind of leadership required are twofold. First, different stages of organizational development require different kinds of culture management. Second, different strategic issues require a focus on different kinds of cultural dimensions. Each of these points is briefly examined below.

LEADERSHIP IN CULTURE CREATION

In a growing organization, leaders externalize their own assumptions and embed them gradually and consistently in the mission, goals, structures, and working procedures of the group. Whether we call these basic assumptions the guiding beliefs, the theories-in-use, the mental models, the basic principles, or the guiding visions on which founders operate, there is little question that they become major elements of the organization's emerging culture (for example, Argyris, 1976; Bennis, 1989; Davis, 1984; Donaldson and Lorsch, 1983; Dyer, 1986; Kotter and Heskett, 1992; Pettigrew, 1979; Schein, 1983).

In a rapidly changing world, the learning leader/founder must not only have vision but must be able to impose it and to develop it further as external circumstances change. Inasmuch as the new members of an organization arrive with prior organizational and cultural experiences, a common set of assumptions can only be forged by clear and consistent messages as the group encounters and survives its own crises. The culture creation leader therefore needs persistence and patience, yet as a learner must be flexible and ready to change.

As groups and organizations develop, certain key emotional issues arise. These have to do with dependence on the leader, with peer relationships, and with how to work effectively. Leadership is needed to help the group identify the issues and deal with them. During this process leaders must often absorb and contain the anxiety that is unleashed when things do not work as they should (Hirschhorn, 1988; Schein, 1983). Leaders may not have the answer, but they must provide temporary stability and emotional reassurance while the answer is being worked out. This anxiety-containing function is especially relevant during periods of learning, when old habits must be given up before new ones are learned. Moreover, if the world

Source: Adapted from *Organizational Culture and Leadership*, Second Edition, by Edgar H. Schein, pp. 374–392. Reprinted by permission of John Wiley & Sons.

is increasingly changing, such anxiety may be perpetual, requiring learning leaders to assume a perpetual supportive role. The traumas of growth appear to be so constant and so powerful that unless a strong leader takes the role of anxiety and risk absorber, the group cannot get through its early stages of growth and fails. Being in an ownership position helps because everyone then realizes that the founder is in fact taking a greater personal financial risk; however, ownership does not automatically create the ability to absorb anxiety. For many leaders this is one of the most important things they have to learn.

When leaders launch new enterprises, they must be mindful of the power they have to impose on those enterprises their own assumptions about what is right and proper, how the world works, and how things should be done. Leaders should not apologize for or be cautious about their assumptions. Rather, it is intrinsic to the leadership role to create order out of chaos, and leaders are expected to provide their own assumptions as an initial road map into the uncertain future. The more aware leaders are of this process, the more consistent and effective they can be in implementing it.

The process of culture creation, embedding, and reinforcement brings with it problems as well as solutions. Many organizations survive and grow but at the same time operate inconsistently or do things that seem contradictory. One explanation of this phenomenon that has been pointed out repeatedly is that leaders not only embed in their organizations what they intend consciously to get across, but they also convey their own inner conflicts and the inconsistencies in their own personal makeup (Schein, 1983; Kets de Vries and Miller, 1984; Miller, 1990). The most powerful signal to which subordinates respond is what catches leaders' attention consistently, particularly what arouses them emotionally. But many of the things to which leaders respond emotionally reflect not so much their conscious intentions as their unconscious conflicts. The organization then either develops assumptions around these inconsistencies and conflicts and they become part of the culture, or the leader gradually loses a position of influence if the behavior begins to be seen as too disruptive or actually destructive. In extreme cases the organization isolates or ejects the founder. In doing so, however, it is not rejecting all of the founder's assumptions but only those that are inconsistent with the core assumptions on which the organization was built.

The period of culture creation, therefore, puts an additional burden on founders—to obtain enough self-insight to avoid unwittingly undermining their own creations. Founding leaders often find it difficult to recognize that the very qualities that made them successful initially, their strong convictions, can become sources of difficulty later on and that they also must learn and grow as their organizations grow. Such insights become especially important when organizations face issues of leadership succession because succession discussions force into the open aspects of the culture that may not have been previously recognized.

What all of this means for leaders of developing organizations is that they must have tremendous self-insight and recognize their own role not only in creating the culture but also their responsibility in embedding and developing culture. Inasmuch as the culture is the primary source of identity for young organizations, the culture creation and development process must be handled sensitively with full understanding of the anxieties that are unleashed when identity is challenged.

LEADERSHIP AT ORGANIZATIONAL MIDLIFE

As the organization develops a substantial history of its own, its culture becomes more of a cause than an effect. As subgroups develop their own subcultures, the opportunities for constructive use of cultural diversity and the problems of integration both become greater. The leader must be able to pay attention to diversity and assess clearly how much of it is useful for further organizational development and how much of it is potentially dysfunctional. The culture is now much less tied to the leader's own personality, which makes it easier to assess objectively, though there are likely to be sacred cows, holdovers from the founding period, that have to be delicately handled.

The leader at this stage must be able to detect how the culture influences the strategy, structure, procedures, and ways in which the group members relate to one another. Culture is a powerful influence on members' perceptions, thinking, and feeling, and these predispositions, along with situational factors, influence members' behavior. Because culture serves an important anxiety-reducing function, members cling to it even if it becomes dysfunctional in relationship to environmental opportunities and constraints.

Leaders at this stage need diagnostic skill to figure out not only what the cultural influences are, but also what their impact is on the organization's ability to change and learn. Whereas founding leaders most need self-insight, midlife leaders most need the ability to decipher the surrounding culture and subcultures. To help the organization evolve into whatever will make it most effective in the future, leaders must also have culture management skills. In some instances this may mean increasing cultural diversity, allowing some of the uniformity that may have been built up in the growth stage to erode. In other instances it may mean pulling together a culturally diverse set of organizational units and attempting to impose new common assumptions on them. In either case the leader needs (1) to be able to analyze the culture in sufficient detail to know which cultural assumptions can aid and which ones will hinder the fulfillment of the organizational mission and (2) to possess the intervention skills to make desired changes happen.

Most of the prescriptive analyses of how to maintain the organization's effectiveness through this period emphasize that the leader must have certain insights, clear vision, and the skills to articulate, communicate, and implement the vision, but these analyses say nothing about how a given organization can find and install such a leader. In U.S. organizations in particular, the outside board members probably play a critical role in this process. If the organization has had a strong founding culture, however, its board may be composed exclusively of people who share the founder's vision. Consequently, real changes in direction may not become possible until the organization experiences serious survival difficulties and begins to search for a person with different assumptions to lead it.

One area to explore further here is the CEO's own role in succession. Can the leader of a midlife organization perceive the potential dysfunctions of some aspects of the culture to a sufficient extent to ensure that his or her successor will be able to move the culture in an appropriate new direction? CEOs have a great deal of power to influence the choice of their successor. Do they use that power wisely in terms of cultural issues? For example, it is alleged that one of the main reasons why Reginald Jones as CEO of General Electric "chose" Jack

Welch to be his successor was because he recognized in Welch a person who would create the kinds of changes that were necessary for GE to remain viable. Similarly, Steve Jobs "chose" John Sculley to head Apple even though at some level he must have sensed that this choice might eventually lead to the kind of conflict that in the end forced Jobs to leave. The ultimate paradox here is that truly learning leaders may have to face the conclusion that they must replace themselves, that they do not have the vision needed to bring the midlife organization into alignment with a rapidly changing world.

LEADERSHIP IN MATURE AND POTENTIALLY DECLINING ORGANIZATIONS

In the mature stage if the organization has developed a strong unifying culture, that culture now defines even what is to be thought of as leadership, what is heroic or sinful behavior, and how authority and power are to be allocated and managed. Thus, what leadership has created now either blindly perpetuates itself or creates new definitions of leadership, which may not even include the kinds of entrepreneurial assumptions that launched the organization in the first place. The first problem of the mature and possibly declining organization, then, is to find a process to empower a potential leader who may have enough insight to overcome some of the constraining cultural assumptions.

What the leader must do at this point in the organization's history depends on the degree to which the culture of the organization has, in fact, enabled the group to adapt to its environmental realities. If the culture has not facilitated adaptation, the organization either will not survive or will find a way to change its culture. If it is to change its culture, it must be led by someone who can, in effect, break the tyranny of the old culture. This requires not only the insight and diagnostic skill to determine what the old culture is, but to realize what alternative assumptions are available and how to start a change process toward their acceptance.

Leaders of mature organizations must, as has been argued repeatedly, make themselves sufficiently marginal in their own organization to be able to perceive its assumptions objectively and nondefensively. They must, therefore, find many ways to be exposed to their external environment and thereby facilitate their own learning. If they cannot learn new assumptions themselves, they will not be able to perceive what is possible in their organizations. Even worse, they may destroy innovative efforts that arise within their organizations if those innovative efforts involve countercultural assumptions.

Leaders capable of such managed culture change can come from inside the organization if they have acquired objectivity and insight into elements of the culture. Such culture objectivity appears to be related to having had a nonconventional career or exposure to many subcultures within the organization (Kotter and Heskett, 1992). However, the formally designated senior managers of a given organization may not be willing or able to provide such culture change leadership. Leadership then may have to come from other boundary spanners in the organization or from outsiders. It may even come from a number of people in the organization, in which case it makes sense to talk of turnaround teams or multiple leadership.

If a leader is imposed from the outside, she or he must have the skill to diagnose accurately what the culture of the organization is, what elements are well adapted and what elements are problematic for future adaptation, and how to change that which needs changing. In other words the leader must be a skilled change manager who first learns what the present state of the culture is, unfreezes it, redefines and changes it, and then refreezes the new assumptions. Talented turnaround managers seem to be able to manage all phases of such changes, but sometimes different leaders will be involved in the different steps over a considerable period of time. They will use all the mechanisms previously discussed in the appropriate combinations to get the job done provided that they have the authority and power to use extreme measures, such as replacing the people who perpetuate the old cultural assumptions.

In summary, leaders play a critical role at each developmental stage of an organization, but that role differs as a function of the stage. Much of what leaders do is to perpetually diagnose the particular assumptions of the culture and figure out how to use those assumptions constructively or to change them if they are constraints.

LEADERSHIP AND CULTURE IN STRATEGY FORMULATION

Many companies have found that they or their consultants can think of new strategies that make sense from a financial, product, or marketing point of view, yet they cannot implement those strategies because such implementation requires assumptions, values, and ways of working that are too far out of line with the organization's existing assumptions. In some cases, the organization cannot even conceive of certain strategic options because they are too out of line with shared assumptions about the mission of the organization and its way of working, what Lorsch (1985) has aptly called "strategic myopia."

. . . We must remember that cultural assumptions are the product of past successes. As a result they are increasingly taken for granted and operate as silent filters on what is perceived and thought about. If the organization's environment changes and new responses are required, the danger is that the changes will not be noticed or, even if noticed, that the organization will not be able to adapt because of embedded routines based on past success. Culture constrains strategy by limiting what the CEO and other senior managers are able to think about and what they perceive in the first place.

One of the critical roles of learning leadership, then, is first of all to notice changes in the environment and then to figure out what needs to be done to remain adaptive. I am defining leadership in this context in terms of the role, not the position. The CEO or other senior managers may or may not be able to fulfill the leadership role, and leadership in the sense that I am defining it can occur anywhere in the organization. However, if real change and learning are to take place, it is probably necessary that the CEO or other very senior managers be able to be leaders in this sense.

Leaders must be somewhat marginal and must be somewhat embedded in the organization's external environment to fulfill this role adequately. At the same time, leaders must be well connected to those parts of the organization that are themselves well connected to the environment—sales, purchasing, marketing, public relations and legal, finance, and R & D. Leaders must be able to listen to disconfirming information coming from these sources and to assess the implications for the future of the organization. Only when they truly understand what is happening and what will be required in the way of organizational change can they begin to take action in initiating a learning process.

Much has been said about the need for vision in leaders, but too little has been said about their need to listen, to absorb, to search the environment for trends, and to build the organization's capacity to learn. Especially at the strategic level, the ability to see and acknowledge the full complexity of problems becomes critical. The ability to acknowledge complexity may also imply the willingness and emotional strength to admit uncertainty and to embrace experimentation and possible errors as the only way to learn. In our obsession with leadership vision, we may have made it possible for learning leaders to admit that their vision is not clear and that the whole organization will have to learn together. Moreover, as I have repeatedly argued, vision in a mature organization only helps when the organization has already been disconfirmed and members feel anxious and in need of a solution. Much of what learning leaders must do occurs before vision even becomes relevant.

To summarize, the critical roles of leadership in strategy formulation and implementation are (1) to perceive accurately and in depth what is happening in the environment, (2) to create enough disconfirming information to motivate the organization to change without creating too much anxiety, (3) to provide psychological safety by either providing a vision of how to change and in what direction or by creating a process of visioning that allows the organization itself to find a path, (4) to acknowledge uncertainty, (5) to embrace errors in the learning process as inevitable and desirable, and (6) to manage all phases of the change process, including especially the management of anxiety as some cultural assumptions are given up and new learning begins. . . .

IMPLICATIONS FOR THE SELECTION AND DEVELOPMENT OF LEADERS

A dynamic analysis of organizational culture makes it clear that leadership is intertwined with culture formation, evolution, transformation, and destruction. Culture is created in the first instance by the actions of leaders; culture is embedded and strengthened by leaders. When culture becomes dysfunctional, leadership is needed to help the group unlearn some of its cultural assumptions and learn new assumptions. Such transformations sometimes require what amounts to conscious and deliberate destruction of cultural elements. This in turn requires the ability to surmount one's own taken-for-granted assumptions, seeing what is needed to ensure the health and survival of the group, and orchestrating events and processes that enable the group to evolve toward new cultural assumptions. Without leadership in this sense, groups will not be able to adapt to changing environmental conditions. Let us summarize what is really needed to be a leader in this sense.

Perception and Insight

First, the leader must be able to perceive the problem, to have insight into himself or herself and into the culture and its dysfunctional elements. Such boundary-spanning perception can be difficult because it requires one to see one's own weaknesses, to perceive that one's own defenses not only help in managing anxiety but can also hinder one's efforts to be effective. Successful architects of change must have a high degree of objectivity about themselves and their own organizations, and such objectivity results from spending portions of their careers in diverse settings that permit them to compare and contrast different cultures. International experience is therefore one of the most powerful ways of learning.

Individuals often are aided in becoming objective about themselves through counseling and psychotherapy. One might conjecture that leaders can benefit from comparable processes such as training and development programs that emphasize experiential learning and self-assessment. From this perspective one of the most important functions of outside consultants or board members is to provide the kind of counseling that produces cultural insight. It is therefore far more important for the consultant to help the leader figure out for himself or herself what is going on and what to do than to provide recommendations on what the organization should do. The consultant also can serve as a "cultural therapist," helping the leader figure out what the culture is and what parts of it are more or less adaptive.

Motivation

Leadership requires not only insight into the dynamics of the culture but the motivation and skill to intervene in one's own cultural process. To change any elements of the culture, leaders must be willing to unfreeze their own organization. Unfreezing requires disconfirmation, a process that is inevitably painful for many. The leader must find a way to say to his or her own organization that things are not all right and, if necessary, must enlist the aid of outsiders in getting this message across. Such willingness requires a great ability to be concerned for the organization above and beyond the self, to communicate dedication or commitment to the group above and beyond self-interest.

If the boundaries of organization become looser, a further motivational issue arises in that it is less and less clear where a leader's ultimate loyalty should lie—with the organization, with industry, with country, or with some broader professional community whose ultimate responsibility is to the globe and to all of humanity.

Emotional Strength

Unfreezing an organization requires the creation of psychological safety, which means that the leader must have the emotional strength to absorb much of the anxiety that change brings with it and the ability to remain supportive to the organization through the transition phase even if group members become angry and obstructive. The leader is likely to be the target of anger and criticism because, by definition, he or she must challenge some of what the group has taken for granted. This may involve closing down the company division that was the original source of the company's growth and the basis of many employees' sense of pride and identity. It may involve laying off or retiring loyal, dedicated employees and old friends. Worst of all, it may involve the message that some of the founder's most cherished assumptions are wrong in the contemporary context. It is here that dedication and commitment are especially needed to demonstrate to the organization that the leader genuinely cares about the welfare of the total organization even as parts of it come under challenge. The leader must remember that giving up a cultural element requires one to take some risk, the risk that one will be very anxious and in the end worse off, and yet the leader must have the strength to forge the way into this unknown territory.

Ability to Change the Cultural Assumptions

If an assumption is to be given up, it must be replaced or redefined in another form, and it is the burden of leadership to make that happen. In other words, the leader must have the ability to induce cognitive redefinition by articulating and selling new visions and concepts. The leader must be able to bring to the surface, review, and change some of the group's basic assumptions. . . .

Ability to Create Involvement and Participation

A paradox of culture change leadership is that the leader must be able not only to lead but also to listen, to emotionally involve the group in achieving its own insights into its cultural dilemmas, and to be genuinely participative in his or her approach to learning and change. The leaders of social, religious, or political movements can rely on personal charisma and let the followers do what they will. In an organization, however, the leader has to work with the group that exists at the moment, because he or she is dependent on the group members to carry out the organization's mission. The leader must recognize that, in the end, cognitive redefinition must occur inside the heads of many members and that will happen only if they are actively involved in the process. The whole organization must achieve some degree of insight and develop motivation to change before any real change will occur, and the leader must create this involvement.

The ability to involve others and to listen to them also protects leaders from attempting to change things that should not be changed. When leaders are brought in from the outside this becomes especially important because some of the assumptions operating in the organization may not fit the leader's own assumptions yet be critical to the organization's success. To illustrate the kinds of mistakes that are possible, we need remember only the period in the Atari Company's history when Warner Communications, the parent company, decided to improve Atari's marketing by bringing in as president an experienced marketing executive from the food industry. This executive brought with him the assumption that the key to success is high motivation and high rewards based on individual performance. He created and imposed an incentive system designed to select the engineers who were doing the best job in inventing and designing new computer games and gave them large monetary rewards. Soon some of the best engineers were leaving, and the company was getting into technical difficulty. What was wrong?

The new executive had created and articulated clear symbols, and everyone had rallied around them. Apparently, what was wrong was the assumption that the incentives and rewards should be based on individual effort. What the president failed to understand, coming from the food industry with its individualistic product management orientation, was that the computer games were designed by groups and teams and that the engineers considered the assignment of individual responsibility to be neither possible nor necessary. They were happy being group members and would have responded to group incentives, but unfortunately, the symbol chosen was the wrong symbol from this point of view. The engineers also noted that the president, with his nontechnical background, was not adept at choosing the best engineers, because their key assumption was that "best" was the product of group effort, not individual brilliance. Given the incompatible assumptions, it is no surprise that the president did not last long. Unfortunately, damage in terms of the loss of employees and in esprit had been done.

Ability to Learn a New Culture

Culture change leaders often have to take over a company in which they did not previously have any experience. If they are to diagnose and possibly change the culture they have entered, it is, of course, mandatory that they first learn what the essence of that culture is. This point raises the question of how much an individual can learn that is totally new. My hypothesis, based on various streams of research on leadership and management, is that leaders can cross boundaries and enter new organizational cultures fairly easily if they stay within a given industry, as defined by a core technology. A manager growing up in one chemical company can probably become the successful CEO of another chemical company and can learn the culture of that company. What appears to be much more difficult is to cross industry or national boundaries, because cognitive frames that are built up early in the manager's career are fundamentally more embedded. The ability of a John Sculley to become a successful leader of Apple is unusual. . . .

In any case, the leader coming into a new organization must be very sensitive to his or her own need to truly understand the culture before assessing it and possibly changing it. A period of learning lasting a year or more, if the situation allows that much time, is probably necessary. If the situation is more critical, the leader could speed up his or her own learning by systematically involving the layers of the organization below him or her in culture deciphering exercises. . . .

SUMMARY AND CONCLUSIONS

It seems clear that the leaders of the future will have to be perpetual learners. This will require (1) new levels of perception and insight into the realities of the world and also into themselves; (2) extraordinary levels of motivation to go through the inevitable pain of learning and change, especially in a world with looser boundaries in which one's own loyalties become more and more difficult to define; (3) the emotional strength to manage their own and others' anxiety as learning and change become more and more a way of life; (4) new skills in analyzing and changing cultural assumptions; (5) the willingness and ability to involve others and elicit their participation; and (6) the ability to learn the assumptions of a whole new organizational culture.

Learning and change cannot be imposed on people. Their involvement and participation are needed diagnosing what is going on, figuring out what to do, and actually doing it. The more turbulent, ambiguous, and out of control the world becomes, the more the learning process will have to be shared by all the members of the social unit doing the learning. If the leaders of today want to create organizational cultures that will themselves be more amenable to learning, they will have to set the example by becoming learners themselves and involving others in the learning process.

The essence of that learning process will be to give organizational culture its due. Can we as individual members of organizations and occupations, as managers, teachers, researchers, and, sometimes, leaders recognize how deeply our own perceptions, thoughts, and feelings are culturally determined? Ultimately, we cannot achieve the cultural humility required to live in a turbulent culturally diverse world unless we can see cultural assumptions within ourselves. In the end, cultural understanding and cultural learning start with self-insight.

REFERENCES

Argyris, C. *Increasing Leadership Effectiveness*. New York: Wiley-Interscience, 1976.

Bennis, W. *On Becoming a Leader*. Reading, Mass.: Addison-Wesley, 1989.

Davis, S. M. *Managing Corporate Culture*. New York: Ballinger, 1984.

Donaldson, G., and Lorsch, J. W. *Decision Making at the Top*. New York: Basic Books, 1983.

Dyer, W. G. Jr. *Culture Change in Family Firms*. San Francisco: Jossey-Bass, 1986.

Hirschhorn, L. *The Workplace Within: Psychodynamics of Organizational Life*. Cambridge, Mass.: MIT Press, 1988.

Kets de Vries, M. F. R., and Miller, D. *The Neurotic Organization: Diagnosing and Changing Counterproductive Styles of Management*. San Francisco: Jossey-Bass, 1984.

Kotter, J. P., and Heskett, J. L. *Corporate Culture and Performance*. New York: Free Press, 1992.

Lorsch, J. W. "Strategic Myopia: Culture as an Invisible Barrier to Change." In R. H. Kilmann, M. J. Saxton, R. Serpa, and others, *Gaining Control of the Corporate Culture*. San Francisco: Jossey-Bass, 1985.

Miller, D. *The Icarus Paradox*. New York: Harper & Row, 1990.

Pettigrew, A. M. "On Studying Organizational Cultures." *Administrative Science Quarterly*, 1979, 24, 570–581.

Schein, E. H. "The Role of the Founder in Creating Organizational Culture." *Organizational Dynamics*, Summer 1983, pp. 13–28.

7
What Makes a Leader?

Daniel Goleman

Every businessperson knows a story about a highly intelligent, highly skilled executive who was promoted into a leadership position only to fail at the job. And they also know a story about someone with solid—but not extraordinary—intellectual abilities and technical skills who was promoted into a similar position and then soared.

Such anecdotes support the widespread belief that identifying individuals with the "right stuff" to be leaders is more art than science. After all, the personal styles of superb leaders vary: some leaders are subdued and analytical; others shout their manifestos from the mountaintops. And just as important, different situations call for different types of leadership. Most mergers need a sensitive negotiator at the helm, whereas many turnarounds require a more forceful authority.

I have found, however, that the most effective leaders are alike in one crucial way: they all have a high degree of what has come to be known as *emotional intelligence*. It's not that IQ and technical skills are irrelevant. They do matter, but mainly as "threshold capabilities"; that is, they are the entry-level requirements for executive positions. But my research, along with other recent studies, clearly shows that emotional intelligence is the sine qua non of leadership. Without it, a person can have the best training in the world, an incisive, analytical mind, and an endless supply of smart ideas, but he still won't make a great leader.

In the course of the past year, my colleagues and I have focused on how emotional intelligence operates at work. We have examined the relationship between emotional intelligence and effective performance, especially in leaders. And we have observed how emotional intelligence shows itself on the job. How can you tell if someone has high emotional intelligence, for example, and how can you recognize it in yourself? In the following pages, we'll explore these questions, taking each of the components of emotional intelligence—self-awareness, self-regulation, motivation, empathy, and social skill—in turn [see Table 1].

EVALUATING EMOTIONAL INTELLIGENCE

Most large companies today have employed trained psychologists to develop what are known as "competency models" to aid them in identifying, training, and promoting likely stars in the leadership firmament. The psychologists have also developed such models for lower-level positions. And in recent years, I have analyzed competency models from 188 companies, most of which were large and global and included the likes

Source: Reprinted by permission of *Harvard Business Review* from "What Makes a Leader?" by Daniel Goleman, 1998.

TABLE 1 • THE FIVE COMPONENTS OF EMOTIONAL INTELLIGENCE AT WORK

	Definition	Hallmarks
Self-Awareness	the ability to recognize and understand your moods, emotions, and drives, as well as their effect on others	self-confidence realistic self-assessment self-deprecating sense of humor
Self-Regulation	the ability to control or redirect disruptive impulses and moods the propensity to suspend judgment — to think before acting	trustworthiness and integrity comfort with ambiguity openness to change
Motivation	a passion to work for reasons that go beyond money or status a propensity to pursue goals with energy and persistence	strong drive to achieve optimism, even in the face of failure organizational commitment
Empathy	the ability to understand the emotional makeup of other people skill in treating people according to their emotional reactions	expertise in building and retaining talent cross-cultural sensitivity service to clients and customers
Social Skill	proficiency in managing relationships and building networks an ability to find common ground and build rapport	effectiveness in leading change persuasiveness expertise in building and leading teams

of Lucent Technologies, British Airways, and Credit Suisse.

In carrying out this work, my objective was to determine which personal capabilities drove outstanding performance within these organizations, and to what degree they did so. I grouped capabilities into three categories: purely technical skills like accounting and business planning; cognitive abilities like analytical reasoning; and competencies demonstrating emotional intelligence such as the ability to work with others and effectiveness in leading change. . . .

When I analyzed all this data, I found dramatic results. To be sure, intellect was a driver of outstanding performance. Cognitive skills such as big-picture thinking and long-term vision were particularly important. But when I calculated the ratio of technical skills, IQ, and emotional intelligence as ingredients of excellent performance, emotional intelligence proved to be twice as important as the others for jobs at all levels.

Moreover, my analysis showed that emotional intelligence played an increasingly important role at the highest levels of the company, where differences in technical skills are of negligible importance. In other words, the higher the rank of a person considered to be a star performer, the more emotional intelligence capabilities showed up as the reason for his or her effectiveness. When I compared star performers with average ones in senior leadership positions, nearly 90% of the difference in their profiles was attributable to emotional intelligence factors rather than cognitive abilities. . . .

SELF-AWARENESS

Self-awareness is the first component of emotional intelligence—which makes sense when one considers that the Delphic oracle gave the advice to "know thyself" thousands of years ago. Self-awareness means having a deep understanding of one's emotions, strengths, weaknesses, needs, and drives. People with strong self-awareness are neither overly critical nor unrealistically hopeful. Rather, they are honest—with themselves and with others.

People who have a high degree of self-awareness recognize how their feelings affect them, other people, and their job performance. Thus, a self-aware person who knows that tight deadlines bring out the worst in him plans his time carefully and gets his work done well in advance. Another person with high self-awareness will be able to work with a demanding client. She will understand the client's impact on her moods and the deeper reasons for her frustration. "Their trivial demands take us away from the real work that needs to be done," she might explain. And she will go one step further and turn her anger into something constructive.

Self-awareness extends to a person's understanding of his or her values and goals. Someone who is highly self-aware knows where he is headed and why; so, for example, he will be able to be firm in turning down a job offer that is tempting financially but does not fit with his principles or long-term goals. A person who lacks self-awareness is apt to make decisions that bring on inner turmoil by treading on buried values. "The money looked good so I signed on," someone might say two years on the job, "but the work means so little to me that I'm constantly bored." The decisions of self-aware people mesh with their values; consequently, they often find work to be energizing.

How can one recognize self-awareness? First and foremost, it shows itself as candor and an ability to assess oneself realistically. People with high self-awareness are able to speak accurately and openly—although not necessarily effusively or confessionally—about their emotions and the impact they have on their work. For instance, one manager I know of was skeptical about a new personal-shopper service that her company, a major department store chain, was about to introduce. Without prompting from her team or her boss, she offered them an explanation: "It's hard for me to get behind the rollout of this service," she admitted, "because I really wanted to run the project, but I wasn't selected. Bear with me while I deal with that." The manager did indeed examine her feelings; a week later, she was supporting the project fully.

Such self-knowledge often shows itself in the hiring process. Ask a candidate to describe a time he got carried away by his feelings and did something he later regretted. Self-aware candidates will be frank in admitting to failure—and will often tell their tales with a smile. One of the hallmarks of self-awareness is a self-deprecating sense of humor.

Self-awareness can also be identified during performance reviews. Self-aware people know—and are comfortable talking about—their limitations and strengths, and they often demonstrate a thirst for constructive criticism. By contrast, people with low self-awareness interpret the message that they need to improve as a threat or a sign of failure.

Self-aware people can also be recognized by their self-confidence. They have a firm grasp of their capabilities and are less likely to set themselves up to fail by, for example, overstretching on assignments. They know, too, when to ask for help. And the risks they take on the job are calculated. They won't ask for a challenge that they know they can't handle alone. They'll play to their strengths. . . .

SELF-REGULATION

Biological impulses drive our emotions. We cannot do away with them—but we can do much to manage them. Self-regulation, which is like an ongoing inner conversation, is the component of emotional intelligence that frees us from being prisoners of our feelings. People engaged in such a conversation feel bad moods and emotional impulses just as everyone else does, but they find ways to control them and even to channel them in useful ways.

Imagine an executive who has just watched a team of his employees present a botched analysis to the company's board of directors. In the gloom that follows, the executive might find himself tempted to pound on the table in anger or kick over a chair. He could leap up and scream at the group. Or he might maintain a grim silence, glaring at everyone before stalking off.

But if he had a gift for self-regulation, he would pick his words carefully, acknowledging the team's poor performance without rushing to any hasty judgment. He would then step back to consider the reasons for the failure. Are they personal—a lack of effort? Are there any mitigating factors? What was his role in the debacle? After considering these questions, he would call the team together, lay out the incident's consequences, and offer his feelings about it. He would then present his analysis of the problem and a well-considered solution.

Why does self-regulation matter so much for leaders? First of all, people who are in control of their feelings and impulses—that is, people who are reasonable—are able to create an environment of trust and fairness. In such an environment, politics and infighting are sharply reduced and productivity is high. Talented people flock to the organization and aren't tempted to leave. And self-regulation has a trickle-down effect. No one wants to be known as a hothead when the boss is known for her calm approach. Fewer bad moods at the top mean fewer throughout the organization.

Second, self-regulation is important for competitive reasons. Everyone knows that business today is rife with ambiguity and change. Companies merge and break apart regularly. Technology transforms work at a dizzying pace. People who have mastered their emotions are able to roll with the changes. When a new change program is announced, they don't panic; instead, they are able to suspend judgment, seek out information, and listen to executives explain the new program. As the initiative moves forward, they are able to move with it. . . .

I want to push the importance of self-regulation to leadership even further and make the case that it enhances integrity, which is not only a personal virtue but also an organizational strength. Many of the bad things that happen in companies are a function of impulsive behavior. People rarely plan to exaggerate profits, pad expense accounts, dip into the till, or abuse power for selfish ends. Instead, an opportunity presents itself, and people with low impulse control just say yes. . . .

The signs of emotional self-regulation, therefore, are not hard to miss: a propensity for reflection and thoughtfulness; comfort with ambiguity and change; and integrity—an ability to say no to impulsive urges.

Like self-awareness, self-regulation often does not get its due. People who can master their emotions are sometimes seen as cold fish—their considered responses are taken as a lack of passion. People with fiery temperaments are frequently thought of as "classic" leaders—their outbursts are considered hallmarks of charisma and power. But when such people make it to the top, their impulsiveness often works against them. In my research, extreme displays of negative emotion have never emerged as a driver of good leadership.

MOTIVATION

If there is one trait that virtually all effective leaders have, it is motivation. They are driven to achieve beyond expectations—their own and everyone else's. The key word here is *achieve*. Plenty of people are motivated by external factors such as a big salary or the status that comes from having an impressive title or being part of a prestigious company. By contrast, those with leadership potential are motivated by a deeply embedded desire to achieve for the sake of achievement.

If you are looking for leaders, how can you identify people who are motivated by the drive to achieve rather than by external rewards? The first sign is a passion for the work itself—such people seek out creative challenges, love to learn, and take great pride in a job well done. They also display an unflagging energy to do things better. People with such energy often seem restless with the status quo. They are persistent with their questions about why things are done one way rather than another; they are eager to explore new approaches to their work. . . .

[There are] two other common traits of people who are driven to achieve. They are forever raising the performance bar, and they like to keep score. Take the performance bar first. During performance reviews, people with high levels of motivation might ask to be "stretched" by their superiors. Of course, an employee who combines self-awareness with internal motivation will recognize her limits—but she won't settle for objectives that seem too easy to fulfill.

And it follows naturally that people who are driven to do better also want a way of tracking progress—their own, their team's, and their company's. Whereas people with low achievement motivation are often fuzzy about results, those with high achievement motivation often keep score by tracking such hard measures as profitability or market share. . . .

Interestingly, people with high motivation remain optimistic even when the score is against them. In such cases, self-regulation combines with achievement motivation to overcome the frustration and depression that come after a setback or failure. . . .

Executives trying to recognize high levels of achievement motivation in their people can look for one last piece of evidence: commitment to the organization. When people love their job for the work itself, they often feel committed to the organizations that make that work possible. Committed employees are likely to stay with an organization even when they are pursued by headhunters waving money.

It's not difficult to understand how and why a motivation to achieve translates into strong leadership. If you set the performance bar high for yourself, you will do the same for the organization when you are in a position to do so. Likewise, a drive to surpass goals and an interest in keeping score can be contagious. Leaders with these traits can often build a team of managers around them with the same traits. And of course, optimism and organizational commitment are fundamental to leadership—just try to imagine running a company without them.

EMPATHY

Of all the dimensions of emotional intelligence, empathy is the most easily recognized. We have all felt the empathy of a sensitive teacher or friend; we have all been struck by its absence in an unfeeling coach or boss. But when it comes to business, we rarely hear people praised, let alone rewarded, for their empathy. The very word seems unbusinesslike, out of place amid the tough realities of the marketplace.

But empathy doesn't mean a kind of "I'm okay, you're okay" mushiness. For a leader, that is, it doesn't mean adopting other people's emotions as one's own and trying to please everybody. That would be a nightmare—it would make action impossible. Rather, empathy means thoughtfully considering employees' feelings—along with other factors—in the process of making intelligent decisions.

For an example of empathy in action, consider what happened when two giant brokerage companies merged, creating redundant jobs in all their divisions. One division manager called his people together and gave a gloomy speech that emphasized the number of people who would soon be fired. The manager of another division gave his people a different kind of speech. He was upfront about his own worry and confusion, and he promised to keep people informed and to treat everyone fairly.

The difference between these two managers was empathy. The first manager was too worried about his own fate to consider the feelings of his anxiety-stricken colleagues. The second knew intuitively what his people were feeling, and he acknowledged their fears with his words. Is it any surprise that the first manager saw his division sink and many demoralized people, especially the most talented, departed? By contrast, the second manager continued to be a strong leader, his best people stayed, and his division remained as productive as ever.

Empathy is particularly important today as a component of leadership for at least three reasons: the increasing use of teams; the rapid pace of globalization; and the growing need to retain talent.

Consider the challenge of leading a team. As anyone who has ever been a part of one can attest, teams are cauldrons of bubbling emotions. They are often charged with reaching a consensus—hard enough with two people and much more difficult as the numbers increase. Even in groups with as few as four or five members, alliances form and clashing agendas get set. A team's leader must be able to sense and understand the viewpoints of everyone around the table. . . .

Globalization is another reason for the rising importance of empathy for business leaders. Cross-cultural dialogue can easily lead to miscues and misunderstandings. Empathy is an antidote. People who have it are attuned to subtleties in body language; they can hear the message beneath the words being spoken. Beyond that, they have a deep understanding of the existence and importance of cultural and ethnic differences. . . .

Finally, empathy plays a key role in the retention of talent, particularly in today's information economy. Leaders have always needed empathy to develop and keep good people, but today the stakes are higher. When good people leave, they take the company's knowledge with them.

That's where coaching and mentoring come in. It has repeatedly been shown that coaching and mentoring pay off not just in better performance but also in increased job satisfaction and decreased turnover. But what makes coaching and mentoring work best is the nature of the relationship. Outstanding coaches and mentors get inside the heads of the people they are helping. They sense how to give effective feedback. They know when to push for better performance and when to hold back. In the way they motivate their protégés, they demonstrate empathy in action. . . .

SOCIAL SKILL

The first three components of emotional intelligence are all self-management skills. The last two, empathy and social skill, concern a person's ability to manage relationships with others. As a component of emotional intelligence, social skill is not as simple as it sounds. It's not just a matter of friendliness, although people with high levels of social skill are rarely mean-spirited. Social skill, rather, is friendliness with a purpose: moving people in the direction you desire, whether that's agreement on a new marketing strategy or enthusiasm about a new product.

Socially skilled people tend to have a wide circle of acquaintances, and they have a knack for finding common ground with people of all kinds—a knack for building rapport. That doesn't mean they socialize continually; it means they work according to the assumption that nothing important gets done alone. Such people have a network in place when the time for action comes.

Social skill is the culmination of the other dimensions of emotional intelligence. People tend to be very effective at managing relationships when they can understand and control their own emotions and can empathize with the feelings of others. Even motivation contributes to social skill. Remember that people who are driven to achieve tend to be optimistic, even in the face of setbacks or failure. When people are upbeat, their "glow" is cast upon conversations and other social encounters. They are popular, and for good reason.

Because it is the outcome of the other dimensions of emotional intelligence, social skill is recognizable on the job in many ways that will by now sound familiar. Socially skilled people, for instance, are adept at managing teams—that's their empathy at work. Likewise, they are expert persuaders—a manifestation of self-awareness, self-regulation, and empathy combined. Given those skills, good persuaders know when to make an emotional plea, for instance, and when an appeal to reason will work better. And motivation, when publicly visible, makes such people excellent collaborators; their passion for the work spreads to others, and they are driven to find solutions.

But sometimes social skill shows itself in ways the other emotional intelligence components do not. For instance, socially skilled people may at times appear not to be working while at work. They seem to be idly schmoozing—chatting in the hallways with colleagues or joking around with people who are not even connected to their "real" jobs. Socially skilled people, however, don't think it makes sense to arbitrarily limit the scope of their relationships. They build bonds widely because they know that in these fluid times, they may need help someday from people they are just getting to know today. . . .

Is social skill considered a key leadership capability in most companies? The answer is yes, especially when compared with the other components of emotional intelligence. People seem to know intuitively that leaders need to manage relationships effectively; no leader is an island. After all, the leader's task is to get work done through other people, and social skill makes that possible. A leader who cannot express her empathy may as well not have it at all. And a leader's motivation will be useless if he cannot communicate his passion to the organization. Social skill allows leaders to put their emotional intelligence to work.

It would be foolish to assert that good-old-fashioned IQ and technical ability are not important ingredients in strong leadership. But the recipe would not be complete without emotional intelligence. It was once thought that the components of emotional intelligence were "nice to have" in business leaders. But now we know that, for the sake of performance, these are ingredients that leaders "need to have."

It is fortunate, then, that emotional intelligence can be learned. The process is not easy. It takes time and, most of all, commitment. But the benefits that come from having a well-developed emotional intelligence, both for the individual and for the organization, make it worth the effort.

8
Leadership as the Legitimation of Doubt

Karl E. Weick

The purpose of this chapter is to develop an allegory for leadership in the twenty-first century, an allegory built around a moment in Warren Bennis's life. . . . Bennis gave an evening lecture at the Harvard School of Education while he was president of the University of Cincinnati. Everything came together in a superb performance. During the upbeat Q and A session after the speech, Bennis was startled when the dean, Paul Ylvisaker, asked quietly, "Warren, do you really love being president of Cincinnati?" Bennis did not have a snappy answer. In fact, he didn't have any answer. After an interminable silence, in a room that quieted dramatically, Bennis finally said, "I don't know." Shortly thereafter, he came to the realization that he loved being a college president but hated doing a college presidency, and left Cincinnati.

Why do I flag this as a moment that can carry the message of leadership for an entire century? Notice what Bennis did not say. He did not say, I can't choose between yes and no. The question of whether he loves being president is not a problem in decision making. It is deeper than that. It is an issue of meaning, direction, and sensemaking. Standing in front of that Harvard audience, Bennis was facing a job, a university, a calling, and his own leadership theories with a mixture of puzzlement, ambivalence, and honesty. Leaders who stand in front of the new millennium and resist the temptation to treat it glibly or breathlessly are in the same position.

I want to argue that, given what Bennis faced, he called this one right. When he said, "I don't know," that was a strong act of leadership, not a weak one. It was strong because it positioned him for the sensemaking that he needed to do, not for the decision making that would come later as a minor by-product of sensemaking. To lead in the future is to be less in thrall of decision making—and more in thrall of sensemaking (Weick, 1995). That is the theme I want to develop.

Think first of the world Bennis faces at the moment of Ylvisaker's question. It is a world that is partly unknowable and unpredictable. It is a world into which people have been thrown. By thrown, I mean that people can't avoid acting, can't step back and reflect on their actions, can't predict the effects of their actions, have no choice but to deal with interpretations whose correctness cannot be settled once and for all, and they can't remain silent. Anything they say shapes both events and themselves. These are the givens that shape sensemaking.

This feeling of thrown-ness, and the need to make sense of it, are just what we would expect if we took seriously the psychological implications of quantum theory and chaos theory. Both of these

Source: From Bennis, *The Future of Leadership: Today's Top Leadership Thinkers Speak to Tomorrow's Leaders*. Reprinted by permission of John Wiley & Sons.

theories suggest that the world is less like a machine and more like shifting patterns of relationships. These patterns are unknowable because any effort to measure them changes them. These patterns are also unpredictable because very small differences in initial conditions can lead very quickly to very large differences in the future state of a system (McDaniel, 1997). In an unknowable, unpredictable world, sensemaking is all we have. Rueben McDaniel put the point this way:

> Because the nature of the world is unknowable (chaos theory and quantum theory) we are left with only sensemaking. Even if we had the capacity to do more, doing more would not help. Quantum theory helps us to understand that the present state of the world is, at best, a probability distribution. As we learn from chaos theory, the next state of the world is unknowable. And so we must pay attention to the world as it unfolds. Therefore, it is a good thing that we can't do more than sensemaking . . . because then we would only be frustrated by our inability to know. But believing enables action, which leads to more sense (sometimes), and taking action leads to more sense (sometimes), and sensemaking connects actions to beliefs (sometimes) [private communication].

It is the combination of thrown-ness, unknowability, and unpredictability that makes having some direction, any direction, the central issue for human beings, and by implication, the central issue for leaders. Sensemaking is about navigating by means of a compass rather than a map. "Maps, by definition, can help only in known worlds—worlds that have been charted before. Compasses are helpful when you are not sure where you are and can get only a general sense of direction" (Hurst, 1995, p. 168). Maps may be the mainstay of performance, but the compass and the compass needle, which function much like human values, are the mainstays of learning and renewal. If people find themselves in a world that is only partially charted, and if leaders also admit that they too don't know, then both are more likely to mobilize resources for direction making rather than for performance.

If I had to convert this broad portrait of leadership challenges into a set of contrasts, they would include the following. As unknowability and unpredictability become more prominent hallmarks of the twenty-first century, we can expect to find conditions such as these:

- Uncertainty will be based less on insufficient facts and more on insufficient questions.
- There will be fewer experts and more novices.
- There will be more of a premium on staying in motion than on detaching and reflecting.
- There will be more migration of decisions to those with the expertise to handle them, and less convergence of decisions on people entitled by rank to make them.
- There will be fewer attempts to capture the big picture and more attempts to capture the big story, with its ongoing dynamic, plot.
- There will be more focus on updating and plausibility and less on forecasting and accuracy.
- There will be more improvisation and fewer routines.
- There will be more humility and less hubris.

THE VALUE OF UNCERTAINTY

If we compress this set of predictions into a singular speculative picture of the effective leader, we can see why that person begins with the assertion, "I don't know." The effective leader is someone who searches for the better question, accepts inexperience, stays in motion, channels decisions to those with the best knowledge of the matter at hand, crafts good stories, is obsessed with updating, encourages improvisation, and is deeply aware of personal ignorance. People who act this way help others make sense of what they are facing. Sensemaking is not about rules and options and decisions. Sensemaking does not presume that there are generic right answers about things like taking risks or following rules. Instead, sensemaking is about how to stay in touch with context.

In the face of all the recent rhetoric about "new rules," we are better off playing up the fact of "newness" and playing down the possibility that this newness will necessarily take the form of rules. What's new is the context. What's new is the need for direction. What's new is a premium on updating. And what's new is the need to fall back on the compass rather than the map. We often run into the image of maps when people reaffirm Count Korzybski's famous caution, *the map is not the territory*. Even though the map never was the territory, and even though people still get confused when they forget this, it is conceivable that the image of maps and territories itself is dated, and the lowly compass may be the better image. Even though the compass is not any closer to the territory than is the map, it is much harder to mistake the compass for the territory. A compass makes it clearer that we are looking for a direction rather than a location. And a compass is a more reliable instrument of navigation if locations on the map are changing. Regardless of whether one has a map or a compass, it is less crucial that people have a specific destination, and more crucial for purposes of sensemaking that they have the capability to act their way into an understanding of where they are, who they are, and what they are doing. While the effective leader may sometimes be able to point to a specific destination that people find compelling, it is more likely that the effectiveness lies in the ability to set in motion a process for direction making.

When bewildered people ask, "What's the story?" the crucial thing is to get them moving, observing, updating, and arguing about feasibility and plausibility. A powerful means to do this is for the leader to answer the question by saying, "I don't know what the story is but let's find out." That reply is more subtle than it sounds. A plausible story is actually not something that one "finds." When the leader says, "let's find out," what the leader really means is, let's create the story. The good story is not simply lying out there waiting to be detected. Instead, the good story comes from experience that is reworked, enacted into the world, and rediscovered as though it were something external. Bennis and the other leaders know that the discovered story is an implanted story, a story whose origins are more internal than they appear.

Let me give an example of what I've been talking about by describing a leader and a leadership style that embodies what I have said. This example comes from my research on the antecedents of wildland firefighting disasters. One of the five best wildland firefighters in the world is Paul Gleason. Much of his fame comes from his work in over five hundred serious fires, as crew chief in charge of nineteen other firefighters from the Interagency Hotshot Crew (the Zig Zag crew). Gleason said that when fighting fires, he prefers to view his leadership efforts as sensemaking rather than decision making. In his words, "If I make a decision it is a possession, I take pride in it, I tend to defend it and not listen to those who question it. If I make sense, then this is more dynamic and I listen and I can change it. A decision is something you polish. Sensemaking is a direction for the next period."

When Gleason perceives his work as decision making, he feels that he postpones action so he can get the decision "right" and that after he makes the decision, he finds himself defending it rather than revising it to suit changing circumstances. Polishing and defending eat up valuable time and encourage blind spots. If, instead, Gleason treats an unfolding fire as a problem in sensemaking, then he gives his crew a direction for some indefinite period, a direction that by definition is dynamic, open to revision at any time, self-correcting, responsive, and with more of its rationale being transparent.

Gleason's commitment to sensemaking is striking. When crews fight fires, they post a lookout whose job is to monitor the relationship between the oncoming fire and the crew and to warn if the distance between the two gets too small. On some of Gleason's especially hazardous fires, where there is danger of rolling rocks or windblown spot fires, he has assigned as many as sixteen people to be lookouts, leaving only four people to actually fight the fire. In the Dude fire near Payson, Arizona, which was an active, dangerous fire, Gleason worked part of the time without gloves so he could get a fuller sense of the weather conditions. He clothed himself as if he didn't know for sure what his surroundings were. It paid off. The first day of fighting this fire, around 1:45 in the afternoon, he felt a few drops of rain on the back of his hands. He knew there were no thunderstorms in the area, inferred that he must be feeling *virga*—condensation from a huge column of smoke that had iced over on top and was about to collapse—and he now knew that it was time to act. He moved firefighters into a safety zone just before the column collapsed. When it did so, it pushed fire in all directions and six people who were some distance from his safety zone were killed.

LEADING BY THE COMPASS

Gleason's example nudges us to think more carefully about what it means to lead when one is thrown into an unknowable, unpredictable context in which the most one can hope for is a plausible direction and plausible updating. Just such a situation is what may have confronted Bennis at Harvard and leaders at the millennium. The nature of leadership when sense is up for grabs has some distinctive properties. I want to suggest that, in the face of doubt, leaders are best served if they focus on animation, improvisation, lightness, authentication, and learning.

Animation

Successful sensemaking is more likely when people stay in motion, have a direction, look closely, update often, and converse candidly. This logic derives from the basic process that is involved. That process is embodied in the rhetorical question, How can we know what we think until we see what we say? People need to act in order to discover what they face, they need to talk in order to discover what they think, and they need to feel in order to discover what it means. The "saying" involves action and animation, the "seeing" involves directed observation, the "thinking" involves the updating of previous thinking, and the "we" that makes all of this happen takes the form of candid dialogue that mixes together trust, trustworthiness, and self-respect.

What is subtle about all of this is that it is surprisingly indifferent to content. In a way, any old prescription, any old change program, any old mantra or guru or text will do, as long as that program *animates people* and gets them moving and generating experiments that uncover opportunities; *provides a direction; encourages updating* through improved situational awareness and closer attention to what is actually happening; and *facilitates respectful interaction* in which trust, trustworthiness, and self-respect (Campbell, 1990) develop equally and allow people to build a stable rendition of what they face. Whether people become animated because of "new economic rules," or total quality, or learning organization, or transformation, or teachable points of view, or action learning, or cultural change, or whatever, they are more or less likely to survive depending on whether their program engages or blocks these components of sensemaking. It is the thrust of this argument that there is nothing special about the context of change programs per se that explains their success or failure. What matters is the extent to which the program triggers sustained animation, direction, attention, and respectful interaction. It is these four activities that make it easier or harder for people to collectively make sense of what they are facing and to deal with it.

Improvisation

When people are thrown into an unknowable, unpredictable environment, there is also a premium on improvisation. Improvisation can be defined as reworking previously experienced material in relation to unanticipated ideas that are conceived, shaped, and transformed under the special conditions of a current performance (adapted from Berliner, 1994, p. 241). Improvisation involves the flexible treatment of preplanned material. It is not about "making something out of nothing." Instead, it is about making something out of previous experience, practice, and knowledge during those moments when people uncover and test intuitive understandings while their ongoing action can still make a difference (Schön, 1987, pp. 26–27). What is noteworthy in improvised action is a certain ad hoc adroitness (Ryle, 1979, p. 129). Improvisation materializes around a simple melody, formula, or theme that provides the pretext for real-time composing and embellishment. Outside the field of music, these melodies are the *directions* that are so important for sensemaking.

The role of the leader during improvisation is suggested by Dan Isenberg's (1985) description of battlefield commanders. On battlefields, commanders often "fight empirically" in order to discover what kind of enemy they are up against. "Tactical maneuvers will be undertaken with the primary purpose of learning more about the enemy's position, weaponry, and strength, as well as one's own strength, mobility, and understanding of the battlefield situation. . . . Sometimes the officer will need to implement his or her solution with little or no problem definition and problem solving. Only after taking action and seeing the results will the officer be able to better define the problem that he or she may have already solved!" (pp. 178–179). Commanders essentially hold a diagnosis lightly and tie their understanding to activity. This is akin to a simple melody that is embellished until a more appropriate melody emerges from the embellishments. A hunch held lightly is a direction to be followed, not a decision to be defended. It is easier to change directions than to reverse decisions, simply because less is at stake.

This is what both Gleason and Bennis have taught us.

Lightness

A leader who says "I don't know" is a lot like a foreman who yells "drop your tools" to wildland firefighters who are trying to outrun an exploding fire. Firefighters who ignore this order and continue to carry heavy tools like chainsaws retreat more slowly. All too often, they are overtaken by the fire and perish. There have been at least twenty-three fatalities just since 1990 where this happened. I think analogous crises occur when a leader says "I don't know" and followers refuse to drop their heavy tools of logic and rationality. Those tools presume that the world is stable, knowable, and predictable, something the leader has disavowed. The leader who says "I don't know" essentially says that the group is facing a new ballgame where the old tools of logic may be its undoing rather than its salvation. To drop these tools is not to give up on finding a workable answer. It is only to give up on one means of answering that is ill-suited to the unstable, the unknowable, the unpredictable. To drop the heavy tools of rationality is to gain access to lightness in the form of intuitions, feelings, stories, experience, active listening, shared humanity, awareness in the moment, capability for fascination, awe, novel words, and empathy. All these nonlogical activities trigger interpretations that have some plausibility and feasibility. And all these activities are made more legitimate when a leader says "I don't know." That admission forces the leader to drop pretense, drop omniscience, drop expert authority, drop a macho posture, and drop monologues. The lightness of listening and exploring is the consequence.

Dropping one's tools to regain lightness and agility is old news. Nowhere is this better stated than in the ancient epigram (Lao Tzu, cited in Muller, 1999, p. 134) that reads:

> In pursuit of knowledge, every day something is acquired;
> In pursuit of wisdom, every day something is dropped.

But old as the ties among dropping and lightness and wisdom may be, they tend to be forgotten in an era where leaders and followers alike are preoccupied with knowledge management, acquisitions, and acquisitiveness. When Bennis says to Ylvisaker, "I don't know," this comment suggests that something more than acquiring the title of president is at stake. When Bennis says he doesn't know, that is a polite way of saying, this isn't about knowledge and acquisitions at all. It is about something different, something more elusive, something more like a quest where the directions are less clear. When any leader suggests that the issue ahead is more about wisdom than knowledge and more about dropping than acquiring, this has an important effect on followers. It makes it legitimate for them to contribute in kind. A leader who drops heavy tools candidly and publicly is more likely to encourage similar acts in others. Having dropped their heavy tools, people are in a better position to watch closely and interact respectively to begin to form some idea of what they do face. The likelihood that this will happen at all depends on their capability for lightness.

Authentication

One of the early pioneers in the study of organizational behavior, Harvard's Fritz Roethlisberger (1977), adds yet another twist to the Bennis prototype for leadership in the future. Roethlisberger was struck by the fact that the vast majority of problems that executives complained about had the same form. He repeatedly heard that many people in organizations were not doing what they should be doing, in spite of numerous policies and standards designed to make sure that workers would do what they should. Accounting people weren't providing the information they were supposed to, supervisors weren't supervising, marketing people weren't working with production people, and so on. In a fascinating conjecture, Roethlisberger said it was as if the organization were undoing all the things the manager did when that person planned, directed, and coordinated. He went on to speculate that the undoing seemed to exhibit the mathematical property of reciprocalness. Thus the relation between the manager and the organization was either like multiplication and division, leaving an identity number of one, or addition and subtraction leaving an identity number of zero. In either case, the executive's contribution was nil. What Roethlisberger wanted to find out was what was responsible for the apparent undoing.

At this point in his discussion, Roethlisberger describes two extended cases where people don't do what they are supposed to be doing. One is the famous Harvard case called the Dashman Company and the other is a real-life experience of one of his students, a stubborn engineer named "Hal" who was appointed superintendent of maintenance shortly after being exposed to Roethlisberger's teaching. In the Dashman case, a newly appointed VP of purchasing, Mr. Post, sends out a directive to twenty decentralized purchasing agents saying that from now on, any purchasing contracts over $10,000 should be cleared with the top office. All twenty agents say they will be pleased to cooperate. But nothing happens. Not a single contract crosses Mr. Post's desk. The case stops with the new VP asking his assistant, Mr. Larson, a veteran of the firm, what he should do. Roethlisberger's students fumble with diagnoses for most of the classroom hour. With thirty seconds left before the bell, Roethlisberger says the following:

> If you stop to think for a moment, none of us knows what the situations in the plants really are, because none of us has gone to the plants to find out. We have just been speculating about what the situations there might be. This applies to Mr. Larson in the case as well as to us in the class. Until these speculations are checked, we may be mistaken. Hence, whatever Mr. Larson can say that might help to move matters in this direction may be the first simple step needed. Perhaps Mr. Larson with one sentence can preview a simple logic for Mr. Post to take the first step. So, dear students, please reflect and ponder until we meet at the next hour about what such a simple one-sentence response to Mr. Post's query, "What should I do now?" should be [pp. 176–177].

The sentence Roethlisberger was reaching for was this one. Mr. Larson might say, in response to Mr. Post's question of what he should do now, "I don't *know;* but perhaps if you or I or both of us went to visit the plants, we might be able to find out" (p. 177; italics in original). Regrettably, even with days to think about it, few of the students came up with this answer. And those who did often deemed the visit a gimmick to get people to cooperate the way they were supposed to. One student, Hal, who thought it was a gimmick, went back to his plant, was promoted to supervisor of maintenance, and assumed his new position. No sooner had he begun the new assignment than the shop steward called and said, "What the hell is going on in your department?" Biting his tongue, and stifling his overwhelming desire to say, "Who the hell do you think you're talking to?" Hal said, "I don't know.

Why don't you come to my office and tell me." The steward came, voiced the grievances, Hal listened, and they worked through their differences.

While these cases may have a quaint 1950s ring to them, set that feeling aside for the moment and look at what is happening. When leaders say "I don't know," this is a nonstereotypical response—they are supposed to know—and the response is truthful; it is factual in the sense that it states what the situation is; it establishes leader credibility in an unknowable world; it invites rather than precludes finding out more; it takes advantage of an immediate point of entry into an ongoing, here-and-now situation; and it strengthens rather than weakens relationships. In terms of the seven conditions for sensemaking (social resources, clear identity, retrospect, cue utilization, update of ongoing impressions, plausibility, and enactment = SIR COPE) the statement "I don't know" is exemplary because it activates all seven. In turn, that means that the relationship has been fully tuned for sensemaking. When a leader says, "I don't know," that seldom stops the conversation. Instead, it invites such follow-on sentences as, I don't know, "but we might know," "but you might know and we need to listen," "but knowing is not the issue here," "but I know how to find out," "but let's talk to see what we do know for sure." Any of these follow-ons authenticate doubt, unknowability, and unpredictability as the point of departure.

Learning

The final and most obvious outcome of leadership acts that begin with not knowing is that they often end with something learned. A particularly vivid example of this point is Winston Churchill's reworking of one of the darkest moments in his life. During World War II Churchill made a colossal error when he failed to realize how vulnerable Singapore was to attack by a Japanese land invasion. This error led to Singapore's downfall. After the collapse Churchill asked four questions: Why didn't I know? Why wasn't I told? Why didn't I ask? Why didn't I tell what I knew? (See Allinson, 1993, pp. 11–12.) Those four questions are questions of interdependence. They are questions of sensemaking. And they are questions that are grounded in doubt. Those four questions take seriously the idea that knowledge is not something people possess in their heads but rather something people do together.

That seems to be the wisdom that lies behind Bennis's answer at Harvard. It is a wisdom that future leaders should take seriously if they want to deal candidly with what they face. It is a wisdom stripped of hubris. The leader willing to say "I don't know" is also a leader willing to admit, in Oscar Wilde's wonderful phrase, "I'm not young enough to know everything" (Kellman, 1999, p. 133).

REFERENCES

Allinson, R. E. (1933). *Global disasters*. Upper Saddle River, N.J.: Prentice-Hall.

Berliner, P. F. (1994). *Thinking in jazz: The infinite art of improvisation*. Chicago: University of Chicago Press.

Campbell, D. T. (1990). Asch's moral epistemology for socially shared knowledge. In I. Rock (Ed.), *The legacy of Solomon Asch: Essays in cognition and social psychology* (pp. 39–52). Hillsdale, N.J.: Erlbaum.

Hurst, D. K. (1995). *Crisis and renewal*. Boston: Harvard Business School Press.

Isenberg, D. (1985). Some hows and whats of managerial thinking: Implications for future army leaders. In J. G. Hunt & J. D. Blair (Eds.), *Leadership on the future battlefield* (pp. 168–181). Dulles, Va.: Pergamon-Brassey's.

Kellman, S. G. (1999). Swan songs. *American Scholar,* 68(4), 111–120.

McDaniel, R. R. Jr. (1997). Strategic leadership: A view from quantum and chaos theories. *Health Care Management Review, 22*(1), 21–37.

Muller, W. (1999). *Sabbath: Restoring the sacred rhythm of rest.* New York: Bantam.

Roethlisberger, F. J. (1977). *The elusive phenomena.* Cambridge, Mass.: Harvard University Press.

Ryle, G. (1979). Improvisation. In G. Ryle, *On thinking* (pp. 121–130). London: Blackwell.

Schön, D. A. (1987). *Educating the reflective practitioner.* San Francisco: Jossey-Bass.

Weick, K. E. (1995). *Sensemaking in organizations.* Thousand Oaks, Calif.: Sage.

9

Efficacy and Effectiveness: Integrating Models of Leadership and Intelligence

Martin M. Chemers

THE ROLE OF INTELLIGENCE IN LEADERSHIP EFFECTIVENESS

Except for one very notable exception, contemporary leadership researchers and theorists have largely ignored the role of intelligence in leadership effectiveness. Among leadership theories of the last thirty or forty years, only Cognitive Resources Theory (Fiedler & Garcia, 1987) regards intelligence as an important variable. This was not always true. Early approaches to the study of leadership were strongly influenced by the apparent success of intelligence tests in the prediction of important outcomes, e.g., performance during military training. Stogdill's (1948) review of leadership traits, which showed that traits alone were not sufficient to predict either leadership emergence or effectiveness, also acknowledged that intelligence was one of the traits with the strongest association with leadership. (About 35% of the studies involving measures of intelligence and leadership revealed a significant relationship between the two variables.)

. . . I will develop the premise that not only is intelligence a useful variable for understanding the processes that underlie effective leadership, but even more, that contemporary intelligence theories can serve as useful models for similar approaches in leadership research. Indeed, there are intriguing parallels in the research histories of the two constructs. Leadership ability, like intellectual ability, was first regarded as a trait that people either had or didn't have, and little attention was paid to situational or environmental factors that might mitigate the utility of particular capabilities.

Later models began to emphasize an interaction between the characteristics of the individual and the nature of the environment with this interaction being the somewhat mechanical fit between stable traits and a relatively static environment. In leadership, this approach might manifest as a hypothesis that one type of leadership behavior (e.g., giving directions versus being emotionally supportive) would be more effective in some situations than in others (e.g., in situations of high versus low clarity and structure).

Finally, contemporary approaches (Sternberg, 1988; Cantor & Kihlstrom, 1987; Chemers, 1997) are moving in the direction of the conceptualization of a more fluid interaction between person and environment with an acknowledgement of the individual's actions in construction and shaping of the environment

Source: "Efficacy and Effectiveness: Integrating Models of Leadership and Intelligence," by Martin Chemers, 2002. Used by permission of Lawrence Erlbaum Associates."

rather than just reacting to it. Thus, rather than a fixed and unchanging capacity, intelligence (or leadership) becomes a set of skills and knowledge that change and develop in interaction with an environment that can, in turn, be shaped and modified to facilitate a good (i.e., effective) fit.

A FUNCTIONAL MODEL OF LEADERSHIP EFFECTIVENESS

Before turning to the application of contemporary intelligence models to leadership theory, it is useful to develop a model of leadership effectiveness that integrates what is currently known about what makes some leaders more effective than others. I will define leadership as "a process of social influence in which one person is able to enlist the aid and support of others in the accomplishment of a common task" (Chemers, 1997, page 1). The important points of this definition are that leadership is social, involves influence, and is centered on a task. The definition is quite simple, but the reality of leadership is very complex.

Part of that complexity is rooted in the nature of organizational functioning. To be effective, an organization must attend two critical demands. First, it must develop a system of rules, norms, and standards that provide the internal order, reliability, and predictability necessary to address recurrent and routine events. Organizations must assign jobs, titles, and offices, meet payrolls, pay suppliers, file governmental reports, etc. However, because organizations also exist within a dynamic environment, they must develop the systems and strategies that foster the sensitivity and flexibility that make it possible to respond to novel challenges. Organizational prosperity (even survival) depends on the appropriate balance between these two somewhat incompatible functions—stability and change.

Organizational effectiveness depends on leadership effectiveness. Leaders must help groups and individuals accomplish the tasks on which the organization's internal stability and external adaptability depend. To do this, leaders must enlist the aid and support of followers, guide and encourage the efforts of those followers, and direct the collective efforts of the team toward task accomplishment. Leadership effectiveness depends on the leader behaving in a manner that (1) elicits the trust and loyalty of followers (image management); (2) motivates followers toward enthusiastic effort (relationship development); and (3) applies the efforts, knowledge, and material resources of the group to mission accomplishment (resource deployment). Although the leadership literature is large, extensive, and somewhat fragmentary, it is the case that considerable agreement exists on the factors that determine these three key elements.

Image Management

It is important to recognize that the decision to act as a follower (i.e., to give up some of one's autonomy and independence of action) represents a social cost that must be balanced by some benefit. The benefit that makes the exchange equitable and attractive occurs when the leader appears able to increase the likelihood that the follower will be able to satisfy personal needs and achieve personal goals.

Hollander's (1958; 1964; Hollander & Julian, 1970) "idiosyncrasy credit" model of status accrual in groups directly addressed this exchange. Hollander showed, both through laboratory and field studies, that when a leader is seen as competent in task-related domains and committed to the group's core values, followers are willing to give the leader greater latitude of action and authority. The task-related competency provides the basis for the leader moving the group toward goal accomplishment, and the loyalty to group values fosters the assurance that the goal pursued by the leader will be one that serves the collective interests of the group. How are such judgments normally made by followers?

Although many researchers have written about leadership attributions, the most integrated and comprehensive treatment of the subject is in the writings of Robert Lord and his associates (Lord, 1985; Lord, Foti, & De Vader, 1984). Lord and Maher's (1991) information processing model posits that leadership is assessed through both recognition and inferential processes. Recognition-based processes are dependent on the implicit theories that each person holds about the traits and characteristics that comprise leadership. The implicit models of "good" leadership result in prototypes (Rosch, 1978; Cantor & Mischel, 1979), sets of characteristics that we consciously or unconsciously associate with the leadership role. When an individual seems (through appearance or behavior) to possess a sufficient number of these characteristics, observers make a generalized attribution (i.e., reach a conclusion) that the individual has leadership capacity. Once a decision is made that an individual is "leaderly," subsequent attention, interpretation, and memory are likely to be consistent with and reinforce the initial judgment.

Inferential attributional processes occur when we ascribe the causes for a group's success to the leader's actions or abilities. The tendency to assign causality as internal to the actor (in this case, the leader) is so pervasive that social psychologists have dubbed it the "fundamental attribution error" (Jones & Nisbett, 1971). Leaders who are associated with successful outcomes are seen as effective, based on the assumption that the leader caused the outcome. Meindl (1990) argues that tendency to credit leaders for anything—good or bad—that happens within an organization is so strong in our culture that it constitutes a "romance of leadership."

Several studies have been done on the particular characteristics that make up the leadership prototype (Lord, Foti, & De Vader, 1984). Although there are some differences between the prototypes for different classes of leaders (i.e., business, military, sports, etc.), there are common elements across these categories. In a simple study reported by Kouzes and Posner (1987), 1,500 managers and workers were asked to describe the characteristics of an outstanding leader they had known. Honesty and competence led the list, with over 80% of the respondents mentioning honesty, reaffirming Hollander's (1964) early results along the same lines.

A consistent theme in the literature on perceptions and attributions of leadership is that such judgments are fraught with biases. Assumptions, implicit theories, and romantic notions may induce observers to see what they are expecting to see and to remember what is consistent with their expectations. Nonetheless, creating the impression of competence and trustworthiness is an essential element of effective leadership, and little influence is possible until a leadership image is established.

Relationship Development

The establishment of a leader's legitimacy through competence and trustworthiness provides the basis for a relationship between leader and follower. The features of a successful leader–follower relationship are threefold. First, the leader must provide the follower with a supervisory context that is motivating and allows the follower to perform effectively. Second, the ability to provide such positive guidance and support depends on accurate judgments of the follower's needs, goals, and capabilities. Finally, the relationship must be equitable and fair.

Research on intrinsic motivation (Deci & Ryan, 1985; Hackman & Oldham, 1976) reveals that tasks are motivating to the extent that they provide one with autonomy, feedback, and an opportunity to engage one's skills and abilities toward meaningful goals. Feedback about performance makes possible a positive self-evaluation for a job well done. Autonomy (i.e., control over one's work) enhances the personal significance of positive feedback. The opportunity to use a variety of skills is interesting, and the entire endeavor is made more meaningful if the goal of the task is important. These characteristics of intrinsic motivation provide the bases for effective supervision.

A leader must provide the follower with direction and guidance that is sufficient to allow the subordinate to perform well and reap the benefits of positive feedback. However, the level of supervisory directiveness is a critical and subtle element. Too little direction might make the task overly ambiguous and difficult, reducing the likelihood of positive feedback. On the other hand, too much direction robs the follower of the autonomy necessary to make the feedback personally meaningful.

Path-goal theory (House, 1971; House & Dessler, 1974) prescribes that two general classes of behavior available to the leader are structuring (i.e., providing direction and task-related feedback) and consideration (i.e., providing emotional support). According to the theory, leader-structuring behavior will have the most positive effects on subordinate morale and performance when the ambiguity or difficulty of the subordinate's task makes direction valuable for goal attainment. Conversely, when the task is well understood by the subordinate, structuring behavior will be seen as overly close monitoring, pushing for performance, and robbing the subordinate of autonomy. Consideration and morale-boosting leader behavior should have their most positive effects when the subordinate's task is aversive by being boring or unpleasant. If the subordinate's task, however, is interesting and engaging, leader consideration will be regarded as unnecessary and distracting. The leader must be familiar with both the demands of the task and the capabilities of the follower to judge how much structuring and consideration would be useful. However, it is more complex than that.

The research findings on path-goal theory are quite mixed. One reason for the lack of consistent findings may be revealed in a study by Griffin (1981). In addition to measuring the nature of the subordinates' tasks, Griffin also measured a subordinate's personality characteristics—"growth need strength," Hackman and Oldham's (1976) measure of an individual's desire for growth and challenge in the workplace. Griffin found that growth need strength (GNS) moderated the predicted relationship between leader behavior and follower motivation and performance. High GNS subordinates, who were energized by difficult and unstructured tasks, responded negatively to leader structuring regardless of task condition, but responded quite positively to leader consideration when the task was highly structured and boring. Low GNS subordinates showed the opposite pattern. Boring tasks did not create as strong a positive reaction to supportive, considerate behavior by the leader, and structuring was well appreciated even when tasks were already fairly structured. Griffin's findings indicate that leaders must be sensitive not only to task features and follower skill levels, but also to followers' personality, needs, and expectations. Accurate judgment becomes a critical part of effective leadership.

The leader–follower relationship is a dynamic one. Subordinates are assigned tasks that they perform well or poorly. Follow-up actions are taken by the leader, and new tasks are assigned. Subordinates are rewarded or chastised; sent for training or given enhanced responsibilities; promoted or not. Thus, another important feature of leadership judgments centers on how the leader interprets this flow of actions and performance. Research by Mitchell and his associates (Green & Mitchell, 1979; Mitchell, Larson, & Green, 1977; Mitchell & Wood, 1980) indicates that attributions about followers by leaders obey many of the principles of classic attribution theory (Jones & Davis, 1965; Kelley, 1967). That is, leaders integrate information about how well the subordinate performed on other tasks, and at other times, and how well other workers perform at similar tasks. Consistent and distinctive performance outcomes (i.e., success or failure that is consistent over time, but different from other workers) are likely to lead to strong attributions about the subordinate's ability, which lead to actions consistent with those judgments.

However, attributional processes in the leadership relationship have some additional features not usually addressed in social psychological studies of person perception. These additional processes are related to the fact that the leader and follower are engaged in a relationship with reciprocal causality and connected outcomes. By this I mean that follower performance may be caused by the leader. Poor leadership is a potential explanation for poor follower performance. Furthermore, poor performance by a follower has important implications for the leader's success and evaluation by superiors.

This mutual dependence makes the subordinate's behavior and performance and subsequent explanations surrounding that performance very important to the leader. This increases the tendency for judgments by the leader to be ego-defensive, self-protective, and occasionally extreme. Because the leader is taking action with respect to the subordinate based on these judgments, biased processes can have serious negative outcomes. Followers who are blamed for failures outside their control are likely to become resentful and problematic employees. The leader–follower relationship can become a descending spiral. This possibility leads to a discussion of the third element of relationship development—equity and fairness.

At base, the leader–follower relationship is a transaction in which the follower provides effort and loyalty to the group and leader in exchange for help in attaining personal goals. Graen (1976; Graen & Cashman, 1975; Graen, Cashman, Ginsburgh, & Schiemann, 1978; Graen & Scandura, 1987) has presented a model of leader–follower exchange that acknowledges the qualitative range of such transactions. Because a leader needs the help of followers to accomplish the leader's and the group's goals, the leader and follower will undergo a perhaps unspoken but important negotiation of the nature of their relationship. The leader may regard a subordinate as a valued partner who is given interesting tasks, made privy to inside information, provided training and development opportunities, and rewarded well, or may be regarded as a "hired hand" who is afforded far less attractive options. Research indicates better leader–follower exchanges are associated with better job-related communication (Graen & Schiemann, 1978) and greater satisfaction (Graen & Ginsburgh, 1977).

Resource Deployment

The successful negotiation of image management and relationship development provides the leader with a legitimate basis for authority that can be used to develop a team of motivated subordinates ready to direct their knowledge, skills, and energy toward mission accomplishment. The actual effectiveness of the team is determined by how successfully the intellectual, motivational, and material resources of the team are utilized to achieve the goal. Like a military commander who must deploy troops, weapons, and materials based on an informed estimate of the enemy's strengths and strategies, an effective leader must deploy the team's resources based on an informed judgment of the critical demands created by the task and mission environment

Resource deployment is achieved on two levels. First, each member of the group must make the most effective use of his or her personal resources, i.e., intelligence, knowledge, skills, etc. Second, the individual efforts of team members must be coordinated and applied to the task environment in a manner that makes the most efficient use of those resources. Both self-deployment and team deployment are strongly influenced by the match between situational variables and team and personal characteristics.

Self-deployment addresses the ability to make the best use of personal resources. The basic premise of the Contingency Model of leadership effectiveness (Fiedler, 1967; Fiedler & Chemers, 1974; 1984) is that leaders function most effectively when their personal orientation or motivational pattern (i.e., toward task versus interpersonal accomplishment) is appropriate to (i.e., "matched" with) the situation. Extensive research (see meta-analyses by Peters, Hartke, & Pohlmann, 1983; Strube & Garcia, 1981) indicates that task-motivated leaders are most effective when the leadership situation (i.e., task, authority, and relationship with subordinates) provides the leader with a stable and predictable leadership environment. Relationship-motivated leaders perform most effectively—i.e., lead groups with high performance and satisfied subordinates—when situational contingencies create an environment of some complexity, ambiguity, and unpredictability.

Applying the Contingency Model to job stress, Chemers, Hays, Rhodewalt, and Wysocki (1985) found that "in-match" leaders reported lower levels of job stress and stress-related illness than did "out-of-match" leaders. Chemers, Ayman, Sorod, and Akimoto (1991) reported that in-match leaders evidenced more positive moods, greater confidence, and greater satisfaction than out-of-match leaders in both laboratory and field studies.

Fiedler and Garcia (1987) extended the logic of the Contingency Model to explain the effective deployment of leaders' cognitive resources (i.e., intelligence and experience) to effective group performance. Studies with the Cognitive Resources Model have indicated that the most effective use of intelligence and experience depends on two factors—the level of stress the leader is experiencing, and the willingness of the leader to provide clear direction to subordinates. Leaders under stress are less able to use their intelligence to solve problems, ostensibly because of the interference of anxiety on thought process, but are able to make good use of highly learned information provided by previous experience in similar situations. We see here the effect of positive and negative emotional states on the ability to make use of personal resources.

Fiedler and Leister (1977) have also shown that unless the leader is active in directing the activities of subordinates, intelligence and experience do not have much impact on the group's success. Fiedler (1993) suggests that match between leadership style and situation is related to the leader's level of directiveness. This notion is consistent with Eagly and Johnson's (1990) conclusions based on a meta-analysis of gender effects in leadership. They found that when a leadership situation was judged to be "congenial" (i.e., a situation in which a leader would be most comfortable) leaders were found to be more directive and judged to be more effective by observers.

Staw and Barsade (1992), who observed M.B.A. students in an assessment center simulation, found leaders with more positive affect to be more effective in the in-basket decision-making task, using more information and making more complex decisions, and were also more likely to be judged as an emergent leader in a leaderless discussion group. Individuals with positive affect are also more likely to take risks (Isen, Nygren, & Ashby, 1988), solve problems creatively (Isen, Daubman, & Nanicki, 1987), and make better decisions (Carnevale & Isen, 1986)—all of which are characteristics that are related to effective leadership.

It appears, then, that confidence plays an important role in the ability of individuals to make the most effective use of personal resources. One contributor to confidence is the degree of fit between the leader's personality, leadership style, gender, or other personal characteristics with features of the task, group, or organizational environment. I will develop this idea a bit more fully in a later section.

Team deployment refers to the effective coordination and application of the individual and collective resources of the team to the accomplishment of the group or organization's mission. The contingency theories (e.g., Fiedler, 1967; Vroom & Yetton, 1973) provide the most relevant explanatory premises for understanding team deployment.

All of the leadership functions discussed in earlier sections are dependent on subjective perceptions. The extent to which the leader looks like a leader (i.e., matches the leadership prototype) or the degree to which the leader's structuring and considerate behavior are seen by the subordinate as appropriate and motivating are influenced primarily by perceptions and judgments that are endogenous to the leader–follower relationship.

However, the strategies and actions that are used to affect the coordination of team resources for task accomplishment have their interface with the more concrete constraints of the external environment. Generally speaking, situations of high predictability make the use of directive, highly structured strategies more likely to yield positive results, while more complex and unpredictable circumstances benefit from the information sharing and creative problem solving made possible by more participative and flexible strategies. For example, Vroom and Yetton (1973) maintain that the wrong decision-making strategy (e.g., the use of autocratic [low follower input], decision making when the leader lacks relevant information and structure) is likely to lead to less efficient use of resources and lower effectiveness. A voluminous literature on the Contingency Model (Fiedler, 1978; Strube & Garcia, 1981) supports the notion that team effectiveness is dependent on the proper match between leadership style and situational factors.

Effective coordination of team resources requires the use of communication and decision-making structures that are compatible with the environment. Successful leaders must make accurate judgments about the nature of the environment and implement strategies that fit.

Transformational Leadership

Leadership researchers have always been interested in that class of exceptionally effective leaders that political historian James McGregor Burns (1978) referred to as "transformational" leaders—i.e., leaders who transcend the "transactional," quid pro quo bases of leadership authority to transform their followers into dedicated agents of collective achievement (Bass, 1985; 1998; Conger, 1989; Conger & Kanungo, 1987; House, 1977; House & Shamir, 1993). Like Weber's (1947) "charismatic" leaders, this class of exceptional leaders is seen as qualitatively different from their more mundane counterparts. I don't find this to be a defensible or useful distinction. Rather, I would argue that so-called transformational leaders are those who exhibit the highest levels of the three elements of image management, relationship development, and resource deployment.

The transformational theories all stress the important role of impression management in eliciting the high levels of follower commitment that define charismatic or transformational leadership. House's (1977) analysis of historical figures with charismatic effects on followers emphasizes the use of image management, such as bold gestures and risk-taking, to establish an image of commitment and trust-evoking dedication to the mission. Conger and Kanungo (1987) place great importance on the leader's technical expertise and "depth of knowledge" for achieving desired objectives. Bass (1985) uses the term "idealized influence" to refer to the leader's image as supremely competent, and "inspirational motivation" to underscore the necessity of stating the group's goal in terms that inspire trust and dedication to the leader and to the mission. House (1977) and House and Shamir (1993) stress that transformational leaders evince extremely high levels of confidence in themselves and their followers. This confidence leads to followers' self-perceptions of competence and subsequently to high expectations and high goals.

Relationship development with its components of judgment and guidance is an important feature of the transformational theories. Bass (1985) argues that transformational leaders employ "individualized consideration" (i.e., a highly personalized understanding of and reaction to follower needs and abilities) to create "intellectual stimulation" (i.e., providing guidance that stretches subordinates to think independently and creatively). This is very similar to the basic elements of relationship development, which are the sensitive understanding of follower needs and abilities in order to provide coaching, and guidance that stretch the follower's capacities and promote growth of knowledge and skills.

Finally, the notion that leaders must coordinate group activities through judgment and process for effective resource deployment is most clearly expressed by Conger and Kanungo (1987), who maintain that an important component of outstanding leadership is the ability to accurately assess the strategic factors affecting the attainment of the leader's vision.

Effective leadership can be conceived of as a continuum from very poor to very excellent. The successful fulfillment of the three elements of image management, relationship development, and resource deployment provides the basis for movement towards the positive pole of that dimension.

THE ROLE OF INTELLIGENCE IN LEADERSHIP EFFECTIVENESS

Leadership research has never been strongly focused on specific skills or knowledge bases that leaders might possess. Since Stogdill's (1948) critical examination of leadership traits, only minimal interest had been shown in intelligence—either as a trait or skill—until Fiedler and Garcia's (1987) presentation of Cognitive Resources Theory. However, in recent years, the conceptualization has moved from a trait to a process. These modern approaches to intelligence hold great promise for illuminating the bases of successful leadership. I will address three of the most prominent of the modern conceptualizations of intelligence and examine how they might contribute to the functional, integrative view of leadership presented previously. The three intelligence models are Sternberg's (1988) Triarchic Theory of Intelligence, Cantor and Kihlstrom's (1987) Social Intelligence Theory, and Salovey and Mayer's (1990; Mayer & Salovey, 1993) Theory of Emotional Intelligence.

Contemporary Models of Intelligence

What sets apart the newer conceptualizations of intelligence from the older "intelligence as stable trait" approaches is the view of intelligence as a process of adaptation. Cognitive skills and knowledge interact with environmental demands in a mutual shaping and development that enhances the adaptive fit of the individual to the environment. Robert Sternberg's Triarchic Theory of Intelligence (1988), which led the way in this approach, regards the individual as possessing internal resources in the form of cognitive abilities, such as specific knowledge and learning strategies that are applied to the solution of problems in the life environment. The relative utility of these internal resources is defined by the degree to which they are appropriate to the environmental demands. By interacting with the environment, the individual develops and refines the resources necessary to be effective, and in the process selects, shapes, and adapts elements of the environment for better fit with existing and developing internal resources. A central process in effective adaptation is turning the novel and unfamiliar into the predictable and routine, which can then be managed for attaining desired goals. The intelligent person, then, is one who can muster current knowledge and ability to relate to the problem environment in a flexible way that allows for the acquisition of new skills and knowledge that help the individual to develop the solutions necessary for goal attainment.

Cantor and Kihlstrom's (1987) Theory of Social Intelligence proceeds from a similar position of intelligence as "problem solving in a context." The socially intelligent person is one who possesses a sophisticated "perceptual readiness" to interpret social life accurately and respond to social situations effectively, i.e., managing interpersonal interactions to attain personal goals. Like Sternberg's "metacomponents," individuals possess internal resources or expertise in the social domain, consisting of concepts, interpretive rules, scripts, etc. These internal resources are applied to "life-task contexts" that afford the opportunity for the individual to accomplish his or her central life tasks. Intelligence becomes the ability to act wisely in human relations and involves the selection and shaping of contexts to provide the best fit with knowledge and abilities. The intelligent person understands the cultural expectations and normative processes governing social interaction and can recognize when and how social rules are applied.

Salovey and Mayer (1990; Mayer & Salovey, 1993) have directed attention to the extent to which emotional as well as cognitive knowledge is an important component of effective mastery of the personal environment. They discuss four types of emotional intelligence: (1) the accurate perception of one's own and others' emotions, (2) the use of emotions to facilitate thinking (i.e., the ability to create task-congruent emotions that help one focus on task demands), (3) emotional knowledge and understanding including empathy and judgment, and (4) regulation of one's emotions to promote personal growth (i.e., self-control, coping with stressful situations). Emotional intelligence contributes to an individual's ability to control oneself and to understand and influence others.

Intelligences as Contributors to Leadership Effectiveness

A reexamination of the key elements of effective leadership affords an opportunity to recognize the role of the various types and aspects of intelligence.

Image management involved the establishment of the credibility and legitimacy of authority by matching subordinate prototype-based expectations for leadership. The strongest components of the leadership prototype across all types of leaders are competence and honesty. A potential leader's ability to match observer expectations depends on two factors: the understanding of what the content of the prototype is, and the capability for presenting the expected behaviors and attitudes. Social intelligence is clearly the basis for the first requirement, and emotional intelligence is a significant contributor to the latter.

Social intelligence includes the knowledge of prototypical characteristics and situational scripts. The socially intelligent person is adept at reading the characteristics of the situation for cues and clues that define the nature of the interpersonal context and the appropriate behaviors for the context. The effective leader knows when a situation requires a formal authority and presentation or a more informal and intimate interactional style. A CEO who attends the corporation's shareholders meeting dressed in jeans and a sweatshirt and gives the annual report while leaning against a table would be as out of place and unconvincing as one who attends the company picnic in a three-piece suit. Social knowledge is a requisite for appearing as a credible leadership figure.

It is also the case that leadership prototypes involve more than appropriate clothing. The projection of competence includes proper attitude, emotions, and demeanor. "Cool under pressure," "calm and self-assured," and "possessing a fire in the belly" have all become common phrases used to describe valued leaders in our culture. Social intelligence contributes to the ability to discern when one should be calm or fiery, but emotional intelligence plays a critical role in the would-be leader's ability to regulate self-control and emotional state to meet situational demands.

If the foregoing descriptions of the uses of intelligence in image management give the impression of a manipulation or insincerity, it would be misleading. Understanding where others "are coming from" and being able to harness and control one's emotions in order to meet the challenges of demanding situations need not imply any insincerity. In the long run, it is the person who is really "calm under pressure" but can "rise to the challenge" that will be recognized and afforded the status to lead.

Relationship development has, as its most central feature, the ability to accurately judge the needs and expectations of followers so that coaching and guidance can be given in a manner that encourages motivation and promotes growth. Again, both social and emotional intelligence are the bases for that ability. Coaching, with its sometimes oppositional components of correction and encouragement, is one of the most subtle and potentially volatile of social interactions. An understanding of the norms surrounding such interactions and a knowledge of the impact of feedback and of how to phrase both praise and criticism is essential for acting effectively in the coaching situation. This ability to understand others and act in ways that are in tune with the feelings of followers is what we mean by the term "consideration."

However, transformational leadership theory (Bass, 1985) makes clear that outstanding leadership goes beyond a generalized knowledge of what considerate behavior is to achieve an "individualized consideration" that is sensitive to the unique personality and situation of a particular follower. We have also discussed the impediments to sensitive understanding of subordinates that are inherent in the leader's own vulnerability to criticism and need to defend self-esteem. It is at this deeper level of understanding that emotional intelligence becomes critical. The leader needs first to control his or her own emotional reactions to the coaching situation, both in terms of anxiety about delivering feedback, as well as in terms of threats to one's own sense of competence. Second, the ability to read and understand the emotions of others, i.e., empathy, forms the basis for truly individualized consideration.

Resource deployment is the facet of leadership that mobilizes and applies the group's collective resources to accomplish the task or mission. At this level, intelligence theories may provide both strikingly apt metaphors as well as useful models for understanding effective leadership. Sternberg's (1988) triarchic model presents intelligence as the employment (or read "deployment") of the individual's internal resources to attain desired goals. To do this, the individual engages the environment in order to both bring to bear existing knowledge and to sample environmental demands to determine what new knowledge or skills must be developed. This interface with the environment is shaped to fit the individual's capabilities just as capabilities are expanded and developed to fit the environment. The hallmark of this process is the turning of the novel and unpredictable aspects of the environment into the well understood and routinely manageable—thus freeing the individual's capabilities to access new novel problems.

If we make a few substitutions in words, we have a very good description of effective leadership. For a group to attain its goals and accomplish its mission, it must bring to bear the individual capabilities, knowledge, skills, and energy of its members to address the demands of the task environment. It begins by selecting and shaping the problem to fit existing knowledge, as well as by activating the learning processes of each individual member. Just as with individual intelligence, the group's immediate goal is to process information and make decisions that turn novel and unpredictable environmental features into routine events that can be reliably and predictably managed to effect solutions.

Although aspects of this metaphor are obvious, some less obvious ideas are brought into relief. The notion of the group as a learning organism reorganizing and expanding knowledge and skills to meet challenges may be more or less explicit in some approaches to organization (Senge, 1990), but those ideas have not been as clearly integrated into leadership theory. Likewise, the idea that effective problem solving is the conversion of novelty into order is not a new concept, but it is relatively new to contemporary leadership theory.

Social and emotional intelligence may also affect the resource deployment process. Clearly, emotional intelligence, i.e., the regulation of one's own emotion and others' emotions, is central to self-deployment—the effective release of personal resources. By managing anxiety, maintaining a positive attitude, and successfully coping with stress, leaders and followers are more able to make use of the resources of knowledge and skill that they possess. In addition, as House and Shamir (1993) point out, the arousal of motives that are appropriate to task performance (e.g., achievement motivation for difficult tasks or "aggression" for competitive situations) enhances ability. Emotional intelligence provides a basis for understanding how a leader's behavior might arouse appropriate moods or motivations in oneself or in one's followers. . . .

LEADERSHIP EFFICACY AND LEADERSHIP PERFORMANCE

Personal Dispositions and Leadership Capabilities

Except for some work on self-esteem (Korman, 1968), the empirical literature on leadership has not reflected a great deal of interest in constructs related to positive affect or self-perception. Comprehensive reviews of leadership trait research (Bass, 1990; Yukl, 1994) reveal just a few studies of confidence, with mixed results. And in most of the studies of leadership confidence (e.g., Kipnis & Lane, 1962), constructs of self-esteem, self-confidence, and self-efficacy were not clearly differentiated from one another.

More qualitative approaches to leadership have touched on these issues. For example, after a loosely structured interview study of 90 outstanding leaders in the public and private sectors, Bennis and Nanus (1985) concluded that all of these individuals shared high levels of self-confidence about their own capabilities and optimism about the outcomes of their actions. Corporate CEOs, political leaders, professional sports coaches, symphony conductors, and others shared the beliefs that (a) they were capable of doing what had to be done (self-efficacy), and (b) if they did what they should do, the environment would respond positively (optimism). In a similar vein, Boyatzis (1982) conducted critical incident interviews with 253 managers preselected on the basis of high effectiveness ratings. Content analyses of the interviews revealed that effective managers demonstrated a strong belief in their own capabilities (self-efficacy) and an internal locus of control.

In purely theoretical analyses, House and Shamir (House, 1977; House & Shamir, 1993; Shamir, House, & Arthur, 1992) have included self-confidence and high expectations for self and followers among the list of traits that have distinguished charismatic leaders throughout history. In other words, traits like confidence and optimism crop up when analysts think about very effective leaders, but these constructs are less prevalent in the empirical work that addresses the more mundane aspects of organizational leadership.

In some empirical studies, positive affect has been found to be associated with better relations between soldiers and their superiors (Solomon, Mikulincer, & Hobfall, 1986). High levels of self-esteem have been related to a greater sense of personal locus of control (Deci & Ryan, 1985), and a greater willingness to assume positions of leadership (Linimon, Barron, & Falbo, 1984). Self-efficacy has been related to work motivation (Gist & Mitchell, 1992) and to better leadership performance under stress (Murphy, 1992).

An extensive literature on self-efficacy (Bandura, 1982; 1997) reveals that perceptions of efficacy can enhance or impair motivation and performance in a variety of ways, e.g., by influencing the kinds of activities in which people choose to engage (Bandura, 1982), the level of the goals they set (Locke, Frederick, Lee, & Bobko, 1984), and their effort and persistence at achieving those goals (Bandura & Cervone, 1983). Self-efficacy judgments are important because they influence not only what skills people perceive themselves to have, but also what they believe they can do with the skills they possess. Self-efficacy beliefs can affect attentional and thinking processes, eliciting either confidence with positive concomitants or debilitating self-doubt (Bandura & Wood, 1989) with a resultant tendency to withdraw or give up (Carver, Peterson, Follansbee, & Scheier, 1983). Bandura and Jourdan (1991) found that M.B.A. students given efficacy-enhancing feedback showed improved performance in a management simulation, decision-making task.

Although these various personal dispositions do not describe a single, unidimensional construct, they do share a focus on the positive effects of confidence in one's ability and positive expectancies about the outcomes of one's actions. In summary, feelings of enhanced self-efficacy should be related to high levels of motivation, which could affect levels of aspiration, goal setting, perseverance in the face of difficulty, and enthusiasm, causing a leader to work harder and longer to achieve group goals. Such feelings might also be contagious to followers, affecting their confidence and related perceptions.

Leadership Efficacy and Effectiveness

Bandura (1982; 1997) has maintained that self-efficacy is quite domain-specific. Therefore, only leadership efficacy, not generalized self-esteem or positive affect, should lead specifically to leadership effectiveness. In a series of recent studies, my colleagues and I (Chemers, Watson, & May, 2000; Watson, Chemers, & Preiser, 1996; Murphy, this volume) have found strong support for the predictive utility of leadership self-efficacy in group and organizational performance.

Chemers, Watson, and May (2000) measured the leadership self-efficacy of approximately 100 cadets enrolled in the Reserve Officer Training Corps (ROTC) at five colleges and universities in southern California and Arizona. Third-year cadets (i.e., juniors) responded to a measure of self-esteem, the Revised Janis-Field Scale (Brockner, 1988); to a measure which asked for their self-evaluation of a number of leadership skills (e.g., decision making, delegation, oral communication) and general leadership capabilities (e.g., "I know how to get a group to work well together"); and to a measure of generalized optimism, the Life Orientations Test (LOT; Scheier & Carver, 1985). The cadets were rated on leadership potential by their military science class instructors (career military officers). Results indicated that leadership efficacy and optimism, but not general self-esteem, were strongly related to the leadership potential ratings.

Follow-up data on these same cadets were collected during their attendance at a U.S. Army six-week summer leadership training camp. Companies of approximately 40 cadets lived in common barracks and rotated through leadership duties. Cadets also underwent extensive training in leadership, as well as in nonleadership skills (e.g., marksmanship, navigation), and participated in highly realistic and demanding leadership simulation exercises. Leadership ratings were obtained from cadet peers, superior officers (regular army), and from simulation observers (Pentagon-trained evaluators). In all analyses, leadership efficacy (but not self-esteem or optimism) was strongly related to leadership ratings by all parties, but not to nonleadership measures. The authors concluded that the leadership efficacy measure provided evidence of strong concurrent (instructor ratings), predictive (summer camp ratings and score), and discriminant (nonleadership measures) validity.

Watson, Chemers, and Preiser (1996) examined the effects of leadership efficacy on collective efficacy and team performance among men's and women's college basketball teams. Small college basketball team members responded to measures of leadership efficacy, individual basketball efficacy, and team collective efficacy prior to the beginning of the basketball season and also identified the player regarded as the team leader. Results indicated that the leadership efficacy of the identified leader (usually the team captain) was strongly predictive of the team's collective efficacy, which, in turn, was strongly predictive of the team's win-loss record during the season. Leaders with high leadership efficacy led more confident and more successful teams. Efficacy was, in fact, a better predictor of performance than more frequently used "objective" measures of talent, such as previous year's win-loss record, number of returning lettered players, or players out for the team. . . .

CONCLUSION

This chapter has presented an integrated theory of leadership that regards effective leadership as grounded in three critical functions. Image management is essential to the development of credibility of the leader and the acceptance of influence by followers and is dependent on follower perceptions of the leader as competent and trustworthy. Relationship development is the basis for the development of a motivated and competent group of followers and is dependent on a leader's ability to recognize follower capabilities and needs, and to provide intrinsically motivating coaching and direction. Finally, resource deployment encompasses a leader's ability to get the most out of individual and collective effort by the appropriate matching of strategy to environment.

An additional thesis of this chapter is that all of these leadership capabilities are dramatically enhanced by a leader's sense of personal efficacy in the leadership role, and in fact, outstanding levels of leadership are not possible without high levels of confidence. Empirical evidence from three major studies supports the value of leadership efficacy as a predictor of leadership, group, and organizational performance as measured in a variety of ways.

The chapter also presents an intriguing hypothesis to guide future research—i.e., that situational self-efficacy (leadership efficacy in this case) is rooted in intelligence, which provides the actor with a sense of personal agency. In particular, social and emotional intelligence may be very highly related to a leader's success at image management and relationship development, and general intelligence to a leader's ability to read and respond to task environments. An exciting direction for future research would be to prove the effects of social and emotional intelligence on leadership efficacy and leadership performance.

REFERENCES

Bandura, A. (1982). Self-efficacy mechanism in human agency. *American Psychologist, 37,* 122–147.

Bandura, A. (1997). *Self-efficacy: The exercise of the self.* New York: W. H. Freeman & Company.

Bandura, A. & Cervone, D. (1983). Self-evaluative and self-efficacy mechanisms governing the motivational effects of goal systems. *Journal of Personality and Social Psychology, 45,* 1017–1028.

Bandura, A. & Jourdan, F. J. (1991). Self-regulatory mechanisms governing the impact of social comparison on complex decision making. *Journal of Personality and Social Psychology, 60,* 941–951.

Bandura, A. & Wood, R. (1989). Effect of perceived controllability and performance standards on self-regulation of complex decision making. *Journal of Personality and Social Psychology, 56,* 805–814.

Bass, B. M. (1985). *Leadership and performance beyond expectations.* New York: Free Press.

Bass, B. M. (1990). *Bass & Stogdill's handbook of leadership: Theory, research, and managerial applications* (3rd ed.). New York: Free Press.

Bass, B. M. (1998). *Transformational leadership: Industry, military, and educational impact.* Mahwah, NJ: Lawrence Erlbaum Associates.

Bennis, W. G. & Nanus, B. (1985). *Leaders: The strategies for taking charge.* New York: Harper & Row.

Boyatzis, R. E. (1982). *The competent manager.* New York: John Wiley.

Brockner, J. (1988). *Self-esteem at work: Research, theory, and practice.* Lexington, MA: D. C. Heath and Company.

Burns, J. M. (1978). *Leadership.* New York: Harper & Row.

Cantor, N. & Kihlstrom, J. F. (1987). *Personality and social intelligence.* Englewood Cliffs, NJ: Prentice-Hall, Inc.

Cantor, N. & Mischel, W. (1979). Prototypes in person perception. In L. Berkowitz (Ed.), *Advances in experimental social psychology* (Vol. 12). New York: Academic Press.

Carnevale, P. J. D. & Isen, A. M. (1986). The influence of positive affect and visual access on the discovery of integrative solutions in bilateral negotiation. *Organizational Behavior and Human Decision Processes, 37,* 1–13.

Carver, C. S., Peterson, L. M., Follansbee, D. J., & Scheier, M. F. (1983). Effects of self-directed attention on performance and persistence among persons high and low in test anxiety. *Cognitive Therapy and Research, 7,* 333–354.

Chemers, M. M. (1997). *An integrative theory of leadership.* Mahwah, NJ: Lawrence Erlbaum Associates.

Chemers, M. M. & Ayman, R. (1985). Leadership orientation as a moderator of the relationship between performance and satisfaction of Mexican managers. *Personality and Social Psychology Bulletin, 11,* 359–367.

Chemers, M. M., Ayman, R., Sorod, B., & Akimoto, S. (1991). Self-monitoring as a moderator of leader-follower relationships. Presented at the International Congress of Psychology. Brussels.

Chemers, M. M., Hays, R., Rhodewalt, F., & Wysocki, J. (1985). A person-environment analysis of job stress: A contingency model explanation. *Journal of Personality and Social Psychology, 49,* 628–635.

Chemers, M. M., Watson, C. B., & May, S. (2000). Dispositional affect and leadership effectiveness: A comparison of self-esteem, optimism, and efficacy. *Personality and Social Psychology Bulletin, 26,* 267–277.

Conger, J. A. (1989). The dark side of the charismatic leader. In J. A. Conger (Ed.), *The charismatic leader.* San Francisco: Jossey-Bass.

Conger, J. A. & Kanungo, R. A. (1987). Towards a behavioral theory of charismatic leadership in organizational settings. *Academy of Management Review, 12,* 637–647.

Deci, E. L. & Ryan, R. M. (1985). *Intrinsic motivation and self-determination in human behavior.* New York: Plenum Press.

Eagly, A. H. & Johnson, B. T. (1990). Gender and leadership style: A meta-analysis. *Psychological Bulletin, 108,* 233–256.

Fiedler, F. E. (1967). *A theory of leadership effectiveness*. New York: McGraw-Hill.

Fiedler, F. E. (1978). The contingency model and the dynamics of the leadership process. In L. Berkowitz (Ed.), *Advances in experimental social psychology*. Vol. 11. New York: Academic Press.

Fiedler, F. E. (1993). The leadership situation and the black box in contingency theories. In M. M. Chemers & R. Ayman (Eds.), *Leadership theory and research: Perspectives and directions*. San Diego: Academic Press.

Fiedler, F. E. & Chemers, M. M. (1974). *Leadership and effective management*. Glenview, IL: Scott, Foresman & Company.

Fiedler, F. E. & Chemers, M. M. (1984). *Improving leadership effectiveness: The Leader Match concept* (2nd ed.). New York: Wiley.

Fiedler, F. E. & Garcia, J. E. (1987). *New approaches to effective leadership: Cognitive resources and organizational performance*. New York: Wiley.

Fiedler, F. E. & Leister, A. F. (1977). Leader intelligence and task performance: A test of the multiple screen model. *Organizational Behavior and Human Performance*, *20*, 1–14.

Gist, M. E. & Mitchell, T. R. (1992). Self-efficacy: A theoretical analysis of its determinants and malleability. *Academy of Management Review*, *17*, 183–211.

Graen, G. (1976). Role-making processes within complex organizations. In M. D. Dunnette (Ed.), *Handbook of industrial and organizational psychology*. Chicago, IL: Rand McNally.

Graen, G. & Cashman, J. (1975). A role-making model of leadership in formal organizations: A developmental approach. In J. G. Hunt and L. L. Larson (Eds.), *Leadership frontiers*. Kent, OH: Kent State University Press.

Graen, G., Cashman, J. F., Ginsburgh, S., & Schiemann, W. (1978). Effects of linking-pin quality on the quality of working life of lower participants: A longitudinal investigation of the managerial understructure. *Administrative Science Quarterly*, *22*, 491–504.

Graen, G. & Ginsburgh, S. (1977). Job resignation as a function of role orientation and leader acceptance: A longitudinal investigation of organizational assimilation. *Organizational Behavior and Human Performance*, *19*, 1–17.

Graen, G. & Scandura, T. A. (1987). Toward a psychology of dyadic organizing. *Research in Organizational Behavior*, 9, 175–208.

Graen, G. & Schiemann, W. (1978). Leader-member agreement: A vertical dyad linkage approach. *Journal of Applied Psychology*, *63(2)*, 206–212.

Green, S. G. & Mitchell, T. R. (1979). Attributional processes of leaders in leader-member interactions. *Organizational Behavior and Human Performance*, *23*, 429–458.

Griffin, R. N. (1981). Relationships among individual, task design, and leader behavior variables. *Academy of Management Journal*, *23*, 665–683.

Hackman, J. R. & Oldham, G. R. (1976). Motivation through the design of work: Test of a theory. *Organizational Behavior and Human Performance*, *16*, 250–279.

Hollander, E. P. (1958). Conformity, status, and idiosyncrasy credit. *Psychological Review*, *65*, 117–127.

Hollander, E. P. (1964). *Leaders, groups, and influence*. New York: Oxford Press.

Hollander, E. P. & Julian, J. W. (1970). Studies in leader legitimacy, influence, and innovation. In L. Berkowitz (Ed.), *Advances in experimental social psychology*. Vol. 5. New York: Academic Press.

House, R. J. (1971). A path-goal theory of leadership. *Administrative Science Quarterly*, *16*, 321–338.

House, R. J. (1977). A 1976 theory of charismatic leadership. In J. G. Hunt & L. L. Larson (Eds.), *Leadership: The cutting edge*. Carbondale, IL: Southern Illinois University Press.

House, R. J. & Dessler, G. (1974). The path-goal theory of leadership: Some post-hoc and a priori tests. In J. G. Hunt & L. L. Larson (Eds.), *Contingency approaches to leadership*. Carbondale, IL: Southern Illinois University Press.

House, R. J. & Shamir, B. (1993). In M. M. Chemers & R. Ayman (Eds.), *Leadership theory and research: Perspective and directions*. San Diego: Academic Press.

Isen, A. M., Daubman, K. A., & Nanicki, G. P. (1987). Positive affect facilitates creative problem solving. *Journal of Personality and Social Psychology*, *51*, 1122–1131.

Isen, A. M., Nygren, J. E., & Ashby, G. F. (1988). The influence of positive affect on the subjective utility of gains and losses: It's not worth the risk. *Journal of Personality and Social Psychology*, *55*, 710–717.

Jones, E. E. & Davis, K. E. (1965). From acts to dispositions: The attribution process in person perception. In L. Berkowitz (Ed.), *Advances in experimental social psychology*. Vol. 2. New York: Academic Press.

Jones, E. E. & Nisbett, R. E. (1971). *The actor and the observer: Divergent perceptions of the causes of behavior*. Morristown, NJ: General Learning Press.

Kelley, H. H. (1967). Attribution theory in social psychology. In D. Levine (Ed.), *Nebraska symposium on motivation*. Lincoln: University of Nebraska Press.

Kipnis, D. & Lane, W. P. (1962). Self-confidence and leadership. *Journal of Applied Psychology, 46*, 291–295.

Korman, A. K. (1968). The prediction of managerial performance: A review. *Personnel Psychology, 21*, 295–322.

Kouzes, J. M. & Posner, B. Z. (1987). *The leadership challenge: How to get extraordinary things done in organizations*. San Francisco: Jossey-Bass.

Linimon, D., Barron, W. W., & Falbo, T. (1984). Gender differences in perceptions of leadership. *Sex Roles, 11*, 1075–1089.

Locke, E. A., Frederick, E., Lee, C., & Bobko, P. (1984). Effect of self-efficacy, goals, and task strategies on task performance. *Journal of Applied Psychology, 69*, 241–251.

Lord, R. G. (1985). An information-processing approach to social perceptions, leadership, and behavioral measurement in organizations. In B. M. Staw & L. L. Cummings (Eds.), *Research in organizational behavior*, Vol. 7. Greenwich, CT: JAI Press.

Lord, R. G., Foti, R. J., & De Vader, C. (1984). A test of leadership categorization theory: Internal structure, information processing, and leadership perceptions. *Organizational Behavior and Human Performance, 34*, 343–378.

Lord, R. G. & Maher, K. J. (1991). *Leadership and information processing: Linking perceptions and performance*. Boston: Unwin Hyman.

Mayer, J. D. & Salovey, P. (1993). The intelligence of emotional intelligence. *Intelligence, 17*, 433–442.

Meindl, J. R. (1990). On leadership: An alternative to the conventional wisdom. In B. A. Staw (Ed.), *Research in organizational behavior* (Vol. 12, pp. 159–203.). New York: JAI Press.

Mitchell, T. R., Larson, J. R., & Green, S. G. (1977). Leader behavior situational moderators in group performance: An attributional analysis. *Organizational Behavior and Human Performance, 18*, 254–268.

Mitchell, T. R. & Wood, R. E. (1980). Supervisor's responses to subordinate poor performance: A test of an attribution model. *Organizational Behavior and Human Performance, 25*, 123–138.

Murphy, S. E. (1992). The contribution of leadership experience and self-efficacy to group performance under evaluation apprehension. Unpublished doctoral dissertation. University of Washington, Seattle.

Peters, L. H., Hartke, D. D., & Pohlmann, J. T. (1983). Fiedler's contingency theory of leadership: An application of the meta-analysis procedure of Schmidt and Hunter. *Psychological Bulletin, 97*, 274–285.

Riggio, R. E., Murphy, S. E., & Pirozzolo, F. J. (2001). *Multiple intelligences and leadership*. Mahwah, NJ: Lawrence Erlbaum Associates.

Rosch, E. (1978). Principles of categorization. In E. Rosch & B. B. Lloyd (Eds.), *Cognition and categorization*. Hillsdale, NJ: Lawrence Erlbaum Associates.

Salovey, P. & Mayer, J. D. (1990). Emotional intelligence. *Imagination, Cognition, and Personality*, 9, 185–211.

Scheier, M. F. & Carver, C. S. (1985). Optimism, coping, and health: Assessment and implications of generalized outcome expectancies. *Health Psychology*, 4, 219–247.

Senge, P. M. (1990). *The fifth discipline: The art and practice of the learning organization*. New York: Doubleday.

Shamir, B., House, R. J., & Arthur, M. B. (1992). The motivational effects of charismatic leadership: A self-concept-based theory. *Organizational Science, 4*, 577–594.

Snyder, C. R., Harris, C., Anderson, J. R., Holleran, S. A., Irving, L. M., Sigmon, S. T., Yoshinobu, L., Gibb, J., Langelle, C., & Harney, P. (1991). The will and the ways: Development and validation of an individual-differences measure of hope. *Journal of Personality and Social Psychology, 60*, 570–585.

Solomon, Z., Mikulincer, M., & Hobfall, S. E. (1986). Effects of social support and battle intensity on loneliness and breakdown during combat. *Journal of Personality and Social Psychology, 51*, 1269–1276.

Staw, B. M. & Barsade, S. G. (1992). Affect and managerial performance: A test of the sadder-but-wiser vs. happier-and-smarter hypothesis. *Administrative Science Quarterly, 38*, 304–331.

Sternberg, R. J. (1988). *The triarchic mind: A new theory of human intelligence*. New York: Viking.

Stogdill, R. M. (1948). Personal factors associated with leadership: A survey of the literature. *Journal of Psychology, 25*, 35–71.

Strube, M. J. & Garcia, J. E. (1981). A meta-analytical investigation of Fiedler's Contingency Model of leadership effectiveness. *Psychological Bulletin*, 90, 307–321.

Vroom, V. H. & Yetton, P. W. (1973). *Leadership and decision-making*. Pittsburgh: University of Pittsburgh Press.

Watson, C. B., Chemers, M. M., & Preiser, N. (1996, June). *Collective efficacy: A multi-level analysis*. Presented at the annual meeting of the American Psychological Society, San Francisco, CA.

Weber, M. (1947). *The theory of social and economic organization*. (A. M. Henderson & T. Parsons, Transls.: T. Parsons, Ed.). New York: Free Press. (Originally published in 1924.)

Yukl, G. (1994). *Leadership in organizations* (3rd. Ed.) Englewood Cliffs, NJ: Prentice-Hall.

CHAPTER II

Motivation

Many factors may, or may not, motivate individual members of our metaphoric orchestra to do their jobs with high enthusiasm and energy. Thundering applause, the sound of the music, relationships with other members of the orchestra, a personal goal, a commitment to parents who paid for an education, the honored first-chair position, a drive to succeed, a monetary reward, public recognition, or even the grateful smile of the conductor—all are possibilities from a potentially limitless number of choices. These motivating factors cause individual musicians to come together to produce, entertain, create, and, potentially, to excel collectively as an orchestra.

How does the conductor keep the musicians motivated, show after show, and season after season? Is the conductor responsible for motivating members of the orchestra, or are the individual musicians responsible because of their personal self-concepts and goals as professionals? What other needs must be met for the musicians to become or remain motivated members of the orchestra? To what extent are the board of directors, the musicians' union, the orchestra's benefactors, and the audience's perception of the orchestra motivating factors? What opportunities for self-development are available within the structure of the orchestra—opportunities that can motivate individuals to grow and improve? Questions such as these have been the concern of motivation theories and research for many decades.

For hundreds of years, the motivation of workers has been the proverbial "pot of gold to be found at the end of the rainbow" for management practitioners and students of organizational behavior. If employees could be motivated to produce just slightly more, the economic rewards to individual organizations and to societies would be immense. Although there always has been consensus about the need for motivated employees, the same cannot be said for beliefs about how to induce higher levels of motivation. Not only have prevailing views (or theories) of motivation changed radically over the course of organizational history, but incompatible theories usually have competed with each other at the same points in time. Some theories of motivation have been developed from empirical research, but most have not. Some theories assume that employees act rationally: Managers simply need to manipulate rewards and punishments rationally, fairly, and consistently. Other theories start from the position that managerial assumptions about employees—which undergird such systems of rewards and punishments—actually stifle employee motivation.

Even today, widely divergent views remain about the essence of motivation in organizations. This chapter attempts to sort, organize, and summarize some of the more important theories that have been proposed over the years. As in all chapters of this book, the readings are organized chronologically. For purposes of perspective, the chapter starts its analysis in the 1760s, at the beginning of the Industrial Revolution.

MOTIVATION THEORY PRIOR TO THE HAWTHORNE STUDIES

Even in the early years of the Industrial Revolution (beginning about 1760), *employee discipline* was one of the most vexing problems confronting managers in the factory system of mass production. Motivating employees and strategic use of negative sanctions were integral tactics for maintaining production and discipline. Prior to the Industrial Revolution, most workers worked under craft traditions or were agrarians and had some degree of independence (Wren, 1972, chap. 3). But the new style factories needed workers who fit into the factory systems' production concept, which was driven by the principle of the *division of labor* (Smith, 1776). Workers had to produce on a schedule not of their own choosing. Expensive machines had to be kept busy. Production shifted from labor-intensive to capital-intensive; and society's basic concept of humans at work changed with this shifting economic base (Haire, 1962). Although some early industrialists reportedly threw periodic feasts in attempts to build company loyalty, reduce absenteeism, and thereby keep production high, the backbone of motivational strategy was the incentive piece-rate system of compensation. Workers were paid for production output rather than for hours at work.

The twentieth-century scientific management movement of Frederick Winslow Taylor, Lillian and Frank Gilbreth, Henry Gantt, and others followed naturally from the piece-rate payment system ethic of the Industrial Revolution factory system of production (see Shafritz & Ott, 2001, chap. 1). Under scientific management principles, motivational methods were rooted in the concept of workers as *rational economic men*. People work for money: Tie compensation to production, and employees produce more (Gantt, 1910). Deal only with individual employees, and try to prevent the formation of groups because they restrict output and lead to unions. Beyond restricting output, Taylor saw productivity limited primarily by workers' ignorance of how to maximize production. To Taylor, scientific study of production process (what he called *scientific management*) was the answer. It would provide for standardization, for the improvement of practices, and for techniques that would reduce worker fatigue. With better procedures and less fatigue, employee income and company profits would increase (Taylor, 1911).

THE HAWTHORNE STUDIES

In 1924 a team of researchers, under the aegis of the National Academy of Sciences' National Research Council, went to the Hawthorne plant of the Western Electric Company near Chicago to study ways for improving productivity. The research team began its work from the perspective—the assumptions, precepts, and principles—of scientific management. Scientific investigative procedures (including control groups) were used to find and identify environmental changes that would increase worker productivity. Their investigations focused on room temperature, humidity, and illumination levels (Pennock, 1930). Interestingly, illumination was included as an experimental variable because scientific management studies by Frederick Winslow Taylor (1911) fifteen years earlier had identified illumination as an easily controlled variable for influencing productivity. The early Hawthorne studies caused confusion. Worker output continued to increase even as illumination decreased.

By 1927 the results were so snarled that Western Electric and the National Research Council were ready to abandon the entire endeavor. In that year, George Pennock, Western Electric's superintendent of inspection, heard Harvard professor Elton Mayo speak at a meeting and invited him to take a team to Hawthorne. Team members eventually included Fritz Roethlisberger, George Homans, and T. N. Whitehead. The results are legendary. However, it was not until the Mayo-led Hawthorne team discarded its rational economic man/scientific management assumptions about people at work that the groundwork was laid for what we have been calling in this volume the field of *organizational behavior*—a perspective with its own very different set of assumptions. (See the *Introduction* to this book.) The long-held assumptions of industrial/organizational psychology, that people could and should be fit to organizations, had been challenged. The process had begun that would render obsolete scientific management's assumptions about people and how to motivate them.

The Hawthorne experiments were the emotional and intellectual wellspring of the organizational behavior perspective and of modern theories of motivation. The Hawthorne experiments showed that complex, interactional variables make the difference in motivating people—things like attention paid to workers as individuals, workers' control over their own work, differences between individuals' needs, management willingness to listen, group norms, and direct feedback.

Fritz J. Roethlisberger, of the Harvard Business School, is the best known chronicler of the Hawthorne studies. Roethlisberger, with William J. Dickson of the Western Electric Company, wrote the most comprehensive account of the Hawthorne studies, *Management and the Worker* (1939). Roethlisberger's chapter, which is reprinted here, "The Hawthorne Experiments," is from his shorter 1941 book, *Management and Morale*.

NEED THEORIES OF MOTIVATION

All discussions of need theories of motivation start with Abraham Maslow. His hierarchy of needs stands alongside the Hawthorne experiments and Douglas McGregor's Theory X and Theory Y as *the* departure points for studying motivation in organizations. An overview of Maslow's basic theory of needs is presented here from his 1943 *Psychological Review* article, "A Theory of Human Motivation." Maslow's theoretical premises can be summarized in a few phrases:

- All humans have needs that underlie their motivational structure.
- As lower levels of needs are satisfied, they no longer "drive" behavior.
- Satisfied needs are not motivators.
- As lower level needs of workers become satisfied, higher order needs take over as the motivating forces.

Maslow's theory has been attacked frequently. Few empirical studies have supported it, and it oversimplifies the complex structure of human needs and motivations (for example, see Wahba & Bridwell, 1973). Several modified needs hierarchies have been proposed over the years that reportedly are better able to withstand empirical testing (for example, Alderfer, 1969). But despite the criticisms and the continuing advances across the spectrum of applied behavioral sciences, Abraham Maslow's theory continues to occupy a most honored and prominent place in organizational behavior and management textbooks.

THEORY X AND THEORY Y

Douglas McGregor's *The Human Side of Enterprise* (1960) is about much more than the motivation of people at work. In its totality, it is a cogent articulation of the basic assumptions of the organizational behavior perspective. Theory X and Theory Y are contrasting basic managerial assumptions about employees, which, in McGregor's words, become self-fulfilling prophesies. Managerial assumptions *cause* employee behavior. Theory X and Theory Y are ways of seeing and thinking about people that in turn affect their behavior. Thus "The Human Side of Enterprise" (1957b, reprinted in this chapter) is a landmark theory of motivation.

Theory X assumptions represent a restatement of the tenets of the scientific management movement. For example, human beings inherently dislike work and will avoid it if possible. Most people must be coerced, controlled, directed, or threatened with punishment to get them to work toward the achievement of organizational objectives; humans prefer to be directed, to avoid responsibility, and will seek security above all else. These assumptions serve as polar opposites to McGregor's Theory Y.

Theory Y assumptions postulate, for example, that people do not inherently dislike work; work can be a source of satisfaction. People will exercise self-direction and self-control if they are committed to organizational objectives. People are willing to seek and to accept responsibility; avoidance of responsibility is not natural, it is a consequence of experiences. The intellectual potential of most humans is only partially utilized at work.

COGNITIVE DISSONANCE AND INEQUITY THEORIES OF MOTIVATION

When two or more people or things around a person are in a state of disharmony, imbalance, or incongruity, that imbalance causes *dissonance* (or discomfort). According to cognitive dissonance theory, people will act—will do something—to reduce or eliminate dissonance. For example, I like two people, "A" and "B," but "A" does not like "B." An imbalance exists that causes dissonance, and I will act to eliminate it. The theory of cognitive dissonance cannot predict what I will do, but it says that I will be motivated to do something. I might try to change "A's" feelings toward "B"; or I might change my feelings about either "A" or "B" and then sever my relationship with the out-of-favor person. Similarly, if I believe that wearing a seat belt will not save my life in the event of a car accident, but I fasten my seat belt anyway because state law says I must, dissonance is created by the incongruity between my belief and my behavior. Cognitive dissonance theory predicts that I will be motivated to reduce or eliminate the dissonance. I might stop wearing a seat belt (for example, by convincing myself that the probability of getting caught violating the law is low or the legal penalty is too minimal to worry about), or, as the authors of the state law hope, I could allow my belief to be altered. If my belief does change, I probably will continue to "buckle up" even if the seat belt law is repealed some day.

Cognitive dissonance theory has many practical managerial applications for motivating employees. For example, management can require workers to do certain things in the hope that attitudes or beliefs will follow—just as in the seat belt example. On the other hand, management can attempt to change people's attitudes or beliefs (Zimbardo & Ebbesen, 1970) in the hope that the resulting cognitive dissonance will motivate a behavior change. In contrast, under cognitive dissonance theories, motivation is *engineered* by intentionally creating dissonance and then not allowing the desired state to change (in the examples used here, beliefs or behavior).

Cognitive dissonance provides the theoretical basis for what are known as equity theories of motivation. Equity theories postulate that workers are motivated to act (for example, to produce more or less) by their perceptions of inequities in the environment, such as between *their* levels of work and compensation and *others'* levels of work and compensation (Mowday, 1983). The theory of cognitive dissonance assumes that a worker performing the same work as another but being paid significantly less will do something to relieve this dissonance. Among the worker's option's are asking for a raise, restricting output, or seeking another job. The 1958 article, "The Motivating Effect of Cognitive Dissonance," by Leon Festinger, the "father" of cognitive dissonance theory, is reprinted in this chapter.

EXPECTANCY THEORY OF MOTIVATION

Expectancy theory holds that people are motivated by two dynamics: how much they want certain rewards (or to avoid negative sanctions) and the expectancy (probability) that their actions will garner the rewards. Victor Vroom (1964, 1969), the most respected expectancy theorist, identifies four classes of variables that comprise expectancy theory:

1. The amounts of particular classes of outcomes such as pay, status, acceptance, and influence, attained by the person.

2. The strength of the person's desire or aversion for outcomes.
3. The amounts of these outcomes believed by the person to be received by comparable others.
4. The amounts of these outcomes the person expected to receive or has received at earlier points in time. (1969, p. 207)

Very simply, expectancy theory claims that people are motivated by calculating how much they want something, how much of it they think they will get, how likely it is their actions will cause them to get it, and how much others in similar circumstances have received.

ANOTHER NEED THEORY

Frederick Herzberg is one of the most widely cited of the numerous students and theorists who studied and wrote about motivation in organizations during the 1960s. Herzberg began construction of his motivation theory with Abraham Maslow's need theory and was also influenced substantially by the Theory X and Theory Y assumptions of Douglas McGregor.

Herzberg's theory of motivation evolved from extensive empirical research. Herzberg and his collaborating researchers would ask people to identify situations when they felt particularly satisfied and dissatisfied with their job (Herzberg, Mausner, & Snyderman, 1959). From thousands of responses, Herzberg developed the motivation-hygiene theory, which can be stated in this way:

- *Motivators* or *satisfiers* are variables centered in the work (or work content) that satisfy self-actualization-type needs (Maslow, 1943) and lead to higher motivation. Examples of Herzberg's motivators include achievement, recognition for achievement, and opportunities for self-development.
- In contrast, *hygiene factors* are maintainers—preventers of dissatisfaction. A few examples of hygiene factors are supervision, administrative practices, and (in most respects) pay.

According to Herzberg's theory, which is described here in his 1968 article, "One More Time: How Do You Motivate Employees?" motivators and hygiene factors are on different dimensions or planes. They are not extreme points on a single scalar continuum. The presence of hygiene factors does not motivate, it only prevents dissatisfaction; and the absence of motivators does not cause employees to be dissatisfied, it only yields nonmotivated employees. If managers want satisfied employees, they should pay attention to hygiene factors, such as pay and working conditions. However, hygiene factors do not "turn employees on"; they only neutralize negative sentiments. To increase motivation, managers must work with motivators.

Herzberg's work has been attacked with great vigor on two fronts. First, numerous behavioral researchers have tried unsuccessfully to replicate his findings, raising serious questions about the validity of his research methods (Vroom, 1964). The second line of criticism directed at Herzberg has essentially been an argument against any and all simplistic, static, one- or two-dimensional theories of motivation, and for more complex, contingency-type theories (Behling, Labovitz, & Kosmo, 1968; Schein, 1980). Despite the sometimes bitter criticisms of motivation-hygiene theory, its popularity continues among management practitioners and trainers. Its greatest weakness—simplicity—also gives it credibility.

SELF-ORIENTED THEORIES

Theories of motivation have traveled down many divergent paths. The quest to understand motivation in organizations brings us back to the fundamental question: What causes individuals to do what they do with different levels of enthusiasm and commitment?

Many long-standing motivation theories provide some answers to this question, but as Leonard, Beauvais, and Scholl (1999) point out in "Work Motivation: The Incorporation of Self-Concept-Based Processes" (reprinted in this chapter), "there is a growing realization that traditional models of motivation do not explain the diversity of behavior found in organizational settings." They seek to unify theories of work motivation into a "metatheory" that blends traditional motivational theories with an understanding of how the self-concept influences behavior in organizations. The theory proposed by Leonard, Beauvais, and Scholl integrates individual traits, competencies, and values and recognizes the various forces that influence the development and perception of self. They argue that there are five primary sources of motivation: "intrinsic processes, extrinsic/instrumental rewards, external self-concept, internal self-concept, and goal internalization." Individuals have dominant sources of motivation that help them to focus their behavior and that will prevail with relative predictability.

The final piece reprinted in this chapter is Edwin Locke's 2001 article, "Self-Set Goals and Self-Efficacy as Mediators of Incentives and Personality." Like Leonard, Beauvais, and Scholl, Locke's focus is self-oriented: "Self-set or personal goals and self-efficacy are the most immediate, motivational determinants of action, and they mediate or link the effects of other motivators." For many years, Locke has been well known for his work on reinforcement and goals theories of motivation, which assume that people respond positively to goals—in other words, that goals motivate. Earlier, Locke (1978) had identified needs and values—not goals—as the most important factors in motivation because they determine goals. In this 2001 article, however, he argues that personal goals and intentions, along with task-specific self-confidence, are the most direct motivational determinants of action. Other factors—including needs, values, motives, personality, and incentives—also need to be considered as situations require.

Locke reviews several studies that investigate the connections between what individuals are trying to do (goals) and the confidence they have in what they can actually do (self-efficacy). He also examines differences between assigned and self-set goals as they relate to behavior and motivation, and the effects of feedback, participation, money, job design, leadership, and personality on goal setting and behavior.

CONCLUSION

In this chapter we present a balanced sampling of the more important theories of motivation. If the result is confusing and inconclusive, we apologize. In many ways, motivation is "the proverbial pot of gold at the end of the rainbow." We may never totally unlock its mysteries. Humans are complicated, ever-changing, and diverse beings. Organizations are complex social systems in which these beings must live and work. Understanding and predicting either is extremely difficult (Schein, 1980, chap. 6 & 11). Discovering universal truths about what motivates people in the context of organizations may be an unrealistic "pot of gold" to seek. On the other hand, much has been learned about what does and does not cause people to "turn on" or "tune out" at work.

REFERENCES

Adams, J. S. (1963). Toward an understanding of inequity. *Journal of Abnormal Social Psychology, 67*, 422–436.

Adams, J. S. (1965). Inequity in social exchange. In L. Berkowitz (Ed.), *Advances in experimental social psychology. Vol. 2* (pp. 267–299). New York: Academic Press.

Alderfer, J. S. (1969). An empirical test of a new theory of human needs. *Organizational Behavior and Human Performance, 4*, 142–175.

Atkinson, J. W., & Raynor, J. O. (1974). *Motivation and achievement*. New York: John Wiley.

Behling, O., Labovitz, G., & Kosmo, R. (1968). The Herzberg controversy: A critical reappraisal. *Academy of Management Journal, 11*(1), 99–108.

Behling, O., & Starke, F. (1973). The postulates of expectancy theory. *Academy of Management Journal, 16*, 373–388.

Campbell, J. P., Dunnette, M. D., Lawler, E. E. III, & Weick, K. E. Jr. (1970). Expectancy theory. In J. P. Campbell, M. D. Dunnette, E. E. Lawler III, & K. E. Weick Jr. (Eds.), *Managerial behavior, performance and effectiveness* (pp. 343–348). New York: McGraw-Hill.

Cohen, A. R., Fink, S. L., Gadon, H., & Willits, R. D. (1988). *Effective behavior in organizations* (4th ed.). Homewood, IL: Richard D. Irwin.

Deci, E. L. (1971). The effects of externally mediated rewards on intrinsic motivation. *Journal of Personality and Social Psychology, 18*, 105–115.

Festinger, L. (1954). Motivations leading to social behavior. In M. R. Jones (Ed.), *Nebraska symposium on motivation*. Lincoln, NE: University of Nebraska Press.

Festinger, L. (1957). *A theory of cognitive dissonance*. Stanford, CA: Stanford University Press.

Festinger, L. (1958). The motivating effect of cognitive dissonance. In G. Lindzey (Ed.), *Assessment of human motives* (pp. 69–86). New York: Holt, Rinehart & Co.

Fink, S. L. (1992). *High commitment workplaces*. New York: Quorum Books.

Gantt, H. L. (1910). *Work, wages, and profit*. New York: Engineering Magazine Company.

Hackman, J. R., & Oldham, G. R. (1976). Motivation through the design of work. *Organizational Behavior and Human Performance, 16*, 250–279.

Haire, M. (1962). The concept of power and the concept of man. In G. B. Strother (Ed.), *Social science approaches to business behavior* (pp. 163–183). Homewood, IL: Richard D. Irwin.

Herzberg, F. (January/February 1968). One more time: How do you motivate employees? *Harvard Business Review, 46*(1).

Herzberg, F., Mausner, B., & Snyderman, B. B. (1959). *The motivation to work*. New York: John Wiley & Sons.

Katzenbach, J. R., & Smith, D. K. (1993). *The wisdom of teams: Creating the high-performance organization*. Boston: Harvard Business School Press.

Kerr, S. (December 1975). On the folly of rewarding A, while hoping for B. *Academy of Management Journal, 18*(4), 769–782.

Lawler, E. E. III, & Porter, L. W. (1963). Perceptions regarding management compensation. *Industrial Relations, 3*, 41–49.

Leonard, N. H., Beauvais, L. L., & Scholl, R. W. (August 1999). Work motivation: The incorporation of self-concept-based processes. *Human Relations, 52*(8), 969–998.

Litwin, G. H., & Stringer, R. A. Jr. (1968). *Motivation and organizational climate*. Boston: Harvard University Press.

Locke, E. A. (July 1978). The ubiquity of the technique of goal setting in theories of and approaches to employee motivation. *Academy of Management Review*, 594–601.

Locke, E. A. (2001). Self-set goals and self-efficacy as mediators of incentives and personality. In M. Erez, U. Kleinbeck, & H. Thierry (Eds.), *Work motivation in the context of a globalizing economy*. Mahwah, NJ: Lawrence Erlbaum.

Maslow, A. H. (1943). A theory of human motivation. *Psychological Review, 50*.

Mayo, E. (1933). *The human problems of an industrial civilization*. New York: Macmillan.

McClelland, D. C. (1961). *The achieving society*. Princeton, NJ: Van Nostrand.

McClelland, D. C. (1966). That urge to achieve. *Think* (published by International Business Machines Corporation), 82–89.

McGregor, D. M. (April 1957a). The human side of enterprise. Address to the Fifth Aniversary Convocation of the School of Industrial Management, Massachusetts Institute of Technology. In *Adventure in thought and action*. Cambridge, MA: M.I.T. School of Industrial Management, 1957. Reprinted in W. G. Bennis, E. H. Schein, & C. McGregor (Eds.), *Leadership and motivation: Essays of Douglas McGregor* (pp. 3–20). Cambridge, MA: The M.I.T. Press, 1966.

McGregor, D. M. (November 1957b). The human side of enterprise. *Management Review*, 22–28, 88–92.

McGregor, D. M. (1960). *The human side of enterprise*. New York: McGraw-Hill.

Mowday, R. T. (1983). Equity theory predictions of behavior in organizations. In R. W. Steers & L. W. Porter (Eds.), *Motivation and work behavior* (3d ed., pp. 91–113). New York: McGraw-Hill.

Organ, D. W., & Bateman, T. (1986). *Organizational behavior: An applied psychological approach* (3d ed.). Plano, TX: Business Publications.

Pennock, G. (1930). Industrial research at Hawthorne. *The Personnel Journal, 8*, 296.

Roethlisberger, F. I. (1941). *Management and morale*. Cambridge, MA: Harvard University Press.

Roethlisberger, F. J., & Dickson, W. J. (1939). *Management and the worker*. Cambridge, MA: Harvard University Press.

Ross, I. C., & Zander, A. (1957). Need satisfactions and employee turnover. *Personnel Psychology, 10*, 327–338.

Schein, E. H. (1980). *Organizational psychology* (3d ed.). Englewood Cliffs, NJ: Prentice-Hall.

Shafritz, J. M., & Ott, J. S. (2001). *Classics of organization theory* (5th ed.). Fort Worth, TX: Harcourt.

Smith, A. (1776). Of the division of labor. In A. Smith, *The wealth of nations* (chapter 1).

Staw, B. M. (1982). Motivation in organizations: Toward synthesis and redirection. In B. M. Staw & G. R. Salancik (Eds.), *New directions in organizational behavior* (pp. 55–95). Malabar, FL: Robert E. Krieger.

Taylor, F. W. (1903). *Shop management*. New York: Harper & Row.

Taylor, F. W. (1911). *The principles of scientific management*. New York: Harper & Row.

Urwick, L. (Ed.). (1956). *The golden book of management*. London, UK: Newman Neame.

Vroom, V. H. (1964). *Work and motivation*. New York: John Wiley.

Vroom, V. H. (1969). Industrial social psychology. In G. Lindzey & E. Aronson (Eds.), *The handbook of social psychology*, Vol. 5 (2d ed., pp. 200–208). Reading, MA: Addison-Wesley.

Vroom, V. H., & Deci, E. L. (Eds.) (1970). *Management and motivation*. Harmondsworth, UK: Penguin Books.

Wahba, M. A., & Bridwell, L. G. (1973). Maslow reconsidered: A review of research on the need hierarchy theory. Boston: *Proceedings of the 1973 meetings of the Academy of Management*.

Wren, D. A. (1972). *The evolution of management thought*. New York: The Ronald Press.

Zaleznik, A., Christensen, C. R., & Roethlisberger, F. J. (1958). *The motivation, productivity and satisfaction of workers: A prediction study*. Cambridge, MA: Harvard University, Graduate School of Business Administration.

Zimbardo, P., & Ebbesen, E. B. (1970). *Influencing attitudes and changing behavior* (rev. printing). Reading, MA: Addison-Wesley.

10
The Hawthorne Experiments

Frederick J. Roethlisberger

There seems to be an assumption today that we need a complex set of ideas to handle the complex problems of this complex world in which we live. We assume that a big problem needs a big idea; a complex problem needs a complex idea for its solution. As a result, our thinking tends to become more and more tortuous and muddled. Nowhere is this more true than in matters of human behavior. It seems to me that the road back to sanity—and here is where my title comes in—lies

1. In having a few simple and clear ideas about the world in which we live.
2. In complicating our ideas, not in a vacuum, but only in reference to things we can observe, see, feel, hear, and touch. Let us not generalize from verbal definitions; let us know in fact what we are talking about.
3. In having a very simple method by means of which we can explore our complex world. We need a tool which will allow us to get the idea from which our generalizations are to be drawn. We need a simple skill to keep us in touch with what is sometimes referred to as "reality."
4. In being "tough-minded," i.e., in not letting ourselves be too disappointed because the complex world never quite fulfills our most cherished expectations of it. Let us remember that the concrete phenomena will always elude any set of abstractions that we can make of them.
5. In knowing very clearly the class of phenomena to which our ideas and methods relate. Now, this is merely a way of saying, "Do not use a saw as a hammer." A saw is a useful tool precisely because it is limited and designed for a certain purpose. Do not criticize the usefulness of a saw because it does not make a good hammer. . . .

It is my simple thesis that a human problem requires a human solution. First, we have to learn to recognize a human problem when we see one; and, second, upon recognizing it, we have to learn to deal with it as such and not as if it were something else. Too often at the verbal level we talk glibly about the importance of the human factor; and too seldom at the concrete level of behavior do we recognize a human problem for what it is and deal with it as such. *A human problem to be brought to a human solution requires human data and human tools*. It is my purpose to use the Western Electric researchers as an illustration of what I mean by this statement, because, if they deserve the publicity and acclaim which they have received, it is because, in my opinion, they have so conclusively demonstrated this point. In this sense they are the road back to sanity in management-employee relations.

Source: Reprinted by permission of the publishers from *Management and Morale* by F. J. Roethlisberger, Cambridge, Massachusetts: Harvard University Press, Copyright © 1941 by the President and Fellows of Harvard College; © 1969 by F. J. Roethlisberger.

EXPERIMENTS IN ILLUMINATION

The Western Electric researches started about sixteen years ago, in the Hawthorne plant, with a series of experiments on illumination. The purpose was to find out the relation of the quality and quantity of illumination to the efficiency of industrial workers. These studies lasted several years, and I shall not describe them in detail. It will suffice to point out that the results were quite different from what had been expected.

In one experiment the workers were divided into two groups. One group, called the "test group," was to work under different illumination intensities. The other group, called the "control group," was to work under an intensity of illumination as nearly constant as possible. During the first experiment, the test group was submitted to three different intensities of illumination of increasing magnitude, 24, 46, and 70 foot candles. What were the results of this early experiment? Production increased in both rooms—in both the test group and the control group—and the rise in output was roughly of the same magnitude in both cases.

In another experiment, the light under which the test group worked was decreased from 10 to 3 foot candles, while the control group worked, as before, under a constant level of illumination intensity. In this case the output rate in the test group went up instead of down. It also went up in the control group.

In still another experiment, the workers were allowed to believe that the illumination was being increased, although, in fact, no change in intensity was made. The workers commented favorably on the improved lighting condition, but there was no appreciable change in output. At another time, the workers were allowed to believe that the intensity of illumination was being decreased, although again, in fact, no actual change was made. The workers complained somewhat about the poorer lighting, but again there was no appreciable effect on output.

And finally, in another experiment, the intensity of illumination was decreased to .06 of a foot candle, which is the intensity of illumination approximately equivalent to that of ordinary moonlight. Not until this point was reached was there any appreciable decline in the output rate.

What did the experimenters learn? Obviously, as Stuart Chase said, there was something "screwy," but the experimenters were not quite sure who or what was screwy—they themselves, the subjects, or the results. One thing was clear: the results were negative. Nothing of a positive nature had been learned about the relation of illumination to industrial efficiency. If the results were to be taken at their face value, it would appear that there was no relation between illumination and industrial efficiency. However, the investigators were not yet quite willing to draw this conclusion. They realized the difficulty of testing for the effect of a single variable in a situation where there were many uncontrolled variables. It was thought therefore that another experiment should be devised in which other variables affecting the output of workers could be better controlled.

A few of the tough-minded experimenters already were beginning to suspect their basic ideas and assumptions with regard to human motivation. It occurred to them that the trouble was not so much with the results or with the subjects as it was with their notion regarding the way their subjects were supposed to behave—the notion of a simple cause-and-effect, direct relationship between certain physical changes in the workers' environment and the responses of the workers to these changes. Such a notion completely ignored the human meaning of these changes to the people who were subjected to them.

In the illumination experiments, therefore, we have a classic example of trying to deal with a human situation in non-human terms. The experimenters had obtained no human data; they had been handling electric-light bulbs and plotting average output curves. Hence their results had no human significance. That is why they seemed screwy. Let me suggest here, however, that the results were not screwy, but the experimenters were— a "screwy" person being by definition one who is not acting in accordance with the customary human values of the situation in which he finds himself.

THE RELAY ASSEMBLY TEST ROOM

Another experiment was framed, in which it was planned to submit a segregated group of workers to different kinds of working conditions. The idea was very simple: A group of five girls were placed in a separate room where their conditions of work could be carefully controlled, where their output could be measured, and where they could be closely observed. It was decided to introduce at specified intervals different changes in working conditions and to see what effect these innovations had on output. . . . Under these conditions of close observation the girls were studied for a period of five years. Literally tons of material were collected. Probably nowhere in the world has so much material been collected about a small group of workers for such a long period of time.

But what about the results? They can be stated very briefly. When all is said and done, they amount roughly to this: A skillful statistician spent several years trying to relate variations to output with variations in the physical circumstances of these five operators. . . . The attempt to relate changes in physical circumstances to variations in output resulted in not a single correlation of enough statistical significance to be recognized by any competent statistician as having any meaning.

Now, of course, it would be misleading to say that this negative result was the only conclusion reached. There were positive conclusions, and it did not take the experimenters more than two years to find out that they had missed the boat. After two years of work, certain things happened which made them sit up and take notice. Different experimental conditions of work, in the nature of changes in the number and duration of rest pauses and differences in the length of the working day and week, had been introduced in this Relay Assembly Test Room. For example, the investigators first introduced two five-minute rests, one in the morning and one in the afternoon. Then they increased the length of these rests, and after that they introduced the rests at different times of the day. During one experimental period they served the operators a specially prepared lunch during the rest. In the later periods, they decreased the length of the working day by one-half hour and then by one hour. They gave the operators Saturday morning off for a while. Altogether, thirteen such periods of different working conditions were introduced in the first two years.

During the first year and a half of the experiment, everybody was happy, both the investigators and the operators. The investigators were happy because as conditions of work improved the output rate rose steadily. Here, it appeared, was strong evidence in favor of their preconceived hypothesis that fatigue was the major factor limiting output. The operators were happy because their conditions of work were being improved, they were earning more money, and they were objects of considerable attention from top management. But then one investigator—one of those tough-minded fellows—suggested that they restore the original conditions of work, that is, go back to a full forty-eight-hour week without rests, lunches and what not. This was Period XII. Then the happy state of affairs, when everything was going along as it theoretically should, went sour. Output, instead of taking the expected nose dive, maintained its high level.

Again the investigators were forcibly reminded that human situations are likely to be complex. In any human situation, whenever a simple change is introduced—a rest pause, for example—other changes, unwanted and unanticipated, may also be brought about. What I am saying here is very simple. If one experiments on a stone, the stone does not know it is being experimented upon—all of which makes it simple for people experimenting on stones. But if a human being is being experimented upon, he is likely to know it. Therefore, his attitudes toward the experiment and toward the experimenters become very important factors in determining his responses to the situation.

Now that is what happened in the Relay Assembly Test Room. To the investigators, it was essential that the workers give their full and wholehearted cooperation to the experiment. They did not want the operators to work harder or easier depending upon their attitude toward the conditions that were imposed. They wanted them to work as they felt, so that they could be sure that the different physical conditions of work were solely responsible for the variations in output. For each of the experimental changes, they wanted subjects whose responses would be uninfluenced by so-called "psychological factors."

In order to bring this about, the investigators did everything in their power to secure the complete cooperation of their subjects, with the result that almost all the practices common to the shop were altered. The operators were consulted about the changes to be made, and, indeed, several plans were abandoned because they met with the disapproval of the girls. They were questioned sympathetically about their reactions to the conditions imposed, and many of these conferences took place in the office of the superintendent. The girls were allowed to talk at work; their "bogey" was eliminated. Their physical health and well-being became matters of great concern. Their opinions, hopes, and fears were eagerly sought. What happened was that in the very process of setting the conditions for the test—a so-called "controlled" experiment—the experimenters had completely altered the social situation of the room. Inadvertently a change had been introduced which was far more important than the planned experimental innovations: the customary supervision in the room had been revolutionized. This accounted for the better attitudes of the girls and their improved rate of work.

THE DEVELOPMENT OF A NEW AND MORE FRUITFUL POINT OF VIEW

After Period XII in the Relay Assembly Test Room, the investigators decided to change their ideas radically. What all their experiments had dramatically and conclusively demonstrated was the importance of employee attitudes and sentiments. It was clear that the responses of workers to what was happening about them were dependent upon the significance these events had for them. In most work situations the meaning of a change is likely to be as important, if not more so, than the change itself. This was the great *éclaircissement,* the new illumination, that came from the research. It was an illumination quite different from what they had expected from the illumination studies. Curiously enough, this discovery is nothing very new or startling. It is something which anyone who has had some concrete experience in handling other people intuitively recognizes and practices.

Whether or not a person is going to give his services whole-heartedly to a group depends, in good part, on the way he feels about his job, his fellow workers, and supervisors—the meaning for him of what is happening about him.

However, when the experimenters began to tackle the problem of employee attitudes and the factors determining such attitudes—when they began to tackle the problem of "meaning"—they entered a sort of twilight zone where things are never quite what they seem. Moreover, overnight, as it were, they were robbed of all the tools they had so carefully forged; for all their previous tools were nonhuman tools concerned with the measurement of output, temperature, humidity, etc., and these were no longer useful for the human data that they now wanted to obtain. What the experimenters now wanted to know was how a person felt, what his intimate thinking, reflections, and preoccupations were, and what he liked and disliked about his work environment. In short, what did the whole blooming business—his job, his supervision, his working conditions—mean to him? Now this was human stuff, and there were no tools, or at least the experimenters knew of none, for obtaining and evaluating this kind of material.

Fortunately, there were a few courageous souls among the experimenters. These men were not metaphysicians, psychologists, academicians, professors, intellectuals, or what have you. They were men of common sense and of practical affairs. They were not driven by any great heroic desire to change the world. They were true experimenters, that is, men compelled to follow the implications of their own monkey business. All the evidence of their studies was pointing in one direction. Would they take the jump? They did.

EXPERIMENTS IN INTERVIEWING WORKERS

A few tough-minded experimenters decided to go into the shops and—completely disarmed and denuded of their elaborate logical equipment and in all humility—to see if they could learn how to get the workers to talk about things that were important to them and could learn to understand what the workers were trying to tell them. This was a revolutionary idea in the year 1928, when this interviewing program started—the idea of getting a worker to talk to you and to listen sympathetically, but intelligently, to what he had to say. In that year a new era of personnel relations began. It was the first real attempt to get human data and to forge human tools to get them. In that year a novel idea was born; dimly the experimenters perceived a new method of human control. In that year the Rubicon was crossed from which there could be no return to the "good old days." Not that the experimenters ever wanted to return, because they now entered a world so exciting, so intriguing, and so full of promise that it made the "good old days" seem like the prattle and play of children.

When these experimenters decided to enter the world of "meaning," with very few tools, but with a strong sense of curiosity and a willingness to learn, they had many interesting adventures. It would be too long a story to tell all of them, or even a small part of them. They made plenty of mistakes, but they were not afraid to learn.

At first, they found it difficult to learn to give full and complete attention to what a person had to say without interrupting him before he was through. They found it difficult to learn not to give advice, not to make or imply moral judgments about the speaker, not to argue, not to be too clever, not to dominate the conversation, not to ask leading questions. They found it difficult to get the person to talk about matters which were important to him and not to the interviewer. But, most important of all, they found it difficult to learn that perhaps the thing most significant to a person was not something in his immediate work situation.

Gradually, however, they learned these things. They discovered that sooner or later a person tends to talk about what is uppermost in his mind to a sympathetic and skillful listener, and they became more proficient in interpreting what a person is saying or trying to say. Of course they protected the confidences given to them and made absolutely sure that nothing an employee said could ever be used against him. Slowly they began to forge a simple human tool—imperfect, to be sure—to get the kind of data they wanted. They called this method "interviewing." I would hesitate to say the number of manhours of labor which went into the forging of this tool. There followed from studies made through its use a gradually changing conception of the worker and his behavior.

A NEW WAY OF VIEWING EMPLOYEE SATISFACTION AND DISSATISFACTION

When the experimenters started to study employee likes and dislikes, they assumed, at first, that they would find a simple and logical relation between a person's likes or dislikes and certain items and events in his immediate work situation. They expected to find a simple connection, for example, between a person's complaint and the object about which he was complaining. Hence, the solution would be easy: Correct the object of the complaint, if possible, and presto! the complaint would disappear. Unfortunately, however, the world of human behavior is not so simple as this conception of it; and it took the investigators several arduous and painful years to find this out. I will mention only a few interesting experiences they had.

Several times they changed the objects of the complaint only to find that the attitudes of the complainants remained unchanged. In these cases, correcting the object of the complaint did not remedy the complaint or the attitude of the person expressing it. A certain complaint might disappear, to be sure, only to have another one arise. Here the investigators were running into so-called "chronic kickers," people whose dissatisfactions were more deeply rooted in factors relating to their personal histories. . . .

Many times they found that people did not really want anything done about the things of which they were complaining. What they did want was an opportunity to talk about their troubles to a sympathetic listener. It was astonishing to find the number of instances in which workers complained about things which had happened many, many years ago, but which they described as vividly as if they had happened just a day before.

Here again, something was "screwy," but this time the experimenters realized that it was their assumptions which were screwy. They were assuming that the meanings which people assign to their experience are essentially logical. They were carrying in their heads the notion of the "economic man," a man primarily motivated by economic interest, whose logical capacities were being used in the service of this self-interest.

Gradually and painfully in the light of the evidence, which was overwhelming, the experimenters had been forced to abandon this conception of the worker and his behavior. Only with a new working hypothesis could they make sense of the data they had collected. The conception of the worker which they developed is actually nothing very new or startling; it is one which any effective administrator intuitively recognizes and practices in handling human beings.

First, they found that the behavior of workers could not be understood apart from their feelings or sentiments. I shall use the word "sentiment" hereafter to refer not only to such things as feelings and emotions, but also to a much wider range of phenomena which may not be expressed in violent feelings or emotions—phenomena that are referred to by such words as "loyalty," "integrity," "solidarity."

Secondly, they found that sentiments are easily disguised, and hence are difficult to recognize and to study. Manifestations of sentiment take a number of different forms. Feelings of personal integrity, for example, can be expressed by a handshake; they can also be expressed, when violated, by a sitdown strike. Moreover, people like to rationalize their sentiments and to objectify them. We are not so likely to say "I feel bad," as to say "The world is bad." In other words, we like to endow the world with those attributes and qualities which will justify and account for the feelings and sentiments we have toward it; we tend to project our sentiments on the outside world.

Thirdly, they found that manifestations of sentiment could not be understood as things in and by themselves, but only in terms of the total situation of the person. To comprehend why a person felt the way he did, a wider range of phenomena had to be explored. The following three diagrams illustrate roughly the development of this point of view.

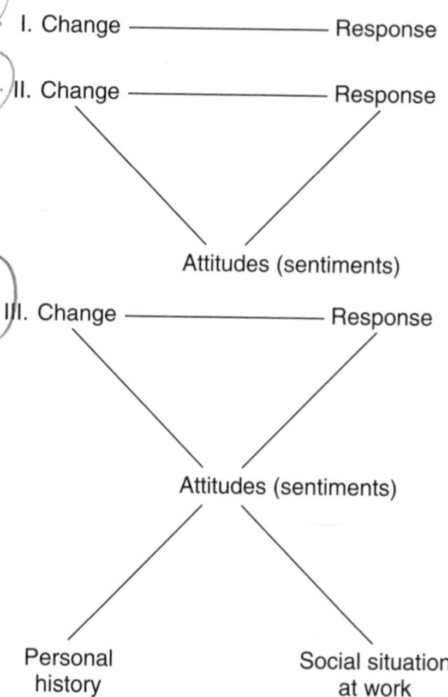

It will be remembered that at first the investigators assumed a simple and direct relation between certain physical changes in the worker's environment and his responses to them. This simple state of mind is illustrated in diagram I. But all the evidence of the early experiments showed that the responses of employees to changes in their immediate working environment can be understood only in terms of their attitudes—the "meaning" these changes have for them. This point of view is represented in diagram II. However, the "meaning" which these changes have for the worker is not strictly and primarily logical, for they are fraught with human feelings and values. The "meaning," therefore, which any individual worker assigns to a particular change depends upon (1) his social "conditioning," or what sentiments (values, hopes, fears, expectations, etc.) he is bringing to the work situation because of his previous family and group associations, and hence the relation of the change to these sentiments; and (2) the kind of human satisfaction he is deriving from his social participation with other workers and supervisors in the immediate work group of which he is a member, and hence the effect of the change on his customary interpersonal relations. This way of regarding the responses of workers (both verbal and overt) is represented in diagram III. It says briefly: Sentiments do not appear in a vacuum; they do not come out of the blue; they appear in a social context. They have to be considered in terms of that context, and apart from it they are likely to be misunderstood.

One further point should be made about that aspect of the worker's environment designated "Social Situation at Work" in diagram III. What is meant is that the worker is not an isolated, atomic individual; he is a member of a group, or of groups. Within each of these groups the individuals have feelings and sentiments toward each other, which bind them together in collaborative effort. Moreover, these collective sentiments can, and do, become attached to every item and object in the industrial environment—even to output. Material goods, output, wages, hours of work, and so on, cannot be treated as things in themselves. Instead, they must be interpreted as carriers of social value.

OUTPUT AS A FORM OF SOCIAL BEHAVIOR

That output is a form of social behavior was well illustrated in a study made by the Hawthorne experimenters, called the Bank Wiring Observation Room. This room contained fourteen workmen representing three occupational groups—wiremen, soldermen, and inspectors. These men were on group piecework, where the more they turned out the more they earned. In such a situation one might have expected that they would have been interested in maintaining total output and that the faster workers would have put pressure on the slower workers to improve their efficiency. But this was not the case. Operating within this group were four basic sentiments, which can be expressed briefly as follows: (1) You should not turn out too much work; if you do, you are a "rate buster." (2) You should not turn out too little work; if you do, you are a "chiseler." (3) You should not say anything to a supervisor which would react to the detriment of one of your associates; if you do, you are a "squealer." (4) You should not be too officious; that is, if you are an inspector you should not act like one.

To be an accepted member of the group a man had to act in accordance with these social standards. One man in this group exceeded the group standard of what constituted a fair day's work. Social pressure was put on him to conform, but without avail, since he enjoyed doing things the others disliked. The best-liked person in the group was the one who kept his output exactly where the group agreed it should be.

Inasmuch as the operators were agreed as to what constituted a day's work, one might have expected rate of output to be about the same for each member of the group. This was by no means the case; there were marked differences. At first the experimenters thought that the differences in individual performance were related to differences in ability, so they compared each worker's relative rank in output with his relative rank in intelligence and dexterity as measured by certain tests. The results were interesting: The lowest producer in the room ranked first in intelligence and third in dexterity; the highest producer in the room was seventh in dexterity and lowest in intelligence. Here surely was a situation in which the native capacities of the men were not finding expression. From the viewpoint of logical, economic behavior, this room did not make sense. Only in terms of powerful sentiments could these individual differences in output level be explained. Each worker's level of output reflected his position in the informal organization of the group.

WHAT MAKES THE WORKER NOT WANT TO COOPERATE

As a result of the Bank Wiring Observation Room, the Hawthorne researchers became more and more interested in the informal employee groups which tend to form within the formal organization of the company, and which are not likely to be represented in the organization chart. They became interested in the beliefs and creeds which have the effect of making each individual feel an integral part of the group and which make the group appear as a single unit, in the social codes and norms of behavior by means of which employees automatically work together in a group without any conscious choice as to whether they will or will not cooperate. They studied the important social functions these groups perform for their members, the histories of these informal work groups, how they spontaneously appear, how they tend to perpetuate themselves, multiply, and disappear, how they are in constant jeopardy from technical change, and hence how they tend to resist innovation. In particular, they became interested in those groups whose norms and codes of behavior are at variance with the technical and economic objectives of the company as a whole. They examined the social conditions under which it is more likely for the employee group to separate itself out in opposition to the remainder of the groups which make up the total organization. In such phenomena they felt that they had at last arrived at the heart of the problem of effective collaboration. They obtained a new enlightenment of the present industrial scene; from this point of view, many perplexing problems became more intelligible.

Some people claim, for example, that the size of the pay envelope is the major demand which the employee is making of his job. All the worker wants is to be told what to do and to get paid for doing it. If we look at him and his job in terms of sentiments, this is far from being as generally true as we would like to believe. Most of us want the satisfaction that comes from being accepted and recognized as people of worth by our friends and work associates. Money is only a small part of this social recognition. The way we are greeted by our boss, being asked to help a newcomer, being asked to keep an eye on a difficult operation, being given a job requiring special skill—all of these are acts of social recognition. They tell us how we stand in our work group. We all want tangible evidence of our social importance. We want to have a skill that is socially recognized as useful. We want the feeling of security that comes not so much from the amount of money we have in the bank as from being an accepted member of a group. A man whose job is without social function is like a man without a country; the activity to which he has to give the major portion of his life is robbed of all human meaning and significance. . . .

In summary, therefore, the Western Electric researchers seem to me like a beginning on the road back to sanity in employee relations because (1) they offer a fruitful working hypothesis, a few simple and relatively clear ideas for the study and understanding of human situations in business; (2) they offer a simple method by means of which we can explore and deal with the complex human problems in a business organization—this method is a human method: it deals with things which are important to people; and (3) they throw a new light on the precondition for effective collaboration. Too often we think of collaboration as something which can be logically or legally contrived. The Western Electric studies indicate that it is far more a matter of sentiment than a matter of logic. Workers are not isolated, unrelated individuals; they are social animals and should be treated as such.

This statement—the worker is a social animal and should be treated as such—is simple, but the systematic and consistent practice of this point of view is not. If it were systematically practiced, it would revolutionize present-day personnel work. Our technological development in the past hundred years has been tremendous. Our methods of handling people are still archaic. If this civilization is to survive, we must obtain a new understanding of human motivation and behavior in business organizations—an understanding which can be simply but effectively practiced. The Western Electric researchers contribute a first step in this direction.

11
A Theory of Human Motivation

Abraham H. Maslow

I. INTRODUCTION

In a previous paper (13) various propositions were presented which would have to be included in any theory of human motivation that could lay claim to being definitive. These conclusions may be briefly summarized as follows:

1. The integrated wholeness of the organism must be one of the foundation stones of motivation theory.
2. The hunger drive (or any other physiological drive) was rejected as a centering point or model for a definitive theory of motivation. Any drive that is somatically based and localizable was shown to be atypical rather than typical in human motivation.
3. Such a theory should stress and center itself upon ultimate or basic goals rather than partial or superficial ones, upon ends rather than means to these ends. Such a stress would imply a more central place for unconscious than for conscious motivations.
4. There are usually available various cultural paths to the same goal. Therefore conscious, specific, local-cultural desires are not as fundamental in motivation theory as the more basic, unconscious goals.
5. Any motivated behavior, either preparatory or consummatory, must be understood to be a channel through which many basic needs may be simultaneously expressed or satisfied. Typically an act has *more* than one motivation.
6. Practically all organismic states are to be understood as motivated and as motivating.
7. Human needs arrange themselves in hierarchies of prepotency. That is to say, the appearance of one need usually rests on the prior satisfaction of another, more prepotent need. Man is a perpetually wanting animal. Also no need or drive can be treated as if it were isolated or discrete; every drive is related to the state of satisfaction or dissatisfaction of other drives.
8. *Lists* of drives will get us nowhere for various theoretical and practical reasons. Furthermore any classification of motivations must deal with the problem of levels of specificity or generalization of the motives to be classified.
9. Classifications of motivations must be based upon goals rather than upon instigating drives or motivated behavior.
10. Motivation theory should be human-centered rather than animal-centered.
11. The situation or the field in which the organism reacts must be taken into account but the field alone can rarely serve as an exclusive explanation for behavior. Furthermore the field itself must be interpreted in terms of the organism. Field theory cannot be a substitute for motivation theory.
12. Not only the integration of organism must be taken into account, but also the possibility of isolated, specific, partial or segmental reactions.

Source: From "A Theory of Human Motivation," by Abraham H. Maslow, *Psychological Review, 50*.
Copyright 1943 by the American Psychological Association.

It has since become necessary to add to these another affirmation.

13. Motivation theory is not synonymous with behavior theory. The motivations are only one class of determinants of behavior. While behavior is almost always motivated, it is also almost always biologically, culturally and situationally determined as well.

The present paper is an attempt to formulate a positive theory of motivation which will satisfy these theoretical demands and at the same time conform to the known facts, clinical and observational as well as experimental. . . . The present theory then must be considered to be a suggested program or framework for future research and must stand or fall, not so much on facts available or evidence presented, as upon researches yet to be done, researches suggested perhaps, by the questions raised in this paper.

II. THE BASIC NEEDS

The "Physiological" Needs. The needs that are usually taken as the starting point for motivation theory are the so-called physiological drives. Two recent lines of research make it necessary to revise our customary notions about these needs, first, the development of the concept of homeostasis, and second, the finding that appetites (preferential choices among foods) are a fairly efficient indication of actual needs or lacks in the body.

Homeostasis refers to the body's automatic efforts to maintain a constant, normal state of the blood stream. Cannon (2) has described this process for (1) the water content of the blood, (2) salt content, (3) sugar content, (4) protein content, (5) fat content, (6) calcium content, (7) oxygen content, (8) constant hydrogen-ion level (acid-base balance) and (9) constant temperature of the blood. Obviously this list can be extended to include other minerals, the hormones, vitamins, etc.

Young in a recent article (21) has summarized the work on appetite in its relation to body needs. If the body lacks some chemical, the individual will tend to develop a specific appetite or partial hunger for that food element. . . .

It should be pointed out again that any of the physiological needs and the consummatory behavior involved with them serve as channels for all sorts of other needs as well. That is to say, the person who thinks he is hungry may actually be seeking more for comfort, or dependence, than for vitamins or proteins. Conversely, it is possible to satisfy the hunger need in part by other activities such as drinking water or smoking cigarettes. In other words, relatively isolable as these physiological needs are, they are not completely so.

Undoubtedly these physiological needs are the most prepotent of all needs. What this means specifically is that, in the human being who is missing everything in life in an extreme fashion, it is most likely that the major motivation would be the physiological needs rather than any others. A person who is lacking food, safety, love, and esteem would most probably hunger for food more strongly than for anything else.

If all the needs are unsatisfied, and the organism is then dominated by the physiological needs, all other needs may become simply nonexistent or be pushed into the background. . . . For the man who is extremely and dangerously hungry, no other interests exist but food. He dreams food, he remembers food, he thinks about food, he emotes only about food, he perceives only food and he wants only food. The more subtle determinants that ordinarily fuse with the physiological drives in organizing even feeding, drinking or sexual behavior, may not be so completely overwhelmed as to allow us to speak at this time (but *only* at this time) of pure hunger drive and behavior, with the one unqualified aim of relief.

Another peculiar characteristic of the human organism when it is dominated by a certain need is that the whole philosophy of the future tends also to change. For our chronically and extremely hungry man, Utopia can be defined very simply as a place where there is plenty of food. He tends to think that, if only he is guaranteed food for the rest of his life, he will be perfectly happy and will never want anything more. Life itself tends to be defined in terms of eating. Anything else will be defined as unimportant. Freedom, love, community feeling, respect, philosophy, may all be waved aside as fripperies which are useless since they fail to fill the stomach. Such a man may fairly be said to live by bread alone.

It cannot possibly be denied that such things are true but their *generality* can be denied. Emergency conditions are, almost by definition, rare in the normally functioning peaceful society. . . .

At once other (and "higher") needs emerge and these, rather than physiological hungers, dominate the organism. And when these in turn are satisfied, again new (and still "higher") needs emerge and so on. This is what we mean by saying that the basic human needs are organized into a hierarchy of relative prepotency.

One main implication of this phrasing is that gratification becomes as important a concept as deprivation in motivation theory, for it releases the organism from the domination of a relatively more physiological need, permitting thereby the emergence of other more social goals. The physiological needs, along with their partial goals, when chronically gratified cease to exist as active determinants or organizers of behavior. They now exist only in a potential fashion in the sense that they may emerge again to dominate the organism if they are thwarted. But a want that is satisfied is no longer a want. The organism is dominated and its behavior organized only by unsatisfied needs. If hunger is satisfied, it becomes unimportant in the current dynamics of the individual. . . .

The Safety Needs. If the physiological needs are relatively well gratified, there then emerges a new set of needs, which we may categorize roughly as the safety needs. . . .

Although in this paper we are interested primarily in the needs of the adult, we can approach an understanding of his safety needs perhaps more efficiently by observation of infants and children, in whom these needs are much more simple and obvious. One reason for the clearer appearance of the threat or danger reaction in infants is that they do not inhibit this reaction at all, whereas adults in our society have been taught to inhibit it at all costs. Thus even when adults do feel their safety to be threatened we may not be able to see this on the surface. Infants will react in a total fashion and as if they were endangered, if they are disturbed or dropped suddenly, startled by loud noises, flashing light, or other unusual sensory stimulation, by rough handling, by general loss of support in the mother's arms, or by inadequate support.[1]

In infants we can also see a much more direct reaction to bodily illnesses of

[1] As the child grows up, sheer knowledge and familiarity as well as better motor development make these "dangers" less and less dangerous and more and more manageable. Throughout life it may be said that one of the main cognitive functions of education is this neutralizing of apparent dangers through knowledge, *e.g.*, I am not afraid of thunder because I know something about it.

various kinds. Sometimes these illnesses seem to be immediately and *per se* threatening and seem to make the child feel unsafe. For instance, vomiting, colic, or other sharp pains seem to make the child look at the whole world in a different way. At such a moment of pain, it may be postulated that, for the child, the appearance of the whole world suddenly changes from sunniness to darkness, so to speak, and becomes a place in which anything at all might happen, in which previously stable things have suddenly become unstable. Thus a child who because of some bad food is taken ill may, for a day or two, develop fear, nightmares, and a need for protection and reassurance never seen in him before his illness.

Another indication of the child's need for safety is his preference for some kind of undisrupted routine or rhythm. He seems to want a predictable, orderly world. For instance, injustice, unfairness, or inconsistency in the parents seems to make a child feel anxious and unsafe. This attitude may be not so much because of the injustice *per se* or any particular pains involved, but rather because this treatment threatens to make the world look unreliable, or unsafe, or unpredictable. Young children seem to thrive better under a system which has at least a skeletal outline of rigidity, in which there is a schedule of a kind, some sort of routine, something that can be counted upon, not only for the present but also far into the future. Perhaps one could express this more accurately by saying that the child needs an organized world rather than an unorganized or unstructured one. . . .

From these and similar observations, we may generalize and say that the average child in our society generally prefers a safe, orderly, predictable, organized world, which he can count on, and in which unexpected, unmanageable or other dangerous things do not happen, and in which, in any case, he has all-powerful parents who protect and shield him from harm.

That these reactions may so easily be observed in children is in a way a proof of the fact that children in our society, feel too unsafe (or, in a word are badly brought up). Children who are reared in an unthreatening, loving family do *not* ordinarily react as we have described above (17). In such children the danger reactions are apt to come mostly to objects or situations that adults too would consider dangerous.[2]

The healthy, normal, fortunate adult in our culture is largely satisfied in his safety needs. The peaceful, smoothly running, "good" society ordinarily makes its members feel safe enough from wild animals, extremes of temperature, criminals, assault and murder, tyranny, etc. Therefore, in a very real sense, he no longer has any safety needs as active motivators. Just as a sated man no longer feels hungry, a safe man no longer feels endangered. . . .

Other broader aspects of the attempt to seek safety and stability in the world are seen in the very common preference for familiar rather than unfamiliar things, or for the known rather than the unknown. The tendency to have some religion or world-philosophy that organizes the universe and the men in it into some sort of satisfactorily coherent, meaningful whole is also in part

[2] A "test battery" for safety might be confronting the child with a small exploding firecracker, or with a bewhiskered face, having the mother leave the room, putting him upon a high ladder, [with] a hypodermic injection, having a mouse crawl up to him, etc. Of course I cannot seriously recommend the deliberate use of such "tests" for they might very well harm the child being tested. But these and similar situations come up by the score in the child's ordinary day-to-day living and may be observed. There is no reason why these stimuli should not be used with, for example, young chimpanzees.

motivated by safety-seeking. Here too we may list science and philosophy in general as partially motivated by the safety needs (we shall see later that there are also other motivations to scientific, philosophical or religious endeavor).

Otherwise, the need for safety is seen as an active and dominant mobilizer of the organism's resources only in emergencies, e.g., war, disease, natural catastrophes, crime waves, societal disorganization, neurosis, brain injury, chronically bad situations. . . .

The Love Needs. If both the physiological and the safety needs are fairly well gratified, then there will emerge the love and affection and belongingness needs, and the whole cycle already described will repeat itself with this new center. Now the person will feel keenly, as never before, the absence of friends, or a sweetheart, or a wife, or children. He will hunger for affectionate relations with people in general, namely, for a place in his group, and he will strive with great intensity to achieve this goal. He will want to attain such a place more than anything else in the world and may even forget that once, when he was hungry, he sneered at love. . . .

One thing that must be stressed at this point is that love is not synonymous with sex. Sex may be studied as a purely physiological need. Ordinarily sexual behavior is multi-determined, that is to say, determined not only by sexual but also by other needs, chief among which are the love and affection needs. Also not to be overlooked is the fact that the love needs involve both giving *and* receiving love.[3]

The Esteem Needs. All people in our society (with a few pathological exceptions) have a need or desire for a stable, firmly based, (usually) high evaluation of themselves, for self-respect, or self-esteem, and for the esteem of others. By firmly based self-esteem, we mean that which is soundly based upon real capacity, achievement and respect from others. These needs may be classified into two subsidiary sets. These are, first, the desire for strength, for achievement, for adequacy, for confidence in the face of the world, and for independence and freedom.[4] Secondly, we have what we may call the desire for reputation or prestige (defining it as respect or esteem from other people), recognition, attention, importance or appreciation.[5] These needs have been relatively stressed by Alfred Adler and his followers, and have been relatively neglected by Freud and the psychoanalysts. More and more today however there is appearing widespread appreciation of their central importance.

Satisfaction of the self-esteem need leads to feelings of self-confidence, worth, strength, capability and adequacy of being useful and necessary in the world. But thwarting of these needs produces feelings of inferiority, of weakness and of helplessness. These feelings in turn give rise to either basic discouragement or else compensatory or neurotic

[3] For further details see (12) and (16, Chap. 5).

[4] Whether or not this particular desire is universal we do not know. The crucial question, especially important today, is "Will men who are enslaved and dominated, inevitably feel dissatisfied and rebellious?" We may assume on the basis of commonly known clinical data that a man who has known true freedom (not paid for by giving up safety and security but rather built on the basis of adequate safety and security) will not willingly or easily allow his freedom to be taken away from him. But we do not know that this is true for the person born into slavery. The events of the next decade should give us our answer. See discussion of this problem in (5).

[5] Perhaps the desire for prestige and respect from others is subsidiary to the desire for self-esteem or confidence in oneself. Observation of children seems to indicate that this is so, but clinical data give no clear support for such a conclusion.

trends. An appreciation of the necessity of basic self-confidence and an understanding of how helpless people are without it can be easily gained from a study of severe traumatic neurosis (8).[6]

The Need for Self-Actualization. Even if all these needs are satisfied, we may still often (if not always) expect that a new discontent and restlessness will soon develop, unless the individual is doing what he is fitted for. A musician must make music, an artist must paint, a poet must write, if he is to be ultimately happy. What a man *can* be, he *must* be. This need we may call self-actualization.

This term, first coined by Kurt Goldstein, is being used in this paper in a much more specific and limited fashion. It refers to the desire for self-fulfillment, namely, to the tendency for him to become actualized in what he is potentially. This tendency might be phrased as the desire to become more and more what one is, to become everything that one is capable of becoming.

The specific form that these needs will take will of course vary greatly from person to person. In one individual it may take the form of the desire to be an ideal mother, in another it may be expressed athletically, and in still another it may be expressed in painting pictures or in inventions. It is not necessarily a creative urge although in people who have any capacities for creation it will take this form.

The clear emergence of these needs rests upon prior satisfaction of the physiological, safety, love and esteem needs. We shall call people who are satisfied in these needs, basically satisfied people, and it is from these that we may expect the fullest (and healthiest) creativeness.[7] Since, in our society, basically satisfied people are the exception, we do not know much about self-actualization, either experimentally or clinically. It remains a challenging problem for research.

The Preconditions for the Basic Need Satisfactions. There are certain conditions which are immediate prerequisites for the basic need satisfactions. Danger to these is reacted to almost as if it were a direct danger to the basic needs themselves. Such conditions as freedom to speak, freedom to do what one wishes so long as no harm is done to others, freedom to express one's self, freedom to investigate and seek for information, freedom to defend one's self, justice, fairness, honesty, orderliness in the group are examples of such preconditions for basic need satisfactions. Thwarting in these freedoms will be reacted to with a threat or emergency response. These conditions are not ends in themselves but they are *almost* so once they are so closely related to the basic needs, which are apparently the only ends in themselves. . . .

We must therefore introduce another hypothesis and speak of degrees of closeness to the basic needs, for we have already pointed out that *any* conscious desires (partial goals) are more or less important as they are more or less close

[6] For more extensive discussion of normal self-esteem, as well as for reports of various researches, see (11).

[7] Clearly creative behavior, like painting, is like any other behavior in having multiple determinants. It may be seen in "innately creative" people whether they are satisfied or not, happy or unhappy, hungry or sated. Also it is clear that creative activity may be compensatory, ameliorative or purely economic. It is my impression (as yet unconfirmed) that it is possible to distinguish the artistic and intellectual products of basically satisfied people from those of basically unsatisfied people by inspection alone. In any case, here too we must distinguish, in a dynamic fashion, the overt behavior itself from its various motivations or purposes.

to the basic needs. The same statement may be made for various behavior acts. An act is psychologically important if it contributes directly to satisfaction of basic needs. The less directly it so contributes, or the weaker this contribution is, the less important this act must be conceived to be from the point of view of dynamic psychology. A similar statement may be made for the various defense or coping mechanisms. Some are very directly related to the protection or attainment of the basic needs; others are only weakly and distantly related. Indeed if we wished, we could speak of more basic and less basic defense mechanisms, and then affirm that danger to the more basic defenses (always remembering that this is so only because of their relationship to the basic needs). . . .

III. FURTHER CHARACTERISTICS OF THE BASIC NEEDS

The Degree of Fixity of the Hierarchy of Basic Needs. We have spoken so far as if this hierarchy were a fixed order but actually it is not nearly as rigid as we may have implied. It is true that most of the people with whom we have worked have seemed to have these basic needs in about the order that has been indicated. However, there have been a number of exceptions.

1. There are some people in whom, for instance, self-esteem seems to be more important than love. This most common reversal in the hierarchy is usually due to the development of the notion that the person who is most likely to be loved is a strong or powerful person, one who inspires respect or fear, and who is self-confident or aggressive. Therefore such people who lack love and seek it may try hard to put on a front of aggressive, confident behavior. But essentially they seek high self-esteem and its behavior expressions more as a means-to-an-end than for its own sake; they seek self-assertion for the sake of love rather than for self-esteem itself.

2. There are other, apparently innately creative people in whom the drive to creativeness seems to be more important than any other counter-determinant. Their creativeness might appear not as self-actualization released by basic satisfaction, but in spite of lack of basic satisfaction.

3. In certain people the level of aspiration may be permanently deadened or lowered. That is to say, the less prepotent goals may simply be lost, and may disappear forever, so that the person who has experienced life at a very low level, *i.e.*, chronic unemployment, may continue to be satisfied for the rest of his life if only he can get enough food.

4. The so-called "psychopathic personality" is another example of permanent loss of the love needs. These are people who, according to the best data available (9), have been starved for love in the earliest months of their lives and have simply lost forever the desire and the ability to give and to receive affection (as animals lose sucking or pecking reflexes that are not exercised soon enough after birth).

5. Another cause of reversal of the hierarchy is that when a need has been satisfied for a long time, this need may be underevaluated. . . .

6. Another partial explanation of *apparent* reversals is seen in the fact that we have been talking about the hierarchy of prepotency in terms of consciously felt wants or desires rather than behavior. Looking at behavior itself may give us the wrong impression. What we have claimed is that the person will *want* the more basic of two needs when deprived in both. There is no necessary implication here that he will act upon his desires. Let us say again that there are many determinants of behavior other than the needs and desires.

7. Perhaps more important than all these exceptions are the ones that involve ideals, high social standards, high values

> and the like. With such values people become martyrs; they will give up everything for the sake of a particular ideal, or value. These people may be understood, at least in part, by reference to one basic concept (or hypothesis) which may be called "increased frustration-tolerance through early gratification." People who have been satisfied in their basic needs throughout their lives, particularly in their earlier years, seem to develop exceptional power to withstand present or future thwarting of these needs simply because they have a strong, healthy character structure as a result of basic satisfaction. They are the "strong" people who can easily weather disagreement or opposition, who can swim against the stream of public opinion and who can stand up for the truth at great personal cost. It is just the ones who have loved and been well loved, and who have had many deep friendships who can hold out against hatred, rejection or persecution.

. . . In respect to this phenomenon of increased frustration tolerance, it seems probable that the most important gratifications come in the first two years of life. That is to say, people who have been made secure and strong in the earliest years, tend to remain secure and strong thereafter in the face of whatever threatens.

Degrees of Relative Satisfaction. So far, our theoretical discussion may have given the impression that these five sets of needs are somehow in a step-wise, all-or-none relationship to each other. We have spoken in such terms as the following: "If one need is satisfied, then another emerges." This statement might give the false impression that a need must be satisfied 100 per cent before the next need emerges. In actual fact, most members of our society who are normal are partially satisfied in all their basic needs and partially unsatisfied in all their basic needs at the same time. A more realistic description of the hierarchy would be in terms of decreasing percentages of satisfaction as we go up the hierarchy of prepotency. For instance, if I may assign arbitrary figures for the sake of illustration, it is as if the average citizen is satisfied perhaps 85 per cent in his physiological needs, 70 per cent in his safety needs, 50 per cent in his love needs, 40 per cent in his self-esteem needs, and 10 per cent in his self-actualization needs.

As for the concept of emergence of a new need after satisfaction of the prepotent need, this emergence is not a sudden, saltatory phenomenon but rather a gradual emergence by slow degrees from nothingness. For instance, if prepotent need A is satisfied only 10 per cent then need B may not be visible at all. However, as this need A becomes satisfied 25 per cent, need B may emerge 5 per cent, as need A becomes satisfied 75 per cent need B may emerge 90 per cent, and so on.

Unconscious Character of Needs. These needs are neither necessarily conscious nor unconscious. On the whole, however, in the average person, they are more often unconscious rather than conscious. . . .

Cultural Specificity and Generality of Needs. This classification of basic needs makes some attempt to take account of the relative unity behind the superficial differences in specific desires from one culture to another. Certainly in any particular culture an individual's conscious motivational content will usually be extremely different from the conscious motivational content of an individual in another society. However, it is the common experience of anthropologists that people, even in different societies, are much more alike than we would think from our first contact with them, and that as we know them better we seem to find more and more of this commonness. . . .

Multiple Motivations of Behavior. . . . Most behavior is multi-motivated. Within the sphere of motivational determinants any behavior tends to be determined by several or *all* of the basic needs simultaneously rather than by only one of them. The latter would be more an exception than the former. Eating may be partially for the sake of filling the stomach, and partially for the sake of comfort and amelioration of other needs. One may make love not only for pure sexual release, but also to convince one's self of one's masculinity, or to make a conquest, to feel powerful, or to win more basic affection. . . .

Multiple Determinants of Behavior. Not all behavior is determined by the basic needs. We might even say that not all behavior is motivated. There are many determinants of behavior other than motives.[8] For instance, one other important class of determinants is the so-called "field" determinants. Theoretically, at least, behavior may be determined by the field, or even by specific isolated external stimuli, as in association of ideas, or certain conditioned reflexes. If in response to the stimulus word "table," I immediately perceive a memory image of a table, this response certainly has nothing to do with my basic needs.

Secondly, we may call attention again to the concept of "degree of closeness to the basic needs" or "degree of motivation." Some behavior is highly motivated, other behavior is only weakly motivated. Some is not motivated at all (but all behavior is determined).

Another important point[9] is that there is a basic difference between expressive behavior and coping behavior (functional striving, purposive goal seeking). An expressive behavior does not try to do anything; it is simply a reflection of the personality. A stupid man behaves stupidly, not because he wants to, or tries to, or is motivated to, but simply because he *is* what he is. . . .

We may then ask, is *all* behavior expressive or reflective of the character structure? The answer is "No." Rote, habitual, automatized, or conventional behavior may or may not be expressive. The same is true for most "stimulus-bound" behaviors.

It is finally necessary to stress that expressiveness of behavior, and goal-directedness of behavior, are not mutually exclusive categories. Average behavior is usually both.

Goals as Centering Principle in Motivation Theory. It will be observed that the basic principle in our classification has been neither the instigation nor the motivated behavior but rather the functions, effects, purposes, or goals of the behavior. It has been proven sufficiently by various people that this is the most suitable point for centering in any motivation theory.[10]

Animal- and Human-Centering. This theory starts with the human being rather than any lower and presumably "simpler" animal. Too many of the findings that have been made in animals have been proven to be true for animals but not for the human being. There is no reason whatsoever why we should start

[8] I am aware that many psychologists and psychoanalysts use the term "motivated" and "determined" synonymously, e.g., Freud. But I consider this an obfuscating usage. Sharp distinctions are necessary for clarity of thought, and precision in experimentation.

[9] To be discussed fully in a subsequent publication.

[10] The interested reader is referred to the very excellent discussion of this point in Murray's *Explorations in Personality* (15).

with animals in order to study human motivation. . . .

Motivation and the Theory of Psychopathogenesis. The conscious motivational content of everyday life has, according to the foregoing, been conceived to be relatively important or unimportant accordingly as it is more or less closely related to the basic goals. A desire for an ice cream cone might actually be an indirect expression of a desire for love. If it is, then this desire for the ice cream cone becomes extremely important motivation. If however the ice cream is simply something to cool the mouth with, or a casual appetitive reaction, then the desire is relatively unimportant. Everyday conscious desires are to be regarded as symptoms, as *surface indicators of more basic needs*. If we were to take these superficial desires at their face value we would find ourselves in a state of complete confusion which could never be resolved, since we would be dealing seriously with symptoms rather than with what lay behind the symptoms.

Thwarting of unimportant desires produces no psychopathological results; thwarting of a basically important need does produce such results. Any theory of psychopathogenesis must then be based on a sound theory of motivation. A conflict or a frustration is not necessarily pathogenic. It becomes so only when it threatens or thwarts the basic needs, or partial needs that are closely related to the basic needs (10).

The Role of Gratified Needs. It has been pointed out above several times that our needs usually emerge only when more prepotent needs have been gratified. Thus gratification has an important role in motivation theory. Apart from this, however, needs cease to play an active determining or organizing role as soon as they are gratified.

What this means is that, e.g., a basically satisfied person no longer has the needs for esteem, love, safety, etc. . . .

It is such considerations as these that suggest the bold postulation that a man who is thwarted in any of his basic needs may fairly be envisaged simply as a sick man. This is a fair parallel to our designation as "sick" of the man who lacks vitamins or minerals. Who is to say that a lack of love is less important than a lack of vitamins? Since we know the pathogenic effects of love starvation, who is to say that we are invoking value-questions in an unscientific or illegitimate way, any more than the physician does who diagnoses and treats pellagra or scurvy? If I were permitted this usage, I should then say simply that a healthy man is primarily motivated by his needs to develop and actualize his fullest potentialities and capacities. If a man has any other basic needs in any active, chronic sense, then he is simply an unhealthy man. He is as surely sick as if he had suddenly developed a strong salt-hunger or calcium hunger.[11]

If this statement seems unusual or paradoxical the reader may be assured that this is only one among many such paradoxes that will appear as we revise our ways of looking at man's deeper motivations. When we ask what man wants of life, we deal with his very essence.

[11] If we were to use the word "sick" in this way, we should then also have to face squarely the relations of man to his society. One clear implication of our definition would be that (1) since a man is to be called sick who is basically thwarted, and (2) since such basic thwarting is made possible ultimately only by forces outside the individual, then (3) sickness in the individual must come ultimately from a sickness in the society. The "good" or healthy society would then be defined as one that permitted man's highest purposes to emerge by satisfying all his prepotent basic needs.

IV. SUMMARY

1. There are at least five sets of goals, which we may call basic needs. These are briefly physiological, safety, love, esteem, and self-actualization. In addition, we are motivated by the desire to achieve or maintain the various conditions upon which these basic satisfactions rest and by certain more intellectual desires.

2. These basic goals are related to each other, being arranged in a hierarchy of prepotency. This means that the most prepotent goal will monopolize consciousness and will tend of itself to organize the recruitment of the various capacities of the organism. The less prepotent needs are minimized, even forgotten or denied. But when a need is fairly well satisfied, the next prepotent ("higher") need emerges, in turn to dominate the conscious life and to serve as the center of organization of behavior, since gratified needs are not active motivators.

Thus man is a perpetually wanting animal. Ordinarily the satisfaction of these wants is not altogether mutually exclusive, but only tends to be. The average member of out society is most often partially satisfied and partially unsatisfied in all of his wants. The hierarchy principle is usually empirically observed in terms of increasing percentages of non-satisfaction as we go up the hierarchy. Reversals of the average order of the hierarchy are sometimes observed. Also it has been observed that an individual may permanently lose the higher wants in the hierarchy under special conditions. There are not only ordinarily multiple motivations for usual behavior, but in addition many determinants other than motives.

3. Any thwarting or possibility of thwarting of these basic human goals, or danger to the defenses which protect them, or to the conditions upon which they rest, is considered to be a psychological threat. With a few exceptions, all psychopathology may be partially traced to such threats. A basically thwarted man may actually be defined as a "sick" man, if we wish.

4. It is such basic threats which bring about the general emergency reactions. . . .

REFERENCES

1. Adler, A. *Social interest*. London: Faber & Faber, 1938.
2. Cannon, W. B. *Wisdom of the body*. New York: Norton, 1932.
3. Freud, A. *The ego and the mechanisms of defense*. London: Hogarth, 1937.
4. Freud, S. *New introductory lectures on psychoanalysis*. New York: Norton, 1933.
5. Fromm, E. *Escape from freedom*. New York: Farrar and Rinehart, 1941.
6. Goldstein, K. *The organism*. New York: American Book Co., 1939.
7. Horney, K. *The neurotic personality of our time*. New York: Norton, 1937.
8. Kardiner, A. *The traumatic neuroses of war*. New York: Hoeber, 1941.
9. Levy, D. M. Primary affect hunger. *Amer. J. Psychiat.*, 1937, 94, 643–652.
10. Maslow, A. H. Conflict, frustration, and the theory of threat. *J. Abnorm. (soc.) Psychol.*, 1943, 38, 81–86.
11. ———. Dominance, personality and social behavior in women. *J. Soc. Psychol.*, 1939, 10, 3–39.
12. ———. The dynamics of psychological security-insecurity. *Character & Pers.*, 1942, 10, 331–344.
13. ———. A preface to motivation theory. *Psychosomatic Med.*, 1943, 5, 85–92.
14. ———, & Mittelmann, B. *Principles of abnormal psychology*. New York: Harper & Bros., 1941.
15. Murray, H. A., et al. *Explorations in personality*. New York: Oxford University Press, 1938.
16. Plant, J. *Personality and the cultural pattern*. New York: Commonwealth Fund, 1937.
17. Shirley, M. Children's adjustments to a strange situation. *J. Abnorm. (soc.) Psychol.*, 1942, 37, 201–217.
18. Tolman, E. C. *Purposive behavior in animals and men*. New York: Century, 1932.
19. Wertheimer, M. Unpublished lectures at the New School for Social Research.
20. Young, P. T. *Motivation of behavior*. New York: John Wiley & Sons, 1936.
21. ———. The experimental analysis of appetite. *Psychol. Bull.*, 1941, 38, 129–164.

12
The Human Side of Enterprise

Douglas Murray McGregor

To a degree, the social sciences today are in a position like that of the physical sciences with respect to atomic energy in the thirties. We know that past conceptions of the nature of man are inadequate and, in many ways, incorrect. We are becoming quite certain that, under proper conditions, unimagined resources of creative human energy could become available within the organizational setting. . . .

MANAGEMENT'S TASK: THE CONVENTIONAL VIEW

The conventional conception of management's task in harnessing human energy to organizational requirements can be stated broadly in terms of three propositions. In order to avoid the complications introduced by a label, let us call this set of propositions "Theory X":

1. Management is responsible for organizing the elements of productive enterprise—money, materials, equipment, people—in the interest of economic ends.
2. With respect to people, this is a process of directing their efforts, motivating them, controlling their actions, modifying their behavior to fit the needs of the organization.
3. Without this active intervention by management, people would be passive—even resistant—to organizational needs. They must therefore be persuaded, rewarded, punished, controlled—their activities must be directed. This is management's task. We often sum it up by saying that management consists of getting things done through other people.

Behind this conventional theory there are several additional beliefs—less explicit, but widespread:

4. The average man is by nature indolent—he works as little as possible.
5. He lacks ambition, dislikes responsibility, prefers to be led.
6. He is inherently self-centered, indifferent to organizational needs.
7. He is by nature resistant to change.
8. He is gullible, not very bright, the ready dupe of the charlatan and the demagogue.

The human side of economic enterprise today is fashioned from propositions and beliefs such as these. Conventional organization structures and managerial policies, practices, and programs reflect these assumptions.

In accomplishing its task—with these assumptions as guides—management has conceived of a range of possibilities.

At one extreme, management can be "hard" or "strong." The methods for directing behavior involve coercion and

Source: Reprinted, by permission of the publisher, from "The Human Side of Enterprise," by Douglas Murray McGregor, 1957, *Management Review*. Copyright 1957 by the American Management Association, New York. All rights reserved.

Note: This article is based on an address by Dr. McGregor before the Fifth Anniversary Convocation of the M.I.T. School of Industrial Management.

threat (usually disguised), close supervision, tight controls over behavior. At the other extreme, management can be "soft" or "weak." The methods for directing behavior involve being permissive, satisfying people's demands, achieving harmony. Then they will be tractable, accept direction.

This range has been fairly completely explored during the past half century, and management has learned some things from the exploration. There are difficulties in the "hard" approach. Force breeds counter-forces: restriction of output, antagonism, militant unionism, subtle but effective sabotage of management objectives. This "hard" approach is especially difficult during times of full employment.

There are also difficulties in the "soft" approach. It leads frequently to the abdication of management—to harmony, perhaps, but to indifferent performance. People take advantage of the soft approach. They continually expect more, but they give less and less. . . .

IS THE CONVENTIONAL VIEW CORRECT?

The social scientist does not deny that human behavior in industrial organization today is approximately what management perceives it to be. He has, in fact, observed it and studied it fairly extensively. But he is pretty sure that this behavior is *not* a consequence of man's inherent nature. It is a consequence rather of the nature of industrial organizations, of management philosophy, policy, and practice. The conventional approach of Theory X is based on mistaken notions of what is cause and what is effect.

Perhaps the best way to indicate why the conventional approach of management is inadequate is to consider the subject of motivation.

PHYSIOLOGICAL NEEDS

Man is a wanting animal—as soon as one of his needs is satisfied, another appears in its place. This process is unending. It continues from birth to death. . . .

A *satisfied need is not a motivator of behavior!* This is a fact of profound significance that is regularly ignored in the conventional approach to the management of people. Consider your own need for air: Except as you are deprived of it, it has no appreciable motivating effect upon your behavior.

SAFETY NEEDS

When the physiological needs are reasonably satisfied, needs at the next higher level begin to dominate man's behavior—to motivate him. These are called *safety needs*. They are needs for protection against danger, threat, deprivation. . . .

The fact needs little emphasis that, since every industrial employee is in a dependent relationship, safety needs may assume considerable importance. Arbitrary management actions, behavior which arouses uncertainty with respect to continued employment or which reflects favoritism or discrimination, unpredictable administration of policy—these can be powerful motivators of the safety needs in the employment relationship *at every level*, from worker to vice president.

SOCIAL NEEDS

When man's physiological needs are satisfied and he is no longer fearful about his physical welfare, his *social needs* become important motivators of his behavior—needs for belonging, for association, for acceptance by his fellows, for giving and receiving friendship and love.

Management knows today of the existence of these needs, but it often assumes quite wrongly that they represent a threat to the organization.

. . . When man's social needs—and perhaps his safety needs, too—are thus thwarted, he behaves in ways which tend to defeat organizational objectives. He becomes resistant, antagonistic, uncooperative. But this behavior is a consequence, not a cause.

EGO NEEDS

Above the social needs—in the sense that they do not become motivators until lower needs are reasonably satisfied—are the needs of greatest significance to management and to man himself. They are the *egoistic needs*, and they are of two kinds:

1. Those needs that relate to one's self-esteem—needs for self-confidence, for independence, for achievement, for competence, for knowledge.
2. Those needs that relate to one's reputation—needs for status, for recognition, for appreciation, for the deserved respect of one's fellows.

. . . The typical industrial organization offers few opportunities for the satisfaction of these egoistic needs to people at lower levels in the hierarchy. The conventional methods of organizing work, particularly in mass-production industries, give little heed to these aspects of human motivation. If the practices of scientific management were deliberately calculated to thwart these needs, they could hardly accomplish this purpose better than they do.

SELF-FULFILLMENT NEEDS

Finally—a capstone, as it were, on the hierarchy of man's needs—there are what we may call the *needs for self-fulfillment*. These are the needs for realizing one's own potentialities, for continued self-development, for being creative in the broadest sense of that term.

It is clear that the conditions of modern life give only limited opportunity for these relatively weak needs to obtain expression. The deprivation most people experience with respect to other lower-level needs diverts their energies into the struggle to satisfy *those* needs, and the needs for self-fulfillment remain dormant.

MANAGEMENT AND MOTIVATION

. . . The man whose needs for safety, association, independence, or status are thwarted is sick just as surely as the man who has rickets. And his sickness will have behavioral consequences. We will be mistaken if we attribute his resultant passivity, his hostility, his refusal to accept responsibility to inherent "human nature." These forms of behavior are *symptoms* of illness—of deprivation of his social and egoistic needs.

The man whose lower-level needs are satisfied is not motivated to satisfy those needs any longer. For practical purposes they exist no longer. Management often asks, "Why aren't people more productive? We pay good wages, provide good working conditions, have excellent fringe benefits and steady employment. Yet people do not seem to be willing to put forth more than minimum effort."

The fact that management has provided for these psychological and safety needs has shifted the motivational emphasis to the social and perhaps to the egoistic needs. Unless there are opportunities *at work* to satisfy these higher-level needs, people will be deprived; and their behavior will reflect this deprivation. Under such conditions, if management continues to focus its attention on physiological needs, its efforts are bound to be ineffective.

People *will* make insistent demands for more money under these conditions. It becomes more important than ever to buy the material goods and services which can provide limited satisfaction of the thwarted needs. Although money has only limited value in satisfying many higher-level needs, it can become the focus of interest if it is the *only* means available.

THE CARROT-AND-STICK APPROACH

The carrot-and-stick theory of motivation (like Newtonian physical theory) works reasonably well under certain circumstances. The *means* for satisfying man's physiological and (within limits) his safety needs can be provided or withheld by management. Employment itself is such a means, and so are wages, working conditions, and benefits. By these means the individual can be controlled so long as he is struggling for subsistence . . . .

. . . And so management finds itself in an odd position. The high standard of living created by our modern technological know-how provides quite adequately for the satisfaction of physiological and safety needs. The only significant exception is where management practices have not created confidence in a "fair break"—and thus where safety needs are thwarted. But by making possible the satisfaction of low-level needs, management has deprived itself of the ability to use as motivators the devices on which conventional theory has taught it to rely—rewards, promises, incentives, or threats and other coercive devices.

The philosophy of management by direction and control—*regardless of whether it is hard or soft*—is inadequate to motivate because the human needs on which this approach relies are today unimportant motivators of behavior. Direction and control are essentially useless in motivating people whose important needs are social and egoistic. Both the hard and the soft approach fail today because they are simply irrelevant to the situation.

People, deprived of opportunities to satisfy at work the needs which are now important to them, behave exactly as we might predict—with indolence, passivity, resistance to change, lack of responsibility, willingness to follow the demagogue, unreasonable demands for economic benefits. It would seem that we are caught in a web of our own weaving.

A NEW THEORY OF MANAGEMENT

For these and many other reasons, we require a different theory of the task of managing people based on more adequate assumptions about human nature and human motivation. I am going to be so bold as to suggest the broad dimensions of such a theory. Call it "Theory Y," if you will.

1. Management is responsible for organizing the elements of productive enterprise—money, materials, equipment, people—in the interest of economic ends.
2. People are *not* by nature passive or resistant to organizational needs. They have become so as a result of experience in organizations.
3. The motivation, the potential for development, the capacity for assuming responsibility, the readiness to direct behavior toward organizational goals are all present in people. Management does not put them there. It is a responsibility of management to make it possible for people to recognize and develop these human characteristics for themselves.
4. The essential task of management is to arrange organizational conditions and

methods of operation so that people can achieve their own goals *best* by directing *their own* efforts toward organizational objectives.

This is a process primarily of creating opportunities, releasing potential, removing obstacles, encouraging growth, providing guidance. It is what Peter Drucker has called "management by objectives" in contrast to "management by control." It does *not* involve the abdication of management, the absence of leadership, the lowering of standards, or the other characteristics usually associated with the "soft" approach under Theory X.

SOME DIFFICULTIES

It is no more possible to create an organization today which will be a full, effective application of this theory than it was to build an atomic power plant in 1945. There are many formidable obstacles to overcome.

The conditions imposed by conventional organization theory and by the approach of scientific management for the past half century have tied men to limited jobs which do not utilize their acceptance of responsibility, have encouraged passivity, have eliminated meaning from work. Man's habits, attitudes, expectations—his whole conception of membership in an industrial organization—have been conditioned by his experience under these circumstances. . . .

Another way of saying this is that Theory X places exclusive reliance upon external control of human behavior, while Theory Y relies heavily on self-control and self-direction. It is worth noting that this difference is the difference between treating people as children and treating them as mature adults. After generations of the former, we cannot expect to shift to the latter overnight.

STEPS IN THE RIGHT DIRECTION

Before we are overwhelmed by the obstacles, let us remember that the application theory is always slow. Progress is usually achieved in small steps. Some innovative ideas which are entirely consistent with Theory Y are today being applied with some success.

Decentralization and Delegation

These are ways of freeing people from the too-close control of conventional organization, giving them a degree of freedom to direct their own activities, to assume responsibility, and, importantly, to satisfy their egoistic needs. . . .

Job Enlargement

This concept, pioneered by IBM and Detroit Edison, is quite consistent with Theory Y. It encourages the acceptance of responsibility at the bottom of the organization; it provides opportunities for satisfying social and egoistic needs. In fact, the reorganization of work at the factory level offers one of the more challenging opportunities for innovation consistent with Theory Y.

Participation and Consultative Management

Under proper conditions, participation and consultative management provide encouragement to people to direct their creative energies toward organizational objectives, give them some voice in decisions that affect them, provide significant opportunities for the satisfaction of social and egoistic needs. The Scanlon Plan is the outstanding embodiment of these ideas in practice.

Performance Appraisal

Even a cursory examination of conventional programs of performance appraisal within the ranks of management will reveal how completely consistent they are with Theory X. In fact, most such programs tend to treat the individual as though he were a product under inspection on the assembly line.

A few companies—among them General Mills, Ansul Chemical, and General Electric—have been experimenting with approaches which involve the individual in setting "targets" or objectives *for himself* and in a *self*-evaluation of performance semiannually or annually. . . .

The individual is encouraged to take a greater responsibility for planning and appraising his own contribution to organizational objectives; and the accompanying effects on egoistic and self-fulfillment needs are substantial.

APPLYING THE IDEAS

The not infrequent failure of such ideas as these to work as well as expected is often attributable to the fact that a management has "bought the idea" but applied it within the framework of Theory X and its assumptions.

Delegation is not an effective way of exercising management by control. Participation becomes a farce when it is applied as a sales gimmick or device for kidding people into thinking they are important. . . .

THE HUMAN SIDE OF ENTERPRISE

The ingenuity and the perseverance of industrial management in the pursuit of economic ends have changed many scientific and technological dreams into commonplace realities. It is now becoming clear that the application of these same talents to the human side of enterprise will not only enhance substantially these materialistic achievements, but will bring us one step closer to "the good society."

13
The Motivating Effect of Cognitive Dissonance

Leon Festinger

COGNITIVE DISSONANCE AS A MOTIVATING STATE

I should like to postulate the existence of *cognitive dissonance* as a motivating state in human beings. Since most of you probably never heard of cognitive dissonance, I assume that so far I have been no more informative than if I had said that I wish to postulate X as a motivating state. I will try, then, to provide a conceptual definition of cognitive dissonance.

Definition of Dissonance. The word "dissonance" was not chosen arbitrarily to denote this motivating state. It was chosen because its ordinary meaning in the English language is close to the technical meaning I want to give it. The synonyms which the dictionary gives for the word "dissonant" are "harsh," "jarring," "grating," "unmelodious," "inharmonious," "inconsistent," "contradictory," "disagreeing," "incongruous," "discrepant." The word, in this ordinary meaning, specifies a relation between two things. In connection with musical tones, where it is usually used, the relation between the tones is such that they sound unpleasant together. In general, one might say that a dissonant relation exists between two things which occur together, if, in some way, they do not belong together or fit together.

Cognitive dissonance refers to this kind of relation between cognitions which exist simultaneously for a person. If a person knows two things, for example, something about himself and something about the world in which he lives, which somehow do not fit together, we will speak of this as cognitive dissonance. Thus, for example, a person might know that he is a very intelligent, highly capable person. At the same time, let us imagine, he knows that he meets repeated failure. These two cognitions would be dissonant—they do not fit together. In general, two cognitions are dissonant with each other if, considering these two cognitions alone, the obverse of one follows from the other. Thus, in the example we have given, it follows from the fact that a person is highly capable that he does not continually meet with failure. . . .

How Cognitive Dissonance Resembles Other Need States. Thus far I have said nothing about the motivating aspects of cognitive dissonance. This is the next step. I wish to hypothesize that the existence of cognitive dissonance is comparable to any other need state. Just as hunger is motivating, cognitive dissonance is motivating. Cognitive dissonance will give rise to activity oriented toward reducing or eliminating the dissonance. Successful reduction of dissonance is rewarding in the same sense that eating when one is hungry is rewarding.

Source: From: "The Motivating Effect of Cognitive Dissonance," by Leon Festinger, from *Assessment of Human Motives*, edited by Gardner Lindzey (New York: Holt, Rinehart & Winston, 1958), pp. 69–85. Reprinted by permission.

In other words, if two cognitions are dissonant with each other there will be some tendency for the person to attempt to change one of them so that they do fit together, thus reducing or eliminating the dissonance. . . .

Data Needed to Demonstrate the Motivating Character of Cognitive Dissonance. Before proceeding, let us consider for a moment the kinds of data one would like to have in order to document the contention that cognitive dissonance is a motivating state. One would like to have at least the following kinds of data:

1. Determination at Time 1 that a state of cognitive dissonance exists. This could be done either by measurement or by experimental manipulation.
2. Determination at Time 2 that the dissonance has been eliminated or reduced in magnitude.
3. Data concerning the behavioral process whereby the person has succeeded in changing some cognition, thus reducing the dissonance.

Actually, the above three items are minimal and would probably not be sufficient to demonstrate cogently the validity of the theory concerning cognitive dissonance. . . .

The kind of data that would be more convincing concerning the motivating aspects of dissonance would be data concerning instances where the dissonance was reduced in the other direction, such as is exemplified in the old joke about the psychiatrist who had a patient who believed he was dead. After getting agreement from the patient that dead men do not bleed, and being certain that the patient understood this, the psychiatrist made a cut on the patient's arm and, as the blood poured out, leaned back in his chair, smiling. Whereupon the patient, with a look of dismay on his face, said, "Well, what do you know, dead men *do* bleed." This kind of thing, if it occurred actually, would be harder to explain in alternative ways.

In other words, one has to demonstrate the effects of dissonance in circumstances where these effects are not easily explainable on the basis of other existing theories. Indeed, if one cannot do this, then one could well ask what the usefulness was of this new notion that explained nothing that was not already understood. . . .

[An] intriguing example of the reduction of dissonance in a startling manner comes from a study I did together with Riecken and Schachter (1956) of a group of people who predicted that, on a given date, a catastrophic flood would overwhelm most of the world. This prediction of the catastrophic flood had been given to the people in direct communications from the gods and was an integral part of their religious beliefs. When the predicted date arrived and passed there was considerable dissonance established in these people. They continued to believe in their gods and in the validity of the communications from them, and at the same time they knew that the prediction of the flood had been wrong. We observed the movement as participants for approximately two months preceding and one month after this unequivocal disproof of part of their belief. The point of the study was, of course, to observe how they would react to the dissonance. Let me give a few of the details of the disproof and how they reacted to it.

For some time it had been clear to the people in the group that those who were chosen were to be picked up by flying saucers before the cataclysm occurred. Some of the believers, these mainly college students, were advised to go home and wait individually for the flying saucer that would arrive for each of them. This was reasonable and plausible, since the data of the cataclysm happened to occur during an academic holiday. Most of the group, including the most central and most heavily committed members, gathered together in the home of the woman who received the messages from the gods to wait together for the arrival of the saucer. For these latter, disproof of the prediction, in the form of evidence that the messages were not valid, began to occur four days before the predicted event was to take place. A message informed them that a saucer would land in the back yard of the house at 4:00 P.M. to pick up the members of the group. With coat in hand they waited, but no saucer came. A later message told them there had been a delay—the saucer would arrive at midnight. Midst absolute secrecy (the neighbors and press must not know), they waited outdoors on a cold and snowy night for over an hour, but still no saucer came. Another message told them to continue waiting, but still no saucer came. At about 3:00 A.M. they gave up, interpreting the events of that night as a test, a drill, and a rehearsal for the real pickup which would still soon take place.

Tensely, they waited for the final orders to come through—for the messages which would tell them the time, place, and procedure for the actual pickup. Finally, on the day before the cataclysm was to strike, the messages came. At midnight a man would come to the door of the house and take them to the place where the flying saucer would be parked. More messages came that day, one after another, instructing them in the passwords that would be necessary in order to board the saucer, in preparatory procedures such as removal of metal from clothing, removal of personal identification, maintaining silence at certain times, and the like. The day was spent by the group in preparation and rehearsal of the necessary procedures and, when midnight came, the group sat waiting in readiness. But no knock came at the door, no one came to lead them to the flying saucer.

From midnight to five o'clock in the morning the group sat there struggling to understand what had happened, struggling to find some explanation that would enable them to recover somewhat from the shattering realization that they would not be picked up by a flying saucer and that consequently the flood itself would not occur as predicted. It is doubtful that anyone alone, without the support of the others, could have withstood the impact of this disproof of the prediction. Indeed, those members of the group who had gone to their homes to wait alone, alone in the sense that they did not have other believers with them, did not withstand it. Almost all of them became skeptics afterward. In other words, without easily obtainable social support to begin reducing the dissonance, the dissonance was sufficient to cause the belief to be discarded in spite of the commitment to it. But the members of the group that had gathered together in the home of the woman who received the messages could, and did, provide social support for one another. They kept reassuring one another of the validity of the messages and that some explanation would be found.

At fifteen minutes before five o'clock that morning an explanation was found that was at least temporarily satisfactory. A message arrived from God which, in effect, said that He had saved the world and stayed the flood because of this group and the light and strength this group had spread throughout the world that night.

The behavior of these people from that moment onwards presented a revealing contrast to their previous behavior. These people, who had been disinterested in publicity and even avoided it, became avid publicity seekers. . . .

There were almost no lengths to which these people would not go to attract publicity and potential believers in the validity of the messages. If, indeed, more and more converts could be found, more and more people who believed in the messages and the things the messages said, then the dissonance between their belief and the knowledge that the messages had not been correct could be reduced. . . .

An Experimental Investigation. In this experiment, we created dissonance in the subjects by inducing them to say something which was at variance with their private opinion. It is clear that this kind of situation does produce dissonance between what the person believes and what he knows he has said. There are also cognitive consonances for the person. His cognitions concerning the things that induced him to make the public statement are consonant with his knowledge of having done it. The total magnitude of the dissonance between all other relevant cognitions taken together and the knowledge of what he has publicly said will, of course, be a function of the number and importance of the dissonances in relation to the number and importance of the consonances. One could, then, manipulate the total magnitude of dissonance experimentally by holding everything constant and varying the strength of the inducement for the person to state something publicly which was at variance with his private opinion. The *stronger* the inducement to do this, the *less* would be the over-all magnitude of dissonance created. . . .

Now for the details of the experiment. I will describe it as it proceeded for the subject, with occasional explanatory comments. Each subject had signed up for a two hour experiment on "measures of performance." The subjects were all students from the Introductory Psychology course at Stanford where they are required to serve a certain number of hours as subjects in experiments. When the student arrived he was met by the experimenter and, with a minimum of explanation, was given a repetitive motor task to work on. . . .

From our point of view, the purpose of this initial part was to provide for each subject an experience which was rather dull, boring, and somewhat fatiguing. The student, however, believed this to be the whole experiment. The explanation of the experiment given to the student was that the experiment was concerned with the effect of preparatory set on performance. He was told that there were two conditions in the experiment, one of these being the condition he had experienced where the subject was told nothing ahead of time. The other condition, the experimenter explained, was one in which the subject, before working on the tasks, was led to expect that they were very enjoyable, very interesting, and lots of fun. The procedure for subjects in this other condition, the experimenter explained, proceeded in the following manner. A person working for us is introduced to the waiting subject as someone who has just finished the experiment and will tell the prospective subject a little about it. This person who works for us then tells the waiting subject that the experiment is very enjoyable, interesting, and lots of fun. In this way, the subjects in the other condition are given the set we want them to have. This concluded the false explanation of the experiment to the student and, in the control group, nothing more was done at this point.

In the experimental groups, however, the experimenter continued by telling the subject that he had a rather unusual proposal to make. It seems that the next subject is scheduled to be in that condition where he is to be convinced in advance that the experiment is enjoyable and a lot of fun. The person who works for us and usually does this, however, although very reliable, could not do it today. We thought we would take a chance and ask him (the student) to do it for us. We would like, if agreeable to him, to hire him on the same basis that the other person was hired to work for us. We would like to put him on the payroll and pay him a lump sum of money to go tell the waiting subject that the experiment is enjoyable, interesting, and fun; and he was also to be on tap for us in case this kind of emergency arises again.

There were two experimental conditions which we actually conducted. The procedure was absolutely identical in both except for the amount of money that the subjects were paid as "the lump sum." In one condition they were paid one dollar for their immediate and possible future services. In the other condition they were paid twenty dollars. When the student agreed to do this, he was actually given the money and he signed a receipt for it. He was then taken into the room where the next subject was waiting and introduced to her by the experimenter, who said that the student had just been a subject in the experiment and would tell her a bit about it. The experimenter then went out, leaving student and the waiting subject together for two and a half minutes. The waiting subject was actually a girl in our employ. Her instructions were very simple. After the student had told her that the experiment was interesting, enjoyable and lots of fun, she was to say something like, "Oh, a friend of mine who took it yesterday told me it was dull and that if I could I should get out of it." After that she was simply supposed to agree with whatever the student said. If, as almost always happened, the student reaffirmed that the experiment was fun, she was to say that she was glad to hear it. . . .

The experimenter then thanked the subject and made a brief speech in which he said that most subjects found the experimental tasks very interesting and enjoyed them, and that, when he thinks about it, he will probably agree. The purpose of this brief speech is to provide some cognitive material which the subject can use to reduce dissonance, assuming that such dissonance exists. The identical speech is, of course, made to the control subjects, too.

The only remaining problem in the experiment was to obtain a measure of what each subject honestly thought privately about the tasks on which he had worked for an hour. It seemed desirable, naturally, to obtain this measure in a situation where the subject would be inclined to be very frank in his statements. . . .

The student was told that someone from Introductory Psychology probably wanted to interview him. The experimenter confessed ignorance about what this impending interview was about but said he had been told that the subject would know about it. Usually at this point the subject nodded his head or otherwise indicated that he did, indeed, know what it was about. The experimenter then took him to an office where the interviewer was waiting, said goodbye to the subject, and left.

The interview itself was rather brief. Four questions were asked, namely, how interesting and enjoyable the experiment was, how much the subject learned from it, how important he thought it was scientifically, and how much he would like to participate in a similar experiment again. The important question, for us, is the first one concerning how interesting and enjoyable the experiment was, since this was the content area in which dissonance was established for the experimental subjects.

Let us look, then, at what the results show. . . .

In the One Dollar experimental condition there is a definite increase over the control group. Here the average rating is +1.35, definitely on the positive side of the scale and significantly different from the control group at the 1 per cent level of confidence. In other words, in the One Dollar condition the dissonance between their private opinion of the experiment and their knowledge of what they had said to the waiting subject was reduced significantly by changing their private opinion somewhat, to bring it closer to what they had overtly said.

But now let us turn our attention to the Twenty Dollar condition. Here the magnitude of dissonance experimentally created was less than in the One Dollar condition because of the greater importance of the cognition that was consonant with what they knew they had done. It seems undeniable that twenty dollars is a good deal more important than one dollar. There should hence be less pressure to reduce the dissonance, and indeed, the average rating for the Twenty Dollar condition is –.05, only slightly above the Control condition and significantly different from the One Dollar condition at the 2 per cent level of confidence.

SUMMARY AND CONCLUSION

This evidence for the validity and usefulness of conceiving cognitive dissonance as motivating is as follows:

1. Evidence that the existence of cognitive dissonance sometimes leads to behavior that appears very strange indeed when viewed only from the standpoint of commonly accepted motives. Here I have had time only to give two examples illustrating this phenomenon.
2. Evidence that the amount of reduction of dissonance is a direct function of the magnitude of dissonance which exists. I illustrated this by describing a laboratory experiment where, under controlled conditions, the magnitude of dissonance was experimentally manipulated.

REFERENCES

Festinger, Leon. *A theory of cognitive dissonance*. Evanston, Ill.: Row-Peterson, 1957.

———, Riecken, H. W., and Schachter, S. *When prophecy fails*. Minneapolis: University of Minnesota Press, 1956.

Janis, I. L., and King, B. T. The influence of role-playing on opinion change. *J. Abnorm. (soc.) Psychol.*, 1954, 49, 211–218.

King, B. T., and Janis, I. L. Comparison of the effectiveness of improvised versus nonimprovised role-playing in producing opinion changes. *Human Relations*, 1956, 9, 177–186.

Prasad, J. A comparative study of rumors and reports in earthquakes. *Brit. J. Psychol.*, 1950, 41, 129–144.

Sinha, D. Behavior in a catastrophic situation: a psychological study of reports and rumors. *Brit. J. Psychol.*, 1952, 43, 200–209.

14
Work and Motivation

Victor H. Vroom

THE NATURE OF MOTIVATION

There are two somewhat different kinds of questions which are typically dealt with in discussions of motivation. One of these is the question of the arousal or energizing of the organism. Why is the organism active at all? What conditions instigate action, determine its duration or persistence and finally its cessation? The phenomena to be explained include the level of activity of the organism and the vigor of amplitude of its behavior. The second question involves the direction of behavior. What determines the form that activity will take? Under what condition will an organism choose one response or another? The problem is to explain the choices made by an organism among qualitatively different behaviors.

The latter question—concerning direction or choice—is probably the more important of the two to the psychologist. . . .

Is all behavior motivated? The answer to this question depends somewhat on the range of processes which are subsumed under the heading of motivation. We will follow the relatively common practice of viewing as motivated only the behaviors that are under central or voluntary control. . . .

To sum up, we view the central problem of motivation as the explanation of choices made by organisms among different voluntary responses. Although some behaviors, specifically those that are not under voluntary control, are defined as unmotivated, these probably constitute a rather small proportion of the total behavior of adult human beings. It is reasonable to assume that most of the behavior exhibited by individuals on their jobs as well as their behavior in the "job market" is voluntary, and consequently motivated.

AN OUTLINE OF A COGNITIVE MODEL

In the remainder of this chapter, we outline a conceptual model which will guide our discussion and interpretation of research in the remainder of the book. The model to be described is similar to those developed by other investigators including Lewin (1938), Rotter (1955), Peak (1955), Davidson, Suppes, and Siegel (1957), Atkinson (1958b), and Tolman (1959). It is basically ahistorical in form. We assume that the choices made by a person among alternative courses of action are lawfully related to psychological events occurring contemporaneously with the behavior. We turn now to consider the concepts in the model and their interrelations.

The Concept of Valence. We shall begin with the simple assumption that, at

Source: Adapted from *Work and Motivation* by Victor Vroom, 1964 pp. 9–33. Copyright 1995 by Jossey-Bass Inc., Publishers. Reprinted by permission.

any given point in time, a person has preferences among outcomes of states of nature. For any pair of outcomes, x and y, a person prefers x to y, prefers y to x, or is indifferent to whether he receives x or y. Preference, then, refers to a relationship between the strength of a person's desire for, or attraction toward, two outcomes. . . . In our system, an outcome is positively valent when the person prefers attaining it to not attaining it (i.e., he prefers x to not x). An outcome has a valence of zero when the person is indifferent to attaining or not attaining it (i.e., he is indifferent to x or not x), and it is negatively valent when he prefers not attaining it to attaining it (i.e., he prefers not x to x). It is assumed that valence can take a wide range of both positive and negative values.

We use the term motive whenever the referent is a preference for a class of outcomes. A positive (or approach) motive signifies that outcomes which are members of the class have positive valence, and a negative (or avoidance) motive signifies that outcomes in the class have negative valence.

It is important to distinguish between the valence of an outcome to a person and its value to that person. An individual may desire an object but derive little satisfaction from its attainment—or he may strive to avoid an object which he later finds to be quite satisfying. At any given time there may be a substantial discrepancy between the anticipated satisfaction from an outcome (i.e., its valence) and the actual satisfaction that it provides (i.e., its value).

There are many outcomes which are positively or negatively valent to persons, but are not in themselves anticipated to be satisfying or dissatisfying. The strength of a person's desire or aversion for them is based not on their intrinsic properties but on the anticipated satisfaction or dissatisfaction associated with other outcomes to which they are expected to lead. People may desire to join groups because they believe that membership will enhance their status in the community, and they may desire to perform their jobs effectively because they expect that it will lead to a promotion.

In effect, we are suggesting that means acquire valence as a consequence of their expected relationship to ends. . . . If an object is believed by a person to lead to desired consequences or to prevent undesired consequences, the person is predicted to have a positive attitude toward it. If, on the other hand, it is believed by the person to lead to undesired consequences or to prevent desired consequences, the person is predicted to have a negative attitude toward it. . . .

We do not mean to imply that all the variance in the valence of outcomes can be explained by their expected consequences. We must assume that some things are desired and abhorred "for their own sake." Desegregation may be opposed "on principle" not because it leads to other events which are disliked, and people may seek to do well on their jobs even though no externally mediated rewards are believed to be at stake.

Without pretending to have solved all of the knotty theoretical problems involved in the determinants of valence, we can specify the expected functional relationship between the valence of outcomes and their expected consequences in the following proposition.

Proposition 1. The valence of an outcome to a person is a monotonically increasing function of the algebraic sum of the products of the valences of all other outcomes and his conceptions of its instrumentality for the attainment of these other outcomes.

In equation form the same proposition reads as follows:

$$V_j = f_j\left[\sum_{k=1}^{n}(V_k I_{jk})\right] (j = 1 \ldots n)$$

$$f_j' > O; I_{jj} = O$$

where V_j = the valence of outcome j

I_{jk} = the cognized instrumentality ($-1 \leq I_{jk} \leq 1$) of outcome j for the attainment of outcome k

The Concept of Expectancy. The specific outcomes attained by a person are dependent not only on the choices that he makes but also on events which are beyond his control. For example, a person who elects to buy a ticket in a lottery is not certain of winning the desired prize. Whether or not he does so is a function of many chance events. Similarly, the student who enrolls in medical school is seldom certain that he will successfully complete the program of study; the person who seeks political office is seldom certain that he will win the election; and the worker who strives for a promotion is seldom certain that he will triumph over other candidates. Most decision-making situations involve some element of risk, and theories of choice behavior must come to grips with the role of these risks in determining the choices that people do make.

Whenever an individual chooses between alternatives which involve uncertain outcomes, it seems clear that his behavior is affected not only by his preferences among these outcomes but also by the degree to which he believes these outcomes to be probable. . . .

Expectancy is an action-outcome association. It takes values ranging from zero, indicating no subjective probability that an act will be followed by an outcome, to 1, indicating certainty that the act will be followed by an outcome. Instrumentally, on the other hand, is an outcome-outcome association. It can take values ranging from -1, indicating a belief that attainment of the second outcome is certain without the first outcome and impossible with it, to $+1$, indicating that the first outcome is believed to be a necessary and sufficient condition for the attainment of the second outcome.

The Concept of Force. It remains to be specified how valences and expectancies combine in determining choices. The directional concept in our model is the Lewinian concept of force. Behavior on the part of a person is assumed to be the result of a field of forces each of which has direction and magnitude. . . .

There are many possible ways of combining valences and expectancies mathematically to yield these hypothetical forces. On the assumption that choices made by people are subjectively rational, we would predict the strength of forces to be a monotonically increasing function of the *product* of valences and expectancies. Proposition 2 expresses this functional relationship.

Proposition 2. The force on a person to perform an act is a monotonically increasing function of the algebraic sum of the products of the valences of all outcomes and the strength of his expectancies that the act will be followed by the attainment of these outcomes.

We can express this proposition in the form of the following equation:

$$F_i = f_i \left[\sum_{j=1}^{n} (E_{ij} V_j) \right] \quad (i = n + 1 \ldots m)$$

$$f_i' > O; \; i \cap j = \Phi, \; \Phi \text{ is the null set}$$

where F_i = the force to perform act i

E_{ij} = the strength of the expectancy ($O \leq E_{ij} \leq 1$) that act i will be followed by outcome j

V_j = the valence of outcome j

It is also assumed that people choose from among alternative acts the one corresponding to the strongest positive (or weakest negative) force. This formulation is similar to the notion in decision theory that people choose in a way that maximizes subjective expected utility.

Expressing force as a monotonically increasing function of the product of valence and expectancy has a number of implications which should be noted. An outcome with high positive or negative valence will have no effect on the generation of a force unless there is some expectancy (i.e., some subjective probability greater than zero) that the outcome will be attained by some act. As the strength of an expectancy that an act will lead to an outcome increases, the effect of variations in the valence of the outcome on the force to perform the act will also increase. Similarly, if the valence of an outcome is zero (i.e., the person is indifferent to the outcome), neither the absolute value nor variations in the strength of expectancies of attaining it will have any effect on forces.

Our two propositions have been stated in separate terms, but are in fact highly related to one another. Insofar as the acts and outcomes are described in different terms the separation is a useful one. We have in the first proposition a basis for predicting the valence of outcomes, and in the second proposition a basis for predicting the actions that a person will take with regard to the outcome. . . .

In practice we will find it useful to maintain the separation between the two propositions by defining sets of actions and sets of outcomes independently of one another. We will use the term action to refer to behavior which might reasonably be expected to be within the repertoire of the person, e.g., seeking entry into an occupation, while the term outcomes will be reserved for more temporally distant events which are less likely to be under complete behavioral control, e.g., attaining membership in an occupation.

TESTING THE MODEL

The model, as outlined so far, is untestable, for its concepts have not been related to observable events. In order to derive empirical hypotheses from the model, we must specify operational definitions for the formal concepts. Some further assumptions must be made which will permit the measurement or experimental manipulation of the concepts. . . .

The only concept in the model that has been directly linked with potentially observable events is the concept of force. We have assumed that the acts performed by a person reflect the relative strength of forces acting upon him. If a person performs act x rather than y the force corresponding to x is assumed to be stronger than y and vice versa.

We have, however, said nothing about observable events that would lead us to infer either that an outcome has a certain valence for a person, or that the strength of a person's expectancy that an act will lead to an outcome has a particular value. It is this kind of problem to which we now turn.

Our approach to this problem is "eclectic." Instead of proposing a single operational definition for each of the concepts, we outline a series of broad approaches to their measurement and/or experimental manipulation.

The Measurement of Valence. What approaches can be taken to the measurement of valence? What observations of behavior need to be made in order to permit us to conclude that one outcome is positively valent and a second negatively valent, or that one is more positively valent than a second?

One approach is to use *verbal reports*. If an individual states that an event is attractive or desirable, it might be assumed to have positive valence. If he states that a second event is unattractive or undesirable, it might be assumed to have negative valence. This procedure can be extended to provide measures of the relative attractiveness or unattractiveness of a series of events or outcomes by requesting the person to make com-

Psychol. Theory. Durham, N.C.: Duke University Press, 1938, 1, No. 4.

McClelland, D. C., Atkinson, J. W., Clark, R. A., and Lowell, E. L. *The achievement motive*. New York: Appleton-Century-Crofts, 1953.

Mosteller, F., and Nogee, P. An experimental measurement of utility. *J. Pol. Econ.*, 1951, 59, 371–404.

Murray, H. A. *Explorations in personality*. New York: Oxford University Press, 1938.

Peak, Helen. Attitude and motivation. In Jones, M. R. (Ed.) *Nebraska symposium on motivation*. Lincoln: University of Nebraska Press, 1955, pp. 149–188.

Preston, M. G., and Baratta, P. An experimental study of the action-value of an uncertain outcome. *Amer. J. Psychol.*, 1948, 61, 183–193.

Rotter, J. B. The role of the psychological situation in determining the direction of human behavior. In Jones, M. R. (Ed.) *Nebraska symposium on motivation*. Lincoln: University of Nebraska Press, 1955, pp. 245–268.

Tolman, E. C. Principles of purposive behavior. In Koch, S. (Ed.) *Psychology: A study of a science*. Vol. 2. New York: McGraw-Hill, 1959, pp. 92–157.

Von Neumann, J., and Morgenstern, O. *Theory of games and economic behavior*. Princeton: Princeton University Press, 1947, 2nd ed.

15

One More Time: How Do You Motivate Employees?

Not By Improving Work Conditions, Raising Salaries, or Shuffling Tasks

Frederick Herzberg

"MOTIVATING" WITH KITA

In lectures to industry on the problem, I have found that the audiences are anxious for quick and practical answers, so I will begin with a straightforward, practical formula for moving people.

What is the simplest, surest, and most direct way of getting someone to do something? Ask him? But if he responds that he does not want to do it, then that calls for a psychological consultation to determine the reason for his obstinacy. Tell him? His response shows that he does not understand you, and now an expert in communication methods has to be brought in to show you how to get through to him. Give him a monetary incentive? I do not need to remind the reader of the complexity and difficulty involved in setting up and administering an incentive system. Show him? This means a costly training program. We need a simple way.

Every audience contains the "direct action" manager who shouts, "Kick him!" And this type of manager is right. The surest and least circumlocuted way of getting someone to do something is to kick him in the pants—give him what might be called the KITA.

There are various forms of KITA, and here are some of them:

Negative Physical KITA. This is a literal application of the term and was frequently used in the past. It has, however, three major drawbacks: (1) it is inelegant; (2) it contradicts the precious image of benevolence that most organizations cherish; and (3) since it is a physical attack, it directly stimulates the autonomic nervous system, and this often results in negative feedback—the employee may just kick you in return. These factors give rise to certain taboos against negative physical KITA. . . .

Negative Psychological KITA. This has several advantages over negative physical KITA. First, the cruelty is not visible; the bleeding is internal and comes much later. Second, since it affects the higher cortical centers of the brain with its inhibitory powers, it reduces the possibility of physical backlash. Third, since the

Source: Reprinted by permission of the *Harvard Business Review*. "One More Time: How Do You Motivate Employees?" by Frederick Herzberg (January/February 1968). Copyright © 1968 by the President and Fellows of Harvard College; all rights reserved.

Author's note: I should like to acknowledge the contribution that Robert Ford of the American Telephone and Telegraph Company has made to the ideas expressed in this paper, and in particular to the successful application of these ideas in improving work performance and the job satisfaction of employees.

number of psychological pains that a person can feel is almost infinite, the direction and site possibility of the KITA are increased many times. Fourth, the person administering the kick can manage to be above it all and let the system accomplish the dirty work. Fifth, those who practice it receive some ego satisfaction (one upmanship), whereas they would find drawing blood abhorrent. Finally, if the employee does complain, he can always be accused of being paranoid, since there is no tangible evidence of an actual attack.

Now, what does negative KITA accomplish? If I kick you in the rear (physically or psychologically), who is motivated? *I* am motivated; you move! Negative KITA does not lead to motivation, but to movement. So:

Positive KITA. Let us consider motivation. If I say to you, "Do this for me or the company and in return I will give you a reward, an incentive, more status, a promotion, all the quid pro quos that exist in the industrial organization," am I motivating you? The overwhelming opinion I receive from management people is "Yes, this is motivation." . . .

Why is it that managerial audiences are quick to see that negative KITA is not motivation while they are almost unanimous in their judgment that positive KITA is motivation? It is because negative KITA is rape, and positive KITA is seduction. But it is infinitely worse to be seduced than to be raped; the latter is an unfortunate occurrence, while the former signifies that you were a party to your own downfall. This is why positive KITA is so popular: it is a tradition; it is in the American way. The organization does not have to kick you; you kick yourself.

MYTHS ABOUT MOTIVATION

With this in mind, we can review some positive KITA personnel practices that were developed as attempts to instill "motivation":

1. *Reducing time spent at work*—This represents a marvelous way of motivating people to work—getting them off the job! We have reduced (formally and informally) the time spent on the job over the last 50 to 60 years until we are finally on the way to the "63-day weekend." An interesting varient of this approach is the development of off-hour recreation programs. The philosophy here seems to be that those who play together, work together. The fact is that motivated people seek more hours of work, not fewer.
2. *Spiraling wages*—Have these motivated people? Yes, to seek the next wage increase. . . .
3. *Fringe benefits*—Industry has outdone the most welfare-minded of welfare states in dispensing cradle-to-the-grave succor. . . .

   These benefits are no longer rewards; they are rights. . . .

   Unless the ante is continuously raised, the psychological reaction of employees is that the company is turning back the clock.
4. *Human relations training*—Over 30 years of teaching and, in many instances, of practicing psychological approaches to handling people have resulted in costly human relations programs and, in the end, the same question: How do you motivate workers? . . .

   The failure of human relations training to produce motivation led to the conclusion that the supervisor or manager himself was not psychologically true to himself in his practice of interpersonal decency. So an advanced form of human relations KITA, sensitivity training, was unfolded.
5. *Sensitivity training*—Do you really, really understand yourself? Do you really, really, really trust the other man? Do you really, really, really, really cooperate? The failure of sensitivity training is now being explained, by those who have become opportunistic exploiters of the technique, as a failure to really

(five times) conduct proper sensitivity training courses. . . .

6. *Communications*—The professor of communications was invited to join the faculty of management training programs and help in making employees understand what management was doing for them. House organs, briefing sessions, supervisory instruction on the importance of communication, and all sorts of propaganda have proliferated until today there is even an International Council of Industrial Editors. But no motivation resulted, and the obvious thought occurred that perhaps management was not hearing what the employees were saying. That led to the next KITA.
7. *Two-way communication*—Management ordered morale surveys, suggestion plans, and group participation programs. Then both employees and management were communicating and listening to each other more than ever, but without much improvement in motivation.

   The behavioral scientists began to take another look at their conceptions and their data, and they took human relations one step further. A glimmer of truth was beginning to show through in the writings of the so-called higher-order-need psychologists. People, so they said, want to actualize themselves. Unfortunately, the "actualizing" psychologists got mixed up with the human relations psychologists, and a new KITA emerged.
8. *Job participation*—Though it may not have been the theoretical intention, job participation often became a "give them the big picture" approach. For example, if a man is tightening 10,000 nuts a day on an assembly line with a torque wrench, tell him he is building a Chevrolet. Another approach had the goal of giving the employee a *feeling* that he is determining, in some measure, what he does on his job. The goal was to provide a *sense* of achievement rather than a substantive achievement in his task. Real achievement, of course, requires a task that makes it possible.
9. *Employee counseling*—The initial use of this form of KITA in a systematic fashion can be credited to the Hawthorne experiment of the Western Electric Company during the early 1930s. At that time, it was found that the employees harbored irrational feelings that were interfering with the rational operation of the factory. Counseling in this instance was a means of letting the employees unburden themselves by talking to someone about their problems. Although the counseling techniques were primitive, the program was large indeed. . . .

Since KITA results only in short-term movement, it is safe to predict that the cost of these programs will increase steadily and new varieties will be developed as old positive KITA reach their satiation points.

HYGIENE VS. MOTIVATORS

Let me rephrase the perennial question this way: How do you install a generator in an employee? A brief review of my motivation hygiene theory of job attitudes is required before theoretical and practical suggestions can be offered. The theory was first drawn from an examination of events in the lives of engineers and accountants. At least 16 other investigations, using a wide variety of populations including some Communist countries, have since been completed, making the original research one of the most replicated studies in the field of job attitudes.

The findings of these studies, along with corroboration from many other investigations using different procedures, suggest that the factors involved in producing job satisfaction and motivation are separate and distinct from the factors that lead to job dissatisfaction. Since separate factors need to be considered, depending on whether job satisfaction or dissatisfaction is being examined, it follows that these two feelings are not opposites of each other. The opposite of job satisfaction is not job dissatisfaction but, rather, *no* job satisfaction; and similarly, the opposite of job dissatisfaction is not job satisfaction, but *no* job dissatisfaction. . . .

Two different needs of man are involved here. One set of needs can be thought of as stemming from his animal nature—the built-in drive to avoid pain from the environment, plus all the learned drives which become conditioned to the basic biological needs. For example, hunger, a basic biological drive, makes it necessary to earn money, and then money becomes a specific drive. The other set of needs relates to that antique human characteristic, the ability to achieve and, through achievement, to experience psychological growth. The stimuli for the growth needs are tasks that induce growth; in the industrial setting, they are the *job content*. Contrariwise, the stimuli inducing pain-avoidance behavior are found in the *job environment*.

The growth or *motivator* factors that are intrinsic to the job are: achievement, recognition for achievement, the work itself, responsibility, and growth or advancement. The dissatisfaction-avoidance or *hygiene* (KITA) factors that are extrinsic to the job include: company policy and administration, supervision, interpersonal relationships, working conditions, salary, status, and security.

A composite of the factors that are involved in causing job satisfaction and job dissatisfaction [is] drawn from samples of 1,685 employees. The results indicate that motivators were the primary cause of satisfaction, and hygiene factors the primary cause of unhappiness on the job. The employees, studied in 12 different investigations, included lower-level supervisors, professional women, agricultural administrators, men about to retire from management positions, hospital maintenance personnel, manufacturing supervisors, nurses, food handlers, military officers, engineers, scientists, housekeepers, teachers, technicians, female assemblers, accountants, Finnish foremen, and Hungarian engineers.

They were asked what job events had occurred in their work that had led to extreme satisfaction or extreme dissatisfaction on their part. Their responses are broken down in the exhibit into percentages of total "positive" job events and of total "negative" job events. . . .

To illustrate, a typical response involving achievement that had a negative effect for the employee was, "I was unhappy because I didn't do the job successfully." A typical response in the small number of positive job events in the Company Policy and Administration grouping was, "I was happy because the company reorganized the section so that I didn't report any longer to the guy I didn't get along with."

As the lower right-hand part of *Exhibit I* shows, of all the factors contributing to job satisfaction, 81% were motivators. And of all the factors contributing to the employees' dissatisfaction over their work, 69% involved hygiene elements.

ETERNAL TRIANGLE

There are three general philosophies of personnel management. The first is based on organizational theory, the second on industrial engineering, and the third on behavioral science.

The organizational theorist believes that human needs are either so irrational or so varied and adjustable to specific situations that the major function of personnel management is to be as pragmatic as the occasion demands. If jobs are organized in a proper manner, he reasons,

EXHIBIT I • FACTORS AFFECTING JOB ATTITUDES, AS REPORTED IN 12 INVESTIGATIONS

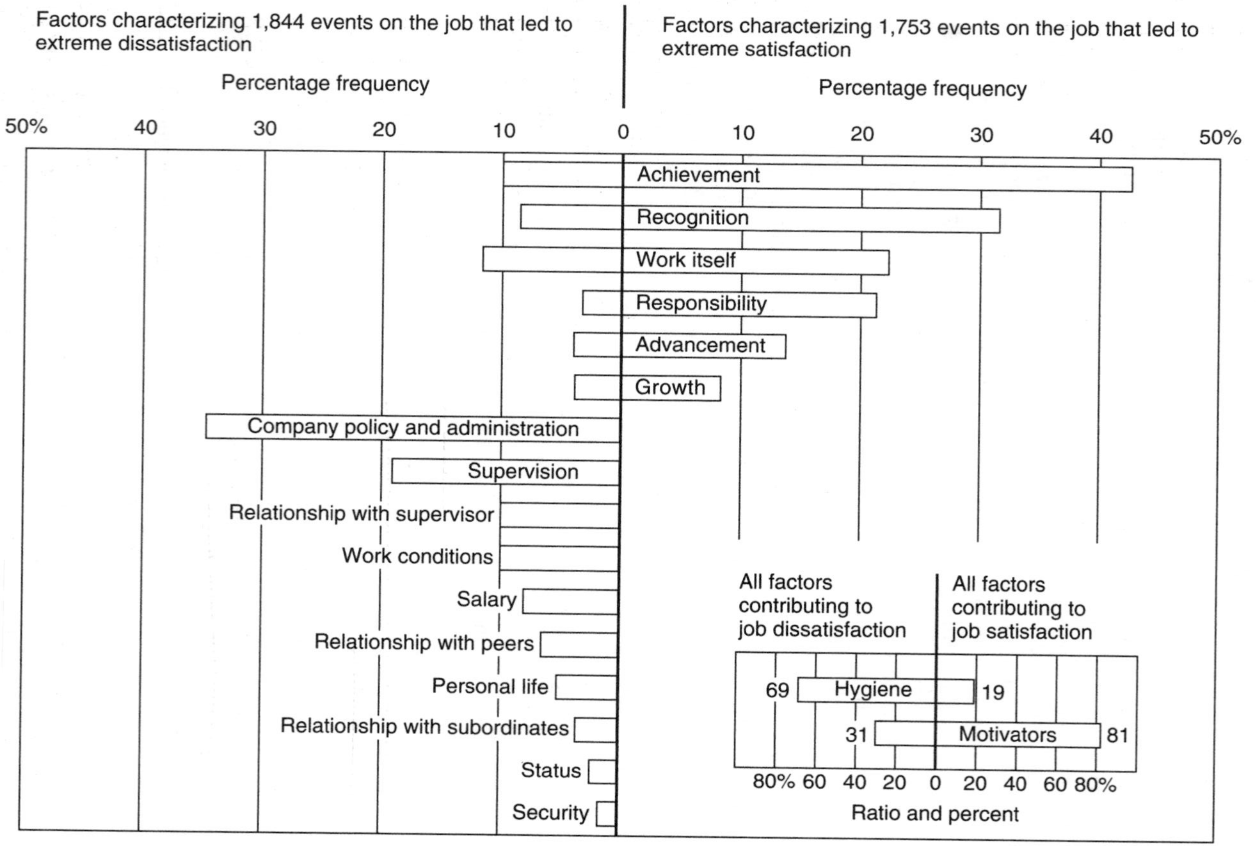

Factors characterizing 1,844 events on the job that led to extreme dissatisfaction

Percentage frequency

Factors characterizing 1,753 events on the job that led to extreme satisfaction

Percentage frequency

50% 40 30 20 10 0 10 20 30 40 50%

Achievement
Recognition
Work itself
Responsibility
Advancement
Growth
Company policy and administration
Supervision
Relationship with supervisor
Work conditions
Salary
Relationship with peers
Personal life
Relationship with subordinates
Status
Security

All factors contributing to job dissatisfaction

All factors contributing to job satisfaction

69 Hygiene 19

31 Motivators 81

80% 60 40 20 0 20 40 60 80%

Ratio and percent

EXHIBIT III • PRINCIPLES OF VERTICAL JOB LOADING

Principle	Motivators Involved
A. Removing some controls while retaining accountability	Responsibility and personal achievement
B. Increasing the accountability of individuals for own work	Responsibility and recognition
C. Giving a person a complete natural unit of work (module, division, area, and so on)	Responsibility, achievement, and recognition
D. Granting additional authority to an employee in his activity; job freedom	Responsibility, achievement, and recognition
E. Making periodic reports directly available to the worker himself rather than to the supervisor	Internal recognition
F. Introducing new and more difficult tasks not previously handled	Growth and learning
G. Assigning individuals specific or specialized tasks, enabling them to become experts	Responsibility, growth, and advancement

content that will produce the motivation, not attitudes about being involved or the challenge inherent in setting up a job. That process will be over shortly, and it is what the employees will be doing from then on that will determine their motivation. A sense of participation will result only in short-term movement.

8. In the initial attempts at job enrichment, set up a controlled experiment. At least two equivalent groups should be chosen, one an experimental unit in which the motivators are systematically introduced over a period of time, and the other one a control group on which no changes are made. For both groups, hygiene should be allowed to follow its natural course for a duration of the experiment. Pre- and post-installation tests of performance and job attitudes are necessary to evaluate the effectiveness of the job enrichment program. The attitude test must be limited to motivator items in order to divorce the employee's view of the job he is given from all the surrounding hygiene feelings that he might have.
9. Be prepared for a drop in performance in the experimental group the first few weeks. The changeover to a new job may lead to a temporary reduction in efficiency.
10. Expect your first-line supervisors to experience some anxiety and hostility over the changes you are making. The anxiety comes from their fear that the changes will result in poorer performance for their unit. Hostility will arise when the employees start assuming what the supervisors regard as their own responsibility for performance. The supervisor without checking duties to perform may then be left with little to do.

After a successful experiment, however, the supervisor usually discovers the supervisory and managerial functions he has neglected, or which were never his because all his time was given over to checking the work of his subordinates. . . .

What has been called an employee-centered style of supervision will come about not through education of supervisors, but by changing the jobs that they do.

CONCLUDING NOTE

Job enrichment will not be a one-time proposition, but a continuous management function. The initial changes, however, should last for a very long period of time. . . .

Not all jobs can be enriched, nor do all jobs need to be enriched. If only a small percentage of the time and money that is now devoted to hygiene, however, were given to job enrichment efforts, the return in human satisfaction and economic gain would be one of the largest dividends that industry and society have ever reaped through their efforts at better personnel management.

The argument for job enrichment can be summed up quite simply: If you have someone on a job, use him. If you can't use him on the job, get rid of him, either via automation or by selecting someone with lesser ability. If you can't use him and you can't get rid of him, you will have a motivation problem.

16

Work Motivation: The Incorporation of Self-Concept-Based Processes

Nancy H. Leonard, Laura L. Beauvais, and Richard W. Scholl

INTRODUCTION

There is growing realization that traditional models of motivation do not explain the diversity of behavior found in organizational settings. While research and theory building in the areas of goal setting, reward systems, leadership, and job design have advanced our understanding of organizational behavior, most of this work is built on the premise that individuals act in ways to maximize the value of exchange with the organization. In addition, some researchers have called attention to the role of dispositions and volitional processes in models of motivation (Kanfer, 1990). Still others have turned to self-theory as an additional explanation of motivated behavior (Bandura, 1982, 1986; Beach & Mitchell, 1990; Gergen, 1984; Schlenker, 1985; Stryker, 1980, 1986; Tajfel & Turner, 1985). This state of the literature has led many researchers to argue that we have a variety of motivation theories with no unifying theme and which are not strongly supported by research (Locke & Henne, 1986). As Klein (1989) has pointed out, the field is replete with "splintered and perplexing" theories of motivation that only create conceptual clutter for researchers and confusion among practitioners who try to apply them to work settings. One way to synthesize existing theories is the development of a metatheory of work motivation which may provide a general framework for linking existing theories (Landy & Becker, 1987). The purpose of this paper is to propose such a metatheory of work motivation.

We will begin by reviewing some traditional theories of motivation, specifically concentrating on their limitations with regard to external validity and ability to generalize across situations. Then we will present self-theory concepts as a way to address these limitations and discuss how the self-concept influences behavior in organizations. Next, we will present a typology of sources of motivation, including the self-concept, which is used to develop propositions for a metatheory of work motivation in organizations. We will conclude with managerial implications and suggestions for future research.

CURRENT THEORIES OF WORK MOTIVATION

Work motivation has been defined as the process by which behavior is energized, directed, and sustained in organi-

Source: From *Human Relations*, 1999. Reprinted by permission of Sage Publications, Ltd.

zational settings (Steers & Porter, 1991). In the literature, there are a number of theories that provide different conceptualizations of the factors that drive this process. In this paper, we refer to these factors as "sources" of motivation.

One early theory which examines different sources of motivation was proposed by deCharmes (1968). He suggests the dichotomy of intrinsic vs. extrinsic motivation to characterize the different loci of causality. Intrinsically motivated behaviors (i.e., those behaviors that occur in the absence of external controls) are said to represent internal causality, whereas behaviors that are induced by external forces are said to represent external causality. Deci (1975) explores the effects of extrinsic rewards on intrinsic motivation and in doing so, sheds some light on the meaning of intrinsic motivation. He suggests that intrinsically motivated behaviors fall into two categories. The first category includes behaviors that individuals engage in to seek out challenging situations. These challenges represent incongruities between stimuli and comparison standards. The second category includes behaviors aimed at reducing these incongruities (i.e., overcoming challenges). Thus, intrinsically motivated behavior, according to Deci, is conceptualized as a continual process of seeking and overcoming challenges.

Another understanding of intrinsic and extrinsic motivation is offered by Katz and Kahn (1978). They argue that the bases of motivation can be categorized in terms of legal compliance, external rewards, and internalized motivation. Internalized motivation is further broken down into *self-expression*, derived directly from role performance, and *internalized values*, resulting when group or organizational goals become incorporated into the value system of the individual. Etzioni (1975) takes a similar view when arguing that organizations induce involvement from their members by one of three means: alienative, calculative, or moral. Alienative and calculative involvement are explained by exchange processes and will be discussed below. Moral involvement is more complex. According to Etzioni, there are two kinds of moral involvement, pure and social. Pure moral involvement is the result of internalization of norms, while social involvement results from sensitivity to pressures of primary groups and their members. Moral involvement is not based on expected satisfaction of needs and may even demand the denial of need satisfaction and the sacrifice of personal pleasure. . . .

The work of these authors points to three sources of motivation: *intrinsic process motivation*, *motivation based on goal internalization*, and *extrinsic or instrumental motivation*. Individuals are motivated by intrinsic process motivation when they perform a behavior just because it is "fun." In other words, the motivation comes from the work itself. Individuals enjoy the work and feel rewarded simply by performing the task. There are no external controls regulating the behavior (deCharms, 1968), and behavior that is challenging (Deci, 1975) may be considered enjoyable to some people. This is what Katz and Kahn refer to as self-expression. Hackman and Oldham's (1976) job characteristics model is based on intrinsic process motivation.

A second source of motivation alluded to by these authors is goal internalization. Behavior is motivated by goal internalization when the individual adopts attitudes and behaviors because their content is congruent with their value system (Kelman, 1958). This is what Katz and Kahn refer to as motivation based on internalized values and Etzioni refers to as pure moral involvement. Some researchers have examined goal internalization as one dimension of organizational commitment (Becker, 1992; O'Reilly & Chatman, 1986).

The third source of motivation is that induced by external forces. Katz and Kahn refer to this type of motivation as legal compliance and external rewards, Etzioni refers to this as alienative or calculative involvement, and deCharms suggests that such behaviors have external causality. The theories of work motivation that focus on extrinsic motivation assume that individuals are "rational maximizer(s) of personal utility" (Shamir, 1990, p. 39). For example, expectancy theory assumes that motivation is a result of calculatively determined probabilities associated with different levels or types of behavior and the valences of the outcomes associated with these behaviors. Equity theory may be considered calculative insofar as it assumes that people cognitively assess their own attitudes and job performance by comparing their input/outcome ratio to that of a referent other. If this ratio indicates an imbalance between inputs and rewards as compared to the referent, then inequity is produced. This inequity causes cognitive dissonance that the individual is motivated to reduce. These cognitive choice or calculative models assume that behaviors are the result of hedonistic processes (i.e., people will behave in ways that maximize positive outcomes and minimize negative outcomes).

Therefore extrinsic or instrumental rewards are a motivating source when individuals believe that the behaviors they engage in will lead to certain outcomes such as pay, promotion, etc. Rooted in the work of Barnard (1938) and March and Simon (1958), the basic assumption is that individuals and organizations participate in an exchange relationship. Expectancy and equity theories are currently accepted models of motivation based on exchange relationships.

Although research over the past 20 years in decision-making, occupational choice, and achievement motivation (see Kanfer, 1990 for an excellent review of this literature) has provided strong support for these calculative models, they cannot account for the full range of motivated behavior. For example, these models do not explain changes in behavior across situations when expectancies and valences remain constant (Atkinson & Birch, 1970). In addition, individuals may differ in the use of expectancy and instrumentality information (Rynes & Lawler, 1983).

In an attempt to address these limitations, some researchers have turned to personality theory as a way to explain behavior which cannot be explained by environmental or situational factors. Psychologists have long postulated that individual dispositions or personalities are significant determinants of behavior. The assumptions underlying this approach are that (1) there are individual differences in ways of behaving; (2) individual behavior is somewhat stable over time; and (3) individual behavior is somewhat consistent across situations (Pervin, 1975). Contrary to the dispositional view, others assert that behavior is determined by situational factors and that similarity in behavior results from similarity of situational circumstances (Davis-Blake & Pfeffer, 1989; Mischel, 1968). The contention is that personality traits have accounted for little variance in behavior across situations. However, some recent writers have begun to shed new light on the predictive validity of the dispositional view (House, Shane, & Herold, 1996). . . .

Today, most researchers take an interactionist view that assumes behavior is a function of both environment and personality (Mitchell & James, 1989; Pervin, 1989). Specifically, these researchers are suggesting that a dynamic reciprocal interaction occurs between the person and the situation. Therefore, models that can explain how people are able to shift from situation to situation, often exhibiting different patterns of behavior while still retaining a recognizable personality structure, need to be developed (House et al., 1996; Pervin, 1975). Self-theories have been proposed as ways of explaining both consistency and variability in individual work behavior across situations.

In recent years, a plethora of self-based theories have been advanced, including social identity theory (Stryker, 1980, 1986; Tajfel & Turner, 1985), self-presentation theory (Beach & Mitchell, 1990; Gergen, 1984; Schlenker, 1985), and self-efficacy theory (Bandura, 1982, 1986). All of these theories are based on the assumption that "human beings have a fundamental need to maintain or enhance the phenomenal self" (Snyder & Williams, 1982 p. 258). Because of this fundamental need, individuals are motivated to behave in ways that are consistent with existing self-perceptions. Thus, these theories may be useful in expanding our notion of motivated behavior in the workplace.

Unfortunately, because of the different streams of research in this area, our knowledge of self-theory is piecemeal in nature and highly disorganized. Further, a proliferation of terms and concepts that often overlap in meaning has resulted. If self-theory is to be useful to organizational behavior researchers, it must do a number of things. First, it must provide a detailed description of the structure and content of the self-concept and an understanding of how it is developed. Second, it must address how the self-concept influences behavior in organizations. In the next section, we will provide an overview of the self-concept in terms of its structural components and developmental processes before explaining how it influences behavior in organizations.

THE STRUCTURE OF THE SELF-CONCEPT

Historically, theoretical models of self-concept can be placed into two broad categories: unidimensional vs. multidimensional perspectives. The unidimensional or nomethetic model is the oldest view of the self-concept (Soares & Soares, 1983). This perspective assumes that the self-concept reflects an individual's global sense of self. Thus, the self-concept is viewed as a stable, additive, or generalized sense of self.

More recent research in social psychology (Greenwald & Pratkanis, 1984; Schlenker, 1980) has conceptualized the self-concept as a multifaceted phenomenon composed of a set of perceptions, images, schemas, and prototypes (Markus & Wurf, 1987; Marsh & Hattie, 1996). There has been a similar movement in sociology where the self is defined in terms of multiple identities (Schlenker, 1985; Stryker, 1980). Kihlstrom, Cantor, and their associates suggest that individuals hold perceptions of themselves in terms of traits and values (Kihlstrom & Cantor, 1984), attributes, experiences, thoughts, and actions (Cantor & Kihlstrom, 1985, 1987), and physical appearance, demographic attributes, and dispositions of various sorts (Kihlstrom et al., 1988). In measuring self-conceptions, Roberts and Donahue (1994) use traits as the metric of self-perception attributes. More specifically, in their view, individuals perceive and describe themselves using a set of traits measured in terms of the "Big Five" dimensions of personality (Goldberg, 1990). Gecas (1982) asserts that the content of the self-concept consists of perceptions of social and personal identities, traits, attributes, and possessions.

Additionally Bandura's (1986, 1991) use of self-efficacy presents a view of the self measured in terms of competencies.

The perspective we advance in this paper is also multidimensional in nature. We propose three general sets of attributes that individuals have perceptions of, which incorporate most of those suggested in earlier research. These include *traits*, *competencies*, and *values*.

Traits. Traits are labels for broad reaction tendencies and express relatively permanent patterns of behavior (Cattell, 1965). Fundamental to this definition is the assumption that people make internal attributions to individuals who consistently demonstrate a particular behavior pattern in different situations or at different times without apparent external reasons. Thus, traits become shorthand labels that we use to describe the repeated behavioral patterns of ourselves and others. For example, we use terms like ambitious, lazy, dependable, and conservative to describe the essential character of individuals, based on multiple observations of their particular patterns of behavior.

Competencies. A second element in the perceived self is competencies. Individuals hold perceptions of what skills, abilities, talents, and knowledge they possess. These can range from very specific skills, such as the ability to run a turret lathe, to more general competencies, such as the leadership skills to create and manage change. Perceptions such as "I am a good problem solver," "I am an excellent golfer," or "I am excellent at building a database" represent this second major defining element of the individual's self-concept.

Values. Values are defined as concepts and beliefs about desirable end states or behaviors that transcend specific situations, guide selection, or evaluation of behavior and events, and are ordered by relative importance (Schwartz & Bilsky, 1990). Individuals demonstrate certain values through their speech and actions.

Thus, the content of individuals' perceptions of self contain traits, competencies, and values. Further, one's concept of self is composed of three interrelated sets of self-perceptions: the *perceived self*, the *ideal self*, and *a set of social identities*. Each of these elements plays a crucial role in understanding how the self-concept relates to energizing, directing, and sustaining organizational behavior. These self-representations are described below.

The Perceived Self

The perceived self describes the set of perceptions that individuals hold about their actual traits, competencies, and values. An individual's perception of these attributes can be described in terms of two separate dimensions, *level* and *strength*. Level of self-perception refers to the degree to which the individual perceives he/she possesses an attribute. Does the individual see himself or herself as highly introverted (trait), or a very good tennis player (competency), or a hard worker (value)? This dimension deals with the issue of where individuals see themselves, relative to their ideal selves which will be described shortly. . . .

The second dimension of the perceived self is the *strength* of the perception, and refers to how strongly the individual holds the perception of attribute level. Individuals with strong perceived selves are relatively firm in their perceptions of an attribute level. A weak perceived self is reflected in individuals who are relatively unsure of an attribute level.

The Ideal Self

While the perceived self describes the set of perceptions individuals hold of their actual traits, competencies, and values, the ideal self represents the set of traits, competencies, and values an individual would like to possess (Rogers, 1959). By possess, we mean that the individual desires to believe that he/she actually has a particular trait, competency, or value, or wants others to believe that he/she has the trait, competency, or value. This view of ideal self is similar to Schlenker's (1985) "idealized image" (i.e., the ultimate person one would like to be) and Bandura's (1991) notion of personal standards.

Social Identities

According to Ashforth and Mael (1989), social identification is a process by which individuals classify themselves and others into different social categories, such as "woman," "Methodist," and "engineer." This classification process serves the functions of segmenting and ordering the social environment and enabling individuals to locate or define themselves in that social environment. Thus, social identification provides a partial answer to the question "Who am I?" Social identities are thus those aspects of individuals' self-concepts that derive from the social categories to which they perceive themselves as belonging (Tajfel & Turner, 1985).

THE DEVELOPMENT OF THE SELF-CONCEPT

Development of Perceived Self

Self-perceptions are determined through interaction with one's environment. Processes of attitude formation, attitude change (Ajzen & Fishbein, 1980), and self-attribution (Jones, 1990) all contribute to the development of a set of self-perceptions. Interaction with one's environment provides feedback relative to one's traits, competencies, and values along with information indicating the social value of these attributes. When feedback is unambiguous, plentiful, and consistent, a set of strongly held self-perceptions is formed. A lack of feedback, or ambiguous or inconsistent feedback, results in weakly held self-perceptions. . . .

Development of the Ideal Self

In the early stages of interaction with a reference group, whether the reference group is the primary group (i.e., the family for a young child) or a secondary group (i.e., one's peers or co-workers), choices and decisions are channeled through the existing social system. As an individual interacts with the reference group, he/she receives feedback from reference group members. If the feedback is positive and unconditional, individuals will internalize the traits, competencies, and values which are important to that reference group. In this case, individuals become *inner-directed*, using these internalized traits, competencies, and values as a measure of their own successes/failures. Internalized competencies and values have been suggested as the basis of the ideal self (Higgins, Klein, & Strauman, 1987) and as an internal standard for behavior (Bandura, 1986). If the individual receives negative feedback or positive but conditional feedback, the individual may not internalize or only partially internalize the traits, competencies, and values of the reference group. This type of individual becomes *other-directed* and will either withdraw from the group or seek constant feedback from group members. . . .

Development of Social Identities

Individuals establish social identities through involvement with reference groups in social situations. Reference groups provide three major functions with respect to social identities: (1) the determination of the profile of traits, competencies, and values for a particular social identity; (2) the establishment and communication of the relative value and status of various social roles or identities; and (3) are the basis of social feedback regarding one's level of these traits, competencies, and values. . . .

Individuals establish at least two types of social identities: a *global or general identity* and *role-specific identities* (Roberts & Donahue, 1994). The global identity is the identity one portrays across all situations, across various roles, and to various reference groups. The global identity exists independently of any specific social or role identity. The reference group for the global identity includes those members of one's primary group, and the traits, competencies, and values which are relevant to the individual are those which are reinforced by the individual's culture. The global identity is formed early in life, and one's family, functioning as a primary reference group, performs the three functions mentioned above.

The global identity provides a starting point for role-specific identities. As the individual matures, the control of the primary group lessens and the individual begins to establish certain role-specific social identities. Role-specific social identities are those identities established for a specific reference group or a specific social role. It is this process of selecting and "earning" the identity that acts to define one's self to various reference groups. By "earning" the identity, we are describing the process whereby the individual meets basic expectations of the reference group (either formal or informal credentialing) necessary to carry out the role.

As an individual begins to interact with reference group members in a role-specific identity, the global identity provides input to this specific identity. However, as an individual remains in a role-specific identity and receives positive feedback from group members, the role-specific identity begins to provide input to the global identity. The reference groups in these social situations (e.g., one's co-workers, friends, etc.) begin to perform the functions which were previously performed by the primary reference group. The individual is now exposed to the traits, competencies and values which are valued by each new reference group. The identity-specific reference groups also provide the social feedback important in the development of the perceived self.

As participation in a social identity continues over time, the reference group itself becomes the basis of identification, and the success or failure of the reference group as a whole becomes a source of feedback for the individual. As defined by social identity theory (Ashforth & Mael, 1989; Tajfel & Turner, 1985), social identification is the perception of oneness with or belongingness to a reference group. When individuals identify with a social reference group, they perceive the fate of the group as their own (Foote, 1951; Tolman, 1943). The more individuals identify with a social identity, the more these individuals vest their self-concepts in that identity. . . .

HOW THE SELF-CONCEPT INFLUENCES BEHAVIOR IN ORGANIZATIONS

In the previous sections we described the structure and development of the self-concept. As the self-concept continues to develop, it becomes a source of motivation in that individuals are motivated to maintain and enhance the internalized view of oneself (Korman, 1970; Gecas, 1982). In this section, we will discuss how the self-concept supplements intrinsic process motivation, extrinsic/instrumental motivation, and goal internalization as sources of motivation.

There have been a number of attempts at developing models of self-concept-based motivation, but none as yet have been integrated into the mainstream of organizational research (Brief & Aldag, 1981; Gecas, 1982; Korman, 1970; Schlenker, 1985; Shamir, 1991; Sullivan, 1989). The sources of self-concept-based motivation, which we will propose, supplement traditional models by suggesting the concept of self as a basis for both calculative or deliberate and noncalculative or reactive explanations of behavior.

Individuals are bombarded with many sorts of information which they often interpret and assign meaning to in terms of their perceived selves. As stated earlier, the information they perceive may or may not have been intended to reflect on an individual's traits, competencies, or values; however, the meaning individuals attribute to this information is often a function of the strength of their self-perceptions and their need for affirmation of the self. Task and/or social feedback provide the stimuli for individual action, and an individual's evaluation of the feedback provides the basis for a behavioral response. We can examine the role of self-concept in explaining organizational behavior from two perspectives: deliberate and reactive processes.

Deliberate Processes

Once a social identity is established, along with its related set of traits, competencies, and values, individuals make choices among behavioral alternatives, set and accept goals, take on projects, and generally direct effort toward obtaining task and social feedback consistent with the self-concept. Using an expectancy theory framework to describe the role of the self-concept, individuals cognitively assess the likelihood of given actions leading to levels and types of task and/or social feedback consistent with their self-perceptions. The valence of this feedback is based on the value or values associated with the role-specific identity as determined by the reference group. In other words, individual behavior is viewed as a choice process engaged in to obtain feedback on traits, competencies, or values which are important in relation to the ideal self (Gecas, 1982; Korman, 1970). The behaviors and tasks one chooses to engage in would be those that are consistent with one's self-perception or are intended to match the ideal self.

Therefore, these processes are deliberate in that individuals consciously act to receive task and social feedback that will confirm or enhance important social identities that make up the self-concept. For example, an individual with a self-perception that she or he is a "conscientious" person would be motivated to get assignments done on time, be at meetings, continue to work on a project until it is complete, and forgo social activities in favor of getting a job done. Individuals identifying with the role of "leader" might exhibit behaviors which they believe are consistent with that role and work toward accomplishment of group goals when such accomplishment can be attributed to their leadership competencies and skills. That is, they are motivated to engage in activities and pursue goals reinforcing their identity as "leader" and its related traits, competencies, and values. When such activities lead to affirmation of an identity, self-perceptions are strengthened.

Reactive Processes

According to the theory of cognitive dissonance (Festinger, 1957), inconsistency between two cognitive elements, whether they represent beliefs, attitudes, or behavior, gives rise to dissonance. Assumed to be unpleasant, the presence of dissonance is said to motivate the individual to change one or more cognitive elements in an attempt to eliminate the unpleasant state. With respect to the self-concept, dissonance occurs when task or social feedback differs from self-perception. When dissonance occurs, individuals react to the situation by utilizing a number of potential adaptive strategies. Thus, these strategies represent reactive processes individuals engage in to preserve self-perceptions.

Adaptive Strategies

Adaptive strategies are the primary mechanisms which individuals use to deal with dissonance (i.e., conflict between their self-perceptions and social or task feedback). The strategies may be cognitive, or they may take the form of cognitive scripts (i.e., patterns for behavior) which people call upon regularly when faced with disconfirming feedback. Therefore, adaptive strategies may or may not be consciously engaged in by the individual. Among a host of potential adaptive behaviors, these strategies would include:

- *Motivation*. Expending greater effort or changing behavior in order to change the feedback in the future.
- *Discounting Feedback*. Seeking out confirming feedback to discount the disconfirming feedback, or discrediting the source of the disconfirming feedback.
- *Changing Feedback*. Presenting evidence and/or arguing that the individual's evaluation was incorrect.
- *Disassociation*. Disassociating oneself from the outcome or behavioral effect. Publicly showing that one was not really trying so that the link between task outcome and traits, competencies, and values is not likely to be made.
- *Association*. Attempting to create a strong perceptual link between task outcome and traits, competencies, and values. Linking oneself to successful or high status organizations or groups.
- *Reaction Formation*. Convincing the world, and oneself, that a particular trait, competency, or value is of no importance.
- *Feedback Avoidance*. Avoiding the opportunity to receive feedback or to subject one's traits, competencies, or values to confirmation.
- *Reducing Status of Others*. Attempting to show that others have lower traits, competencies, or values than oneself.
- *Reducing Personal Responsibility*. Attempting to show that a particular outcome or behavioral effect was the result of forces outside the individual's control and should not be attributed to the traits, competencies, or values of the target individual.

Both deliberate and reactive processes explain the underlying mechanisms by which the self-concept influences behavior. Now we turn to a discussion of two major types of self-concept-based motivation: external and internal sources.

External Self-Concept-Based Motivation

Self-concept motivation is externally based when the individual is primarily other-directed. In this case, the ideal self is derived by adopting the role expectations of reference groups. The individual attempts to meet the expectations of others by behaving in ways that will elicit social feedback consistent with self-perceptions. When positive task feedback is obtained, the individual finds it necessary to communicate these results to members of the reference group. The individual behaves in ways which satisfy reference group members, first to gain acceptance, and after achieving that, to gain status. These two needs for acceptance and status are similar to McClelland's (1961) need for affiliation and need for power. The individual is motivated to continually strive for the acceptance and status of reference group members. This status orientation usually leads to an ordinal standard of self-evaluation. This type of motivation is also similar to Etzioni's (1975) social moral involvement.

Internal Self-Concept-Based Motivation

Self-concept motivation will be internally based when the individual is primarily inner-directed. Internal self-concept motivation takes the form of the individual setting internal standards that become the basis for the ideal self. The individual tends to use fixed rather than ordinal standards of self-measurement as he/she attempts to first reinforce perceptions of competency, and later achieve higher levels of competency. This need for achieving higher levels of competency is similar to what McClelland (1961) refers to as a high need for achievement. The motivating force for individuals who are inner-driven and motivated by their self-concept is task feedback. It is important to these individuals that their efforts are vital in achieving outcomes and that their ideas and actions are instrumental in performing a job well. It is not important that others provide reinforcing feedback as is true for other-directed individuals. . . .

Individuals experience both internally and externally based self-concept motivation to varying degrees. Whether or not an individual will be motivated by his or her self-concept and whether the source of that motivation is internal or external, are dependent on a number of things. As discussed above, an individual may have a high or low self-concept, strong or weakly held self-perceptions and utilize a fixed or ordinal standard of evaluation. In order to demonstrate how the proposed self-concept-based sources of motivation can increase our understanding of organizational behavior, we will discuss two of these types in detail.

The first type characterizes individuals who have an other-directed, high self-concept which is weakly held, and who utilize an ordinal standard of evaluation. These individuals are highly competitive and self-presentation is important. They have a need to put their fingerprints on success and to dissociate themselves from failure. A prime concern for these individuals is establishing blame when failure occurs or establishing credits for group successes. These individuals are status- and power-oriented with a strong need for external or social affirmation.

A second type represents individuals who have an inner-directed, high self-concept which is weakly held and utilize a fixed standard of evaluation. These individuals set high standards for themselves. Each project is a test of their competency. They seek task feedback and involve themselves in projects that test competencies and allow for this type of feedback. They must have ownership (control) over project outcomes. While they have a high self-concept, it is not strongly held and thus they need to continually seek feedback through task performance.

Table I provides detailed descriptions of 16 potential types of self-concept-based motivation by considering the dimensions of inner- and other-directed, high and low self-perceptions, strongly and weakly held perceptions, and fixed and ordinal standards of evaluation. All types may not be represented in the general population, but are presented to show the potential diversity of self-concept-based motivation processes. These descriptions, although logically deducted from our model, are highly speculative at this stage of our theory building, and will need to be empirically examined for their external validity. . . .

A METATHEORY OF THE INTEGRATED SOURCES OF MOTIVATION

Intrinsic process motivation, extrinsic or instrumental motivation, and goal internalization have been discussed extensively in previous literature and are generally accepted among researchers as valid sources of work motivation. However, as pointed out earlier these three sources have not always been able to account for the variety of behavior observed among employees. We have proposed the self-concept as an additional source of motivation, specifically concentrating on the internal and external types. If internal and external self-concepts are valid bases of motivation, distinct from the other sources, then they must be able to independently explain motivation and behavior. In this section, we are proposing a metatheory of sources of motivation which we believe provides a unifying framework for future work motivation research.

Based on the research literature cited and our theory of the self-concept, the following propositions are offered:

> *Proposition 1*. There are five basic sources of motivation: intrinsic process, extrinsic/instrumental rewards, external self-concept, internal self-concept, and goal internalization.
>
> *Proposition 2*. Individuals can be characterized by motivational profiles which reflect the relative strength of each of the five sources.
>
> *Proposition 3*. For every individual, there is a dominant source of motivation that acts as focus or lens by which they make decisions and channel behavior.
>
> *Proposition 4*. When two or more sources of motivation within an individual conflict, the dominant source will prevail.
>
> *Proposition 5*. Individuals have different motivational source profiles in different situations or with regard to different identities.

Specific propositions relating to choice of tasks and response to feedback are offered below for each of the five sources of motivation. In order to more clearly understand how these sources of motivation aid in our understanding of behavior, we will illustrate how an individual with each of the five dominant sources of motivation may behave within a team decision-making process.

Intrinsic Process Motivation

Individuals primarily motivated by intrinsic process will only engage in activities which they consider fun. These individuals are often diverted from tasks that are relevant to goal attainment in order to pursue tasks which are intrinsically more enjoyable. Thus, as long as team tasks are enjoyable, these individuals will be motivated to continue working effectively in the context of the team. Since they are relatively indifferent to task and social feedback, such feedback will not serve to motivate continued performance on the part of the intrinsically motivated person. Therefore, the following proposition is advanced.

> *Proposition 6*. When faced with alternative tasks, individuals dominated by intrinsic process motivation will choose the task which is more enjoyable and the behavior will be sustained until the task is no longer enjoyable.

Extrinsic/Instrumental Motivation

Individuals primarily motivated by this source must see that the attainment of group goals leads to a greater level of extrinsic rewards. Bonuses based on goal attainment, gainsharing, and group performance-based awards all potentially have the power to provide instrumental motivation toward group goals. In the situation of pure instrumental motivation, members resolve conflict

TABLE I • TYPES OF SELF-CONCEPT-BASED BEHAVIORS

	High		Low	
	Strong	Weak	Strong	Weak
Inner Ordinal	Strives to achieve high goals relative to others (e.g., the best, first, smartest, etc.). Relies on task feedback and involves oneself in projects that reinforce important TCV's [traits, competencies, values]. Does not need to take personal credit for successes if goals are achieved. Does not change self-perceptions of important TCV's upon task failure. Does not respond to positive or negative feedback from others regarding performance related to important TCV's.	Strives to achieve high goals relative to others (e.g., the best, first, smartest, etc.) Relies on task feedback and involves oneself in projects that reinforce important TCV's. Needs to successfully complete tasks relative to others to strengthen one's self-perceptions. May disassociate oneself from the outcome of a project if high standards of performance are not met or if one does not perform well relative to others.	Strives toward low to moderate goals/standards relative to others. Relies on task feedback for performance evaluation. Ignores or discounts positive feedback on task performance. Uses negative feedback on task performance to confirm one's low self-perceptions.	Strives toward low to moderate goals/standards relative to others. Relies on task feedback for performance evaluation. Positive feedback on task performance may encourage future higher goal setting and performance. Ignores or discounts negative task feedback. Disassociates oneself from project outcomes or denigrates the task.
Fixed	Strives to achieve high, fixed goals/standards that reflect important TCV's. Relies on task feedback and involves oneself in projects that reinforce important TCV's. Does not need to take personal credit for successes if goals are achieved. Does not change self-perceptions of important TCV's upon task failure. Does not respond to positive or negative feedback from others regarding performance related to important TCV's.	Strives to achieve high, fixed goals/standards that reflect important TCV's. Relies on task feedback and involves oneself in projects that reinforce important TCV's. Needs to successfully complete tasks to strengthen one's self-perceptions. May disassociate oneself from the outcome of a project if high standards of performance are not met.	Strives toward low to moderate fixed goals/standards. Relies on task feedback for performance evaluation. Ignores or discounts positive feedback on task performance. Uses negative feedback on task performance to confirm one's low self-perceptions.	Strives toward low to moderate fixed goals/standards. Relies on task feedback for performance evaluation. Positive feedback on task performance may encourage future higher goal setting and performance. Ignores or discounts negative task feedback. Disassociates oneself from project outcomes or denigrates the task.

Other Ordinal	Strives to achieve high goals relative to others (e.g., the best, first, smartest, etc.). Is status and power oriented. Relies on social feedback to reinforce strongly held perceptions of important TCV's. Ignores or discounts feedback from others that does not support the self-concept. Discredits or reduces the status of others who provide negative feedback.	Strives to achieve high goals relative to others (e.g., the best, first, smartest, etc.). Is status and power oriented. Relies on social feedback and involves oneself in highly visible projects. Needs to be recognized by others for success to strengthen self-perceptions. Needs to be disassociated from feedback to avoid others' possible negative evaluation. Discredits or reduces the status of others who provide negative feedback.	Strives toward low to moderate goals/standards relative to others. Relies on social feedback for performance evaluation. Ignores or discounts positive feedback on performance from others. Uses negative feedback on performance from others to confirm one's low self-perceptions.	Strives toward low to moderate fixed goals/standards relative to others. Relies on social feedback for performance valuation. Positive feedback from others may encourage future higher goal setting and performance. Ignores or discounts negative feedback from others. Discredits the person who provides negative feedback.
Fixed	Strives to achieve high, fixed goals/standards that reflect important TCV's. Relies on social feedback to reinforce strongly held perceptions of important TCV's. Ignores or discounts feedback from others that does not support the self-concept. Discredits or reduces the status of others who provide negative feedback.	Strives to achieve high, fixed goals/standards that reflect important TCV's. Relies on social feedback and involves oneself in highly visible projects. Needs to be recognized by others for successes to strengthen self-perceptions. Needs to be disassociated from failure to avoid others' possible negative evaluation. Discredits or reduces the status of others who provide negative feedback.	Strives toward low to moderate fixed goals/standards. Relies on social feedback for performance evaluation. Ignores or discounts positive feedback on performance from others. Uses negative feedback on performance from others to confirm one's low self-perceptions.	Strives toward low to moderate fixed goals/standards. Relies on social feedback for performance evaluation. Positive feedback from others may encourage future higher goal setting and performance. Ignores or discounts negative feedback from others. Discredits the person who provides negative feedback.

among alternative courses of action by determining the actions, tasks, or procedures most likely to lead to goal attainment and thus, to their extrinsic benefit. Commitment to a course of action will only exist when members cannot agree on which course of action is likely to be the most effective, and some members cannot be convinced that strategies other than their own preferred strategy are at least as likely to be successful. Task and social feedback is used to reflect on the instrumentality and expectancy probabilities associated with the behavior. Therefore, the following proposition is advanced.

> *Proposition 7.* When faced with alternative tasks, individuals dominated by extrinsic/instrumental motivation will engage in the task that provides the greatest potential for extrinsic rewards, and the behavior will be sustained as long as the likelihood of attaining those rewards remains.

External Self-Concept

This is the dominant source of motivation when an individual has a high, weak, ordinal self-concept. This type of motivation can take two forms: that based on personal social identity and that based on being associated publicly with a successful group (i.e., public attributions of success extend to the individual). With regard to the first form, the individual desires and works toward organizational success because he/she bases an important social identity on being a member of the team or organization. In other words, membership in a successful team or organization leads to acceptance or high status in the eyes of others, which is motivating to this type of individual. With regard to the second form, the individual's identity (i.e., traits, competencies, and values) is publicly tied to the outcomes of the group. When the group is successful, that success is tied to the skills and competencies of the individual. In other words, individuals strive for group success in order to publicly validate their self-perceptions.

In both cases, motivation is high when individuals perceive success or failure will be attributed to them personally. It is not only important that the group is successful in meeting its goals, but that it is the members' technical, behavioral, or conceptual skills that are responsible for this success. Therefore, when a conflict arises between two plans or courses of action, the individual tied to the goal through externally based self-concept motivation is expected to remain strongly committed to his or her plan. Such individuals will have a difficult time giving "credit" for success to others. One's reputation is one of the driving forces behind this form of motivation. Therefore, the following proposition is advanced.

> *Proposition 8.* When faced with alternative tasks, individuals dominated by external self-concept-based motivation will engage in tasks that provide them with affirmative social feedback relative to others, concerning their traits, competencies, and values in their important identities. Behavior will be sustained as long as relative, positive social feedback is forthcoming, and if affirming social feedback relative to others is not received, the behavior will end.

Internal Self-Concept

This is the dominant source of motivation when an individual has a high, weak, fixed self-concept. Similar to external self-concept, these individuals must be able to tie or attribute group success to their individual identity. However, in this case, it is more important that the individual himself or herself perceives that this relationship exists, and less important that others identify and reinforce it. Bandura's (1986) notion of personal standard is a key to understanding individuals motivated through this source.

When a conflict arises between two plans or courses of action within a team, individuals dominated by internal self-concept-based motivation will remain strongly committed to that plan or course of action that provides feedback on valued traits, competencies, and values. These individuals do not need to take "credit" for successful outcomes, but must believe internally that success is due to their efforts. One's sense of mastery is one of the driving forces behind this source of motivation. We advance the following proposition.

> *Proposition* 9. When faced with alternative tasks, individuals dominated by internal self-concept-based motivation will engage in tasks that provide them with affirmative task feedback about their traits, competencies, and values in their important identities. Behavior will be sustained as long as positive task feedback is forthcoming, and if affirming feedback is not received, the behavior will end.

Goal Internalization

Individuals primarily motivated by goal internalization accept group goals because the attainment of such goals is important to the individual. These goals will be pursued independent of their extrinsic benefits, their ability to provide for attribution of success to members, or their ability to provide individual, personal credit to members through goal attainment. Task and social feedback are used to measure progress toward attainment of the goal.

When conflict among courses of action arise, these individuals will commit themselves to plans that are most likely to attain group goals. Attaining credit for success, either in one's own or in others' eyes, is not important. Achieving internalized values and goals of the team or organization is the driving force behind this source of motivation. Thus, the following proposition is advanced.

> *Proposition 10*. When faced with alternative tasks, individuals dominated by goal-internalization motivation will choose to engage in tasks that have the greatest potential of achieving the group's or organization's goal. Behavior will be sustained as long as progress toward the goal continues.

DISCUSSION AND IMPLICATIONS FOR FUTURE DIRECTIONS

In this paper, we have proposed a metatheory of motivation incorporating traditional theories of motivation and self-concept theory. Expanding current theories of motivation to include the self-concept allows us to account for both situationally inconsistent behavior as well as the overall stability or cross-situational consistency of behavior. We do this by proposing that individuals possess situationally based motivation profiles that feature a dominant source. This dominant source directs an individual's behavior in a given situation and explains how choices among conflicting courses of action are resolved. We believe that this metatheory provides a more realistic portrayal of motivation as well as a basis for future theory building and research.

This new theory provides a number of areas of future research. First, it is important to test the propositions outlined above. To accomplish that, reliable and valid measures of the five sources of motivation need to be developed. Not only will measures need to distinguish between the five sources, but also they must be sensitive enough to be able to identify a dominant source in a variety of situations. Specifically, the possibility that different motivational profiles exist for different social identities needs to be explored. This theory may also be examined from the perspective of the interpretive paradigm through the use of observational research, projective techniques, or in-depth case analysis of individuals in multiple work settings.

An interesting and rich area of research arises if we consider the possibility that the five sources of motivation provide the basis for a developmental model of motivation. This is, do individuals progress through stages of "motivational development" as they mature both psychologically and socially? It may be that individuals begin to engage in particular behaviors because they are simply enjoyable. As they mature over time and begin to experience the consequences that different behavioral responses elicit, individuals may learn to perform certain behaviors for the extrinsic rewards, acceptance, status, or sense of personal achievement they provide. Perhaps only at advanced stages of psychosocial development do individuals become motivated to engage in and sustain activities based on internalized goals and values of organizations and societies. Investigation of such a developmental perspective will require longitudinal studies that examine the motivational histories of people, keeping track of their profiles and dominant sources to determine if and how they change over time.

The self-concept-based theory of motivation we have outlined in this paper also provides rich avenues for research. First, we believe we have incorporated most of the self-constructs that have been proposed in the literature in our formulation of the self-concept. However, there may be other constructs that we have overlooked. The role of self-esteem, in particular, may need further exploration (Korman, 1970). We believe that self-esteem comes into play when the individual evaluates the gap between the ideal and perceived selves and experiences the cognitive and affective responses associated with the adaptive strategies outlined earlier. However, given the importance of self-esteem concepts in the literature (Campbell & Fairey, 1985; Rosenthal & Rosnow, 1991), it may entail a broader development than that given in our model.

Second, at this point in the development of our model, we have only speculated on the general motivational properties of the self-concept in terms of the inner- and other-directed dimensions. The motivational consequences of the variety of self-concept types specified in Table I are highly speculative in the model's current development. Critically, all 16 types may not actually exist in the population. Future research needs to determine the likely number of kinds of types that normatively describe the general population and the effects of such types on motivational efforts. To do this requires that we develop good measures of the dimensions of self-concept and apply them in studies that cover a wide range of employees in a wide range of situations.

The metatheory proposed in this paper also has some practical implications for those interested in work motivation. For example, an understanding of how the various sources of motivation affect employees' choices regarding the direction, level of effort, and persistence of behavior is crucial in areas such as team management, conflict resolution, leadership, and organizational change. This knowledge may make managers wary of the "one size fits all" approaches to motivational success. By gaining an understanding of the sources of motivation described in this paper, managers will better be able to design inducement systems which are closely linked to individual differences in sources of motivation. For instance, inducement systems can be designed to elicit desired employee behavior based on particular sources of motivation. The most commonly studied inducement systems are the reward, task, managerial, and social inducement systems. The reward system involves the design and implementation of formal reward systems in the organization, such as compensation and promotional systems. The task inducement system is involved with the motivational aspects of job and task design. The managerial inducement system derives its motivational properties from aspects of leadership style. Finally, the motivational impact of the work group or the organization as a social and cultural system defines the social inducement system. As an example, changes in pay or the reward system may elicit desired behaviors from employees who are motivated by extrinsic reward, but may not elicit the desired behavior from those whose dominant source of motivation is internal self-concept. Likewise, changes in the task system which increase autonomy, task significance, task feedback, task identity, and skill variety might elicit the desired behavior from the individual motivated by intrinsic process and not from the individual motivated by external self-concept. In addition, transformational leadership styles may be highly effective with goal internalized individuals, but less effective with employees dominated by either intrinsic process or instrumental sources of motivation. . . .

In the area of organizational change and development, this model has the potential to help managers understand why organizational change efforts often fail to produce the expected organizational outcomes. Change agents and managers must recognize the variety of forces which motivate employees in order to design interventions which stimulate motivation to change or lead to resistance to change. For example, individuals who are inner-directed may be more responsive to participative rather than autocratic leadership when the organization is evolving from an individual to a team-based environment. Participative leadership allows for input into the decision process and thus more direct feedback from the task, whereas autocratic leadership lacks this direct input from the task. On the other hand, socioemotional leadership may work best for the external individual because of the provision for social feedback in making such a change.

The metatheory that we have proposed is an attempt to organize and synthesize what we know about motivation into a parsimonious framework. We believe that it offers practitioners a valid and useful framework for managing an increasingly diverse population of employees.

REFERENCES

Ajzen, I., & Fishbein, M. *Understanding attitudes and predicting social behavior.* Englewood Cliffs, NJ: Prentice-Hall, 1980.

Ashford, B. E., & Mael, F. Social identity theory and the organization. *Academy of Management Review,* 1989, *14,* 20–39.

Atkinson, J. W., & Birch, D. *The dynamics of action.* New York: Wiley, 1970.

Bandura, A. Self-efficacy mechanism in human agency. *American Psychologist,* 1982, *37,* 122–147.

Bandura, A. *Social foundations of thought and action: A social cognitive theory.* Englewood Cliffs, NJ: Prentice-Hall, 1986.

Bandura, A. Social cognitive theory of self regulation. *Organizational Behavior and Human Decision Processes,* 1991, *50,* 248–287.

Barnard, C. *The functions of the executive.* Cambridge, MA: Harvard University Press, 1938.

Beach, L. R., & Mitchell, T. R. Image theory: A behavioral theory of decision making in organizations. In B. Staw and L. L. Cummings (Eds.), *Research in organizational behavior.* JAI Press, Greenwich, CT, 1990.

Becker, T. E. Foci and bases of commitment: Are they distinctions worth making? *Academy of Management Journal*, 1992, *35*, 232–244.

Brief, A. P., & Aldag, R. J. The self in organizations: A conceptual review. *Academy of Management Review*, 1981, *6*, 75–88.

Campbell, T. D., & Fairey, P. J. Effects of self-esteem, hypothetical explanations, and verbalization of expectancies on future performance. *Journal of Personality and Social Psychology*, 1985, *48*, 1097–1111.

Cantor, N., & Kihlstrom, J. F. Social intelligence: The cognitive basis of personality. *Review of Personality and Social Psychology*, 1985, *6*, 15–33.

Cantor, N., & Kihlstrom, J. F. *Personality and social intelligence*. Englewood Cliffs, NJ: Prentice-Hall, 1987.

Cattell, R. B. *The scientific analysis of personality*. Baltimore, MD: Penguin, 1965.

deCharms, R. *Personal causation: The internal affective determinants of behavior*. New York: Academic Press, 1968.

Davis-Blake, A., & Pfeffer, J. Just a mirage: The search for dispositional effects in organizational research. *Academy of Management Review*, 1989, *14*, 385–400.

Deci, E. L. *Intrinsic motivation*. New York: Plenum, 1975.

Etzioni, A. *Comparative analysis of complex organizations* (enlarged ed.). New York: MacMillan Publishing Co., 1975.

Festinger, L. *A theory of cognitive dissonance*. Stanford, CA: Stanford University Press, 1957.

Foote, N. N. Identification as the basis for a theory of motivation. *American Sociological Review*, 1951, *16*, 14–21.

Gecas, V. The self concept. *Annual Review of Sociology*, 1982, *8*, 1–33.

Gergen, K. J. Theory of the self: Impasse and evaluation. In L. Berkowitz (Ed.), *Advances in experiential social psychology*. Orlando: Academic Press, 1984, pp. 49–115.

Gerhardt, B. How important are dispositional factors as determinants of job satisfaction? Implications for job design and other personnel programs. *Journal of Applied Psychology*, 1987, *72*, 366–373.

Goldberg, L. R. An alternative description of personality: The big-five factor structure. *Journal of Personality and Social Psychology*, 1990, *59*, 1216–1229.

Greenwald, A. G., & Pratkanis, A. R. The self. In R. S. Wyer and T. S. Srull (Eds.), *Handbook of social cognition*. Hillsdale, NJ: Erlbaum, 1984.

Hackman, J. R., & Oldham, G. R. Motivation through the design of work: Test of a theory. *Organizational Behavior and Human Performance*, 1976, *16*, 250–279.

Higgins, E. T., Klein, R. L., & Strauman, T. J. Self discrepancies: Distinguishing among self-states, self-state conflicts, and emotional vulnerabilities. In K. Yardley and T. Hones (Eds.), *Self and identity: Psychosocial contributions*. New York: Wiley, 1987, pp. 173–186.

House, R. J., Shane, S. A., & Herold, D. M. Rumors of the death of dispositional research are vastly exaggerated. *Academy of Management Review*, 1996, *21*, 203–224.

Jones, E. E. *Interpersonal perception*. New York: W. H. Freeman, 1990.

Jones, E. E., & Gerard, H. B. *Foundations of social psychology*. New York: Wiley, 1967/1990.

Kanfer, R. Motivation and individual differences in learning: An integration of developmental, differential, and cognitive perspectives. *Learning and Individual Differences*, 1990, *2*, 219–237.

Katz, D., & Kahn, R. L. *The social psychology of organizations* (2nd. ed.). New York: Wiley, 1978.

Kelman, H. The induction of action and attitude change. In G. Nielson (Ed.), *Proceedings of the XIV International Congress of Applied Psychology*, 1958, pp. 81–110.

Kihlstrom, J. F., & Cantor, N. Mental representations of the self. *Advances in Experimental Social Psychology*, 1984, *17*, 1–47.

Kihlstrom, J. F., Albright, J. S., Klein, S. B., Cantor, N., Chew, B. R., & Niedenthal, P. M. Information processing and the study of the self. *Advances in Experimental Social Psychology*, 1988, *21*, 145–180.

Klein, H. J. An integrated control theory model of work motivation. *Academy of Management Review*, 1989, *14*, 150–172.

Korman, A. K. Toward a hypothesis of work behavior. *Journal of Applied Psychology*, 1970, *56*, 31–41.

Landy, F. J., & Becker, L. J. Motivation theory reconsidered. *Research in Organizational Behavior*, 1987, *9*, 1–38.

Locke, E. A., & Henne, D. Work motivation theories. In C. L. Cooper and I. Robertson (Eds.), *International review of industrial and organizational psychology*. Chichester, England: Wiley, 1986, pp. 1–35.

March, J., & Simon, H. *Organizations*. New York: Wiley, 1958.

Markus, H., & Wurf, E. The dynamic self-concept: A social psychological perspective. *Annual Review of Psychology*, 1987, *38*, 299–337.

Marsh, H. W., & Hattie, J. Theoretical perspectives on the structure of self-concept. In B. A. Bracken (Ed.), *Handbook of self-concept: Developmental, social, and clinical considerations*. New York: Wiley, 1996.

McClelland, D. C. *The achieving society*. Princeton, NJ: Van Nostrand Reinhold, 1961.

Mischel, W. *Personality and assessment*. New York: Wiley, 1968.

Mitchell, T. R., & James, L. R. Conclusions and future directions. *Academy of Management Review*, 1989, *14*, 401–407.

O'Reilly, C. III, & Chatman, J. Organizational commitment and psychological attachment: The effects of compliance, identification, and internalization of prosocial behavior. *Journal of Applied Psychology*, 1986, *71*, 492–499.

Pervin, L. A. *Personality: Theory, assessment & research*. New York: Wiley, 1975.

Pervin, L. A. Persons, situations, interactions: The history of a controversy and a discussion of theoretical models. *Academy of Management Review*, 1989, *14*, 350–360.

Roberts, B. W., & Donahue, E. M. One personality, multiple selves: Integrating personality and social roles. *Journal of Personality*, 1994, *62*, 199–218.

Rogers, C. R. A theory of therapy, personality, and interpersonal relationships as developed in the client-centered framework. In S. Koch (Ed.), *Psychology: A study of a science*. New York: McGraw-Hill, 1959, pp. 184–256.

Rosenthal, R., & Rosnow, R. L. *Essentials of behavioral research. Methods and data analysis*. New York: McGraw-Hill, 1991.

Rynes, S., & Lawler, J. A. A policy-capturing investigation of the role of expectancies in decisions to pursue job alternatives. *Journal of Applied Psychology*, 1983, *68*, 620–631.

Schlenker, B. R. *Impression management: The self-concept, social identity, and interpersonal relations*. Monterey, CA: Brooks/Cole, 1980.

Schlenker, B. R. Identities, identification, and relationships. In V. Derlega (Ed.), *Communication, intimacy, and close relationships*. New York: Academic Press, 1985.

Schlenker, B. R. Identity and self-identification. In B. R. Schlenker (Ed.), *The self and social life*. New York: McGraw-Hill, 1985, pp. 15–99.

Schwartz, S. H., & Bilsky, W. Toward a theory of the universal content and structure of values: Extensions and cross-cultural replications. *Journal of Personality and Social Psychology*, 1990, *58*, 878–891.

Shamir, B. Calculations, values and identities: The sources of collective work motivation. *Human Relations*, 1990, *43*, 313–332.

Shamir, B. Meaning, self and motivation in organizations. *Organizational Studies*, 1991, *12*, 405–424.

Sims, H. P., Jr., & Lorenzi, P. *The new leadership paradigm: Social learning and cognition in organizations*. Newbury Park, CA: Sage, 1992.

Snyder, R. A., & Williams, R. R. Self theory: An integrative theory of work motivation. *Journal of Occupational Psychology*, 1982, *55*, 257–267.

Soares, A. T., & Soares, L. M. *Components of Students' Self-Related Cognitions*. Paper presented at the American Educational Research Association Annual Meeting, Montreal, 1983 (ERIC Document Reproduction Service No. ED 228 317).

Steers, R. M., & Porter, L. W. *Motivation and work behavior*. New York: McGraw-Hill, 1991.

Stryker, S. *Symbolic interactionism: A social structural version*. Menlo Park, CA: Benjamin/Cummings, 1980.

Stryker, S. Identity theory: Developments and extensions. In K. Yardley and T. Hones (Eds.), *Self and identity*. New York: Wiley, 1986.

Sullivan, J. J. Self theories and employee motivation. *Journal of Management*, 1989, *15*, 345–363.

Tajfel, H., & Turner, J. C. The social identity theory of intergroup behavior. In S. Worchel and W. G. Austin (Eds.), *Psychology of intergroup relations*. Chicago: Nelson-Hall, 1985, pp. 7–24.

Tolman, E. C. Identification and the post-war world. *Journal of Abnormal and Social Psychology*, 1943, *38*, 141–148.

17

Self-Set Goals and Self-Efficacy as Mediators of Incentives and Personality

Edwin A. Locke

In a provocative report published in 1935, C. A. Mace made the following observation:

> So, generally, whatever incentive or incentive conditions may be employed, the performance of any task is throughout controlled by some specific intention. . . . Supervision, verbal encouragement or reproof, the prescription of standards and so forth, are of value, just in so far as, directly or indirectly, they control the specific intention which is operative in the performance of the given task. (Mace, 1935, p. 2)

It has taken more than 50 years for Mace's idea to be taken seriously enough to be systematically tested. Based on Mace, as well as on Ryan (1970), I hypothesized the role of goals and intentions as causal mediators of incentives in Locke (1968b). More recently (Locke, 1991), I proposed an enlarged mediation model focused around the concept of the "motivation hub." A hub is a "center of activity." In the context of motivation theory it refers to the place where the action is, or, more precisely, that part of the motivation sequence that is closest to action. By closest I mean closest in time and in causal influence. The hub in Locke (1991) was part of a proposed "motivation sequence" model that started with needs and values and ended with rewards and satisfaction. My focus here is on the first several links of the model—those going from needs and incentives to action. This part of the model (which is modified slightly from Locke, 1991) is shown [in Figure 1].

THE MEDIATION-LINKING MODEL

This model asserts that self-set or personal goals (which is what Mace meant by intentions) and self-efficacy (which refers to task-specific self-confidence) are the most immediate, motivational determinants of action (Bandura, 1986; Locke & Latham, 1990), and that they mediate or link the effects of other motivators. For the purpose of this paper, I am treating goal commitment as part of the motivation hub. (It is true, of course, that goals themselves are mediated by various mechanisms [attention, effort, and persistence], but these core mechanisms are activated relatively automatically in response to goals.) Previously (Locke, 1991), I discussed two motivational elements hypothesized to be mediated by goals and self-efficacy: needs and values (or motives), both of which are internal factors. Here I have added two more elements to the model: personality, which reflects values and motives as well as personal style, and

Source: From *Work Motivation in the Context of a Globalizing Economy*. Reprinted by permission of Lawrence Erlbaum Assoc.

FIGURE 1 • MOTIVATION HUB

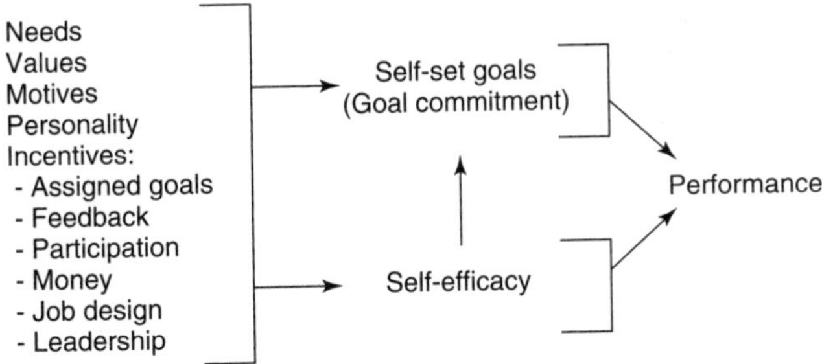

incentives, which are external inducements to action (e.g., feedback, participation, job characteristics, leadership, and money incentives).

The basic assumption of the hub model is that self-set goals and self-efficacy, which are task and situationally specific, take into account or reflect the other motivational elements in the context of the specific situation at hand. Consider, for example, values. Values may affect how individuals choose and "frame" situations. Individuals who highly value achievement, for example, should be more likely to: look for situations in which they can achieve, conclude that tasks and situations they encounter are pertinent to achievement or opportunities for achievement, look for ways to measure their accomplishments, set high achievement goals, and be highly committed to these goals as compared to individuals who do not value achievement highly. What goals are set also will be affected by the individual's perceived self-efficacy for the task at hand.

The principle is the same for external incentives; they can also help to frame situations. For example, individuals who value money highly should be more likely to look for money-making opportunities, think of ways to turn situations into opportunities for making money, set higher goals for money and for achievements that will gain money (depending again on their self-efficacy) and be more committed to such goals than individuals who do not value it. (Observe here that, to be effective, external incentives must appeal to values.) Leaders can motivate followers through framing. By communicating an inspiring vision that appeals to their values and expressing high confidence in followers, leaders can convince them that high performance is important and that they are capable of achieving it (Kirkpatrick & Locke, 1996).

As shown in the hub model, goals and goal commitment will be affected not only by values and incentives, but by the individual's degree of self-efficacy for the specific task involved (Bandura, 1986). Self-efficacy may also be affected by external factors (e.g., participation; Latham, Winters, & Locke, 1994) and, like goals, has a direct effect on performance.

Several limitations of the proposed model must be noted. An obvious limitation is that the model does not explicitly include cognition (e.g., knowledge, skills, task strategies). Knowledge and skill, of course, are known to affect action over and above the effects of motivational variables—assuming some motivation is present. The hub model in no way denies such factors, but, because of its focus on motivation, it does not specify them. Self-efficacy, of course, is a cognitive judgment, an estimate of capacity for performing, but it functions as a motivator of action (Bandura, 1986). A related cognitive element is volition, the choice to think or not to think (Binswanger, 1991). How and if a person thinks can affect every part of the model (Locke, 1991).

A second limitation of the model is that it does not take into account subconscious motivation, that is, motives that affect action independent of conscious awareness, including conscious goal setting and self-efficacy. In other words, subconscious motivation may bypass the hub altogether. For example, it may affect arousal or direction of attention without affecting conscious goals. Another alternative is possible, however. A person might be unaware of certain subconsciously held values and yet these values still might affect the person's conscious goals or self-efficacy beliefs. The precondition of relevant studies on the topic of subconscious motivation is the measurement of such motives in task-performance settings—a very difficult undertaking.

A third limitation of the model is that it does not address emotions as direct determinants of action. The full causal sequence model (Locke, 1991) places emotions at the end of the causal sequence, as consequences of value appraisals of events and situations, including one's own performance and the rewards that it produces. This, however, does not preclude the possibility that emotions, once experienced, can affect subsequent performance. Whether these operate through or around the hub is an interesting research question. Similarly, the model does not incorporate moods, which are enduring emotional states.

Thus the model is best viewed as a working hypothesis with obvious limitations. The model does not specify whether goals or self-efficacy will be the more critical link in a given case. Despite being conceptually distinct, the two concepts represent two complementary aspects of motivation: what individuals are trying to accomplish and the confidence that they can accomplish it. These are often highly correlated. In this chapter I will summarize studies that have tested the basic mediation idea. This will give some indication of its basic viability. . . .

Assigned Goals

Locke and Latham (1990) argue that assigned goals affect performance through their effects on personal goals and on self-efficacy. Although assigned and self-set goals are typically correlated, there may be discrepancies between them because individuals are not always fully committed to what others ask them to accomplish. Assigned goals can also affect self-efficacy, for example, because assigning difficult goals is an expression of confidence and may constitute a form of Pygmalion effect (Eden, 1990) or persuasion (Bandura, 1986). Self-efficacy may affect performance both directly and through its effects on personal goals.

Meyer and Gellatly (1988) found that assigned goals also supply to subjects normative information that they use when setting their goals. In two laboratory studies they found that the effects of assigned goal difficulty on performance were fully mediated: by personal goals, and by performance expectancies (efficacy) via a path from perceived norms. Another laboratory study, by Meyer, Schact-Cole, and Gellatly (1988), also found a mediation effect. Two of the laboratory studies reported by Earley and Lituchy (1991) found that personal goals and self-efficacy substantially, but not totally, mediated the significant effects of experimenter-assigned goal difficulty on performance.

In quite a different type of study, conducted in a field setting, Zimmerman, Bandura, and Martinez-Pons (1992) found that 9th- and 10th-grade students' personal grade goals fully mediated the effects of their parents' grade goals (that is, the grades their parents wanted them to get) on actual grade performance. Although self-efficacy also affected grade performance, it did not mediate the effects of the parents' goals.

Feedback

Feedback, by which I mean here, knowledge of results (KR)—that is, knowledge of how you are doing on a task—was the most studied incentive with respect to the issue of mediation at the time Locke and Latham (1990) published their integration of the goal-setting literature. Locke and Bryan (1966) found no effect of degree of KR on the performance of subjects working on a complex computation task, but when the subjects were resorted according to the level of the performance goals they reported trying for, there was a significant relationship between goal level and performance.

A better-designed study by Locke and Bryan (1968) found a significant main effect of KR (versus no KR) using the same computation task. However, subjects in the KR condition set significantly harder goals than those in the no-KR condition. When goal difficulty was partialed out the KR effect was vitiated, thus indicating complete mediation of the KR effect by goals.

A third study (Locke, 1968a) replicated this finding using a reaction-time task. Both degree of KR and goal difficulty were varied. These variables were highly correlated with each other and with performance when one experimental group given full KR and low (easy) goals was excluded from the analysis. When this group was included, it had the effect of partialing out a high, preexisting (and artifactual) correlation between degree of KR and goal level among subjects in the remaining conditions. When this was done, the effect of KR was eliminated, whereas the goal effect remained significant.

A number of studies gave subjects feedback on two or more performance dimensions but assigned goals for only one dimension or outcome or measured what outcomes subjects set goals for. In all cases performance improved only on the dimensions for which goals were set (e.g., Locke & Bryan, 1969; see Locke & Latham, 1990, for a summary). These studies show that KR only improves performance to the extent that goals single out which performance dimension requires improvement.

Some feedback, of course, is necessary for goal setting to be effective (Locke & Latham, 1990), but the key finding here is that KR alone does not directly cause better performance. KR, of course, must be distinguished from task knowledge (knowledge of how to perform the task effectively), which does have a direct effect on performance. . . .

Participation

The topic of participation in decision-making, or pdm, has a long contentious history (e.g., see Locke & Latham, 1990, and Locke, Alavi, & Wagner, 1997, for summaries). I will only be concerned here with the small portion of it relevant to goal mediation. Erez, Earley, and Hulin (1985) varied both degree of pdm and whether the subjects set or did not set personal goals in a laboratory study involving making up class schedules. Pdm subjects significantly outperformed those given assigned goals in Phase I of the study. However, this effect was mediated by degree of goal acceptance (commitment). Acceptance was significantly related to performance and, when entered before pdm in the regression, vitiated its effects. This could be considered a weak mediation finding, however, in that the R^2 reduction was very small and was not tested for significance.

The other study relevant to pdm is Study 3 of Latham, Erez, and Locke (1988), which used the same task as Erez, Earley, and Hulin (1985). There were three goal conditions: tell, tell and sell, and participative. For low-ability subjects, there was a significant effect of goal condition, with pdm leading to higher performance than telling the subjects what goal to aim for. This effect, however, was fully mediated by goal commitment and self-efficacy, which were higher in the pdm condition.

The two studies above suggest that to the extent that pdm does motivate higher performance, it may do so partly through its effects on goal commitment and self-efficacy. This does not preclude pdm effects on goal level as well. Latham and Yukl (1975) found that uneducated woods workers set higher goals in a pdm than in an assigned goal condition and that the pdm workers showed higher productivity, but they did not conduct a formal mediation analysis.

Recent research suggests that there are strong (though contingent—Scully, Kirkpatrick, & Locke, 1995) cognitive benefits of pdm (Locke, Alvai, & Wagner, 1997). These cognitive effects of pdm, which also raise self-efficacy (e.g., Latham, Winters, & Locke, 1994), may be more significant and reliable than its motivational effects. It is intriguing to consider the probability that self-efficacy may help mediate both the motivational and cognitive benefits of pdm.

Money Incentives

A number of studies have examined the role of goals and goal commitment in mediating the effects of money incentives, but the results have been inconsistent. On the negative side, Latham, Mitchell, and Dossett (1978), Pritchard and Curtis (1973) and Reidel, Nebeker, and Cooper (1988) all found that incentives affected performance even when goal level and goal commitment were controlled or partialed out. Furthermore, the first two studies did not even find an effect of incentives on commitment. Reidel, Nebeker, and Cooper (1988) did find an effect of incentives on both goal level and commitment, but, as noted, these did not fully mediate the incentive effect. None of these studies used a validated measure of goal commitment, and none used self-efficacy as a mediator.

On the positive side, Wright (1989) found evidence for mediation in which incentives affected personal goals and commitment, which in turn affected performance. However, there was no initial effect of incentives on performance. In a later study, Wright (1992) found that an interactive goal-incentive effect on performance was mediated by goal commitment.

One factor to consider about the above studies is that no one of them met the following four criteria: (a) significant incentive effects or goal-incentive interactions were obtained; (b) a validated commitment measure was used (e.g., the Hollenbeck scale); (c) personal goals were measured after the experimental inductions were made; (d) self-efficacy was measured. Although (a) is not obligatory according to Guzzo and Hanges' (1997) definition of mediation, (b), (c), and (d) are needed in order to include all the potential mediators that constitute the motivation hub. The inclusion of self-efficacy is especially critical, because

Bandura (1986) has found consistently that incentives are not effective unless people believe they have the capacity to take the actions required to earn them.

A recent study by Lee, Locke, and Phan (1997), however, did meet these four criteria. Three types of incentives (piece rate, bonus, and hourly) were crossed with three levels of assigned goals. A significant interaction in the second trial following performance feedback (given after the first trial) was found in line with an earlier study by Mowen, Middlemist, and Luther (1981): Under piece-rate pay, performance was higher with hard than with medium assigned goals, but under bonus pay performance was higher with medium than with hard goals. Although commitment was not significantly affected by the experimental treatments, personal (self-set) goals and self-efficacy (which were significantly correlated with commitment) were. Furthermore, goals and self-efficacy completely mediated the interaction effect. For example, when subjects tried to attain hard to impossible assigned goals, personal goals and self-efficacy dropped or failed to increase under bonus pay but increased under piece-rate pay. These results indicate that with a proper design, mediation effects for money incentives can be obtained.

Job Design

Job design, especially job enrichment, has been studied for several decades (Hackman & Oldham, 1980). The results indicate that enriched jobs characteristically raise the level of job satisfaction (Oldham, 1996), but, their effect on performance is more problematic, especially when actual productivity rather than satisfaction-related actions such as absenteeism and turnover are considered (Kirkpatrick, 1992). Kirkpatrick conducted a laboratory study using a proofreading task in an attempt to isolate the performance-enhancing elements of job design. Both autonomy and responsibility were manipulated. Manipulated responsibility enhanced the level of personal goals (measured directly and in terms of anticipated satisfaction with various levels of performance) and goal commitment. Personal goals, in turn, enhanced performance. Goal commitment was only related to satisfaction. Although manipulated responsibility strongly affected experienced responsibility, the latter was unrelated to performance. These results suggest that it may be motivation hub variables (goals in this case) rather than critical intervening states (Hackman & Oldham, 1980) that link job redesign to motivational performance improvements.

Charismatic Leadership

Charismatic or transformational leadership is a hot topic in the leadership literature today, but most relevant studies have been correlational in design. There is some question as to the mechanisms by which this style produces beneficial organizational outcomes, if it does. Kirkpatrick and Locke (1996) designed a laboratory study, using a clerical task used by a real organization, that isolated three elements of this leadership style: vision, charismatic personality style (divorced from vision content), and task information (which is akin to intellectual stimulation). They found that vision was the most potent of the three components. Vision (which stressed quality) significantly affected both personal goal level for quality and self-efficacy for quality, which in turn significantly affected quality of task performance. Goal commitment was not related to performance. Task strategy information, a cognitive variable, followed a partial mediation model; it affected performance quantity through its effects on quantity goals and efficacy, and also directly. Vision had the most potent effects on a variety of attitude measures, e.g., trust in the leader, congruence between own beliefs and vision, inspiration, and perceived charisma. Charismatic personality style had few effects of any kind. These results . . . suggest that, in leadership, substance (vision content) counts more than style and that vision operates, in part, through its effects on goals and self-efficacy.

Of course, there are other mediators of leadership that must be considered, e.g., communication, reward system, selection, training, team building, structuring, etc. Many of these are highly cognitive, but even these, as we found was the case with task strategy information, may operate in part through the hub variables.

Personality

Whereas there are relatively few relevant studies, and sometimes only one, relevant to the previous six categories, there have been at least eight studies of hub variables as mediators of personality effects. The first of these was a laboratory study conducted by Matsui, Okada, and Kakuyama (1982), who found that a self-report measure of achievement motivation was significantly related to performance on a perceptual speed task. This effect was fully mediated by the difficulty or level of the goals the subjects set for themselves on the task.

Taylor, Locke, Lee, and Gist (1984) examined the relationship between the Type A personality style and the scholarly productivity of university faculty. The significant association between Type A scores and productivity was fully mediated by three variables: productivity goals, self-efficacy, and one task strategy—working on multiple projects rather than completing them one at a time. The Type A subscale that was mainly responsible for the results entailed job involvement. (In recent years, the definition of the Type A syndrome has changed to emphasize hostility or anger as the core component).

In a set of three studies conducted by Earley and Lituchy (1991), they found that trait efficacy was significantly associated with personal goals and task-specific self-efficacy, which in turn were related to performance

Johnson and Perlow (1992) found that need for mastery, a component of self-reported need for achievement, was significantly related to goal commitment which, in turn, was significantly related to performance on a complex laboratory task. Personal goals and self-efficacy were not measured.

Barric, Mount, and Strauss (1993) conducted a field study using sales personnel. They found that conscientiousness (one of the "big-five" personality dimensions) was associated with both sales volume and performance ratings by supervisors. . . . The association of conscientiousness with sales volume was partly mediated by autonomous goal setting (setting goals on one's own), and the association with performance ratings was partially mediated by goal commitment. Since mediation was not complete, obviously other causal variables must have been involved, including ability. Notably, self-efficacy was not measured in this study.

Mone, Baker, and Jeffries (1995) found that college students' self-esteem, although unrelated to grades, was significantly associated with personal (grade) goals and self-efficacy, which in turn predicted course performance.

Lerner and Locke's (1995) study occurred in a sports-exercise context. Students in P.E. classes were given hard or easy goals to meet on a sit-up task. Half the subjects competed with a standard (assigned goal) and half competed with a "stooge" who performed at the level of the assigned goal. The students' scores on a previously validated sports orientation questionnaire, which measured traits such as competitiveness and goal orientation, were significantly associated with sit-up performance. This association was completely mediated by personal (self-set) goals and self-efficacy. Goal commitment was significantly related to performance, self-set goals, and self-efficacy, but did not explain any performance variance beyond that attributable to the other two mediators.

The final study (Gellatly, 1996) was a laboratory investigation using a simple arithmetic task. A Conscientiousness factor was significantly related to performance. This effect was completely mediated by expectancy (which was actually a measure of self-efficacy) and two personal goal measures. One was a direct goal item and the other was a measure of expected satisfaction with various levels of performance (valence). Notably, of the six Conscientiousness subscales, only three were significantly associated with performance and with the mediators: cognitive structure, order, and impulsiveness (—). The subscales were not defined.

SUBCONSCIOUS MOTIVATION

Only one study to date has examined both conscious goals and subconscious motives as predictors of performance. Howard and Bray (personal communication), based on reanalyses of the data in their 25-year longitudinal study of AT&T managers (Howard & Bray, 1988), found that a one-item interview question in year 1, which asked the hirees how many levels they wanted to progress in the company, was strongly related to subsequent promotion over the next 25 years. In contrast, McClelland's managerial TAT measures were unrelated to promotion except for one subscale (need for affiliation), which predicted promotion weakly (and negatively) for nontechnical managers only. There was no interaction between the conscious and the subconscious measures. Obviously, further studies of this type would be useful, but the problem will be finding subconscious measures that are valid predictors.

CONCLUSION

Although only a limited number of relevant studies have been done to date, there is considerable support for the thesis that the effects of incentives and personality affect performance at least partly through "hub" variables, i.e., personal goals or goal commitment, and self-efficacy.

To our surprise, in those studies in which goal commitment was measured along with personal goals and self-efficacy, commitment does not explain any performance variance over and above that attributable to personal goals and self-efficacy. Typically, commitment is significantly related to goals and efficacy, indicating that they may act as a proxy for commitment. More committed people set higher goals and have higher self-efficacy than less committed people (or vice versa).

A qualification to the hub model that will need exploration is that it may not operate effectively in certain conditions. For example, Cervone and Wood (1995) found that when neither assigned goals nor feedback were present, personal goals and self-efficacy did not predict performance. Cervone, Jiwani, and Wood (1991) found that even when feedback was given but assigned goals were not, personal goals and self-efficacy did not predict performance. These results are somewhat puzzling in that one wonders what *was* regulating performance in such cases. Obviously this issue needs to be explored further.

Finally, as our knowledge develops, it will be necessary to bring relevant cognitive variables (knowledge, skill) into the model in order to provide a more comprehensive explanatory framework. However, since I am a believer in grounded (i.e., inductively developed) theory (Locke, 1996), I prefer to postpone this task until we have more data.

REFERENCES

Bandura, A. (1986). *Social foundations of thought and action*. Englewood Cliffs, NJ: Prentice-Hall.

Barrick, M. R., Mount, M. K., & Strauss, J. P. (1993). Conscientiousness and performance of sales representatives: Test of the mediating effects of goal setting. *Journal of Applied Psychology, 78*, 715–722.

Binswanger, H. (1991). Volition as cognitive self-regulation. *Organizational Behavior & Human Decision Processes, 50*, 154–178.

Cervone, D., Jiwani, N., & Wood, R. (1991). Goal setting and the differential influence of self-regulatory processes on complex decision-making performance. *Journal of Personality and Social Psychology, 61*, 257–266.

Cervone, D., & Wood, R. (1995). Goals, feedback, and the differential influence of self-regulatory processes on cognitively complex performance. *Cognitive Therapy and Research, 19*, 519–545.

Earley, P. C., & Lituchy, T. R. (1991). Delineating goal and efficacy effects: A test of three models. *Journal of Applied Psychology, 76*, 81–98.

Eden, D. (1990). *Pygmalion in management*. Lexington, MA: Lexington Books.

Erez, M., Earley, P. C., & Hulin, C. L. (1985). The impact of participation on goal acceptance and performance: A two-step model. *Academy of Management Journal, 28*, 50–66.

Gellatly, I. (1996). Conscientiousness and task performance: Test of a cognitive process model. *Journal of Applied Psychology, 81*, 474–482.

Guzzo, R. A., & Hanges, P. J. (1997). *Reconsidering the traditional criteria for establishing mediator variables*. Unpublished manuscript, Department of Psychology, University of Maryland.

Hackman, J. R., & Oldham, G. R. (1980). *Work redesign*. Reading, MA: Addison-Wesley.

Howard, A., & Bray, D. (1988). *Managerial lives in transition*. New York: Guilford Press.

Johnson, D. S., & Perlow, R. (1992). The impact of need for achievement components on goal commitment and performance. *Journal of Applied Social Psychology, 22*, 1711–1720.

Kirkpatrick, S. A. (1992). *The effect of psychological variables on the job characteristics–work outcomes relations*. Paper presented at Eastern Academy of Management.

Kirkpatrick, S. A., & Locke, E. A. (1966). Direct and indirect effects of three core charismatic leadership components on performance and attitudes. *Journal of Applied Psychology, 81*, 36–51.

Latham, G. P., Erez, M., & Locke, E. A. (1988). Resolving scientific disputes by the joint design of crucial experiments: Applications to the Erez-Latham dispute regarding participation in goal setting. *Journal of Applied Psychology, 73*, 753–772.

Latham, G. P., Mitchell, T. R., & Dossett, D. L. (1978). Importance of participative goal setting and anticipated rewards on goal difficulty and job performance. *Journal of Applied Psychology, 63*, 163–171.

Latham, G. P., Winters, D. C., & Locke, E. A. (1994). Cognitive and motivational effects of participation: A mediator study. *Journal of Organizational Behavior, 15*, 49–63.

Latham, G. P., & Yukl, G. A. (1975). Assigned versus participative goal setting with educated and uneducated woods workers. *Journal of Applied Psychology, 60*, 299–302.

Lee, T. W., Locke, E. A., & Phan, S. H. (1997). Explaining the assigned goal-incentive interaction: The role of self-efficacy and personal goals. *Journal of Management, 23*, 541–559.

Lerner, B. S., & Locke, E. A. (1995). The effects of goal setting, self-efficacy, competition, and personal traits on the performance of an endurance task. *Journal of Sport and Exercise Psychology, 17*, 138–152.

Locke, E. A. (1968a). Effects of knowledge of results, feedback in relation to standards and goals on reaction-time performance. *American Journal of Psychology, 81*, 566–574.

Locke, E. A. (1968b). Toward a theory of task motivation and incentives. *Organizational Behavior and Human Performance, 3*, 157–189.

Locke, E. A. (1991). The motivation sequence, the motivation hub and the motivation core. *Organizational Behavior and Human Decision Processes, 50,* 288–299.

Locke, E. A. (1996). Using programmatic research to build a grounded theory. In P. Frost & S. Taylor (Eds.), *Rhythms of academic life.* Thousand Oaks, CA: Sage.

Locke, E. A., Alavi, M., & Wagner, J. (1997). Participation in decision-making: An information exchange approach. In G. R. Ferris (Ed.), *Research in personnel and human resource management* (Vol. 15). Greenwich, CT: JAI Press.

Locke, E. A., & Bryan, J. F. (1966). The effects of goal setting, rule-learning and knowledge of score on performance. *American Journal of Psychology, 79,* 451–457.

Locke, E. A., & Bryan, J. F. (1968). Goal setting as a determinant of the effect of knowledge of score on performance. *American Journal of Psychology, 81,* 398–406.

Locke, E. A., & Bryan, J. F. (1969). The directing function of goals in task performance. *Organizational Behavior & Human Performance, 4,* 35–42.

Locke, E. A., & Latham, G. P. (1990). *A theory of goal setting and task performance.* Englewood Cliffs, NJ: Prentice-Hall.

Mace, C. A. (1935). Incentives—Some experimental studies. *Industrial Health Research Report No. 72* (Great Britain).

Matsui, T., Okada, A., & Kakuyama, T. (1982). Influence of achievement need on goal setting, performance, and feedback effectiveness. *Journal of Applied Psychology, 67,* 645–648.

Meyer, J. P., & Gellatly, I. R. (1988). Perceived performance norm as a mediator in the effect of assigned goal on personal goal and task performance. *Journal of Applied Psychology, 73,* 410–420.

Meyer, J. P., Schact-Cole, B., & Gellatly, I. R. (1988). An examination of the cognitive mechanisms by which assigned goals affect task performance and reactions to performance. *Journal of Applied Social Psychology, 18,* 390–408.

Mone, M. A., Baker, D. D., & Jeffries, F. (1995). Predictive validity and time dependency of self-efficacy, self-esteem, personal goals and academic performance. *Educational and Psychological Measurement, 55,* 716–727.

Mowen, J. C., Middlemist, R. D., & Luther, D. (1981). Joint effects of assigned goal level and incentive structure on task performance: A laboratory study. *Journal of Applied Psychology, 66,* 598–603.

Oldham, G. (1996). Job design. In C. Cooper & I. Robertson (Eds.), *International review of industrial and organizational psychology.* Chichester, UK: Wiley.

Pritchard, R. D., & Curtis, M. I. (1973). The influence of goal setting and financial incentives on task performance. *Organizational Behavior and Human Performance, 10,* 175–183.

Reidel, J. A., Nebeker, D. M., & Cooper, B. L. (1988). The influence of monetary incentives on goal choice, goal commitment, and task performance. *Organizational Behavior and Human Decision Processes, 42,* 155–180.

Ryan, T. A. (1970). *International behavior.* New York: Ronald Press.

Scully, J. A., Kirkpatrick, S. A., & Locke, E. A. (1995). Locus of knowledge as a determinant of the effects of participation on performance, affect and perceptions. *Organizational Behavior and Human Decision Processes, 61,* 276–288.

Taylor, M. S., Locke, E. A., Lee, C., & Gist, M. E. (1984). Type A behavior and faculty productivity: What are the mechanisms? *Organizational Behavior and Human Performance, 34,* 402–418.

Wright, P. M. (1989). Test of the mediating role of goals in the incentive-performance relationship. *Journal of Applied Psychology, 74,* 699–705.

Wright, P. M. (1992). An examination of the relationships among monetary incentives, goal level, goal commitment and performance. *Journal of Management, 18,* 677–693.

Zimmerman, B., Bandura, A., & Martinez-Pons, M. (1992). Self-motivation for academic attainment: The role of self-efficacy beliefs and personal goal setting. *American Educational Research Journal, 29,* 663–676.

CHAPTER III

Individuals in Teams and Groups

Orchestras consist of individual musicians who must work together effectively in sections—a wind section, a brass section, and a string section, among others. Great musicians don't produce great orchestral music. Individuals must be molded into cohesive teams that have a common mission and an understanding and appreciation of what the conductor (formal leader) and the other musicians (individuals) and sections (groups or teams) will be doing at all moments in a performance. Orchestras need highly talented individuals who are also "team players."

This tension between individualism and organizational needs is a core issue for all work groups and teams. Membership in a group always involves a willingness to subsume some individualism for the benefit of an organization's larger purposes. In this chapter, we focus on how organizations accomplish their purposes by blending the skills and creativity of individuals into effective efforts of groups and networks of groups.

People are social beings at work as well as at play. We form and associate in groups, and groups create their own norms, values, sentiments, membership criteria, roles, and aspirations. Most work groups also develop shared beliefs and attitudes about such things as the nature of the relationship between members and their employing organization, expectations about levels of work output and pay, what it takes to get ahead, and positive and negative consequences of trusting the organization or exhibiting loyalty to it.

Deciding whether to become a member of a group usually poses an *approach-avoidance conflict* for people. Joining has plus and minus connotations. Groups are a primary way people satisfy their desire for affiliation, their need for belonging. People working with and near each other form bonds—relationships—of friendship, camaraderie, and conversation. Yet group membership always requires relinquishing some individuality—of personal identity and freedom of behavior—at least temporarily. Although groups vary, most demand some degree of conforming behavior, of acquiescence to "claims" made by other members or by the group, as one "price" of membership and thus for satisfying affiliation wants. As the result, decisions to join groups at work often are made with tentativeness and feelings of ambiguity.

The formation of groups in the workplace is more than just a way for people to satisfy their desires for affiliation. Ever since the days of the Industrial Revolution, workplace organizations have been constructed on the foundation principles of *specialization* and *division of labor* (Smith, 1776). In our complex organizations of today, few jobs can be done from start to finish by one person. Specialization allows an organization to use people's skills and efforts more systematically and to focus their knowledge and energy on a limited number of tasks. Employee learning curves are minimized.

With division of labor, people who perform a set of specialized functions are organizationally clustered in work groups, work groups in units or branches, branches in divisions or departments, divisions in companies or agencies, and so forth. Work groups attract people with like backgrounds; for example, professional training, socialization, and experience as accountants, teachers, production managers, or human resources managers; or, perhaps, people from similar sociodemographic backgrounds, for example, from "old line" New England families, or particular ethnic groups. All such shared backgrounds involve the socialization of people into common value/belief/behavior systems. We learn how to think and act like doctors, teachers, accountants, or credit managers, and like Texans, New Yorkers, or Southern Californians.

Virtually all groups, and particularly purposeful, specialized, organizational groups, develop their own sets of norms (behavioral rules), values, stories, heroes, sagas, legends, myths, beliefs about their realities, and assumptions about things like the nature of their organizational environment and appropriate relations with other groups. When a group becomes institutionalized in an organization, such as a production unit or a branch office, these shared beliefs, values, and assumptions become the essence of an organizational subculture (Martin & Siehl, 1983). Most group subcultures have a resemblance to the overall organizational culture but also contain unique elements that form through the impact of events, circumstances, and personalities, including (Ott, 1989, chap. 4)

- The nature or type of business in which the organization is engaged
- The *psychological script* or basic personality of the founder or other dominant early leaders
- The general culture of the society where the organization is located

A specific group subculture develops from the learning members accumulate through their shared successes and failures experienced in solving problems that threatened the survival of the group and its identity or independence (Schein, 1992).

Putting aside the question of why work groups have at least partially unique subcultures, the fact remains that they usually are distinctive. Then, considering the normal loyalties that groups demand and the affiliational needs they meet, it becomes easy to understand why *ingroups* and *outgroups* and feelings of *we* and *they* and *we* versus *they* are so characteristic of life in organizations.

Group dynamics is the subfield of organization behavior "dedicated to achieving knowledge about the nature of groups, the laws of their development, and their interrelations with individuals, other groups, and larger institutions" (Cartwright &

Zander, 1968, p. 5). Kurt Lewin, perhaps the most influential social psychologist of this century (Marrow, 1969), is widely credited with creating and naming this field in which he was a most influential contributor.

Lewin's group dynamics perspective was subsumed under the general heading *field theory*, which holds that a person's behavior is a function of the individual and her or his immediate environment—the group and the organizational context. (Excerpts from Lewin's chapter, "Group Decision and Social Change," are in Chapter VI.) For much of the decade of the 1940s, Lewin and his associates at the Massachusetts Institute of Technology's Research Center for Group Dynamics introduced concepts like *fields*, *force fields*, and *field forces* into the study of human behavior, focusing on things such as resistance to change and the effects of leadership on group performance. Perhaps Lewin's greatest single contribution, however, was to move the focus of behavioral theory and research from individuals to groups.

But the field of group dynamics has been more than Kurt Lewin. It has represented the first comprehensive pulling together of theories, research methods, and empirical findings from myriad social sciences. It is the acquisition of "knowledge about the . . . psychological and social forces associated with groups. . . . It refers to a field of inquiry dedicated to achieving knowledge about the nature of groups, the laws of their development, and their interrelations with individuals, other groups, and larger institutions" (Cartwright & Zander, 1968, p. 9). Group dynamics is the accumulated contributions of many notable social scientists including R. F. Bales (1950), Dorwin Cartwright and Alvin Zander (1968), George Homans (1950), Jake Moreno (1934), T. M. Newcomb (1943), M. Sherif (1936), and William F. Whyte (1943, 1948).

Although definitions of a *group* vary, there is less disagreement here than there is about definitions of most other concepts of organizational behavior, such as *leader* and *motivation*. Usually, the term *group* refers to what is more technically known as a *primary group*—a group small enough to permit face-to-face interaction among its members and which remains in existence long enough for some personal relations, sentiments, and feelings of identification or belongingness to develop. Schein (1980) uses the term *psychological group* to mean much the same thing: "Any number of people who [1] interact with one another, [2] are psychologically aware of one another, and [3] perceive themselves to be a group" (p. 145). Over the years, many labels have been used to describe different types of groups, but for understanding organizational behavior, the most important types of groups probably are these (Ivancevich & Matteson, 2002, pp. 314–316):

- *Formal groups:* Groups that are formally sanctioned, usually for the purpose of accomplishing tasks. Employees are assigned to formal groups based on their position in the organization. There are two basic types of formal groups:
  - *Command groups:* Formal groups that are specified in the organization chart—groups that include supervisors and the people who report directly to them. Groups of this type are the *building blocks* of organiza-

tion structure: for example, a production work group, the staff of a small branch office, a product marketing group, or a military flight crew.

- *Task groups:* Formally sanctioned task-oriented groups with short lives. Employees who work together to complete a particular project or task, such as solving a problem or capitalizing on a specific opportunity, and then are disbanded. Examples include task forces and committees.

- *Informal groups:* Natural groupings of people in the work situation. People who associate voluntarily, primarily to satisfy social needs. Although informal groups at work may have goals and tasks (for example, ethnic support groups, investment clubs, and luncheon bridge groups), their primary reasons for existence are friendship, affiliation, and shared interests. Although informal groups seldom are formally sanctioned, they are extremely important to the working of organizations. Their norms, values, beliefs, and expectations have significant impacts on work-related behavior and attitudes.

Groups in organizations of all types are of high importance and interest to students and practitioners of organizational behavior, both for what happens *in* them (and why) and what happens *between* them. Thus, this chapter contains seven important readings about diverse aspects of group and intergroup dynamics.

Groups cannot be discussed without considering important variables that are the subjects of other chapters, most importantly leadership, motivation, and the organizational context. However, to avoid repetition, subjects that are the topics of other chapters are introduced only tangentially here.

DYNAMICS IN GROUPS

Dorwin Cartwright and Alvin Zander's contribution here is the introductory chapter "Origins of Group Dynamics" from their landmark volume, *Group Dynamics* (1968). Cartwright and Zander define group dynamics as "a field of inquiry dedicated to advancing knowledge about the nature of groups, the laws of their development, and their interrelations with individuals, other groups, the laws of their development, and their interrelations with individuals, other groups, and larger institutions." The distinguishing characteristics of group dynamics—what separates group dynamics from numerous other groups of behavioral sciences that have investigated groups over the years—are these:

1. Emphasis on theoretically significant empirical research; conceptual theories and personal observations are not adequate.
2. Interest in the dynamics and interdependence of phenomena; the dynamics are more important than static elements, single-variable theories, and structural schemes.
3. Broad interdisciplinary relevance; the importance of incorporating methods and knowledge from all of the social sciences, including sociology, psychology, and cultural anthropology.

4. "Potential applicability of its findings in efforts to improve the functioning of groups and their consequences on individuals and society"; the results must be useful in social practice.

"Origins of Group Dynamics" provides a thorough analysis of the historical development of the field including the positive impetus provided by advancements in other professions, most notably group psychotherapy, education, and social group work, and social research techniques such as controlled observation and sociometry. Cartwright and Zander are *the* premiere chroniclers of group dynamics, and "Origins of Group Dynamics" remains the outstanding overview of this field.

INTERGROUP DYNAMICS

Robert Blake, Herb Shepard, and Jane Mouton's chapter, "Foundations and Dynamics of Intergroup Behavior" (1964, reprinted here), approaches conflict within and among groups. Blake, Shepard, and Mouton identify sets of forces that affect behavior between two or more members of an organization: formal roles and responsibilities, personal backgrounds, and the roles they feel themselves to be in as representatives of particular groups in the organization. This three-forces framework is used to distinguish between conflict in organizations that is caused by personal matters and conflict that is caused by intergroup matters. The authors offer three alternative sets of assumptions about intergroup disagreement and discuss strategies for managing disagreement under each: (1) disagreement is inevitable and permanent, (2) conflict can be avoided since interdependence between groups is unnecessary, and (3) agreement and maintaining interdependence is possible.

In "An Intergroup Perspective on Group Dynamics" (1987, included in this chapter), Clayton P. Alderfer proposes a theory of intergroup relations that incorporates individual, interpersonal, group, intergroup, and organizational relations interpretations. Alderfer argues that an intergroup perspective "can explain a broader range of phenomena than just what go on at the intersection of two or more groups." His theory relates the status of intergroup relations to the larger organizational system in which groups are embedded. It has application in a wide variety of organizational problems and opportunities, including "the development of effective work teams, the definition and management of organizational culture, the analysis and implementation of affirmative action, and the teaching of organizational behavior in management schools."

"Cultural Diversity in Organizations: Intergroup Conflict" (1993), by Taylor Cox Jr., is a chapter from his groundbreaking book, *Cultural Diversity in Organizations: Theory, Research & Practice*. Cox suggests that a great deal of interpersonal conflict in organizations may be analyzed from an intergroup perspective, because "group identities are an integral part of the individual personality. Therefore, much of what is commonly referred to as 'personality clash' may actually be a manifestation of group identity-related conflict." Five sources of intergroup conflict are particularly important in the context of cultural diversity in organizations: competing goals, competition for resources, cultural differences, power discrepancies, and assimilation versus preservation of microcultural identity. Cox concludes with a listing of approaches for managing intergroup conflict in organizations and an assessment of the sources of diversity-related conflict that each of the approaches is most effective in addressing.

In "Why Teams: Leading to the High-Performance Organization" (reprinted here), Jon R. Katzenbach and Douglas K. Smith explain that there is far more to the "wisdom of teams" than they had expected when setting out to write their landmark 1993 book, *The Wisdom of Teams*. For example, teamwork is indeed desirable, but it needs to be seen as a means not an end. "Performance is the crux of the matter for teams," and when it is, any team "will deliver results well beyond what individuals acting alone in nonteam working situations could achieve." The strong emphasis on individualism in the United States can destroy the potential of teams, but it shouldn't and doesn't need to. Effective organizations use a carefully blended mix of individual and team performance approaches to enhance performance.

Katzenbach and Smith identify three widespread sources of reluctance to the use of teams in organizations: "a lack of conviction that a team or teams can work better than other alternatives; personal styles, capabilities, and preferences that make teams risky or uncomfortable; and weak organizational performance ethics that discourage the conditions in which teams flourish." They also discuss the characteristics of teams in high-performance organizations—"where the best companies are headed." They conclude with predictions that "future organization designs will seek structures simpler and more flexible than the heavily layered command-and-control hierarchies that have dominated the twentieth century. . . . [and] they . . . emphasize teams as the key performance unit of the company."

TEAMS AND TEAMWORK

Productivity in private and public sector organizations has become the overriding issue in corporate boardrooms as well as in the legislative corridors of power. Virtually all of the "new" approaches to management being advocated—the attempts to find solutions to the "productivity problem"—have blended traditional and experimental management methods with new forms of employee involvement and participative management. For the past two decades we have witnessed a never-ending series of "new" management approaches, particularly approaches that emphasize organizational flexibility through the development and empowerment of individuals and work groups.

"Japanese management," with its long-term commitment to employees and its emphasis on communications through quality circles (Ouchi 1981; Pascale & Athos, 1981), was the first major participative/empowerment approach to clearly emerge from the post–World War II Japanese industrial experience. In the 1970s, impressive productivity gains were attributed primarily to highly goal-oriented group activity within organizations (Hyde, 1991). For the most part, quality circles—voluntary work groups that attempt to recommend solutions to organizational problems—have been merged into and given way to successively more comprehensive management approaches, including these:

- The "search for excellence" (Peters & Waterman, 1982)
- The "M-form society" (Ouchi, 1984)
- "Total quality management" or "TQM" (Crosby, 1984; Deming, 1986, 1993; Juran, 1992)
- "Reinventing government" (Gore, 1993; Osborne & Gaebler, 1992)
- "Sociotechnical systems" or "Quality of Work Life (QWL)" (Weisbord, 1991)
- "Productivity management" (Hyde, 1991; M.I.T. Commission on Industrial Productivity, 1989)
- "Organizational architecture" (Nadler, Gerstein, & Shaw, 1992)
- "Reengineering," "process reengineering," or "business reengineering" (Hammer & Champy, 1993)

These management approaches share some common elements but also differ in emphasis, assumptions, and specific methods—as well as in their commitment to individual and work team empowerment. For example, "reengineering" is a radical change strategy, not an incremental "grassroots" employee involvement approach. Reengineering literally means what its name implies. "When someone asks us for a quick definition of business reengineering, we say that it means 'starting over.' It *doesn't* mean tinkering with what already exists or making incremental changes that leave basic structures intact. . . . It involves going back to the beginning and inventing a better way of doing work" (Hammer & Champy, 1993, p. 31).

In contrast to reengineering's radical change approach, Quality of Work Life (QWL) has as its central themes dignity, meaning of work and life, and community in the workplace. "We hunger for community in the workplace and are a great deal more productive when we find it. To feed this hunger in ways that preserve democratic values of individual dignity, opportunity for all, and mutual support is to harness energy and productivity beyond imagining" (Weisbord, 1991, p. xiv).

"Organizational architecture," an approach that uses physical architecture as an analogy for how managers should manage, falls between process reengineering and QWL. Principles of architecture that are applicable to this new-style management of organizations include these (Gerstein, 1992, pp. 14, 15):

- Architecture is a "practical art." "Ordinary people" are its consumers. Because people have to work and live in that which is created, the ultimate test of any architecture is its utility measured in human terms.
- Architecture provides a framework for the conduct of life, not a specification for what that life should be. Architecture should facilitate, guide, and provide a context; it should not provide a blueprint for conduct.
- Unlike a painting that is produced by a single artist, architecture is produced by large numbers of people working together to achieve the vision of the architect.

Organizational architecture can be seen as the art of forming organizational space to meet human needs and aspirations. "Organizational architects work in the 'behavioral space' . . . creating opportunities for action, which we often call *empowerment*, and creating constraints to action which are central to the organizational architect's job" (Gerstein, 1992, p. 15). Thus, proponents of organizational architecture apply principles from applied physical sciences and art to the empowerment—and steering—of work teams and individuals.

Despite their differences, process reengineering, organizational architecture, and QWL all share common elements, including an acknowledged need for organizations to be more flexible and innovative; recognition that people who actually do the work are the most knowledgeable about it and often have the best ideas about how to improve it; and an unwavering belief that major productivity gains cannot be achieved in bureaucracies that are top heavy with rules and administrators.

Virtually all of these flexibility- and productivity-increasing management approaches assume that groups provide individuals with opportunities for personal and professional growth and development, self-expression and creativity, and work satisfaction. They also assume that these opportunities cannot become available to workers in traditional hierarchical organizations. Also essential to the approaches, however, is the assumption that groups can and will provide structure and discipline for individuals at work. Therefore, organizations that permit empowerment do not need multiple levels and layers of supervisors and managers to coordinate, control, and monitor production and the behavior of individual workers. Work groups can and will accept responsibility for their processes and products—as well as the behavior of other group members.

Ruth Wageman explains why self-managing work teams often do not live up to performance expectations in "Critical Success Factors for Creating Superb Self-managing Teams" (1997, reprinted here). Dysfunctional teams "are not surprising when one considers that, in many U.S. companies, teamwork is an 'unnatural act.'" Organizations in the United States have long histories of hierarchical decision making that cause team members to "balk at the idea of relying on one another to get work done." Her study of self-managing work teams at Xerox Corporation found that how teams are set up and supported is more important for team success than day-to-day behavior of team leaders or coaches. Thus, the critical team success factors are mostly structural, including, for example, "clear, engaging direction"; work assignments that are designed for teams—that are real team tasks; team rewards that reflect superior team self-management; and authority to manage the work without interference. "Leaders do have an important role in the life of teams—but that role differs at various stages in the team's life" and thus changes as teams mature.

The bureaucratic-hierarchical form of organization developed in the nineteenth century Industrial Age of Adam Smith when people had to work together in the same physical place. In the information era of the twenty-first century, organizations "made up of virtual teams and networks of teams . . . rather than the pyramid—[have] become the conceptual model for how people work together." In a cutting-edge article, "Virtual Teams: The New Way to Work" (reprinted here),

Jessica Lipnack and Jeffrey Stamps (1999) explore crucial issues that are of high importance and concern for managers and students of twenty-first-century organizations. They compare the new "networks of organizations, networks of companies, and networks of nations" with Buckminster Fuller's geodesic domes made up of "many tetrahedrons joined together at key intersections." Virtual teams of individuals who may be dispersed around the globe are connected or networked through telecommunications in this newest stage in the evolution of organizations. To take advantage of advances in communication technology, many traditional hierarchical organizations are adopting more horizontal and more wheel-like or hub-and-spoke-like designs that include virtual teams. Networked organizations of virtual teams, however, pose enormous new challenges that require "a new kind of management, and a new kind of leadership." Teams with common purposes may cross boundaries of "languages, cultures, governments, distances, and the mysterious nuances of human behavior" that are "staggering in [their] complexity." Lipnack and Stamps propose a model and principles for virtual teams that are created from Robert Putnam's (2000) three essential factors for developing social capital: trust, reciprocity, and dense social networks.

REFERENCES

Alderfer, C. P. (1987). An intergroup perspective on group dynamics. In J. W. Lorsch (Ed.), *Handbook of organizational behavior* (pp. 190–222). Englewood Cliffs, NJ: Prentice-Hall.

Asch, S. E. (1951). Effects of group pressure upon the modification and distortion of judgments. In H. S. Guetzkow (Ed.), *Groups, leadership, and men* (pp. 177–190). Pittsburgh, PA: Carnegie Press.

Bales, R. F. (1950). *Interaction process analysis: A method for the study of small groups*. Reading, MA: Addison-Wesley.

Barzelay, M. (1992). *Breaking through bureaucracy: A new vision for managing in government*. Berkeley, CA: University of California Press.

Bennis, W. G. (1999). The secrets of great groups. In F. Hesselbein & P. M. Cohen (Eds.), *Leader to leader* (pp. 315–322). New York: The Peter Drucker Foundation for Nonprofit Management; and San Francisco: Jossey-Bass.

Blake, R. R., Shepard, H. A., & Mouton, J. S. (1964). *Managing intergroup conflict in industry*. Houston: Gulf.

Cartwright, D., & Zander, A. (Eds.). (1968). *Group dynamics: Research and theory* (3d ed.). New York: Harper & Row.

Cohen, A. R., Fink, S. L., Gadon, H., & Willits, R. D. (1988). *Effective behavior in organizations* (4th ed.). Homewood, IL: Richard D. Irwin.

Cox, T. H. Jr. (1993). *Cultural diversity in organizations: Theory, research & practice*. San Francisco: Berrett-Koehler.

Crosby, P. B. (1979). *Quality is free*. New York: McGraw-Hill.

Crosby, P. B. (1984). *Quality without tears*. New York: McGraw-Hill.

Daft, R. L., Bettenhausen, K. R., & Tyler, B. B. (1993). Implications of top managers' communication choices for strategic decisions. In G. P. Huber & W. H. Glick (Eds.), *Organi-*

zational change and redesign: Ideas and insights for improving performance (pp. 112–146). New York: Oxford University Press.

Davis, S. M., & Lawrence, P. R. (1977). *Matrix*. Reading, MA: Addison-Wesley.

Deming, W. E. (1986). *Out of the crisis*. Cambridge, MA: Massachusetts Institute of Technology Press.

Deming, W. E. (1993). *The new economics*. Cambridge, MA: Massachusetts Institute of Technology Press.

Fink, S. L. (1992). *High commitment workplaces*. New York: Quorum Books.

Gerstein, M. S. (1992). From machine bureaucracies to networked organizations: An architectural journey. In D. A. Nadler, M. S. Gerstein, & R. B. Shaw (Eds.), *Organizational architecture: Designs for changing organizations* (pp. 11–38). San Francisco: Jossey-Bass.

Gore, A. (1993). *The Gore report on reinventing government*. New York: Times Books.

Gouldner, A. (1960). The norm of reciprocity. *American Sociological Review, 25*, 161–178.

Hackman, J. R., & Oldham, G. R. (1980). *Work redesign*. Reading, MA: Addison-Wesley.

Hammer, M., & Champy, J. (1993). *Reengineering the corporation*. New York: Harper-Collins.

Harvard Business Review. (Eds.). (1994). *Differences that work: Organizational excellence through diversity*. Boston: Harvard Business Review Publishing Corporation.

Homans, G. C. (1950). *The human group*. New York: Harcourt, Brace.

Hyde, A. C. (1991). Productivity management for public sector organizations. In J. S. Ott, A. C. Hyde, & J. M. Shafritz (Eds.), *Public management: The essential readings*. Chicago: Nelson-Hall.

Ivancevich, J. M., & Matteson, M. T. (2002). *Organizational behavior and management* (6th ed.). Homewood, IL: Irwin.

Janis, I. L. (November 1971). Groupthink. *Psychology Today*, 44–76.

Juran, J. M. (1992). *Juran on quality by design*. New York: The Free Press.

Juran, J. M., & Gryna, F. M. (Eds.). (1988). *Juran's quality control handbook* (4th ed.). New York: McGraw-Hill.

Katzenbach, J. R., & Smith, D. K. (1993). *The wisdom of teams: Creating the high-performance organization*. Boston: Harvard Business School Press.

Lawler, E. E. III, Mohrman, S. A., & Ledford, G. E. Jr. (1992). *Employee involvement and total quality management*. San Francisco: Jossey-Bass.

Lewin, K. (1943). Forces behind food habits and methods of change. *Bulletin of the National Research Council, 108*, 35–65.

Lewin, K. (June 1947). Frontiers in group dynamics: Concept, method and reality in social science; Social equilibria and social change. *Human Relations, 1*(1).

Lewin, K. (1951). *Field theory in social science*. New York: Harper & Row.

Lewin, K. (1952). Group decision and social change. In G. E. Swanson, T. N. Newcomb, & E. L. Hartley (Eds.), *Reading in social psychology* (rev. ed., pp. 207–211). New York: Holt, Rinehart & Winston.

Lindzey, G. W. (Ed.). (1954). *The handbook of social psychology*. Cambridge, MA: Addison-Wesley.

Lipnack, J., & Stamps, J. (January/February, 1999). Virtual teams: The new way to work. *Strategy & Leadership, 27*(1), 14–19.

Marrow, A. J. (1969). *The practical theorist: The life and work of Kurt Lewin*. New York: Basic Books.

Martin, J., & Siehl, C. (Autumn, 1983). Organizational culture and counterculture: An uneasy symbiosis. *Organizational Dynamics*, 52–64.

M.I.T. Commission on Industrial Productivity. (1989). *Made in America: Regaining the productive edge*. Cambridge, MA: Massachusetts Institute of Technology Press.

Mitroff, I. I. (1987). *Business not as usual*. San Francisco: Jossey-Bass.

Moreno, J. L. (1934). *Who shall survive? A new approach to human interrelations*. Washington, D.C.: Nervous and Mental Disease Publishing Co.

Nadler, D. A., Gerstein, M. S., & Shaw, R. B. (Eds.). (1992). *Organizational architecture: Designs for changing organizations*. San Francisco: Jossey-Bass.

Newcomb, T. M. (1943). *Personality and social change*. New York: Dryden.

Osborne, D., & Gaebler, T. (1992). *Reinventing government*. Reading, MA: Addison-Wesley.

Ott, J. S. (1989). *The organizational culture perspective*. Belmont, CA: Wadsworth.

Ouchi, W. G. (1981). *Theory Z: How American business can meet the Japanese challenge*. Reading, MA: Addison-Wesley.

Ouchi, W. G. (1984). *The M-form society: How American teamwork can recapture the competitive edge*. Reading, MA: Addison-Wesley.

Pascale, R. T., & Athos, A. G. (1981). *The art of Japanese management*. New York: Simon & Schuster.

Peters, T. J., & Waterman, R. H. Jr. (1982). *In search of excellence*. New York: Harper & Row.

Pfeffer, J. (1981). *Power in organizations*. Boston: Pitman Publishing Company.

Pondy, L. R. (1967). Organizational conflict: Concepts and models. *Administrative Science Quarterly, 12*, 296–320.

Putnam, R. D. (2000). *Bowling alone: The collapse and revival of American community*. New York: Simon & Schuster.

Roy, D. F. (1960). "Banana time": Job satisfaction and informal interaction. *Human Organization, 18*, 158–168.

Schein, E. H. (1980). *Organizational psychology* (3d ed.). Englewood Cliffs, NJ: Prentice-Hall.

Schein, E. H. (1992). *Organizational culture and leadership* (2d ed.). San Francisco: Jossey-Bass.

Seashore, S. E. (1954). *Group cohesiveness in the industrial work group*. Ann Arbor: University of Michigan Press.

Shafritz, J. M., & Ott, J. S. (Eds.). (2001). *Classics of organization theory* (5th ed.). Belmont, CA: Wadsworth.

Sherif, M. (1936). *The psychology of social norms*. New York: Harper.

Sherif, M., Harvey, O. J., White, B. J., & Sherif, C. (1961). *Intergroup conflict and cooperation: The robbers' cave experiment*. Norman, OK: University Book Exchange.

Smith, A. (1776). *The wealth of nations* (chap. 1, Of the division of labor).

Strauss, G. (1962). Tactics of lateral relationship: The purchasing agent: *Administrative Science Quarterly, 7*, 161–186.

Thibaut, J., & Kelly, H. (1959). *The social psychology of groups*. New York: John Wiley.

Thorndike, E. L. (1935). *The psychology of wants, interests, and attitudes*. New York: Appleton-Century.

Wageman, R. (Summer, 1997). Critical success factors for creating superb self-managing teams. *Organizational Dynamics, 26*(1), 49–61.

Walton, R. E., & Dutton, J. M. (March, 1969). The management of interdepartmental conflict: A model and review. *Administrative Science Quarterly, 14*(1).

Walton, R. E., Dutton, J. M., & Fitch, H. G. (1966). A study of conflict in the process, structure, and attitudes of lateral relationships. In A. H. Rubenstein & C. J. Haberstroh (Eds.), *Some theories of organization* (rev. ed., pp. 444–465). Homewood, IL: Richard D. Irwin.

Weisbord, M. R. (1991). *Productive workplaces: Organizing and managing for dignity, meaning, and community*. San Francisco: Jossey-Bass.

Whyte, W. F. Jr. (1943). *Street corner society*. Chicago: University of Chicago Press.

Whyte, W. F. Jr. (1948). *Human relations in the restaurant industry*. New York: McGraw-Hill.

Zander, A. (1971). *Motives and goals in groups*. New York: Academic Press.

Zander, A. (1982). *Making groups effective*. San Francisco: Jossey-Bass.

18

Foundations and Dynamics of Intergroup Behavior

Robert R. Blake, Herbert A. Shepard, and Jane S. Mouton

BEHAVIOR AT THE INTERPERSONAL LEVEL

When a man speaks as a group representative, his behavior is to some extent dictated by the fact that he is a member of that group. In contrast, when a man speaks from the framework of his job responsibilities, he speaks only for himself. In the latter case, disagreement between the parties is a *personal* matter. . . .

FACTORS INFLUENCING THE RESOLUTION OF A DISPUTE WHEN DISAGREEMENT IS AN INTERGROUP MATTER

Significant differences appear when a person's interactions with another are dictated by his membership in or leadership of a group. Under these conditions, *the individual is not free* in the same sense as the person who acts independently out of job description or rank alone. Now the person's behavior is determined by many additional factors.[1]

The Dynamics of Group Interplay in Resolution of Disputes

In situations where an individual is interacting with another and both are representatives of groups, additional forces, quite complex, come into play. Acting as an individual, a man is free to change his mind on the basis of new evidence. But as a group representative, if he changes his thinking or position from that of his group's and capitulates to an outside point of view, *he is likely to be perceived by them as a traitor.*[2] On the other hand, if as a representative, he is able to persuade a representative of the other group to capitulate to his point of view, *his group receives him as a hero.* In other words, when a man is acting as a representative of one group in disagreement with another, the problem is no longer a personal affair. It is an *intergroup* problem. And as such, it can become a significant factor in accounting for his actions—as we will see.

Group Responsibilities of Individual Members

Often, men are quite aware that they have responsibilities as group representatives as well as individual job responsibilities. But formal organizational practices and attitudes often prevent this awareness from being discussed or from being openly considered.

Source: From *Foundations and Dynamics of Intergroup Behavior,* by Robert R. Blake, Herbert A. Shepard, and Jane S. Mouton, Gulf Publishing Company, 1964, pp. 1–17. Reprinted by permission of Scientific Methods.

As an example, consider the situation where the Vice President of sales speaks with the Vice President of operations. Formal organizational theory commonly assumes that each man speaks for himself, out of the background of his individual job and responsibilities. In practice, however, each may be keenly aware that he is representing the goals, values and convictions of his own group, and furthermore, when he speaks for them, he also speaks for himself. When problems between sales and operations seem difficult to resolve, it is not, as a rule, a sign of rigidity, incompetence, or personality conflict.[3] Rather, it is more likely to be a product of the complex task of seeking resolutions which will not violate the attitudes, values, and interests of the many other persons that each represents.

Incompatible Group Norms, Goals and Values

Just as formal organizational theory, as written, recognizes only that the individual speaks for himself out of his job responsibilities, similarly it may fail to recognize other facts of organizational life. Formal organization theory assumes that the goals, norms and procedures of different functional groups in the organization are, by definition, similar, complementary or identical. . . .

There is increasing recognition, however, that neither of these circumstances accurately describes many situations in modern industrial life. This recognition has led to an acknowledgment that men, in fact, are group representatives within the framework of an organization. In turn, it has led to an awareness and appreciation of how an individual acting as a member, or as a leader, of a group, is confronted with a host of additional problems.[4] These problems must be dealt with in terms of their genuine complexities if unity of organizational purpose is to be achieved.

The roots of these complex problems which group representatives face are characteristic of groups and of individuals. As will be seen, group membership is complicated further by the characteristics of intergroup relations. After looking briefly at these characteristics of groups, we will turn our attention to the dynamics of intergroup relations.

THE STRUCTURE AND PROCESS OF GROUPS-IN-ISOLATION

There are a number of ways of describing the characteristics of groups-in-isolation which we should consider prior to dealing with industrial intergroup relations.[5, 6]

Regulation of the Interdependent Behavior of Members of Groups-in-Isolation

Fundamentally, a group consists of a number of individuals bound to each other in some stage or degree of interdependence or shared "stake." Their problem is to guarantee the survival of the group in order to attain some *purpose or goal*. Taking for granted that the group's goals are clearly understood by its members, the interdependence among individuals, then, must be regulated to insure partial or entire achievement of these goals.

The Emergence of Group Structure, Leadership and Normative Rules

The need to regulate interdependence leads to three further properties of groups. When these properties emerge in group life they become additional forces which influence individual behavior. Let us look at each of these.

1. *Group Structure*. A differentiation of individual roles often is needed to

accomplish group objectives. Differentiation inevitably results in some individuals who have varying degrees of power to influence the actions of others. The result is that some group members carry greater weight than others in determining the direction of group action, its norms, values and attitudes.

2. *Leadership*. When the power system among members of an informal group is crystallized, it is common to speak of *that individual with the most power as the leader*. In some groups, he is boss, or supervisor; other members are subordinates. The leader is looked to by the members for guidance and direction. The power and influence of the leader varies according to his ability to aid the group in achieving its goals.[7] Where the leader is appointed by a more powerful group rather than being selected by his own group, the above generalizations must be qualified. For instance, if the goals of the subordinate group clash with those of the group by which he is appointed, he will be received not as leader, but as a representative of a different group.

3. *Normal Rules Guiding Behavior*. Along with the emerging set of power relations is the evolution of a normal set of "rules of the game," which specifies the conditions of interaction between group members. In other words, varying degrees of familiarity, influence, interaction and other relationships between members are sanctioned by the group according to an individual's role and position in the group hierarchy. Deviations from the rules and procedures by a member can lead to subtle but potent pressures by his fellow members to insure that the deviant "swings back into line."[7] Such pressures act quite differently on each person as a function of his status and personality, but they do act.

Identification with One's Group

The preceding three characteristics of group formation and operation—goals, leadership and norms—lead to varying degrees of identification with one's group. When feelings of identification are strong, the group is said to have high morale; it is highly cohesive.[8] The opposite is true when feelings of identification with group goals are low. Under circumstances of unacceptable power distribution or inappropriate norms, for example, the result is feelings of low morale, demoralization, low cohesion or possibly alienation. The greater the sense of identification a member has with his group, the greater are the pressures on him to follow, at times blindly, the direction and will of the group position.[9, 10]

These are all common properties of organized groups. A representative of a group, whether leader or member, is compelled to acknowledge in some way these group properties as he comes in contact with members of other groups whose interests support or violate those of his own. For a representative to agree to actions which other members feel are contrary to group goals can result in his being seen to have acted in a betraying way, or in poor faith. On the other hand, acting effectively against opposition and in support of group purpose and goals, and consistent with internal norms and values, insures retention or enhancement of his status.[11]

THE RELATIONSHIP OF THE ORGANIZATION FRAMEWORK TO INDIVIDUAL AND GROUP RELATIONS

The internal properties of a group are only one of the significant matters involved in understanding and managing intergroup relations. When the actions of individuals and groups are viewed within the framework of a complex organization, we can identify additional determinants of behavior.[12]

A Framework of Interdependent Organizational Subgroups

Consider the following circumstances in a large and complex organization: the total membership of the organization is subdivided into many smaller groups. Each subgroup has its own leadership and its rules and regulations. Each has its own goals which may or may not be in accord with overall organizational goals.[13] Each operates with its own degree of cohesion which varies with feelings of failure or accomplishment.[14] In an organization, these groups are interdependent with one another. They may be interdependent in performing a complex task requiring coordination of effort, in geographical proximity, or in terms of the reward system of the organization. Differences among them immediately become apparent to members.

Comparison Between Groups. Perception of differences between groups leads spontaneously to a comparison and to a "we-they" orientation.[5] Attention quickly focuses on similarities and differences. Furthermore, these spontaneous comparisons are intensified by the tendency of higher levels of authority to evaluate and reward by group comparison. For example, group incentive plans, awarding of plaques or other symbols of organization success to the highest selling group, the group with the highest safety record, and so forth, all tend to highlight group differences.[15] Thus, in a sense, "winning" and "losing" groups are held up for all to see. The organization's rationale is that a spirit of competition is a "healthy" motivating force for achieving organizational ends.[16, 17]

On the other hand, these comparisons sometimes lead to the discovery of common values and mutually supportive opportunities which can result in greater intergroup cohesion. When this happens, it is possible to achieve an intergroup atmosphere that can lead to effective problem-solving and cooperation. Feelings of shared responsibility may then lead to identification with overall organizational goals, and to heightened recognition of similarities with resulting reduction of differences and tensions between them.[18]

Pitfalls of Comparisons Across Groups. There is no assurance, however, that comparisons between groups inevitably lead to favorable outcomes. Instead, in the process of comparison, groups may discover discrepancies in treatment and privileges,[19] points of view, objectives, values, and so on. Then a different process unfolds. Comparisons tend to become invidious.[5] Differences are spotlighted and come to the focus of attention. Distortions in perception occur which favor the ingroup and deprecate the outgroup.[20, 21, 22] Each group finds in the other's performances an obstacle to attaining some or all of its own goals. When this situation extends beyond some critical point, each group may view the other as a threat to its own survival. At this point, disagreements are seen as permanent and inevitable, and the only possible resolution seems to lie in defeat of the other group in order to gain one's own objectives. Then all of the tools of common power struggles are brought into play.[23]

The manner in which representatives of groups interact, then, is colored by the background and history of agreements or disagreements of the groups they represent. The forces involved are powerful. The individual group's representative does not act only in terms of his job description or his specific background of training. Nor does he act solely within the context of his position within the group. Rather, he must be governed to some extent, depending on circumstances, by pre-existing relationships between the group he represents and the opposing group or representative of it that he is addressing.

Evaluated in terms of the forces acting in intergroup life, effective management of intergroup relations is a dimension of management that requires more analysis, more theory, and more skills than has been traditional in industrial life. To gain the necessary perspective, managers must focus not only on effective methods of resolving intergroup differences, but also on dysfunctional methods which lead to undesirable and disruptive side effects. Many dysfunctional methods for resolving conflicts have become common. These common practices have become embedded in the traditions of groups and organizations and must be understood to avoid their unthoughtful repetition.

THREE BASIC ASSUMPTIONS TOWARD INTERGROUP DISAGREEMENT

Three basic assumptions or attitudes toward intergroup disagreements and its management can be identified.

1. Disagreement Is Inevitable and Permanent

One identifiable basic assumption is that disagreement is inevitable and permanent. When *A* and *B* disagree, the assumption is that the disagreement must be resolved in favor of *A* or in favor of *B*, one way or the other. Under this assumption there seems to be no other alternative. If two points of view are seen to be mutually exclusive, and if neither party is prepared to capitulate, then any of three major mechanisms of resolution may be used:

A. *Win-lose* power struggle to the point of capitulation by one group.
B. Resolution through a *third-party* decision.
C. Agreement *not* to determine the outcome, namely, *fate* arbitration.

2. Conflict Can Be Avoided Since Interdependence Between Groups Is Unnecessary

A second orientation to intergroup relations rests on the assumption that while intergroup disagreement is not inevitable, neither is intergroup agreement possible. If these assumptions can be made, then interdependence is not necessary. Hence, when points of conflict arise between groups, they can be resolved by reducing the interdependence between parties. This reduction of interdependence may be achieved in three ways.

A. One group withdrawing from the scene of action.
B. Maintaining, or substituting *indifference* when it appears there is a conflict of interest.
C. *Isolating* the parties from each other; or the parties isolating themselves.

All of these (A, B, and C) share in common the maintenance of independence, rather than any attempt to achieve interdependence.

3. Agreement and Maintaining Interdependence Is Possible

The third orientation to intergroup disagreement is that agreement is possible and that a means of resolving it must be found. Resolving conflict in this way is achieved by smoothing over the conflict while retaining interdependence. For example, visible though trivial reference may be made to overall organizational goals to which both parties are in some degree committed. Then attention is shifted away from real issues with surface harmony maintained. Alternatively, agreement may be achieved by bargaining, trading, or compromising. In a general sense, this is splitting the difference that separates the parties while at the same time retaining their interdependence. Finally, an effort may be made to resolve the disagreement by a genuine problem-solving approach. Here the effort is not devoted to determining who is right and who is wrong. Nor is it devoted to yielding something to gain something. Rather, a genuine effort is made to discover a creative resolution of fundamental points of difference.

As mentioned earlier, each of these three orientations is related to another dimension which determines the specific approach to be used in managing disagreement. This dimension might be pictured as extending from a *passive* attitude or low stakes to an *active* orientation involving high stakes.

FRAMEWORK FOR VIEWING INTERGROUP CONFLICT

Figure 1 pictures the possibilities within each of the three major orientations just described. These orientations (three vertical columns in Figure 1) are:

1. Conflict inevitable. Agreement impossible.
2. Conflict not inevitable, yet agreement not possible.
3. Agreement possible in spite of conflict.

At the bottom of each orientation is the method of resolution likely to be used where stakes in the outcome are low. The middle shows mechanisms employed where stakes in the outcome are moderate, and the upper end shows mechanisms likely to be adopted where stakes in the outcome of the conflict are high.

All the approaches in the left-hand orientation (column) *presume a condition of win-lose between the contesting parties*. Fate strategies come into force when stakes in the outcome are low, arbitration when the stakes are moderate, and win-lose power struggles when the stakes are high.

The right-hand vertical column of the graph reflects three opposite approaches to resolving disagreement. These approaches assume that though disagreement is present, agreement can be found. The most passive orientation here is identified as "smoothing over." This approach involves such well-known cultural phenomena as efforts to achieve intergroup cohesion and co-existence without really solving problems. The assumption is that somehow or another, peaceful co-existence will arise and that people will act in accordance with it.

The more active agreement contains the element of splitting differences. This is a more positive (active) approach than smoothing over differences, but it leaves much to be desired for it often produces only temporary resolution.

In the upper right-hand corner is the orientation of problem solving. This position identifies the circumstances under which the contesting parties search out the rationale of their agreements as well as the bases of their disagreements. It also identifies the causes for reservations and doubts of both parties. Here, the parties work toward the circumstances which will eliminate reservations. This climate affords the opportunity to actively explore means for achieving true agreement on issues without "smoothing over" or compromising differences. . . .

SUMMARY

As a group member, whether leader or member, *an individual is a representative of his group* whenever he interacts with others in different groups, provided the

FIGURE 1 • THE THREE BASIC ASSUMPTIONS TOWARD INTERGROUP DISAGREEMENTS AND THEIR MANAGEMENT

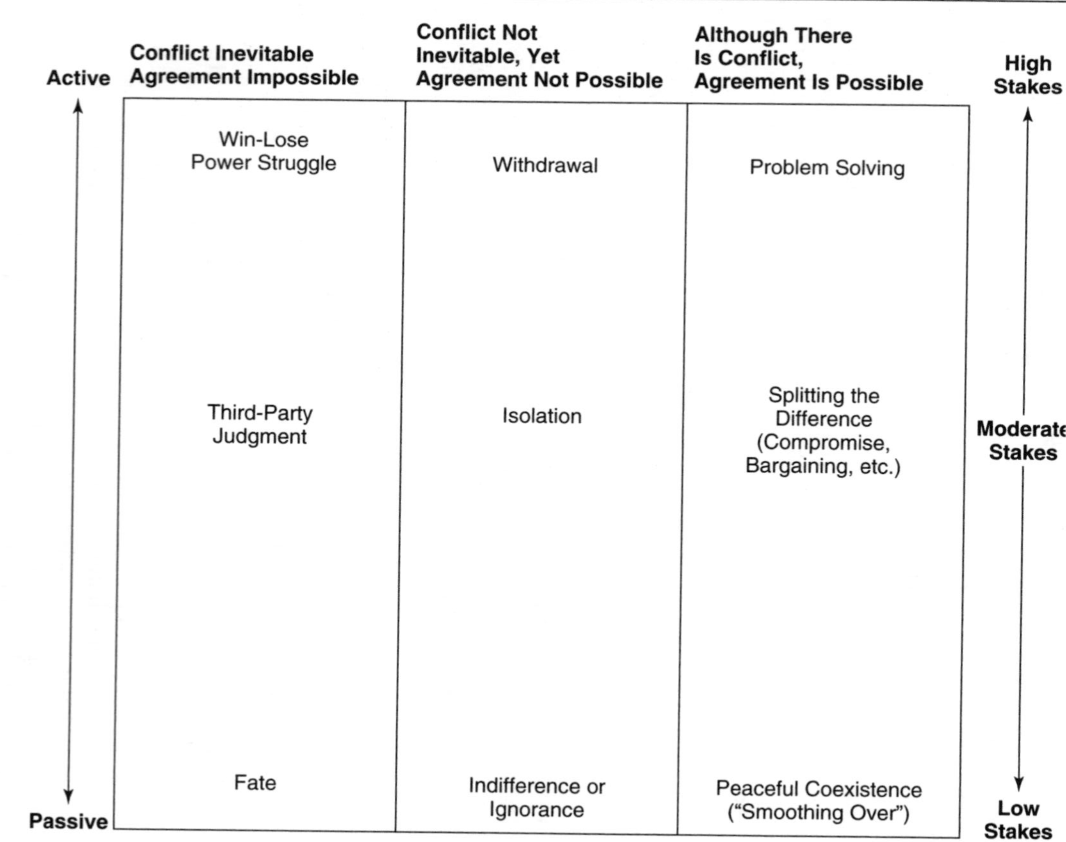

groups are in some way interdependent. As a representative, a group member's opinions and attitudes are shaped by the goals, norms and values he shares with others of his group. Normal rules of conduct and the expectations of others in his group do not allow him to act independently of his group's interests when areas of disagreement arise between his group and another.

Large organizations are composed of many small groups. Because of the size, complexity and nature of present-day organizations, group comparisons, particularly of an invidious character, are bound to occur. Under such circumstances, differences, rather than similarities and commonness of purpose, are highlighted, with conflict the inevitable result. The result is that organizational needs for interdependence and cooperation among groups are not met as well as they might have been, had managerial personnel applied greater understanding to intergroup relations.

Three basic orientations to intergroup disagreement, in combination with these different degrees of "stake in the outcome," and their accompanying approaches for achieving resolution were outlined. . . .

REFERENCES

1. Sheppard, H. L. "Approaches to Conflict in American Industrial Sociology." *Brit. J. Sociol.*, 5, 1954, 324–341.
2. Blake, R. R. "Psychology and the Crisis of Statesmanship." *Amer. Psychologist*, 14, 1959, 87–94. Blake, R. R. and Mouton, J. S., *Group Dynamics—Key to Decision Making*. Houston: Gulf Publishing Co., 1961, 87.
3. Faris, R. E. L. "Interaction Levels and Intergroup Relations." In. M. Sherif (Ed.), *Intergroup Relations and Leadership*. New York: John Wiley and Sons, Inc., 1962, 24–45.
4. Stogdill, R. M. Intragroup-Intergroup Theory and Research. In M. Sherif (Ed.), *Intergroup Relations and Leadership*. New York: John Wiley and Sons, Inc., 1962, 48–65.
5. Sherif, M. and Sherif C. *Outline of Social Psychology* (revised). New York: Harper & Bros., 1956.
6. Cartwright, D. and Zander, A. *Group Dynamics: Research and Theory* (2nd edition). Evanston, Ill.: Row, Peterson, & Co., 1960.
7. Hamblin, R. L., Miller, K. and Wiggins, J. A. "Group Morale and Competence of the Leader," *Sociometry*, 24 (3), 1961, 295–311.
8. Sherif, M. and Sherif, C. W. *Outline of Social Psychology* (revised), *op. cit.*
9. Cartwright, D. and Zander, A. *Group Dynamics: Research and Theory* (1st edition). Evanston, Ill.: Row, Peterson & Co., 1953.
10. Gerard, H. B. "The Anchorage of Opinion in Face to Face Groups," *Human. Relat.*, 7, 1954, 313–325; and Kelley, H. H. and Volkart, E. H., "The Resistance to Change of Group Anchored Attitudes," *Amer. Sociol. Rev.*, 17, 1952, 453–465.
11. Pryer, M. W., Flint, A. W., and Bass, B. M. "Group Effectiveness and Consistency of Leadership," *Sociometry*, 25 (4), 1962, 391; and Sherif, M. and Sherif, C. W. *Outline of Social Psychology* (revised), *op. cit.*
12. Arensberg, C. H. "Behavior and Organization: Industrial Studies." In J. H. Rohrer and M. Sherif (eds.), *Social Psychology at the Crossroads*. New York: Harper & Bros., 1951.
13. Cooper, H. C. "Perception of Subgroup Power and Intensity of Affiliation with a Large Organization." *Amer. Sociol. Rev.*, 26, (2) 1961, 272–274.
14. Wolman, B. B. "Impact of Failure on Group Cohesiveness," *J. Soc. Psychol.*, 51, 1960, 409–418.
15. Sherif, M. and Sherif, C. W. *Outline of Social Psychology* (revised), *op. cit.*
16. Sayles, L. R. "The Impact of Incentives on Intergroup Relations: Management and Union Problem," *Personnel*, 28, 1952, 483–490.
17. Spriegel, W. R. and Lansburgh, R. H. *Industrial Management* (5th edition). New York: John Wiley, 1955; and Strauss, G. and Sayles, L. R. *Personnel*. Englewood Cliffs, N.J.: Prentice-Hall, 1960.
18. Sherif, M. "Superordinate Goals in the Reduction of Intergroup Conflict." *Amer. J. Sociol.*, 43, 1958, 394–356.
19. Strauss, G. "Group Dynamics and Intergroup Relations." In W. F. White (Ed.), *Money and Motivation*. New York: Harper & Bros., 1955, 90–96.

20. Sherif, M. and Sherif, C. W. *Outline of Social Psychology* (revised), *op. cit.*

21. Cohen, A. R. "Upward Communication in Experimentally Created Hierarchies," *Human Relat.*, 11, 1958, 41–53; Kelley, H. H. "Communication in Experimentally Created Hierarchies," *Human Relat.*, 4, 1951, 39–56; and Thibaut, J. "An Experimental Study of the Cohesiveness of Under-Privileged Groups," *Human Relat.*, 3, 1950, 251–278.

22. Blake, R. R. and Mouton, J. S. "Comprehension of Own and Outgroup Position Under Intergroup Competition," *J. Confl. Resolut.*, 5 (3), 1961, 304–310.

19
Origins of Group Dynamics

Dorwin Cartwright and Alvin Zander

Whether one wishes to understand or to improve human behavior, it is necessary to know a great deal about the nature of groups. . . .

What, then, is group dynamics? The phrase has gained popular familiarity since World War II but, unfortunately, with its increasing circulation its meaning has become imprecise. According to one rather frequent usage, group dynamics refers to a sort of political ideology concerning the ways in which groups should be organized and managed. This ideology emphasizes the importance of democratic leadership, the participation of members in decisions, and the gains both to society and to individuals to be obtained through cooperative activities in groups. The critics of this view have sometimes caricatured it as making "togetherness" the supreme virtue, advocating that everything be done jointly in groups that have and need no leader because everyone participates fully and equally. A second popular usage of the term group dynamics has it refer to a set of techniques, such as role playing, buzz-sessions, observation and feedback of group process, and group decision, which have been employed widely during the past decade or two in training programs designed to improve skill in human relations and in the management of conferences and committees. These techniques have been identified most closely with the National Training Laboratories whose annual training programs at Bethel, Maine, have become widely known. According to the third usage of the term group dynamics, it refers to a field of inquiry dedicated to achieving knowledge about the nature of groups, the laws of their development, and their interrelations with individuals, other groups, and larger institutions.

. . . [We] shall limit our usage of the term group dynamics to refer to the field of inquiry dedicated to advancing knowledge about the nature of group life.

Group dynamics, in this sense, is a branch of knowledge or an intellectual specialization. Being concerned with human behavior and social relationships, it can be located within the social sciences. And yet it cannot be identified readily as a subpart of any of the traditional academic disciplines. . . .

In summary, then, we have proposed that group dynamics should be defined as a field of inquiry dedicated to advancing knowledge about the nature of groups, the laws of their development, and their interrelations with individuals, other groups, and larger institutions. It may be identified by four distinguishing characteristics: (*a*) an emphasis on theoretically significant empirical research, (*b*) an interest in dynamics and the interdependence among phenomena,

Source: From *Group Dynamics*, 3rd ed., by Dorwin Cartwright and Alvin Zander, pp. 4–21. Copyright © 1968 by Dorwin Cartwright and Alvin Zander. Reprinted by permission of HarperCollins Publishers, Inc.

(*c*) a broad relevance to all the social sciences, and (*d*) the potential applicability of its findings in efforts to improve the functioning of groups and their consequences on individuals and society. Thus conceived, group dynamics need not be associated with any particular ideology concerning the ways in which groups should be organized and managed nor with the use of any particular techniques of group management. In fact, it is a basic objective of group dynamics to provide a better scientific basis for ideology and practice.

CONDITIONS FOSTERING THE RISE OF GROUP DYNAMICS

Group dynamics began, as an identifiable field of inquiry, in the United States toward the end of the 1930s. Its origination as a distinct specialty is associated primarily with Kurt Lewin (1890–1947) who popularized the term group dynamics, made significant contributions to both research and theory in group dynamics, and in 1945 established the first organization devoted explicitly to research on group dynamics. Lewin's contribution was of great importance, but, as we shall see in detail, group dynamics was not the creation of just one person. It was, in fact, the result of many developments that occurred over a period of several years and in several different disciplines and professions. Viewed in historical perspective, group dynamics can be seen as the convergence of certain trends within the social sciences and, more broadly, as the product of the particular society in which it arose. . . .

A SUPPORTIVE SOCIETY

. . . In the 1930s significant resources were being allotted to the social sciences. The dramatic use of intelligence testing during World War I had stimulated research on human abilities and the application of testing procedures in school systems, industry, and government. "Scientific management," though slow to recognize the importance of social factors, was laying the groundwork for a scientific approach to the management of organizations. The belief that the solution of "social problems" could be facilitated by systematic fact-finding was gaining acceptance. . . . Thus, when the rapid expansion of group dynamics began after World War II, there were important segments of American society prepared to provide financial support for such research. Support came not only from academic institutions and foundations but also from business, the Federal Government, and various organizations concerned with improving human relations.

DEVELOPED PROFESSIONS

. . . Before considering the social scientific background of group dynamics, we will describe briefly some of the developments within the professions that facilitated its rise.

By the 1930s a large number of distinct professions had come into existence in the United States, probably more than in any other country. Many of these worked directly with groups of people, and as they became concerned with improving the quality of their practice they undertook to codify procedures and to discover general principles for dealing with groups. It gradually became evident, more quickly in some professions than in others, that generalizations from experience can go only so far and that systematic research is required to produce a deeper understanding of group life. Thus, when group dynamics began to emerge as a distinct field, the leaders of some of the professions were well prepared to foster the idea that systematic research on group life could make a significant contribution to their professions. As a result, several professions helped to create a favorable atmosphere for the financing of group dynamics research, provided from their accumulated experience a broad systematic conception of group functioning from which hypotheses for research could be drawn, afforded facilities in which research could be conducted, and furnished the beginnings of a technology for creating and manipulating variables in experimentation on groups. Four professions played an especially important part in the origin and growth of group dynamics.

1. Social Group Work
2. Group Psychotherapy
3. Education
4. Administration

DEVELOPED SOCIAL SCIENCE

. . . A basic premise of group dynamics is that the methods of science can be employed in the study of groups. This assumption could be entertained seriously only after the more general belief had gained acceptance that man, his behavior, and his social relations can be properly subjected to scientific investigation. . . . Not until the last decades of the nineteenth century were there many people actually observing, measuring, or conducting experiments on human behavior. The first psychological laboratory was established only in 1879.

The Reality of Groups. An important part of the early progress in school science consisted in clarifying certain basic assumptions about the reality of social phenomena. The first extensions of the scientific method of human behavior occurred in close proximity to biology. Techniques of experimentation and measurement were first applied to investigations of the responses of organisms to stimulation of the sense organs and to modification of responses due to repeated stimulation. There was never much doubt about the "existence" of individual organisms, but when attention turned to groups of people and to social institutions, a great confusion arose. Discussion of these matters invoked terms like "group mind," "collective representations," "collective unconscious," and "culture." And people argued heatedly as to whether such terms refer to any real phenomena or whether they are mere "abstractions" or "analogies." On the whole, the disciplines concerned with institutions (anthropology, economics, political science, and sociology) have freely attributed concrete reality to supra-individual entities, whereas psychology, with its interest in the physiological bases of behavior, has been reluctant to admit existence to anything other than the behavior of organisms. But in all these disciplines there have been conflicts between "institutionalists" and "behavioral scientists."

It may appear strange that social scientists should get involved in philosophical considerations about the nature of reality. As a matter of fact, however, the social scientist's view of reality makes a great deal of difference to his scientific behavior. In the first place, it determines what things he is prepared to subject to empirical investigation. Lewin pointed out this fact succinctly in the following statement (22, 190):

> Labeling something as "nonexistent" is equivalent to declaring it "out of bounds" for the scientist. Attributing "existence" to an item automatically makes it a duty of the scientist to consider this item as an object of research; it includes the necessity of considering its properties as "facts" which cannot be neglected in the total

> system of theories; finally, it implies that the terms with which one refers to the item are acceptable as scientific "concepts" (rather than as "mere words").

Secondly, the history of science shows a close interaction between the techniques of research which at any time are available and the prevailing assumptions about reality. Insistence on the existence of phenomena that cannot at that time be objectively observed, measured, or experimentally manipulated accomplishes little of scientific value if it does not lead to the invention of appropriate techniques of empirical research. . . .

Development of Techniques of Research. Of extreme importance for the origin of group dynamics, then, was the shaping of research techniques that could be extended to research on groups. This process, of course, took time. It began in the last half of the nineteenth century with the rise of experimental psychology. Over the subsequent years more and more aspects of human experience and behavior were subjected to techniques of measurement and experimentation. . . . These advances were important, of course, not only for the rise of group dynamics but for progress in all the behavioral sciences.

Within this general development we may note three methodological gains contributing specifically to the rise of group dynamics.

> 1. Experiments on individual behavior in groups. As noted above, research in group dynamics is deeply indebted to experimental psychology for the invention of techniques for conducting experiments on the conditions affecting human behavior. But experimental psychology did not concern itself, at first, with social variables; it was only toward the beginning of the present century that a few investigators embarked upon experimental research designed to investigate the effects of social variables upon the behavior of individuals.
>
> 2. Controlled observation of social interaction. . . . The first serious attempts to refine methods of observation, so that objective and quantitative data might be obtained, occurred around 1930 in the field of child psychology. A great amount of effort went into the construction of categories of observation that would permit an observer simply to indicate the presence or absence of a particular kind of behavior or social interaction during the period of observation. Typically, reliability was heightened by restricting observation to rather overt interactions whose "meaning" could be revealed in a short span of time and whose classification required little interpretation by the observer. Methods were also developed for sampling the interactions of a large group of people over a long time so that efficient estimates of the total interaction could be made on the basis of more limited observations. By use of such procedures and by careful training of observers quantitative data of high reliability were obtained. The principal researchers responsible for these important advances were Goodenough (**15**), Jack (**19**), Olson (**34**), Parten (**35**), and Thomas (**44**).
>
> 3. Sociometry. . . . Of the many devices for obtaining information from group members one of the earliest and most commonly used is the sociometric test, which was invented by Moreno (**30**). Although based essentially on subjective reports of individuals, the sociometric test provides quantifiable data about patterns of attractions and repulsions existing in a group. The publication by Moreno (**30**) in 1934 of a major book based on experience with the test and the establishment in 1937 of a journal, *Sociometry*, ushered in a prodigious amount of research employing the sociometric test and numerous variations of it.

The significance of sociometry for group dynamics lay both in the provision of a useful technique for research on groups and in the attention it directed to such features of groups as social position, patterns of friendship, subgroup formation, and, more generally, informal structure.

BEGINNINGS OF GROUP DYNAMICS

By the mid-1930s conditions were ripe within the social sciences for a rapid advance in empirical research on groups. And, in fact, a great burst of such activity did take place in America just prior to the entry of the United States into World War II. This research, moreover, began to display quite clearly the characteristics that are now associated with work in group dynamics. Within a period of approximately five years several important research projects were undertaken, more or less independently of one another but all sharing these distinctive features. We now briefly consider four of the more influential of these.

EXPERIMENTAL CREATION OF SOCIAL NORMS

In 1936 Sherif (**42**) published a book containing a systematic theoretical analysis of the concept *social norm* and an ingenious experimental investigation of the origin of social norms among groups of people. Probably the most important feature of this book was its bringing together of ideas and observations from sociology and anthropology and techniques of laboratory experimentation from experimental psychology. . . .

In formulating his research problem, Sherif drew heavily upon the findings of Gestalt psychology in the field of perception. He noted that this work had established that there need not necessarily be a fixed point-to-point correlation between the physical stimulus and the experience and behavior it arouses. The frame of reference a person brings to a situation influences in no small way how he sees that situation. Sherif proposed that psychologically a social norm functions as such a frame of reference. Thus, if two people with different norms face the same situation (for example, a Mohammedan and a Christian confront a meal of pork chops), they will see it and react to it in widely different ways. For each, however, the norm serves to give meaning and to provide a stable way of reacting to the environment.

Having thus related social norms to the psychology of perception, Sherif proceeded to ask how norms arise. It occurred to him that he might gain insight into this problem by placing people in a situation that had no clear structure and in which they would not be able to bring to bear any previously acquired frame of reference or social norm. . . .

. . . Sherif's experiment consisted of placing subjects individually in the darkened room and getting judgments of the extent of apparent motion. He found that upon repeated test the subject establishes a range within which his judgments fall and that this range is peculiar to each individual. Sherif then repeated the experiment, but this time having groups of subjects observe the light and report aloud their judgments. Now he found that the individual ranges of judgment converged to a group range that was peculiar to the group. In additional variations Sherif was able to show that (**42**, 104):

> When the individual, in whom a range and a norm within that range are first developed in the individual situation, is put into a group situation, together with other individuals who also come into the situation with their own ranges and norms established in their own individual sessions, the ranges and norms tend to converge.

Moreover, "when a member of a group faces the same situation subsequently *alone*, after once the range and norm of his group have been established, he perceives the situation in terms of the range and norm that he brings from the group situation" (**42**, 105).

Sherif's study did much to establish the feasibility of subjecting group phenomena to experimental investigation. . . . And his research helped establish among psychologists the view that certain properties of groups have reality, for, as he concluded, "the fact that the norm thus established is peculiar to the group suggests that there is a factual psychological basis in the contentions of social psychologists and sociologists who maintain that new and supra-individual qualities arise in the group situations" (**42**, 105).

SOCIAL ANCHORAGE OF ATTITUDES

During the years 1935–39, Newcomb (**32**) was conducting an intensive investigation of the same general kind of problem that interested Sherif but with quite different methods. Newcomb selected a "natural" rather than a "laboratory" setting in which to study the operation of social norms and social influence processes, and he relied primarily upon techniques of attitude measurement, sociometry, and interviewing to obtain his data. Bennington College was the site of his study, the entire student body were his subjects, and attitudes toward political affairs provided the content of the social norms. . . .

Newcomb's study showed that the attitudes of individuals are strongly rooted in the groups to which people belong, that the influence of a group upon an individual's attitudes depends upon the nature of the relationship between the individual and the group, and that groups evaluate members, partially at least, on the basis of their conformity to group norms. Although most of these points had been made in one form or another by writers in the speculative era of social science, this study was especially significant because it provided detailed, objective, and quantitative evidence. It thereby demonstrated, as Sherif's study did in a different way, the feasibility of conducting scientific research on important features of group life.

GROUPS IN STREET CORNER SOCIETY

The sociological and anthropological background of group dynamics is most apparent in the third important study of this era. In 1937 W. F. Whyte moved into one of the slums of Boston to begin a three and one-half year study of social clubs, political organizations, and racketeering. His method was that of "the participant observer," which had been most highly developed in anthropological research. More specifically, he drew upon the experience of Warner and Arensberg which was derived from the "Yankee City" studies. In various ways he gained admittance to the social and political life of the community and faithfully kept notes of the various happenings that he observed or heard about. In the resulting book, Whyte (**51**) reported in vivid detail on the structure, culture, and functioning of the Norton Street gang and the Italian Community Club. The importance of these social groups in the life of their members and in the political structure of the larger society was extensively documented. . . .

The major importance of this study for subsequent work in group dynamics was three-fold: (*a*) It dramatized, and described in painstaking detail, the great significance of groups in the lives of individuals and in the functioning of larger social systems. (*b*) It gave impetus to the interpretation of group properties and processes in terms of interactions among individuals. (*c*) It generated a number of hypotheses concerning the relations among such variables as initiation of interaction, leadership, status, mutual obligations, and group cohesion. These hypotheses have served to guide much of Whyte's later work on groups as well as the research of many others.

EXPERIMENTAL MANIPULATION OF GROUP ATMOSPHERE

By far the most influential work in the emerging study of group dynamics was that of Lewin, Lippitt, and White (**23, 25**, Chap. 25). Conducted at the Iowa Child Welfare Research Station between 1937 and 1940, these investigations of group atmosphere and styles of leadership accomplished a creative synthesis of the various trends and developments considered above. . . .

The basic objective of this research was to study the influences upon the group as a whole and upon individual members of certain experimentally induced "group atmospheres," or "styles of leadership." Groups of ten- and eleven-year-old children were formed to meet regularly over a period of several weeks under the leadership of an adult, who induced the different group atmospheres. In creating these groups care was taken to assure their initial comparability; by utilizing the sociometric test, playground observations, and teacher interviews, the structural properties of the various groups were made as similar as possible; on the basis of school records and interviews with the children, the backgrounds and individual characteristics of the members were equated for all the groups; and the same group activities and physical setting were employed in every group.

The experimental manipulation consisted of having the adult leaders behave in a prescribed fashion in each experimental treatment, and in order to rule out the differential effects of the personalities of the leaders, each one led a group under each of the experimental conditions. Three types of leadership, or group atmosphere, were investigated: democratic, autocratic, and laissez-faire. . . . Each group, moreover, developed a characteristic level of aggressiveness, and it was demonstrated that when individual members were transferred from one group to another their aggressiveness changed to approach the new group level. An interesting insight into the dynamics of aggression was provided by the rather violent emotional "explosion" which took place when some of the groups that had reacted submissively to autocratic leadership were given a new, more permissive leader. . . .

Of major importance for subsequent research in group dynamics was the way in which Lewin formulated the essential purpose of these experiments. The problem of leadership was chosen for investigation, in part, because of its practical importance in education, social group work, administration, and political affairs. Nevertheless, in creating the different types of leadership in the laboratory the intention was not to mirror or to simulate any "pure types" that might exist in society. The purpose was rather to lay bare some of the more important ways in which leader behavior may vary and to discover how various styles of leadership influence the properties of groups and the behavior of members. As Lewin put it (**21**, 74), the purpose "was not to duplicate any given autocracy or democracy or to study an 'ideal' autocracy or democracy, but to create set-ups which would give insight into the underlying group dynamics." This statement, published in 1939, appears to be the earliest use by Lewin of the phrase group dynamics.

It is important to note rather carefully how Lewin generalized the research problem. He might have viewed this research primarily as a contribution to the technology of group management in social work or education. Or he might have placed it in the context of research on leadership. Actually, however, he stated the problem in a most abstract way as one of learning about the underlying dynamics of group life. He believed that it was possible to construct a coherent body of empirical knowledge about the nature of group life that would be meaningful when specified for any particular kind of group. Thus, he envisioned a general theory of groups that could be brought to bear on such apparently diverse matters as family life, work groups, classrooms, committees, military units, and the community. Furthermore, he saw such specific problems as leadership, status, communication, social norms, group atmosphere, and intergroup relations as part of the general problem of understanding the nature of group dynamics. . . .

SUMMARY

Group dynamics is a field of inquiry dedicated to advancing knowledge about the nature of groups, the laws of their development, and their interrelations with individuals, other groups, and larger institutions. It may be identified by its reliance upon empirical research for obtaining data of theoretical significance, its emphasis in research and theory upon the dynamic aspects of group life, its broad relevance to all the social sciences, and the potential applicability of its findings to the improvement of social practice. . . .

By the end of the 1930s several trends converged with the result that a new field of group dynamics began to take shape. The practical and theoretical importance of groups was by then documented empirically. The feasibility of conducting objective and quantitative research on the dynamics of group life was no longer debatable. And the reality of groups had been removed from the realm of mysticism and placed squarely within the domain of empirical social science. Group norms could be objectively measured, even created experimentally in the laboratory, and some of the processes by which they influence the behavior and attitudes of individuals had been determined. The dependence of certain emotional states of individuals upon the prevailing group atmosphere had been established. And different styles of leadership had been created experimentally and shown to produce marked consequences on the functioning of groups. After the interruption imposed by World War II, rapid advances were made in constructing a systematic, and empirically based, body of knowledge concerning the dynamics of group life.

REFERENCES

1. Allport, F. H. *Social psychology*. Boston: Houghton Mifflin, 1924.
2. Allport, G. W. The historical background of modern social psychology. In G. Lindzey (Ed.), *Handbook of social psychology*. Cambridge, Mass.: Addison-Wesley, 1954. Pp. 3–56.
3. Bach, G. R. *Intensive group psychotherapy*. New York: Ronald Press, 1954.
4. Bales, R. F. *Interaction process analysis*. Cambridge, Mass.: Addison-Wesley, 1950.
5. Barnard, C. I. *The functions of the executive*. Cambridge, Mass.: Harvard Univ. Press, 1938.
6. Bavelas, A. Morale and training of leaders. In G. Watson (Ed.), *Civilian morale*. Boston: Houghton Mifflin, 1942.
7. Bion, W. R. Experiences in groups. I–VI. *Human Relations*, 1948–1950, **1,** 314–320, 487–496; **2,** 13–22, 295–303; **3,** 3–14, 395–402.
8. Bogardus, E. S. Measuring social distance. *Journal of Applied Sociology*, 1925, 9, 299–308.
9. Busch, H. M. *Leadership in group work*. New York: Association Press, 1934.

10. Chapple, E. D. Measuring human relations: An introduction to the study of interaction of individuals. *Genetic Psychology Monographs*, 1940, **22,** 3–147.
11. Coyle, G. L. *Social process in organized groups*. New York: Rinehart, 1930.
12. Dashiell, J. F. Experimental studies of the influence of social situations on the behavior of individual human adults. In C. C. Murchison (Ed.), *Handbook of social psychology*. Worcester, Mass.: Clark Univ. Press, 1935. Pp. 1097–1158.
13. Follett, M. P. *The new state, group organization, the solution of popular government*. New York: Longmans, Green, 1918.
14. Follett, M. P. *Creative experience*. New York: Longmans, Green, 1924.
15. Goodenough, F. L. Measuring behavior traits by means of repeated short samples. *Journal of Juvenile Research*, 1928, **12,** 230–235.
16. Gordon, K. Group judgments in the field of lifted weights. *Journal of Experimental Psychology*, 1924; **7,** 398–400.
17. Haire, M. Group dynamics in the industrial situation. In A. Kornhauser, R. Dubin, & A. M. Ross (Eds.), *Industrial conflict*. New York: McGraw-Hill, 1954. Pp. 373–385.
18. Homans, G. C. *The human group*. New York: McGraw-Hill, 1954. Pp. 373–385.
19. Jack, L. M. An experimental study of ascendent behavior in preschool children. *Univ. of Iowa Studies in Child Welfare*, 1934, **9,** (3).
20. Lewin, K. Forces behind food habits and methods of change. *Bulletin of the National Research Council*, 1943, **108,** 35–65.
21. Lewin, K. *Resolving social conflicts*. New York: Harper, 1948.
22. Lewin, K. *Field theory in social science*. New York: Harper, 1951.
23. Lewin, K., Lippitt, R., & White, R. Patterns of aggressive behavior in experimentally created "social climates." *Journal of Social Psychology*, 1939, **10,** 271–299.
24. Likert, R. A technique for the measurement of attitudes. *Archives of Psychology*, 1932, No. 140.
25. Lippitt, R. An experimental study of authoritarian and democratic group atmospheres. *Univ. of Iowa Studies in Child Welfare*, 1940, **16** (3), 43–195.
26. Marrow, A. J. *Making management human*. New York: McGraw-Hill, 1957.
27. Mayo, E. *The human problems of an industrial civilization*. New York: Macmillan, 1933.
28. Moede, W. *Experimentelle massenpsychologie*. Leipzig: S. Hirzel, 1920.
29. Moore, H. T. The comparative influence of majority and expert opinion. *American Journal of Psychology*, 1921, **32,** 16–20.
30. Moreno, J. L. *Who shall survive?* Washington, D.C.: Nervous and Mental Diseases Publishing Co., 1934.
31. Myrdal, G. *An American dilemma*. New York: Harper, 1944.
32. Newcomb, T. M. *Personality and social change*. New York: Dryden, 1943.
33. Newstetter, W., Feldstein, M., & Newcomb, T. M. *Group adjustment, a study in experimental sociology*. Cleveland: Western Reserve Univ., School of Applied Social Sciences, 1938.
34. Olson, W. C., & Cunningham, E. M. Time-sampling techniques. *Child Development*, 1934, **5,** 41–58.
35. Parten, M. B. Social participation among preschool children. *Journal of Abnormal and Social Psychology*, 1932, **27,** 243–269.
36. Radke, M., & Klisurich, D. Experiments in changing food habits. *Journal of American Dietetics Association*, 1947, **23,** 403–409.
37. Redl, F., & Wineman, D. *Children who hate*. Glencoe, Ill.: Free Press, 1951.
38. Roethlisberger, F. J., & Dickson, W. J. *Management and the worker*. Cambridge, Mass.: Harvard Univ. Press, 1939.
39. Scheidlinger, S. *Psychoanalysis and group behavior*. New York: Norton, 1952.
40. Shaw, C. R. *The jack roller*. Chicago: Univ. of Chicago Press, 1939.
41. Shaw, M. E. A comparison of individuals and small groups in the rational solution of complex problems. *American Journal of Psychology*, 1932, **44,** 491–504.
42. Sherif, M. *The psychology of social norms*. New York: Harper, 1936.
43. Slavson, S. R. *Analytic group psychotherapy*. New York: Columbia Univ. Press, 1950.
44. Thomas, D. S. An attempt to develop precise measurement in the social behavior field. *Sociologus*, 1933, **9,** 1–21.
45. Thomas, W. I., & Znaniecki, F. *The Polish peasant in Europe and America*. Boston: Badger, 1918.
46. Thrasher, F. *The gang*. Chicago: Univ. of Chicago Press, 1927.

47. Thurstone, L. L. Attitudes can be measured. *American Journal of Sociology*, 1928, **33,** 529–554.

48. Thurstone, L. L., & Chave, E. J. *The measurement of attitude*. Chicago: Univ. of Chicago Press, 1929.

49. Triplett, N. The dynamogenic factors in pacemaking and competition. *American Journal of Psychology*, 1897, **9,** 507–533.

50. Watson, G. B. Do groups think more effectively than individuals? *Journal of Abnormal and Social Psychology*, 1928, **23,** 328–336.

51. Whyte, W. F. Jr. *Street corner society*. Chicago: Univ. of Chicago Press, 1943.

52. Whyte, W. H. Jr. *The organization man*. New York: Simon and Schuster, 1956.

53. Wilson, A. T. M. Some aspects of social process. *Journal of Social Issues*, 1951 (Suppl. Series 5).

54. Wilson, G., & Ryland, G. *Social group work practice*. Boston: Houghton Mifflin, 1949.

20
An Intergroup Perspective on Group Dynamics

Clayton P. Alderfer

INTRODUCTION

The study of intergroup relations brings to bear a variety of methods and theories from social science on a diverse set of difficult social problems (Allport 1954; Merton 1960; Sherif and Sherif 1969; Van Den Berge 1972; Pettigrew 1981). Taken literally, intergroup relations refer to activities *between* and *among* groups. Note that the choice of preposition is significant. Whether people observe groups only two at a time or in more complex constellations has important implications for action and for understanding. Intergroup concepts can explain a broader range of phenomena than just what goes on at the intersection of two or more groups. The range of concern is from how individuals think as revealed in studies of prejudice and stereotyping to how nation states deal with each other in the realm of international conflict. A central feature of virtually all intergroup analysis is the persistently problematic relationship between individual people and collective social processes. . . .

A THEORY OF INTERGROUP RELATIONS AND ORGANIZATIONS

In the two preceding sections I sought to establish two metatheoretical points. The first was to establish intergroup theory in general as a way of thinking about problems of human behavior; the aim was to distinguish intergroup theory from nonintergroup theory. The second was to determine dimensions on which particular versions of intergroup theory varied from one another; the objective was to differentiate among versions of intergroup theories. This section now presents a particular version of intergroup theory.

According to the dimensions of difference among intergroup theories, it has the following properties:

1. The group is the primary level of analysis.
2. Groups appear embedded in social systems.
3. The orientation toward research is clinical.
4. Concepts from the theory apply to researchers as well as to respondents. . . .

Definition of Groups in Organizations

Within the social psychology literature there is no shortage of definitions of groups, but there is also no clear consensus among those who propose definitions (Cartwright and Zander, 1968). Because much work leading to these definitions has been done by social psychologists studying internal properties of groups in laboratories, the resulting

Source: From *Handbook of Organizational Behavior*, Jay W. Lorsch, ed., Prentice-Hall, Inc., 1987. Reprinted by permission of the author. This research was sponsored by the Organizational Effectiveness Research Programs, Office of Naval Research (Code 442OE, Contract No. N00014-82-K-0715).

concepts have been comparatively limited in recognizing the external properties in groups. Looking at groups in organizations, however, produces a definition that gives more balanced attention to both functional and external properties.

> A human group is a collection of individuals (1) who have significantly interdependent relations with each other. (2) who perceive themselves as a group, reliably distinguishing members from nonmembers, (3) whose group identity is recognized by nonmembers, (4) who, as group members acting alone or in concert, have significantly interdependent relations with other groups, and (5) whose roles in the group are therefore a function of expectations from themselves, from other group members, and from nongroup members (Alderfer 1977a).

This idea of a group begins with individuals who are interdependent, moves to the sense of the group as a significant social object whose boundaries are confirmed from inside and outside, recognizes that the group as a whole is an interacting unit through representatives or by collective action, and returns to the individual members whose thoughts, feelings, and actions are determined by forces within the individual and from both members and nongroup members. This conceptualization of a group makes every individual member into a group representative wherever he or she deals with members of other groups and treats transactions among individuals as at least, in part, intergroup events (Rice 1969; Smith 1977).

Figure 1 shows an "intergroup transaction between individuals." This is another way of reconceptualizing what may usually be thought of as an interpersonal transaction. In the diagram, there are three classes of forces corresponding to intrapersonal, intragroup, and intergroup dynamics. The general point is that any exchange between people is subject to all three kinds of forces; most people (including behavioral scientists) tend to understand things mainly in intrapersonal or interpersonal terms. Which class of forces becomes most dominant at any time depends on how the specific dimensions at each level of analysis differentiate the individuals. Suppose I_1 is a male engineering supervisor and I_2 is a female union steward. Intrapersonally I_1 prefers abstract thinking and demonstrates persistent difficulty in expressing feelings; I_2 prefers concrete thinking and shows ease in expressing feelings. G_1 is a predominantly male professional group that communicates to I_1 that he at all times should stay in control and be rational. G_2 is a predominantly female clerical group that communicates to I_2 that she should be more assertive about the needs of the G_2s. The I-G $_{1\text{-}2}$ relationship includes ten years of labor-management cooperation punctuated by a series of recent strike (from the labor side) and termination (from the management side) threats. The tradition in much of behavioral-science intervention is to focus on the I dynamics and to give little or no attention to G or I-G forces (Argyris 1962; Walton 1969).

By viewing transactions between individuals from an intergroup perspective, an observer learns to examine the condition of each participant's group, the relationship of the participants to their groups, and the relationship between groups represented by participants as well as their personalities in each "interpersonal" relationship. . . .

Properties of Intergroup Relations

Research on intergroup relations has identified a number of properties characteristic of intergroup relations, regardless of the particular groups or the specific

FIGURE 1 • INTERGROUP TRANSACTION BETWEEN INDIVIDUALS

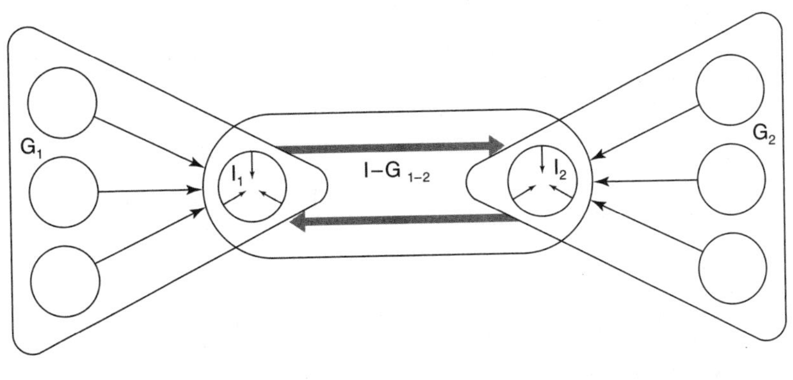

setting where the relationship occurs (Sumner 1906; Coser 1956; Van Den Berge 1972; Levine and Campbell 1972; Billig 1976; Alderfer 1977a). These phenomena include

1. Group boundaries. Group boundaries, both physical and psychological, determine who is a group member and regulate transactions among groups by variations in their permeability (Alderfer 1977b). Boundary permeability refers to the ease with which boundaries can be crossed.

2. Power differences. Groups differ in the types or resources they can obtain and use (Lasswell and Kaplan 1950). The variety of dimensions on which there are power differences and the degree of discrepancy among groups on these dimensions influence the degree of boundary permeability among groups.

3. Affective patterns. The permeability of group boundaries varies with the polarization of feeling among the groups; that is, to the degree that group members split their feelings so that mainly positive feelings are associated with their own group and mainly negative feelings are projected onto other groups (Sumner 1906; Coser 1956; Levine and Campbell 1972).

4. Cognitive formations, including "distortions." As a function of power differences and affective patterns, groups tend to develop their own language (or elements of language, including social categories), condition their members' perceptions of objective and subjective phenomena, and transmit sets of propositions—including theories and ideologies—to explain the nature of experiences encountered by members and to influence relations with other groups (Sherif and Sherif 1969; Blake, Shepard, and Mouton 1964; Tajfel 1970; Billig 1976).

5. Leadership behavior. The behavior of group leaders and of members representing a group reflects the boundary permeability, power differences, affective patterns, and cognitive formations of their group in relation to other groups. The behavior of group representatives, including formally designated leaders, is both cause and effect of the total pattern of intergroup behavior in a particular situation.

Group Relations in Organizations

Every organization consists of a large number of groups, and every organization member represents a number of these groups in dealing with other people in the organization. The full set of groups in an organization can be divided into two broad classes: identity groups and organizational groups. An identity group may be thought of as a group whose members share some common biological characteristic (such as gender), have participated in equivalent historical experiences (such as migration), currently are subjected to similar social forces (such as unemployment), and as a result have consonant world views. The coming together of world views by people who are in the same group occurs because of their having like experiences *and* developing shared meanings of these experiences through exchanges with other group members. As people enter organizations they carry with them their ongoing membership in identity groups based on variables such as their ethnicity, gender, age, and family. An organizational group may be conceived of as one whose members share (approximately) common organizational positions, participate in equivalent work experiences, and, as a consequence, have consonant organizational views. Organizations assign their members to organizational groups based on division of labor and hierarchy of authority. One critical factor in understanding intergroups in organizations is that identity-group membership and organizational-group membership are frequently highly related. Depending on the nature of the organization and the culture in which it is embedded, certain organizational groups tend to be populated by members of particular identity groups. In the United States, for example, upper-management positions tend to be held by older white males, and certain departments and ranks tend to be more accepting of females and minorities than others (Loring and Wells 1972; Purcell and Cavanagh 1972).

Considering the definition of a human group given above, we can observe how both identity groups and organizational groups fit the five major criteria. First, identity-group members have significant interdependencies because of their common historical experiences, and organizational groups, because of their equivalent work or organizational experiences, which result in their sharing similar fates even though members may be unaware of their relatedness or even actively deny it. Second, organization-group and identity-group members can reliably distinguish themselves as members from nonmembers on the basis of either identity factors (ethnicity, gender, etc.) or of location in the organization. However, the precision of this identification process can vary, depending on both the permeability of group boundaries and the fact that many groups overlap significantly, with individuals having multiple group memberships. A similar point applies to the third definitional characteristic, the ability of nonmembers to recognize members; this again will vary, depending on the permeability of the group's boundaries. The less permeable the boundaries, the more easily recognizable are members. The fourth and fifth aspects of the definition are highly linked when applied to identity and organizational groups. For example, members may be more or less aware of the extent to which they are acting, or being seen, as group representatives when relating to individuals from other groups. Every person has a number of identity- and organizational-group memberships. At any given moment an individual may be simultaneously a member of a large number, if not all, of these groups. However, which group will be focal at the moment will depend on who else representing which other groups is present and what identity-group and organizational-group issues are critical in the current intergroup exchanges. A white person in a predominantly black organization, for example, can rarely escape representing "white people" at some level, regardless of performance. But the same white person placed in a predominantly white organization will not be seen as representing "white people," but rather some other group, such as a particular hierarchical level. Rarely are individuals "just people" when they act in organizations. When there are no other group representatives present, individuals may experience themselves as "just people" in the context of their own group membership, but this subjective experience will quickly disappear when the individual is placed in a multiple-group setting. How group members relate to each other within their group, and to the expectations placed upon them by others, is highly dependent on the nature of both the intragroup and intergroup forces active at the time. . . .

Organizational Groups. The essential characteristic of organizational groups is that individuals belong to them as a function of negotiated exchange between the person and the organization. Often the exchange is voluntary, as when a person decides to work to earn a living or volunteers to work for a community agency. But the exchange may also be involuntary, as when children must attend school, draftees must join the military, and convicted criminals must enter a prison. Regardless of whether the exchange about entry is voluntary or involuntary, becoming an organizational member assigns a person to membership in both a task group and a hierarchical group. A person who stops being an organization member, for whatever reason, also gives up membership in the task and hierarchical groups. In this way task-group and hierarchical group memberships differ from identity-group affiliations.

Task-group membership arises because of the activities (or, in some unusual cases, such as prisons or hospitals, inactivities) members are assigned to perform. The activities typically have a set of objectives, role relationships, and other features that shape the task-group members' experiences. As a result, people develop a perspective on their own group, other groups, and the organization as a whole, which in turn shapes their behavior and attitudes.

Membership in task groups also tends to be transferable from one organization to another because people can carry the knowledge and skills necessary to perform particular tasks with them if they leave one system and attempt to join another. As a function of developing and maintaining certain knowledge and skills, people may belong to known professional or semiprofessional organizations outside their employing (or confining) organizations. Support from these "outside interest groups" may help people achieve more power within the system where they are working, and it may make it more possible for them to leave one system and join another.

Hierarchical-group membership is assigned by those in the system with the authority to determine rank in the system. The determination of a member's hierarchical position in an organization is typically a carefully controlled, and often highly secret, process. One's place in the hierarchy determines one's legitimate authority, decision-making autonomy, scope of responsibility, and frequently, access to benefits of membership. Group effects of the hierarchy arise from the nature of the work required of people who occupy the different levels, from the various personal attributes that the work calls for from incumbents, and from the relations that develop between people who occupy different positions in the hierarchy (Smith 1982; Oshry 1977). . . .

No one who belongs to an organization escapes the effects of hierarchy. Finer differentiations than the three offered here (e. g., upper upper, lower middle, etc.) can be made, but the same basic structure will be repeated within the microcosm of finer distinctions. The effects of hierarchy are "system" characteristics; anyone occupying a particular position in the hierarchy will tend to show the traits associated with that level.

Figure 2 provides a schematic to show the intersection of identity and organization groups. There is an inevitable tension between the two classes of the groups as long as there are systematic processes that allocate people to organization groups as a function of their identity groups. Sometimes these processes are called "institutional discrimination." (Thought question: how many 30-year-old [age group too young] Greek [ethnic group nondominant] women do you know of who are presidents of major corporations?) There is usually enough tension among organization groups to occupy the emotional energies of the top group, who have the task of managing group boundaries and transactions. Thus, unless there are special forces to strengthen the boundaries of identity groups within organizations (i.e., give them more authority), the inclination of those in senior positions will be to manage only in terms of organization groups. The manner in which an organization is embedded in its environment and the relations among identity groups in that environment will affect the degree to which management processes respond to identity *and* organization groups or just to organization groups. . . .

Embedded-Intergroup Relations

Any intergroup relationship occurs within an environment shaped by the suprasystem in which it is embedded. In observing an intergroup relationship one has several perspectives.

FIGURE 2 • IDENTITY AND ORGANIZATION GROUPS

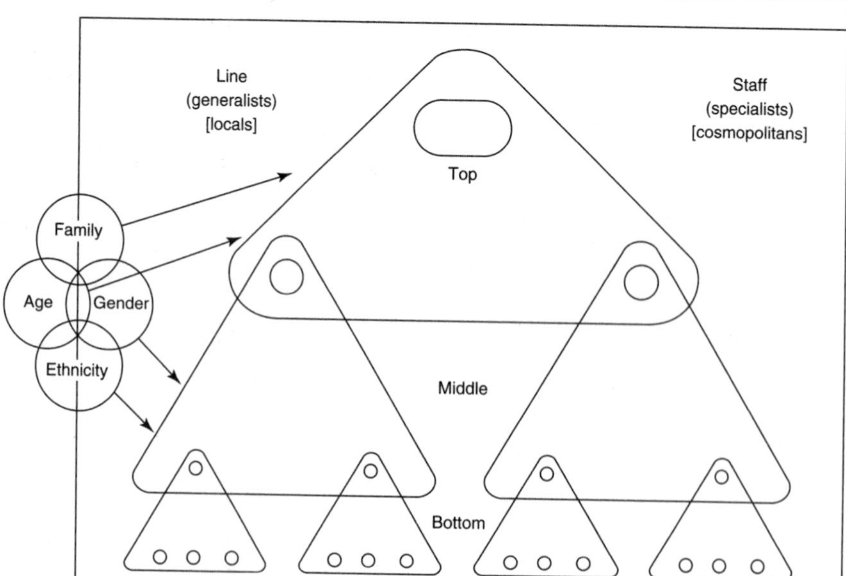

1. The effects on individuals who represent the groups in relation to one another
2. The consequences for subgroups within groups as the groups deal with one another
3. The outcomes for groups as a whole when they relate to significant other groups
4. The impact of suprasystem forces on the intergroup relationship in question

Regardless of which level one observes, the phenomenon of "interpenetration" among levels will be operating. Individuals carry images of their own and other groups as they serve in representational roles (Berg 1978; Wells 1980). Subgroup splits within face-to-face groups reflect differing degrees of identification and involvement with the group itself, which are in turn shaped by the relationship of the group as a whole to other groups. Then the group as a whole develops a sense—which may be more or less unconscious—of how its interests are cared for or abused by the suprasystem. The concept of embedded-intergroup relations applies to both identity and task groups (Alderfer and Smith 1982). . . .

Figure 3 shows how intergroup dynamics might be exhibited in the dynamics within a ten-person work group. The work group has four subgroups identified by dashed lines. Viewed exclusively from the perspective of intragroup dynamics, the work group is affected only by the individual and subgroup processes inside the group. An intergroup perspective, however, suggests that the subgroups inside the work group represent memberships in groups that exist beyond the boundaries of the work unit as indicated by the dotted lines. Suppose I_3 is a new female group leader, having recently joined the group from outside; I_1 and I_2 are men closely associated with the former male group leader; I_4, I_5, and I_6 are junior male members of the work team; and I_7, I_8, $I_9$and I_{10} are junior female members of the work team. During the period of transition, and probably subsequent to it as well, embedded-intergroup theory would predict that the relationship between the new female leader and the senior men would be affected by the authority of women in the total system, and that the relationship between the junior men and junior women in the work group would be changed by the group as a whole gaining a female leader. . . .

APPLICATION OF THE INTERGROUP THEORY TO SELECTED PROBLEMS

As a general perspective on group behavior in organizations, the intergroup theory may be used to address a variety of human problems. In this concluding section . . . I selected each of the problems because it has been a subject of my attention during the last several years. The problems are,

> understanding organizational culture; responding to minorities and white women in predominantly white male organizations.

Understanding Organizational Culture

As investigators and consultants have shifted their concerns from small groups to the organization as a whole, there has been a corresponding search for concepts that offer the possibility of giving a holistic formulation to the total system. The notion of an organizational culture has, in part, emerged from this quest.[1] From the standpoint of this paper, the key question is What sort of

[1] The concept of organizational culture serves other functions as well, and not all organizational culture researchers are concerned with viewing organizations holistically.

FIGURE 3 • INTERGROUP DYNAMICS EMBEDDED IN A SMALL GROUP

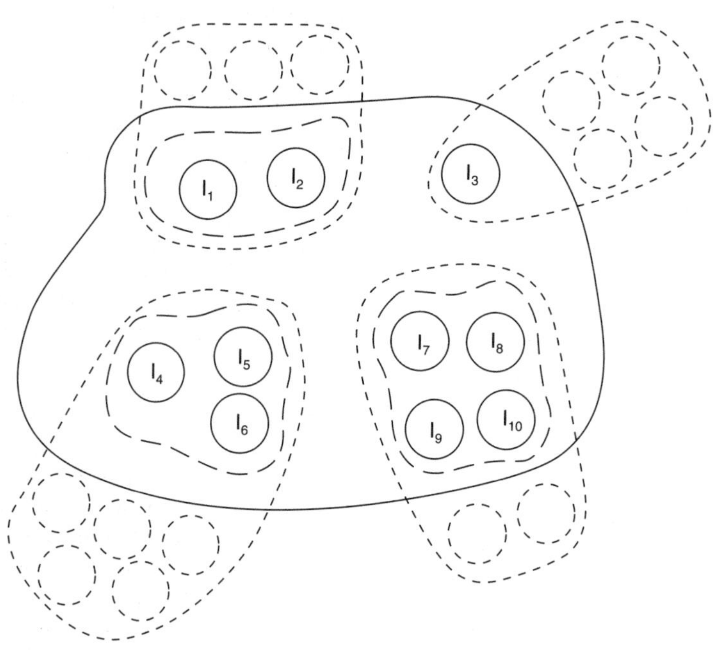

intellectual conversation might occur between the theorist of organizational culture and the intergroup theorist? . . .

Martin and Siehl (1982) . . . use the concept of subculture. In their case, they propose the notion of a "counterculture" formed around a charismatic figure who provides a sensitively balanced set of assumptions and behaviors that offer an alternative to the dominant culture. Their empirical material is drawn from the activities of John DeLorean when he was a senior executive with General Motors.

The notion of subcultures, of course, suggests an intergroup perspective, but it does not explicitly propose that view. Rather, the term *sub*culture implies that the diversity of cultures is really *sub*ordinate to the main culture, or perhaps, that subculture is the theorist's way of accommodating to data that are obviously present but do not quite fit a "one-group" view of cultural dynamics. What if the idea of organizational culture were viewed as a multiple-group phenomenon?

A study by McCollom (1983) provides data that were gathered and analyzed from a multiple-group perspective. Her work is especially interesting because she initially expected to find a single culture but emerged from her research to write about the cultures of the BCD School. Her own words state,

> I began this study expecting to be able to identify a culture which typified BCD. Instead, I found a number of distinct subcultures residing in the major groups in the School (students, faculty, and staff). The interaction of these cultures seemed to

> produce an organizational culture that was far from homogeneous. In fact, conflict between the groups seemed to become part of the culture of the whole system (e.g., the generally held expectation that the staff and faculty would disagree). My hypothesis is that the relative power of each of the groups over time in the organization is a major factor in determining the culture.

This statement exemplifies an intergroup view of organizational culture. It makes the culture of the whole system a product of the cultures of key groups in the system *in interaction with one another.* In McCollom's study the predominant pattern of interaction between at least two of these groups was conflictual. Conflict, however, need not be the major style of intergroup transaction for the organization culture to be usefully conceptualized as a dynamic intergroup pattern.

An important difference between the work of McCollom and that of . . . Martin and Siehl (1982) may be their own roles and group memberships in relation to the cultures they described. . . . Martin and Siehl were outsiders who read published materials about GM and DeLorean and who interviewed people who had been close to the scene. McCollom was a member of the organizations she studied and was committed to examining the perspectives her group memberships gave her on the system she studied. It is likely that . . . Martin and Siehl were prevented from fully seeing the multiple-group qualities of the organizations they studied, because they permitted themselves to become mainly associated with just one group. I suggest again that the intergroup relationships of investigators and how those relationships are managed are likely to shape the data they obtain and the concepts derived from those findings. . . .

Responding to White Women and Minorities in Predominantly White Male Organizations

An intergroup perspective on affirmative action notably heightens the complexity of thinking and of action. Perhaps the beginning is to recognize and to accept that a white male is not only an individual but also a group condition (see Figure 1). The term *affirmative action* interpreted progressively means recognizing and changing the exclusively white-male domination of a large proportion of U.S. institutions. Acknowledging only the individual difference among white men (or any other group) and denying the group effects seriously limits what can be understood and what can be done. These limits often serve the material interests of certain groups and individuals—perhaps especially white men but also individual white women and individual members of minority groups who unconsciously or consciously have decided to cope with their group's position by using white men as models (see Davis and Watson 1982; Davis 1983; Joseph and Lewis 1981).

However, once one begins to take a multiple-group perspective, the answers do not come easily nor do the actions become obvious. In fact, there is probably an increase in group-level psychic pain associated with an increase in consciousness about both the historical and contemporary relations of one's own group to other groups. For some, there may be a wish that all oppressed groups can unite in challenging the oppressor group of white males. But then new awareness develops. An historical examination of the relation between white women and blacks reveals some periods of serious cooperation *and also* many evidences of deep-seated racism in the (white) women's movement (Joseph and Lewis 1981; Davis 1983). History also includes episodes when black men spoke against immediately developing voting rights for women (Davis 1983). Contemporary research shows evidence of black women ready to capitalize on the difficulties of black men in order to advance in predominantly white male corporate cultures (Davis and Watson 1982) and of white women in totally female interracial organizations apparently oblivious to racial dynamics unless directly confronted with the issues (Van Steenberg 1983). . . .

CONCLUSION

Intergroup perspectives began to shape the understanding of human behavior from the beginning of the twentieth century. Scholars reflecting upon such diverse events as political revolution, tribal warfare, labor-management relations, and mental illness showed an awareness of group-to-group relations in their thinking and action. In the last thirty years, numerous intergroup theories have evolved and shaped methodological traditions. Currently, these theory-method combinations can be distinguished by their relative focus on group-level concepts, attention to groups in context or in isolation, acceptance of interventionist behavior by researchers, and tendency toward examining the individual and group behavior of investigators.

Intergroup theory provides interpretations for individual, interpersonal, group, intergroup, and organizational relations. The version of intergroup theory given here uses a definition of group that is concerned with both internal and external properties. It explains intergroup dynamics in terms of group boundaries, power, affect, cognition, and leadership behavior. It examines the nature of identity and organization groups. It relates the state of intergroup relations to the suprasystem in which they are embedded. It presents an understanding of the changing relations among interdependent groups and their representatives through the operation of parallel and unconscious processes.

The theory relates to a wide array of social and organizational problems, including the development of effective work teams, the definition and management of organizational culture, the analysis and implementation of affirmative action, and the teaching of organizational behavior in management schools.

The most important implication of intergroup theory may be the reorientation it offers to those who study and teach about human behavior in groups and organizations. Mannheim was among the most prominent of twentieth-century scholars who connected the sociology of knowledge with the group memberships of writers.

> Accordingly, the products of cognitive process are already . . . differentiated because not every possible aspect of the world comes within the purview of the members of a group, but only those out of which difficulties and problems for the group arise. And even this common world (not shared by any outside groups in the same way) appears differently to subordinate groups within the larger group. It appears differently because the subordinate groups and strata in a functionally differentiated society have a different experiential approach . . . (Mannheim 1936, 29).

Intergroup theory proposes that both organization groups (e.g., being a researcher versus being a respondent) and identity groups (e.g., being a person of particular gender, age, ethnicity and family) affect one's intergroup relations and thereby shape one's cognitive formations. The body of data supporting this general proposition grows as changes in society broaden the range of identity groups who have access to research roles (see Balmary 1981; Eagly and Carli 1981; Herman 1891), and consequently the content of "well-established" empirical generalizations and conceptual frameworks are called into question. These new developments affect research and development as well as clinical methods. None of the accepted methods in their implementation escapes potential intergroup effects between researchers and respondents. Investigators who accept this idea cannot avoid questioning the part they and their groups play in the knowledge-making process. Understanding one's intergroup relationships may become a key ingredient for all who wish to study people effectively.

REFERENCES

Alderfer, C. P. 1977a. "Group and Intergroup Relations." In *Improving Life at Work*, ed. J. R. Hackman and J. L. Suttle, pp. 227–96. Santa Monica: Goodyear.

———. 1977b. "Improving Organizational Communication through Long-Term, Intergroup Intervention." *Journal of Applied Behavioral Science* 13:193–210.

Alderfer, C. P., and K. K. Smith. 1982. "Studying Intergroup Relations Embedded in Organizations." *Administrative Science Quarterly* 27:35–65.

Allport, G. W. 1954. *The Nature of Prejudice*. New York: Doubleday.

Argyris, C. 1962. *Interpersonal Competence and Organizational Effectiveness*. Homewood, Ill.: Richard D. Irwin.

Balmary, M. 1981. *Psychoanalyzing Psychoanalysis*. Baltimore: Johns Hopkins University Press.

Berg, D. N. 1978. "Intergroup Relations in Out Patient Psychiatric Facility." Ann Arbor, Mich.: University of Michigan.

Billig, M. 1976. *Social Psychology and Intergroup Relations*. London: Academic Press.

Blake, R. R., H. A. Shepard, and J. Mouton. 1964. *Managing Intergroup Conflict in Industry*. Houston: Gulf.

Cartwright, D., and A. Zander. 1968. *Group Dynamics*. 3d ed. Evanston, Ill.: Row-Peterson.

Coser, L. A. 1956. *The Functions of Social Conflict*. Glencoe, Ill.: Free Press.

Davis, A. Y. 1983. *Women, Race, and Class*. New York: Vintage Books.

Davis, G., and G. Watson. 1982. *Black Life in Corporate America*. Garden City, N.Y.: Anchor Press/ Doubleday.

Eagly, A. H., and L. L. Carli. 1981. "Sex of Researchers and Sex-Typed Communications as Determinants of Sex Differences in Influenceability: A Meta-Analysis of Social Influence Studies." *Psychological Bulletin* 90:1–20.

Herman, J. L. 1981. *Father-Daughter Incest*. Cambridge, Mass.: Harvard University Press.

Joseph, G. I., and J. Lewis. 1981. *Common Differences: Conflicts in Black and White Feminist Perspectives*. Garden City, N.Y.: Anchor Press/Doubleday.

Lasswell, H. D., and A. Kaplan. 1950. *Power and Society*. New Haven: Yale.

Levine, R. A., and D. T. Campbell. 1972. *Ethnocentrism*. New York: Wiley.

Loring, R., and T. Wells. 1972. *Breakthrough: Women into Management*. New York: Van Nostrand Reinhold.

Mannheim, Karl. 1936. *Ideology and Utopia*. New York: Harcourt Brace Jovanovich.

Martin, J., and C. Siehl. 1982. "Organizational Culture and Counterculture: An Uneasy Symbiosis." Working paper, Stanford University.

McCollom, M. 1983. "Organizational Culture: A Case Study of the BCD School." Yale School of Organization and Management Working Paper.

Merton, R. K. 1960. "The Ambivalences of LeBon's *The Crowd*." In *The Crowd*, ed. G. LeBon, pp. v–xxxix. New York: Viking.

Oshry, B. 1977. *Power and Position*. Boston: Power and Systems Training.

Pettigrew, T. P. 1981. "Extending the Stereotype Concept." In *Cognitive Processes in Stereotyping and Intergroup Behavior*, ed. D. Hamilton, pp. 303–32. Hillsdale, N.J.: Lawrence Erlbaum Associates.

Purcell, T. V., and G. F. Cavanagh. 1972. *Blacks in the Industrial World*. New York: Free Press.

Rice, A. K. 1969. "Individual, Group, and Intergroup Processes." *Human Relations* 22:565–84.

Sherif, M., and C. Sherif. 1969. *Social Psychology*. New York: Harper and Row.

Singer, E. 1965. *Key Concepts in Psychotherapy*. New York: Random House.

Smith, K. K. 1977. "An Intergroup Perspective on Individual Behavior." In *Perspectives on Behavior in Organizations*. 2d ed., ed. J. R. Hackman, E. E. Lawler, and L. W. Porter, pp. 397–407. New York: McGraw-Hill.

———. 1982. *Groups in Conflict: Prisons in Disguise*. Dubuque, Iowa: Kendall-Hunt.

Sumner, W. J. 1906. *Folkways*. New York: Ginn.

Tajfel, H. 1970. "Experiments in Intergroup Discrimination." *Scientific American* 223:96–102.

Van Den Berge, P., ed. 1972. *Intergroup Relations*. New York: Basic Books.

Van Steenberg, V. 1983. "Within White Group Differences on Race Relations at CTCGS." Yale School of Organization and Management Working Paper.

Walton, R. E. 1969. *Interpersonal Peacemaking*. Reading, Mass.: Addison-Wesley.

Wells, L. J. 1980. "The Group-as-a-Whole." In *Advances in Experimental Social Processes*, vol. 2, ed. C. P. Alderfer and C. L. Cooper, pp. 165–200. London: Wiley.

21

Cultural Diversity in Organizations: Intergroup Conflict

Taylor Cox Jr.

INTERGROUP CONFLICT DEFINED

Although writers have offered numerous different definitions of conflict, they seem to agree that conflict is an overt expression of tensions between the goals or concerns of one party and those of another. Thus the core of conflict is opposing interests of the involved parties (Rummell, 1976). In this chapter we are concerned with conflict between groups. Since all groups are composed of individuals and conflict behavior is frequently enacted by individuals, intergroup conflict may be conceived as a special case of interpersonal conflict. Intergroup conflict in the context of cultural diversity has two distinguishing features: (1) group boundaries and group differences are involved, and (2) the conflict is directly or indirectly related to culture group identities.

Concerning the second point, there are at least two reasons why a great deal of observed interpersonal conflict may be analyzed from an intergroup perspective. First, group identities are an integral part of the individual personality. Therefore, much of what is commonly referred to as "personality clash" may actually be a manifestation of group identity-related conflict. Second, there are clear cases in which the basis of conflict is endemic to the groups as well as, or instead of, the individuals involved. For example, considerable conflict has arisen in parts of Florida and California over the extent to which education will be conducted exclusively in English. The main parties to the conflict are Hispanic Americans (the majority of whom are bilingual but have Spanish as their first language) and non-Hispanic Americans, who by and large are monolingual English speakers. In this instance, the source of the conflict itself has roots in the different culture identities of the parties.

Also in the context of cultural diversity in organizations, it may be useful to note that intergroup conflict occurs between the majority group and the various minority groups represented as well as among the minority groups themselves. In the following section, sources of intergroup conflict in the context of cultural diversity in organizations will be addressed.

SOURCES OF INTERGROUP CONFLICT

As indicated in the definition above, the core element of conflict is opposing interests. A study of literature on intergroup dynamics in organizations reveals

Source: Reprinted with permission of the publisher. *Cultural Diversity in Organizations: Theory, Research & Practice*, Copyright © 1993 by Taylor H. Cox Jr., Berret-Koehler Publishers, Inc., San Francisco, CA 94104.

myriad issues, attitudes, and behaviors around which opposing interest may develop (Alderfer, Alderfer, Tucker, & Tucker, 1980; Landis & Boucher, 1987; Arnold & Feldman, 1986; Daft & Steers, 1986). In the context of cultural diversity in organizations, however, five stand out to me as particularly important. They are:

1. Competing goals
2. Competition for resources
3. Cultural differences
4. Power discrepancies
5. Assimilation versus preservation of microcultural identity . . .

Competing Goals

As previously indicated, common goals is one of the defining characteristics of culture groups. Indeed, this characteristic applies to groups of any kind. In multicultural social systems, the various groups represented may develop competing goals which then become the basis of intergroup conflict. This insight into intergroup conflict has been addressed extensively by Campbell (1965) and by Sherif (1966) in their discussions of "realistic group conflict theory. . . ."

. . . The point to be made here is that organizational functions are often characterized by very different systems of norms, goal priorities, work styles, and so on. In other words, they may be viewed as having different occupational cultures. The difference in cultures between them, partly manifested in different goals, sets the stage for intergroup conflict.

Competition for Resources

A second source of intergroup conflict is disagreement about the allocation of resources. In some cases, such as conflict between American Indians and white Americans, the bases of these conflicts are embedded in the history of intergroup relations. In other cases, such as tensions between men and women over access to executive jobs, the conflict is more directly embedded in organizational issues. Several examples will be offered.

Intergroup conflict over resources is illustrated by a recent consulting project I was involved in at a plant site of a large international telecommunications company. Several years ago, the plant hired a significant number of Laotian immigrants. Subsequently there was a major downsizing in which several hundred employees were relocated or lost their jobs. Many of the local Laotian workers survived these cuts. In interviews with African American, Hispanic American, and white American workers at the plant, all of whom are native-born, a great deal of resentment was expressed toward the plant's management and toward the Laotians themselves over the loss of jobs to "outsiders." The Laotians that I talked to were also aware of this resentment and held a certain amount of hostility of their own toward what they regarded as unfair treatment by the native-born Americans. The conflict had persisted over a period of several years and was a hindrance to the effective functioning of self-managed workteams that the plant was trying to implement.

The resource in contention in the above example (jobs) is frequently a source of intergroup conflict related to diversity. This can be seen, for example, in the recent events in European cities where immigrants, most of them non-white, are increasingly being harassed by natives who view them as unwelcome outsiders who are threatening their access to employment (see, for example, "Germans," 1991). It has also been identified as a major source of conflict between black and white Americans as well as between blacks and other racioethnic minorities. . . .

Cultural Differences

Intergroup conflict between diverse groups may also occur because of misunderstandings and misperceptions that are related to the different worldviews of culture groups. For example, Alderfer and Smith (1982) and Daft and Steers (1986) are among those citing cognitive differences between groups as a primary source of potential conflict. Alderfer and Smith describe the nature of these differences in the following way: "[Groups] condition their members' perceptions of objective and subjective phenomena and transmit a set of propositions . . . to explain the nature of experiences encountered by members to influence relations with other groups" (p. 40).

Alderfer and Smith provide one of the most startling examples of different cognitive orientations between groups from their data on perceptions of race relations in a large organization. In a study of 2,000 managers in a large corporation, they found that perceptions between whites and blacks were dramatically different. For example, they found that while 62 percent of black men and 53 percent of black women agreed that qualified whites were promoted in the company more rapidly than equally qualified blacks, the percent agreement among whites was only 4 and 7 percent respectively for men and women. They also asked the same subjects if they agreed that qualified blacks are promoted more rapidly than equally qualified whites. Here the percentages tended to be reversed, with agreement by only 12 to 13 percent of blacks versus 75 to 82 percent of whites. Since the statements are mutually exclusive, these data give a striking portrayal of how members of different groups in the same organization can see events very differently. Another revealing finding from this study concerns perceptions of nature of two support groups in the organization. The Black Managers Association was composed of black managers of all organization levels and restricted its membership to blacks. The Foreman's Club was composed of first-level supervisors, nearly all of whom were white; however, membership was open to anyone at the specified organization level. Nearly half of the white women (45 percent) and more than half of the white men (64 percent) viewed the Black Managers Association as "essentially a racist organization." This compared to only 25 and 16 percent respectively for black women and men. Alternatively, a majority of blacks (both men and women) viewed the Foreman's Club as essentially racist, while less than 20 percent of whites held this view. One could argue that the difference in eligibility criteria between two support groups left the Black Managers Association more vulnerable to charges of racism, but the point here is to note how differently whites and blacks viewed the two organizations.

These types of organizational support groups have become increasingly common in recent years (Cox, 1991) and therefore these data are relevant to one of the most ubiquitous consequences of cultural diversity in organizations. I contend that it is not the existence of such organizational support groups per se that creates conflict but rather the differences in how they are perceived. Reconciling such differences in perceptions therefore is a critical challenge for organization development work related to cultural diversity. . . .

Power Discrepancies

Majority groups as defined in this book hold advantages over minority groups in the power structure of organizations. As numerous writers have noted, this discrepancy of power is a primary source of potential conflict (Landis & Boucher, 1987; Alderfer & Smith, 1982; Randolph & Blackburn, 1989). The logic of this is straightforward. Stated simply, the "power approach" argues that intergroup hostility and antagonism are natural results of competition between groups for control of the economic, political, and social structures of social systems (Giles & Evans, 1986). On a general level, a core manifestation of the power perspective is tension between minority groups and the majority group over whether to change or preserve the status quo. . . .

. . . The power approach to explaining intergroup conflict is illustrated in tensions between majority and minority group members over the use of affirmative action in promotion decisions. Most minority group members are favorable toward affirmative action as one method to promote a redistribution of power in organizations, while many majority group members oppose it as an unwarranted and misguided policy of reverse discrimination. . . . Suffice to say, however, majority group backlash against affirmative action and similar practices are among the most serious forms of intergroup conflict in organizations. . . .

Minority Group Density. Minority group density refers to the percentage representation of a minority group in the total population of a social system. A considerable amount of research in the political science and social science fields has addressed the effects of minority group density on majority-minority relations in diverse groups (Blalock, 1967; Giles & Evans, 1986). Much of the research has focused on how minority group density affects the behavior of majority group members toward minorities. Specifically of interest has been the "minority-group-size-inequality hypothesis" (MGSI) which holds that majority group members tend to lower levels of support for, and increase levels of discrimination against, minorities when their percentage representation increases beyond a certain, relatively low, threshold (Blalock, 1967; Blau, 1977). The essence of the argument is that majority members are far less favorable toward minorities when their numbers are relatively large because they perceive them as a threat to their established power.

Blalock's empirical data on the MGSI hypothesis were largely taken from records of voting behavior among whites, and on educational and economic inequality between blacks and whites in the southern United States. He concluded that the level of educational and economic disadvantage for blacks, and the level of support of politically conservative candidates among whites, was systematically related to the percentage representation of blacks in the local area. Consistent with the MGSI hypothesis, Blalock concluded that the aforementioned conditions were more favorable toward blacks in those areas where they had small representations (Blalock, 1967). . . .

A second example is Ott's study (1989) of 297 women in two Dutch police departments. Ott found that male attitudes toward the presence of women shifted from neutral to negative when their numbers reached a critical mass (15–20 percent).

In another relevant study, Hoffman (1985) examined communications patterns in ninety-six groups with varying percentages of black and white government-agency supervisors. He predicted that communication would improve in higher-density groups because there would be less isolation and stereotyping of blacks in groups where they represented a larger percentage of the group. He found, however, that only formal communications such as in staff meetings increased in the higher-density groups. Communication on the interpersonal level actually declined as the percent non-white increased. . . .

Collectively the theory and research of MGSI provide considerable support for the idea that the distribution of power is key to majority-minority group conflict. Promotion decisions are a primary mechanism by which organizations define participation in the formal influence structure, and therefore changes here simultaneously pose a threat to the existing power structure and an opportunity for those who are relatively powerless.

Conformity Versus Identity Affirmation

The final source of interconflict to be discussed here is the tension between majority and minority group members over the preservation of minority group identity. One perspective on this source of conflict that I have found very useful is provided by Ashforth and Mael (1989) in their discussion of high-status versus low-status groups in organizations: "The identity of a low-status group is implicitly threatened by a high-status group. . . . A high-status group, however, is less likely to feel threatened and thus less in need of positive affirmation. Accordingly, while a low-status group may go to great lengths to differentiate itself from a high-status group, the latter may be relatively unconcerned about such comparisons and form no strong impression about the low-status group. This indifference of the high status group is, perhaps, the greatest threat to the identity of the low-status group because the latter's identity remains socially unvalidated" (p. 33).

Status is not defined by the authors but, based on the examples they give, appears to be closely related to the relative power and prestige of groups. Thus the majority in an organization has higher status than minority groups by definition. Having made this clarification, we can identify several important insights in the above quotation. First, it points out that minority groups will usually be much more aware of, and more concerned with, the preservation of group identity than majority group members will. Not feeling a need for "positive affirmation" themselves, they often will not understand or appreciate that members of minority groups do feel this need. The constant efforts of minority groups to affirm themselves may annoy majority group members, who view these efforts as needless differentiations that serve no useful purpose. A prime example of this in organizations is the reaction of majority group members to support groups formed by minority group members. . . . Many majority group members view these organizations with disdain. The difference in perspective regarding the need for, and desirability of, such groups often becomes the focus of intergroup tensions.

The prevalence of minority support groups throughout history attests to the fact that minority group members in majority organizations often feel a need to form such groups and their purposes are often expressly understood to include protection against a perceived threat to survival of the group (i.e., the groups are to some degree a reaction to being in a lower-status situation). Thus, in the groups of which I have been a member or had occasion to observe, the role of the group in identity affirmation has been explicitly acknowledged. On the other hand, my experience has been that majority group members often fail to realize that their opposition to minority support groups is, in part, a result of their insensitivity to the identity threat that minorities feel. The last statement of the Ashforth and Mael quotation gets at this. They refer to the indifference of the high-status group toward efforts of minority groups to differentiate and affirm themselves. As suggested previously, I have observed numerous cases where the attitude has gone beyond indifference to a hostility toward efforts of the minority group to differentiate itself. The refusal by members of a majority group to acknowledge the need for support groups leaves differences unvalidated, which minorities are quite sensitive to but majorities, by and large, are not. Thus Ashforth and Mael have hit upon an important, albeit subtle, insight into sources of intergroup conflict in organizations related to identity preservation. . . .

A final example of intergroup conflict related to identity preservation is the frequent disagreement over the use of non-majority-group languages in organizations. In my own work, this was illustrated most recently in interviews at the plant site of a large telecommunications company, referred to earlier, that employs a significant number of Laotians. Considerable tensions between Laotian and non-Laotian members of the organization existed. As previously reported, some of this was due to conflict over jobs. However, a second dimension was the preference among many of the non-Laotian members for the use of English only in communications in the workplace. Some Laotians felt that this represented an unwarranted denial of their opportunity for cultural expression as well as simply a loss of communication facility when conversing with others who knew their native language. The basis of concern among some about the use of the Laotian language revolved around a discomfort with not being able to understand proximate communication, even when it was directed to someone else, and a concern that it tended to interfere with developing English language skills. . . .

APPROACHES TO MANAGING INTERGROUP CONFLICT

Thus far in this chapter I have reviewed five primary sources of intergroup conflict related to cultural diversity in organizations. There is no question that the potential for increased conflict is a possible downside of increased diversity in workgroups. However, since diversity in many situations is a fact of life and not a choice, and since the potential benefits of diversity appear to be greater than the potential costs (Cox & Blake, 1991), the challenge for organizations is to manage the conflict. In this final section, I will briefly discuss suggestions for minimizing diversity-related intergroup conflict.

Management writers have identified common approaches to the resolution of intergroup conflict in organizations (Arnold & Feldman, 1986; Randolph & Blackburn, 1989). Table 1 shows a list of the most commonly mentioned strategies, along with my assessment of the sources of diversity-related conflict that they are most effective in addressing.

Competing Goals

As Table 1 indicates, most of the strategies offer some potential for addressing conflict resulting from competing goals. I will discuss two examples. Competing goals between marketing and manufacturing might be addressed by restructuring the organization into cross-functional workteams whose organizational rewards depend upon collaboration and joint outcomes. One of the most promising resolution techniques is to get both departments to focus attention on superordinate organizational goals such as profits and market share rather than on those of their individual

TABLE 1 • MANAGING CONFLICT IN DIVERSE WORKGROUPS

Resolution Strategies	Source of Conflict				
	Competitive Goals	Resources	Cultural Differences	Power Discrepancies	Identity Affirmation
Collaboration/negotiation/bargaining	X			X	X
Alter situation/context (e.g., organization redesign)	X	X		X	X
Procedures/rules/policies		X		X	X
Alter personnel			X		X
Alter/redefine the issues of contention	X		X	X	
Hierarchical appeal	X				
Smoothing (emphasize similarities, play down conflict)	X				
Superordinate goals	X	X			
Structured interactions	X	X	X	X	X
Integrative problem solving (mediation + compromise)	X				X

departments. As a final example, bargaining and mediation have historically been used to resolve competing interests of management and labor groups, although not always successfully, especially in recent years.

An application of superordinate goals and of smoothing that seems especially pertinent to gender, racioethnic, and nationality diversity in organizations is to capitalize on the shared group identity of the common employer. To do this successfully, minority as well as majority members of organizations have to identify with the employer and have some degree of confidence that goals of the organization and those of the microculture group are compatible if not mutually supportive.

Competition for Resources

As noted earlier, one of the most common manifestations of resource competition in the context of cultural diversity is competition over jobs. Obviously a great deal of conflict potential is eliminated when jobs are more plentiful. Thus to the extent that overall job opportunities can be expanded, the climate of intergroup relations will be improved immeasurably. Unfortunately, the expansion of resources is often not possible, especially in the short term.

In many organizations, hiring policies—such as Xerox's Balanced Workforce Plan—attempt to formally acknowledge group identities such as gender, racioethnicity, and nationality in regulating the competition for jobs. The goal is to ensure equal competition, although, as noted in previous chapters, the reaction to such plans among majority group members often heightens intergroup conflict related to job competition. Xerox has been somewhat successful at minimizing and resolving conflict related to their plan partly by paying a lot of attention to how the plan has been communicated.

The utility of superordinate goals for resolving resource-based conflict can be illustrated by considering the case of two departments vying for a larger share of a limited training budget. If both can be encouraged to plan on the basis of the training priorities of the overall organization, it may help to resolve the conflict.

Finally, as with all of the sources of conflict, structured interaction to discuss the points of contention, gain a better appreciation of the other party's perspective, and promote mutual understanding is a potentially valuable tool for resolving conflict based on resource competition.

Cultural Differences

Here I recommend three strategies for conflict resolution related to cultural differences, beginning with altering personnel. One way to achieve this goal is by educating existing personnel to obtain a better knowledge of cultural differences. Another way is to hire and promote persons with tolerant and flexible personalities who will productively support cultural-diversity change initiatives in the organization. Stated simply, people who are more tolerant and accepting of difference will produce less conflict when confronted with cultural differences than people who are not. The problem of intergroup conflict is partly due to emotional or affective reactions of individuals.

Redefining issues can also aid in cultural conflict resolution. An example of this is promoting the mindset that cultural differences present opportunities rather than problems to be solved. For example, Blau (1977) argues that increased intergroup experience stimulates intellectual endeavors. One way that this kind of redefinition is illustrated in the language of organizational relations is in the preference for the "valuing" of diversity rather than "tolerating" diversity.

Structured interaction is also usable in resolving conflict related to cultural differences. An example is the use of interdepartmental task forces. Although such groups normally have a specific work task to accomplish, time may be spent initially on activities designed to help representatives of the various departments get to know the culture of the departments better. Familiarity with the language and norms of the other groups is likely to facilitate the work on the task. Even informal meetings may be of great value. For example, during a recent consulting project with a research and development firm, several engineers and scientists spoke about how some of them had used cross-disciplinary meetings as a means of gaining understanding about the differences between their functions and how they viewed their role in the overall mission of the firm. These persons reported that the meetings had proved valuable in reducing misconceptions between the groups and that joint projects and cross-functional communications had increased as a result.

Power Discrepancies

The earlier discussion of this factor made it clear that power differences between majority and minority members of organizations are perhaps the most deadly of the conflict sources. Power discrepancies are sometimes resolved by negotiations, such as those currently under way between the government of South Africa and the African National Congress over representation of Black and White South Africans in the new government under a democratic model. Power differences may also be resolved by policies, such as designated representation of minority groups in government bodies. For example, a minimum of four seats are reserved for Maoris in the New Zealand legislature.

Another policy with obvious power redistribution objectives is affirmative action in promotion decisions. Although controversial, there is no denying the impact of affirmative action in changing and diversifying the authority structure of an organization. The substantial results of Xerox's Balanced Workforce Plan and U.S. West's Pluralism Performance Effort are two cases in point.

An example of an organization redesign to assist in resolving intergroup power conflicts is the creation of diverse groups of advisers to give direct input to senior management. U.S. West and Equitable Life Insurance are examples of companies that have created these. To the extent that such groups address issues beyond diversity, they hold the potential to make modest shifts in the power structure of organizations, even though they do not change the fundamental authority hierarchy per se.

It may also be useful to redefine issues as a means of conflict reduction. For example, what is the primary motive for using affirmative action in promotion decisions? Is it to right the wrongs of past discrimination, to address the discrimination of the present, to meet social responsibility objectives, or to meet economic responsibilities of the organization? . . . I submit that how these questions are answered, and the extent to which their answers are understood and embraced by members of organizations, has much to do with the success in resolving power-based conflict in organizations.

Finally, planned interactions between groups to discuss the existence of power discrepancies, their effects, and what to do about them are advised for majority-minority situations of all kinds.

Conflict over Conformity Versus Affirmative Identity

In this last category, a number of strategies are indicated in Table 1 as potentially effective. First, since some combination of assimilation to majority group norms and preservation of microculture norms is expected, the techniques of negotiation and compromise seem at least theoretically relevant. One example is the extent to which organizations adapt the work environment to accommodate a particular disability of an employee or potential employee. In many instances the level of accommodation will not eliminate all barriers to full participation. However, some compromise may be reached that reduces the potential for conflict between persons with disabilities seeking accommodation and fully able members who may feel that the cost of accommodations places an undue burden on the financial and social resources of the firm.

In some instances, mediation may be of help in resolving intergroup differences related to conformity. One example is when consultants on workforce diversity are asked to assist in improving relations between identity-based employee support groups and the senior management of organizations. This work includes increasing awareness among senior management of the importance of identity affirmation by members of minority groups, as well as increasing sensitivity among support-group members of senior management concerns over the existence and purposes of these groups.

An example of a structural/environmental change that organizations can make to alter conflict potential related to conformity is the selection of a mode of acculturation. . . . But suffice it to say here that an organization's choice of whether to approach acculturation using a pluralism or a traditional assimilation model has many implications for the identity-based conflict under discussion here.

Another type of identity-related conflict that was discussed above is disagreement over the use of alternative languages. Organizations may wish to address this type of conflict by establishing a policy statement about the use of alternative languages in the workplace that is sensitive to the concerns of both groups. Companies such as Esprit De Corp., Economy Color Card, and Pace Foods are examples of firms that have taken what I consider to be a sound approach by supporting the learning of alternative languages by English-only speakers and formal use of non-English languages under some conditions such as in published policy manuals (Cox, 1991).

Concerning altering personnel, the same points made earlier in this section about cultural differences apply here. Intolerant, narrow-minded people will tend to expand the scope of behaviors for which pressure is applied to conform to the norms of the majority group. It is true that restricting the hiring of persons in minority groups to those who do not have a strong concern with the preservation of microcultural identity may eliminate some potential intergroup conflict by creating a more culturally homogeneous organization. This approach is not recommended, however, because it is out of step with worldwide labor-force demographic trends and because it brings other, unaffordable costs, such as the loss of divergent cultural perspectives to enhance problem solving.

REFERENCES

Alderfer, C. P., Alderfer, C. J., Tucker, L., & Tucker, R. (1980). Diagnosing race relations in management. *Journal of Applied Behavioral Science*, *16*, 135–166.

Alderfer, C. P., & Smith, K. K. (1982), Studying intergroup relations embedded in organizations. *Administrative Science Quarterly*, *27*, 5–65.

Arnold, H., & Feldman, D. (1986). *Organizational behavior*. New York: McGraw-Hill.

Ashforth, B., & Mael, F. (1989). Social identity theory and the organization. *Academy of Management Review*, *14*(1), 20–39.

Blalock, H. Jr. (1967). *Toward a theory of minority-group relations*. New York: Wiley.

Blau, P. M. (1977). A macrosociological theory of social structure. *American Journal of Sociology*, *83*, 26–54.

Campbell, D. T. (1965). Ethnocentric and other altruistic motives. In D. Levine (Ed.), *Nebraska symposium on motivation* (pp. 283–311). Lincoln: University of Nebraska Press.

Cox, T. H. (1991). The multicultural organization. *The Executive*, *5*(2), 34–47.

Cox, T. H., & Blake, S. (1991). Managing cultural diversity: Implications for organizational competitiveness. *The Executive*, 5(3), 45–56.

Daft, R., & Steers, R. (1986). *Organizations: A micro/macro approach*. Glenview, IL: Scott-Foresman.

Germans try to stem right wing attacks against foreigners. (1991, December 4). *Wall Street Journal*.

Giles, M. W., & Evans, A. (1986). The power approach to intergroup hostility. *Journal of Conflict Resolution*, 30(3), 469–486.

Hoffman, E. (1985). The effect of race ratio composition on the frequency of organizational communication. *Social Psychology Quarterly*, 48(1), 17–26.

Landis, D., & Boucher, J. (1987). Themes and models of conflict. In J. Boucher, D. Landis, & K. A. Clark (Eds.), *Ethnic conflict: International perspectives* (pp. 18–32). Newbury Park, CA: Sage.

Ott, E. M. (1989). Effects of the male-female ratio. *Psychology of Women Quarterly, 13*, 41–57.

Randolph, W. A., & Blackburn, R. S. (1989). *Managing organizational behavior*. Homewood, IL: Richard D. Irwin.

Rummell, R. J. (1976). *Understanding conflict and war*. New York: Wiley.

Sherif, M. (1966). *Group conflict and cooperation*. London: Routledge & Kegan Paul.

22

Why Teams: Leading to the High-Performance Organization

Jon R. Katzenbach and Douglas K. Smith

Teams have existed for hundreds of years, are the subject of countless books, and have been celebrated throughout many countries and cultures. Most people believe they know how teams work as well as the benefits teams offer. Many have had first-hand team experiences themselves, some of which were rewarding and others a waste of time. Yet, as we explored the use of teams, it became increasingly clear that the potential impact of single teams, as well as the collective impact of many teams, on the performance of large organizations is woefully underexploited—despite the rapidly growing recognition of the need for what teams have to offer. Understanding this paradox and the discipline required to deal with it are central to the basic lessons we learned about team performance. . . .

There is much more to the wisdom of teams than we ever expected, which we highlight in the following summary of key lessons we have learned about teams and team performance.

1. **Significant performance challenges energize teams regardless of where they are in an organization.** No team arises without a performance challenge that is meaningful to those involved. Good personal chemistry or the desire to "become a team," for example, can foster teamwork values, but teamwork is not the same thing as a team. Rather, a common set of demanding performance goals that a group considers important to achieve will lead, most of the time, to both performance and a team. Performance, however, is the primary objective *while a team remains the means, not the end.*

Performance is the crux of the matter for teams. Its importance applies to many different groupings, including teams who recommend things, teams who make or do things, and teams who run or manage things. Each of these three types of teams do face unique challenges. Teams that make or do things often need to develop new skills for managing themselves as compared to teams elsewhere in organizations. Teams that recommend things often find their biggest challenge comes when they make the handoff to those who must implement their findings. Finally, groups who run or manage things must address hierarchical obstacles and turf issues more than groups who recommend, make, or do things. But notwithstanding such special issues, any team—if it focuses on performance regardless of where it is in an organization or what it does—will deliver results well beyond what individuals acting alone in nonteam working situations could achieve.

2. **Organizational leaders can foster team performance best by building a strong performance ethic rather than by establishing a team-promoting environ-**

Source: From "The Wisdom of Teams" © 1993 by the Harvard Business School Publishing Corp. Reprinted by permission.

ment alone. A performance focus is also critical to what we learned about how leaders create organizational environments that are friendly to teams. In fact, too many executives fall into the trap of appearing to promote teams for the sake of teams. They talk about entire organizations becoming a "team" and thereby equate teams with teamwork. Or they reorganize their companies around self-managing teams, and risk putting the number of officially designated teams as an objective ahead of performance. They sometimes loosely refer to their own small group at the top as a team when most people in the organization recognize they are anything but a team.

Real teams are much more likely to flourish if leaders aim their sights on performance results that balance the needs of customers, employees, and shareholders. Clarity of purpose and goals have tremendous power in our ever more change-driven world. Most people, at all organizational levels, understand that job security depends on customer satisfaction and financial performance, and are willing to be measured and rewarded accordingly. What is perhaps less well appreciated, but equally true, is how the opportunity to meet clearly stated customer and financial needs enriches jobs and leads to personal growth.

Most of us really do want to make a difference. Naturally, organization policies, designs, and processes that promote teams can accelerate team-based performance in companies already blessed with strong performance cultures. But in those organizations with weak performance ethics or cultures, leaders will provide a sounder foundation for teams by addressing and demanding performance than by embracing the latest organization design fad, including teams themselves.

3. **Biases toward individualism exist but need not get in the way of team performance.** Most of us grow up with a strong sense of individual responsibility. Parents, teachers, coaches, and role models of all kinds shape our values based on individual accomplishment. Rugged individualism is credited with the formation of our country and our political society. These same values carry through in our corporate families, where all advancement and reward systems are based on individual evaluations. Even when teams are part of the picture, it is seldom at the expense of individual achievement. We are taught to play fair, but "Always look out for number one!" And, most of us have taken this to heart far more deeply than sentiments such as "We're all in this together" or "If one fails, we all fail."

Self-preservation and individual accountability, however, can work two ways. Left unattended, they can preclude or destroy potential teams. But recognized and addressed for what they are, especially if done with reference to how to meet a performance challenge, individual concerns and differences become a source of collective strength. Teams are not antithetical to individual performance. Real teams always find ways for each individual to contribute and thereby gain distinction. Indeed, when harnessed to a common team purpose and goals, our need to distinguish ourselves as individuals becomes a powerful engine for team performance. Nothing we learned in looking at dozens of teams supports an argument for the wholesale abandonment of the individual in favor of teams. Nor does our book present such an either/or proposition.

4. **Discipline—both within the team and across the organization—creates the conditions for team performance.** Any group seeking team performance itself, like any leader seeking to build strong performance standards across his organization, must focus sharply on performance. For organizational leaders, this entails making clear and consistent demands that reflect the needs of customers, shareholders, and employees, and then holding themselves and the organization relentlessly accountable. Out of such demands come the most fruitful conditions for teams. An analogous lesson also applies to teams. . . . Groups become teams through *disciplined action*. They *shape* a common purpose, *agree* on performance goals,

define a common working approach, *develop* high levels of complementary skills, and *hold* themselves mutually accountable for results. And, as with any effective discipline, they never stop doing any of these things.

THE NEED FOR TEAMS

We believe that teams—real teams, not just groups that management calls "teams"—should be the basic unit of performance for most organizations, regardless of size. In any situation requiring the real-time combination of multiple skills, experiences, and judgments, a team inevitably gets better results than a collection of individuals operating within confined job roles and responsibilities. Teams are more flexible than larger organizational groupings because they can be more quickly assembled, deployed, refocused, and disbanded, usually in ways that enhance rather than disrupt more permanent structures and processes. Teams are more productive than groups that have no clear performance objectives because their members are committed to deliver tangible performance results. Teams and performance are an unbeatable combination.

The record of team performance speaks for itself. Teams invariably contribute significant achievements in business, charity, schools, government, communities, and the military. Motorola, recently acclaimed for surpassing its Japanese competition in producing the world's lightest, smallest, and highest-quality cellular phones with only a few hundred parts versus over a thousand for the competition, relied heavily on teams to do it. So did Ford, which became America's most profitable car company in 1990 on the strength of its Taurus model. At 3M, teams are critical to meeting the company's well-known goal of producing half of each year's revenues from product innovations created in the prior five years. General Electric has made self-managing worker teams a centerpiece of its new organization approach.

Nonbusiness team efforts are equally numerous. The Coalition's dramatic Desert Storm victory over Iraq in the Gulf War involved many teams. A team of active duty officers and reservists, for example, lay at the heart of moving, receiving and sustaining over 300,000 troops and 100,000 vehicles with more than 7,000,000 tons of equipment, fuel, and supplies between the late 1990 buildup through and beyond the end of hostilities in 1991. At Bronx Educational Services, a team of staff and trustees shaped the first nationally recognized adult literacy school. A team of citizens in Harlem founded and operated the first Little League there in over forty years.

We do not argue that such team achievements are a new phenomenon. But we do think there is more urgency to team performance today because of the link between teams, individual behavioral change, and high performance. A "high-performance organization" consistently outperforms its competition over an extended period of time, for example, ten years or more. It also outperforms the expectations of its key constituents: customers, shareholders, and employees. Few people today question that a new era has dawned in which such high levels of performance depend on being "customer driven," delivering "total quality," "continuously improving and innovating," "empowering the workforce," and "partnering with suppliers and customers." Yet these require specific behavioral changes in the entire organization that are difficult and unpredictable for any single person, let alone an entire company, to accomplish. By contrast, we have observed that the same team dynamics that promote performance also support learning and behavioral change, and do so more effectively than larger organizational units or individuals left to their own devices. Consequently, we believe teams will play an increasingly essential part in first creating and then sustaining high-performance organizations.

Change, of course, has always been a management challenge. But, until recently, when executives spoke of managing change, they referred to "normal" change—that is, new circumstances well within the scope of their existing management approaches. Managers deal with this kind of change every day. It is a fundamental part of their job, and includes raising prices, handling disgruntled customers, dealing with stubborn unions, replacing people, and even shifting strategic priorities. Many people, however, would agree that change today has taken on an entirely different meaning. While all managers continue to have to deal with "normal" change, more and more they must also confront "major" change that requires a lot of people throughout the company—including those across the broad base of the organization—to become very good at behaviors and skills they are not very good at now. The days of viewing change as primarily concerned with strategic decisions and management reorganizations have vanished. . . .

Several well-known phenomena explain why teams perform well. First, they bring together complementary skills and experiences that, by definition, exceed those of any individual on the team. This broader mix of skills and know-how enables teams to respond to multifaceted challenges like innovation, quality, and customer service. Second, in jointly developing clear goals and approaches, teams establish communications that support real-time problem solving and initiative. Teams are flexible and responsive to changing events and demands. As a result, teams can adjust their approach to new information and challenges with greater speed, accuracy, and effectiveness than can individuals caught in the web of larger organizational connections.

Third, teams provide a unique social dimension that enhances the economic and administrative aspects of work. Real teams do not develop until the people in them work hard to overcome barriers that stand in the way of collective performance. By surmounting such obstacles together, people on teams build trust and confidence in each other's capabilities. They also reinforce each other's intentions to pursue their team purpose above and beyond individual or functional agendas. Overcoming barriers to performance is how groups become teams. Both the meaning of work and the effort brought to bear upon it deepen, until team performance eventually becomes its own reward.

Finally, teams have more fun. This is not a trivial point because the kind of fun they have is integral to their performance. The people on the teams we met consistently and without prompting emphasized the fun aspects of their work together. Of course this fun included parties, hoopla, and celebrations. But any group of people can throw a good party. What distinguishes the fun of teams is how it both sustains and is sustained by team performance. For example, we often see a more highly developed sense of humor on the job within the top-performing teams because it helps them deal with the pressures and intensity of high performance. And we inevitably hear that the deepest, most satisfying source of enjoyment comes from "having been part of something larger than myself."

Behavioral change also occurs more readily in the team context. Because of their collective commitment, teams are not as threatened by change as are individuals left to fend for themselves. And, because of their flexibility and willingness to enlarge their solution space, teams offer people more room for growth and change than do groups with more narrowly defined task assignments associated with hierarchical job assignments. Finally, because of their focus on performance, teams motivate, challenge, reward, and support individuals who are trying to change the way they do things.

As a result, in the kinds of broad-based change that organizations increasingly confront today, teams can help concentrate the direction and quality of top-down leadership, foster new behaviors, and facilitate cross-functional activities. When teams work, they represent the best proven way to convert embryonic visions and values into consistent action patterns because they rely on people working together. They also are the most practical way to develop a shared sense of direction among people throughout an organization. Teams can make hierarchy responsive without weakening it, energize processes across organizational boundaries, and bring multiple capabilities to bear on difficult issues.

In fact, most models of the "organization of the future" that we have heard about—"networked," "clustered," "nonhierarchical," "horizontal," and so forth—are premised on *teams surpassing individuals as the primary performance unit in the company*. According to these predictions, when management seeks faster, better ways to best match resources to customer opportunity or competitive challenge, the critical building block will be at the team, not individual, level. This does not mean that either individual performance or accountability become unimportant. Rather, the challenge for management increasingly becomes that of balancing the roles of individuals and teams versus displacing or favoring one over the other. In addition, the individual's role and performance will become more a matter for teams, instead of hierarchies of managers, to exploit; that is, in many cases teams, not managers, will figure out what the individuals on those teams should be doing and how they are performing.

RESISTANCE TO TEAMS

Such predictions about teams, however, induce a lot of skepticism. We believe the argument for greater focus on teams is compelling, and most people we have interviewed agree. Yet when it comes to using the team approach for themselves or those they manage, most of these same people are reluctant to rely on teams. Notwithstanding the evidence of team performance all around us, the importance of teams in managing behavioral change and high performance, and the rewards of team experiences in everyday lives, many people undervalue, forget, or openly question the team option when confronting their own performance challenges. We cannot fully explain this resistance; there probably are as many reasons and emotions as there are people. Moreover, we do not suggest that such resistance is either "bad" or "good." We do, however, think that it is powerful because it is grounded in deeply held values of individualism that neither can nor should be entirely dismissed.

Three primary sources for people's reluctance about teams stand out: a lack of conviction that a team or teams can work better than other alternatives; personal styles, capabilities, and preferences that make teams risky or uncomfortable; and weak organizational performance ethics that discourage the conditions in which teams flourish.

1. **Lack of conviction.** Some people do not believe that teams, except in unusual or unpredictable circumstances, really do perform better than individuals. Some think that teams cause more trouble than they are worth because the members waste time in unproductive meetings and discussions, and actually generate more complaints than constructive results. Others think that teams are probably useful from a human relations point of view, but are a hindrance when it comes to work, productivity, and decisive action. Still others believe that concepts of teamwork and empowerment applied broadly to an organization supersede the need to worry or be disciplined about the performance of specific small groups of people.

On the one hand, most people share a lot of constructive common sense about teams but fail to rigorously apply it. People know, for example, that teams rarely work without common goals; yet far too many teams casually accept goals that are neither demanding, precise, realistic, nor actually held *in common*. On the other hand, the very popularity of the word "team" courts imprecision. People rarely use "team" with much concern for its specific meaning to them in the context they face. As a consequence, most people remain unclear over what makes a real team. A team is not just any group working together. Committees, councils, and task forces are not necessarily teams. Groups do not become teams simply because someone labels them as teams. The complete workforce of any large and complex organization is never a team. Entire organizations can believe in and practice teamwork, but teamwork and teams differ.

Most executives outspokenly advocate teamwork. And they should. Teamwork represents a set of values that encourage behaviors such as listening and constructively responding to points of view expressed by others, giving others the benefit of the doubt, providing support to those who need it, and recognizing the interests and achievements of others. When practiced, such values help all of us communicate and work more effectively with one another and, therefore, are good and valuable behaviors. Obviously, teamwork values help teams perform. They also promote our performance as individuals and the performance of the entire organization. In other words, teamwork values—by themselves—are not exclusive to teams, nor are they enough to ensure team performance.

Teams are discrete units of performance, not a positive set of values. And they are a unit of performance that differs from the individual or the entire organization. A team is a small group of people (typically fewer than twenty) with complementary skills committed to a common purpose and set of specific performance goals. Its members are committed to working with each other to achieve the team's purpose and hold each other fully and jointly accountable for the team's results. Teamwork encourages and helps teams succeed; but teamwork alone never makes a team. Consequently, when senior executives call for the entire organization to be a "team," they really are promoting teamwork values. However well intended, such ambiguities can cause unproductive confusion. Moreover, those who describe teams as vehicles primarily to make people feel good or get along better not only confuse teamwork with teams, but also miss the most fundamental characteristic that distinguishes real teams from nonteams—a relentless focus on performance.

Teams thrive on performance challenges; they flounder without them. Teams cannot exist for long without a performance-driven purpose to both nourish and justify the team's continuing existence. Groups established for the sake of becoming a team, job enhancement, communication, organizational effectiveness, or even excellence rarely become real teams, as demonstrated by the bad feelings left in many companies after experimenting with quality circles. While quality represents an admirable aspiration, quality circles often fail to connect specific, achievable performance objectives with the collaborative effort of those in the circle.

Ignoring performance, we suspect, also explains much of the evidence about apparent team failures. Peter Drucker, for example, has cited the difficulties GM, P&G, and Xerox, among others, have had in overshooting the mark with "team-building" efforts. Without question, teams and team efforts sometimes fail. But more often than not, such failures lie in not adhering to the discipline of what makes teams successful. In other words, unclear thinking and practice explain more about such disappointments than whether teams are appropriate units of performance to get something done. Regardless of their cause, however, such unrewarding personal experiences in groups labeled as teams weaken people's conviction about teams even further. Many of us who have observed, participated in, or watched the best intentions at team-building exercises get quickly forgotten or scorned have grown cynical, cautious, or even hostile to teams.

2. **Personal discomfort and risk.** Many people fear or do not like to work in teams. Some are true loners who contribute best when left to work quietly on their own. Some research scientists, university professors, and specialized consultants fit this pattern. Most people's discomfort with teams, however, is because they find the team approach too time-consuming, too uncertain, or too risky.

"My job is tough enough," goes one recurring comment, "without having to worry about meeting and getting along with a bunch of people I don't even know that well, or I do know and I'm not sure I like all that much. I just don't have that kind of time to invest." In this view, teams represent a risky extra burden that can slow down individual accomplishment and advancement. Some people are uncomfortable about speaking up, participating, or being otherwise conspicuous in group settings. Some are afraid of making commitments that they might not be able to keep. And many people just do not like the idea of having to depend on others, having to listen or agree to contrary points of view, or having to suffer the consequences of other people's mistakes. These concerns particularly afflict managers who find it difficult to be part of a team when they are not the leader.

Few people deny the benefit of teamwork values or the potentially useful performance impact of teams. But, at their core, most people have values that favor individual responsibility and performance over any form of group, whether it be a team or otherwise. Our parents, teachers, ministers, and other elders emphasize individual responsibility as paramount from our earliest days onward. We grow up under a regimen that measures (academic grades), rewards (allowances), and punishes (trips to the principal's office) individual—not collective—performance. Whenever we want to "get something done," our first thought is that of holding an individual responsible.

It is hardly surprising, then, to discover strong anxieties among individuals faced with joining a team. It is not that teams and teamwork are absent from our culture. From *The Three Musketeers* through *The Dirty Dozen* and *Star Trek*, we have read about, listened to, and watched stories of famous teams accomplishing the improbable. Most sports we follow are team sports. And our parents and other teachers have also instructed us in, and expected us to practice, teamwork values. But for most of us, these admirable notions, however potentially rewarding, forever remain secondary to our responsibilities as individuals. Individual responsibility and self-preservation remain the rule; shared responsibility based on trusting others is the exception. A reluctance to take a risk and submit one's fate to the performance of a team, therefore, is almost inbred.

3. **Weak organizational performance ethics.** The reluctance to commit one's own fate to a team pervades most organizations with weak performance ethics. Such companies lack compelling purposes that appeal rationally and emotionally to their people. Their leaders fail to make clear and meaningful performance demands to which they hold the organiza-

tion and, most important, themselves accountable. To the organization at large, such behavior manifests more concern about internal politics or external public relations than a commitment to a clear set of goals that balances the expectations of customers, shareholders, and employees. At the worst, such environments undermine the mutual trust and openness upon which teams depend. There is a built-in expectation that any decision of consequence must be made at the top or, at a minimum, be approved by enough other layers that the implementor of that decision is well-covered. Politics displace performance as the daily focus. And, inevitably, those politics play on individual insecurities that, in turn, further erode the conviction and courage to invest in a team approach. Bad team experiences become self-fulfilling prophecies.

Modifying the strong natural emphasis on individual accountability will, of course, be necessary as teams become more important. Yet *replacing individually focused management structures and approaches with team-oriented designs will matter little, or even do damage, unless the organization has a robust performance ethic*. If it does, then shifting the organization's emphasis away from individual toward team can enrich both the number and performance of teams—particularly if management also is disciplined about how it deals with team situations. But all the team-promoting policies in the world will fall short if the teams are not convinced that performance truly matters. Some teams, of course, will always emerge—beyond all reasonable expectation. But they will remain the exception. Because of the all-important link between teams and performance, companies with weak performance ethics will always breed resistance to teams themselves.

CONCLUSION

Teams are *not* the solution to everyone's current and future organizational needs. They will not solve every problem, enhance every group's results, nor help top management address every performance challenge. Moreover, when misapplied, they can be both wasteful and disruptive. Nonetheless, teams usually do outperform other groups and individuals. They represent one of the best ways to support the broad-based changes necessary for the high-performing organization. And executives who really believe that behaviorally based characteristics like quality, innovation, cost effectiveness, and customer service will help build sustainable competitive advantage will give top priority to the development of team performance.

To succeed, however, they and others must also pay a lot of attention to why most people approach teams cautiously. In large part, this resistance springs from undeniable experiences and convictions about individual responsibility and the risks involved in trusting other people. Teams, for example, do demand a merging of individual accountability with mutual accountability. Teams also do require lots of time together; indeed, it is folly to assume that teams can perform without investing time to shape and agree upon a common purpose, set of goals, and working approach. Moreover, few groups become real teams without taking risks to overcome constraints imposed by individual, functional, and hierarchical boundaries. And team members do depend on one another in pursuit of common performance.

No wonder, then, that many of us only reluctantly entrust critical issues to team resolution. We all fool ourselves if we think well-meaning aspirations to "work better as a team" will be enough to dispel the resistance to teams. Building the performance of teams throughout an organization that needs to perform better, we argue, is mandatory. But doing so also poses a far more serious challenge than any of us would like to admit.

The good news is that there is a discipline to teams that, if rigorously followed, can transform reluctance into team performance. Moreover, while some of the elements of this discipline are counterintuitive and must be learned—for example, that "becoming a team" is not the primary goal—most of it builds on commonsense ideas like the importance of goal setting and mutual accountability. Furthermore, this discipline applies equally well to teams that run things, teams that recommend things, and teams that make or do things. What works at the front lines also works in the executive suite.

The bad news is that, like all disciplines, the price of success is strict adherence and practice. Very few people lose weight, quit smoking, or learn the piano or golf without constant practice and discipline. Very few small groups of people become teams without discipline as well. Extracting team performance is challenging. Long-standing habits of individualism, rampant confusion about teams and teamwork, and seemingly adverse team experiences all undercut the possibilities teams offer at the very moment that team performance has become so critical. Groups do not become teams just because we tell them to; launching hundreds of teams will not necessarily produce real teams in the right places; and building teams at the top remains among the most difficult of tests. Yet the fact remains that potential teams throughout most organizations usually can perform much better than they do. We believe this untapped potential literally begs for renewed attention, especially from the top. We also believe the key to such performance is in recognizing the wisdom of teams, having the courage to try, and then applying the discipline to learn from the experience. . . .

TEAMS AND THE HIGH-PERFORMANCE ORGANIZATION

We believe that focusing on both performance and the teams that deliver it will materially increase top management's prospects of leading their companies to become high-performance organizations. Again, we do *not* contend that teams are the only answer to this aspiration. They are, however, a very important piece of the puzzle—particularly because the dynamics that drive teams mirror the behaviors and values necessary to the high-performance organization and because teams are, simply stated, so practical.

More agreement exists today about the capabilities of high-performance organizations than about the specific organizational forms and management approaches that will support them. No one, including us, argues over the value of such company attributes as being "customer-driven," "informated," "focused on total quality" and having "empowered work forces" that "continuously improve and innovate." Behind these lie a set of six characteristics, only one of which—balanced performance results—is ever overlooked in discussions of where the best companies are headed. The six include:

1. **Balanced performance results. . . .** [T]he primary standard for the "new paradigm" organization ought to be performance itself. Companies that consistently outperform the competition over an extended period, say ten years, are high-performance organizations—regardless of how they get there. One can argue with the yardstick of a decade. Perhaps, for example, the only true high-performing organizations outperform competition in perpetuity. But we find it hard to question performance as the key criterion of a high-performance organization.

At one level, performance as a characteristic of the high-performance organization is obvious. But it often goes unstated—thereby leaving people assuming that the other characteristics of high-performance are ends rather than means to an end. One group of executives we know illustrates this point. When challenged to articulate the characteristics that would make their company qualify as a "high-performance organization," they ticked off every attribute on every list we know except one—none of them suggested a specific performance achievement.

Of equal importance is a balanced performance ethic that benefits the primary constituencies of any large business organization: customers, employees, and shareholders/owners. Proven high performers such as Levi Strauss, Procter & Gamble, Hewlett-Packard, and Goldman, Sachs are all well known for their balanced performance aspirations. They are relentless in delivering superior results to employees, customers, and shareholders. It is no accident that they attract the best people, serve enviable customer groups, and sustain the highest earnings. Equally relevant are the balanced performance goals of companies placing the highest emphasis on creating new paradigm, high-performance organizations for the future. Recognized organizational change leaders such as General Electric, Motorola, and American Express's IDS each are explicit about achieving performance results of multidimensions.

2. **Clear, challenging aspirations.** Whether it goes under the name of "vision," "mission," "strategic intent," or "directional intensity," the company's purpose must reflect clear and challenging aspirations that will benefit all of its key constituencies. Too many vision statements are just that: a written attempt by top management to meet the well-accepted "vision requirement." They may be read by all, and may even be immortalized in plaques on the wall, but they have no real emotional meaning to people down the line whose behaviors and values they are supposed to influence. The purpose, meaning, and performance implications of visions must communicate, to all who matter, that they will benefit both rationally and emotionally from the company's success.

Reaching for the stars is not just an idealistic notion. Past, present, and future high performers make "meanings" as well as money. Thus, for example, "being the best" is a common phrase in high-performing organizations, although it means different things in different places. . . . Whatever the meaning that goes beyond the money, it makes people proud to be a part of a demanding and challenging total effort.

3. **Committed and focused leadership.** High-performance organizations follow leaders who themselves almost evangelically pursue performance. Through their time, attention, and other symbolic behavior, such leaders express a constant focus on where the company is headed and an unrelenting dedication to the communication, involvement, measurement, and experimentation required to get there. Truly committed leaders inspire confidence throughout the organization that the pursuit of performance is the single best path to economic and personal fulfillment.

Such leadership, of course, does not require teams at the top. But the power in such teams is undeniable because of how well the members keep each other committed and focused. Moreover, when an organization confronts . . . major change, it is hard to imagine success without the committed and focused leadership provided by a real team at the top. . . .

4. **An energized work force dedicated to productivity and learning.** The "learning," "adaptive," "self-directed," and "evergreen" characteristics of high-performance organizations depend on a critical mass of people who are turned on to winning as well as to the change that winning requires. Performance in a constantly changing world demands change. And change, in turn, must be understood and tested before it can be mastered. Few companies can afford a work force caught

in the trap of " it's not my job" or "not invented here" attitudes. Rather, the people of the organization must share an eagerness to ask questions, to experiment with new approaches, to learn from results, and to take responsibility for making changes happen.

No major company we know is pursuing an energized, productive work force without the conscious use of teams. . . . Productivity and learning across the base of an organization means teams—plain and simple.

5. **Skill-based sources of competitive advantage.** Companies should always seek and make best use of intrinsically valuable assets like access to natural resources, control over powerful distribution channels, strong brand names, and patents and other government licenses. People generally agree, however, that most industries have entered an era in which sustainable competitive advantage will favor those who develop the core skills and core competencies that allow them to win a battle that now depends more on "movement than position." Indeed, innovation, customer-driven service, total quality, and continuous improvement are examples of the capabilities companies need for high performance.

Core skills invariably depend on team skills. To re-engineer work flows based on customer needs, for example, requires teams that integrate across functional boundaries. Whenever adding value depends on the real-time blending of multiple skills, experiences, and judgments, a team performance challenge exists. And teams provide an excellent (often unsurpassed) crucible for on-the-job skill development.

6. **Open communications and knowledge management.** A number of observers from academia, business, and the press believe that knowledge has become as scarce and important a factor of production as capital and labor. Few seriously doubt that information technology is critical to high performance. But that "technology" includes more than the hardware and software behind what some people call a new industrial revolution. It also includes the shared values and behavioral norms that foster open communications and knowledge management. For example, one commentator has suggested that in "information era organizations," there are no guards, only guides. In order to "informate" company performance, the right information must get to the right people at the right time to affect performance. Moreover, those people must hold themselves accountable for their results. Otherwise, empowerment is dangerous.

We have seen how teams promote open communications and knowledge management. . . . But, as we have noted several times, real teams *always* seek fresh facts and share information both within the team and with others beyond. Real teams communicate and learn whatever is necessary to get their job done; team "doors" are always open. Moreover, through the "extended team" influence, the communications and knowledge management of others work better.

Leading thinkers have come forth with a variety of intriguing images of what high-performance organizations with these characteristics and capabilities will actually look like. Peter Drucker pictures it as an "orchestra," Quinn Mills as "clusters," Robert Waterman as an "ad hocracy," and Ram Charan as "networked." Even one of us has a favorite entry, the "horizontal organization." Notwithstanding the range of concepts, however, these people seem to agree on three things. First, future organization designs will seek structures simpler and more flexible than the heavily layered command-and-control hierarchies that have dominated the twentieth century. Second, they strike a balance in favor of organizing work and behavior around processes instead of functions or tasks. And third, they all emphasize teams as the key performance unit of the company.

23
Critical Success Factors for Creating Superb Self-Managing Teams

Ruth Wageman

Self-managing teams are fast becoming the management practice of choice for organizations that wish to become more flexible, push decision making to the front lines, and fully use employees' intellectual and creative capacities. Indeed, claims for the astounding potential of teamwork in general and self-managing teams in particular are abundant and increasing. Partisans of teamwork claim that organizations need teams to compete; and the proliferation of manufacturing teams, cross-functional teams, quality teams, and the like suggest that managers are listening.

The central principle behind self-managing teams is that the teams themselves, rather than managers, take responsibility for their work, monitor their own performance, and alter their performance strategies as needed to solve problems and adapt to changing conditions. This way of running an organization's day-to-day activities is said to:

- enhance the company's performance, because those closest to the customer and best able to respond to customer demands have the authority to meet those demands;
- enhance organizational learning and adaptability, because members of self-managing teams have the latitude to experiment with their work and to develop strategies that are uniquely suited to tasks; and
- enhance employees' commitment to the organization, because self-managing teams offer wider participation in and ownership of important organizational decisions.

Clearly, self-managing teams have the potential to make a multifaceted contribution to an organization's competitiveness.

WHY, THEN, MIXED RESULTS?

What sounds straightforward in principle—a change in authority—turns out to be troublesome in practice. While numerous examples of the gains to performance, learning, and commitment attributed to self-managing teams are offered in evidence of their value, an increasing number of organizations are becoming disenchanted with the idea. Managers observe slow and sometimes nonexistent progress in team members' efforts to take on responsibility for decisions that previously belonged to managers. They note that many teams continue to operate much as they always have: Members divide their work and do it independently, showing little inclination to join in a collective effort to

Source: From *Organizational Dynamics*, Vol. 26, Summer 1997. Reprinted by permission of Elsevere Science.

improve their work strategies, take responsibility for difficult decisions, or solve problems.

These dysfunctions are not surprising when one considers that, in many U.S. companies, teamwork is an "unnatural act." These organizations have long histories of hierarchical decision making cemented with a work ethic based on individual achievement. Given this culture and context, team members will balk at the idea of relying on one another to get work done.

For all their claimed promise, then, many self-managing teams never contribute to organization performance and adaptability—because they never operate as intended. This raises a critical question for many organizations: How can managers get teams to take on self-management and ensure that those teams will perform superbly—especially if this means bucking a long history of manager-directed, individualistic work?

CASE IN POINT: CUSTOMER SERVICE TEAMS AT XEROX

This is precisely the question that faced the Xerox Corporation's Customer Service organization. "Working solo" was part of this unit's culture. In fact, the customer service engineers (CSEs) were hired, in part, because of their ability to work alone, independently, and without supervision.

For many years, each individual CSE handled specific territories and customer accounts. This changed when the unit's senior management created interdependent self-managing teams, each composed of multiple CSEs who would share responsibility for the team's collective customers. Moreover, the groups would be responsible for more than simply fixing equipment—they would design maintenance procedures for their many kinds of machines, analyze and monitor the machines' performance levels, manage the costs of their work, and solve the problems created by unpredictable customer needs.

In many cases, management intended the groups to go even further in the decisions they made: Teams would select their own members, provide peer feedback, and assist in the design of support systems. The Xerox teams provide the main point of contact between the company and its customers—and their effectiveness is critical to the company's ultimate success.

How well do these self-managed service teams actually function? In general, the results are quite positive. But a closer look shows that the teams vary in the degree to which they have embraced self-management and matured into the proactive problem-solving units they were intended to be. Consider two examples, selected from our observations of the Xerox teams.

One team of veteran CSEs approached their machine maintenance responsibilities in a way that was distinctively different from the other groups. When our researchers asked what was going on, a team member explained that they were running an experiment. The team was attempting to increase the time certain copier parts lasted by cleaning related machine areas more frequently. Each team member was trying this process on several machines and recording the length of time that the parts lasted. If the experiment proved successful, they could make substantial savings in parts expenses.

This same team conducted a team meeting after work hours, giving our researchers an opportunity to see its problem-solving dynamics in action. A team member who had been absent earlier in the day explained that he was actually on vacation and had come in just for the meeting. We asked if this happened often. "When we need to," he replied. "We're in charge of our own schedules, so we have to make our vacation plans work with no decrease in care for our customers. All of us have come in on vacation days at some time or another when the call rate got too high for the rest of the team to handle."

We observed a second team, also composed of veteran CSEs, as it reviewed performance data at a group meeting. This team's leader (first-line manager) presented graphical data indicating problems with machine reliability—customers often had to call back to fix repeated problems. What was the team going to do about it? He put this question on the table, then left the meeting, expecting that the group would analyze and solve the problem.

Once the leader had gone, however, the conversation took a different tack. Some team members focused on problems with the data: "It's more than a month old. Who knows if that's even accurate anymore?" Others laid the problem at the feet of their customers: "Some of these call-backs are for trivial problems, and at least one of those machines was abused." Still others chose not to participate in the conversation: "Those aren't my customers."

While these critiques of the data and the customers may have been accurate, the conversation avoided any focus on what could be done—even on how to get better data or how to manage their customers better to prevent machine abuse.

While both teams had responsibility for managing their own work, the degree to which real self-management was expressed in their actual behavior varied dramatically. Members of teams that are genuinely managing themselves show three basic characteristics in the way they approach their work:

- They take personal responsibility for the outcomes of their team's work.
- They monitor their own work performance, actively seeking data about how well they are performing.
- They alter their performance strategies as needed, creating suitable solutions to work problems.

All these signs were visible in the first team discussed above, and all were absent in the second.

A QUESTION OF LEVERAGE: DESIGN OR COACHING?

How can leaders help their teams become more like the first team? Where should they concentrate their resources and energy to help guide their teams toward effective, proactive self-management? A fast-growing body of advice centers on two basic influences: (1) how the team is set up and supported, and (2) how the team's leader (or coach) behaves in his or her day-to-day interactions with the team.

. . . Many consulting practices, skill-assessment instruments, and training courses address how the role of the manager/leader needs to change, from directing and controlling the work to coaching the team as it decides how best to get its work done.

Just how important is high-quality coaching relative to high-quality team design? To find out, we conducted an in-depth examination of 43 self-managing teams in the Xerox service organization. The researchers looked at both the basic design features of the teams and the day-to-day actions of the team leaders to see which of these had the greater impact on effective team self-management. The study sought to answer the following question: "If we have limited resources (such as time and money), what critical few factors should we focus on to increase the chances our self-managing teams will be superb?"

A Close Look at the Differences

To launch the research, we first asked Xerox managers to identify teams that were either superb or ineffective. Superb teams (a) consistently met the needs of their customers, (b) appeared to be operating with increasing effectiveness over time, and (c) were made up of members who were engaged in and satisfied with their work. Ineffective teams (a) frequently failed to meet customer needs, (b) appeared to be operating increasingly poorly over time, and (c) were made up of members who were alienated from or dissatisfied with their work.

The researchers then assessed a wide variety of team features to determine which most strongly differentiated between the superb and the ineffective. Each self-managing team participated in a two-hour interview, describing their history, their work, and the context in which they operated. Their first-line managers provided extensive descriptions of how these teams were set up and supported. Finally, each team member completed an extensive survey describing the team, its interactions, and its environment.

Team self-management was measured by assessing such behaviors as the degree to which the team monitored its own performance and acted to improve its work strategies without waiting for direction.

Researchers also measured a range of coaching behaviors, some of which were expected to promote self-management, others to undermine it. Appropriate coaching included sending cues that the team was responsible for its own performance, providing timely feedback and information, and helping the team develop problem-solving strategies. Ineffective coaching included intervening in the team's day-to-day work and providing solutions to team problems.

Design factors covered a wide range of features, including team composition, team size, the design of the task, the design of the reward system, and many others. (See Exhibit 1 for a list of the full range of potential influences assessed.)

These measures allowed a direct test of the question, Which makes a bigger difference in team self-management and performance: how well leaders coach their teams, or how well the teams are designed and supported?

CRITICAL INGREDIENTS FOR TEAM SELF-MANAGEMENT

. . . The quality of a team's design, our data showed, actually had a larger effect on its level of self-management than coaching—by a wide margin. Well-designed teams show far stronger signs of self-managing than poorly designed teams. While high-quality coaching does influence how well a team manages itself, it does so to a much smaller degree.

For team leaders, a most important finding to note is the joint effect of design and coaching. Exhibit 2 shows how quality of design and coaching work together to influence team self-management. The first diagram shows the influence of high-quality coaching on well-designed vs. poorly designed teams. Note that good coaching had a far more powerful effect on well-designed teams than on poorly designed ones. The implication is that teams whose leaders are good coaches are better self-managers only when the team structures are well designed.

Teams that had many of the critical design features in place became even more self-managing when their leaders provided effective coaching—for example, helping the team build its problem-solving repertoire. Poorly designed teams hardly responded at all to good coaching. Leaders who tried to help a poorly designed team had almost no impact on the team's ability to self-manage, despite the fact that the lead-

EXHIBIT 1 • POTENTIAL INFLUENCES ON TEAM SELF-MANAGEMENT MEASURED IN THE RESEARCH

Design Features

1. Clear, engaging direction
2. Task interdependence
3. Authority to manage the work
4. Performance goals
5. Skill diversity of team members
6. Demographic diversity of team members
7. Team size
8. Length of time the team has had stable membership
9. Group rewards
10. Information resources
11. Availability of training
12. Basic material resources

Coaching Behaviors

Potential positive influences:

1. Providing reinforcers and other cues that the group is responsible for managing itself
2. Appropriate problem-solving consultation
3. Dealing with interpersonal problems in the team through team-process consultation
4. Attending team meetings*
5. Providing organization-related data*

Potential negative influences:

1. Signaling that individuals (or the leader/manager) were responsible for the team's work
2. Intervening in the task
3. Identifying the team's problems
4. Overriding group decisions**

* Because all leaders engaged in this behavior, it was impossible to determine whether it influenced team behavior.

** Because very few leaders engaged in this behavior, it was impossible to determine whether it influenced team effectiveness.

ers followed the principles of effective coaching.

Moreover, ineffective coaching had a much more detrimental effect on poorly designed teams than on well-designed teams. At the same time, coaching errors (such as intervening in the team's work and overriding decisions) had very little negative impact on well-designed teams. These teams were robust enough to remain highly self-managing in spite of a leader's blunders—whereas poorly designed teams were hindered by such errors. (The second panel in Exhibit 2 shows the influence of poor coaching on well-designed vs. poorly designed teams.)

These findings suggest that the first step in creating effective self-managing teams is to get the team designed right. Only then does it make sense to tackle the hands-on coaching and counseling that are part of a leader's day-to-day interactions with the team. To have the greatest possible influence, then, a team leader needs:

1. knowledge of the design factors that most strongly influence the effectiveness of self-managing teams;
2. the diagnostic skills to tell which factors are present and which are absent; and
3. the ability to act—to put the missing factors in place.

The following discussion addresses each of these three issues. We first focus on the seven critical success factors that the study revealed had the most impact. To address the second issue, we present

EXHIBIT 2 • HOW TEAM DESIGN AND QUALITY OF COACHING AFFECT TEAM SELF-MANAGEMENT

High-Quality Coaching	Team Design: High-Quality	Team Design: Poor Quality
Little	Moderate to High Self-Management	Low Self-Management
A great deal	Very High Self-Management	Low Self-Management

Poor-Quality Coaching	Team Design: High-Quality	Team Design: Poor Quality
Little	Moderate to High Self-Management	Low Self-Management
A great deal	Moderate to High Self-Management	Very Low Self-Management

a set of diagnostic questions to help assess whether a particular factor is in place for a team. To address the third area, the discussion of critical factors includes examples of actions leaders took to put high-quality design factors in place.

CRITICAL SUCCESS FACTORS

Seven features emerged as the ones most likely to be seen in superb teams and not in ineffective teams. Collectively, they were strongly related to a wide range of performance measures such as customer satisfaction, speed of response to customer calls, and expense management.

Moreover, each factor is something that team leaders can influence. That is, first-line managers can determine whether or not their teams have each supportive feature and can take action to get the missing ingredients in place. The seven success factors are discussed in descending order of importance.

Factor 1: Clear, Engaging Direction

Superb teams, far more than ineffective ones, have a clear and engaging direction—a sense of why the group exists and what it is trying to accomplish. One team, for example, stated its mission as follows: "This team exists to keep customers so pleased with Xerox that they will remain with Xerox; and the team aims to do so in a way that uses Xerox resources as efficiently as possible." This statement of direction is exemplary for the following reasons:

1. It is clear and simple. That is, it contains only a few objectives. . . .
2. It specifies the ends, but not the means. That is, it is clear about the team's purpose but it does not say how the team should get there. . . .

Two common errors in setting direction emerged from the study: (1) failing to set any direction at all and (2) setting a direction that is all about means—the how—but doesn't specify ends—the why. . . .

Factor 2: A Real Team Task

A self-managing team requires work that is designed to be done by a team. That is, basic elements of the work should require members to work *together* to complete significant tasks. Spending time together as a whole team is critical—especially in organizations where members have little experience with teamwork.

In the Xerox customer service teams, the basic task elements included sharing responsibility for all its customers (vs. having customers assigned to specific individuals), managing expenses, designing basic work practices, and solving problems. Groups with real team tasks do all these things collectively. That is, they have no individual territories—rather, members respond to calls from any of the team's customers (often consulting about which member should handle a particular call). They design their work practices collectively and monitor members' compliance with those practices; they meet every week or two; they are fully cross-trained and are thus able to help each other at any time; and they are given a group budget, with only group-level information about expenses—that is, they manage the parts budget as a group.

Two common task design errors are (1) creating a "team-in-name-only"; or worse, (2) designing a task that only occasionally requires a real team. The first error involves designating some group of individuals a team without changing the nature of the work. . . .

The second design error—creating a task that sometimes requires significant team activity, sometimes significant individual activity—results in what can be called a "hybrid" task. In this study, a typical hybrid task design asked the team to handle one set of activities as a team (for example, members designed their work practices as a collective, met occasionally, and managed expenses for the group as a whole) and another set of tasks individually (for example, members had specific customers and product specialties).

Hybrid task designs create difficulties for teams because they send mixed signals to the group about whether or not this really is a team. The pull in both directions—to operate alone and to operate as a team—leaves these groups floundering, as some members attend more to their solo tasks than to collective activities. Moreover, hybrid designs prevent a group from investing significant time in learning how to operate effectively as a team. And when members work together only periodically, they discover that much of their "together" time is more difficult and less effective than their "solo" time. In the end, both team members and their leaders may be convinced that teamwork is not such a good idea after all.

. . . Self-managing teams need a task that is defined as a team task, that is measured as a team task, and that requires the members to spend a great deal of time accomplishing something together. A task designed this way creates the opportunity—indeed, the necessity—of learning how to operate effectively as a unit.

Factor 3: Rewards for Team Excellence

This study, as well as previous research, shows that team rewards (not individual or mixed rewards) are strongly associated with superior team self-management. In our study, teams were considered to have team rewards if at least 80 percent of the available rewards were distributed equally among team members. The exceptions to this were (1) small rewards from the leader that are given to individual team members for actions that supported the team and (2) rewards given to the team as a whole but distributed differentially by team members themselves.

The use of mixed rewards—about half provided to individuals and half to the team—emerged as the most common error in reward system design. Leaders tend to provide mixed rewards for the same reason they create "hybrid" tasks—they assume that it is best to introduce team members gradually to the idea of being fully dependent on each other. Like hybrid tasks, mixed rewards send mixed signals to the team and undermine its ability to operate as an effective unit.

. . . Some lingering discomfort remains in many companies—among managers and employees alike—about "group-only" rewards. But, contrary to what many managers believe, rewards that are about 50/50 individual/group are associated with the lowest team performance.

Factor 4: Basic Material Resources

These are the physical materials the team needs: the tools, appropriate meeting space, access to computing services, and other resources that make it possible for the team to work in a timely, proactive, and effective fashion. Teams that had such resources readily available strongly outperformed teams that did not. My observations suggest that leaders are sometimes reluctant to provide resources to struggling teams, under the premise that "they haven't learned to manage them yet." But this very lack of resources may be among the factors demoralizing the team and preventing it from embracing self-management. . . .

Factor 5: Authority to Manage the Work

Authority to manage the work means that the team—and not the leader—has decision rights over basic work strategies. . . .Teams with the prerogative to make these decisions themselves, without interference from their leader, strongly outperformed those that did not.

While many of these decisions might "officially" belong to the team, some leaders frequently intervened—for example, by monitoring call rates during the day or asking a team member to take a particular call. These interventions compromise a team's sense of ownership for the work. Moreover, when things go wrong, they can easily attribute the cause to their leaders rather than to themselves. Leaders' ambivalence about the teams' authority erodes the very purpose of having self-managed teams.

By contrast, the leaders of the more effective teams explicitly addressed the teams' authority and the boundaries around it. And they made it clear that they were available for consultation—but that the ultimate decision-making authority for solving work problems belonged to the team. . . .

Factor 6: Team Goals

This critical success factor refers to whether the team has performance goals that are congruent with the organization's objectives. Unlike the team's statement of its overall purpose, goals are specific (often quantified) descriptions of work the team is to accomplish within a specific time frame. In this study, we classified a team as having such goals if members could articulate what they wanted to accomplish as a team by some clear deadline: "maintaining 100 percent customer satisfaction this year," or "improving our customer satisfaction performances by 2.5 percent and our parts expense performance by 5 percent this year." . . .

Factor 7: Team Norms That Promote Strategic Thinking

Norms are the informal rules that guide team members' behavior. Our findings showed that norms which promote strategic thinking about work issues were related to team effectiveness. Self-managing teams, unlike manager-led teams, require an outward focus on the part of team members—they must be aware of their environment, able to detect problems, and accustomed to developing novel ways of working.

This kind of forward thinking may not come naturally to teams, especially if members shoulder greater responsibility than they ever had before. But group norms that promote proactive strategic thinking are very important for effective team self-management.

Superb teams encourage members to (1) experiment with new ways to work more effectively, (2) seek best practices from other teams and other parts of the organization, (3) take action to solve problems without waiting for direction, and (4) discuss differences in what each member has to contribute to the work. These are all ways in which the team encourages a proactive stance toward problems and increases its responsiveness to changing demands.

Norms emerge naturally in teams, regardless of whether a leader attempts to guide their development. However, norms that are left to emerge on their own often do not support strategic planning. Leaders can—and should—help appropriate norms develop. . . .

. . . [W]hen a leader gets the other six critical success factors in place, norms that supported active problem-solving and strategic thinking tend to take hold more quickly and to be more carefully maintained by team members. Tackling the other six factors first greatly increased the chances that a leader was successful in building appropriate team norms.

ON COACHING WELL

For many team leaders, the struggle to learn how to coach effectively has been a difficult one. It requires new behaviors that differ widely from their old habits of directing and coordinating work. Such habits are difficult to unlearn. For these leaders, the study findings on team design should come as good news: Once their teams are designed well, leaders have the latitude to experiment with their own behavior and learn how to coach effectively. If their teams are set up right, a leader's coaching errors will not harm the teams much. . . .

. . . Among the leader behaviors that helped a team were:

- providing rewards and other signals that the team is responsible for managing itself (e.g., rewarding the team for solving a problem; spending more time in interaction with the group as a whole, rather than with individuals); and
- broadening the team's repertoire of problem-solving skills (e.g., teaching the team how to use a problem-solving process; facilitating problem-solving discussions without imposing one's own view of a solution).

These behaviors underscored the team's responsibility for its own outcomes, motivated the team to tackle problems as a group, and enhanced members' basic self-management skills.

Among the coaching behaviors that undermined a team were:

- signaling that individuals (or the manager/leader) were responsible for managing the team (e.g., by spending more time with individuals than with the team; by running team meetings rather than coaching the team on how to run its own meetings effectively); and
- intervening in the task in ways that undermined the team's authority (e.g., monitoring team actions and assigning a team member a particular responsibility; dealing directly with a team's customer without involving the team; and overriding a team decision—even if it seemed to be a poor one).

Coaching behaviors do influence whether the team takes responsibility for its work and monitors and manages its own performance. . . .

THE ROLE OF THE LEADER

. . . Do leaders matter? The findings of this study might be taken to imply that leaders don't matter much. A better interpretation is that our emphasis on a leader's day-to-day coaching is misplaced. After all, setting up a team right in the first place and ensuring that it has the needed resources are critical leadership functions. The elements of team design discussed here are all features that a leader or first-line manager can and should influence.

Exhibit 3 presents a guide to help leaders determine where their leadership is most needed to get their teams set up right. . . .

On Leadership and Timing

Leaders do have an important role in the life of teams—but that role differs at various stages in the team's life. It is useful to look back at the critical success factors to see how the leader's role changes as he or she takes action to get all the pieces in place.

Role 1: Designer (critical success factors one through five). This role is most critical when the team is first launched.

EXHIBIT 3 • CRITICAL SUCCESS FACTORS: DIAGNOSTIC QUESTIONS FOR TEAM LEADERS

1. ***Clear direction***
   Can team members articulate a clear direction, shared by all members, of the basic purpose that the team exists to achieve?
2. ***A real team task***
   Is the team assigned collective responsibility for all the team's customers and major outputs?
   Is the team required to make collective decisions about work strategies (rather than leaving it to individuals)?
   Are members cross-trained, able to help each other?
   Does the team get team-level data and feedback about its performance?
   Is the team required to meet frequently, and does it do so?
3. ***Team rewards***
   Counting all reward dollars available, are more than 80 percent available to teams only, and not to individuals?
4. ***Basic material resources***
   Does the team have its own meeting space?
   Can the team easily get basic materials needed for the work?
5. ***Authority to manage the work***
   Does the team have the authority to decide the following (without first receiving special authorization)?
   - How to meet client demands
   - Which actions to take, and when
   - Whether to change their work strategies when they deem necessary
6. ***Team goals***
   Can the team articulate specific goals?
   Do these goals stretch their performance?
   Have they specified a time by which they intend to accomplish these goals?
7. ***Strategy norms***
   Do team members encourage each other to detect problems without the leader's intervention?
   Do members openly discuss differences in what members have to contribute to the team?
   Do members encourage experimentation with new ways of operating?
   Does the team actively seek to learn from other teams?

The leader's action at this stage is to set a direction for the performing unit, design a team task and a team reward system, make sure the team has the basic material resources it needs to do the work, and establish the team's authority over and its responsibility for its performance strategies. These actions serve to get a team started in the right direction and with the right supports for high-quality performance.

Role 2: Midwife (critical success factors six and seven). This role becomes important after the team is launched; it is best played at natural break-points in the team's work. In this role, the leader works with the team to establish appropriate performance goals. Goals represent measurable aims that specify how a team will take on its work in ways that fulfill its overall direction. Consequently, the critical factors related to task and direction must be firmly in place.

The leader also helps establish norms about strategic thinking, thus influencing how the team uses its resources and authority. In shaping these norms, the leader is helping the team develop work strategies that use the team's decision-making power over how it operates. . . .

Role 3: Coach. Finally, the coaching role takes over—and continues throughout the life of the team. With the critical success factors in place, the team is now positioned to take full advantage of high-quality coaching. This means that the time and energy a leader invests in day-to-day coaching will be resources well used, not wasted effort. . . .

CONCLUSION

The seven critical success factors matter for anyone leading a team—from front-line managers leading shop-floor teams to senior managers launching problem-solving groups. Indeed, the messages here may be especially critical for senior managers. Putting the success factors in place may require organization-wide changes—in reward systems, in work design, in resources available to teams. Because it is middle and senior managers who have the most opportunity and authority to change these design features, it is particularly critical that they be aware of what teams require throughout the organization. Putting these factors in place gives the organization the greatest possible chance of getting the creativity, flexibility, and responsiveness that are the whole point of building self-managing teams.

24
Virtual Teams: The New Way to Work

Jessica Lipnack and Jeffrey Stamps

THE AGE OF THE NETWORK

The 21st century organization is made up of virtual teams and networks of teams. The network—rather than the pyramid—becomes the conceptual model for how people work together to accomplish the goals of the enterprise. A physical model of a networked organization would look like one of Buckminster Fuller's geodesic domes—many tetrahedrons joined together at key intersections. One of the interesting things about the geodesic dome is that it's the only built structure in the universe that gets stronger as it gets larger. A networked organization can increase in effectiveness as it grows. In team-based organizations, networks can help teams avoid a sense of fragmentation and isolation. Networks can even extend beyond the boundaries of a single organization. There are networks of organizations, networks of companies, and networks of nations.

Virtual teams and networked organizations are the latest stage in the evolution of organization. . . .

The networked organization will not wipe out all the old forms. Rather, it includes them and adds new capabilities. When hierarchies formed, we didn't lose the ability to work in small groups. A complex, networked organization will, in fact, involve hierarchy, bureaucracy, and small groups, as well as distinctly networked relationships. The key is to select the best form of organization for a particular kind of work.

Hierarchy is a fundamental principle of organization in the universe. Our cells, organs, organisms, and communities are all based on hierarchies. We don't want to lose the structure, but we need to change the one-way paths of information, which create bottlenecks.

A hierarchy alone is a tall structure without much of a horizontal base. Bureaucracies are formed as organizations spread out and work is divided into specialized departments. This lateral extension helps to create a stronger structure, which is able to grow larger and handle more complexity. But this organization is still quite vulnerable to change. In particular, any pressure on the top of the structure could cause the whole thing to collapse.

The easiest way to transition from hierarchy/bureaucracy to a networked organization is to add links to connect the various functions. The result is a strong but flexible geodesic structure based on connected tetrahedrons—a structure better able to resist the impact of change. Bureaucratic specialization is not going away, but the new links allow communication to flow horizontally as

Source: Reprinted by permission of the author.

EXHIBIT 1 • ORGANIZATION CHART OF EASTMAN CHEMICAL COMPANY

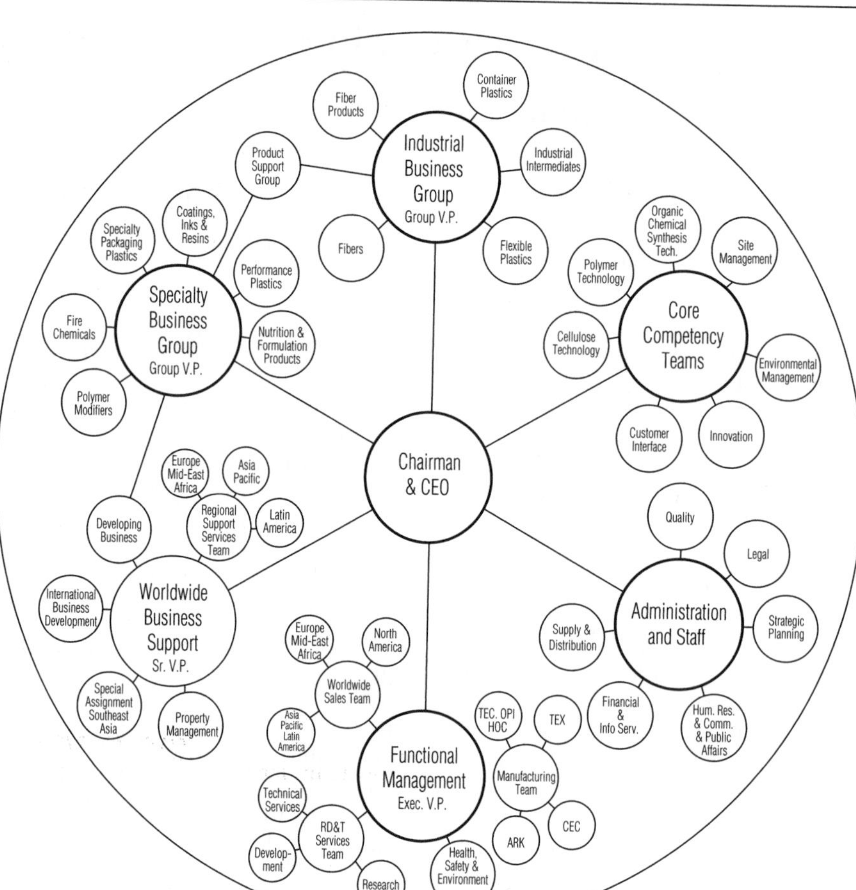

well as vertically, and precious time is saved. Gradually, a new form of organization will emerge.

All four of these ways of organizing coexist in many organizations. Exhibit 1 shows the organization chart of Eastman Chemical Company. It's not a metaphor for the organization chart—it's the actual way the company's chief executive, Earnest Deavenport, drew it.

The hierarchy is in the hub-and-spoke design. It has the same logic as a tree diagram, but putting it in a wheel gives it a very different sense. The bureaucracy is there in that each of the circles has a different name and focuses on a specific purpose. The thick outer line defines the boundary of the organization. The white space in the chart is where all the connections are, and that's what makes it a networked organization. Communication goes directly between the people who need the information and the people who have it.

Eastman uses self-managed teams at all levels. For example, the presidents of each of the manufacturing facilities have formed a Presidents' Council, and the role of executive vice president for manufacturing rotates every quarter. They have assembled an information system that keeps everyone up to date as the responsibility passes from one person to the next.

One of the earliest companies to move in this direction where information flows quickly is Buckman Labs, a specialty chemical company located in Memphis. . . .

. . . [I]f a customer had a problem, Buckman Labs typically would send its most experienced person out to the customer's site to work on it. For a company that does business all over the world, this became very costly. The solution was to put all 1,200 people at Buckman Labs online. That was 10 years ago, and the technology they used was CompuServe—not Lotus Notes, not web pages, not even live chats on CompuServe, but CompuServe forums. The discussions went on 24 hours a day, and problems were solved quickly. Even with what we would today consider primitive technology for this purpose, Buckman Labs was able to become an around-the-clock, global organization.

THE EMERGENCE OF VIRTUAL TEAMS

In today's business environment, teams have been accepted as the smart way to organize for flexible and cost-effective operations. With recent advances in technology, however, team members no longer must be housed in one location in order to work together. They can become virtual teams—teams with a common purpose that use technology to cross time zones, distance, and the boundaries of organizations. . . .

Telecommunications in the global economy has brought new partners and ways of working to millions of people. Colleagues can sleep in different time zones and still be members of the same team. This is true, but it's not easy. The explosion of links across every conceivable boundary is staggering in its complexity as languages, cultures, governments, distances, and the mysterious nuances of human behavior all play their parts.

When NCR was spun off by AT&T, it used virtual teams to achieve its turnaround. In 1996, NCR brought out its WorldMark enterprise computer server, machines so massive that they may weigh 10 or 12 tons. Involving over 1,000 people in 17 primary locations, the WorldMark project housed internal groups situated in five U.S. states, Ireland, India, and China. Outside partners were in six other locations. Unbelievably, given the number of players and their diverse locations, the project was completed on budget and ahead of schedule.

Three things made the WorldMark project successful. First, everyone involved understood what the project was about—there was a clear mission, and it was well communicated. Second, they had common work processes. Everyone knew how to set goals, describe the tasks and the ultimate results, and create schedules to work toward those results. And finally, they had superb communications.

The virtual team worked together on a daily basis even though they were a continent apart. The engineers were connected by a high-speed, full-bandwidth, continuously available, audio, video, and data link that they affectionately nicknamed "the Worm Hole." (A worm hole is an intergalactic phenomenon found in science fiction—a portal of instant transport from one place in the universe to another.) NCR's Worm

Hole is made possible by a switched T1 line, a very high speed telecommunications link that connects three videoconferencing rooms separated by thousands of miles.

In the Worm Hole, each screen serves a different purpose. One shows the people at the other location, a second serves as an overhead projector to display materials being used, and a third allows a standard PC to facilitate information sharing and distribution. At their frequent meetings, team members discuss strategy, argue points, solve problems, make presentations, exchange documents, use flip charts, and share files. They work not only with each other, but also with colleagues in many other locations. Using this technology, it took the team 11 months to develop NCR's next generation computer system.

When Sun Microsystems had some quality problems a few years ago, Scott McNealy, Sun's chief executive, invited the CEOs of Federal Express, Motorola, and Xerox to offer suggestions. In every case, the CEOs said that what made a difference in their companies was teams.

At that time, Sun was the archetype of the cowboy/cowgirl mentality—the brilliant engineer working alone, never in teams. To address its problems, employees were invited to form teams to investigate the 32 top "customer dissatisfiers." Seventy boundary-crossing virtual teams were formed, and they were highly effective in solving the problems. Each team had an executive sponsor, clear guidelines about what needed to be done to be successful, and a fantastic technology infrastructure.

Virtual teams are a type of small group. They differ from other small groups in forms of communication, number of relationships, and in the ability to create in a global context. The technology is here today that allows people to work together at a distance just as though they were next door to one another in an office setting. Successful virtual teams, however, depend more on people than they do on technology. . . . The technology won't work unless the people issues are addressed first. Working in a virtual environment requires a new kind of organization, a new kind of management, and a new kind of leadership.

A MODEL FOR VIRTUAL TEAMS

The basic principles that underlie all of our case examples have three facets: purpose, people, and links. . . .

Purpose. Purpose is very important to any form of organization. But it is critical to virtual organizations and teams because purpose is the glue that holds them together. Hierarchy has the power to hire and fire. Bureaucracy has rules, regulations, constitutions, and laws. But truly networked organizations and virtual teams often have only purpose. For example, a team that's pulled together because several companies are in an alliance together has no common reporting structure. They will stay together only if their shared purpose is robust and agreed upon by all the members of the team.

In a virtual team, purpose goes beyond a mission statement that is put on the wall and forgotten. Purpose must be translated into action steps that become the basis for the work people will do together. It requires cooperative goals, interdependent tasks, and concrete results. Teams exist to produce results. Without cooperative goals, the project will never get started. And if the tasks are all independent, then a team is unnecessary. Virtual teams are usually created because one person or one organization can't get the desired results alone.

People. People are the core of virtual teams. But there are key factors that must be considered. The first is independence. Everyone in the virtual team must be autonomous and self-reliant but still able to be interdependent. They must know how to be "me," while simultaneously holding on to being "we."

The second aspect is shared leadership. At some point, each member of the virtual team will play a leadership role, depending on where the team is in the process. Leadership will shift, depending on the task at hand. Each person brings a particular set of skills and expertise that will be called upon in the process.

The third aspect is integrated levels. Virtual teams are not only horizontally articulated teams; they must connect up and down in the organization.

Links. Links are connections—not just technology. These connections may be through face-to-face conversation or through communication technologies. But the connections themselves are totally passive. Results require interaction of some kind. Over time, these interactions will produce relationships, and if they are trusting relationships they will endure. Relationships make the organization. What makes the information age different is not the relationships or interactions, it's the digital technologies.

Digital technologies offer a fantastic cornucopia of interactive capabilities. We are now beginning to explore how these technologies might affect the way we organize ourselves. We won't lose other forms of communication; we'll just add to them. There are things you can do face-to-face that you can't do at a distance, such as build trust quickly. Once you determine the purpose and the people you can decide which linkages are most useful for tying these people together to accomplish the work they've agreed upon.

. . . Virtual teams are small systems, while networks tend to be much larger systems. But all of these characteristics will be present in all successful, distributed organizations.

SOCIAL CAPITAL: THE OTHER BOTTOM LINE

There is a double bottom line in the work of any team. There's a task result or outcome that is usually visible and obvious, and there is a social outcome, based on the team's interactions. The social effect may not be apparent in the quality of the task outcome. In one team, there may have been really unpleasant interactions—a lot of loud talk, banging of heads, and long nights. In another team, the same result may have been achieved through cooperation, collaboration, and mutual assistance, making the entire experience a very positive one. The next time a teaming opportunity arises, those who went through a bad experience may decide they never want to be part of another team, while those who had a good experience are apt to participate and, in fact, will be more effective because they have built relationships and learned how to work as a team.

These contrasting team experiences have either increased or decreased the organization's social capital. Increased social capital means there is increased capability to do work. In the reverse situation, capacity has been taken away. It is impossible not to have some impact. The team experience will either add to or deplete the organization's existing stock of "relationship resources." James Coleman first developed the concept of social capital in the early '80s.[1] Today social capital is recognized as a valuable addition to an organization's total resources, which include physical property, financial capital, and human capital.

According to Harvard history professor Robert Putnam, three things are necessary to develop social capital: trust, reciprocity, and dense social networks.[2]

- *Trust* is No. 1. All else flows from it. Often, seemingly irrelevant, unrelated-to-work conversations among employees build trust that will make their working relationships more effective in the future.
- *Reciprocity* means give and take. It is not necessary in the immediate moment; rather, people need the sense that giving will eventually result in receiving.
- Research shows that in communities where people are well-connected in *dense social networks*, they tend to be healthier and more economically stable. The same holds true for organizations.

Companies like Eastman Chemical are deliberately working to increase their levels of trust. In the early 1980s, Eastman conducted a survey to determine the level of trust within the company, and its leaders were shocked to find that trust was very low. According to the survey, the No. 1 item that accounted for that low level of trust was the company's use of the Hay compensation system that used the normal, bell-shaped curve to determine pay and reward. Here was a company that hired the best and the brightest and then immediately told half of them that they were underperformers and would be paid accordingly. The pay system was radically reformed.

Eastman also had a suggestion box program through which an individual could win up to $25,000 for a successful idea, but it created competition among employees instead of collaboration. So the individual-suggestion box was discontinued. Teams were asked to work together on suggestions and were rewarded accordingly.

There are also hazards in giving team rewards. First, the teams themselves can become unproductively competitive. Second, who's to say who exactly contributed to a given team's success? There's an apocryphal story about Hewlett-Packard, in which the leader of a team that had a tremendous success was purported to have sent an e-mail inviting everyone who contributed to the team's success to come to dinner. They were expecting about 50 responses, and instead they got 1,500. They had to rent a football field. Teams have porous boundaries, and many people throughout the organization may consider themselves to be a part.

Social capital is built in small groups and internal organizations, but it doesn't stop there, AnnaLee Saxenian has compared Silicon Valley with the Route 128 area in Boston.[3] Both of these regions have had to respond to threats to their dominance: The PC challenge to minicomputers in Boston and the Japanese semiconductor challenge to the chip industry in the Valley. The Valley not only came back, it became the unquestioned world leader in this industry, while the economy around Route 128 has never regained its 1980's level of prominence. It is recovering today, thanks to a burgeoning telecommunications industry.

What made the difference? Saxenian says the difference was social capital writ large. In the Valley, organizations were more open—people could move easily from Sun to Apple to Silicon Graphics. They competed very vigorously, but they also traded ideas. In the East, companies are more insular and vertically oriented. In the heyday of the Digital Equipment Corporation, an employee who left the company was considered a traitor—an outcast. This attitude closed doors and prevented the formation of social capital.

We are only at the beginning of our understanding of virtual teams and their impact on organizations of the future. We believe that, in time, virtual teams will become the accepted way to work. Virtual teams and networks—effective, value-based, swiftly reconfiguring, high-performance, cost-sensitive, and decentralized—will profoundly reshape our world.

NOTES AND REFERENCES

1. James S. Coleman, "Social Capital in the Creation of Human Capital," *American Journal of Sociology* (1988 Supplement), S98.
2. Robert S. Putnam, *Making Democracy Work: Civic Traditions in Modern Italy* (Princeton, N.J.: Princeton University Press, 1993).
3. AnnaLee Saxenian, *Regional Advantage: Culture and Competition in Silicon Valley and Route 128* (Cambridge: Harvard University Press, 1994).

CHAPTER IV

Effects of the Work Environment on Individuals

Individual levels of performance, creativity, and even personal satisfaction or dissatisfaction of musicians are highly influenced by the organizational environment. "Environment" is an imprecise term that includes many factors. The orchestra's organizational structure, its financial health, communication patterns among musicians and between individual musicians and the business office, methods of coordinating among the sections, the style and temperament of the musical and business executives, the work norms, the presence or absence—and strength—of a musicians union, and the particular tastes of the orchestra's patrons all are parts of the "work environment." The work environment affects the psychological state, the attitudes, and the performance of individual musicians.

In this chapter, our analysis of organizational behavior moves away from individuals and small groups to address organizational structures, systems, culture, and behavioral norms. Although gifted individual musicians are the building blocks for any orchestra, the orchestra's organizational behavior cannot be understood without also looking beyond the individuals (the "trees") to the work environment (the "forest").

In 1959, Warren Bennis observed that such classical organizational theorists as Frederick Winslow Taylor, Henry Gantt, and Henri Fayol (see Shafritz & Ott, 2001, chap. I) were fixated on structural variables (such as the chain of command, centralization and decentralization, and span of control) to the extent that they almost seem to think about "organizations without people." In contrast, the human relations–oriented organizational behaviorists of the late 1950s and 1960s were so enamored with people and groups (with personal growth, group development, sensitivity training groups, and human relations training) that they seemed to think only about "people without organizations." Bennis's observation was equally applicable to the early industrial/organizational psychologists—to the pre-Hawthorne and pre-Theory X and Theory Y value system–based social scientists who worked with organizational behavior, but not from an organizational behavior perspective (see the *Introduction*). However, between the 1930s and the 1950s and 1960s, organizational behavior reversed its field and in the process almost forgot (or at least ignored) the substantial influences that organization systems and structures have on the people and groups in and around them.

Many things in the organizational context influence and are influenced by organizational behavior. To list only a few:

- *The type of business in which an organization is engaged.* The business of banking places different demands on and yields different rewards to employees than does making and marketing new television game shows.
- *The legal relationship between an organization and people who work for it.* Typically, there are different impacts on organizational behavior in, for example, a family-owned business, a publicly held investor-owned company, a nonprofit arts organization, and a government agency.
- *The nature of the perceived relationships between an organization and its environment at large.* The prevailing perception in some organizations seems to be that they exist in a hostile world where the media, general public, other types of organizations (such as government agencies, legislatures, or private corporations), and sometimes even clientele or customers (as well as direct competitors) all are immediate or potential enemies or threats. In contrast, the prevailing view in other organizations is more one of the organization existing in harmony with its environment.

The structure of the organization is also an important component. When someone refers to *organization structure*, usually he or she is talking about the relatively stable relationships among the positions or groups of positions (such as the units, divisions, and departments) that comprise an organization, along with the organized procedures and methods that define how things are designed for work to flow through it. Structure is the design of an organization, its units, and its production processes. It is the set of specific patterns of differentiation and integration of tasks and activities in an organization (Thompson, 1967; Miles, 1980). *Differentiation* is the (conceptual) dividing up of a total system into its component parts (units, groups, and people), which perform specialized tasks. (In essence, differentiation is a more sophisticated way of saying "division of labor.") *Integration* is how the divided-up parts and specialized tasks are linked together to form a coordinated whole.

To be more concrete, a widely read article by Lyman Porter and Edward Lawler (1965) identifies the properties of organization structure that, according to an extensive search of the then-published literature, most affect individual and group attitudes and on-the-job behavior. Their list of structural properties includes the following:

- *Organization levels* (the number of levels and in which one—or how high—one is situated)
- *Line* or *staff roles* of organization units
- *Span of control*
- *Size of units*
- *Size of the total organization*
- *Organization shape* (flat or tall)
- *Centralized* or *decentralized authority* and responsibility

The structure—an organization's shape, size, procedures, production technology, position descriptions, reporting arrangements, and coordinating relationships—affects the feelings and emotions, and therefore the behavior, of the people and groups inside them. There are incongruencies between the needs of a mature personality and of formal organization—between the growth trends of healthy people and the requirements of organizations (Argyris, 1957b). The impacts of structure on behavior partially result from the unique functions structure performs. In each organization, structure defines the unique ways labor is divided, how specialized roles and functions are to be coordinated (related to each other and to other organizational levels and functions), how information is to flow among people and groups, and how the system of controls (how tasks are measured, evaluated, and altered) is to work (Organ & Bateman, 1986). Structure establishes how *roles, expectations*, and *resource allocations* are defined for people and groups in any given organization. Structure is a primary reason organizational behavior differs from mere behavior, and thus why organizational behavior developed as a separate field of study within the applied behavioral sciences.

Structure, however, is only one of several forces that affect the behavior of people in organizations. Attitudes and behaviors also are shaped by *peer group pressure* (Asche, 1951; Janis, 1971); *group norms*—the standards that develop are shared and enforced by the members of groups (Cohen, Fink, Gadon, & Willits, 1988, chap. 3; Feldman, 1984; Roy, 1960); the particular blending of social and technical aspects of work tasks—the *sociotechnical systems* (Thorsrud, 1968; Trist, 1960; Trist & Bamforth, 1951); and the *organizational culture* (Ott, 1989; Schein, 1992; Whyte, 1956).

To an extent, all formal and informal groups (see Chapter III) require and expect people to conform to norms—prescriptions for behavior. Norms are behavioral blueprints that provide organizations with coherence. Acceptance of and adherence to group norms permit people to know what to expect from each other and to predict what other members will do in different circumstances. Norms cause people to behave in patterned and predictable ways; "because their behaviors are guided by common expectations, attitudes and understandings . . . norms are strong stabilizers of organizational behavior" (Schmuck, 1971, pp. 215–216). Norms establish some conformity, stability, and predictability—states that are both necessary and desirable.

On the other hand, too much adherence to norms causes overconformance and can hurt or destroy individualism (Merton, 1957; Whyte, 1956). Potential damage, though, is not limited to individuals who work in organizations. Excessive conformity also can result in organizational rigidity. Organizations must be open to divergent information, viewpoints, realities, and value systems. Indeed, organizations must seek diversity and reward individuals and groups who succeed in injecting diversity into strategic decision processes (Cox, 1993).

The readings in this chapter examine ways in which structure, sociotechnical systems, group norms and pressures to conform, and organizational culture influence the behavior of individuals and groups in organizations. The focus is on how norms, structures of relationships, group pressures, sociotechnical systems, and organizational culture combine to shape organizational behavior. Several of the selections also examine ways in which the forces that lead to conformity potentially damage individuals and organizations.

The first reading describes research in the problematic area of group effects on individuals' decisions. In "Effects of Group Pressure Upon the Modification and Distortion of Judgments," Solomon Asch (1951) describes his famous investigations into ways individuals cope when a group's majority opinion is directly contrary to the facts of a situation. Asch put lone experimental subjects (college students) in rooms with people who had been instructed to give blatantly wrong answers to factual questions. Only the experimental subjects did not know what was going on. Although a slim majority of experimental subjects retained their independence and reported the facts accurately, a sizable minority of subjects *altered their judgment to match that of the majority*. When faced with a group opinion that was obviously wrong, they were not willing to report their observations as they saw them. They changed their judgments. Asch attributes people's decisions to retain independence of judgment or to yield to the majority to several factors. The two most important factors are these:

- The size of the majority and the extent of unanimity among members of the majority
- Identifiable, enduring differences among individuals, particularly character differences involving social relations

Asch's experiments provide dramatic evidence of group impacts on people in organizations. From a managerial perspective, they show why it is extremely important to focus attention on the group's beliefs, values, composition, and activities. Nevertheless, for the most part, informal groups are outside of the formal organization's direct sphere of influence.

Sociotechnical systems commonly refers to the interactive relationships or the *fit* between work technology, organization structure, and social interactions of the workplace. Most sociotechnical system studies involve investigations of how work processes (technology) and work teams (social systems) can be structured (organization) to maximize productivity and at the same time satisfy employees' desires for affiliation and, in some work settings, needs for safety that only close groups can provide. The Tavistock Institute of London has been closely identified with sociotechnical systems research and consulting since the 1950s. The best known of the Tavistock sociotechnical systems studies have been set in British coal mines (Trist & Bamforth, 1951; Trist, Higgin, Murray, & Pollock, 1965) and weaving mills of India (Rice, 1953). These studies became the forerunners of many widely publicized sociotechnical systems–style work reorganization efforts, such as in the Scandinavian automobile industry (Thorsrud, 1968); "Procter & Gamble's plant in Lima, Ohio; Alcan's cold rolling mill in Quebec; Shell's refinery in Teesport, England; and Norsk Hydro's fertilizer plant in Porsgrunn, Norway" (Walton, 1975, p. 117).

Eric Trist, Kenneth Bamforth, and their associates at the Tavistock Institute studied the links between work technology, organization structure, and social structure. In their famous 1951 article, "Some Social and Psychological Consequences of the Longwall Method of Coal-Getting" (reprinted in this chapter), Trist and

Bamforth found that management's attempts to increase coal mining productivity by moving to the longwall method (a technology analogous to mass production) had negative repercussions. At the time of its introduction in the late 1940s, the longwall method of coal-getting represented a major technological improvement. Prior to that time, coal had been mined by self-selecting, highly mutually supportive, self-regulating small groups (often pairs) who performed the entire cycle of extraction operations. The pairs faced grave dangers together working far under the earth, watched out for each other, and jointly decided when to change working places and procedures in the face of dangers. The pair system also provided each man with someone to talk with about fears and anxieties.

The longwall method changed everything. Miners no longer worked in long-established small groups. They worked in long lines, using new machinery that required them to face the wall, with a substantial distance between each man. When work pressure increased, there was no close associate to talk with about stress and anxiety or even people close enough for bantering. Introduction of the new structural and technological systems destroyed important social systems; hence, as Trist and Bamforth note, productivity and morale became major problems: "It is difficult to see how these problems can be solved effectively without restoring responsible autonomy to primary groups throughout the system and ensuring that each of these groups has a satisfying subwhole as its work task, and some scope for flexibility in workpace." The longwall coal study, along with several other sociotechnical system studies that appeared at about the same time (for example, Jaques, 1950; Rice, 1953; Rice, Hill, & Trist, 1950), represented a major turning point in the *practice* of organizational behavior. The coal companies listened to the workers (through the reporting of the behavioral scientists) and modified the technical system to mesh with the workers' social system needs.

In "Bureaucratic Structure and Personality," Robert Merton (1940, 1957) analyzes how one form of organization structure—*bureaucracy*—impinges on the personalities of people who work inside them. Merton uses "bureaucracy" to mean the pervasive form of organization that Max Weber (1922) described in *Wirtschat und Gesellschaft*. In this use, bureaucracy is neither an epithet per se, nor is it limited in applicability to government agencies. According to Merton, bureaucracy exerts constant pressures on people to be methodical and disciplined, to conform to patterns of obligations. These pressures eventually cause people to adhere to rules as an end rather than a means—as a matter of blind conformance. Bureaucratic structure also stresses depersonalized relations and power and authority gained by virtue of organizational position rather than by thought or action. Without question, Merton sees bureaucratic structure as more than *affecting* organizational behavior and thinking: it also *determines and controls it*. As a form of organization, bureaucracy has its advantages: order, predictability, stability, professionalism, and consistency (Shafritz & Ott, 2001, chap. I). Nevertheless, the behavioral consequences of bureaucratic structure are mostly negative, including reduced organizational flexibility and efficiency and, adapting a phrase coined by Merton, eventually "bureaupathological personalities" of members.

Twenty years after Solomon Asch's experiments, Irving Janis (1971) published the equally well-known study, "Groupthink," which is reprinted in this chapter. Like Asch, Janis explores pressures for conformance—the reasons social conformity is encountered frequently in groups. But unlike Asch's experimental use of college students, Janis looked at high-level decision makers in times of real major fiascos: the 1962 Bay of Pigs, the 1950 decision to send General MacArthur to the Yalu River, and the 1941 failure to prepare for the attack on Pearl Harbor. *Groupthink* is "the mode of thinking that persons engage in when *concurrence seeking* becomes so dominant in a cohesive in-group that it tends to override realistic appraisal of alternative courses of action . . . the desperate drive for consensus at any cost that suppresses dissent among the mighty in the corridors of power." Janis identifies eight symptoms of groupthink that are relatively easy to observe:

- An illusion of invulnerability
- Collective construction of rationalizations that permit group members to ignore warnings or other forms of negative feedback
- Unquestioning belief in the morality of the ingroup
- Strong, negative, stereotyped views about the leaders of enemy groups
- Rapid application of pressure against group members who express even momentary doubts about virtually any illusions the group shares
- Careful, conscious, personal avoidance of deviation from what appears to be a group consensus
- Shared illusions of unanimity of opinion
- Establishment of *mindguards*—people who "protect the leader and fellow members from adverse information that might break the complacency they shared about the effectiveness and morality of past decisions"

Janis concludes with an assessment of the negative influence of groupthink on executive decision making (including overestimation of the group's capability and self-imposed isolation from new or opposing information and points of view), and some preventive and remedial steps for groupthink.

Porter, Lawler, and Hackman's chapter, "Social Influences on Work Effectiveness" (reprinted in this chapter), from their 1975 book *Behavior in Organizations*, analyzes in depth how groups and other members of a person's role set exert influence on individuals in organizations, and how these social influences affect work effectiveness. This piece focuses particularly on the "notion that the nature and degree of such social influences depend crucially on the type of work being performed and thus on the demands that the work makes on the person." The chapter specifically examines dysfunctional aspects of eliminating deviance from group norms, why high group cohesiveness can be dysfunctional, and ways that groups influence individual work effectiveness. "The point is that the people who surround an individual at work can facilitate as well as hinder . . . performance effectiveness—and that any serious attempt to diagnose the social environment in the interest of improving work performance should explicitly address unrealized possibilities for enhancing performance as well as issues for which remedial action may be required."

In "Organization Theory and Structural Perspectives on Management" (reprinted in this chapter), Jeffrey Pfeffer (1991) argues that studies of organizational behavior have overemphasized individual variables and tended to ignore the influence of structural variables. He builds a persuasive argument by demonstrating that structural position—including network location, physical location, and one's demographic relationship to others—affects organizational behaviors that have been studied extensively but almost exclusively from an individualistic perspective. "In spite of the fact that we know that organizations are relational entities in which individuals interact and compare themselves with others, many of our analyses take the individual alone as the unit of analysis and do not attempt to incorporate notions of social structure into either theory or empirical research. . . . A concern with structural effects can enrich the analysis of even individual-level outcomes such as satisfaction, turnover, performance, and salary." Pfeffer thus seeks to convince us of the usefulness of the structural perspective (including social relations and organizational influence) for understanding organizational behavior.

The readings in Chapter IV conclude with an insightful examination of one specific type of influence on the behavior of individuals—when people believe an organization has violated its commitment to them. These commitments are known as *psychological contracts*, unwritten sets of expectations between all members of an organization and the various supervisors, managers, and others in the organization. In "Psychological Contracts in Organizations: Violating the Contract" (reprinted in this chapter), Denise M. Rousseau (1995) states that people in organizations often fail to live up to the terms of psychological contracts but claims that "how people interpret the circumstances of this failure determines whether they *experience* a violation" of a contract. People subjectively feel that a psychological contract has been violated "when failure to keep a commitment *injures* or causes damages that the contract was designed to avoid. . . . A major 'problem' in contract violation is understanding why some events, seemingly at odds with a contract, do not provoke adverse reactions, but other events that appear innocuous engender outrage and anger." When an employee feels that a contract has been violated, the response may take many forms. "Violated contracts promote mistrust, anger, and attrition and change the way people behave in subsequent interactions. . . . The aftermath of contract violation can be seen in declining corporate loyalty and increased litigation." Thus, trust erodes when people believe psychological contracts have been violated. "The strength and quality of the relationship [between an individual and the organization] not only affects the extent to which violation is tolerated or leads to dissolution of the contract but also affects the ability of the parties to repair the relationship."

REFERENCES

Argyris, C. (1957a). *Personality and organization*. New York: Harper.

Argyris, C. (1957b). The individual and organization: Some problems of mutual adjustment. *Administrative Science Quarterly*, *2*, 1–24.

Asch, S. E. (1951). Effects of group pressure upon the modification and distortion of judgments. In, H. S. Guetzkow (Ed.), *Groups, leadership, and men* (pp. 177–190). Pittsburgh: Carnegie Press.

Bell, N. E., & Staw, B. M. (1989). People as sculptors versus sculpture: The roles of personality and personal control in organizations. In M. B. Arthur, D. T. Hall, & B. S. Lawrence (Eds.), *Handbook of career theory* (pp. 232–241). Cambridge, UK: Cambridge University Press.

Cohen, A. R., Fink, S. L., Gadon, H., & Willits, R. D. (1988). *Effective behavior in organizations* (4th ed.). Homewood, IL: Irwin.

Cox, T. H. Jr. (1993). *Cultural diversity in organizations: Theory, research & practice*. San Francisco: Berrett-Koehler.

Dill, W. R. (1958). Environment as an influence on managerial autonomy. *Administrative Science Quarterly, 2*, 409–443.

Feldman, D. C. (January, 1984). The development and enforcement of group norms. *Academy of Management Review*, 47–53.

Janis, I. L. (1971). Groupthink. *Psychology Today*, 44–76.

Jaques, E. (1950). Collaborative group methods in a wage negotiation situation (The Glacier Project—I). *Human Relations*, 3(3).

Kahn, W. A. (1990). Psychological conditions of personal engagement and disengagement at work. *Academy of Management Journal*, 33(4), 692–724.

Katz, D., & Kahn, R. L. (1966). *The social psychology of organizations*. New York: John Wiley.

Merton, R. K. (1957). Bureaucratic structure and personality. In R. K. Merton, *Social theory and social structure* (rev. & enl. ed.). New York: The Free Press. A revised version of an article of the same title that appeared in *Social Forces, 18* (1940).

Miles, R. H. (1980). *Macro organizational behavior*. Santa Monica, CA: Goodyear Publishing.

Mills, T. (October, 1976). Altering the social structure in coal mining: A case study. *Monthly Labor Review*, 3–10.

Organ, D. W., & Bateman, T. (1986). *Organizational behavior: An applied psychological approach* (3d ed.). Plano, TX: Business Publications.

Ott, J. S. (1989). *The organizational culture perspective*. Belmont, CA: Wadsworth.

Pfeffer, J. (1991). Organization theory and structural perspectives on management. *Journal of Management, 17*(4), 789–803.

Porter, L. W., & Lawler, E. E. III (1965). Properties of organization structure in relation to job attitudes and job behavior. *Psychological Bulletin*, 64(1), 23–51.

Porter, L. W., & Lawler, E. E. III (1964). The effects of tall vs. flat organization structures on managerial job satisfaction. *Personnel Psychology, 17*, 135–148.

Porter, L. W., Lawler, E. E. III, & Hackman, J. R. (1975). Social influences on work effectiveness. In L. W. Porter, E. E. Lawler III, & J. R. Hackman, *Behavior in organizations* (pp. 403–422). New York: McGraw-Hill.

Rice, A. K. (1953). Productivity and social organization in an Indian weaving shed: An examination of some aspects of the sociotechnical system of an experimental automatic loom shed. *Human Relations*, 6, 297–329.

Rice, A. K., Hill, J. M. M., & Trist, E. L. (1950). The representation of labour turnover as a social process (The Glacier Project—II). *Human Relations*, 3(4).

Rousseau, D. M. (1995). *Psychological contracts in organizations: Understanding written and unwritten agreements*. Thousand Oaks, CA: Sage.

Roy, D. F. (1960). "Banana time": Job satisfaction and informal interaction. *Human Organization, 18*, 158–168.

Schein, E. H. (1980). *Organizational psychology* (3d ed.). Englewood Cliffs, NJ: Prentice-Hall.

Schein, E. H. (1992). *Leadership and organizational culture* (2d ed.). San Francisco: Jossey-Bass.

Schmuck, R. A. (1971). Developing teams of organizational specialists. In R. A. Schmuck & M. B. Miles (Eds.), *Organization development in schools* (pp. 213–230). Palo Alto, CA: National Press Books.

Shafritz, J. M., & Ott, J. S. (2001). *Classics of organization theory* (5th ed.). Fort Worth, TX: Harcourt College.

Thayer, F. C. (1981). *An end to hierarchy and competition: Administration in the post–affluent world* (2d ed.). New York: New Viewpoints.

Thompson, J. D. (1967). *Organizations in action*. New York: McGraw-Hill.

Thorsrud, D. E. (1968). Sociotechnical approach to job design and organization development. *Management International Review, 8,* 120–131.

Tocqueville, A. de (1847). *Democracy in America*. New York: Walker.

Trist, E. L. (1960). *Socio-technical systems*. London: Tavistock Institute of Human Relations.

Trist, E. L., & Bamforth, K. (1951). Some social and psychological consequences of the longwall method of coal-getting. *Human Relations, 4,* 3–38.

Trist, E. L., Higgin, G. W., Murray, H., & Pollock, A. B. (1965). *Organizational choice*. London: Tavistock Institute of Human Relations.

Walton, R. E. (1975). From Hawthorne to Topeka and Kalmar. In E. L. Cass & F. G. Zimmer (Eds.), *Man and work in society* (pp. 116–129). New York: Western Electric Co.

Weber, M. (1922). Bureaucracy. In H. Gerth & C. W. Mills (Eds.), *Max Weber: Essays in sociology*. Oxford, U.K.: Oxford University Press.

Whyte, W. F. (1961). *Men at work*. Homewood, IL: The Dorsey Press.

Whyte, W. H. Jr. (1956). *The organization man*. New York: Simon & Schuster.

Worthy, J. C. (1950). Organizational structure and employee morale. *American Sociological Review, 15,* 169–179.

25

Effects of Group Pressure Upon the Modification and Distortion of Judgments

Solomon E. Asch

. . . Our immediate object was to study the social and personal conditions that induce individuals to resist or to yield to group pressures when the latter are perceived to be *contrary to fact*. The issues which this problem raises are of obvious consequence for society; it can be of decisive importance whether or not a group will, under certain conditions, submit to existing pressures. Equally direct are the consequences for individuals and our understanding of them, since it is a decisive fact about a person whether he possesses the freedom to act independently, or whether he characteristically submits to group pressures. . . .

Basic to the current approach has been the axiom that group pressures characteristically induce psychological changes *arbitrarily*, in far-reaching disregard of the material properties of the given conditions. This mode of thinking has almost exclusively stressed the slavish submission of individuals to group forces, has neglected to inquire into their possibilities for independence and for productive relations with human environment, and has virtually denied the capacity of men under certain conditions to rise above group passion and prejudice. It was our aim to contribute to a clarification of these questions, important both for theory and for their human implications, by means of direct observation of the effects of groups upon the decisions and evaluations of individuals.

THE EXPERIMENT AND FIRST RESULTS

To this end we developed an experimental technique which has served as the basis for the present series of studies. We employed the procedure of placing an individual in a relation of radical conflict with all the other members of a group, of measuring its effect upon him in quantitative terms, and of describing its psychological consequences. A group of eight individuals was instructed to judge a series of simple, clearly structured perceptual relations—to match the length of a given line with one of three unequal lines. Each member of the group announced his judgments publicly. In the midst of this monotonous "test" one individual found himself suddenly contradicted by the entire group, and this contradiction was repeated again and again in the course of the experiment. The group in question had, with the exception of one member, previously met with the experimenter and received instructions to respond at certain points with wrong—and unanimous—judgments. The errors of

Source: From "Effects of Group Pressure Upon the Modification and Distortion of Judgments" by Solomon E. Asch, in *Groups, Leadership, and Men*, edited by Harold S. Guetzkow (Pittsburgh: Carnegie Press, 1951, pp. 177–190). Reprinted by permission from Carnegie Mellon University.

the majority were large (ranging between ½″ and 1¾″) and of an order not encountered under control conditions. The outstanding person—the critical subject—whom we had placed in the position of a *minority of one* in the midst of a *unanimous majority*—was the object of investigation. He faced, possibly for the first time in his life, a situation in which a group unanimously contradicted the evidence of his senses.

This procedure was the starting point of the investigation and the point of departure for the study of further problems. Its main features were the following: (1) The critical subject was submitted to two contradictory and irreconcilable forces—the evidence of his own experience of an utterly clear perceptual fact and the unanimous evidence of a group of equals. (2) Both forces were part of the immediate situation; the majority was concretely present, surrounding the subject physically. (3) The critical subject, who was requested together with all others to state his judgments publicly, was obliged to declare himself and to take a definite stand vis-à-vis the group. (4) The situation possessed a self-contained character. The critical subject could not avoid or evade the dilemma by reference to conditions external to the experimental situation. (It may be mentioned at this point that the forces generated by the given conditions acted so quickly upon the critical subjects that instances of suspicion were rare.)

The technique employed permitted a simple quantitative measure of the "majority effect" in terms of the frequency of errors in the direction of the distorted estimates of the majority. At the same time we were concerned from the start to obtain evidence of the ways in which the subjects perceived the group, to establish whether they became doubtful, whether they were tempted to join the majority. Most important, it was our object to establish the grounds of the subject's independence or yielding—whether, for example, the yielding subject was aware of the effect of the majority upon him, whether he abandoned his judgment deliberately or compulsively. To this end we constructed a comprehensive set of questions which served as the basis of an individual interview immediately following the experimental period. Toward the conclusion of the interview each subject was informed fully of the purpose of the experiment, of his role and of that of the majority. The reactions to the disclosure of the purpose of the experiment became in fact an integral part of the procedure. We may state here that the information derived from the interview became an indispensable source of evidence and insight into the psychological structure of the experimental situation, and in particular, of the nature of the individual differences. Also, it is not justified or advisable to allow the subject to leave without giving him a full explanation of the experimental conditions. The experimenter has a responsibility to the subject to clarify his doubts and to state the reasons for placing him in the experimental situation. When this is done most subjects react with interest and many express gratification at having lived through a striking situation which has some bearing on wider human issues.

Both the members of the majority and the critical subjects were male college students. We shall report the results for a total of fifty critical subjects in this experiment. In Table 1 we summarize the successive comparison trials and the majority estimates. The quantitative results are clear and unambiguous.

1. There was a marked movement toward the majority. One-third of all the estimates in the critical group were errors identical with or in the direction of the distorted estimates of the majority.

TABLE I • LENGTHS OF STANDARD AND COMPARISON LINES

Trials	Length of Standard Line (in inches)	Comparison Lines (in inches)			Correct Response	Group Response	Majority Error (in inches)
		1	2	3			
1	10	8¾	10	8	2	2	–
2	2	2	1	1½	1	1	–
3	3	3¾	4¼	3	3	1*	+ ¾
4	5	5	4	6½	1	2*	−1.0
5	4	3	5	4	3	3	–
6	3	3¾	4¼	3	3	2*	+1¼
7	8	6¼	8	6¾	2	3*	−1¼
8	5	5	4	6½	1	3*	+1½
9	8	6¼	8	6¾	2	1*	−1¾
10	10	8¾	10	8	2	2	–
11	2	2	1	1½	1	1	–
12	3	3¾	4¼	3	3	1*	+ ¾
13	5	5	4	6½	1	2*	−1.0
14	4	3	5	4	3	3	–
15	3	3¾	4¼	3	3	2*	+1¼
16	8	6¼	8	6¾	2	3*	−1¼
17	5	5	4	6½	1	3*	+1½
18	8	6¼	8	6¾	2	1*	−1¾

*Starred figures designate the erroneous estimates by the majority.

The significance of this finding becomes clear in the light of the virtual absence of errors in control groups the members of which recorded their estimates in writing. . . .

2. At the same time the effect of the majority was far from complete. The preponderance of estimates in the critical group (68 per cent) was correct despite the pressure of the majority.
3. We found evidence of extreme individual differences. There were those in the critical group subjects who remained independent without exception, and there were those who went nearly all the time with the majority. (The maximum possible number of errors was 12, while the actual range of errors was 0–11.) One-fourth of the critical subjects was completely independent; at the other extreme, one-third of the group displaced the estimates toward the majority in one-half or more of the trials.

The differences between the critical subjects in their reactions to the given conditions were equally striking. There were subjects who remained completely confident throughout. At the other extreme were those who became disoriented, doubt-ridden, and experienced a powerful impulse not to appear different from the majority. . . .

A FIRST ANALYSIS OF INDIVIDUAL DIFFERENCES

On the basis of the interview data described earlier, we undertook to differentiate and describe the major forms of reaction to the experimental situation, which we shall now briefly summarize.

Among the *independent* subjects we distinguished the following main categories:

1. Independence based on *confidence* in one's perception and experience. The most striking characteristic of these subjects is the vigor with which they withstand the group opposition. Though they are sensitive to the group, they show a resilience in coping with it, which is expressed in their continuing reliance on their perception and the effectiveness with which they shake off the oppressive group opposition.

2. Quite different are those subjects who are independent and *withdrawn*. These do not react in a spontaneously emotional way, but rather on the basis of explicit principles concerning the necessity of being an individual.

3. A third group of independent subjects manifest considerable tension and *doubt*, but adhere to their judgments on the basis of a felt necessity to deal adequately with the task.

The following were the main categories of reaction among the *yielding* subjects, or those who went with the majority during one-half or more of the trials.

1. *Distortion of perception* under the stress of group pressure. In this category belong a very few subjects who yield completely, but are not aware that their estimates have been displaced or distorted by the majority. These subjects report that they came to perceive the majority estimates as correct.

2. *Distortion of judgment*. Most submitting subjects belong to this category. The factor of greatest importance in this group is a decision the subjects reach that their perceptions are inaccurate, and that those of the majority are correct. These subjects suffer from primary doubt and lack of confidence; on this basis they feel a strong tendency to join the majority.

3. *Distortion of action*. The subjects in this group do not suffer a modification of perception nor do they conclude that they are wrong. They yield because of an overmastering need not to appear different from or inferior to others, because of an inability to tolerate the appearance of defectiveness in the eyes of the group. These subjects suppress their observations and voice the majority position with awareness of what they are doing.

The results are sufficient to establish that independence and yielding are not psychologically homogeneous, that submission to group pressure (and freedom from pressure) can be the result of different psychological conditions. It should also be noted that the categories described above, being based exclusively on the subjects' reactions to the experimental conditions, are descriptive, not presuming to explain why a given individual responded in one way rather than another. The further exploration of the basis for the individual differences is a separate task upon which we are now at work.

EXPERIMENTAL VARIATIONS

The results described are clearly a joint function of two broadly different sets of conditions. They are determined first by the specific external conditions, by the particular character of the relation between social evidence and one's own experience. Second, the presence of pronounced individual difference points to the important role of personal factors, of factors connected with the individual's character structure. We reasoned that there are group conditions which would produce independence in all subjects, and that there probably are group conditions which would induce intensified yielding in many, though not in all. Accordingly we followed the procedure of *experimental variation*, systematically altering the quality of social evidence by means of systematic variation of group conditions. . . .

The Effect of Nonunanimous Majorities

Evidence obtained from the basis experiment suggested that the condition of being exposed *alone* to the opposition of a "compact majority" may have played a decisive role in determining the course and strength of the effects observed. Accordingly we undertook to investigate in a series of successive variations the effects of *nonunanimous* majorities. The technical problem of altering the uniformity of a majority is, in terms of our procedure, relatively simple. In most instances, we merely directed one or more members of the instructed group to deviate from the majority in prescribed ways. It is obvious that we cannot hope to compare the performance of the same individual in two situations on the assumption that they remain independent of one another. At best we can investigate the effect of an earlier upon a later experimental condition. . . . The following were some of the variations we studied:

1. *The presence of a "true partner."* (a) In the midst of the majority were *two* naive, critical subjects. The subjects were separated, spatially, being seated in the fourth and eighth positions, respectively. Each therefore heard his judgment confirmed by one other person (provided the other person remained independent), one prior to, the other subsequently to announcing his own judgment. In addition, each experienced a break in the unanimity of the majority. There were six pairs of critical subjects. (b) In a further variation the "partner" to the critical subject was a member of the group who had been instructed to respond correctly throughout. This procedure permits the exact control of the partner's responses. The partner was always seated in the fourth position; he therefore announced his estimates in each case before the critical subject.

The results clearly demonstrate that a disturbance of the unanimity of the majority markedly increased the independence of the critical subjects. The frequency of pro-majority errors dropped to 10.4 per cent of the total number of estimates in variation (a), and to 5.5 per cent in variation (b). These results are to be compared with the frequency of yielding to the unanimous majorities in the basic experiment, which was 32 per cent of the total number of estimates. It is clear that the presence in the field of *one other* individual who responded correctly was sufficient to deplete the power of the majority, and in some cases to destroy it. This finding is all the more striking in the light of other variations which demonstrate the effect of even small minorities provided they are unanimous. Indeed, we have been able to show that a unanimous majority of three is, under the given conditions, far more effective than a majority of eight containing one dissenter. That critical subjects will under these conditions free themselves of a majority of seven and join forces with one other person in the minority is, we believe, a result significant for theory. It points to a fundamental psychological difference between the condition of being alone and having a minimum of human support. It further demonstrates that the effects obtained are not the result of a summation of influences proceeding from each member of the group; it is necessary to conceive the results as being relationally determined.

2. *Withdrawal of a "true partner."* What will be the effect of providing the critical subject with a partner who responds correctly and then withdrawing him? The critical subject started with a partner who responded correctly. The partner was a member of the majority who had been instructed to respond correctly and to "desert" to the majority in the middle of the experiment. This procedure permits the observation of the same subject in the course of transition from one condition to another. The withdrawal of the partner produced a powerful and unexpected result. We had assumed that the critical subject, having gone through the experience of opposing the majority with a minimum of support, would maintain his independence when alone. Contrary to this expectation, we found that the experience of having had and then lost a partner restored the majority effect to its full force, the proportion of errors rising to

28.5 per cent of all judgments, in contrast to the preceding level of 5.5 per cent. Further experimentation is needed to establish whether the critical subjects were responding to the sheer fact of being alone, or to the fact that the partner abandoned them.

3. *Late arrival of a "true partner."* The critical subject started as a minority of one in the midst of a unanimous majority. Toward the conclusion of the experiment one member of the majority "broke" away and began announcing correct estimates. This procedure, which reverses the order of conditions of the preceding experiment, permits the observation of the transition from being alone to being a member of a pair against a majority. It is obvious that those critical subjects who were independent when alone would continue to be so when joined by another partner. The variation is therefore of significance primarily for those subjects who yielded during the first phase of the experiment. The appearance of the late partner exerts a freeing effect, reducing the level to 8.7 per cent. Those who had previously yielded also became markedly more independent, but not completely so, continuing to yield more than previously independent subjects. The reports of the subjects do not cast much light on the factors responsible for the result. It is our impression that having once committed himself to yielding, the individual finds it difficult and painful to change his direction. To do so is tantamount to a public admission that he has not acted rightly. He therefore follows the precarious course he has already chosen in order to maintain an outward semblance of consistency and conviction.

4. *The presence of a "compromise partner."* The majority was consistently extremist, always matching the standard with the most unequal line. One instructed subject (who, as in the other variations, preceded the critical subject) also responded incorrectly, but his estimates were always intermediate between the truth and the majority position. The critical subject therefore faced an extremist majority whose unanimity was broken by one more moderately erring person. Under these conditions the frequency of errors was reduced but not significantly. However, the lack of unanimity determined in a strikingly consistent way the *direction* of the errors. The preponderance of the errors, 75.7 per cent of the total, was moderate, whereas, in a parallel experiment in which the majority was unanimously extremist (*i.e.*, with the "compromise" partner excluded), the incidence of moderate errors was reduced to 42 per cent of the total. As might be expected, in a unanimously moderate majority, the errors of the critical subjects were without exception moderate.

The Role of Majority Size

To gain further understanding of the majority effect, we varied the size of the majority in several different variations. The majorities, which were in each case unanimous, consisted of 16, 8, 4, 3, and 2 persons, respectively. In addition, we studied the limited case in which the critical subject was opposed by one instructed subject. . . .

With the opposition reduced to one, the majority effect all but disappeared. When the opposition proceeded from a group of two, it produced a measurable though small distortion, the errors being 12.8 per cent of the total number of estimates. The effect appeared in full force with a majority of three. Larger majorities of four, eight, and sixteen did not produce effects greater than a majority of three.

The effect of a majority is often silent, revealing little of its operation to the subject, and often hiding it from the experimenter. To examine the range of effects it is capable of inducing, decisive variations of conditions are necessary. An indication of one effect is furnished by the following variation in which the conditions of the basic experiment were simply reversed. Here the majority, consisting of a group of sixteen, was naive;

in the midst of it we placed a single individual who responded wrongly according to instructions. Under these conditions the members of the naive majority reacted to the lone dissenter with amusement and disdain. Contagious laughter spread through the group at the droll minority of one. Of significance is the fact that the members lack awareness that they draw their strength from the majority, and that their reactions would change radically if they faced the dissenter individually. In fact, the attitude of derision in the majority turns to seriousness and increased respect as soon as the minority is increased to three. These observations demonstrate the role of social support as a source of power and stability, in contrast to the preceding investigations which stressed the effect of withdrawal of social support, or to be more exact, the effects of social opposition. Both aspects must be explicitly considered in a unified formulation of the effects of group conditions on the formation and change of judgments.

The Role of the Stimulus-Situation

It is obviously not possible to divorce the quality and course of the group forces which act upon the individual from the specific stimulus-conditions. Of necessity the structure of the situation molds the group forces and determines their direction as well as their strength. Indeed, this was the reason that we took pains in the investigations described above to center the issue between the individual and the group around an elementary and fundamental matter of fact. And there can be no doubt that the resulting reactions were directly a function of the contradiction between the objectively grasped relations and the majority position. . . .

We have also varied systematically the structural clarity of the task, including in separate variations judgments based on mental standards, In agreement with other investigators, we find that the majority effect grows stronger as the situation diminishes in clarity. Concurrently, however, the disturbance of the subjects and the conflict-quality of the situation decrease markedly. We consider it of significance that the majority achieves its most pronounced effect when it acts most painlessly.

SUMMARY

We have investigated the effects upon individuals of majority opinions when the latter were seen to be in a direction contrary to fact. By means of a simple technique we produced a radical divergence between a majority and a minority, and observed the ways in which individuals coped with the resulting difficulty. Despite the stress of the given conditions, a substantial proportion of individuals retained their independence throughout. At the same time a substantial minority yielded, modifying their judgments in accordance with the majority. Independence and yielding are a joint function of the following major factors: (1) The character of the stimulus situation. Variations in structural clarity have a decisive effect: With diminishing clarity of the stimulus-conditions the majority effect increases. (2) The character of the group forces. Individuals are highly sensitive to the structural qualities of group opposition. In particular, we demonstrated the great importance of the factor of unanimity. Also, the majority effect is a function of the size of group opposition. (3) The character of the individual. There were wide, and indeed, striking differences among individuals within the same experimental situation. The hypothesis was proposed that these are functionally dependent on relatively enduring character differences, in particular those pertaining to the person's social relations.

BIBLIOGRAPHY

1. Asch, S. E. Studies in the principles of judgments and attitudes: II. Determination of judgments by group and by ego-standards. *J. soc. Psychol.*, 1940, *12*, 433–465.
2. ———. The doctrine of suggestion, prestige and imitation in social psychology. *Psychol. Rev.*, 1948, *55*, 250–276.
3. Asch, S. E., Block, H., and Hertzman, M. Studies in the principles of judgments and attitudes. I. Two Basic principles of judgment. *J. Psychol.*, 1938, *5*, 219–251.
4. Coffin, E. E. Some conditions of suggestion and suggestibility: A study of certain attitudinal and situational factors influencing the process of suggestion. *Psychol. Monogr.* 1941, 53, No. 4.
5. Lewis, H. B. Studies in the principles of judgments and attitudes: IV. The operation of prestige suggestion. *J. soc. Psychol.*, 1941, *14*, 229–256.
6. Lorge, I. Prestige, suggestion, and attitudes. *J. soc. Psychol.*, 1936, *7*, 386–402.
7. Miller, N. E. and Dollard, J. *Social Learning and Imitation*. New Haven: Yale University Press, 1941.
8. Moore, H. T. The comparative influence of majority and expert opinion. *Amer. J. Psychol.*, 1921, *32*, 16–20.
9. Sherif, M. A study of some social factors in perception. *Arch. Psychol.*, N. Y. 1935, No. 187.
10. Thorndike, E. L. *The Psychology of Wants, Interests, and Attitudes*. New York: D. Appleton-Century Company, Inc., 1935.

26

Some Social and Psychological Consequences of the Longwall Method of Coal-Getting[1]

An Examination of the Psychological Situation and Defences of a Work Group in Relation to the Social Structure and Technological Content of the Work System

Eric L. Trist and K. W. Bamforth[2]

INTRODUCTION: A PERSPECTIVE FROM RECENT INNOVATIONS

A number of innovations in work organization at the coal-face have been making a sporadic and rather guarded appearance since the change-over of the industry to nationalization. During the past two years the authors have been following the course of these developments. Though differing from each other, they have had the common effect of increasing productivity, at least to some extent, and sometimes the increase reported has reached a level definitely above the upper limit customarily achieved by good workmen using similar equipment under conventional conditions. They have been accompanied by impressive changes in the social quality of the work-life of face teams. Greater cohesiveness has appeared in groups, and greater personal satisfaction has been reported by individuals. Decreases have also been indicated in sickness and absenteeism.

In the account to follow, the longwall method will be regarded as a technological system expressive of the prevailing outlook of mass-production engineering and as a social structure consisting of the occupational roles that have been institutionalized in its use. These interactive technological and sociological patterns will be assumed to exist as forces having psychological effects in the life-space of the face-worker, who must either take a

[1] The study reported here is one part of a larger project on which the Tavistock Institute of Human Relations has for some time been engaged, concerned with the conditions likely to increase the effectiveness of the "dissemination of information" about new social techniques developed in industry. This project was initiated by the Human Factors Panel of the Committee on Industrial Productivity set up by the Lord President of the Council under the Scientific Adviser to the Government. It has been administered by the Medical Research Council. No responsibility, however, attaches to either of these bodies for the contents of this paper, a shortened version of which has been discussed by the Medical Research Subcommittee of the National Coal Board.

[2] The field work necessary for this study has been lessened by the fact that Mr. K. W. Bamforth was himself formerly a miner and worked at the coal-face for 18 years.

Source: From "Some Social and Psychological Consequences of the Longwall Method of Coal-Getting" by E. L. Trist and K. W. Bamforth in *Human Relations*, 4 (1951). Reprinted by permission of Sage Publications.

role and perform a task in the system they compose or abandon his attempt to work at the coal-face. His own contribution to the field of determinants arises from the nature and quality of the attitudes and relationships he develops in performing one of these tasks and in taking one of these roles. Together, the forces and their effects constitute the psycho-social whole which is the object of study.

THE CHARACTER OF THE PRE-MECHANIZED EQUILIBRIUM AND THE NATURE OF ITS DISTURBANCE

1. Hand-Got Systems and the Responsible Autonomy of the Pair-Based Work Group

The outstanding feature of the social pattern with which the pre-mechanized equilibrium was associated is its emphasis on small group organization at the coal-face. The groups themselves were interdependent working pairs to whom one or two extra individuals might be attached. It was common practice for two colliers—a hewer and his mate—to make their own contract with the colliery management and to work their own small face with the assistance of a boy "trammer." This working unit could function equally well in a variety of engineering layouts both of the advance and retreat type, whether step-wise or direct. Sometimes it extended its numbers to seven or eight, when three or four colliers, and their attendant trammers, would work together.[3]

A primary work-organization of this type has the advantage of placing responsibility for the complete coal-getting task squarely on the shoulders of a single, small, face-to-face group which experiences the entire cycle of operations within the compass of its membership. For each participant the task has total significance and dynamic closure. Though the contract may have been in the name of the hewer, it was regarded as a joint undertaking. Leadership and "supervision" were internal to the group, which had a quality of *responsible autonomy*. The capacity of these groups for self-regulation was a function of the wholeness of their work task, this connection being represented in their contractual status. A whole has power as an independent detachment, but a part requires external control.

Within these pair-based units was contained the full range of coal-face skills; each collier being an all-round workman, usually able to substitute for his mate. Though his equipment was simple, his tasks were multiple. The "underground skill" on which their efficient and safe execution depended was almost entirely person-carried. He had craft pride and artisan independence. These qualities obviated status difficulties and contributed to responsible autonomy.

Choice of workmates posed a crucial question. These choices were made by the men themselves, sociometrically, under full pressure of the reality situation and with long-standing knowledge of each other. Stable relationships tended to result, which frequently endured over many years. In circumstances where a man was injured or killed, it was not uncommon for his mate to care for his family. These work relationships were often reinforced by kinship ties, the contract system and the small group autonomy allowing a close but spontaneous connection to be maintained between family and occupation, which avoided tying

[3] Hand-got methods contained a number of variants, but discussion of these is beyond present scope.

the one to the other. In segregated mining communities the link between kinship and occupation can be oppressive as well as supportive; against this danger, "exogamous" choice was a safeguard. But against too emotional a relationship, more likely to develop between non-kin associates, kinship barriers were in turn a safeguard. . . .

2. The Adaptability of the Small Group to the Underground Situation

Being able to work their own short faces continuously, these pair, or near pair, groups could stop at whatever point may have been reached by the end of a shift. The flexibility in work pace so allowed had special advantages in the underground situation; for when bad conditions were encountered, the extraction process in a series of stalls could proceed unevenly in correspondence with the uneven distribution of these bad conditions, which tend to occur now in one and now in another section along a seam. Even under good conditions, groups of this kind were free to set their own targets, so that aspirations levels with respect to production could be adjusted to the age and stamina of the individuals concerned.

In the underground situation external dangers must be faced in darkness. Darkness also awakens internal dangers. The need to share with others anxieties aroused by this double threat may be taken as self-evident. In view of the restricted range of effective communication, these others have to be immediately present. Their number therefore is limited. These conditions point to the strong need in the underground worker for a role in a small primary group.

A second characteristic of the underground situation is the wide dispersal of particular activities, in view of the large area over which operations generally are extended. The small groups of the hand-got systems tended to become isolated from each other even when working in the same series of stalls; the isolation of the group, as of the individual, being intensified by the darkness. Under these conditions there is no possibility of continuous supervision, in the factory sense, from any individual external to the primary work group.

The small group, capable of responsible autonomy, and able to vary its work pace in correspondence with changing conditions, would appear to be the type of social structure ideally adapted to the underground situation. It is instructive that the traditional work systems, evolved from the experience of successive generations, should have been founded on a group with these attributes. . . .

3. The Counter Balance of the Large Undifferentiated Collectivity

The psychological disadvantages of a work system, the small group organization of which is based on pair relationships, raises issues of a far-reaching kind only recently submitted to study in group dynamics (2). It would appear that the self-enclosed character of the relationship makes it difficult for groups of this kind to combine effectively in differentiated structures of a somewhat larger social magnitude, though this inability does not seem to hold in respect of much larger collectivities of a simpler mass character. . . .

In the pre-mechanized pattern, the pair-based primaries and the large relatively undifferentiated collectivities composed a dynamically interrelated system that permitted an enduring social balance. The intense reciprocities of the former, with their personal and family significance, and the diffuse identifications of the latter, with their community and class connectedness, were mutually supportive. The face teams could bear the responsibility of their autonomy through the security of their dependence on the united collectivity of the pit.

Difficulties arose largely from rivalries and conflicts between the various pairs and small teams. . . . All this was accepted as part of the system.

Inter-team conflict provided a channel for aggression that preserved intact the loyalties on which the small group depended. In the large group, aggression received structured expression in trade union resistance. If the struggle was harsh, it was at least direct and understandable. It was not the insidious kind that knocked the bottom out of life, leaving those concerned without a sense of a scheme in things—the "anomie" described by Halliday (1) after the transition to the longwall. The system as a whole contained its bad in a way that did not destroy its good. The balance persisted, albeit that work was of the hardest, rewards often meagre, and the social climate rough at times and even violent.

4. Mechanization and the Problem of Intermediate Organization

With the advent of coal-cutters and mechanical conveyors, the degree of technological complexity of the coal-getting task was raised to a different level. Mechanisation made possible the working of a single long face in place of a series of short faces. . . .

The associated characteristics of mechanized complexity, and of largeness as regards the scale of the primary production unit, created a situation in which it was impossible for the method to develop as a technological system without bringing into existence a work relationship structure radically different from that associated with hand-got procedures. The artisan type of pair, composed of the skilled man and his mate, assisted by one or more labourers, was out of keeping as a model for the type of work group required. Need arose for a unit more of the size and differentiated complexity of a small factory department. A structure of intermediate social magnitude began therefore to emerge. The basic pattern round which the work relationships of the longwall production unit were organized became the cycle group of 40–50 men, their shot-firer and shift "deputies," who were responsible to the pit management for the working as a whole. Only in relation to this total cycle group could various smaller subgroups secure function and acquire social form.

This centring of the new system on a differentiated structure of intermediate social magnitude disturbed the simple balance that had existed between the very small and very large traditional groups, and impaired the quality of responsible autonomy. The psychological and sociological problems posed by the technological needs of the longwall system were those with respect to which experience in the industry was least, and towards which its traditions were antithetical. . . .

5. The Lack of Recognition of the Nature of the Difficulties

Anyone who has listened to the talk of older miners who have experienced in their own work-lives the change-over to the longwall cannot fail to be impressed by the confused mourning for the past that still goes on in them together with a dismay over the present coloured by despair and indignation. To the clinical worker the quality of these talks has at times a ring that is familiar. Those with rehabilitation experience will recognize it as similar to the quality of feeling expressed by rehabilitees when ventilating the aftermath in themselves of an impairment accepted as irreversible.

THE STRESS OF MASS PRODUCTION IN THE UNDERGROUND SITUATION

1. The Interaction of Bad Conditions and Bad Work

Differentiated, rigidly sequenced work systems, organized on mass-production lines to deal with large quantities of material on a multi-shift cycle, are a basic feature of the factory pattern. . . . It [is] virtually impossible to establish the kind of constant background to the task that is taken for granted in the factory. A very large variety of unfavourable and changing environmental conditions is encountered at the coal-face, many of which are impossible to predict. Others, though predictable, are impossible to alter.

2. The Strain of Cycle Control

. . . In view of the darkness and the spread out character of the work, there is no possibility of close supervision. Responsibility for seeing to it that bad work is not done, however bad the conditions, rests with the face-workers themselves. But the responsible autonomy of some, especially, of the occupational subgroups has been impaired in the longwall method. This problem will be taken up in succeeding sections.

As a result, management complain of lack of support from the men, who are accused of being concerned only with their own fractional tasks and unwilling to take broader cycle responsibility. The parallel complaint of the workers is of being driven and tricked by management, who are resented as outsiders—intermittent visitors and "stick" men, who interfere without sharing the hard, physical work and in-group life of the face. . . .

The strain of cycle control tends to produce a group "culture" of angry and suspicious bargaining over which both management and men are in collusion. There is displacement both upwards and downwards of the tensions generated. The "hell" that breaks loose in the under-manager's office when news comes in that the fillers are unlikely to fill off in one or more faces resounds through the pit.

3. The Norm of Low Productivity

In all work at the coal-face two distinct tasks are simultaneously present; those that belong to the production cycle being always to some extent carried out in the background of a second activity arising from the need to contend with interferences, actual or threatened, emanating from the underground situation.

. . . The crises of cycle stoppages and the stress of the deputy's role are but symptoms of a wider situation characterized by the establishment of a norm of low productivity, as the only adaptive method of handling, in the contingencies of the underground situation, a complicated, rigid, and large-scale work system, borrowed with too little modification from an engineering culture appropriate to the radically different situation of the factory. . . .

THE SPECIAL SITUATION OF THE FILLING SHIFT

1. Isolated Dependence

Relationships between members of the filling shift are characterized by an absence of functional interdependence, which arises from the absence of role differentiation in the twenty identical tasks performed by the shift aggregate. . . .

The effect of the introduction of mechanized methods of face preparation and conveying, along with the retention of manual filling, has been not only to isolate the filler from those with whom he formerly shared the coal-getting task as a whole, but to make him one of a large aggregate serviced by the same small group of preparation workers. In place of an actually present partner, who belonged to him solely as the second member of an interdependent pair, he has acquired an "absent group," whom he must share with nineteen others. . . .

The absent, internally disconnected group on which he is dependent takes no functional cognizance of the existence of the filler as an individual. In view of the far-reaching community, as well as work, separation that exists between the preparation and the filling shifts (produced by the time-table arrangements), actual cognizance tends also to be minimal. . . .

2. Unequal Men with Equal Stints Under Unequal Conditions

The fillers, as has been shown, have no secure relationships in face of the differential incidence of the bad conditions they may encounter or of the bad work they may inherit from the preparation workers on whom they are dependent. The men who face these unequal conditions are themselves unequal; but the lengths of face they clear are the same. . . .

The local arrival of certain types of bad conditions, such as rolls that move across the face, can be anticipated, so that anxiety piles up. . . . As regards bad work left by the other shifts, the filler is in the situation of never knowing what he may find, so that anxiety of a second kind arises that tends to produce chronic uncertainty and irritation. There is little doubt that these two circumstances contribute to the widespread incidence of psycho-somatic and kindred neurotic disorders among those concerned.

The degree of stress arising when men experience the full weight of this situation could have been explored only in a therapeutic relationship. But many instances were given of neurotic episodes occurring on shift—of men sitting in their lengths in stony silence, attacking their coal in towering rage, or leaving the face in panic. In a situation of dependent isolation with the odds unequal both as regards his own resources and what is required of him, the individual inevitably erects protective defences, and these are elaborated and shared in the work group. An account of the main pattern of group defences will now be given. These defences are reactive rather than adaptive. Their effectiveness therefore is only partial. But without them life at the longwall would be intolerable for all but those whose level of personal adjustment is rather better than that attained by most individuals in the course of their development.

FOUR TYPES OF GROUP DEFENCE

1. Informal Organization

The functional isolation of the filler within his own group, which leaves him "officially" alone with his "coals," is met by an attempt to develop informal, small-group organization in which private arrangements to help each other out are made among neighbours, in twos, threes, or fours. But these solely interpersonal arrangements are undependable and open to manipulation for anti-social and competitive as well as for mutually protective ends. A number of isolates is left over. The total face group is incapable, except defensively, of acting as a socially responsible whole, since not even private allegiances are owed outside the small informal groups. These in turn are without responsible autonomy; the absence of institutionalized mutual obligation means that there are no statutory group tasks, and each individual can be held ultimately responsible only for clearing his own length. Internal "rows" the more easily break up the informal "coalitions," whose morale tends to be of the clique type. . . .

Isolates, it appears, are either individualists—who "won't even share timber"—or men with bad reputations, with whom others refuse to work. Amongst these are the unconscientious—who "won't help out at the end of a shift" and who are frequently absent—and the helpless—who "cannot learn to look after themselves under bad conditions." Others, whose stamina is deficient (whether through age, illness, or neurosis) and whose lengths are often uncleared in consequence, are dropped from the informal groups.

Only to a very limited extent, therefore, does his informal group organization meet the filler's need for a secure role in a primary group within his own shift. In view of the extent of his dependence on the performance of those in the other two shifts, his need for this foundation is greater than that of any of the other occupational groups, while the resources available to him are fewer.

2. Reactive Individualism

His small group failing, the filler is thrown on to himself and against others. The second defence against isolation is the development of a reactive individualism, in which a reserve of personal secrecy is apt to be maintained. Among his own shift mates there is competitive intrigue for the better places—middle positions are avoided; from these "it is a long way to creep"—and for jobs in workings where conditions are good there is a scramble.

On some faces described to the writers, fear of victimization was rife, particularly in the form of being sent to work in a "bad place"; the deputy being more easily turned into a persecutor in view of the guilt arising from the intrigue and deception which the men practised both against him and against each other. Against the deputy, advantage is taken of the scope afforded in the underground situation for petty deception over such matters as time of leaving the pit, or the "measure that is sent up" (amount of coal filled on to the conveyor). With the deputy, however, men are also prepared to enter into alliance against each other, often for very good reasons—to stop mates from going absent and by so doing throwing more work on to the others.

As regards outside groups, practice of bribing members of the other shifts in the hope of getting a "good deal" in one's own length were mentioned by several informants. Tobacco is taken to the cutter; gummers are stood a pint on Sunday. These practices are to be regarded as symptoms of a state of affairs rather than as widespread in themselves.

The effect of this defensive individualism is to reduce the sense of secure identification in the larger pit collectivity, which was the second principle on which the older equilibrium was based. . . .

The competition, intrigue, unwillingness to put allegations to the test and the reserve of personal secrecy, are parts of one pattern. Whatever their personal wishes, men feel under pressure to be out for themselves, since the social structure in which they work denies them membership in any group that can legitimize interdependence. In this respect reactive individualism makes a basic interpretation of the social structure of the filling shift and is the only form of authorized behaviour.

3. Mutual Scapegoating

Fillers almost never see those who work on the "back shifts," and this absence of contact gives full scope for mutual and irresponsible scapegoating. When there is a crisis, and the filling shift is unable to fill off, the "buck" is passed to the other shifts—or vice versa if disorganization has occurred elsewhere. It is frequently also passed to the deputy, who is blamed for not finding substitutes, and to repair men, brought in, but too old to stand the pace.

For these to pass the buck back to the fillers is fruitless. As they do not exist as a responsible whole, they, as a group, are not there to take the blame, and the individual filler can always exempt himself. Since bad conditions and bad work interact so closely, it is usually difficult to point blame specifically. Mutual scapegoating is a self-perpetuating system, in which nothing is resolved and no one feels guilty. For all concerned to remain in collusion with such a system is a defence which allows each to make his "anonymous contribution" to the "group mentality," (2) which sabotages both the goal of cycle productivity and the needs of the individual for a membership in a satisfying work-group. So far as this pattern obtains, all strike at each other in a mock war in which no one is hurt yet all suffer.

This defence can also be seen as a "back-handed" attempt to recover the supportive unity lost through reactive individualism in a way that is consistent with it. For all to be "in the bad" together is at least a way of being together. . . .

Not that the system is felt as entirely bad since it is the means by which a living is earned. Moreover, under present conditions this living is a good one, both in terms of wages and of community status. But the benefits which these "goods" bring are not realized in the work activities of the group. They lie outside the work system, which is tolerated as a means to external ends rather than accepted also as an end in itself, worthy of whole-hearted pursuit in virtue of the internal satisfactions it affords. . . .

4. Self-Compensatory Absenteeism

Withdrawal is the fourth form of defence, complementing mutual scapegoating, and absenteeism is to be regarded as a recognized social technique within this pattern. . . .

When conditions on a face deteriorate, especially in ways that are predictable, absenteeism among fillers sometimes piles up to a point where the remainder have to stay down an extra two or three hours in order to clear the face. Should this situation repeat itself for more than a day or two, those coming on shift often meet at the pit-head baths before presenting themselves for work. If less than a certain number arrive, all go home.

Absenteeism of this self-compensatory type, though carried out as an act of aggrieved defiance against a system, felt in these circumstances as persecutory, is an attempt on the part of the individual to prolong his work life at the coal-face. For without the respite of occasional absences, he feels that he would soon become unable to carry on. In view of the accentuated differences both in wages and in status between face workers and repair, haulage, or surface personnel, the goal of remaining at the coal-face for as long as possible would appear to operate as a powerful motivational force in determining the behaviour of the ordinary face-worker. . . .

This, and the other three defences discussed, play a dynamically interrelated part in forming the culture[4] of the work group, though naturally the intensity to which the pattern is present varies widely, and there are faces where the group atmosphere remains for long periods relatively immune from these influences. There are apt, however, to be "fair-weather" faces.

The danger is that habituation to working in a bad system has the compensation of enabling those concerned to leave too much both of their own and of their group's "badness" *in the system*. It then ties them to it through the fact that it does this, despite their hatred of it. As well as its faults, it is their own hatred that they hate in the system—and there is usually stubborn refusal to recognize such projections in work—no less than in therapy-groups. A characteristic of faces with a bad group atmosphere is the protesting yet excited collusion of all concerned with the state of affairs. This is in contrast to the more independently critical and realistic attitude of those in groups where the pattern is less complete and less intense.

[4] The concept of "culture" as a psycho-social technique developed by a group in a structurally determined situation has been outlined by Trist, "Culture as a Psycho-Social Process," contributed to a symposium on The Concept of Culture, British Association, Section (H), Anthropology and Archeology, Birmingham Meeting, 1950. This viewpoint develops that of Curle, and Curle and Trist, "Transitional Communities and Social Reconnection," *Human Relations*, Vol. I, No. 1, pp. 42–68, and No. 2, pp. 240–288; and is akin to that of Ruesch, "Experiments in Psychotherapy, II: Individual Social Techniques," *The Journal of Social Psychology*, 1949, 29, 3–28; and Ruesch and Bateson, "Structure and Process in Social Relations," *Psychiatry*, 1949, Vol. XII, 2, pp. 105–124.

REFERENCES

1. Halliday, J. L. *Psychosocial Medicine: A Study of the Sick Society*, Heinemann, London, 1949.
2. Bion, W. R. "Experiences in Groups, III," *Human Relations*, Vol. II, No. 1, January, 1949, pp. 13–22.

27

Bureaucratic Structure and Personality

Robert K. Merton

THE STRUCTURE OF BUREAUCRACY

The ideal type of . . . formal organization is bureaucracy and, in many respects, the classical analysis of bureaucracy is that by Max Weber.[1] As Weber indicates, bureaucracy involves a clear-cut division of integrated activities which are regarded as duties inherent in the office. A system of differentiated controls and sanctions is stated in the regulations. The assignment of roles occurs on the basis of technical qualifications which are ascertained through formalized, impersonal procedures (*e.g.*, examinations). Within the structure of hierarchically arranged authority, the activities of "trained and salaried experts" are governed by general, abstract, and clearly defined rules which preclude the necessity for the issuance of specific instructions for each specific case. The generality of the rules requires the constant use of *categorization*, whereby individual problems and cases are classified on the basis of designated criteria and are treated accordingly. The pure type of bureaucratic official is appointed, either by a superior or through the exercise of impersonal competition; he is not elected. A measure of flexibility in the bureaucracy is attained by electing higher functionaries who presumably express the will of the electorate (*e.g.*, a body of citizens or a board of directors). The election of higher officials is designed to affect the purposes of the organization, but the technical procedures for attaining these ends are carried out by continuing bureaucratic personnel.[2]

Most bureaucratic offices involve the expectation of life-long tenure, in the absence of disturbing factors which may decrease the size of the organization. Bureaucracy maximizes vocational security.[3] The function of security of tenure, pensions, incremental salaries and regularized procedures for promotion is to ensure the devoted performance of official duties, without regard for extraneous pressures.[4] The chief merit of bureaucracy is its technical efficiency, with a premium placed on precision, speed, expert control, continuity, discretion, and optimal returns on input. The structure is one which approaches the complete elimination of personalized relationships and nonrational considerations (hostility, anxiety, affectual involvements, etc.).

With increasing bureaucratization, it becomes plain to all who would see that man is to a very important degree controlled by his social relations to the instruments of production. This can no longer seem only a tenet of Marxism, but a stubborn fact to be acknowledged by all, quite apart from their ideological persuasion. Bureaucratization makes

Source: Reprinted with permission of The Free Press, a Division of Simon & Schuster, from *Social Theory and Social Structure*, revised and enlarged edition, by Robert K. Merton. Copyright © 1957 by The Free Press, renewed 1985 by Robert K. Merton.

readily visible what was previously dim and obscure. More and more people discover that to work, they must be employed. For to work, one must have tools and equipment. And the tools and equipment are increasingly available only in bureaucracies, private or public. Consequently, one must be employed by the bureaucracies in order to have access to tools in order to work and in order to live. It is in this sense that bureaucratization entails separation of individuals from the instruments of production, as in modern capitalistic enterprise or in state communistic enterprise (of the midcentury variety), just as in the postfeudal army, bureaucratization entailed complete separation from the instruments of destruction. Typically, the worker no longer owns his tools nor the soldier, his weapons. And in this special sense, more and more people become workers, either blue collar or white collar or stiff shirt. So develops, for example, the new type of scientific worker, as the scientist is "separated" from his technical equipment—after all, the physicist does not ordinarily own his cyclotron. To work at his research, he must be employed by a bureaucracy with laboratory resources.

Bureaucracy is administration which almost completely avoids public discussion of its techniques, although there may occur public discussion of its policies.[5] This secrecy is confirmed neither to the public nor to private bureaucracies. It is held to be necessary to keep valuable information from private economic competitors or from foreign and potentially hostile political groups. . . .

THE DYSFUNCTIONS OF BUREAUCRACY

The transition to a study of the negative aspects of bureaucracy is afforded by the application of Veblen's concept of "trained incapacity," Dewey's notion of "occupational psychosis" or Warnotte's view of "professional deformation." Trained incapacity refers to that state of affairs in which one's abilities function as inadequacies or blind spots. Actions based upon training and skills which have been successfully applied in the past may result in inappropriate responses *under changed conditions*. An inadequate flexibility in the application of skills, will, in a changing milieu, result in more or less serious maladjustments.[6] . . .

Dewey's concept of occupational psychosis rests upon much the same observations. As a result of their day to day routines, people develop special preferences, antipathies, discriminations and emphases.[7] (The term psychosis is used by Dewey to denote a "pronounced character of the mind.") These psychoses develop through demands put upon the individual by the particular organization of his occupational role. . . .

For reasons which we have already noted, the bureaucratic structure exerts a constant pressure upon the official to be "methodical, prudent, disciplined." If the bureaucracy is to operate successfully, it must attain a high degree of reliability of behavior, an unusual degree of action. Hence, the fundamental importance of discipline which may be as highly developed in a religious or economic bureaucracy as in the army. Discipline can be effective only if the ideal patterns are buttressed by strong sentiments which entail devotion to one's duties, a keen sense of the limitation of one's authority and competence, and methodical performance of routine activities. The efficacy of social structure depends ultimately upon infusing group participants with appropriate attitudes and sentiments. As we shall see, there are definite arrangements in the bureaucracy for inculcating and reinforcing these sentiments.

At the moment, it suffices to observe that in order to ensure discipline (the necessary reliability of response), these sentiments are often more intense than is technically necessary. There is a margin of safety, so to speak, in the pressure exerted by these sentiments upon the bureaucrat to conform to his patterned obligations, in much the same sense that added allowances (precautionary overestimations) are made by the engineer in designing the supports for a bridge. But this very emphasis leads to a transference of the sentiments from the *aims* of the organization onto the particular details of behavior required by the rules. Adherence to the rules, originally conceived as a means, becomes transformed into an end-in-itself; there occurs the familiar process of *displacement of goals* whereby "an instrumental value becomes a terminal value."[8] Discipline, readily interpreted as conformance with regulations, whatever the situation, is seen not as a measure designed for specific purposes but becomes an immediate value in the life-organization of the bureaucrat. This emphasis, resulting from the displacement of the original goals, develops into rigidities and an inability to adjust readily. Formalism, even ritualism, ensues with an unchallenged insistence upon punctilious adherence to formalized procedures.[9] This may be exaggerated to the point where primary concern with conformity to the rules interferes with the achievement of the purposes of organization, in which case we have the familiar phenomenon of the technicism or red tape of the official. An extreme product of this process of displacement of goals is the bureaucratic virtuoso, who never forgets a single rule binding his action and hence is unable to assist many of his clients.[10] . . .

STRUCTURAL SOURCES OF OVERCONFORMITY

Thus far, we have treated the ingrained sentiments making for rigorous discipline simply as data, as given. However, definite features of the bureaucratic structure may be seen to conduce to these sentiments. The bureaucrat's official life is planned for him in terms of a graded career, through the organizational devices of promotion by seniority, pensions, incremental salaries, etc., all of which are designed to provide incentives for disciplined action and conformity to the official regulations.[11] The official is tacitly expected to and largely does adapt his thoughts, feelings and actions to the prospect of this career. But *these very devices* which increase the probability of conformance also lead to an over-concern with strict adherence to regulations which induces timidity, conservatism, and technicism. Displacement of sentiments from goals onto means is fostered by the tremendous symbolic significance of the means (rules).

Another feature of the bureaucratic structure tends to produce much the same result. Functionaries have the sense of a common destiny for all those who work together. They share the same interests, especially since there is relatively little competition in so far as promotion is in terms of seniority. In-group aggression is thus minimized and this arrangement is therefore conceived to be positively functional for the bureaucracy. However, the *esprit de corps* and informal social organization which typically develops in such situations often leads the personnel to defend their entrenched interests rather than to assist their clientele and elected higher officials. . . .

In a stimulating paper, Hughes has applied the concepts of "secular" and "sacred" to various types of division of labor; "the sacredness" of caste and *Stände* prerogatives contrasts sharply, with the increasing secularism of occupational differentiation in our society.[12] However, as our discussion suggests, there may ensue, in particular vocations and in particular types of organization, the *process of sanctification* (viewed as the counterpart of the process of secularization). This is to say that through sentiment-formation, emotional dependence upon bureaucratic symbols and status, and affective involvement in spheres of competence and authority, there develop prerogatives involving attitudes of moral legitimacy which are established as values in their own right, and are no longer viewed as merely technical means for expediting administration. One many note a tendency for certain bureaucratic norms, originally introduced for technical reasons, to become rigidified and sacred, although, as Durkheim would say, they are *laïque en apparence*.[13] Durkheim has touched on this general process in his description of the attitudes and values which persist in the organic solidarity of a highly differentiated society.

PRIMARY VERSUS SECONDARY RELATIONS

Another feature of the bureaucratic structure, the stress on depersonalization of relationships, also plays its part in the bureaucrat's trained incapacity. The personality pattern of the bureaucrat is nucleated about this norm of impersonality. Both this and the categorizing tendency, which develops from the dominant role of general, abstract rules, tend to produce conflict in the bureaucrat's contacts with the public or clientele. Since functionaries minimize personal relations and resort to categorization, the peculiarities of individual cases are often ignored. But the client who, quite understandably, is convinced of the special features of *his* own problem often objects to such categorical treatment. Stereotyped behavior is not adapted to the exigencies of individual problems. The impersonal treatment of affairs which are at times of great personal significance to the client gives rise to the charge of "arrogance" and "haughtiness" of the bureaucrat. . . .

Still another source of conflict with the public derives from the bureaucratic structure. The bureaucrat, in part irrespective of his position with*in* the hierarchy, acts as a representative of the power and prestige of the entire structure. In his official role he is vested with definite authority. This often leads to an actually or apparently domineering attitude, which may only be exaggerated by a discrepancy between his position within the hierarchy and his position with reference to the public.[14] Protest and recourse to other officials on the part of the client are often ineffective or largely precluded by the previously mentioned *esprit de corps* which joins the officials into a more or less solidary in-group. This source of conflict *may* be minimized in private enterprise since the client can register an effective protest by transferring his trade to another organization within the competitive system. But with the monopolistic nature of the public organization, no such alternative is possible. Moreover, in this case, tension is increased because of a discrepancy between ideology and fact: the governmental personnel are held to be "servants of the people," but in fact they are often superordinate, and release of tension can seldom be afforded by turning to other agencies for the necessary service.[15] This tension is in part attributable to the confusion of the status of bureaucrat and client; the client may consider himself socially superior to the official who is at the moment dominant.[16]

. . . The conflict may be viewed, then, as deriving from the introduction of inappropriate attitudes and relationships. Conflict with*in* the bureaucratic structure arises from the converse situation, namely, when personalized relationships are substituted for the structurally required impersonal relationships. This type of conflict may be characterized as follows.

The bureaucracy, as we have seen, is organized as a secondary, formal group. The normal responses involved in this organized network of social expectations are supported by affective attitudes of members of the group. Since the group is oriented toward secondary norms of impersonality, any failure to conform to these norms will arouse antagonism from those who have identified themselves with the legitimacy of these rules. Hence, the substitution of personal for impersonal treatment within the structure is met with widespread disapproval and is characterized by such epithets as graft, favoritism, nepotism, apple-polishing, etc. These epithets are clearly manifestations of injured sentiments.[17] The function of such virtually automatic resentment can be clearly seen in terms of the requirements of bureaucratic structure.

Bureaucracy is a secondary group structure designed to carry on certain activities which cannot be satisfactorily performed on the basis of primary group criteria.[18] Hence behavior which runs counter to these formalized norms becomes the object of emotionalized disapproval. This constitutes a functionally significant defence set up against tendencies which jeopardize the performance of socially necessary activities. . . .

PROBLEMS FOR RESEARCH

A large number of specific questions invite our attention. To what extent are particular personality types selected and modified by the various bureaucracies (private enterprise, public service, the quasi-legal political machine, religious orders)? Inasmuch as ascendancy and submission are held to be traits of personality, despite their variability in different stimulus-situations, do bureaucracies select personalities of particularly submissive or ascendant tendencies? And since various studies have shown that these traits can be modified, does participation in bureaucratic office tend to increase ascendant tendencies? Do various systems of recruitment (*e.g.*, patronage, open competition involving specialized knowledge or general mental capacity, practical experience) select different personality types?[19] Does promotion through seniority lessen competitive anxieties and enhance administrative efficiency? A detailed examination of mechanisms for imbuing the bureaucratic codes with affect would be instructive both sociologically and psychologically. Does the general anonymity of civil service decisions tend to restrict the area of prestige-symbols to a narrowly defined inner circle? Is there a tendency for differential association to be especially marked among bureaucrats?

The range of theoretically significant and practically important questions would seem to be limited only by the accessibility of the concrete data. . . .

NOTES

1. Max Weber, *Wirtschaft und Gesellschaft* (Tübingen: J. C. B. Mohr, 1922), Pt. III, chap. 6; 650–678. For a brief summary of Weber's discussion, see Talcott Parsons, *The Structure of Social Action*, esp. 506 ff. For a description, which is not a caricature, of the bureaucrat as a personality type, see C. Rabany, "Les types sociaux: le fonctionnaire," *Revue générale d'administration* 88 (1907), 5–28.
2. Karl Mannheim, *Ideology and Utopia* (New York: Harcourt Brace Jovanovich, 1936), 18n., 105 ff. See also Ramsay Muir, *Peers and Bureaucrats* (London: Constable, 1910), 12–13.
3. E. G. Cahen-Salvador suggests that the personnel of bureaucracies is largely constituted by those who value security above all else. See his "La situation matérielle et morale des

fonctionnaires," *Revue politique et parlementaire* (1926), 319.

4. H. J. Laski, "Bureaucracy," *Encyclopedia of the Social Sciences*. This article is written primarily from the standpoint of the political scientist rather than that of the sociologist.
5. Weber, *op. cit.*, 671.
6. For a stimulating discussion and application of these concepts, see Kenneth Burke, *Permanence and Change* (New York: New Republic, 1935), pp. 50 ff.; Daniel Warnotte, "Bureaucratie et Fonctionnarisme," *Revue de l'Institut de Sociologie* 17, (1937), 245.
7. *Ibid.*, 58–59.
8. This process has often been observed in various connections. Wundt's *heterogony of ends* is a case in point; Max Weber's *Paradoxie der Folgen* is another. See also MacIver's observations on the transformation of civilization into culture and Lasswell's remark that "the human animal distinguishes himself by his infinite capacity for making ends of his means." See Merton, "The unanticipated consequences of purposive social action," *American Sociological Review* 1 (1936), 894–904. In terms of the psychological mechanisms involved, this process has been analyzed most fully by Gordon W. Allport, in his discussion of what he calls "the functional autonomy of motives." Allport emends the earlier formulations of Woodworth, Tolman, and William Stern, and arrives at a statement of the process from the standpoint of individual motivation. He does not consider those phases of the social structure which conduce toward the "transformation of motives." The formulation adopted in this paper is thus complementary to Allport's analysis; the one stressing the psychological mechanisms involved, the other considering the constraints of the social structure. The convergence of psychology and sociology toward this central concept suggests that it may well constitute one of the conceptual bridges between the two disciplines. See Gordon W. Allport, *Personality* (New York: Henry Holt & Co., 1937), chap. 7.
9. See E. C. Hughes, "Institutional office and the person," *American Journal of Sociology*, 43, (1937), 404–413; E. T. Hiller, "Social structure in relation to the person," *Social Forces* 16 (1937), 34–44.
10. Mannheim, *Ideology and Utopia*, 106.
11. Mannheim, *Mensch and Gesellshaft*, 32–33. Mannheim stresses the importance of the "Lebensplan" and the "Amtskarriere." See the comments by Hughes, *op. cit.*, 413.
12. E. C. Hughes, "Personality types and the division of labor," *American Journal of Sociology* 33, (1928), 754–768. Much the same distinction is drawn by Leopold von Wiese and Howard Becker, *Systematic Sociology* (New York: John Wiley & Sons, 1932), 22–25 *et passim*.
13. Hughes recognizes one phase of this process of sanctification when he writes that professional training "carries with it as a by-product assimilation of the candidate to a set of professional attitudes and controls, *a professional conscience and solidarity. The profession claims and aims to become a moral unit.*" Hughes, *op. cit.*, 762, (italics inserted). In this same connection, Sumner's concept of *pathos*, as the halo of sentiment which protects a social value from criticism, is particularly relevant, inasmuch as it affords a clue to the mechanism involved in the process of sanctification. See his *Folkways*, 180–181.
14. In this connection, note the relevance of Koffka's comments on certain features of the pecking-order of birds. "If one compares the behavior of the bird at the top of the pecking list, the despot, with that of one very far down, the second or third from the last, then one finds the latter much more cruel to the few others over whom he lords it than the former in this treatment of all members. As soon as one removes from the group all members above the penultimate, his behavior becomes milder and may even become very friendly. . . . It is not difficult to find analogies to this in human societies, and therefore one side of such behavior must be primarily the effects of the social groupings, and not of individual characteristics." K. Koffka, *Principles of Gestalt Psychology* (New York: Harcourt Brace Jovanovich, 1935), 668–9.
15. At this point the political machine often becomes functionally significant. As Steffens and others have shown, highly personalized relations and the abrogation of formal rules (red tape) by the machine often satisfy the needs of individual "clients" more fully than the formalized mechanism of governmental bureaucracy.
16. As one of the unemployed men remarked about the clerks at the Greenwich Employment Exchange: "'And the bloody blokes wouldn't have their jobs if it wasn't for us men out of a job either. That's what gets me about their holding their noses up.'" Bakke, *op. cit.*, 80. See also H. D. Lasswell and G.

Almond, "Aggressive behavior by clients towards public relief administrators," *American Political Science Review* 28 (1934), 643–55.

17. The diagnostic significance of such linguistic indices as epithets has scarcely been explored by the sociologist. Sumner properly observes that epithets produce "summary criticisms" and definitions of social situations. Dollard also notes that "epithets frequently define the central issues in a society," and Sapir has rightly emphasized the importance of context of situations in appraising the significance of epithets. Of equal relevance is Linton's observation that "in case histories the way in which the community felt about a particular episode is, if anything, more important to our study than the actual behavior. . . ." A sociological study of "vocabularies of encomium and opprobrium" should lead to valuable findings.

18. *Cf*. Ellsworth Faris, *The Nature of Human Nature* (New York: McGraw-Hill, 1937), 41 ff.

19. Among recent studies of recruitment to bureaucracy are: Reinhard Bendix, *Higher Civil Servants in American Society* (Boulder: University of Colorado Press, 1949); Dwaine Marwick, *Career Perspectives in a Bureaucratic Setting* (Ann Arbor: University of Michigan Press, 1945); R. K. Kelsall, *Higher Civil Servants in Britain* (London: Routledge & Kegan Paul, 1955); W. L. Warner and J. C. Abegglen, *Occupational Mobility in American Business and Industry* (Minneapolis: University of Minnesota Press, 1955).

28

Groupthink: The Desperate Drive for Consensus at Any Cost

Irving L. Janis

"How could we have been so stupid!" President John F. Kennedy asked after he and a close group of advisers had blundered into the Bay of Pigs invasion. For the last two years I have been studying that question, as it applies not only to the Bay of Pigs decision-makers but also to those who led the United States into such other major fiascos as the failure to be prepared for the attack on Pearl Harbor, the Korean War stalemate and the escalation of the Vietnam War.

Stupidity certainly is not the explanation. The men who participated in making the Bay of Pigs decision, for instance, comprised one of the greatest arrays of intellectual talent in the history of American Government—Dean Rusk, Robert McNamara, Douglas Dillon, Robert Kennedy, McGeorge Bundy, Arthur Schlesinger Jr., Allen Dulles and others.

It also seemed to me that explanations were incomplete if they concentrated only on disturbances in the behavior of each individual within a decision-making body: temporary emotional states of elation, fear, or anger that reduce a man's mental efficiency, for example, or chronic blind spots arising from a man's social prejudices or idiosyncratic biases.

I preferred to broaden the picture by looking at the fiascos from the standpoint of group dynamics as it has been explored over the past three decades, first by the great social psychologist Kurt Lewin and later in many experimental situations by myself and other behavioral scientists. My conclusion after poring over hundreds of relevant documents—historical reports about formal group meetings and informal conversations among the members—is that the groups that committed the fiascos were victims of what I call "groupthink."

"Groupy." In each case study, I was surprised to discover the extent to which each group displayed the typical phenomena of social conformity that are regularly encountered in studies of group dynamics among ordinary citizens. For example, some of the phenomena appear to be completely in line with findings from social-psychological experiments showing that powerful social pressures are brought to bear by the members of a cohesive group whenever a dissident begins to voice his objections to a group consensus. Other phenomena are reminiscent of the shared illusions observed in encounter groups and friendship cliques when the members simultaneously reach a peak of "groupy" feelings.

Source: Reprinted with permission from *Psychology Today Magazine*, Copyright © 1971 (Sussex Publishers, Inc.).

Above all, there are numerous indications pointing to the development of group norms that bolster morale at the expense of critical thinking. One of the most common norms appears to be that of remaining loyal to the group by sticking with the policies to which the group has already committed itself, even when those policies are obviously working out badly and have unintended consequences that disturb the conscience of each member. This is one of the key characteristics of groupthink.

1984. I use the term groupthink as a quick and easy way to refer to the mode of thinking that persons engage in when *concurrence-seeking* becomes so dominant in a cohesive ingroup that it tends to override realistic appraisal of alternative courses of action. Groupthink is a term of the same order as the words in the newspeak vocabulary George Orwell used in his dismaying world of *1984*. In that context, groupthink takes on an invidious connotation. Exactly such a connotation is intended, since the term refers to a deterioration in mental efficiency, reality testing and moral judgments as a result of group pressures.

The symptoms of groupthink arise when the members of decision-making groups become motivated to avoid being too harsh in their judgments of their leaders' or their colleagues' ideas. They adopt a soft line of criticism, even in their own thinking. At their meetings, all the members are amiable and seek complete concurrence on every important issue, with no bickering or conflict to spoil the cozy, "we-feeling" atmosphere.

Kill. Paradoxically, soft-headed groups are often hard-hearted when it comes to dealing with outgroups or enemies. They find it relatively easy to resort to dehumanizing solutions—they will readily authorize bombing attacks that kill large numbers of civilians in the name of the noble cause of persuading an unfriendly government to negotiate at the peace table. They are unlikely to pursue the more difficult and controversial issues that arise when alternatives to a harsh military solution come up for discussion. Nor are they inclined to raise ethical issues that carry the implication that *this fine group of ours, with its humanitarianism and its high-minded principles, might be capable of adopting a course of action that is inhumane and immoral*.

Norms. There is evidence from a number of social-psychological studies that as the members of a group feel more accepted by the others, which is a central feature of increased group cohesiveness, they display less overt conformity to group norms. Thus we would expect that the more cohesive a group becomes, the less the members will feel constrained to censor what they say out of fear of being socially punished for antagonizing the leader or any of their fellow members.

In contrast, the groupthink type of conformity tends to increase as group cohesiveness increases. Groupthink involves nondeliberate suppression of critical thoughts as a result of internalization of the group's norms, which is quite different from deliberate suppression on the basis of external threats of social punishment. The more cohesive the group, the greater the inner compulsion on the part of each member to avoid creating disunity, which inclines him to believe in the soundness of whatever proposals are promoted by the leader or by a majority of the group's members.

In a cohesive group, the danger is not so much that each individual will fail to reveal his objections to what the others propose but that he will think the proposal is a good one, without attempting to carry out a careful, crucial scrutiny of the pros and cons of the alternatives. When groupthink becomes dominant, there also is considerable suppression of deviant thoughts, but it takes the form of each person's deciding that his misgivings are not relevant and should be set aside, that the benefit of the doubt regarding any lingering uncertainties should be given to the group consensus.

Stress. I do not mean to imply that all cohesive groups necessarily suffer from groupthink. All ingroups may have a mild tendency toward groupthink, displaying one or another of the symptoms from time to time, but it need not be so dominant as to influence the quality of the group's final decision. Neither do I mean to imply that there is anything necessarily inefficient or harmful about group decisions in general. On the contrary, a group whose members have properly defined roles, with traditions concerning the procedures to follow in pursuing a critical inquiry, probably is capable of making better decisions than any individual group member working alone.

The problem is that the advantages of having decisions made by groups are often lost because of powerful psychological pressures that arise when the members work closely together, share the same set of values and, above all, face a crisis situation that puts everyone under intense stress.

The main principle of groupthink, which I offer in the spirit of Parkinson's Law, is this: *The more amiability and esprit de corps there is among the members of a policy-making ingroup, the greater the danger that independent critical thinking will be replaced by groupthink, which is likely to result in irrational and dehumanizing actions directed against outgroups.*

Symptoms. In my studies of high-level governmental decision-makers, both civilian and military, I have found eight main symptoms of groupthink.

1. INVULNERABILITY. Most or all of the members of the ingroup share an illusion of invulnerability that provides for them some degree of reassurance about obvious dangers and leads them to become over-optimistic and willing to take extraordinary risks. It also causes them to fail to respond to clear warnings of danger.

The Kennedy ingroup, which uncritically accepted the Central Intelligence Agency's disastrous Bay of Pigs plan, operated on the false assumption that they could keep secret the fact that the United States was responsible for the invasion of Cuba. Even after news of the plan began to leak out, their belief remained unshaken. They failed even to consider the danger that awaited them: a worldwide revulsion against the U.S. . . .

2. RATIONALE. As we see, victims of groupthink ignore warnings; they also collectively construct rationalizations in order to discount warnings and other forms of negative feedback that, taken seriously, might lead the group members to reconsider their assumptions each time they recommit themselves to past decisions. Why did the Johnson ingroup avoid reconsidering its escalation policy when time and again the expectations on which they based their decisions turned out to be wrong? James C. Thompson, Jr., a Harvard historian who spent five years as an observing participant in both the State Department and the White House, tells us that the policymakers avoided critical discussion of their prior decisions and continually invented new rationalizations so that they could sincerely recommit themselves to defeating the North Vietnamese.

In the fall of 1964, before the bombing of North Vietnam began, some of the policymakers predicted that six weeks of air strikes would induce the North Vietnamese to seek peace talks. When someone asked, "What if they don't?" the answer was that another four weeks certainly would do the trick. . . .

3. MORALITY. Victims of groupthink believe unquestioningly in the inherent morality of their ingroup; this belief inclines the members to ignore the ethical or moral consequences of their decisions.

Evidence that this symptom is at work usually is of a negative kind—the things that are left unsaid in group meetings. At least two influential persons had doubts about the morality of the Bay of Pigs adventure. One of them, Arthur Schlesinger Jr., presented his strong objections in a memorandum to President Kennedy and Secretary of State Rusk but suppressed them when he attended meetings of the Kennedy team. The other, Senator J. William Fulbright, was not a member of the group, but the President invited him to express his misgivings in a speech to the policymakers. However, when Fulbright finished speaking the President moved on to other agenda items without asking for reactions of the group.

David Kraslow and Stuart H. Loory, in *The Secret Search for Peace in Vietnam*, report that during 1966 President Johnson's ingroup was concerned primarily with selecting bomb targets in North Vietnam. They based their selections on four factors—the military advantage, the risk to American aircraft and pilots, the danger of forcing other countries into the fighting, and the danger of heavy civilian casualties. At their regular Tuesday luncheons, they weighed these factors the way school teachers grade examination papers, averaging them out. Though evidence on this point is scant, I suspect that the group's ritualistic adherence to a standardized procedure induced the members to feel morally justified in their destructive way of dealing with the Vietnamese people—after all, the danger of heavy civilian casualties from U.S. air strikes was taken into account on their checklists.

4. STEREOTYPES. Victims of groupthink hold stereotyped views of the leaders of enemy groups: they are so evil that genuine attempts at negotiating differences with them are unwarranted, or they are too weak or too stupid to deal effectively with whatever attempts the ingroup makes to defeat their purposes, no matter how risky the attempts are.

Kennedy's groupthinkers believed that Premier Fidel Castro's air force was so ineffectual that obsolete B-26s could knock it out completely in a surprise attack before the invasion began. They also believed that Castro's army was so weak that a small Cuban-exile brigade could establish a well-protected beach-head at the Bay of Pigs. In addition, they believed that Castro was not smart enough to put down any possible internal uprisings in support of the exiles. They were wrong on all three assumptions. Though much of the blame was attributable to faulty intelligence, the point is that none of Kennedy's advisers even questioned the CIA planners about these assumptions. . . .

5. PRESSURE. Victims of groupthink apply direct pressure to any individual who momentarily expresses doubts about any of the group's shared illusions or who questions the validity of the arguments supporting a policy alternative favored by the majority. This gambit reinforces the concurrence-seeking norm that loyal members are expected to maintain.

President Kennedy probably was more active than anyone else in raising skeptical questions during the Bay of Pigs meetings, and yet he seems to have encouraged the group's docile, uncritical acceptance of defective arguments in favor of the CIA's plan. At every meeting, he allowed the CIA representatives to dominate the discussion. He permitted them to give their immediate refutations in response to each tentative doubt that one of the others expressed, instead of asking whether anyone shared the doubt or wanted to pursue the implications of the new worrisome issue that had just been raised. And at the most crucial meeting, when he was calling on each member to give his vote for or against the plan, he did not call on Arthur Schlesinger, the one man there who was known by the President to have serious misgivings.

Historian Thomson informs us that whenever a member of Johnson's ingroup began to express doubts, the group used subtle social pressures to "domesticate" him. To start with, the dissenter was made to feel at home provided that he lived up to two restrictions: (1) that he did not voice his doubts to outsiders, which would play into the hands of the opposition; and

(2) that he kept his criticisms within the bounds of acceptable deviation, which meant not challenging any of the fundamental assumptions that went into the group's prior commitments. One such "domesticated dissenter" was Bill Moyers. When Moyers arrived at a meeting, Thomson tells us, the President greeted him with, "Well, here comes Mr. Stop-the Bombing."

6. SELF-CENSORSHIP. Victims of groupthink avoid deviating from what appears to be group consensus; they keep silent about their misgivings and even minimize to themselves the importance of their doubts.

As we have seen, Schlesinger was not at all hesitant about presenting his strong objections to the Bay of Pigs plan in a memorandum to the President and the Secretary of State. But he became keenly aware of his tendency to suppress objections at the White House meetings. "In the months after the Bay of Pigs, I bitterly reproached myself for having kept so silent during those crucial discussions in the cabinet room," Schlesinger writes in *A Thousand Days*, "I can only explain my failure to do more than raise a few timid questions by reporting that one's impulse to blow the whistle on this nonsense was simply undone by the circumstances of the discussion."

7. UNANIMITY. Victims of groupthink share an illusion of unanimity within the group concerning almost all judgments expressed by members who speak in favor of the majority view. This symptom results partly from the preceding one, whose effects are augmented by the false assumption that any individual who remains silent during any part of the discussion is in full accord with what the others are saying.

When a group of persons who respect each other's opinions arrives at a unanimous view, each member is likely to feel that the belief must be true. This reliance on consensual validation within the group tends to replace individual critical thinking and reality testing, unless there are clear-cut disagreements among the members. In contemplating a course of action such as the invasion of Cuba, it is painful for the members to confront disagreements within their group, particularly if it becomes apparent that there are widely divergent views about whether the preferred course of action is too risky to undertake at all. Such disagreements are likely to arouse anxieties about making a serious error. Once the sense of unanimity is shattered, the members no longer can feel complacently confident about the decision they are inclined to make. Each man must then face the annoying realization that there are troublesome uncertainties and he must diligently seek out the best information he can get in order to decide for himself exactly how serious the risks might be. This is one of the unpleasant consequences of being in a group of hardheaded, critical thinkers.

To avoid such an unpleasant state, the members often become inclined, without quite realizing it, to prevent latent disagreements from surfacing when they are about to initiate a risky course of action. The group leader and the members support each other in playing up the areas of convergence in their thinking, at the expense of fully exploring divergencies that might reveal unsettled issues. . . .

8. MINDGUARDS. Victims of groupthink sometimes appoint themselves as mindguards to protect the leader and fellow members from adverse information that might break the complacency they shared about the effectiveness and morality of past decisions. At a large birthday party for his wife, Attorney General Robert F. Kennedy, who had been constantly informed about the Cuban invasion plan, took Schlesinger aside and asked him why he was opposed. Kennedy listened coldly and said, "You may be right or you may be wrong, but the President has made his mind up. Don't push it any further. Now is the time for everyone to help him all they can. . . ."

Products. When a group of executives frequently displays most or all of these interrelated symptoms, a detailed study of their deliberations is likely to reveal a number of immediate consequences. These consequences are, in effect, products of poor decision-making practices because they lead to inadequate solutions to the problems under discussion.

First, the group limits its discussions to a few alternative courses of action (often only two) without an initial survey of all the alternatives that might be worthy of consideration.

Second, the group fails to reexamine the course of action initially preferred by the majority after they learn of risks and drawbacks they had not considered originally.

Third, the members spend little or no time discussing whether there are nonobvious gains they may have overlooked or ways of reducing the seemingly prohibitive costs that made rejected alternatives appear undesirable to them.

Fourth, members make little or no attempt to obtain information from experts within their own organizations who might be able to supply more precise estimates of potential losses and gains.

Fifth, members show positive interest in facts and opinions that support their preferred policy, they tend to ignore facts and opinions that do not.

Sixth, members spend little time deliberating about how the chosen policy might be hindered by bureaucratic inertia, sabotaged by political opponents, or temporarily derailed by common accidents. Consequently, they fail to work out contingency plans to cope with foreseeable setbacks that could endanger the overall success of their chosen course.

Support. The search for an explanation of why groupthink occurs has led me through a quagmire of complicated theoretical issues in a murky area of human motivation. My belief, based on recent social psychological research, is that we can best understand the various symptoms of groupthink as a mutual effort among the group members to maintain self-esteem and emotional equanimity by providing social support to each other, especially at times when they share responsibility for making vital decisions.

Even when no important decision is pending, the typical administrator will begin to doubt the wisdom and morality of his past decisions each time he receives information about setbacks, particularly if the information is accompanied by negative feedback from prominent men who originally had been his supporters. It should not be surprising, therefore, to find that individual members strive to develop unanimity and esprit de corps that will help bolster each other's morale, to create an optimistic outlook about the success of pending decisions, and to reaffirm the positive value of past policies to which all of them are committed.

Pride. Shared illusions of invulnerability, for example, can reduce anxiety about taking risks. Rationalizations help members believe that the risks are really not so bad after all. The assumption of inherent morality helps the members to avoid feelings of shame or guilt. Negative stereotypes function as stress-reducing devices to enhance a sense of moral righteousness as well as pride in a lofty mission.

The mutual enhancement of self-esteem and morale may have functional value in enabling the members to maintain their capacity to take action, but it has maladaptive consequences insofar as concurrence-seeking tendencies interfere with critical, rational capacities and lead to serious errors of judgment. . . .

Remedies. To counterpoint my case studies of the major fiascos, I have also investigated two highly successful group enterprises, the formulation of the Marshall Plan in the Truman Administration and the handling of the Cuban missile crisis by President Kennedy and his advisers. I have found it instructive to examine the steps Kennedy took to change his group's decision-making processes. These changes ensured that the mistakes made by his Bay of Pigs ingroup were not repeated by the missile-crisis ingroup, even though the membership of both groups was essentially the same.

The following recommendations for preventing groupthink incorporate many of the good practices I discovered to be characteristic of the Marshall Plan and missile crisis groups:

1. The leader of a policy-forming group should assign the role of critical evaluator to each member, encouraging the group to give high priority to open airing of objections and doubts. This practice needs to be reinforced by the leader's acceptance of criticism of his own judgments in order to discourage members from soft-pedaling their disagreements and from allowing their striving for concurrence to inhibit critical thinking.

2. When the key members of a hierarchy assign a policy-planning mission to any group within their organization, they should adopt an impartial stance instead of stating preferences and expectations at the beginning. This will encourage open inquiry and impartial probing of a wide range of policy alternatives.

3. The organization routinely should set up several outside policy-planning and evaluation groups to work on the same policy question, each deliberating under a different leader. This can prevent the insulation of an ingroup.

4. At intervals before the group reaches a final consensus, the leader should require each member to discuss the group's deliberations with associates in his own unit of the organization—assuming that those associates can be trusted to adhere to the same security regulations that govern the policy-makers—and then to report back their reactions to the group.

5. The group should invite one or more outside experts to each meeting on a staggered basis and encourage the experts to challenge the views of the core members.

6. At every general meeting of the group, whenever the agenda calls for an evaluation of policy alternatives, at least one member should play devil's advocate, functioning as a good lawyer in challenging the testimony of those who advocate the majority position.

7. Whenever the policy issue involves relations with a rival nation or organization, the group should devote a sizable block of time, perhaps an entire session, to a survey of all warning signals from the rivals and should write alternative scenarios on the rivals' intentions.

8. When the group is surveying policy alternatives for feasibility and effectiveness, it should from time to time divide into two or more subgroups to meet separately under different chairmen, and then come back together to hammer out differences.

9. After reaching a preliminary consensus about what seems to be the best policy, the group should hold a "second-chance" meeting at which every member expresses as vividly as he can all his residual doubts, and rethinks the entire issue before making a definitive choice.

How. These recommendations have their disadvantages. To encourage the open airing of objections, for instance, might lead to prolonged and costly debates when a rapidly growing crisis requires immediate solution. It also could cause rejection, depression and anger. A leader's failure to set a norm might create cleavage between leader and members that could develop into a disruptive power struggle if the leader looks on the emerging consensus as anathema. Setting up outside evaluation groups might increase the risk of security leakage. Still, inventive executives who know their way around the organizational maze probably can figure out how to apply one or another of the prescriptions successfully, without harmful side effects. . . .

In this era of atomic warheads, urban disorganization and ecocatastrophes, it seems to me that policymakers should collaborate with behavioral scientists and give top priority to preventing groupthink and its attendant fiascos.

29

Social Influences on Work Effectiveness

Lyman W. Porter, Edward E. Lawler III, and J. Richard Hackman

CONDITIONS WITHIN GROUPS THAT MODERATE THEIR IMPACT ON WORK EFFECTIVENESS

Before proceeding to consider (in the next section) the ways that groups can influence the work effectiveness of individuals, we should first take into account certain conditions within groups that can affect how much and what kind of impact they will have. Uppermost among these are a group's characteristic reactions to deviance and the degree of cohesiveness that exists within the group.

Deviance and Group Effectiveness

The experimental work on how groups react to members who engage in behaviors which are inconsistent with group norms . . . reveals a fairly primitive type of group process. Caricatured a bit, the process operates as follows: Uniformity, conformity to norms, and adherence to one's role is the rule. When someone steps out of line, other members provide him with potent doses of discretionary stimuli designed to persuade or coerce him back to "normal." This pressure continues until the would-be deviant (1) gives in and ceases expressing his deviant thoughts or exhibiting his deviant behavior; (2) is psychologically or bodily rejected by the group or becomes institutionalized by the group as the "house deviant"; or (3) finally convinces the other group members of the rightness of his thoughts or the appropriateness of his behavior.

The more the group has control of discretionary stimuli which are important to group members, the more it can effectively eliminate most appearances of deviance on the part of its members. The members, in such circumstances, may faithfully behave in accord with their roles in the group, refrain from violating group norms, and express their endorsement of the "right" attitudes and beliefs. And from all visible indicators, at least in the short term, everything seems well with the group.

Dysfunctional Aspects of Eliminating Deviance from Group Norms

It can be argued, however, that this pattern of dealing with deviance is highly dysfunctional for the long-term effectiveness of a group, for at least two reasons (Hackman, 1975). First, if members comply primarily because of the application of pressure from the group (or the expected application of that pressure), the result may be public compliance *at*

Source: Lyman W. Porter, Edward E. Lawler III, and J. Richard Hackman, "Social Influences on Work Effectiveness." Pages 404–422 in Porter, Lawler and Hackman, *Behavior in Organizations* (McGraw-Hill, 1975). Reprinted by permission of the publisher.

the expense of private acceptance and personal commitment to what is being done (cf. Kelman, 1961; Kiesler, 1969; pp. 279–295). And when a group is heavily populated by individuals who are saying and doing one thing but thinking and feeling another, high effectiveness in the long haul is unlikely.

Second, to the extent that a group uses its control of discretionary stimuli to swiftly extinguish any signs of deviance, it loses the opportunity to explore the usefulness and ultimate validity of the very attitudes, beliefs, norms and roles it is enforcing. For example, if compliance to a given norm about work behavior is enforced so effectively that deviance from that norm virtually never occurs, the group will be unable to discover whether that norm is actually helpful or detrimental to the achievement of the goals of the group. In essence, it may be that an unexamined norm is not worth enforcing—at least if high group effectiveness is aspired to in the long run.

Despite these and other dysfunctions of excessive pressures against deviance, the research literature suggests that groups have a strong tendency to stamp out (or at least sweep under the rug) behaviors which are not congruent with traditional standards of acceptability in the group. Apparently groups rarely attempt to work through the more basic problems of why people deviate from the group, what the consequences of such deviance for the group are, and how deviance can be most effectively dealt with for the good of both individual members and the group as a whole. . . .

It is emotionally quite stressful and difficult for group members to deal openly with core questions of conformity, deviation, and interpersonal relationships in a group. Indeed, research (Bion, 1959; Argyris, 1969) suggests that it may be impossible for a group to break out of a traditional pattern of interpersonal behavior without outside professional assistance. Even with such assistance, it may take a great deal of time and effort before a group can overcome the basic assumptions which guided its early behavior and develop into an effective and truly independent work group (Bion, 1959). When a group becomes able to make more open and conscious choices about the use of those discretionary stimuli under its control to deal with issues of conformity and deviance, the long-term effectiveness of the group should be greatly enhanced.

Why High Group Cohesiveness Can Be Dysfunctional

In general, as the cohesiveness of a work group increases, the overall level of member conformity to the norms of the group would also be expected to increase—for two different but mutually reinforcing reasons: First, . . . there tend to be stronger group-generated pressures toward uniformity and conformity in groups which are highly cohesive than in groups which are not (cf. Festinger et al., 1950). And second, group members are likely to value especially strongly the interpersonal rewards which are available in highly cohesive groups—precisely because of the strong positive feelings members have for one another in such groups. Therefore, group members are unlikely to risk losing those rewards by ignoring or defying pressures to conform to group norms. And, in fact, research evidence confirms that conformity is especially high in cohesive groups (cf. Tajfel, 1969; pp. 334–347; Lott & Lott, 1965, pp. 292–296; Hackman, 1975).

The problem is that conformity to group norms which occurs in highly cohesive groups may *not* be functional for group or individual productivity. Indeed, cohesiveness may be strongly dysfunctional for effectiveness in some situations for several reasons, which are discussed below.

Deviance Is Dealt with Ineffectively. As noted previously, groups tend in general to stamp out deviant behavior on the part of individual group members—rather than use such deviance to increase either the learning of individual group members or the capability of the group as a whole to respond effectively to a changing or turbulent state of affairs. Since pressures toward uniformity are highest in highly cohesive groups, the risk of quick and ill-considered elimination of all appearances of deviance in the group also are likely to be highest in cohesive groups—even though exploration of such deviant behaviors might actually be helpful to the group in the long run.

Norms Are Strong, but Their Direction May Be Negative. While it is generally true that cohesive groups are able to effectively control members such that their behavior closely approximates that specified by the group norm, the *direction* of the group norm itself (i.e., toward high versus low performance) has been found to be unrelated to the level of cohesiveness (Schachter, 1951; Berkowitz, 1954; Seashore, 1954; Darley et al., 1952).

For example, in several studies (e.g., Schachter, 1951; Berkowitz, 1954) conditions of high versus low cohesiveness and high- versus low-productivity norms were created by experimental manipulation. It was found that member productivity was indeed closer to the group norm in the high- than in the low-cohesiveness groups—for both the high- *and* the low-production norms. There have been similar findings in industrial situations using survey techniques (Seashore, 1954). In this study of over 200 work groups in a machinery factory, no correlation was found between cohesiveness and productivity—but, as would be expected, when cohesiveness was high, the amount of *variation* in the productivity of group members was low, and vice versa.

Groupthink May Develop. One of the seeming advantages of having a great deal of uniformity or conformity in a group is that members do not have to deal with the thorny interpersonal problems which can arise when members behave in nonuniform ways—e.g., when each member of a work group is allowed to select his own level of production and the levels selected turn out to vary a good deal from member to member. This "group-maintenance" function of uniformity may be especially important to members of highly cohesive groups, since members of such groups typically value strongly the rewards controlled by their fellows—and would be particularly upset to receive negative interpersonal reactions from them.

It has been suggested, however, that as a group becomes excessively close-knit and develops a strong feeling of "we-ness," it becomes susceptible to a pattern of behavior known as "groupthink" (Janis, 1972). Among the several symptoms of groupthink are an excessive concern with maintaining uniformity among members, a marked decrease in the openness of the group to discrepant or unsettling information (from sources either inside or outside the group), and a simultaneous unwillingness to examine seriously and process such negative information if it ever is brought to the attention of the group.

These social processes may often serve immediate group-maintenance functions and help perpetuate the warm and cohesive feelings which characterize the group. In addition, however, they result in an increased likelihood that the group, in a spirit of goodwill and shared confidence, will develop and implement a course of action which is grossly inappropriate and ineffective. It has been shown (Janis, 1972), for example, how the groupthink phenomenon may have contributed substantially to a number of historical fiascoes planned and executed by groups of government officials (e.g., the Bay of Pigs invasion and Britain's appeasement policy toward Hitler prior to World War II).

Should Cohesiveness Be Avoided?

It might appear from the above discussion that high cohesiveness of groups in organizations is something that should be avoided—to minimize the possibility of enforced low-production norms in work settings or the likelihood that groupthink-like phenomena will develop among decision makers. Such a conclusion would be a very pessimistic one: low cohesiveness among members of work groups or decision-making groups would indeed lower the possibility of obtaining the negative outcomes mentioned but also would require that the positive potential of cohesive groups be forgone as well—such as the increased capability of such groups to regulate behavior so as to *increase* the attainment of group and organizational goals.

The question, then, becomes how the norms of highly cohesive groups can be changed such that they encourage careful examination of the task environment (including negative or unsettling information which may be present), exploration of interpersonal issues, which may be impairing group performance, and high rather than low levels of group and member productivity. Although presently little is known about what factors affect the kinds of norms developed by work groups in organizations (cf. Vroom, 1969, pp. 226–227), two general approaches to the problem are discussed briefly below.

Fostering Intergroup Competition. One frequently espoused tactic for developing simultaneously high work-group cohesiveness and commitment to organizational goals can be referred to as the "best damn group in the whole damn organization ploy." Many managers realize that if they can get their subordinates, as a group, to experience themselves in competition with other groups in the organization, a kind of team spirit often develops which results in high group cohesiveness and great member commitment to be the "best" in whatever it is that defines the competition. And, in fact, there is considerable research evidence that when groups enter into competitive relationships with other groups, internal cohesiveness and high individual task commitment do increase—often dramatically (cf. Sherif, 1965; Blake & Mouton, 1964).

The problem is that such intergroup competitiveness often actually works against the best interests of the total organization in the long run. For example, in the interest of "winning," information which really should be shared *among* groups for optimal organizational functioning often is withheld—and at times even misinformation is communicated up and down the line in a way intended to make sure that "our group looks best." The pervasive line-staff and interdepartment (e.g., sales versus production) conflicts in contemporary organizations often reflect exactly this type of intergroup competition.

One common means of attempting to overcome such problems of dysfunctional intergroup competition within organizations (while maintaining high commitment within groups) is to introduce or make especially salient a superordinate goal which all groups share. Research evidence does support the idea that a superordinate goal can reduce or eliminate hostilities between groups

(Sherif, 1965). And, in fact, many business organizations use the idea of the superordinate goal in their attempts to get employees in diverse groups to pull together for the good of the organization as a whole—for example, by prominently posting the number of trunkets sold this month by one's own company versus the number sold by the chief competitor. The problem, of course, is that it is not likely that a lower-level employee who hates his job and feels he is grossly and unfairly underpaid is going to *care* very much about whether or not his own organization is ahead in the trunket-selling competition—regardless of the attempts of the company employee-relations department to make that competition an organizing theme of the company.

Basing Cohesiveness on Task Rather Than Social Rewards. It may be that one of the major reasons for the failure of many cohesive groups to work as effectively as they might toward group and organizational goals has to do with the basis of the cohesiveness itself—i.e., the reasons why the group members have a strong desire to stick together.

In virtually all the research which has been discussed here, cohesiveness was based upon the *interpersonal rewards* present or potentially present in the group. The "stake" of most group members in such situations, then, would be to refrain from behaviors that might disrupt the interpersonal satisfactions which are obtained from group membership. The control of the group over its members in such cases rests largely upon its capability to provide or withhold such valued social satisfactions. In the groupthink situation, for example, such control results in interpersonal strategies characterized by lessened vigilance for new and potentially disruptive information, acceptance of the views of "high-status others" as the doctrine of the group, and suppression of any interpersonal unpleasantries—all of which can severely impair the work effectiveness of the group.

If the basis for the cohesiveness were a shared commitment to the *task* of the group (instead of a commitment to maintaining the interpersonal rewards received in the group), the picture might change considerably. The criterion for when to accept information and direction from others in the group, for example, might change from something like "Will questioning what is being said by the leader risk my being rejected or ridiculed by the group?" to "Will such questioning contribute to our succeeding in the task?" Conformity, then, should remain high in such groups, but the norms to which conformity is enforced would focus on facilitating the group's task performance activities rather than on maintaining interpersonal comfortableness. This change in orientation also would bear on the question of the *direction* of norms for individual production in work groups: if one of the major reasons for the cohesiveness of the group were a shared commitment to succeeding in the task, then that commitment should in most cases lead to group norms oriented toward high rather than low task effectiveness. . . .

The problem in attempting to develop task-based cohesiveness in real-world work groups is twofold. First, many tasks (and perhaps most production tasks) in organizations are not such as to generate genuine group commitment. Instead, the reverse may often be true: the task may be so uninteresting that the group accepts as an alternative a task of "getting" management or of avoiding hard work. In such cases, the power resident in the group cohesiveness may be exceptionally dysfunctional for organizational goals. Second, it is quite difficult, even for objectively important tasks, for group members to overcome their orientation to interpersonal rewards and rejections. The group of Kennedy advisors during the Bay of Pigs crisis, for example, certainly had an important task; but the heavy investment of each member toward remaining a member of the high-status, high-prestige group apparently was so strong that "not rocking the interpersonal boat" overwhelmed "doing the task well" as a behavioral criterion for most group members.

Thus, while there appears to be much to be said for the development of tasks which can provide a strong positive basis for group cohesiveness, few guidelines for designing such tasks currently exist. The crux of the problem, it seems, is to create conditions such that the rewards from genuinely shared task activities become as salient and as attractive to group members as are the more skin-surface interpersonal satisfactions, which, unfortunately, currently typify relationships within most "cohesive" groups in organizations.

WAYS GROUPS INFLUENCE INDIVIDUAL WORK EFFECTIVENESS

Now we are in a position to turn to the question of *how* groups can in fact have an impact on how hard and how well their members work. . . . The major direct determinants of the work behavior of organization members can be summarized in terms of four major classes of variables:

1. The job-relevant knowledge and skills of the individual
2. The level of psychological arousal the individual experiences while working
3. The performance strategies the individual uses doing his work
4. The level of effort the individual exerts in doing his work

Which (or which combination) of the four classes of variables can contribute substantially to increased individual work *effectiveness*, of course, very much depends upon the nature of the task or job being performed. On a routine and simple clerical job, for example, where the sole performance criterion is quantity of acceptable output, only effort is likely to be of real importance in influencing measured work effectiveness. On a more complex job, where there are many ways to go about performing it (e.g., most managerial jobs), the performance *strategies* used may critically influence effectiveness. For yet other jobs, arousal and/or the job-relevant skills of the individual may be critical.* . . .

Group Influences by Affecting Member Knowledge and Skills

Performance on many tasks and jobs in organizations is strongly affected by the job-relevant knowledge and skills of the individuals who do the work. Thus, even if an employee has both high commitment toward accomplishing a particular piece of work and a well-formed strategy about how to go about doing it, the implementation of that plan can be constrained or terminated if he does not know how to carry it out, or if he knows how but is incapable of doing so. While ability is relevant to the performance of jobs at all levels in an organization, its

* The characteristics of tasks or jobs which identify which classes of variables are of most importance in determining work effectiveness have been termed "critical task contingencies," i.e., those contingencies which specify what behaviors are critical to effective or successful performance for the job in question. Depending upon what the critical task contingencies are for a given task or job, it is possible to determine on an a priori basis which variables must be dealt with in any attempt to improve performance effectiveness on that job. This notion is developed more completely by Hackman (1975).

impact probably is somewhat reduced for lower-level jobs. The reason is that such jobs often are not demanding of high skill levels. Further, to the extent that organizational selection, placement, and promotion practices are adequate, *all* jobs should tend to be occupied by individuals who possess the skills requisite for adequate performance.

. . . The impact of groups on member performance effectiveness by improving member knowledge and skill probably is one of the lesser influences groups can have—both because employees on many jobs tend already to have many or all of the skills needed to perform them effectively and because there are other sources for improving skills which may be more useful and more potent than the work group, such as formal job training programs and self-study programs.

Group Influences by Affecting Member Arousal Level

It was shown in the last chapter how a group can substantially influence the level of psychological arousal experienced by a member—through the mere presence of the other group members and by those others sending the individual messages which are directly arousal-enhancing or arousal-depressing. The conditions under which such group-promoted changes in arousal level will lead to increased performance effectiveness, however, very much depend upon the type of task being worked on (Zajonc, 1965).

In this case, the critical characteristics of the job have to do with whether the initially *dominant task responses* of the individual are likely to be correct or incorrect. Since the individual's output of such responses is facilitated when he is in an aroused state, arousal should improve performance effectiveness on well-learned tasks (so-called performance tasks) in which the dominant response is correct and needs merely to be executed by the performer. By the same token, arousal should impair effectiveness for new or unfamiliar tasks (learning tasks) in which the dominant response is likely to be incorrect. . . .

Groups can, of course, increase member arousal in ways other than taking an evaluative stance toward the individual. Strongly positive, encouraging statements also should increase arousal in some performance situations—for example, by helping the individual become personally highly committed to the group goal, and making sure he realizes that he is a very important part of the team responsible for reaching that goal. What must be kept in mind, however, is that such devices represent a double-edged sword: while they may facilitate effective performance for well-learned tasks, they may have the opposite effect for new and unfamiliar tasks.

What, then, can be said about the effects on performance of group members when their presence (and interaction) serves to *decrease* the level of arousal of the group member—as, for example, when individuals coalesce into groups under conditions of high stress? When the other members of the group are a source of support, comfort, or acceptance to the individual (and serve to decrease his arousal level), it would be predicted that performance effectiveness would follow a pattern exactly opposite to that described above: the group would impair effectiveness for familiar or well-learned performance tasks (because arousal helps on these tasks, and arousal is being lowered) and facilitate effectiveness for unfamiliar or complicated learning tasks (because in this case arousal is harmful, and it is being lowered).

. . . As the group becomes increasingly threatening, evaluative, or strongly encouraging, effectiveness should increase for performance tasks and decrease for learning tasks. When the group is experienced as increasingly supportive, comforting, or unconditionally accepting, effectiveness should decrease for performance tasks and increase for learning tasks. And when no meaningful relationship at all is experienced by the individual between himself and the group, performance should not be affected. While some of these predictions have been tested and confirmed in small group experimental settings, others await research. . . .

It is well known that overly routine jobs can decrease a worker's level of arousal to such an extent that his performance effectiveness is impaired. It seems quite possible, therefore, that the social environment of workers on such jobs can be designed so as to compensate partially for the deadening effects of the job itself and thereby lead to an increment in performance on well-learned tasks.

Finally (as discussed in a subsequent section), the supervisor probably has a more powerful effect on the level of arousal of a worker than any other single individual in his immediate social environment. By close supervision (which usually results in the worker's feeling more or less constantly evaluated), supervisors can and do increase the level of arousal experienced by workers. While this may, for routine jobs, have some potential for improving performance effectiveness, it also is quite likely that the worker's negative reactions to being closely supervised ultimately will result in his attention being diverted from the job itself and focused instead on ways he can either get out from "under the gun" of the supervisor or somehow get back at the supervisor to punish him for his unwanted close supervision.

Group Influences by Affecting Level of Member Effort and Member Performance Strategies

The level of effort a person exerts in doing his work and the performance strategies he follows are treated together here because both variables are largely under the performer's *voluntary* control.

Direct Versus Indirect Influences on Effort and Strategy. Throughout this book we have used a general "expectancy theory" approach to analyze those aspects of a person's behavior in organizations which are under his voluntary control. From this perspective, a person's choices about his effort and work strategy can be viewed as hinging largely upon (1) his *expectations* regarding the likely consequences of his choices and (2) the degree to which he *values* those expected consequences. Following this approach, it becomes clear that the group can have both a direct and an indirect effect on the level of effort a group member exerts at his job and his choices about performance strategy.

The *direct* impact of the group on effort and strategy, of course, is simply the enforcement by the group of its own norms regarding what is an "appropriate" level of effort to expend on the job and what is the "proper" performance strategy. We previously discussed in some detail how groups use their control of discretionary stimuli to enforce group norms, and thereby affect such voluntary behaviors. Thus, if the group has established a norm about the level of member effort or the strategies members should use in going about their work, the group can control individual behavior merely by making sure that individual members realize that their receipt of valued group-controlled rewards is contingent upon their behaving in accord with the norm.

The *indirect* impact of the group on the effort and performance strategies of the individual involves the group's control of information regarding the state of the organizational environment outside the boundaries of the group. Regardless of any norms the group itself may have about effort or strategy, it also can communicate to the group member "what leads to what" in the broader organization, and thereby affect the individual's *own* choices about his behavior. . . .

Moreover . . . groups can affect the *personal preferences and values* of individual members—although such influences tend to occur relatively slowly and over a long period of time. When such changes do occur, the level of desire (or the valence) individuals have for various outcomes available in the organizational setting will change as well. And as the kinds of outcomes valued by the individual change, his behavior also will change to increase the degree to which the newly valued outcomes are obtained at work. The long-term result can be substantial revision of the choices made by the individual about the work he will expend and the performance strategies he will use at work.

It should be noted, however, that such indirect influences on member effort and performance strategy will be most potent early in the individual's tenure in the organization when he has not yet had a chance to develop through experience his own personal "map" of the organization. When the individual becomes less dependent upon the group for data about "what leads to what" and "what's good" in the organization, the group may have to revert to direct norm enforcement to maintain control of the work behavior of individual members.

In summary, the group can and does have a strong impact on both the level of effort exerted by its members and the strategies members use in carrying out their work. This impact is realized both directly (i.e., by enforcement of group norms) and indirectly (i.e., by affecting the beliefs and values of the members). When the direct and indirect influences of a group are congruent—which is often the case—the potency of the group's effects on its members can be quite strong. For example, if at the same time that a group is enforcing its *own* norm of, say, moderately low production, it also is providing a group member with data regarding the presumably *objective* negative consequences of hard work in the particular organization, the group member will experience two partially independent and mutually reinforcing influences aimed at keeping his rate of production down.

Effort, Strategy, and Performance Effectiveness. What, then, are the circumstances under which groups can improve the work *effectiveness* of their members through influences on individual choices about level of effort and about strategy? Again, the answer depends upon the nature of the job. Unless a job is structured so that effort level or performance strategy actually can make a real difference in work effectiveness, group influences on effort or strategy will be irrelevant to how well individual members perform.

Strategy: In general, groups should be able to facilitate member work effectiveness by influencing strategy choices more for complex jobs than for simple, straightforward, or routine ones. The reason is that on simple jobs, strategy choices usually cannot make much of a difference in effectiveness; instead, how well one does is determined almost entirely by how hard one works. On jobs characterized by high variety and autonomy, on the other hand, the work strategy used by the individual usually is of considerable importance in determining work effectiveness. By helping an individual develop and implement an appropriate work strategy—of where and how to put in his effort—the group should be able to substantially facilitate his effectiveness.

Effort: In the great majority of organizational settings, most jobs are structured such that the harder one works, the more effective his performance is likely to be. Thus, group influences on the effort expended by members on their jobs are both very pervasive and very potent determiners of individual work effectiveness. There are, nevertheless, some exceptions to this generalization: the success of a complicated brain operation, for example, is less likely to depend upon effort expended than it is upon the strategies used and the job-relevant knowledge and skills of the surgeon.

When either effort or strategy or both are in fact important in determining performance effectiveness, the individual has substantial personal control over how well he does in his work. In such cases, the degree to which the group facilitates (rather than hinders) individual effectiveness will depend jointly upon (1) the degree to which the group has accurate information regarding the task and organizational contingencies which are operative in that situation and makes such information available to the individual and (2) the degree to which the norms of the group are congruent with those contingencies and reinforce them.

Participation. One management practice which in theory should contribute positively to meeting both of the above conditions is the use of group participation in making decisions about work practices. Participation has been widely advocated as a management technique, both on ideological grounds and as a direct means of increasing work effectiveness. And, in fact, some studies have shown that participation can lead to higher work effectiveness (e.g., Coch & French, 1948; Lawler & Hackman, 1969). In the present framework, participation should contribute to increased work effectiveness in two different ways.

> 1. Participation can increase the amount and the accuracy of information workers have about work practices and the environmental contingencies associated with them. . . .
>
> 2. Participation can increase the degree to which group members feel they "own" their work practices—and therefore the likelihood that the group will develop a norm of support for those practices. In the participative groups in the study cited above, for example, the nature of the work-related communication among members changed from initial "shared warnings" about management and "things management proposes" to helping members (especially new members) come to understand and believe in "our plan." In other words, as group members come to experience the work or work practices *as under their own control or ownership*, it becomes more likely that informal group norms supportive of effective behavior vis-à-vis those practices will develop. Such norms provide a striking contrast to the "group protective" norms which often emerge when control is perceived to be exclusively and unilaterally under management control.

We can see, then, that group participative techniques can be quite facilitative of individual work effectiveness—but only under certain conditions:

> 1. The topic of participation must be relevant to the work itself. There is no reason to believe that participation involving task-irrelevant issues (e.g., preparing for the Red Cross Bloodmobile visit to the plant) will have facilitative effects on work productivity. While such participation may indeed help increase the cohesiveness of the work group, it

clearly will not help group members gain information or develop norms which are facilitative of high work effectiveness. Indeed, such task-irrelevant participation may serve to direct the attention and motivation of group members *away from* work issues and thereby even lower productivity (cf. French, Israel, & As, 1960).

2. The objective task and environmental contingencies in the work setting must actually be supportive of more effective performance. That is, if through participation group members learn more about what leads to what in the organization, then it is increasingly important that there be real and meaningful positive outcomes which result from effective performance. If, for example, group members gain a quite complete and accurate impression through participation that "hard work around here pays off only in backaches," then increased effort as a consequence of participation is most unlikely. If, on the other hand, participation results in a new and better understanding that hard work can lead to increased pay, enhanced opportunities for advancement, and the chance to feel a sense of personal and group accomplishment, then increased effort should be the result.

3. Finally, the work must be such that increased effort (or a different and better work strategy) objectively can lead to higher work effectiveness. If it is true—as argued here—that the main benefits of group participation are (1) increased understanding of work practices and the organizational environment and (2) increased experienced "ownership" by the group of the work and work practices, then participation should increase productivity only when the *objective determinants of productivity are under the voluntary control of the worker.* There is little reason to expect, therefore, that participation should have a substantial facilitative effect on productivity when work outcomes are mainly determined by the level of skill of the worker and/or by his arousal level (rather than effort expended or work strategy used) or when outcomes are controlled by objective factors in the environment over which the worker can have little or no control (e.g., the rate or amount of work which is arriving at the employee's station).

Implications for Diagnosis and Change

This section has focused on ways that the group can influence the performance effectiveness of individual group members. While it has been maintained throughout that the group has a substantial impact on such performance effectiveness, it has been emphasized that the nature and extent of this impact centrally depends upon the characteristics of the work being done.

To diagnose and change the direction or extent of social influences on individual performance in an organization, then, the following three steps might be taken.

1. An analysis of the task or job would be made to determine which of the four classes of variables (i.e., skills, arousal, strategies, effort) objectively affect measured performance effectiveness. This might be done by posing this analytical question: "If skills (or arousal, or effort, or strategies) were brought to bear on the work differently than is presently the case, would a corresponding difference in work effectiveness be likely to be observed as a consequence?" By scrutinizing each of the four classes of variables in this way, it usually is possible to identify which specific variables are objectively important to consider for the job. In many cases, of course, more than one class of variables will turn out to be of importance.

2. After one or more "target" classes of variables have been identified, the work group itself would be examined to unearth any ways in which the group was blocking effective individual performance. It might be determined, for example, that certain group norms were impeding the expression and use of various skills which individuals potentially could bring to bear on

their work. Or it might turn out that the social environment of the worker created conditions which were excessively (or insufficiently) arousing for optimal performance on the task at hand. For effort and strategy, which are under the voluntary control of the worker, there are two major possibilities to examine: (a) that norms are enforced in the group which coerce individuals to behave in ineffective ways or (b) that the group provides information to the individual members about task and environmental contingencies in an insufficient or distorted fashion, resulting in their making choices about their work behavior which interfere with task effectiveness. . . .

3. Finally, it would be useful to assess the group and the broader social environment to determine if there are ways that the "people resources" in the situation could be more fully utilized in the interest of increased work effectiveness. That is, rather than focusing solely on ways the group may be blocking or impeding performance effectiveness, attention should be given as well to any unrealized *potential* which resides in the group. It could turn out, for example, that some group members would be of great help to others in increasing the level of individual task-relevant skills, but these individuals have never been asked for help. Alternatively, it might be that the group could be assisted in finding new and better ways of ensuring that each group member has available accurate and current information about those tasks and environmental contingencies which determine the outcomes of various work behaviors.

The point is that the people who surround an individual at work can facilitate as well as hinder his performance effectiveness—and that any serious attempt to diagnose the social environment in the interest of improving work performance should explicitly address unrealized possibilities for enhancing performance as well as issues for which remedial action may be required.

What particular organizational changes will be called for on the basis of such a diagnosis—or what techniques should be used to realize these changes—will, of course, largely depend upon the particular characteristics of the organization and of the resources which are available there. The major emphasis of this section has been that there is *not* any single universally useful type of change or means of change—and that, instead, intervention should always be based on a thorough diagnosis of the existing social, organizational, and task environment. Perhaps especially intriguing in this regard is the prospect of developing techniques of social intervention which will help groups see the need for (and develop the capability of) making such interventions *on their own* in the interest of increasing the work effectiveness of the group as a whole. . . .

BIBLIOGRAPHY

Argyris, C. The incompleteness of social psychological theory: Examples from small group, cognitive consistency and attribution research. *American Psychologist*, 1969, **24**, 893–908.

Berkowitz, L. Group standards, cohesiveness and productivity. *Human Relations*, 1954, **7**, 509–519.

Bion, W. R. *Experiences in groups*. New York: Basic Books, 1959.

Blake, R. R., & Mouton, J. S. *The Managerial Grid*. Houston: Gulf, 1964.

Coch, L., & French, J. R. P. Jr. Overcoming resistance to change. *Human Relations*, 1948, **1**, 512–532.

Darley, J., Gross, N., & Martin, W. Studies of group behavior: Factors associated with the productivity of groups. *Journal of Applied Psychology*, 1952, **36**, 396–403.

Festinger, L. Informal social communication. *Psychological Review*, 1950, **57**, 271–282.

Festinger, L., Schachter, S., & Back, K. *Social pressures in informal groups*. Stanford: Stanford University Press, 1950.

French, J. R. P. Jr., Israel, J., & As, D. An experiment on participation in a Norwegian factory. *Human Relations*, 1960, **13**, 3–19.

Hackman, J. R. Group influences on individuals in organizations. In M. D. Dunnette (Ed.), *Handbook of industrial and organizational psychology*. Chicago: Rand-McNally, 1975.

Janis, I. L. *Victims of groupthink: A psychological study of foreign-policy decisions and fiascos*. Boston: Houghton Mifflin, 1972.

Kelman, H. C. Processes of opinion change. *Public Opinion Quarterly*, 1961, **25,** 57–58.

Kiesler, C. A. Group pressure and conformity. In J. Mills (Ed.), *Experimental social psychology*. New York: Macmillan, 1969.

Lawler, E. E., & Hackman, J. R. The impact of employee participation in the development of pay incentive plans: A field experiment. *Journal of Applied Psychology*, 1969, **53,** 467–471.

Lott, A. J., & Lott, B. E. Group cohesiveness as interpersonal attraction: A review of relationships with antecedent and consequent variables. *Psychological Bulletin*, 1965, **64,** 259–309.

Schachter, S. Deviation, rejection and communication. *Journal of Abnormal and Social Psychology*, 1951, **46,** 190–207.

Seashore, S. *Group cohesiveness in the industrial work group*. Ann Arbor: Institute for Social Research, University of Michigan, 1954.

Sherif, M. Formation of social norms: The experimental paradigm. In H. Proshansky and B. Seidenberg (Eds.), *Basic studies in social psychology*. New York: Holt, Rinehart & Winston, 1965.

Tajfel, H. Social and cultural factors in perception. In G. Lindzey and E. Aronson (Eds.), *The handbook of social psychology* (2nd ed.). Reading, Mass.: Addison-Wesley, 1969.

Vroom, V. H. Industrial social psychology. In G. Lindzey & E. Aronson (Eds.), *The handbook of social psychology* (2nd ed.). Reading, Mass.: Addison-Wesley, 1969.

Zajonc, R. B. Social facilitation. *Science*, 1965, **149,** 269–274.

30

Organization Theory and Structural Perspectives on Management

Jeffrey Pfeffer

The unique and important contribution of organization theory to the study of management is, at least potentially, its focus on social structure and the effects of such structure on organizations and the people within them. This focus on structure tends to direct attention away from the characteristics of individuals, such as their personalities, attitudes, backgrounds, or beliefs, and toward the enduring properties of the relations among actors that both constrain and enable action to occur. . . .

We proceed by first defining and illustrating what we mean by structural analysis, including contrasting it with alternative ways of understanding behavior. We then examine several domains of research activity to illustrate how a focus on structure and structural effects can help us understand phenomena of substantial interest and importance.

THE CONCEPT OF STRUCTURAL EFFECTS

Blau (1977: 1) has written, "The fundamental fact of social life is precisely that it is social—that human beings do not live in isolation but associate with other human beings. . . . The study of social structure . . . centers attention on the distribution of people among different positions and their social associations."

The question posed by the study of structural effects is how position in the social structure, as well as the characteristics of that structure, affect outcomes of interest. In this regard, it is important to note that structure is more than the formal organization chart, although the formal structure of an organization is obviously an important measure and cause of differentiated positions. Organizational structure, defined as the patterning of relationships among task-relevant roles, is one, but only one, source of structure, and a source of role differentiation and differential association that has effects through processes of social comparison, interaction, and physical propinquity.

Blau and Scott (1962) were among the earliest to assess the effects of social structure in organizational settings. The question they posed was this: "How can we distinguish between the influence of individual attitudes on behavior and the social constraints effected by group values and norms?" (Blau & Scott, 1962: 100). In particular, they wanted to distinguish between the effect of the group on individual attitudes and beliefs, through processes of informational social influence or conformity, from the influence of the group on the member's conduct regardless of his or her own attitudes or values. . . .

Source: Reprinted with permission from the *Journal of Management* 1991 (17:4).

The ensuing period has witnessed progress on both the measurement of social structure and empirical estimating of its effects. Blau and Schwartz (1984: 9), for instance, defined social structure as the differences among people and particularly the differences in social position among them. . . .

Social structure, then, refers not only to the patterning of social or task-related interactions (although this is clearly one element or dimension of structure), but also to the patterning of relations among any consequential social attributes such as income, tenure in the organization, or gender. Social structure is clearly measured by aggregating from the characteristics of individuals, but because it describes the relationship among them, it is a property of the aggregate and not of any individual within it. For example, income inequality, whether measured by the coefficient of variation or some other indicator like the Gini index, is obviously computed from individual incomes. But inequality in wages within some department or organization is a characteristic of the larger social unit, and one can not ask how unequal an individual's wages are.

The exploration of structural effects on behavior has also progressed, although not as rapidly as one might have presumed because this is a form of analysis and theoretical explanation that is not widely followed (e.g., Mayhew, 1980; 1981). As one example of this line of inquiry, Blau and Schwartz (1984) explored patterns of intermarriage along racial, occupational, ethnic background, and birth region dimensions in a sample of metropolitan areas. . . . Blau and Schwartz (1984) demonstrated that in spite of the presumed preference for within-group contact, the relative size of various demographic groups affected the observed rate of intermarriage. Individual preferences were exercised within structural constraints, and these constraints (in this instance operationalized as the relative size of various demographic groups) had significant explanatory power in accounting for variations in rates of intermarriage.

Kanter's (1977b) work on the effect of proportions on group life represents another example of the effect of social structure on the attitudes and behavior of individuals. She argued that people in token status, in which they were a very small proportion of the group, would experience heightened pressure, would be more visible, and would be seen as being typical of their group. Spangler, Gordon, and Pipkin (1978) studied women in two law schools, one in which they constituted about one third of the class, and one in which they were only one fifth of the class. When women composed a larger proportion of the class, they participated in class discussion more and were less likely to choose a "female" law specialty (e.g., divorce law). Pfeffer (1983) reviewed other studies on the effects of numbers and proportions on social life, including evidence that the size of youth cohorts affects both the amount of juvenile delinquency and the proportion of persons who become delinquent (Maxim, 1985), that the size of birth cohorts affects economic well-being of cohort members and consequences of economic well-being such as fertility and divorce (Easterlin, 1980), and that the relative number of men and women affect marriage customs such as the provision of dowries and monogamy (Guttentag & Secord, 1983). What each of these studies shows is that social behavior is a function not only of individual attributes and characteristics, which include attitudes and preferences, but also of the distribution of individuals in social space. This distribution results in constraints and social forces that affect behavior.

If one structural effect derives from the relative size of various groups in a social setting, another such effect derives from the physical dimensions of that setting. Structure involves the patterning of interaction, and such interaction is produced in part because of the effects of physical space and geography. The effects of spatial arrangements on social behavior such as friendship patterns and amount of socializing were explored by Festinger, Schachter, and Back (1950), and the importance of physical aspects of organizations has been noted by Pfeffer (1982) and Davis (1984). Hatch (1987) has shown that the openness and physical proximity produced by the physical setting affects the time that managers spend on social interaction and on tasks.

Social structure also refers to the patterns of communication among people. Thompson (1967) defined structure as the patterning of relationships, and these relationships are determined in part by the formal organization chart, by the nature of task and social interdependence, and by physical distance and other factors. These relationships can be represented as networks and are consequential because they affect how information, opportunities, and other resources diffuse through some population, as well as the power of people who occupy differing network positions. Brass (1984) and Krackhardt (1990) both found that structural centrality was related to individual power. Studies of the diffusion of innovations have argued that the diffusion process is structured by the pattern of social relationships that affect how information and evaluation of the innovation spreads through the population. Most diffusion theories adopt a social contagion perspective (Burt, 1987) that argues that ideas or products diffuse through actual social contact, much as in epidemiological studies of disease. There is, however, an alternative form of social contagion, in which adopters are influenced not by social contact but by observation of others in equivalent positions, who are competitors for status, for instance. Burt's (1987) reanalysis of the classic Coleman, Katz, and Menzel (1966) study of the diffusion of tetracycline found that structurally equivalent physicians—those who shared similar relations with others in their environment and who were equivalent to early adopters—also tended to prescribe the antibiotic early. . . . What the results from the Burt (1987) study suggest is that this mimetic diffusion will follow a process in which structurally equivalent social actors imitate each other.

It is important to note that beginning with Blau and Scott (1962) and continuing to the present, structural approaches to analyzing organizational behavior have always examined not only the measurement and determinants of structure (e.g., how to adequately measure wage inequality and what its causes are) but also the effects of structure, where such effects are often effects on individual behaviors and attitudes. What distinguishes structural analysis, then, is not so much the dependent variables or even the level of analysis, but the causes or the independent variables that provide the explanation. Thus, for instance, instead of or in addition to measuring vocational preferences, individual needs, and personal values to account for women students' choices of elective courses and career specialties in law school, a structural account would focus on the proportion of women in the school, what women in structurally equivalent positions were doing, and what students in contact with the individual in question were doing. Moreover, I would not claim that structural forces inevitably or invariably are more important than individual differences. . . . The argument is simply that because organizations are social and relational entities, it is often useful to seek understanding and explanation of behavior in the structural properties of the organization.

In the remainder of the paper, I explore how such a focus on structural effects can help enrich our analysis of issues that have long been treated primarily as reflecting almost purely individual factors—job attitudes, turnover, performance on the job, and wages. In each instance, I briefly illustrate what a structural perspective can suggest about additional ideas and analytic strategies to explore these outcomes.

JOB ATTITUDES

There have been literally thousands of studies of job satisfaction and other attitudes toward work, and these have been reviewed elsewhere (e.g., Locke, 1976; Miller, 1980). As we have argued previously (Salancik & Pfeffer, 1977), much if not all of that literature looks to individual psychology to understand job satisfaction. . . .

A structural approach to the issue of job attitudes would look to the environment and to the possibility of social contagion as a source of affective reactions to the work environment. One example of this type of approach is the social information processing model articulated by Salancik and Pfeffer (1978) and subsequently investigated by numerous others (see, e.g., Thomas & Griffen, 1983, for a review). The empirical research suggests that one's own attitudes are affected by the expressed opinions of others in the environment. For instance, in one of the earliest studies, O'Reilly and Caldwell (1979) indicated that both job satisfaction and even perceptions of job characteristics could be affected by having a confederate of the experimenter make favorable or unfavorable comments about the work environment. Griffen (1983) replicated this effect in a field setting, in which managers, trained in how to provide positive social cues, had an effect on perceptions of task characteristics and the work environment.

That we are affected by the opinions of others, in a process of informational social influence (Cialdini, 1984; Deutsch & Gerard, 1955) is not that startling, although it does suggest looking outside of the individual to understand his or her reactions to the job. In addition to the direct informational social influence so often studied, another form of social structural effect is important—that deriving from social comparison. We learn about our preferences and about our environment directly from others. At the same time, we compare our own outcomes to those received by others around us to determine how well we are doing in a comparative sense, and therefore, how satisfied we should be. Stouffer, Suchman, Devinney, Star, and Williams (1949) used the idea of social comparison to attempt to explain why soldiers who, by most objective standards, lived under better conditions on occasion were less happy with their situation than others who seemed to be worse off. They argued that it was not the objective conditions that mattered, but one's conditions compared to those with whom one compared oneself. Theories examining the effects of pay on both satisfaction and behavior also have occasionally argued for the importance of social comparison processes (Adams, 1963, 1965; Deutsch, 1985). These theories have most frequently been examined in laboratory experiments (Mowday, 1983; but see Telly, French, & Scott,

1971) because researchers seldom collect field data in a way that permits social comparison effects to be assessed. In an extension of these ideas to the domain of job characteristics, Oldham and his associates (Oldham & Miller, 1979; Oldham et al., 1982) examined how individuals' reactions to job characteristics were affected by the job characteristics of their co-workers. They found that reactions to the job environment were affected by whether others in the immediate environment had jobs that were either more or less attractive. Persons who were comparatively disadvantaged in terms of the characteristics of their job were less satisfied than those who had better jobs compared to others in their immediate environment, even when the task characteristics themselves were taken into account.

The problem with theories incorporating social comparison processes is that the question of the choice of the comparison other is left unresolved. One of the criticisms of the original Stouffer et al. (1949) study was that in any instance, it is possible to imagine some people who are better off and others who are worse off than the focal group. Thus, one can always account, after the fact, for a feeling of either satisfaction or dissatisfaction by relying on the appropriate choice of a social comparison. But this is where structural methods and perspectives can add analytic power. The issue of availability or proximity is emphasized in these approaches, and methods are provided to measure propinquity, a factor Smith (1980) has emphasized in determining the choice of comparison others.

Two general predictions emerge from adopting a structural approach. First, we would predict that job attitudes would be a consequence, in part, of social contagion processes. People who are in contact with others will come to share their attitudes and perceptions of the work environment, and people who are structurally equivalent (connected to the same others even if not in direct contact) will come to share the same attitudes. Whether direct contact or structural equivalence is more important for affecting attitudes is an empirical question. Second, we would predict greater uniformity in job attitudes the greater the amount of contact and connectedness, and the more similar are those being studied to each other. Thus, structural factors should help us understand both the content of attitudes as well as their variation within a social unit. . . .

TURNOVER

The subject of turnover is also well studied (e.g., Bluedorn, 1982). Turnover has most often been examined, again, as the consequence of an individual decision process, with the individual acting in isolation. Thus, for instance, research has found that turnover is negatively related to tenure in the organization because such tenure entails making commitments (Salancik, 1977; Sheldon, 1971) and often represents more investment in the organization. Turnover is negatively related to salary (Mobley, 1982; Price, 1977), because the higher a person's salary, the less likely it is that he or she can find a better opportunity elsewhere. Thus, there is less likelihood of a person searching for an alternative job, and less likelihood of finding a more financially attractive alternative, the higher the individual's salary. . . . Virtually all of the dominant models of turnover conceptualize it as an individual decision, without considering the effects of social structure.

Some exceptions to this astructural approach do exist. Krackhardt and Porter (1986), for instance, explicitly modelled turnover as a process that was socially influenced. Gathering data on friendship and interaction patterns in fast food restaurants, these authors found that turnover was clustered in both time and social space. As soon as some of the friendship group began to leave, the others followed quickly. Thus, turnover tended to snowball, and turnover patterns followed patterns of social interaction.

Researchers have examined turnovers as a consequence of demographic similarity, arguing that because interaction is likely to follow cohort lines, and integration is a function of interaction, demography would affect turnover. . . .

The evidence appears consistent with the view that turnover is structured. The more central the person that leaves, the more likely it is that others will also leave. There is a social contagion effect, and it is likely that people who are both socially proximate as well as structurally equivalent to those leaving are more likely to leave, although (as in the case of other diffusion studies) it will require empirical research to assess the relative effects of social contact versus structural equivalence. Persons who are demographically more similar to the dominant group are less likely to leave, and turnover is higher in organizations that have bimodal or heterogeneous demographic distributions. Although the explicit role of network position in all of this has not often been examined, the Krackhardt and Porter study of turnover as a snowball effect provides an illustration of how to proceed along this road.

To the extent that social structure affects turnover, it is possible both to identify groups and individuals within those groups that are potentially most at risk and possibly to make an effort to compensate for the tendency to leave. Such compensation might entail instituting more integrating activities such as social events and devoting managerial time and attention to the groups and individuals most at risk. It is also clear that differential efforts to retain people may be warranted because if more central individuals leave there will be comparatively more turnover as a consequence. Evaluating potential actions such as increasing someone's salary, therefore, might include an assessment of the individual's structural centrality, in both a communication and social distance sense, to ascertain how potentially disruptive the loss of the person would be.

As in the case of attitudes, there are likely to be important social comparison effects that affect turnover. In particular, the effects of salary, job attributes, and other rewards received from the work place operate, in part, only in comparison to others in the environment. For instance, studying turnover among high level academic administrators, Pfeffer and Davis-Blake (in press) found no main effect for salary on turnover, when other factors were statistically controlled. However, salary as a proportion of the average salary paid to occupants of the particular job in the sample as a whole did significantly predict turnover. The higher a given individual's salary compared to the average salary paid for that position, the less likely the person was to leave the position. And there was an interaction between the dispersion of salaries within the set of administrators within the college or university and the individual's own salary that affected turnover. Lower salaried individuals were more likely to leave when confronted with highly dispersed salary distributions, which left them comparatively worse off, and were less likely to leave when in a system of more equal salaries. Conversely, higher salaried individuals were less likely to leave in more dispersed distributions, because it was in those settings that they fared comparatively better. One would make similar predictions concerning the effects of the distribution of other organizational rewards.

JOB PERFORMANCE

Vroom (1964) argued that performance was a function of ability times motivation, a formulation that remains the dominant perspective to this day. Obviously, ability and motivation both matter, but what the Vroom approach overlooks is the fact that both ability and motivation are partly endogenous and, along with performance, are partly socially determined. Begin by considering academic productivity, which has the advantages of fairly clear measurability and of low task interdependence compared to that found in many work contexts. Long and McGinnis (1981), in a longitudinal study of academic chemists, asked the critical question: Does research productivity affect one's academic placement, or does one's placement affect one's academic productivity? Their results suggest that the observed correlation between research performance and the prestige of one's academic placement is produced, at least for their sample, almost entirely by the effect of employment context on performance: there was virtually no evidence that performance affected one's placement, and this was in a field that is paradigmatically highly developed. . . .

Why might there be this effect of placement on productivity? There are a number of plausible, and not mutually exclusive, reasons. First, some environments have more resources, including reduced teaching load, better laboratory facilities, better research assistants, and so forth. Second, there are research norms or cultures that develop, and these encourage or discourage one from working hard on research. In other words, there are social facilitation and social competition effects that may operate in some environments to increase effort and output. Third, some environments in which there are productive scholars provide others in that environment with better quality advice and assistance on issues ranging from how to get research grants to how to get published, to more knowledge about technical and theoretical issues.

Similar effects occur in other settings as well. Obtaining advice and assistance from one's colleagues may be critical in learning on the job, and the availability of this advice and assistance depends both on the quality of one's colleagues and one's relationship to them. It is quite likely that observed correlations between communication centrality and ability and performance (e.g., Blau, 1955) occur both because centrality accrues to those who have more expertise to offer and because occupying a central position in a system of interaction can, in fact, make one more expert and able. For jobs that require learning by doing and a high degree of information and coordination with others, it is clear that performance is a product both of one's own individual qualities and of one's relationship to the social structure and the content of one's social environment. As yet another example of this, Dalton (1959) relates the case of a black, appointed to supervise a group of white workers in a plant in the South in the 1950s. The manager was unsuccessful, and ultimately resigned his position, because of the resistance and outright sabotage of the men he was supervising. . . .

SALARIES

The explanation of variation in individual income has, again, tended to proceed from consideration of individual attributes. . . .

An alternative view of how wages are affected by social structures would emphasize the importance of social comparison processes and the operation of social networks that serve to diffuse both information and salaries, as well as job opportunities (e.g., Granovetter, 1974). For instance, O'Reilly, Main, and Crystal (1988) conducted a study that is a model of this kind of reasoning and analysis. They wanted to explore the determinants of CEO salaries. They reasoned that director compensation committees would work from a comparative frame—to someone earning a great deal of money, a high salary would look comparatively smaller than it would to someone earning less. Because directors on compensation committees are invariably outside directors who serve as high level executives (CEOs) in their own firms, O'Reilly et al. reasoned that the higher the salaries these committee members earned in their own executive capacities, the higher the salaries they would bestow upon the CEO in the firm for which they were setting compensation. Controlling for both firm size and financial performance, O'Reilly and his associates did observe an effect of compensation committee salaries earned in their own executive roles on the salaries of CEOs.

There are industry effects on salaries, and these effects cannot be fully accounted for by variation in industry profitability, riskiness, regulation, and so forth (O'Reilly et al., 1988). Following the line of argument we have been developing, we would suggest that there will be stronger industry effects on salaries in industries in which there is more interfirm communication and in which there are higher levels of both social contact and structural equivalence. The centrality of both directors, executives, and firms, measured in network terms, could be employed to analyze the effects of structure on salary in a way that would add more precision to the type of analysis done by O'Reilly and his colleagues.

Our discussion to this point has focused primarily on interfirm social structure and its effect on wages. Stronger effects of the kind we have described may actually be observed within rather than across organizational boundaries. Social comparison processes operate within organizations, and these processes follow both demographic and communication contours. For instance, Pfeffer and Langton (1998) and Pfeffer and Davis-Blake (1990) both observed more wage dispersion in demographically heterogeneous organizations. . . . Pfeffer and Davis-Blake (1990) also observed that the proliferation of job titles tended to be associated with more wage dispersion. Different job titles legitimate paying different people differently. Indeed, one of the reasons for title proliferation may be to justify differential treatment, as in separating jobs by gender (Baron & Bielby, 1986), which then can be used to rationalize paying women and men differently.

It is also the case that communication structures may affect the wage determination process. For instance, Pfeffer and Langton (1988) found that there was less wage dispersion in academic departments in which there was more social contact and more task-related interaction among the faculty. Social integration and social cohesion made paying more differentiated wages less acceptable and desired. Pfeffer and Konrad (in press) found that an individual's power, related in part to his or her place in the structure of social communication both within and outside of academic departments, increased wages. Also, communication frequency increased the economic return to both research productivity and experience. Granovetter (1974) observed that individuals who found jobs through social contacts tended to find better jobs (i.e., jobs that paid higher salaries) than those who used only formal means or direct applications to find jobs. Again, then, there is evidence that social structure affects economic returns as well as returns to various forms of human capital. Where one is located in the structure, both demographically and in terms of communication structure, matters for how well one does.

DISCUSSION

The study of organizations has most frequently started from the individual as the unit of observation. The problem, however, is that "the analysis must move from the individual level of observation to the system level where the problem of interest usually lies" (Huber, 1990: 2). How to do so is often problematic, and much of the study of organizations remains insensitive to this issue. In spite of the fact that we know that organizations are relational entities, in which individuals interact and compare themselves with others, many of our analyses take the individual alone as the unit of analysis and do not attempt to incorporate notions of social structure into either theory or empirical research. Blau and Schwartz (1984: 8) have noted that people are "affected by the social environment because the other people in their environment determine the options people have in establishing social relations." These social relations have consequences for how people perceive their environment as well as how successfully they perform it.

We have tried to indicate how a concern with structural effects can enrich the analysis of even individual-level outcomes such as satisfaction, turnover, performance, and salary. In our review, we have seen that both demography and social interaction are likely to be important. Although there are some suggestive findings in the literature about the usefulness of this approach, such as the studies of turnover and CEO compensation, virtually none of the existing studies really use the full range of methodological techniques available to analyze structure. In that sense, there is much to be accomplished empirically.

But, there is also much to be accomplished theoretically. We have barely scratched the surface in our attempts to analyze the effects of structure on organizations. . . . A focus on structural effects requires us to gather different forms of data, sensitive to structural position, if we are to really develop this line of inquiry.

Such research seems to be well worth the effort. The social environment, when it has been examined, has been seen to be a potent factor determining outcomes ranging from task perceptions to turnover. Because organizations are social settings, it seems only reasonable to use macro-structural perspectives and techniques to explore at least some aspects of these settings.

REFERENCES

Adams, J. S. 1963. Toward an understanding of inequity. *Journal of Abnormal and Social Psychology*, 67: 422–436.

Adams, J. S. 1965. Inequity in social exchange. In L. Berkowitz (Ed.), *Advances in experimental social psychology*, 2: 267–299. New York: Academic Press.

Baron, J. N., & Bielby, W. T. 1986. The proliferation of job titles in organizations. *Administrative Science Quarterly*, 31: 561–586.

Blau, P. M. 1955. *The dynamics of bureaucracy*. Chicago: University of Chicago Press.

Blau, P. M. 1977. *Inequality and heterogeneity*. New York: Free Press.

Blau, P. M., & Schwartz, J. E. 1984. *Crosscutting social circles: Testing a macrostructural theory of intergroup relations*. New York: Academic Press.

Blau, P., & Scott, W. R. 1962. *Formal organizations*. San Francisco: Chandler.

Bluedorn, A. C. 1982. The theories of turnover: Causes, effects and meaning. In S. B. Bacharach (Ed.), *Research in the sociology of organizations*. 1: 75–128. Greenwich, CT: JAI Press.

Brass, D. J. 1984. Being in the right place: A structural analysis of individual influence in an organization. *Administrative Science Quarterly*, 29: 518–539.

Burt, R. S. 1987. Social contagion and innovation: Cohesion versus structural equivalence. *American Journal of Sociology*, 92: 1287–1335.

Cialdini, R. B. 1984. *Influence: How and why people agree to things*. New York: William Morrow.

Coleman, J. S., Katz, E., & Menzel, H. 1966. *Medical innovation*. New York: Bobbs-Merrill.

Dalton, M. 1959. *Men who manage*. New York: John Wiley.

Davis, T. R. V. 1984. The influence of the physical environment in offices. *Academy of Management Review*, 9: 271–283.

Deutsch, M. 1985. *Distributive justice: A social psychological perspective*. New Haven, CT: Yale University Press.

Deutsch, M., & Gerard, H. 1955. A study of normative and informational social influences on individual judgment. *Journal of Abnormal and Social Psychology*, 51: 629–636.

Easterlin, R. A. 1980. *Birth and fortune: The impact of numbers on personal welfare*. New York: Basic Books.

Festinger, L., Schachter, S., & Back, K. 1950. *Social pressures in informal groups*. Stanford, CA: Stanford University Press.

Granovetter, M. S. 1974. *Getting a job: A study of contacts and careers*. Cambridge, MA: Harvard University Press.

Griffen, R. W. 1983. Objective and social sources of information in task redesign: A field experiment. *Administrative Science Quarterly*, 28: 184–200.

Guttentag, M., & Secord, P. F. 1983. *Too many women? The sex ratio question*. Beverly Hills, CA: Sage.

Hatch, M. J. 1987. Physical barriers, task characteristics, and interaction activity in research and development firms. *Administrative Science Quarterly*, 32: 387–399.

Huber, J. 1990. Macro-micro links in gender stratification. *American Sociological Review*, 55: 1–10.

Kanter, R. M. 1977b. Some effects of proportions on group life: Skewed sex ratios and responses to token women. *American Journal of Sociology*, 82: 965–990.

Krackhardt, D. 1990. Assessing the political landscape: Structure, cognition, and power in organizations. *Administrative Science Quarterly*, 35: 342–369.

Krackhardt, D., & Porter, L. W. 1986. The snowball effect: Turnover embedded in communication networks. *Journal of Applied Psychology*, 71: 50–55.

Locke, E. A. 1976. The nature and causes of job satisfaction. In M. D. Dunnette (Eds.), *Handbook of industrial and organizational psychology*: 1297–1349. Chicago: Rand McNally.

Long, J. S., & McGinnis, R. 1981. Organizational context and scientific productivity. *American Sociological Review*, 46: 422–442.

Maxim, P. S. 1985. Cohort size and juvenile delinquency: A test of the Easterlin hypothesis. *Social Forces*, 63: 661–681.

Mayhew, B. H. 1980. Structuralism versus individualism: Part I, shadowboxing in the dark. *Social Forces*, 59: 335–375.

Mayhew, B. H. 1981. Structuralism versus individualism: Part II, ideological and other obfuscations. *Social Forces*, 59: 627–648.

Miller, J. 1980. Individual and occupational determinants of job satisfaction. *Sociology of Work and Occupations*, 7: 337–366.

Mobley, W. H. 1982. *Employee turnover: Causes, consequences, and control*. Reading, MA: Addison-Wesley.

Mowday, R. F. 1983. Equity theory predictions of behavior in organizations. In R. M. Steers & L. W. Porter (Eds.), *Motivation and work behavior* (3rd ed.): 91–113. New York: McGraw-Hill.

Oldham, G. R., & Miller, H. E. 1979. The effects of significant other's job complexity on employee relations to work. *Human Relations*, 32: 247–260.

Oldham, G. R., Nottenburg, G., Kassner, M. W., Ferris, G., Fedor, D., & Masters, M. 1982. The selection and consequences of job comparisons. *Organizational Behavior and Human Performance*, 29: 84–111.

O'Reilly, C. A., & Caldwell, D. 1979. Informational influence as a determinant of perceived task characteristics and job satisfaction. *Journal of Applied Psychology*, 64: 157–165.

O'Reilly, C. A. III, Main, B. G., & Crystal, G. S. 1988. CEO compensation as tournament and social comparison: A tale of two theories. *Administrative Science Quarterly*, 33: 257–274.

Pfeffer, J. 1982. *Organizations and organization theory*. Marshfield, MA: Pitman.

Pfeffer, J. 1983. Organizational demography. In L. L. Cummings & B. M. Staw (Eds.), *Research in organizational behavior*, 5. Greenwich, CT: JAI Press.

Pfeffer, J., & Davis-Blake, A. 1990. Determinants of salary dispersion in organizations. *Industrial Relations*, 29: 38–57.

Pfeffer, J., & Davis-Blake, A. in press. Salary dispersion and turnover among college administrators. *Industrial and Labor Relations Review*.

Pfeffer, J., & Konrad, A. in press. The effects of individual power on earnings. *Work and Occupations*.

Pfeffer, J., & Langton, N. 1988. Wage inequality and the organization of work: The case of academic departments. *Administrative Science Quarterly*, 33: 588–606.

Price, J. L. 1977. *The study of turnover*. Ames, IA: Iowa State University Press.

Salancik, G. R. 1977. Commitment and the control of organizational behavior and belief. In B. M. Staw & G. R. Salancik (Eds.), *New directions in organizational behavior*, 1–54. Chicago: St. Clair Press.

Salancik, G. R., & Pfeffer, J. 1977. An examination of need-satisfaction models of job attitudes. *Administrative Science Quarterly*, 22: 427–456.

Salancik, G. R., & Pfeffer, J. 1978. A social information processing approach to job attitudes and task design. *Administrative Science Quarterly*, 23: 224–253.

Sheldon, M. E. 1971. Investments and involvements as mechanisms producing commitment to the organization. *Administrative Science Quarterly*, 16: 143–150.

Smith, P. B. 1980. *Group processes and personal change*. New York: Harper & Row.

Spangler, E., Gordon, M. A., & Pipkin, R. M. 1978. Token women: An empirical test of Kanter's hypothesis. *American Journal of Sociology*, 85: 160–170.

Stouffer, S. A., Suchman, E. A., Devinney, L. S., Star, S. A., & Williams, R. M. 1949. Adjustment during army life. *The American Soldier*, 1. Princeton, NJ: Princeton University Press.

Telly, C. S., French, W. L., & Scott, W. G. 1971. The relationship of inequity to turnover among hourly workers. *Administrative Science Quarterly*, 16: 164–172.

Thomas, J., & Griffen, R. 1983. The social information processing model of task design: A review of the literature. *Academy of Management Review*, 8: 672–682.

Thompson, J. D. 1967. *Organizations in action*. New York: McGraw-Hill.

Vroom, V. H. 1964. *Work and motivation*. New York: John Wiley.

31

Psychological Contracts in Organizations

Violating the Contract

Denise M. Rousseau

> "They promised me a job in marketing and here I am doing telephone sales."
>
> "The company promised that no one would be fired out of the training program—that all of us were "safe" until placement. In return for this security, we accepted lower pay. The company subsequently fired four people from the training program."
>
> "Original representations of the company's financial and market strength [were] clearly fraudulent."
>
> *Quotes from recently hired employees*

Contract violation can run the gamut from subtle misperceptions to stark breaches of good faith. In organizations, violated contracts are at the heart of many lawsuits brought by customers (Kaufmann & Stern, 1988) and employees (Bies & Tyler, 1993). Although potentially damaging to reputations, careers, and relationships, violations also appear to be both frequent and survivable.

The basic facts of contract violation, detailed in this chapter, are these:

- Contract violation is commonplace.
- Violated contracts lead to adverse reactions by the injured party.
- Failure to fulfill a contract need not be fatal to the relationship.

. . .

WHAT IS CONTRACT VIOLATION?

In the strictest sense, violation is a failure to comply with the terms of a contract. But, given the subjective nature of psychological contracts, how people interpret the circumstances of this failure determines whether they *experience* a violation. Violation takes three forms (Table 1). *Inadvertent* violation occurs when both parties are able and willing to keep their bargain, but divergent interpretations lead one party to act in a manner at odds with the understanding and interests of the other. Two people who misunderstand the time of a meeting will inadvertently fail to honor their mutual commitment to attend. *Disruption* to the contract occurs when circumstances make it impossible for one or both parties to fulfill their end of the contract, despite the fact that they are willing to do so. A plant closing forced by a hurricane can prevent an employer from providing work. Similarly, a car accident can keep an employee from showing up to work on time. *Reneging* or *breach of contract* occurs when one side, otherwise capable of performing the contract, refuses to do so. A sales representative who agrees to stay on the job

Source: From *Psychological Contracts in Organizations*. Reprinted by permission of Sage Publications, Inc.

TABLE 1 • SOURCES OF EXPERIENCED VIOLATION

Inadvertent	Able and willing (divergent interpretations made in good faith)
Disruption	Willing but unable (inability to fulfill contract)
Breach of contract	Able but unwilling (reneging)

for three years when hired may quit after 6 months. Whether the victim understands the source of violation to be unwillingness or inability to comply has a tremendous impact on how violation is experienced and what victims do in response (Bies & Moag, 1986).

Given the subjectivity of contract terms, a contract could hardly exist without some inadvertent violation. Because contracts are continually being created and sustained, we can assume that organizations, members, suppliers, and customers make accommodations for many inadvertent violations. Misunderstandings may be ignored, some remedied by rationalization. A person who has been passed over for a promised promotion may decide that next time it will be her turn. Victims do not interpret all instances of noncompliance as violation; thus we cannot understand violation simply as noncompliance. If contract terms are in the eye of the beholder, then violation will be as well. Subjectivity might make it easier to *feel* that violation has occurred but harder to *know* if it has. Some contract failures result not from an actual break but from a failure to communicate.

It is our thesis that experienced violation occurs when failure to keep a commitment *injures* or causes damages that the contract was designed to avoid. Failure to keep commitments can be based on opportunism, negligence, or failure to cooperate. . . . Opportunism, negligence, and failure to cooperate are the bases of contract violation.

A bank manager who wants to spend more time with his family leaves a high-demand/high-pay job with one bank for another with a smaller financial institution. The major attraction of the new bank for the manager is its low-pressure environment, which is played up by the officers who recruit him. Within two weeks of taking the job, the manager learns that the smaller firm is starting an aggressive marketing campaign he is expected to head, which will keep him away from his family for even longer hours than before. Damages include increased stress and family conflict along with loss of reputation if he tries to change jobs again soon. The sense of betrayal and entrapment this manager feels exacerbates his personal costs from the organization's actions. If the bank manager was deliberately misled, the violation is based on opportunism. If critical information was denied him because recruiters were ill-informed themselves, this is an example of negligence. And if a new strategic plan was made without his input, this constitutes a failure to cooperate. In any case, the circumstances can feel like betrayal.

Although contracts can be violated in innumerable ways, there are a number of common forms (Table 2). Recruiters may overpromise a job's opportunity for challenge, growth, or development, but at the same time eager job seekers may read

TABLE 2 • SOURCES OF VIOLATION BY CONTRACT MAKERS AND SYSTEMS

Sources	Violations
Contract makers:	
recruiters	• unfamiliar with actual job
	• overpromise
managers	• say one thing, do another
coworkers	• failure to provide support
mentors	• little follow-through
	• few interactions
top management	• mixed messages
Systems:	
compensation	• changing criteria
	• reward seniority, low job security
benefits	• changing coverage
career paths	• dependent on one's manager
	• inconsistent application
performance review	• not done on time
	• little feedback
training	• skills learned not tied to job
documentation	• stated procedures at odds with actual practice

into a promise what they want to hear. Managers, coworkers, or executives who say one thing and do another all can engender violation. . . . Then there is the phenomenon of mixed messages, where different contract makers express divergent intentions. A mission statement can convey that the organization rewards employees based on merit ("commitment to excellence") while the compensation system is based on seniority. Different contract sources may each convey mutually exclusive promises.

The *experience* of violation appears to be quite common. A longitudinal study of M.B.A. alumni reported that over half experienced a violation of a preemployment commitment within the first two years on the job (Robinson & Rousseau, 1994). The types of violations reported ran the gamut of employment conditions, from pay and promotion opportunities to the nature of the work and the quality and character of coworkers and the organization itself. . . . Changes in personnel (new managers or top executives) were frequently at the root of these other changes. However, despite the high rate of reported violations, M.B.A.s reported that some of these violations were repaired by actions they and their employer have taken. Others reported that even though they disputed what had happened between them and their employer, their contract was still basically fulfilled. The differences between violation and contract fulfillment can be analyzed by examining the dynamics of contract violation.

HOW CONTRACT VIOLATION OCCURS: A MODEL

To understand the dynamics of contract violation, we need a model to explain instances such as these:

FIGURE 1 • A MODEL OF CONTRACT VIOLATION

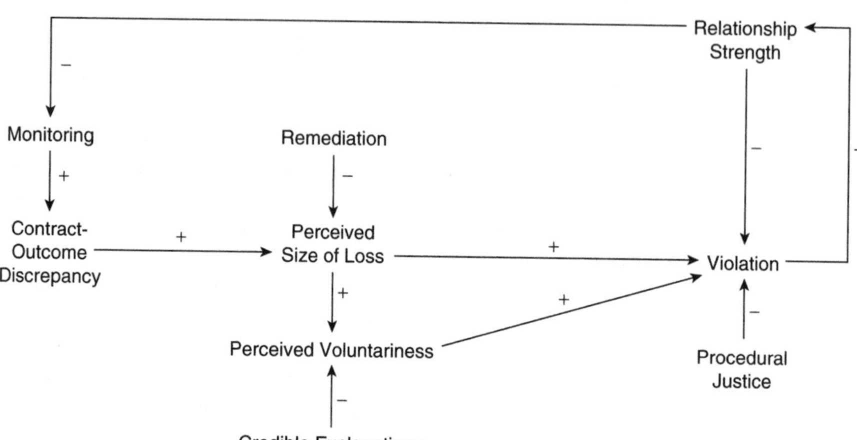

- A sales representative whose lucrative accounts are reassigned reacts angrily. Meanwhile, another sales rep readily accepts the same change.
- One customer receives a replacement for a damaged shipment and is pleased with the service while another remains outraged at the supplier's unreliability.
- One plant's closing leads to angry protests in the city in which it is located, but another's leads the local newspapers to praise the company.

A major "problem" in contract violation is understanding why some events, seemingly at odds with a contract, do not provoke adverse reactions, but other events that appear innocuous engender outrage and anger. . . . [A] model is proposed (Figure 1) to account for the dynamics of contract violation.

Contract-Outcome Discrepancy

Contract violation begins with the perception of a discrepancy between a relied-upon outcome (e.g., a choice assignment, extra support) and the actual outcome that occurs. But not all discrepancies are noticed and not all that are noticed are perceived as violations. What turns contract-outcome discrepancy into a violation? Three basic factors increase the likelihood that a discrepancy will be interpreted as a violation: monitoring, size of loss, and relationship strength.

Monitoring. Monitoring is the indirect seeking of information by scrutinizing the behavior of others (Clark & Reis, 1988). . . . Some discrepancies are more likely than others to be noticed. People pay particular attention to the behavior of others when they feel a special need for information. Unless someone is watching the clock, a coworker's arrival five minutes late can go unnoticed. But if that coworker's lateness is chronic and a source of frustration to others, people are more likely to note when the tardy individual arrives.

Unless a person is actively comparing outcomes with his or her understanding of the contract, many discrepancies may go unrecognized. If no one checks an employee's work to see if it is up to standard, the employee may come to believe that the quality he or she has been giving is good enough. Unless we have reason to check the employee's work, we may not do so, and thus discrepancies pass by unnoticed—and continue. The extent to which people monitor the behaviors of others affects the *experience* of violation. Monitoring in the form of quality control may not occur until a particularly poor performance occurs. Other things being equal, larger discrepancies are more likely to be noticed than smaller ones.

Perceived Size of Loss. The perceived size of the loss is an important factor in determining whether the victim perceives a contract-outcome discrepancy as a contract violation. Not only are large discrepancies more salient, but we interpret them differently than small ones. In making judgments regarding the amount of harm done, people tend to attribute more responsibility for events such as accidents that produce severe rather than mild consequences. . . . [P]erception of contract violation is likely to be greater when one party's actions engender considerable harm to another party. Failure to deliver a promised promotion may not be seen as violating a contract if other benefits accrue to the promisee or if a sense of good faith is maintained before the delayed promotion is obtained. However, when there has been a history of trouble in the relationship (e.g., between employee and organization, work group and team leader, or customer and supplier), monitoring is more likely to occur. Once trust has eroded, minute discrepancies can take on a special, aversive significance.

Relationship Strength: The Context of Violation. When a contract is violated, the relationship on which it rests can ultimately be damaged too. . . . [T]he relationship's strength and especially its history influence the experience of violation. If there is a history of adversarial behavior, grievances, or other symptoms of mistrust, victims are more likely to perceive any adverse event as intentional. Repeat offenders are treated more harshly by the criminal justice system than first-timers. . . . The person, not the situation, is seen as responsible for any wrongdoing. Trust once lost is not easily restored. Good relationships tend to manifest high tolerance of the behaviors of others, even when they result in discrepant outcomes. However, troubled relationships often go from bad to worse.

Organizations and individuals may both go through cycles of escalating violation, because each may be inclined to perceive adverse events as part of a larger pattern of untrustworthy conduct. The escalation cycle is brought about because people who perceive their relationships as troubled react differently to adverse events than those in more stable relationships. Healthy relations relax monitoring, but troubled relationships fuel it (Clark & Reis, 1988). . . . Not surprising, because troubled relations lead to monitoring, monitoring tends to identify many more *negative* judgments than positive ones. It is difficult to pass a test when one is unaware of being tested; thus many secret tests are failed by the testee. . . .

In sum, several factors operate on the experience of a discrepancy between contract terms and actual outcomes:

- Monitoring increases the number of observed discrepancies in contract performance.
- Larger contract-outcome discrepancies are more likely to be seen as violations than smaller ones.
- In troubled relationships, small discrepancies between contract outcome are more likely to be seen as violations than they are in healthy relationships.

CHANGING THE MEANING OF A LOSS: THE FUNCTION OF REMEDIATION AND CREDIBLE EXPLANATION

Because violations are injurious and often willful, strategies for reducing the experience of violation target both the actual losses incurred as well as the perception of these losses. The following example illustrates such a strategy. In England, the palace announced that Queen Elizabeth II was no longer permitting her staff the perks they had historically enjoyed. As part of a plan "to rationalize and streamline" palace pay and administrative costs, the 350 staff members no longer would be allowed to take home, for their own consumption, miniature bottles of alcohol drawn from the royal bar stocks. Instead of the spirits, staff were given an extra $45 in their pay packet. Servants once given free bars of bath soap received an annual stipend instead. Senior courtiers lost the privilege of buying a new suit on the queen's account for every other trip they made with her. According to the *New York Times* ("In Her Majesty's Service," 1993): "The palace insisted that none of its workers would be worse off as a result of the changes, even though the new cash allotments would be taxable" (p. 6).[1]

. . . The palace example illustrates several strategies for managing the size of reliance losses incurred by the contract violation: (a) reducing actual losses by substitution (e.g., money in exchange for gifts), (b) reducing perceived losses (e.g., downplaying the tax liability), (c) recognizing the symbolic features of the contract (e.g., continuing to offer the Christmas pudding), and (d) offering a credible explanation or justification for the actions taken (e.g., streamlining the household and cutting costs).

Remediation. Remedies substitute one outcome for another and thus can be thought of as forms of "buyout." In some fashion, remedies are a way of honoring the spirit if not the letter of a contract. Reliance losses often will not result in termination of the contract if remediation of comparable value is offered. . . .

Substitution is actually a common form of contract keeping. Early retirements often occur along with beefed-up benefits packages for veteran employees. Workers with obsolete skills are retrained. A vendor loans a customer a personal computer while the one he purchased is being repaired. All these substitutions can be seen as cushioning reliance losses. The closer the cushion comes to the perceived value of the original contract term, the better the deal is honored. Thus a psychological contract of long-term employment with an employer can be honored during a period of downsizing if efforts are taken to insure the worker's long-term employability somewhere else.

Nevertheless, substitution strategies for reducing losses (e.g., money for the queen's soap) can change the *meaning* or nature of the relationship. The symbolic value of being able to take home some of the queen's special household items conveys a sense of closeness to the royal family, but additional cash puts the household staff on more formal footing. Efforts made to manage actual and perceived losses can be thought of as *remedies* for reliance losses. Increasing a servant's pay can serve to reduce the resources (household goods) lost by the change. Keeping the traditional Christmas pudding might mitigate the status losses that monetary buyouts can create in relational contracts. When substitutions are used as remedies, the troublesome issue of comparable value arises. Can we reduce the value of a bar of soap to "mere" money? Obviously, the answer is "yes" in most cases. But doesn't it matter that the soap belongs to the Queen of England, or that employees have become accustomed to a position of special trust and privilege? Symbolic value makes the equation of one resource with another problematic. . . .

The difference between remedies honoring the spirit of a contract and remedial efforts that fail is evident in the way in which remedies have been applied in plant closings. Based on their study of plant closings in the automobile industry, Yoder and Staudohar (1985) argue:

> The impact on workers of plant closings is fourfold: (1) their jobs are lost; (2) the old job experiences are not readily transferable to new jobs in growing industries; (3) their new jobs typically provide pay and benefits that are significantly reduced from previous levels; and (4) they and their families experience high levels of anxiety and stress. During the period of transition to new jobs, displaced workers usually need help in such areas as retraining, counseling, job search, and income maintenance. Thus, management and public policies are judged by their effectiveness in cushioning adversity. (pp. 45–46)

Yoder and Staudohar contrast shutdowns at GM and Ford. In the 1980s, assembling cars and trucks in California was no longer economically feasible in light of the diminished market and long distances involved in shipping parts. Faced with the same market pressures, GM and Ford conducted plant closings in distinct ways that yielded different outcomes. . . .

The GM Fremont plant was closed indefinitely in 1982. Employees were given 3 weeks' notice. With a history of labor-management dispute since the plant's opening, neither the union nor individual nonmanagerial employees were involved in the planned shutdown. At the time of closing, with no plans for retraining or other postshutdown support, employees believed that the closing was temporary. Employees who did not know their job loss was permanent waited for GM to reopen. Only a few sought retraining. Postemployment programs, largely offered by state and federal agencies, were not well coordinated. Little retraining occurred, and existing programs emphasized finding jobs without offering retraining. Local television and newspapers accused GM of abandoning its workers. Two years later, less than half of GM's former employees had found jobs. Dysfunctional behavior was also evident in the aftermath of the plant closing. Community records indicate that eight employees committed suicide following the plant closing. There was a 240% increase in reported child abuse in the community at large.

In contrast, the Milpitas plant of the Ford Motor Company, with a history of cooperative union-management relations, announced its closing 6 months in advance. Employees were told that the closing was permanent and a joint union-management planning process was begun. Planning entailed development of skill testing and job placement programs within the plant along with stress counseling. The program emphasized retraining and developed employability plans for individual workers. Production continued to the last day at a relatively high rate. The final car off the assembly line was donated by Ford to the city of Milpitas in recognition of its support. A little over a year later, 63% of employees had found new jobs. . . .

The history of long-term employment in both of these organizations makes it likely that employees would believe in a relational contract. Ford offered employees the opportunity of employability elsewhere along with a variety of efforts designed to reverse the adversities of job loss. By cushioning employees from present stresses and future losses, the organization in effect can honor the spirit if not the letter of its contract with employees. . . .

Voluntariness. Any event at odds with the perceiver's understanding of a contract can be interpreted as a violation. A breach of contract occurs when one party reneges on the agreement despite his or her ability to fulfill it. From the perspective of the victim, there may be a fine line between ability and inability to fulfill the contract. How the perpetrator acts cues the potential victim as to whether to interpret a given behavior as a violation. Behavior, both before and after the violation, matters in the interpretation of an event as contract breaking.

If the circumstances inhibiting contract completion are perceived to be under the control of the perpetrator, victims are more likely to experience a breach of contract. . . . If the company's owners are seen as having acted in bad faith, the . . . worker and his peers may believe that their contract has been broken. Similarly, escalating workloads may cause an employee to unwillingly miss deadlines or turn in poor quality work. However, if that person missed opportunities to plan or to organize better, disappointed colleagues may still blame the poor performer. "You knew we might get last minute requests," they might ask, "so why did you wait until today to start the work I gave you last week?" It is a truism that we judge others by their behavior and ourselves by our intentions. However, attributions regarding the intentions of others are fundamental to the experience of violation.

Credible Explanations. Whether the potential contract violator is perceived as responsible for the occurrence of an adverse outcome is a function of the information available to victims. Perceived voluntariness is based on the attribution of intent. What would-be violators convey to victims can shape their understanding of motives and circumstances. . . . People who don't receive the expected raise, special assignment, or other opportunity look for explanations to help them understand and adjust to their losses. Much of how people make sense of losses stems from what perpetrators communicate to victims. A corporation that gives an account of its actions can reduce its culpability by

Communicating positive intentions

Providing information on constraints (economic, external competition, and so on) or other extenuating circumstances that limit available courses of action.

Causal accounts claiming mitigating circumstances create a perception of fairness because they attempt to eliminate "worst case scenario" interpretations of a decision maker's intentions (Schlenker, 1980). Bies and Shapiro (1993) use the example of a journal editor who remains silent as to why there has been a delay in the manuscript review process. If that editor continues to offer authors no explanation, they may expect the worst, that is, that he is unfair and even prejudiced against them. But if an account is offered explaining that the delay was due to a vacation or misaddressed letters, feelings of unfairness are reduced, and the behavior appears more inadvertent than deliberate. Credible accounts that claim mitigating circumstances reduce perceptions of unfairness and volition. . . .

PROCEDURAL JUSTICE

People make distinctions between outcomes that favor their own self-interest and outcomes that are fair (Lind & Tyler, 1988). Although contract discrepancies work against the self-interest of the victim, people do react more favorably when the decision-making process behind the discrepancies is perceived as fair. If an employee notices a discrepancy or loses a dispute that leads to a negative outcome, the decision will be perceived as more legitimate and understandable when the process used was believed to be fair.

Procedural justice refers to the fairness of the decision-making processes underlying the allocation of outcomes or the resolution of disputes. Although *distributive justice* refers to the fairness of the outcomes, and contract violations are, by definition, unfair in distributive terms, procedural justice affects the magnitude of violation. Fairness in processes has been characterized by six procedural rules (Bies & Moag, 1986; Levinthal, 1988):

- *Consistency:* Allocative procedures should be consistent across people and over time.
- *Bias suppression:* Personal self-interest and blind allegiance to narrow preconceptions should be prevented.
- *Accuracy:* Decisions must be based on good information and informed opinion.
- *Correctability:* Opportunities must exist to modify or reverse decisions based on inaccurate information.
- *Representativeness:* Allocation process must represent the concerns of all important subgroups and individuals.
- *Ethicality:* Allocation process must be compatible with prevailing moral and ethical standards.

Losses experienced by individuals will seem more serious and generate more adverse reactions when others have been or are treated differently. If an organization that gave notice before previous layoffs does not for a subsequent layoff, the experienced violation will deepen. On the other hand, careful attention to due process, especially those specified in personnel manuals and handbooks, is essential to creating a sense of consistency.

Bias is manifested in losses that seem to unduly benefit particular individuals or where forms of prejudice are evident. Family businesses that give preferential treatment to a low-performing family member over a nonfamily employee who contributes highly breach the bias suppression rule.

When employees are to be terminated for cause or punished for substandard contributions, the quality of the performance data on which such a decision is made influences the accuracy associated with the decision. Performance-based decisions such as merit pay or terminations-for-cause necessitate high-quality performance appraisals (e.g., well-informed raters, including bosses and peers, who employ the measures consistently).

Correctability implies that if the decision is based on false, inaccurate, or limited information, it can be reversed or altered. Decisions to terminate many employees for business-necessity reasons do not usually offer the option of correctability, because job loss occurred regardless of performance. However, when there is a merit basis for the decision, fair procedures permit people to voice their objections, argue their case, and exercise the opportunity to reverse unfair decisions.

Representativeness is a special concern when losses are borne unequally across organizational subgroups. The outcry over executive-level pay raises at General Motors in the face of flat wages for union workers is a potential violation of the representativeness rule. To avoid such inequality, and the resulting perception of violation, companies might use across-the-board cuts in pay for all employees, including management, when economic difficulties precipitate such cuts. An example is Hewlett-Packard, which cut payroll costs through use of the 4-day workweek across the board, from senior management to production workers.

The ethicality rule is a sort of "mother of all rules." The way in which decisions are made must be consistent with ethical standards, which change over time and with the prevalence of contract violations in the larger society. . . . The prevalence of contract breakdowns can provide available justification for subsequent violations. Contract violation may lower the subsequent standards to which people hold themselves accountable both within an existing relationship as well as in a larger society where such actions become commonplace. In effect, behaviors involved in honoring or breaching a contract may themselves shape the moral context of subsequent decisions.

Adherence to procedures affects the quality of treatment victims and witnesses perceive. The quality of treatment a person receives in the context of a violation can reflect on one's social standing: in the organization, among peers, and in the individual's broader personal life (Wade-Benzoni, 1993). Information about one's standing in a group is often communicated by the quality of the treatment received, especially from those in authority (Tyler & Lind, 1992). When one is treated with dignity and shown respect (e.g., through soliciting opinions, creating an opportunity for correctability or recourse), social standing is enhanced (Bies & Moag, 1986). Disrespectful treatment, especially by a boss, carries the implication that the person is not a full member of the group. These effects are enhanced when losses are made public, for example, when family and coworkers become aware of them (Wade-Benzoni, 1993). Public losses make incidents harder to dismiss or forget, especially when isolated individuals are affected, as in the case of the firing of an individual as contrasted with a large-scale termination. Violations can humiliate victims when they involve public losses, public attributions of personal wrongdoing or negligence, and disrespectful treatment (e.g., denial of a promised promotion without possibility of corrective action or voice).

Creating Just Procedures. Procedural justice involves a number of practices. First and foremost, procedures must exist for promoting consistency, accuracy, and correctability. Compliance with prespecified routines, such as procedures specified in employee handbooks governing terminations-for-cause, enhances the sense of fairness, particularly among witnesses but also for those directly involved in the process. . . .

Established procedures are especially important when substandard performance by one contract party is the basis for termination of the contract. When subjectivity exists in contract terms (occurring more often in relational agreements than in transactional ones), understanding performance standards and one's own level of compliance is critical to a felt fair process. . . .

Procedural justice mechanisms have both positive and negative aspects. On the upside, use of procedures is critical to protecting people from inadvertent contract breach (e.g., due to misunderstandings of performance terms). Procedures can establish more dignified treatment of people who are disciplined by allowing them recourse, voice, and the opportunity to change. But their downside is the escalation of both expectations and bureaucratization. Growth of formalized procedures (e.g., grievance mechanisms) has the effect of creating higher aspirations and expectations for the employer among employees (Selznick, 1969). Employees perceive managers to have obligations to act ethically (Folger & Bies, 1989) and, as a consequence of rising expectations, managers have to meet higher standards of fairness, thus increasing the potential for even greater perceived unfairness (Folger, 1977). . . .

Procedural justice mechanisms protect the interests of contract parties by providing a means for enforcing sanctions (e.g., against poor-performing employees, who themselves are in effect contract violators) in a way that seems fair to both victims and witnesses. . . .

When is a discrepancy a violation? The three instances this chapter opened with involved contract discrepancies with very different outcomes:

• A sales representative whose lucrative accounts are reassigned reacts angrily, but another rep readily accepts the same change. Both reassignments occurred in metropolitan Chicago due to an organizational restructuring aimed at creating sales areas based on customer needs rather than geography. The second sales rep had been participating in ongoing training in support of a new strategy that could potentially position him to advance within the company. The first rep had no such preparation.

• One customer receives a replacement for a damaged shipment and is pleased with the service, but another remains outraged at the supplier's unreliability. Not surprising, service recovery works well for the first customer, who has a long history of quality service from this vendor, but fails with the second, who recently has put up with a series of shipping problems due to the vendor's ongoing poor interdepartmental coordination.

• One plant's closing leads to angry protests in the city in which it is located, but another's leads the local newspapers to praise the company. As in the case of Yoder and Staudohar's (1985) discussion of Ford's and GM's different plant closing strategies, an abrupt, indefinite closing generates much greater loss for employees than a closing that is announced well in advance and supported by programs that assist employees in coping with the change.

These instances demonstrate how events before, during, and after the appearance of contract discrepancies shape whether they eventually turn into violations.

WHEN IS VIOLATION MOST LIKELY?

Based on the above discussion of contract dynamics, we can conclude that violation is most likely when the following occur:

- There is a history of conflict and low trust in the relationship.
- Social distance exists between the parties such that one does not understand the perspective of the other.
- An external pattern of violations exists (e.g., an era of business retrenchment).
- Incentives to breach contracts are very high or perpetrators perceive themselves to have no alternatives (e.g., organizational crises).
- One party places little value in the relationship (e.g., alternative parties are relatively available and there are few sunk costs).

. . .

WHEN A CONTRACT IS VIOLATED

Responses to violation take many forms. Violated contracts promote mistrust, anger, and attrition (Robinson & Rousseau, 1994) and change the way people behave in subsequent interactions (Rousseau et al., 1992). The aftermath of contract violation can be seen in declining corporate loyalty (Hirsch, 1987) and increased litigation (Bies & Tyler, 1993). Managers decry the decline of employee loyalty, but at the same time the workforce has been counseled to eschew reliance on job security and employer commitments, and to "pack its own" parachute instead (Hirsch, 1987). In both instances, there is the suggestion of contract violation and

FIGURE 2 • RESPONSES TO VIOLATION

	Constructive	Destructive
Active	Voice	Neglect/Destruction
Passive	Loyalty/Silence	Exit

the implication that at least one party has failed to keep its side of the bargain.

Types of Responses

Whether organizations and individuals choose to end their relationship, resolve their dispute, sue, or suffer in silence is a function of both situational factors and the predispositions of the parties. Previous research on responses to the more general phenomenon of dissatisfaction has largely focused on four courses of action: exit, voice, loyalty, and destruction. Although studied in various combinations (e.g., Hirschman's, 1970, *Exit, Voice, and Loyalty*) and labels (e.g., Farrell's, 1983, exit, voice, loyalty, and neglect), these courses of action reflect two essential dimensions (Farrell, 1983; Robinson, 1992): active-passive and constructive-destructive (Figure 2).

These responses to violation can be induced by both personal predispositions and situational factors. Personal characteristics predisposing the victim to believe that the relationship is valuable or can be saved should promote relationship-building behaviors of either voice or loyalty. Without this belief, behaviors that undermine the relationship—exit or destruction—are more likely. . . . Situational factors promoting certain behaviors and inhibiting others also affect responses to violation. Social learning and the presence of behavioral models tend to induce certain types of behaviors. Thus employees in organizations where other victims have left might be inclined to leave themselves. Similarly, individuals who have observed others successfully complain about their treatment might themselves be inclined to complain (Robinson, 1992). It is likely that the culture of the organization shapes the type of violation responses people make. A very bureaucratic organization that stifles communication and deviant behavior probably engenders little voice and more neglect and disloyalty. An open, communal organization might foster more overt complaints as well as attempts to repair the contract by communicating with superiors.

Exit is voluntary termination of the relationship. Employers can terminate workers whose performance does not meet standards (e.g., too frequently tardy, absent, or careless), and workers can quit an untrustworthy or unreliable employer (e.g., one that fails to deliver promised training or promotions). Exit is most likely in employment with transactional terms, where its costs are relatively low. . . . Both active and destructive, exit terminates the relationship. The vast majority of people quitting jobs within the first two years of employment report that their employer had violated commitments it had made (Robinson & Rousseau, 1994). . . .

However, it should be pointed out that violations don't always lead to exit. Robinson and Rousseau (1994) found that although 79% of leavers reported violated contracts, so too did 52% of stayers. While enduring violation, stayers can manifest three forms of response: voice, loyalty/silence, or neglect/destruction.

Voice refers to the actions victims take to remedy the violation. Any attempt to change the objectionable features in the situation, such as complaints to one's boss or to human resources, or the filing of a grievance, are efforts made to remedy or compensate for the violation while remaining in the relationship. . . . Voice in contract violation focuses on (a) reducing losses and (b) restoring trust.

As a response to dissatisfaction, voice often has been associated with relationship-threatening alternatives, where members in effect burn their bridges (e.g., whistle-blowing). Voice in response to contract violation is an active, constructive effort and is manifested in a number of ways. In a study of M.B.A. alumni, there were three major types of employee voice behaviors: talking with superiors, threats, and changes in behavior (Rousseau et al., 1992).

Talking with superiors was the most frequent type of voice:[2]

> I discussed my disappointment with my boss and also with my mentor. I was assured that, although I did not receive a bonus, my performance was above average. I was promoted and received a salary increase 6 months later.
>
> They moved me to a more challenging job . . . after I asked them to do so. This required two formal requests for a transfer.
>
> [My boss and I] had a heated discussion face to face. He took notes on what I felt I needed to have in order to complete the transition. He carried through 110%.
>
> I am in the process of negotiating with higher management. . . . I do have places to go with my concerns and have never felt the need to remain silent.

Some complaints obtain some sort of substitution:

> They said the situation was out of their hands and gave me a substantial salary increase.
>
> Management attempted to rationalize the decision to explain it was a capricious process and then gave me a larger bonus to assuage my discontent.
>
> Their system of training has come around a little . . . but they do not place as high a priority on training as they first told me.

Some complaints elicit no response:

> My boss paid lip service to making changes, but nothing actually occurred.
>
> Senior management listens to me very well and then does nothing.
>
> I went through all the necessary channels and have met with no success.
>
> They just said no.

Voice can take the form of a threat in a smaller number of cases:

> I threatened to leave based on my work assignment, training, and development opportunities. I was given new assignments, more training, and was allowed to stretch for development . . . however, I believe that happened primarily because of my director; another director probably would have let me leave.
>
> I had to appeal my case and threaten legal action to get my record changed to a layoff from firing and also to get a settlement.

In a few instances, a change in the victim's behavior generates a response:

> I was unhappy with the situation and my performance reflected it. The decision was made by [my] managers to reverse the situation. I now report to the marketing manager with a dotted line reporting relationship with the financial manager [a reversal of the previous situation].

Exit was the final resort for some:

> First there was a confrontation on my part to bring the problem forth, then following further unkept promises, I left the company [giving over a month's notice].
>
> . . .

Voice is most likely when

1. A positive relationship and trust exist
2. Voice channels exist
3. Other people are using voice
4. People believe that they can influence the other contract party

Silence is a form of nonresponse. Manifested as loyalty or as avoidance, silence reflects a willingness to endure or accept unfavorable circumstances. Silence can imply pessimism, in terms of believing that one has no available alternatives. Or silence can reflect loyalty—optimistically waiting for conditions to improve (Rusbult, Farrell, Rogers, & Mainous, 1988). As a passive, constructive response, silence serves to perpetuate the existing relationship.

> I started spending more time with my family and worrying less about what was happening at work.
>
> The last few years have really changed things with new owners and little investment back into the business. Where else could I go?

Silence is likely when

1. There are no voice channels or established ways of complaining or communicating violations
2. No available alternative opportunities exist elsewhere

Neglect, which entails passive negligence or active destruction, is a complex form of response. It can involve neglect of one's duties to the detriment of the interests of the other party. Passive-aggressive employee behavior, as in work slowdowns or providing customers with poor service, is a form of neglect, as is an organization's failure to invest in certain employees while developing others. Even when passive, neglect reflects erosion of the relationship between the parties. *Destruction* involves more active examples of counterproductive behaviors, including vandalism, theft, and interpersonal aggression (e.g., violence at work).

Neglect/destruction is most likely when

1. There is a history of conflict, mistrust, and violation
2. No voice channels exist
3. Other people demonstrate neglect or destruction

VIOLATION ISN'T THE END OF THE CONTRACT

Exit is only one of many results of contract violation. The fact that so many people with violated contracts remain with their employer suggests that although violation may be based on a discrete event (e.g., a willful breach of contract terms), a contract's fulfillment is more a matter of degree. When Robinson and Rousseau (1994) asked employees to indicate *whether* their contact had been violated, using a yes/no format, a total of 55% indicated "yes." However, when respondents were asked if their contract had ultimately been fulfilled by their employer, a large proportion (73%) indicated that their employer had honored its commitments at least moderately well. Among those employees reporting a violation at some point in the first two years of employment, 48% indicated that their contract had been honored at least somewhat by their employer. . . . Extent of contract keeping was affected by what benefits the employee received (e.g., if not the promotion as scheduled, then one later) as well as whether the violation was an isolated incident or part of a larger pattern.

These findings suggest that although violation is a discrete event, contract fulfillment is not. Rather, fulfillment is a continuum shaped by both the quality of the relationship and the postviolation behavior of both victim and perpetrator.

SUMMARY

Contract violation erodes trust. It undermines the employment relationship, yielding both lower employee contributions (e.g., performance and attendance) and lower employer investments (e.g., retention and promotion). How people respond to violation is largely a function of attributions made regarding the violator's motives, the behavior of the violator, and the scope of losses incurred. To understand how events are experienced as violations, it is necessary to take into account the perspective of the victim and the behavior of the perpetrator. For the prospective victim, the experience of violation is heightened when

- Losses seem greater (experienced violation is a matter of degree rather than a discrete event)
- The event occurs in a context where it poses a threat to the relationship between the parties (e.g., a history of previous breach or conflict)
- The violation event appears to be voluntary, as opposed to inadvertent, accidental, or due to forces beyond the violator's control
- No evidence of good faith efforts to avoid violation (the appearance of irresponsibility or neglect) is perceived by the victim

The strength and quality of the relationship not only affects the extent to which violation is tolerated or leads to dissolution of the contract but also affects the ability of the parties to repair the relationship. How people are treated following violation can repair the relationship or exacerbate its problems.

NOTES

1. Schmidt, 1993, p. 6. Copyright © 1993 by *The New York Times*. Reprinted with permission.
2. The following quotations were obtained from the M.B.A. alumni constituting the sample also used in Rousseau et al. (1992), Robinson, Kraatz, and Rousseau (1994), and Robinson and Rousseau (1994). The quotes appear here for the first time.

REFERENCES

Bies, R. J., & Moag, J. S. (1986). Interactional justice: Communication criteria of fairness. In M. H. Bazerman, R. Lewicki, & B. Sheppard (Eds.), *Research on negotiations in organizations* (Vol. 1, pp. 43–55). Greenwich, CT: JAI Press.

Bies, R. J., & Shapiro, D. L. (1993). Interactional fairness judgements: The influence of causal accounts. *Social Justice Research, 1*, 199–218.

Bies, R. J., & Tyler, T. R. (1993). The "litigation mentality" in organizations: A test of alternative psychological explanations. *Organization Science*, *4*, 352–366.

Clark, M. S., & Ries, H. T. (1988). Interpersonal processes in close relationships. *Annual Review of Psychology*, *39*, 609–672.

Farrell, D. (1983). Exit, voice, loyalty and neglect as responses to job dissatisfaction: A multidimensional scaling study. *Academy of Management Journal*, *26*, 596–607.

Folger, R. (1977). Distributive and procedural justice: Combined impact of "voice" and improvement on experienced inequity. *Journal of Personality and Social Psychology*, *35*, 2253–2261.

Folger, R., & Bies, R. J. (1989). Managerial responsibilities and procedural justice. *Employee Rights and Responsibilities Journal*, *2*, 79–90.

Hirsch, P. M. (1987). *Pack your own parachute*. Reading, MA: Addison-Wesley.

Hirschman, A. O. (1970). *Exit, voice, and loyalty*. Cambridge, MA: Harvard University Press.

In her majesty's service, but without free soap. (1993, October 2). *New York Times*, p. 6.

Kaufmann, P. J., & Stern, L. W. (1988). Relational exchange norms, perceptions of unfairness, and retained hostility in commercial litigation. *Journal of Conflict Resolution*, *32*, 534–552.

Levinthal, D. (1988). A survey of agency models of organizations. *Journal of Economic Behavior and Organization*, 9, 153–185.

Lind, E. A., & Tyler, T. R. (1988). *The social psychology of procedural justice*. New York: Plenum.

Robinson, S. L. (1992). *Responses to dissatisfaction*. Unpublished dissertation, Northwestern University, Kellogg Graduate School of Management.

Robinson, S. L., Kraatz, M. S., & Rousseau, D. M. (1994). Changing obligations and the psychological contract: A longitudinal study. *Academy of Management Journal*, *37*, 137–152.

Robinson, S. L., & Rousseau, D. M. (1994). Violating the psychological contract: Not the exception but the norm. *Journal of Organizational Behavior*, *15*, 245–259.

Rousseau, D. M., Robinson, S. L., & Kraatz, M. S. (1992, May). *Renegotiating the psychological contract*. Paper presented at the Society for Industrial Organizational Psychology meetings, Montreal.

Rusbult, C., Farrell, D., Rogers, G., & Mainous, A. (1988). Impact of exchange variables on exit, voice, loyalty and neglect: An integrative model of response to declining job satisfaction. *Academy of Management Journal*, *31*, 599–627.

Schlenker, B. R. (1980). *Impression management: The self-concept, social identity, and interpersonal relations*. Belmont, CA: Brooks/Cole.

Selznick, P. (1969). *Law, society, and industrial justice*. New York: Russell Sage.

Tyler, T. R., & Lind, E. A. (1992). A relational model of authority in groups. In M. P. Zanna (Ed.), *Advances in experimental social psychology* (Vol. 25, pp. 115–192). New York: Academic Press.

Wade-Benzoni, K. (1993). *Humiliation in the workplace*. Unpublished manuscript, Northwestern University, Kellogg Graduate School of Management.

Yoder, D., & Staudohar, P. D. (1985, Summer). Management and public policy in plant closure. *Sloan Management Review*, *26*(4), 45–58.

CHAPTER V

Power and Influence

Power and influence are key aspects of behavior in all organizations. The orchestra members must recognize and understand this fact of organizational life if they hope to be effective contributors to its success. Acceptance of the conductor's authority, interpersonal influence, coalition building and dynamics within and between the sections, and action (or inaction) all affect the orchestra's ability to perform positively or negatively.

Imagine a situation in which members of the string section deliberately slow their tempo in an attempt to influence the actions of the other musicians. Whatever their purpose may be, and like it or not, the strings are using their political skills and group cohesiveness to enhance their own power—perhaps to the detriment of others. The musicians in the other sections and the conductor must decide whether to resist or go along with the string section. They must assess the purpose and strategy behind the maneuver and decide on their course of action. An orchestra, like any other type of organization, is not immune from issues of power and influence—nor should it be.

Power is the latent ability to influence others' actions, thoughts, or emotions. It is the potential to get people to do things the way you want them done—a social energy waiting to be used, to be transformed into influence or, as in the words of R. G. H. Siu, to be transformed from *potential power* into *kinetic power*. Power is influence over the beliefs, emotions, and behaviors of people and, according to Siu, "potential power is the capacity to do so, but kinetic power is the act of doing so. . . . One person exerts power over another to the degree that he is able to exact compliance as desired" (1979, p. 31).

As we have seen throughout this book, almost everything necessary for understanding organizational behavior is related to everything else, and *power* is no exception. The subject of power in organizations is inseparable from the topics and issues that have been the focus of several earlier chapters.

As a concept of organizational behavior, *power* is associated with several other organizational subjects that many people find distasteful. First, for most of us, power suggests an ability to overcome resistance. This "black side" of power is behind Rosabeth Moss Kanter's (1979) observation: "Power is America's last dirty word. It is easier to talk about money—and much easier to talk about sex—than it is to talk about power. People who have it deny it; people who want it do not want to appear hungry for it; and people who engage in its machinations do so secretly" (p. 65). Second, power owes much of its existence to feelings of dependence. Power exists only when there is an unequal relationship between two people—where one of the two is dependent upon the other (Emerson, 1962).

THE ORGANIZATIONAL CONTEXT

Power starts with structural issues. Although individual skill determines the effectiveness of the use of power, power is not fundamentally an issue of person or personality. "Power is first and foremost a structural phenomenon, and should be understood as such" (Pfeffer, 1981, p. x). *Specialization* and *division of labor*, two related subjects that were discussed rather extensively in the *Introduction*, are the most fundamental causes of dependence among individuals and organizational units. With division of labor, people in organizations are dependent upon others for all sorts of things that are needed to accomplish their tasks: they are dependent for timely completion of prior tasks, accurate information, materials and supplies, competent people, and political support.

In this chapter we assert that structure establishes how *roles, expectations*, and *resource allocations* are defined for people and groups in any given organization. Thus, the structural forces caused by specialization and division of labor are extended (by the vital importance of these three functions of structure) to the people and groups in organizations. The functions of structure in the establishment of organizational roles, expectations, and resource allocations make it very clear why power is first and foremost a structural phenomenon, and why effective use of power in organizations is crucial for success. Jeffrey Pfeffer emphasizes this point in his "Preface" to *Power in Organizations* (1981): "Those persons and those units that have the responsibility for performing the more critical tasks in the organization have a natural advantage in developing and exercising power in the organization" (p. x). Resource allocation decisions have enormous impacts on a person's (or group's) ability to do its job, to "shine" or "excel." Structure affects resource allocations. A primary reason for using power is to affect resource allocations, and resource allocations affect the balance of power in organizations; these variables are inseparable. Power cannot be understood independent of the structural context, and vice versa.

INTERGROUP DYNAMICS

Organizations are complex systems that often can be visualized most clearly as grids or spider webs of overlapping, interwoven, and competing *coalitions* of individuals, formal groups, and informal groups, each having its own interests, beliefs, values, preferences, perspectives, and perceptions. The coalitions compete with each other continuously for scarce organizational resources. Conflict is inevitable. Influence—and the power and political activities through which influence is acquired and maintained—is the primary "weapon" for use in competition and conflicts. Thus, power, politics, and influence are critically important and permanent facts of organizational life.

Power relations are permanent features of organizations primarily because specialization and the division of labor result in many interdependent organizational units with varying degrees of importance. The units compete with each other for scarce resources—as well as with the transitory coalitions. As James D. Thompson points out in *Organizations in Action* (1967), lack of balance in the interdependence among units sets the stage for the use of power relations.

LEADERSHIP

Leadership involves "an interpersonal process through which one individual influences the attitudes, beliefs, and especially the behavior of one or more other people" (see Chapter I). The parallels and overlappings among issues of *leadership* and of *power in organizations* are obvious, and this chapter emphasizes the parallels and explains the overlappings.

Historically, power in organizations and authority were viewed as being essentially synonymous. Such "classical era" students of organization as Max Weber (1922) and Henri Fayol (1949, 1916) simply *assumed* that power and formal rules (promulgated and enforced by those in authority) flow downward through people who occupy offices to successively lower levels in hierarchical organizations. Even today, proponents of the "modern structural perspective of organization theory" (see Shafritz & Ott, 2001, chap. IV) tend to see authority as the source of power in organizations (or, at least the primary source). From this perspective, *leader, supervisor*, and *manager* mean the same thing: people who possess power by virtue of the authority inherent in the organizational position they occupy. Power is legitimized by virtue of a person being in such a position. In fact, the aptly descriptive phrases *legitimate power* and *legitimate authority* gained common usage and still are seen and heard occasionally in today's management literature.

In contrast, most organizational behavioralists see power in a very different light. For example, in today's organizational world John Kotter (1985) argues that the gap is increasing between the power one needs to get the job done and the power that automatically comes with the job (authority). Most organizational behavioralists view authority as only one of many available sources of organizational power, and power is aimed in *all* directions—not just down through the hierarchy. For example, Robert W. Allen and Lyman W. Porter divide their 1983 book of readings on *Organizational Influence Processes* into three major parts: downward influence (authority), lateral influence, and upward influence.

Authority-based power is far from being the only form of power in organizations. In fact, other forms of power and influence often prevail over authority-based power. Several of this chapter's selections identify different sources of power in organizations (particularly the second reading, "The Bases of Social Power," by John R. P. French and Bertram Raven), so only a few are listed here as examples:

- *Control over scarce resources*, for example, office space, discretionary funds, current and accurate information, and time and skill to work on projects

- *Easy access to others who are perceived as having power*, important customers or clients, members of the board of directors, or someone else with formal authority or who controls scarce resources
- *A central place in a potent coalition*
- *Ability to "work the organizational rules,"* such as knowing how to get things done or to prevent others from getting things done
- *Credibility*, for example, that one's word can be trusted.

The more that leadership issues in organizations are separated or differentiated from management issues, the more closely they become aligned with power issues—issues that extend beyond authority issues.

SELECTIONS IN THIS CHAPTER

The readings on power that comprise this chapter span almost thirty-five years and address a spectrum of issues associated with power and behavior in organizations. The first, Dorwin Cartwright's "Power: A Neglected Variable in Social Psychology" (1959), is adapted from an address he delivered to the Society for the Psychological Study of Social Issues in 1953. The article is not organization-specific. Rather, it defines the historical place of power in the field of social psychology originating with "metaphysical era social psychologists" including Hobbes (1651) and Nietzsche (1912). However, as Cartwright says, "twentieth century social psychologists have been 'soft' on power," preferring to avoid it or to study it only in "safe or weak populations—witness the classical stature of research on pecking order among chickens and on dominance among children." Cartwright identifies leading social issues (phenomena that are social psychological in nature) that "cannot be adequately understood without the concept of power." They include leadership and social roles, public opinion, rumor, propaganda, prejudice, attitude change, morale, communications, race relations, and conflicts of value. Cartwright concludes that these phenomena raise questions about power in society that cannot be answered with our existing systems of knowledge.

"The Bases of Social Power," by John R. P. French and Bertram Raven (1959), reprinted here, accepts Cartwright's challenge head on. In their often-cited analysis, French and Raven start from the premise that power and influence involve relations between at least two agents (they limit their definition of agents to individuals) and theorize that the reaction of the *recipient agent* is the more useful focus for explaining the phenomena of social influence and power. The core of French and Raven's piece, however, is their identification of five bases or sources of social power: reward power, the perception of coercive power, legitimate power (organizational authority), referent power (through association with others who possess power), and expert power (power of knowledge or ability).

French and Raven examine the effects of power derived from the five different bases on *attraction* (the recipient's sentiment toward the agent who uses power) and *resistance* to the use of power. Their investigations show that the use of power from the different bases has different consequences. For example, coercive power typically decreases attraction and causes high resistance, whereas reward power increases attraction and creates minimal levels of resistance. In what amounts to one of the earliest looks at ethical limits on the use of power, they conclude that "the more legitimate the coercion (is perceived to be) the less it will produce resistance and decreased attraction."

David Mechanic's influential 1962 *Administrative Science Quarterly* article, "Sources of Power of Lower Participants in Complex Organizations" (reprinted here), examines sources of influence and power that can be aimed at targets who possess more formal authority than the potential "influencer" possesses. As John Kotter (1977) explains, power requires feelings of dependence, and lower-level organization members have an array of tools with which to make others dependent on them. These tools include expertise, effort and interest, attractiveness (or charisma), location and position in the organization, membership in intra- and interorganizational coalitions, and knowledge of rules. All of this is a more formal way of saying something that we all know—some people are treated like prima donnas or "get away with murder" in organizations because they have some special skills that give them power in the context of their organizations. "Hawkeye" and "Trapper," from the *MASH* movie and television series, are ready examples. If they had not been badly needed surgeons at the battlefront, they would have been court-martialed years before.

From Dorwin Cartwright, French and Raven, and David Mechanic, it is a fifteen-year leap to Gerald Salancik and Jeffrey Pfeffer's 1977 widely respected analysis, "Who Gets Power—And How They Hold on to It: A Strategic-Contingency Model of Power." This article also reflects the field of organizational behavior's tremendous strides during the 1970s in accepting power as a legitimate subject for serious investigation.

Salancik and Pfeffer see power as one of the few mechanisms available for aligning an organization with the realities of its environment. Their assertion rests on the premise that power is derived from being essential to an organization's functional needs. According to Salancik and Pfeffer's notion (which they label *strategic-contingency theory*), power accrues to individuals and subunits that handle an organization's most critical problems. Effective use of power allows those subunits that are engaged in critical activities to "place allies in key positions," "control scarce critical resources," and thereby enhance the probability of their survival and expansion. Subunits engaged in critical functions prosper, and those engaged in noncritical functions wither, and the organization realigns itself. Because the most critical contingencies organizations face involve the environmental context, this power allocating process explains how organizations constantly readjust themselves with the needs of their external worlds.

Salancik and Pfeffer believe power is shared in organizations "out of necessity more than out of concern for principles of organizational development or participatory democracy." It is shared out of structural-functional need. To repeat an earlier quotation: "Power is first and foremost a structural phenomenon, and should be understood as such."

Strategic-contingency theory has far-reaching consequences. If the use of power by subunits helps organizations align themselves with their critical needs, then suppression of the use of power—for example, to reduce unwanted *politics* and *conflicts*—reduces organizational adaptability. Thus, in the current literature of organizational behavior, one seldom sees the phrase "conflict resolution." It has been almost totally replaced with the concept of "conflict management"—using conflict (and power struggles) constructively for the organization's benefit.

"Who Gets Power—And How They Hold on to It" contains a second very important contribution to the understanding of power in organizations. Salancik and Pfeffer identify three contextual conditions under which the use of power by members of subunits can be expected to determine how important decisions are decided. (For Salancik and Pfeffer, "important decisions" usually are resource allocation decisions.) These contextual decisions are identified as follows:

- The degree of resource scarcity
- The criticalness of the resources to subunits' core activities
- The level of uncertainty existing about what or how an organization should do

When these conditions are linked with Salancik and Pfeffer's identification of subunits that are most likely to get and hold on to power, it is possible to predict an organization's decision processes (under certain circumstances) by using a power perspective of organizational behavior. When clear-cut criteria do not exist, the use of power to control resource allocation decisions is likely to be most effective.

In the final reading reprinted in this chapter, "Managing with Power," Jeffrey Pfeffer (1992) discusses power and influence as they relate to decision making and implementation. Pfeffer claims that we often attempt to avoid the "social realities of power and influence," which causes us to "lose our chance to understand these critical social processes and to train managers to cope with them." Avoidance results in the "almost trained or produced incapacity of anyone except the highest-level managers to take action and get things accomplished."

We live in a society that favors individualism to the point that interdependence is often minimized and "cooperation may even be considered cheating." Without cooperation and coordination in organizations, however, success becomes a challenge. Pfeffer also notes that we are taught that there are right and wrong answers to problems from a very young age. In organizations, solutions to problems are rarely so clear. Most decisions are complex. "It is critical that organizational members develop the fortitude to continue when confronted by adversity, and the insight about how to turn situations around. The most important skill may be managing the consequences of decisions."

Organizations need leaders who are not afraid to exercise power and influence. Political leaders understand that this is required for success, and members of organizations need to reach this same understanding. Organizations need a strongly shared vision, culture, and common goals to strive for, and these cannot be developed without the strategic use of power and influence to build consensus.

Pfeffer concludes with a reminder that managing effectively requires recognition of competing interests as they relate to points of concern and the understanding that power is needed to get things done. The more we recognize and understand the importance of power in organizations, the more likely we are to be effective in implementing decisions and bringing success to our organizations.

CONCLUSION

Power and influence are integral aspects of organizational behavior. Their contributions to understanding the behavior of people in organizations can be understood only in relationship to leadership, group and intergroup dynamics, the organizational context, and motivational structures. In 1959, Dorwin Cartwright wrote about power as a neglected variable in social psychology. In 1979, Rosabeth Moss Kanter called power "America's last dirty word," a word and a concept that people in organizations (and elsewhere) try to avoid. But power is a subject that cannot and should not be avoided. The importance of power will become even clearer in Chapter VI, *Organizational Change*.

REFERENCES

Allen, R. W., Madison, D. L., Porter, L. W., Renwick, P. A., & Mayes, B. T. (1979). Organizational politics: Tactics and characteristics of its actors. *California Management Review, 22*, 77–83.

Allen, R. W., & Porter, L. W. (Eds.) (1983). *Organizational influence processes*. Glenview, IL: Scott, Foresman.

Cartwright, D. (1959). Power: A neglected variable in social psychology. In D. Cartwright (Ed.), *Studies in social power* (pp. 1–14). Ann Arbor, MI: University of Michigan, Institute for Social Research.

Emerson, R. M. (1962). Power-dependence relations. *American Sociological Review, 27*, 31–40.

Fayol, H. (1949). *General and industrial management* (C. Storrs, Trans.). London: Pitman Publishing Co. (Original work published 1916)

French, J. R. P., & Raven, B. (1959). The bases of social power. In D. Cartwright & A. Zander (Eds.), *Studies in social power* (pp. 150–167). Ann Arbor, MI: University of Michigan, Institute for Social Research.

Haire, M. (1962). The concept of power and the concept of man. In G. B. Strother (Ed.), *Social science approaches to business behavior* (pp. 163–183). Homewood, IL: Richard D. Irwin.

Hobbes, T. (1651). *Leviathan*. Reprinted in 1904, Cambridge, UK; University Press.

Kanter, R. M. (July–August, 1979). Power failure in management circuits. *Harvard Business Review, 57*, 65–75.

Korda, M. (1975). *Power*. New York: Ballantine Books.

Kotter, J. P. (March–April, 1976). Power, success, and organizational effectiveness. *Organizational Dynamics*, 27–40.

Kotter, J. P. (July–August, 1977). Power, dependence, and effective management. *Organizational Dynamics*, 125–136.

Kotter, J. P. (1985). *Power and influence*. New York: Free Press.

March, J. G. (1962). The business firm as a political coalition. *Journal of Politics, 24*, 662–678.

Mayes, B. T., & Allen, R. W. (1977). Toward a definition of organizational politics. *Academy of Management Review, 2*, 672–678.

McClelland, D., & Burnham, D. (March–April, 1976). Power is the great motivator. *Harvard Business Review*, 100–110.

Mechanic, D. (December, 1962). Sources of power of lower participants in complex organizations. *Administrative Science Quarterly, 7*(3), 349–364.

Mintzberg, H. (1983). *Power in and around organizations*. Englewood Cliffs, NJ: Prentice-Hall.

Nietzsche, F. (1912). *Der Wille zur Macht*. Book 3, sec. 702. In F. Nietzsche, *Werke* (Vol. 16). Leipzig: Alfred Kroner.

Perrow, C. (1970). Departmental power and perspectives in industrial firms. In M. N. Zald (Ed.), *Power in organizations* (pp. 59–89). Nashville, TN: Vanderbilt University Press.

Pfeffer, J. (1981). *Power in organizations*. Marshfield, MA: Pitman Publishing Co.

Pfeffer, J. (1992). *Managing with power: Politics and influence in organizations*. Boston: Harvard Business School Press.

Porter, L. W., Allen, R. W., & Angle, H. L. (1981). The politics of upward influence in organizations. In L. L. Cummings & B. M. Staw (Eds.), *Research in organizational behavior* (vol. 3, pp. 408–422). Greenwich, CT: JAI Press.

Robbins, S. P. (1976). *The administrative process: Integrating theory and practice*. Englewood Cliffs, NJ: Prentice-Hall.

Salancik, G. R., & Pfeffer, J. (1977). Who gets power—and how they hold on to it: A strategic-contingency model of power. *Organizational Dynamics, 5*, 2–21.

Sennett, R. (1980). *Authority*. New York: Alfred A. Knopf.

Shafritz, J. M., & Ott, J. S. (2001). *Classics of organization theory* (5th ed.). Fort Worth, TX: Harcourt.

Siu, R. G. H. (1979). *The craft of power*. New York: John Wiley.

Thompson, J. D. (1967). *Organizations in action*. New York: McGraw-Hill.

Tushman, M. L. (April, 1977). A political approach to organizations: A review and rationale. *The Academy of Management Review, 2*, 206–216.

Weber, M. (1922). Bureaucracy. In H. Gerth & C. W. Mills (Eds.), *Max Weber: Essays in sociology*. Oxford, U.K.: Oxford University Press.

Yates, D. Jr. (1985). *The politics of management*. San Francisco: Jossey-Bass.

32

Power: A Neglected Variable in Social Psychology[1]

Dorwin Cartwright

Twentieth century social psychology can be traced back to the earliest philosophers, but its complexion is largely determined by developments in this century. Prior to World War I social psychology had failed by and large to meet those requirements of an abstract, positive science which Comte had laid down about the middle of the nineteenth century. Today, in sharp contrast, the spirit of positivism holds sway, and the only problems deemed worthy of attention are those susceptible to objective observation and, preferably, quantification. But this gain has not been made without cost, for scientific status has been achieved by neglecting any phenomena which do not lend themselves readily to the operation of science. . . .

Power is such a phenomenon. This topic received considerable attention in the metaphysical era of social psychology. The classic reference is Hobbes **(8)** who in 1651 analyzed the motivation for power and some of its social consequences. More recent discussions, still in the metaphysical era, are those of Nietzsche **(21)** and Adler **(1)**. Many other philosophical and speculative treatments could, of course, be cited. . . .

Both early social psychology and modern society recognize the importance of power. If, however, we examine social psychology since the beginning of its scientific epoch, we search in vain for any concentrated attack on the problem. Surely this constitutes a weakness of modern social psychology. We can only conclude that twentieth century social psychologists have been "soft" on power. Direct investigation has been evaded in many ways. One mode of evasion has been to study power in safe or weak populations—witness the classical stature of research on pecking order among chickens and on dominance among children. Another has been to convert the problem of power into one of attitudes, expectations, and perceptions. Thus, there is more interest in authoritarianism than authority; expectations are made the critical element in the notion of role rather than behavioral restrictions or compulsions; prestige is studied because it can be investigated apart from any specific situation of interpersonal interaction and influence.

It is not here suggested that social psychologists have been cowardly; the fact is that the softer aspects of power have been more accessible to investigation.

[1] This chapter is based on the presidential address delivered at the 1953 annual meeting of the Society for the Psychological Study of Social Issues.

Source: Dorwin Cartwright, "Power: A Neglected Variable in Social Psychology," in *Studies in Social Power*, edited by Dorwin Cartwright (Ann Arbor, MI: Institute for Social Research, The University of Michigan, 1959), pp. 1–14. Reprinted by permission of the publisher.

Nor is it implied that these softer aspects are irrelevant or psychologically uninteresting. The complaint is, rather, that power is often seen as essentially not a psychological problem. When asked about power the social psychologist has typically referred the question to the political scientist, sociologist, or economist; or, worse, he has given answers based upon purely personal values. . . .

SOME ILLUSTRATIVE PROBLEMS INVOLVING POWER

To document the point it is necessary to show how power is inevitably a part of the accepted phenomena of social psychology. This task is made difficult by the fact that there is considerable ambiguity concerning the boundaries of the field. Nevertheless, it is possible to identify certain phenomena (problem areas) as essentially social psychological in nature. Allport **(2)** has provided a list of these, not intended to be exhaustive, which contains the following: leadership, public opinion, rumor, propaganda, prejudice, attitude change, morale, communications, race relations, and conflicts of value. We shall attempt to show that phenomena of this sort cannot be adequately understood without the concept of power.

Leadership and Social Roles

Empirical research has progressively forced a restatement of the problem of leadership from that of identifying personal traits of the leader to one of determining the causes and consequences of leadership behavior. In this analysis concepts like "social situation," "position," "function," and "role" have come to the fore. As long as leadership was viewed only as a particular combination of personality traits, properties of the social system could easily be ignored. A major advance in the study of leadership therefore came with the abandonment of this narrow point of view, mistakenly labeled "psychological." . . .

The gradually accumulating evidence from studies such as these fosters a dim view of supervisory training schemes which ignore the power structure of the organization; any theory of leadership which ignores power cannot be viewed more favorably.

If we turn our attention to the general theory of role, we are forced to conclude that here too power is inevitably involved. Since recent work on role, especially that of Newcomb **(20)**, has broadened the scope of social psychology and increased its ability to deal with important phenomena in an integrated fashion, the significance of this conclusion is far-reaching. . . .

Strodtbeck **(24, 25)** has devised an ingenious experimental method for determining the relative influence of roles. He has used this method to study the roles of husband, wife, and son in different cultures. The procedure is to place members of a family in a situation where they will have a difference of opinion and then to record the ensuing events. He finds, for example, that among Navajos the wife wins 46 arguments to the husband's 34. But among Mormons it is husband 42 to 29! The son seldom wins except by forming coalitions. This research of Strodtbeck and that of others makes it clear that even in groups having no formal table of organization the power of one person to influence another depends upon the role he occupies.

The program of investigations by Shartle, Stogdill, Hemphill and others in the Ohio State Leadership Studies **(23)** is providing important documentation for our theories of role. In their work the concept of responsibility is assuming fundamental importance; each member of an organization is responsible for the performance of certain activities and is responsible to certain other individuals. Positions in an organization can be described in terms of these two aspects of responsibility. What people in the organization do, with whom they interact, whom they like, from whom they receive recognition, and so forth—all these factors depend to a high degree upon the nature of the responsibility structure. Members of the organization may vary in the extent to which they accept this structure, but if a member does accept it, his behavior is then guided by certain other people and organizational requirements. Stated differently, the whole organizational structure acquires power over the member and consequently certain other people have power over him, the specific persons depending upon his position in the organization.

This raises the ancient sociological problem which Jaques **(14)** has analyzed in some detail and has referred to as the "sanctioning of authority." It seems that a group member cannot simply proclaim a new position of power with himself as the occupant. The authority of a position must be sanctioned by others if it is to possess power. In one of the earliest experiments upon the process of interpersonal influence, Frank **(7)** found that when students agreed to be subjects they automatically gave such authority to the role of experimenter that he could not get them to resist his efforts to have them perform very disagreeable tasks. He finally had to instruct them to resist before he could measure the relative effectiveness of his different techniques of pressure! In a study on changing mothers' behavior toward their children, Brim **(5)** found that mothers were more likely to try out advice given by a doctor the more they attributed high prestige to the role of doctor. Much of the research on the effects of prestige and credibility, it would seem, can best be interpreted in terms of the sanctioning of the authority of certain roles.

This line of theorizing raises an important question: what determines whether a person accepts the authority of a position occupied by others (or even by himself)? Although there is no research which answers this question directly, the work relating group cohesiveness to strength of group standards (discussed below) suggests that if the authority structure of a group is functionally equivalent to the standards of a group, then the more strongly members are attracted to the group the more will they accept its authority structure. This hypothesis could readily be tested.

The personality characteristics of individuals may also be expected to influence their readiness to sanction the authority of a role. Much of the work on authoritarianism can be interpreted as dealing with this problem. Another provocative approach is represented by the research of Jeanne and Jack Block **(4)** who, though not investigating directly the sanctioning of authority of a role, do show how the amount of influence exerted by a role on a person is related to certain of his personality characteristics. . . . The results show compliance to be related to (a) a trichotomy on "ego control" into over-controllers, appropriate controllers, and under-controllers; (b) scores on the California test of ethnocentrism; and (c) speed of establishing norms in an experiment on autokinetic movement. The Blocks propose that conforming to a suggestion from an authority is the expression of a more general "structuring" approach to an unpredictable environment. This predisposition, in turn, may be viewed as part of a larger syndrome of ego control which they term "over-control." The results of this one study do not, of course, tell us whether these over-controllers tend to accept the authority of all roles which might claim authority or whether they are inclined to give sanction only to certain sorts of potentially authoritative roles.

An experiment by Hoffman **(9)** should also be mentioned in this connection. He, too, related behavior in an experimental setting to personality variables. In his study, subjects were dichotomized into conformers and nonconformers on the basis of conformity to an announced group average of judgments of perceived distance. His results show that the conformers scored significantly higher on such measures as parental dominance, inability to tolerate impulses, overconcern for the well-being of parents, and strict moralism. . . .

This brief overview of research on role raises doubt that such soft properties as expectations and perceptions adequately characterize the actual phenomena of role. The harder properties of power are inextricably a part of the phenomena referred to by the concept of role.

Communication

If we turn to research on communication, we find that power must be recognized here, too. In fact, it is the power aspect of communication which gives the concept such a central place in current social psychological theory. Communication is the mechanism by which interpersonal influence is exerted. Without communication there would be no group norms, group goals, or organized group action. Let us examine the evidence for these conclusions.

First, it is perfectly obvious as soon as one bothers to raise the question that all communications are not equally influential. This, of course, has been known for a long time, and there is a respectable literature on the effectiveness of different kinds of content in communications. We are not so well supplied, however, with findings concerning the way in which the relations between communicator and recipient influence the effectiveness of communication. The work of Hovland and Weiss **(10)** and Kelman and Hovland **(17)** on source credibility dramatizes the importance of treating separately the content of a communication and its source. They have shown that the so-called "sleeper effect" depends upon the more rapid decay over time of the effects of the source than of the content. . . .

A program of research conducted at the Research Center for Group Dynamics adds further insight into the nature of communication. First, Festinger, Schachter, and Back **(6)** and Back **(3)** show that a communication between people in a group to which they are strongly attracted is more effective than a similar communication between people in a less attractive group. . . .

Second, the direction and content of the flow of communication in an organized group or community are not indifferent to the social position of the people involved. Orders, for example, seldom flow up a power hierarchy, but certain other types of communication are quite likely to do so. The studies by Hurwitz, Zander, and Hymovitch **(12)**, Jackson **(13)**, Kelley **(16)**, and others are beginning to reveal how upward communication may serve an individual as a substitute for upward locomotion in a power hierarchy, how a person may use communication as a device for minimizing the dangers of hostile actions by those in higher positions, and how a person of superior power may tailor the content and direction of his communications to maintain the belief among others that his superior behavior justifies his position. Thus, we must specify the power relations among people to understand either the frequency and content of communications passing among them or the authority of such communications.

Third, even the study of rumor cannot safely ignore the power situation. . . . Rumors are especially likely to flourish among people who see that their fates are in other people's hands.

If communication is to be a basic concept of social psychology, so too is power.

Interpersonal and Intergroup Relations

A few years ago the Research Center for Group Dynamics was asked by a group of junior high school teachers to help them understand better the sources of conflict and irritation in the relations among teachers, parents, and students. A project was organized by Jenkins and Lippitt **(15)** which included interviews with a sample of each of these populations. Respondents were asked to indicate what they believed were the things that each group did that each other group liked (for example, "What are the things that parents do that teachers like?"). They were also asked parallel questions to indicate disliked behavior.

Consider, first, the teacher-student relationship. Of all categories of teacher behavior, the one having most significance for students is that the teacher be fair. This seems to imply that the teacher is a sort of judge who hands down decisions of importance, thus making fairness a matter of real concern. When we examine the other side of the relationship and consider the responses of teachers, we get further confirmation of the teacher's power over students. Seventy-three percent of the teachers mention as important student behavior "being respectful" and "accepting the teacher as authority." Forty-two percent mention "obedience."

The relations between parents and students turn out to be much the same, but with different realms of behavior coming under the control of parents. Complaints about parents consists of a long list of things "they won't let us do" and of other things "they make us do." Though parents tend not to mention the importance of obedience and respect as much as teachers, the students nonetheless report that parents do place major emphasis upon compliance to parental authority.

More subtle is the finding concerning teacher-parent relations. Here it is clear that teachers have strong needs for friendship with adults and for acceptance as members of the community. Parents chiefly control the fate of teachers in this respect; they can give or withhold gratification of these needs. This relation is, moreover, one way; there is no indication that parents would feel deprived without the friendship, recognition, or acceptance of teachers. Knowledge of this asymmetrical power relation is essential for understanding the behavior, attitudes, and feelings of teachers and parents.

Experience with intergroup discrimination and prejudice points the same lesson. Can we really hope to explain these phenomena or to build programs of social action solely with such variables as authoritarianism, ethnocentrism, displaced aggression, and attitude? How do these concepts help to understand the substantial improvement of conditions for Negroes in the automobile industry following certain union policy-decisions or the presence of a nonsegregated dining room at Montgomery, Alabama—on the Air Force Base? Kurt Lewin **(18)** recognized the importance of power in intergroup relations when he asserted that "discrimination against minorities will not be changed as long as forces are not changed which determine the decisions of the gatekeepers" (p. 186). With such a perspective, social psychologists will take more than passing notice of such findings as that of Hunter **(11)** in his study of the power structure of Regional City—a medium sized city with a Negro population of nearly one-third the total. Through various devices he was able to construct a list of 40 people who could safely be called the city's most powerful; the approval of these people is required for the success of any community project. Those who wish to better intergroup relations in this city might be well advised to work with this group. They should know, however, that not a single Negro is on this list of influential people. (Only 3 could be considered even nominees on a list of 175.) . . .

Social Determinants of Emotional Adjustment

The importance of the concept of power for social psychology may be illustrated with respect to one other social problem. What determines the mental health or illness of individuals? While it is clear that physiological determinants are important, it is now known that social situations differ significantly in their impact upon the emotional adjustment of all those involved in them. Perhaps one of the clearest demonstrations of such influences was provided by the experiment of Lewin, Lippitt, and White **(19)** on different styles of leadership. Here it was found that the aggressiveness of a given child depended upon the style of leadership provided by the adult in charge of the group. Although the different styles of leadership studied in this experiment differed from one another in a number of ways, it appears that the most critical aspects of leadership were the size of the space of free movement allowed the children and whether the leader's power was used to support or obstruct the behavior of the children. The leader's use of power basically affected the emotional climate of the group.

In any social situation, and especially in hierarchical ones, certain people have power to help or hinder the goal-directed behavior of others. Emotional security depends rather directly upon the magnitude of this power and upon the benevolence of its use. . . .

Consistent with this general conception of the relation between security and power are the findings of a rather different sort of experiment conducted by Pepitone **(22)**. He placed boys in a situation where the achievement of an attractive object was under the control of a panel of three judges. After a standardized interaction between the boy and the panel, each boy was asked to rate the relative power and relative benevolence of each member of the panel. In this setting Pepitone found perceptual distortions designed, as it were, to minimize the threatening power of the panel members—if a member was rated as powerful, his benevolence was rated higher; and if he was rated as malevolent, his power was rated lower.

From the findings of research of the sort reported here it seems clear that the impact of social situations upon emotional adjustment will be adequately understood only if power is explicitly recognized.

SUMMARY

This brief overview of the field of social psychology leads to four conclusions:

1. A major deficiency of the theories of social psychology is that they have been soft on power.
2. The important social problems which demand our attention raise questions about power—questions which our systematic knowledge cannot answer.
3. Quite apart from any practical considerations, a social psychological theory

without the concept of power (or its equivalent) is incomplete. Such concepts as communication, role, attitude, expectation, and norm cannot by themselves account realistically for the processes of influence to which they refer, nor can they deal effectively with social change and resistance to change.

4. A concerted attack on the problem of power should produce a major advance in the field of social psychology. Such an advance will consist of an improved understanding of the proper subject-matter of social psychology and a reorganization of its conceptual systems.

REFERENCES

1. Adler, A. A study of organ inferiority and its psychic compensations. *Trans. Nerv. ment. Dis. Monogr. Ser.*, 1917, **24.**
2. Allport, G. W. The historical background of modern social psychology. In G. Lindzey (Ed.), *Handbook of social psychology*. Cambridge: Addison-Wesley, 1954, 3–56.
3. Back, K. W. Influence through social communication. *J. abnorm. soc. Psychol.*, 1951, **46,** 9–23.
4. Block, J., & Block, J. An interpersonal experiment on reactions to authority. *Hum. Relat.*, 1952, **5,** 91–98.
5. Brim, O. G. Jr. The acceptance of new behavior in child-rearing. *Hum. Relat.*, 1954, **7,** 473–491.
6. Festinger, L., Schachter, S., & Back, K. W. *Social pressures in informal groups*. New York: Harper, 1950.
7. Frank, J. D. Experimental study of personal pressures and resistance: I. Experimental production of resistance. *J. gen. Psychol.*, 1944, **30,** 23–41.
8. Hobbes, T. *Leviathan*. Reprint of 1st (1651) Ed., Cambridge: Univer. Press, 1904.
9. Hoffman, M. L. Some psychodynamic factors in compulsive conformity. *J. abnorm. soc. Psychol.*, 1953, **48,** 383–393.
10. Hovland, C. I., & Weiss, W. The influence of source credibility on communication effectiveness. *Pub. Opin. Quart.*, 1952, **15,** 635–650.
11. Hunter, F. *Community power structure*. Chapel Hill: Univer. North Carolina Press, 1953.
12. Hurwitz, J. I., Zander, A. F., & Hymovitch, B. Some effects of power on the relations among group members. In D. Cartwright & A. Zander (Eds.), *Group dynamics: Research and theory*. Evanston: Row, Peterson, 1953, pp. 483–492.
13. Jackson, J. M. Analysis of interpersonal relations in a formal organization. Unpublished doctor's dissertation, Univer. Michigan, 1952.
14. Jaques, E. *The changing culture of a factory*. London: Tavistock, 1951.
15. Jenkins, D., & Lippitt, R. *Interpersonal perceptions of teachers, students and parents*. Washington: Nat. Train. Labor. Group Devel., 1951.
16. Kelley, H. H. Communication in experimentally created hierarchies. *Hum. Relat.*, 1951, **4,** 39–56.
17. Kelman, H. C., & Hovland, C. I. "Reinstatement" of the communicator in delayed measurement of opinion change. *J. abnorm. soc. Psychol.*, 1953, **48,** 327–335.
18. Lewin, K. *Field theory in social science*. New York: Harper, 1951.
19. Lewin, K., Lippitt, R., & White, R. K. Patterns of aggressive behavior in experimentally created "social climates." *J. soc. Psychol.*, 1939, **10,** 271–299.
20. Newcomb, T. *Social psychology*. New York: Dryden, 1950.
21. Nietzsche, F. *Der Wille zur Macht*. Book 3, sec. 702. In Nietzsche's complete *Werke*, vol. 16. Leipzig: Alfred Kröner, 1912.
22. Pepitone, A. Motivational effects in social perception. *Hum. Relat.*, 1950, **3,** 57–76.
23. Stogdill, R. M. Leadership, membership and organization. *Psychol. Bull.*, 1950, **47,** 1–14.
24. Strodtbeck, F. L. Husband-wife interaction over revealed differences. *Amer. social. Rev.*, 1951, **16,** 468–473.
25. Strodtbeck, F. L. The family as a three-person group. *Amer. social. Rev.*, 1954, **19,** 23–29.

33

The Bases of Social Power

John R. P. French Jr. and Bertram Raven

The processes of power are pervasive, complex, and often disguised in our society. Accordingly one finds in political science, in sociology, and in social psychology a variety of distinctions among different types of social power or among qualitatively different processes of social influence (**1, 6, 14, 18, 19, 23, 24, 29, 32**). Our main purpose is to identify the major types of power and to define them systematically so that we may compare them according to the changes which they produce and the other effects which accompany the use of power. The phenomena of power and influence involve a dyadic relation between two agents which may be viewed from two points of view: (a) What determines the behavior of the agent who exerts power? (b) What determines the reactions of the recipient of this behavior? We take this second point of view and formulate our theory in terms of the life space of P, the person upon whom the power is exerted. In this way we hope to define basic concepts of power which will be adequate to explain many of the phenomena of social influence, including some which have been described in other less genotypic terms. . . .

POWER, INFLUENCE, AND CHANGE

Psychological Change

Since we shall define power in terms of influence, and influence in terms of psychological change, we begin with a discussion of change. We want to define change at a level of generality which includes changes in behavior, opinions, attitudes, goals, needs, values and all other aspects of the person's psychological field. We shall use the word "system" to refer to any such part of the life space.[1] Following Lewin (**22**, p. 305) the state of a system at time 1 will be noted $s_1(a)$.

Psychological change is defined as any alteration of the state of some system *a* over time. The amount of change is measured by the size of the difference between the states of a system *a* at time 1 and at time 2: $ch(a) = s_2(a) - s_1(a)$.

Change in any psychological system may be conceptualized in terms of psychological forces. But it is important to note the change must be coordinated to the resultant force of all the forces operating at the moment. Change in an

[1] The word "system" is here used to refer to a whole or a part of the whole.

Source: John R. P. French Jr. and Bertram Raven, "The Bases of Social Power," in *Studies in Social Power*, edited by Dorwin P. Cartwright (Ann Arbor, MI: Institute for Social Research, The University of Michigan, 1959), pp. 150–167. Reprinted by permission of the publisher.

opinion, for example, may be determined jointly by a driving force induced by another person, a restraining force corresponding to anchorage in a group opinion, and an own force stemming from the person's needs.

Social Influence

Our theory of social influence and power is limited to influence on the person, P, produced by a social agent, O, where O can be either another person, a role, a norm, a group or a part of a group. We do not consider social influence exerted on a group.

The influence of O on system *a* in the life space of P is defined as the resultant force on system *a* which has its source in an act of O. This resultant force induced by O consists of two components: a force to change the system in the direction induced by O and an opposing resistance set up by the same act of O.

By this definition the influence of O does not include P's own forces nor the forces induced by other social agents. Accordingly the "influence" of O must be clearly distinguished from O's "control" of P. O may be able to induce strong forces on P to carry out an activity (i.e., O exerts strong influence on P); but if the opposing forces induced by another person or by P's own needs are stronger, then P will locomote in an opposite direction (i.e., O does not have control over P). Thus psychological change in P can be taken as an operational definition of the social influence of O on P only when the effects of other forces have been eliminated. . . .

Commonly social influence takes place through an intentional act on the part of O. However, we do not want to limit our definition of "act" to such conscious behavior. Indeed, influence might result from the passive presence of O, with no evidence of speech, or overt movement. A policeman's standing on a corner may be considered an act of an agent for the speeding motorist. Such acts of the inducing agent will vary in strength, for O may not always utilize all of his power. The policeman, for example, may merely stand and watch or act more strongly by blowing his whistle at the motorist.

The influence exerted by an act need not be in the direction intended by O. The direction of the resultant force on P will depend on the relative magnitude of the induced force set up by the act of O and the resisting force in the opposite direction which is generated by that same act. In cases where O intends to influence P in a given direction, a resultant force in the same direction may be termed positive influence whereas a resultant force in the opposite direction may be termed negative influence. . . .

Social Power

The strength of power of O/P in some system *a* is defined as the maximum potential ability of O to influence P in *a*.

By this definition influence is kinetic power, just as power is potential influence. It is assumed that O is capable of various acts which, because of some more or less enduring relation to P, are able to exert influence on P.[2] O's power is measured by his maximum possible influence, though he may often choose to exert less than his full power.

[2] The concept of power has the conceptual property of *potentiality*; but it seems useful to restrict this potential influence to more or less enduring power relations between O and P by excluding from the definition of power those cases where the potential influence is so momentary or so changing that it cannot be predicted from the existing relationship. Power is a useful concept for describing social structure only if it has a certain stability over time; it is useless if every momentary social stimulus is viewed as actualizing social power.

An equivalent definition of power may be stated in terms of the resultant of two forces set up by the act of O: one in the direction of O's influence attempt and another resisting force in the opposite direction. Power is the maximum resultant of these two forces:

$$\text{Power of O/P(a)} = (f_{a,x} - f_{a,x})^{max}$$

where the source of both forces is an act of O.

Thus the power of O with respect to system *a* of P is equal to the maximum resultant force of two forces set up by any possible act of O: (a) the force which O can set up on the system *a* to change in the direction x, (b) the resisting force,[3] in the opposite direction. Whenever the first component force is greater than the second, positive power exists; but if the second component force is greater than the first, then O has negative power over P. . . .

For certain purposes it is convenient to define the range of power as the set of all systems within which O has power of strength greater than zero. A husband may have a broad range of power over his wife, but a narrow range of power over his employer. We shall use the term "magnitude of power" to denote the summation of O's power over P in all systems of his range.

The Dependence of s(a) on O

We assume that any change in the state of a system is produced by a change in some factor upon which it is functionally dependent. That state of an opinion, for example, may change because of a change either in some internal factor such as a need or in some external factor such as arguments of O. Likewise, the maintenance of the same state of a system is produced by the stability or lack of change in the internal and external factors. In general, then, psychological change and stability can be conceptualized in terms of dynamic dependence. Our interest is focused on the special case of dependence on an external agent, O **(25)**.

In many cases the initial state of the system has the character of a quasistationary equilibrium with a central force field around $s_1(a)$ **(22,** p. 106). In such cases we may derive a tendency toward retrogression to the original state as soon as the force induced by O is removed.[4]

Consider the example of three separated employees who have been working at the same steady level of production despite normal, small fluctuations in the work environment. The supervisor orders each to increase his production, and the level of each goes up from 100 to 115 pieces per day. After a week of producing at the new rate of 115 pieces per day, the supervisor is removed for a week. The production of employee A immediately returns to 100 but B and C return to only 110 pieces per day. Other things being equal, we can infer that A's new rate was completely dependent on his supervisor whereas the new rate of B and C was dependent on the supervisor only to the extent of 5 pieces. Let us further assume that when the supervisor returned, the production of B and of C returned to 115 without further orders from the supervisor. Now another

[3] We define resistance to an attempted induction as a force in the opposite direction which is set up by the same act of O. It must be distinguished from opposition, which is defined as existing opposing forces which do not have their source in the same act of O. For example, a boy might resist his mother's order to eat spinach because of the manner of the induction attempt, and at the same time he might oppose it because he didn't like spinach.

[4] Miller **(33)** assumes that all living systems have this character. However, it may be that some systems in the life space do not have this elasticity.

month goes by during which B and C maintain a steady 115 pieces per day. However, there is a difference between them: B's level of production still depends on O to the extent of 5 pieces whereas C has come to rely on his own sense of obligation to obey the order of his legitimate supervisor rather than on the supervisor's external pressure for the maintenance of his 115 pieces per day. Accordingly, the next time the supervisor departs, B's production again drops to 110 but C's remains at 115 pieces per day. In cases like employee B, the degree of dependence is contingent on the perceived probability that O will observe the state of the system and note P's conformity **(5, 6, 11, 12, 19).** The level of observability will in turn depend on both the nature of the system (e.g., the difference between a covert opinion and overt behavior) and on the environmental barriers to observation (e.g., O is too far away from P). . . .

THE BASES OF POWER

By the basis of power we mean the relationship between O and P which is the source of that power. It is rare that we can say with certainty that a given empirical case of power is limited to one source. Normally, the relation between O and P will be characterized by several qualitatively different variables which are bases of power (**24,** Chapter 11). Although there are undoubtedly many possible bases of power which may be distinguished, we shall here define five which seem especially common and important. These five bases of O's power are: (1) reward power, based on P's perception that O has the ability to mediate rewards for him; (2) coercive power, based on P's perception that O has the ability to mediate punishments for him; (3) legitimate power, based on the perception by P that O has a legitimate right to prescribe behavior for him; (4) referent power, based on P's identification with O; (5) expert power, based on the perception that O has some special knowledge or expertness. . . .

Reward Power

Reward power is defined as power whose basis is the ability to reward. The strength of the reward power of O/P increases with the magnitude of the rewards which P perceives that O can mediate for him. Reward power depends on O's ability to administer positive valences and to remove or decrease negative valences. The strength of reward power also depends upon the probability that O can mediate the reward, as perceived by P. A common example of reward power is the addition of a piecework rate in the factory as an incentive to increase production.

The new state of the system induced by a promise of reward (for example, the factory worker's increased level of production) will be highly dependent on O. Since O mediates the reward, he controls the probability that P will receive it. Thus P's new rate of production will be dependent on his subjective probability that O will reward him for conformity minus his subjective probability that O will reward him even if he returns to his old level. Both probabilities will be greatly affected by the level of observability of P's behavior. . . .

The utilization of actual rewards (instead of promises) by O will tend over time to increase the attraction of P toward O and therefore the referent power of O over P. As we shall note later, such referent power will permit O to induce changes which are relatively independent. Neither rewards nor promises will arouse resistance in P, provided P considers it legitimate for O to offer rewards.

The range of reward power is specific to those regions within which O can reward P for conforming. The use of rewards to change systems within the range of reward power tends to increase reward power by increasing the probability attached to future promises. However, unsuccessful attempts to exert reward power outside the range of power would tend to decrease the power; for example, if O offers to reward P for performing an impossible act, this will reduce for P the probability of receiving future rewards promised by O.

Coercive Power

Coercive power is similar to reward power in that it also involves O's ability to manipulate the attainment of valences. Coercive power of O/P stems from the expectation on the part of P that he will be punished by O if he fails to conform to the influence attempt. Thus negative valences will exist in given regions of P's life space, corresponding to the threatened punishment by O. The strength of coercive power depends on the magnitude of the negative valence of the threatened punishment multiplied by the perceived probability that P can avoid the punishment by conformity, i.e., the probability of punishment for nonconformity minus the probability of punishment for conformity **(11)**. Just as an offer of a piece-rate bonus in a factory can serve as a basis for reward power, so the ability to fire a worker if he falls below a given level of production will result in coercive power.

Coercive power leads to dependent change also; and the degree of dependence varies with the level of observability of P's conformity. An excellent illustration of coercive power leading to dependent change is provided by a clothes presser in a factory observed by Coch and French **(3)**. As her efficiency rating climbed above average for the group, the other workers began to "scapegoat" her. That the resulting plateau in her production was not independent of the group was evident once she was removed from the presence of the other workers. Her production immediately climbed to new heights.[5] . . .

The distinction between these two types of power is important because the dynamics are different. The concept of "sanctions" sometimes lumps the two together despite their opposite effects. While reward power may eventually result in an independent system, the effects of coercive power will continue to be dependent. Reward power will tend to increase the attraction of P toward O; coercive power will decrease this attraction **(11, 12)**. The valence of the region of behavior will become more negative, acquiring some negative valence from the threatened punishment. The negative valence of punishment would also spread to other regions of the life space. Lewin **(21)** has pointed out this distinction between the effects of rewards and punishment. In the case of threatened punishment, there will be a resultant force on P to leave the field entirely. Thus, to achieve conformity, O must not only place a strong negative valence in certain regions through threat of punishment, but O must also introduce restraining forces, or other strong valences, so as to prevent P from withdrawing completely from O's range of coercive power. Otherwise, the probability of receiving the punishment, if P does not conform, will be too low to be effective.

[5] Though the primary influence of coercive power is dependent, it often produces secondary changes which are independent. Brainwashing, for example, utilizes coercive power to produce many primary changes in the life space of the prisoner, but these dependent changes can lead to identification with the aggressor and hence to secondary changes in ideology which are independent.

Legitimate Power

There has been considerable investigation and speculation about socially prescribed behavior, particularly that which is specific to a given role or position. Linton **(23)** distinguishes group norms according to whether they are universals for everyone in the culture, alternatives (the individual having a choice as to whether or not to accept them), or specialties (specific to given positions). Whether we speak of internalized norms, role prescriptions and expectations **(27)**, or internalized pressures **(15)**, the fact remains that each individual sees certain regions toward which he should locomote, some regions toward which he should not locomote, and some regions toward which he may locomote if they are generally attractive for him. This applies to specific behaviors in which he may, should, or should not engage; it applies to certain attitudes or beliefs which he may, should, or should, or should not hold. The feeling of "oughtness" may be an internalization from his parents, from his teachers, from his religion, or may have been logically developed from some idiosyncratic system of ethics. He will speak of such behaviors with expressions like "should," "ought to," or "has a right to." In many cases, the original source of the requirement is not recalled.

Though we have oversimplified such evaluations of behavior with a positive-neutral-negative trichotomy, the evaluation of behaviors by the person is really more one of degree. This dimension of evaluation, we shall call "legitimacy." Conceptually, we may think of legitimacy as a valence in a region which is induced by some internalized norm or value. This value has the same conceptual property as power, namely, an ability to induce force fields (**22,** pp. 40–41). . . .

Legitimate power of O/P is here defined as that power which stems from internalized values in P which dictate that O has a legitimate right to influence P and that P has an obligation to accept this influence. We note that legitimate power is very similar to the notion of legitimacy of authority which has long been explored by sociologists, particularly by Weber **(33)**, and more recently by Goldhammer and Shils **(14)**. However, legitimate power is not always a role relation: P may accept an induction from O simply because he had previously promised to help O and he values his word too much to break the promise. In all cases, the notion of legitimacy involves some sort of code or standard, accepted by the individual, by the virtue of which the external agent can assert his power. We shall attempt to describe a few of these values here.

Bases for legitimate power. Cultural values constitute one common basis for the legitimate power of one individual over another. O has characteristics which are specified by the culture as giving him the right to prescribe behavior for P, who may not have these characteristics. These bases, which Weber **(33)** has called the authority of the "eternal yesterday," include such things as age, intelligence, caste, and physical characteristics. In some cultures, the aged are granted the right to prescribe behavior for others in practically all behavior areas. In most cultures, there are certain areas of behavior in which a person of one sex is granted the right to prescribe behavior for the other sex.

Acceptance of the social structure is another basis for legitimate power. If P accepts as right the social structure of his group, organization, or society, especially the social structure involving a hierarchy of authority, P will accept the legitimate authority of O who occupies a superior office in the hierarchy. Thus legitimate power in a formal organization is largely a relationship between offices rather than between persons. And the acceptance of an office as *right* is a basis for legitimate power—a judge has a right to levy fines, a foreman should assign work, a priest is justified in prescribing religious beliefs, and it is the management's prerogative to make certain decisions **(10)**. However, legitimate power also involves the perceived right of the person to hold the office.

Designation by a legitimizing agent is a third basis for legitimate power. An influencer O may be seen as legitimate in prescribing behavior for P because he has been granted such power by a legitimizing agent whom P accepts. Thus a department head may accept the authority of his vice-president in a certain area because that authority has been specifically delegated by the president. An election is perhaps the most common example of a group's serving to legitimize the authority of one individual or office for other individuals in the group. The success of such legitimizing depends upon the acceptance of the legitimizing agent and procedure. In this case it depends ultimately on certain democratic values concerning election procedures. The election process is one of legitimizing a person's right to an office which already has a legitimate range of power associated with it.

Range of legitimate power of O/P. The areas in which legitimate power may be exercised are generally specified along with the designation of that power. A job description, for example, usually specifies supervisory activities and also designates the person to whom the jobholder is responsible for the duties described. Some bases for legitimate authority carry with them a very broad range. Culturally derived bases for legitimate power are often especially broad. It is not uncommon to find cultures in which a member of a given caste can legitimately prescribe behavior for all members of lower castes in practically all regions. More common, however, are instances of legitimate power where the range is specifically and narrowly prescribed. A sergeant in the army is given a specific set of regions within which he can legitimately prescribe behavior for his men.

The attempted use of legitimate power which is outside of the range of legitimate power will decrease the legitimate power of the authority figure. Such use of power which is not legitimate will also decrease the attractiveness of O **(11, 12, 28)**.

Legitimate power and influence. The new state of the system which results from legitimate power usually has high dependence on O though it may become independent. Here, however, the degree of dependence is not related to the level of observability. Since legitimate power is based on P's values, the source of the forces induced by O include both these internal values and O. O's induction serves to activate the values and to relate them to the system which is influenced, but thereafter the new state of the system may become directly dependent on the values with no mediation by O. Accordingly this new state will be relatively stable and consistent across varying environmental situations since P's values are more stable than his psychological environment. . . .

Referent Power

The referent power of O/P has its basis in the identification of P with O. By identification, we mean a feeling of oneness of P with O, or a desire for such an identity. If O is a person toward whom P is highly attracted, P will have a feeling of membership or a desire to join. If P is already closely associated with O, he will want to maintain this relationship **(30, 32)**. P's identification with O can be established or maintained if P behaves, believes, and perceives as O does. Accordingly O has the ability to influence P, even though P may be unaware of this referent power. A verbalization of such power by P might be, "I am like O, and therefore I shall behave or believe as O does," or "I want to be like O, and I will be more like O if I behave or believe as O does." The stronger the identification of P with O the greater the referent power of O/P. . . .

We must try to distinguish between referent power and other types of power which might be operative at the same time. If a member is attracted to a group and he conforms to its norms only because he fears ridicule or expulsion from the group for nonconformity, we would call this coercive power. On the other hand, if he conforms in order to obtain praise for conformity, it is a case of reward power. . . . Conformity with majority opinion is sometimes based on a respect for the collective wisdom of the group, in which case it is expert power. It is important to distinguish these phenomena, all grouped together elsewhere as "pressures toward uniformity," since the type of change which occurs will be different for different bases of power.

The concepts of "reference group" **(31)** and "prestige suggestion" may be treated as instances of referent power. In this case, O, the prestigeful person or group, is valued by P; because P desires to be associated or identified with O, he will assume attitudes or beliefs held by O. Similarly a negative reference group which O dislikes and evaluates negatively may exert negative influence on P as a result of negative referent power.

It has been demonstrated that the power which we designate as referent power is especially great when P is attracted to O **(2, 7, 8, 9, 13, 19, 24)**. In our terms, this would mean that the greater the attraction, the greater the identification, and consequently the greater the referent power. In some cases, attraction or prestige may have a specific basis, and the range of referent power will be limited accordingly: a group of campers may have great referent power over a member regarding campcraft, but considerably less effect on other regions **(24)**. However, we hypothesize that the greater the attraction of P toward O, the broader the range of referent power of O/P. . . .

Expert Power

The strength of the expert power of O/P varies with the extent of the knowledge or perception which P attributes to O within a given area. Probably P evaluates O's expertness in relation to his own knowledge as well as against an absolute standard. In any case, expert power results in primary social influence on P's cognitive structure and probably not on other types of systems. Of course changes in the cognitive structure can change the direction of forces and hence of locomotion, but such a change of behavior is secondary social influence. Expert power has been demonstrated experimentally **(8, 26)**. Accepting an attorney's advice in legal matters is a common example of expert influence; but there are many instances based on much less knowledge, such as the acceptance by a stranger of directions given by a native villager.

Expert power, where O need not be a member of P's group, is called "informational power" by Deutsch and Gerard **(4)**. This type of expert power must be distinguished from influence based on the content of communication as described by Hovland et al. **(16, 17, 19, 20)**. The influence of the content of a communication upon an opinion is presumably a secondary influence produced after the *primary* influence (i.e., the acceptance of the information). Since power is here defined in terms of the primary changes, the influence of the content on a related opinion is not a case of expert power as we have defined it, but the initial acceptance of the validity of the content does seem to be based on expert power or referent power. . . .

The range of expert power, we assume, is more delimited than that of referent power. Not only is it restricted to cognitive systems but the expert is seen as having superior knowledge or ability in very specific areas, and his power will be limited to these areas, though some "halo effect" might occur. Recently, some of our renowned physical scientists have found quite painfully that their expert power in physical sciences does not extend to regions involving international politics. Indeed, there is some evidence that the attempted exertion of expert power outside of the range of expert power will reduce that expert power. An undermining of confidence seems to take place.

SUMMARY

We have distinguished five types of power: referent power, expert power, reward power, coercive power, and legitimate power. These distinctions led to the following hypotheses.

1. For all five types, the stronger the basis of power the greater the power.
2. For any type of power the size of the range may vary greatly, but in general referent power will have the broadest range.
3. Any attempt to utilize power outside the range of power will tend to reduce the power.
4. A new state of a system produced by reward power or coercive power will be highly dependent on O, and the more observable P's conformity the more dependent the state. For the other three types of power, the new state is usually dependent, at least in the beginning, but in any case the level of observability has no effect on the degree of dependence.
5. Coercion results in decreased attraction of P toward O and high resistance; reward power results in increased attraction and low resistance.
6. The more legitimate the coercion the less it will produce resistance and decreased attraction.

REFERENCES

1. Asch, S. E. *Social psychology*. New York: Prentice-Hall, 1952.
2. Back, K. W. Influence through social communication. *J. abnorm. soc. Psychol.*,1951, **46,** 9–23.
3. Coch, L., & French, J. R. P., Jr. Overcoming resistance to change. *Hum. Relat.*, 1948, **1,** 512–532.
4. Deutsch, M., & Gerard, H. B. A study of normative and informational influences upon individual judgment. *J. abnorm. soc. Psychol.*, 1955, **51,** 629–636.
5. Dittes, J. E., & Kelley, H. H. Effects of different conditions of acceptance upon conformity to group norms. *J. abnorm. soc. Psychol.*, 1956, **53,** 100–107.
6. Festinger, L. An analysis of compliant behavior. In Sherif, M., & Wilson, M. O., (Eds.), *Group relations at the crossroads*. New York: Harper, 1953, 232–256.
7. Festinger, L. Informal social communication. *Psychol. Rev.*, 1950, **57,** 271–282.
8. Festinger, L., Gerard, H. B., Hymovitch, B., Kelley, H. H., & Raven, B. H. The influence process in the presence of extreme deviates. *Hum. Relat.*, 1952, **5,** 327–346.
9. Festinger, L., Schachter, S., & Back, K. The operation of group standards. In Cartwright, D., & Zander, A. *Group dynamics: research and theory*. Evanston: Row, Peterson, 1953, 204–223.
10. French, J. R. P., Jr., Israel, Joachim, & Ås Dagfinn. "Arbeidernes medvirkning i industribedriften. En eksperimentell undersøkelse." Institute for Social Research, Oslo, Norway, 1957.
11. French, J. R. P., Jr., Levinger, G., & Morrison, H. W. The legitimacy of coercive power. In preparation.
12. French, J. R. P., Jr., & Raven, B. H. An experiment in legitimate and coercive power. In preparation.

13. Gerard, H. B. The anchorage of opinions in face-to-face groups. *Hum. Relat.*, 1954, **7,** 313–325.

14. Goldhammer, H., & Shils, E. A. Types of power and status. *Amer. J. Sociol.*, 1939, **45,** 171–178.

15. Herbst, P. G. Analysis and measurement of a situation. *Hum. Relat.*, 1953, **2,** 113–140.

16. Hovland, C. I., Lumsdaine, A. A., & Sheffield, F. D. *Experiments on mass communication*. Princeton: Princeton Univer. Press, 1949.

17. Hovland, C. I., & Weiss, W. The influence of source credibility on communication effectiveness. *Publ. Opin. Quart.*, 1951, **15,** 635–650.

18. Jahoda, M. Psychological issues in civil liberties. *Amer. Psychologist*, 1956, **11,** 234–240.

19. Kelman, H. Three processes of acceptance of social influence: compliance, identification and internalization. Paper read at the meetings of the American Psychological Association, August 1956.

20. Kelman, H., & Hovland, C. I. "Reinstatement" of the communicator in delayed measurement of opinion change. *J. abnorm. soc. Psychol.*, 1953, **48,** 327–335.

21. Lewin, K. *Dynamic theory of personality*. New York: McGraw-Hill, 1935, 114–170.

22. Lewin, K. *Field theory in social science*. New York: Harper, 1951.

23. Linton, R. *The cultural background of personality*. New York: Appleton-Century-Crofts, 1945.

24. Lippitt, R., Polansky, N., Redl, F., & Rosen, S. The dynamics of power. *Hum. Relat.*, 1952, **5,** 37–64.

25. March, J. G. An introduction to the theory and measurement of influence. *Amer. polit. Sci. Rev.*, 1955, **49,** 431–451.

26. Moore, H. T. The comparative influence of majority and expert opinion. *Amer. J. Psychol.*, 1921, **32,** 16–20.

27. Newcomb, T. M. *Social psychology*. New York: Dryden, 1950.

28. Raven, B. H., & French, J. R. P., Jr. Group support, legitimate power, and social influence. *J. Person.*, 1958, **26,** 400–409.

29. Russell, B. *Power: A new social analysis*. New York: Norton, 1938.

30. Stotland, E., Zander, A., Burnstein, E., Wolfe, D., & Natsoulas, T. Studies on the effects of identification. University of Michigan, Institute for Social Research. Forthcoming.

31. Swanson, G. E., Newcomb, T. M., & Hartley, E. L. *Readings in social psychology*. New York: Henry Holt, 1952.

32. Torrance, E. P., & Mason, R. Instructor effort to influence: an experimental evaluation of six approaches. Paper presented at USAF-NRC Symposium on Personnel, Training, and Human Engineering. Washington, D.C., 1956.

33. Weber, M. *The theory of social and economic organization*. Oxford: Oxford Univer. Press, 1947.

34

Sources of Power of Lower Participants in Complex Organizations

David Mechanic

It is not unusual for lower participants[1] in complex organizations to assume and wield considerable power and influence not associated with their formally defined positions within these organizations. In sociological terms they have considerable personal power but no authority. Such personal power is often attained, for example, by executive secretaries and accountants in business firms, by attendants in mental hospitals, and even by inmates in prisons. The personal power achieved by these lower participants does not necessarily result from unique personal characteristics, although these may be relevant, but results rather from particular aspects of their location within their organizations.

INFORMAL VERSUS FORMAL POWER

Clarification of Definitions

The purpose of this paper is to present some hypotheses explaining why lower participants in organizations can often assume and wield considerable power which is not associated with their positions as formally defined within these organizations. For the purposes of this analysis the concepts "influence," "power," and "control" will be used synonymously. Moreover, we shall not be concerned with type of power, that is, whether the power is based on reward, punishment, identification, power to veto, or whatever.[2] Power will be defined as *any force that results in behavior that would not have occurred if the force had not been present*. We have defined power as a force rather than a relationship because it appears that much of what we mean by power is encompassed by the normative framework of an organization, and thus any analysis of power must take into consideration the power of norms as well as persons.

I shall also argue, following Thibaut and Kelley,[3] that power is closely related

[1] The term "lower participants" comes from Amitai Etzioni, A *Comparative Analysis of Complex Organizations* (New York, 1961) and is used by him to designate persons in positions of lower rank: employees, rank-and-file, members, clients, customers, and inmates. We shall use the term in this paper in a relative sense denoting position vis-à-vis a higher-ranking participant.

[2] One might observe, for example, that the power of lower participants is based primarily on the ability to "veto" or punish. For a discussion of bases of power, see John R. P. French Jr. and Bertram Raven, "The Bases of Social Power," in D. Cartwright and A. Zander, eds., *Group Dynamics* (Evanston, Ill., 1960) pp. 607–623.

[3] John Thibaut and Harold H. Kelley, *The Social Psychology of Groups* (New York, 1959). For a

Source: Reprinted from "Sources of Power of Lower Participants in Complex Organizations," by David Mechanic, published in *Administrative Science Quarterly*, Volume 7 #3 (December 1962), pp. 349–365, by permission of *Administrative Science Quarterly*.

to dependence. To the extent that a person is dependent on another, he is potentially subject to the other person's power. Within organizations one makes others dependent upon him by controlling access to information, persons, and instrumentalities, which I shall define as follows:

a. *Information* includes knowledge of the organization, knowledge about persons, knowledge of the norms, procedures, techniques, and so forth.
b. *Persons* include anyone within the organization or anyone outside the organization upon whom the organization is in some way dependent.
c. *Instrumentalities* include any aspect of the physical plant of the organization or its resources (equipment, machines, money, and so on).

Power is a function not only of the extent to which a person controls information, persons, and instrumentalities, but also of the importance of the various attributes he controls.[4] . . .

A Classic Example

Like many other aspects of organizational theory, one can find a classic statement of our problem in Weber's discussion of the political bureaucracy. Weber indicated the extent to which bureaucrats may have considerable power over political incumbents, as a result, in part, of their permanence within the political bureaucracy, as contrasted to public officials, who are replaced rather frequently.[5] Weber noted how the low-ranking bureaucrat becomes familiar with the organization—its rules and operations, the work flow, and so on—which gives him considerable power over the new political incumbent, who might have higher rank but is not as familiar with the organization. While Weber does not directly state the point, his analysis suggests that bureaucratic permanence has some relationship to increased access to persons, information, and instrumentalities. To state the hypothesis suggested somewhat more formally:

H1 Other factors remaining constant, organizational power is related to access to persons, information, and instrumentalities.

H2 Other factors remaining constant, as a participant's length of time in an organization increases, he has increased access to persons, information, and instrumentalities. . . .

IMPLICATIONS OF ROLE THEORY FOR THE STUDY OF POWER

Role theorists approach the question of influence and power in terms of the behavioral regularities which result from established identities within specific social contexts like families, hospitals, and business firms. The underlying premise of most role theorists is that a large proportion of all behavior is brought about through socialization within specific organizations, and much behavior is routine and established through learning the traditional modes of adaptation in dealing with specific tasks. Thus the positions persons occupy in an organization account for much of their behavior. Norms and roles serve as mediating forces in influence processes.

While role theorists have argued much about vocabulary, the basic premises underlying their thought have been

similar emphasis on dependence, see Richard M. Emerson, "Power-Dependence Relationships," *American Sociological Review*, 28(1962), 31–41.

[4] Although this paper will not attempt to explain how access may be measured, the author feels confident that the hypotheses concerned with access are clearly testable.

[5] Max Weber, "The Essentials of Bureaucratic Organization: An Ideal-Type Construction," in Robert Merton *et al.*, *Reader in Bureaucracy* (Glencoe, Ill., 1952), pp. 18–27.

rather consistent. The argument is essentially that knowledge of one's identity or social position is a powerful index of the expectations such a person is likely to face in various social situations. Since behavior tends to be highly correlated with expectations, prediction of behavior is therefore possible. The approach of role theorists to the study of behavior within organizations is of particular merit in that it provides a consistent set of concepts which is useful analytically in describing recruitment, socialization, interaction, and personality, as well as the formal structure of organizations. Thus the concept of role is one of the few concepts clearly linking social structure, social process, and social character. . . .

It should be clear that lower participants will be more likely to circumvent higher authority, other factors remaining constant, when the mandates of those in power, if not the authority itself, are regarded as illegitimate. Thus as Etzioni points out, when lower participants become alienated from the organization, coercive power is likely to be required if its formal mandates are to be fulfilled.[6]

Moreover, all organizations must maintain control over lower participants. To the extent that lower participants fail to recognize the legitimacy of power, or believe that sanctions cannot or will not be exercised when violations occur, the organization loses, to some extent, its ability to control their behavior. Moreover, in-so-far as higher participants can create the impression that they can or will exert sanctions above their actual willingness to use such sanctions, control over lower participants will increase. It is usually to the advantage of an organization to externalize and impersonalize controls, however, and if possible to develop positive sentiments toward its rules.

In other words, an effective organization can control its participants in such a way as to make it hardly perceivable that it exercises the control that it does. It seeks commitment from lower participants, and when commitment is obtained, surveillance can be relaxed. On the other hand, when the power of lower participants in organizations is considered, it often appears to be clearly divorced from the traditions, norms, and goals and sentiments of the organization as a whole. Lower participants do not usually achieve control by using the role structure of the organization, but rather by circumventing, sabotaging, and manipulating it.

SOURCES OF POWER OF LOWER PARTICIPANTS

The most effective way for lower participants to achieve power is to obtain, maintain, and control access to persons, information, and instrumentalities. To the extent that this can be accomplished, lower participants make higher-ranking participants dependent upon them. Thus dependence together with the manipulation of the dependency relationship is the key to the power of lower participants.

A number of examples can be cited which illustrate the preceding point. Scheff, for example, reports on the failure of a state mental hospital to bring about intended reform because of the opposition of hospital attendants.[7] He noted that the power of hospital attendants was largely a result of the dependence of ward physicians on attendants. This dependence resulted from the physician's short tenure, his lack of interest in administration, and the large amount

[6] Etzioni, *op. cit.*

[7] Thomas J. Scheff, Control over Policy by Attendants in a Mental Hospital, *Journal of Health and Human Behavior*, 2 (1961), 93–105.

of administrative responsibility he had to assume. An implicit trading agreement developed between physicians and attendants, whereby attendants would take on some of the responsibilities and obligations of the ward physician in return for increased power in decision-making processes concerning patients. Failure of the ward physician to honor his part of the agreement resulted in information being withheld, disobedience, lack of co-operation, and unwillingness of the attendants to serve as a barrier between the physician and a ward full of patients demanding attention and recognition. When the attendant withheld co-operation, the physician had difficulty in making a graceful entrance and departure from the ward, in handling necessary paper work (officially his responsibility), and in obtaining information needed to deal adequately with daily treatment and behavior problems. When attendants opposed change, they could wield influence by refusing to assume responsibilities officially assigned to the physician.

Similarly, Sykes describes the dependence of prison guards on inmates and the power obtained by inmates over guards.[8] He suggests that although guards could report inmates for disobedience, frequent reports would give prison officials the impression that the guard was unable to command obedience. The guard, therefore, had some stake in ensuring the good behavior of prisoners without use of formal sanctions against them. The result was a trading agreement whereby the guard allowed violations of certain rules in return for co-operative behavior. A similar situation is found in respect to officers in the Armed Services or foremen in industry. To the extent that they require formal sanctions to bring about co-operation, they are usually perceived by their superiors as less valuable to the organization. For a good leader is expected to command obedience, at least, if not commitment.

FACTORS AFFECTING POWER

Expertise

Increasing specialization and organizational growth has made the expert or staff person important. The expert maintains power because high-ranking persons in the organization are dependent upon him for his special skills and access to certain kinds of information. One possible reason for lawyers obtaining many high governmental offices is that they are likely to have access to rather specialized but highly important means to organizational goals.[9]

We can state these ideas in hypotheses, as follows:

H3 Other factors remaining constant, to the extent that a low-ranking participant has important expert knowledge not available to high-ranking participants, he is likely to have power over them.

Power stemming from expertise, however, is likely to be limited unless it is difficult to replace the expert. This leads to two further hypotheses:

H4 Other factors remaining constant, a person difficult to replace will

[8] Gresham M. Sykes, "The Corruption of Authority and Rehabilitation," in A. Etzioni, ed., *Complex Organizations* (New York, 1961), pp. 191–197.

[9] As an example, it appears that 6 members of the cabinet, 30 important subcabinet officials, 63 senators, and 230 congressmen are lawyers (*New Yorker*, April 14, 1962, p. 62). Although one can cite many reasons for lawyers holding political posts, an important one appears to be their legal expertise.

> have greater power than a person easily replaceable.
>
> *H5* Other factors remaining constant, experts will be more difficult to replace than non-experts. . . .

The application of our hypothesis about expertise is clearly relevant if we look at certain organizational issues. For example, the merits of medical versus lay hospital administrators are often debated. It should be clear, however, that all other factors remaining unchanged, the medical administrator has clear advantage over the lay administrator. Where lay administrators receive preference, there is an implicit assumption that the lay person is better at administrative duties. This may be empirically valid but is not necessarily so. The special expert knowledge of the medical administrator stems from his ability legitimately to oppose a physician who contests an administrative decision on the basis of medical necessity. Usually hospitals are viewed primarily as universalistic in orientation both by the general public and most of their participants. Thus medical necessity usually takes precedence over management policies, a factor contributing to the poor financial position of most hospitals. The lay administrator is not in a position to contest such claims independently, since he usually lacks the basis for evaluation of the medical problems involved and also lacks official recognition of his competence to make such decisions. If the lay administrator is to evaluate these claims adequately on the basis of professional necessity, he must have a group of medical consultants or a committee of medical men to serve as a buffer between medical staff and the lay administration.

As a result of growing specialization, expertise is increasingly important in organizations. As the complexity of organizational tasks increases, and as organizations grow in size, there is a limit to responsibility that can be efficiently exercised by one person. Delegation of responsibility occurs, experts and specialists are brought in to provide information and research, and the higher participants become dependent upon them. Experts have tremendous potentialities for power by withholding information, providing incorrect information, and so on, and to the extent that experts are dissatisfied, the probability of organizational sabotage increases.

Effort and Interest

The extent to which lower participants may exercise power depends in part on their willingness to exert effort in areas where higher-ranking participants are often reluctant to participate. Effort exerted is directly related to a degree of interest one has in an area.

> *H6* Other factors remaining constant, there is a direct relationship between the amount of effort a person is willing to exert in an area and the power he can command.

For example, secretarial staffs in universities often have power to make decisions about the purchase and allocation of supplies, the allocation of their services, the scheduling of classes, and, at times, the disposition of student complaints. Such control may in some instances lead to sanctions against a professor by polite reluctance to furnish supplies, ignoring his preferences for the scheduling of classes, and giving others preference in the allocation of services. While the power to make such decisions may easily be removed from the jurisdiction of the lower participant, it can only be accomplished at a cost—the willingness to allocate time and effort to the decisions dealing with these matters. To the extent that responsibilities are delegated to lower participants, a certain degree of power is likely to accompany the responsibility. Also, should the lower participant see his perceived rights in jeopardy, he may sabotage the system in various ways. . . .

When an organization gives discretion to lower participants, it is usually trading the power of discretion for needed flexibility. The cost of constant surveillance is too high, and the effort required too great; it is very often much easier for all concerned to allow the secretary discretion in return for cooperation and not too great an abuse of power.

> *H7* Other factors remaining constant, the less effort and interest high-ranking participants are willing to devote to a task, the more likely are lower participants to obtain power relevant to this task.

Attractiveness

Another personal attribute associated with the power of low-ranking persons in an organization is attractiveness or what some call "personality." People who are viewed as attractive are more likely to obtain access to persons, and, once such access is gained, they may be more likely to succeed in promoting a cause. But once again dependence is the key to the power of attractiveness, for whether a person is dependent upon another for a service he provides, or for approval or affection, what is most relevant is the relational bond which is highly valued.

> *H8* Other factors remaining constant, the more attractive a person, the more likely he is to obtain access to persons and control over these persons.

Location and Position

In any organization the person's location in physical space and position in social space are important factors influencing access to persons, information, and instrumentalities.[10] Propinquity affects the opportunities for interaction, as well as one's position within a communication network. Although these are somewhat separate factors, we shall refer to their combined effect as centrality[11] within the organization.

> *H9* Other factors remaining constant, the more central a person is in an organization, the greater is his access to persons, information, and instrumentalities.

Some low participants may have great centrality within an organization. An executive's or university president's secretary not only has access, but often controls access in making appointments and scheduling events. Although she may have no great formal authority, she may have considerable power.

Coalitions

It should be clear that the variables we are considering are at different levels of analysis; some of them define attributes of persons, while others define attributes of communication and organization. Power processes within organizations are particularly interesting in that there

[10] There is considerable data showing the powerful effect of propinquity on communication. For summary, see Thibaut and Kelley, *op. cit.*, pp. 39–42.

[11] The concept of centrality is generally used in a more technical sense in the work of Bavelas, Shaw, Gilchrist, and others. For example, Bavelas defines the central region of a structure as the class of all cells with the smallest distance between one cell and any other cell in the structure, with distance measured in link units. Thus the most central position in a pattern is the position closest to all others. Cf. Harold Leavitt, "Some Effects of Certain Communication Patterns on Group Performance," in E. Maccoby, T. N. Newcomb, and E. L. Hartley, eds., *Reading in Social Psychology* (New York, 1958), p. 559.

are many channels of power and ways of achieving it.

In complex organizations different occupational groups attend to different functions, each group often maintaining its own power structure within the organization. Thus hospitals have administrators, medical personnel, nursing personnel, attendants, maintenance personnel, laboratory personnel, and so on. Universities, similarly, have teaching personnel, research personnel, administrative personnel, maintenance personnel, and so on. Each of these functional tasks within organizations often becomes the sphere of a particular group that controls activities relating to the task. While these tasks usually are coordinated at the highest levels of the organization, they often are not coordinated at intermediate and lower levels. It is not unusual, however, for coalitions to form among lower participants in these multiple structures. A secretary may know the man who manages the supply of stores, or the person assigning parking stickers. Such acquaintances may give her the ability to handle informally certain needs that would be more time-consuming and difficult to handle formally. Her ability to provide services informally makes higher-ranking participants in some degree dependent upon her, thereby giving her power, which increases her ability to bargain on issues important to her.

Rules

In organizations with complex power structures, lower participants can use their knowledge of the norms of the organization to thwart attempted change. In discussing the various functions of bureaucratic rules, Gouldner maintains that such rules serve as excellent substitutes for surveillance, since surveillance in addition to being expensive in time and effort arouses considerable hostility and antagonism.[12] Moreover, he argues, rules are a functional equivalent for direct, personally given orders, since they specify the obligations of workers to do things in specific ways. Standardized rules, in addition, allow simple screening of violations, facilitate remote control, and to some extent legitimize punishment when the rule is violated. The worker who violates a bureaucratic rule has little recourse to the excuse that he did not know what was expected, as he might claim for a direct order. Finally, Gouldner argues that rules are "the 'chips' to which the company staked the supervisors and which they could use to play the game";[13] that is, rules established a punishment which could be withheld, and this facilitated the supervisors' bargaining power with lower participants.

While Gouldner emphasizes the functional characteristics of rules within an organization, it should be clear that full compliance to all the rules at all times will probably be dysfunctional for the organization. Complete and apathetic compliance may do everything but facilitate achievement of organizational goals. Lower participants who are familiar with an organization and its rules can often find rules to support their contention that they not do what they have been asked to do, and rules are also often a rationalization for inaction on their part. The following of rules becomes especially complex when associations and unions become involved, for there are then two sets of rules to which the participant can appeal.

What is suggested is that rules may be chips for everyone concerned in the game. Rules become the "chips" through

[12] Alvin W. Gouldner, *Patterns of Industrial Bureaucracy* (Glencoe, Ill., 1954).

[13] *Ibid.*, p. 173.

which the bargaining process is maintained. Scheff, as noted earlier, observed that attendants in mental hospitals often took on responsibilities assigned legally to the ward physician, and when attendants refused to share these responsibilities the physician's position became extremely difficult.[14]. . . .

Given the time-consuming formal chores of the physician, and his many other duties, he usually worked out an arrangement with the ward personnel, particularly the charge (supervisory attendant), to handle these duties. On several wards, the charge called specific problems to the doctor's attention, and the two of them, in effect, would have a consultation. The charge actually made most of the decisions concerning dosage change in the back wards. Since the doctor delegated portions of his formal responsibilities to the charge, he was dependent on her good will toward him. If she withheld her co-operation, the physician had absolutely no recourse but to do all the work himself.[15]. . .

There are occasions, of course, when rules are regarded as illegitimate by lower participants, and they may disregard them. Gouldner observed that, in the mine, men felt they could resist authority in a situation involving danger to themselves.[16] They did not feel that they could legitimately be ordered to do anything that would endanger their lives. It is probably significant that in extremely dangerous situations organizations are more likely to rely on commitment to work than on authority. Even within nonvoluntary groups dangerous tasks are regarded usually as requiring task commitment, and it is likely that commitment is a much more powerful organizational force than coercive authority. . . .

[14] Scheff, *op. cit.*

[15] *Ibid.*, p. 97.

[16] Gouldner, *op. cit.*

35

Who Gets Power—And How They Hold on to It: A Strategic-Contingency Model of Power

Gerald R. Salancik and Jeffrey Pfeffer

Power is held by many people to be a dirty word or, as Warren Bennis has said, "It is the organization's last dirty secret."

This article will argue that traditional "political" power, far from being a dirty business, is, in its most naked form, one of the few mechanisms available for aligning an organization with its own reality. However, institutionalized forms of power—what we prefer to call the cleaner forms of power: authority, legitimization, centralized control, regulations, and the more modern "management information systems"—tend to buffer the organization from reality and obscure the demands of its environment. Most great states and institutions declined, not because they played politics, but because they failed to accommodate to the political realities they faced. Political processes, rather then being mechanisms for unfair and unjust allocations and appointments, tend toward the realistic resolution of conflicts among interests. And power, while it eludes definition, is easy enough to recognize by its consequences—the ability of those who possess power to bring about the outcomes they desire.

The model of power we advance is an elaboration of what has been called strategic-contingency theory, a view that sees power as something that accrues to organizational subunits (individuals, departments) that cope with critical organizational problems. Power is used by subunits, indeed, used by all who have it, to enhance their own survival through control of scarce critical resources, through the placement of allies in key positions, and through the definition of organizational problems and policies. Because of the processes by which power develops and is used, organizations become both more aligned and more misaligned with their environments. This contradiction is the most interesting aspect of organizational power, and one that makes administration one of the most precarious of occupations.

WHAT IS ORGANIZATIONAL POWER?

You can walk into most organizations and ask without fear of being misunderstood, "Which are the powerful groups or people in this organization?" Although many organizational informants may be *unwilling* to tell you, it is unlikely they will be *unable* to tell you. Most people do not require explicit definitions to know what power is.

Power is simply the ability to get things done the way one wants them to be done. For a manager who wants an in-

Source: Reprinted by permission of the publisher from *Organizational Dynamics* (Winter 1977), © 1977 American Management Association, New York. All rights reserved.

creased budget to launch a project that he thinks is important, his power is measured by his ability to get that budget. For an executive vice-president who wants to be chairman, his power is evidenced by his advancement toward his goal.

People in organizations not only know what you are talking about when you ask who is influential but they are likely to agree with one another to an amazing extent. . . .

WHERE DOES ORGANIZATIONAL POWER COME FROM?

Earlier we stated that power helps organizations become aligned with their realities. This hopeful prospect follows from what we have dubbed the strategic-contingencies theory of organizational power. Briefly, those subunits most able to cope with the organization's critical problems and uncertainties acquire power. In its simplest form, the strategic-contingencies theory implies that when an organization faces a number of lawsuits that threaten its existence, the legal department will gain power and influence over organizational decisions. Somehow other organizational interest groups will recognize its critical importance and confer upon it a status and power never before enjoyed. This influence may extend beyond handling legal matters and into decisions about product design, advertising production, and so on. Such extensions undoubtedly would be accompanied by appropriate, or acceptable, verbal justifications. In time, the head of the legal department may become the head of the corporation, just as in times past the vice-president for marketing had become the president when market shares were a worrisome problem and, before him, the chief engineer, who had made the production line run as smooth as silk.

Stated in this way, the strategic-contingencies theory of power paints an appealing picture of power. To the extent that power is determined by the critical uncertainties and problems facing the organization and, in turn, influences decisions in the organization, the organization is aligned with the realities it faces. In short, power facilitates the organization's adaptation to its environment—or its problems. . . .

Ignoring Critical Consequences

When organizational members are not aware of the critical contingencies they face, and do not share influence accordingly, the failure to do so can create havoc. In one case, an insurance company's regional office was having problems with the performance of one of its departments, the coding department. From the outside, the department looked like a disaster area. The clerks who worked in it were somewhat dissatisfied; their supervisor paid little attention to them, and they resented the hard work. Several other departments were critical of this manager, claiming that she was inconsistent in meeting deadlines. The person most critical was the claims manager. He resented having to wait for work that was handled by her department, claiming that it held up his claims adjusters. Having heard the rumors about dissatisfaction among her subordinates, he attributed the situation to poor supervision. He was second in command in the office, and therefore took up the issue with her immediate boss, the head of administrative services. They consulted with the personnel manager and the three of them concluded that the manager needed leadership training to improve her relations with her subordinates. The coding manager objected, saying it was a waste of time, but agreed to go along with the training and also agreed to give more priority to the claims department's work. Within a week after the training, the results showed that her workers were happier but that the performance of her department had decreased, save for the people serving the claims department.

About this time, we began, quite independently, a study of influence in this organization. We asked the administrative services director to draw up flow charts of how the work of one department moved on to the next department. In the course of the interview, we noticed that the coding department began or interceded in the work flow of most of the other departments and casually mentioned to him, "The coding manager must be very influential." He said, "No, not really. Why would you think so?" Before we could reply, he had recounted the story of her leadership training and the fact that things were worse. We then told him that it seemed obvious that the coding department would be influential from the fact that all the other departments depended on it. It was also clear why productivity had fallen. The coding manager took the training seriously and began spending more of her time raising her workers' spirits than she did worrying about problems of all the departments that depended on her. Giving priority to the claims area only exaggerated the problem, for their work was getting done at the expense of the work of the other departments. Eventually the company hired a few more clerks to relieve the pressure in the coding department and performance returned to a more satisfactory level.

Originally we got involved with this insurance company to examine how the influence of each manager evolved from his or her department's handling of critical organizational contingencies. We reasoned that one of the most important contingencies faced by all profit-making organizations was that of generating income. Thus we expected managers would be influential to the extent to which they contributed to this function. Such was the case. The underwriting managers, who wrote the policies that committed the premiums, were the most influential; the claims managers, who kept a lid on the funds flowing out, were a close second. Least influential were the managers of functions unrelated to revenue, such as mailroom and payroll managers. And contrary to what the administrative services manager believed, the third most powerful department head (out of 21) was the woman in charge of the coding function, which consisted of rating, recording, and keeping track of the codes of all policy applications and contracts. Her peers attributed more influence to her than could have been inferred from her place on the organization chart. And it was not surprising, since they all depended on her department. The coding department's records, their accuracy and speed with which they could be retrieved, affected virtually every other operating department in the insurance office. The underwriters depended on them in getting the contracts straight; the typing department depended on them in preparing the formal contract document; the claims department depended on them in adjusting claims; and accounting depended on them for billing. Unfortunately, the "bosses" were not aware of these dependences, . . . while the coding manager, who was a hardworking but quiet person, did little to announce her importance.

The cases of this plant and office illustrate nicely a basic point about the source of power in organizations. The basis for power in an organization derives from the ability of a person or subunit to take or not take actions that are desired by others. . . . Whether power is used to influence anything is a separate issue. We should not confuse this issue with the fact that power derives from a social situation in which one person has a capacity to do something and another person does not, but wants it done.

POWER SHARING IN ORGANIZATIONS

Power is shared in organizations, and it is shared out of necessity more than out of concern for principles of organizational development or participatory democracy. Power is shared because no one person controls all the desired activities in the organization. While the factory owner may hire people to operate his noisy machines, once hired they have some control over the use of the machinery. And thus they have power over him in the same way he has power over them. Who has more power over whom is a mooter point than that of recognizing the inherent nature of organizing as a sharing of power. . . .

Because power derives from activities rather than individuals, an individual's or subgroup's power is never absolute and derives ultimately from the context of the situation. The amount of power an individual has at any one time depends, not only on the activities he or she controls, but also on the existence of other persons or means by which the activities can be achieved and on those who determine what ends are desired and, hence, on what activities are desired and critical for the organization. One's own power always depends on other people for these two reasons. Other people, or groups or organizations, can determine the definition of what is a critical contingency for the organization and can also undercut the uniqueness of the individual's personal contribution to the critical contingencies of the organization.

Perhaps one can best appreciate how situationally dependent power is by examining how it is distributed. In most societies, power organizes around scarce and critical resources. Rarely does power organize around abundant resources. In the United States, a person doesn't become powerful because he or she can drive a car. There are simply too many others who can drive with equal facility. In certain villages in Mexico, on the other hand, a person with a car is accredited with enormous social status and plays a key role in the community. In addition to scarcity, power is also limited by the need for one's capacities in a social system. While a racer's ability to drive a car around a 90° turn at 80 mph may be sparsely distributed in a society, it is not likely to lend the driver much power in the society. The ability simply does not play a central role in the activities of the society.

The fact that power revolves around scarce and critical activities, of course, makes the control and organization of those activities a major battleground in struggles for power. Even relatively abundant or trivial resources can become the bases for power if one can organize and control their allocation and the definition of what is critical. Many occupational and professional groups attempt to do just this in modern economies. Lawyers organize themselves into associations, regulate the entrance requirements for novitiates, and then get laws passed specifying situations that require the services of an attorney. Workers had little power in the conduct of industrial affairs until they organized themselves into closed and controlled systems. In recent years, women and blacks have tried to define themselves as important and critical to the social system, using law to reify their status. . . .

The power to define what is critical in an organization is no small power. Moreover, it is key to understanding why organizations are either aligned with their environments or misaligned. If an organization defines certain activities as critical when in fact they are not critical, given the flow of resources coming into the organization, it is not likely to survive, at least in its present form.

Most organizations manage to evolve a distribution of power and influence that is aligned with the critical realities they face in the environment. The environment, in turn, includes both the internal environment, the shifting situational contexts in which particular decisions get made, and the external environment that it can hope to influence but is unlikely to control.

THE CRITICAL CONTINGENCIES

The critical contingencies facing most organizations derive from the environmental context within which they operate. This determines the available needed resources and thus determines the problems to be dealt with. That power organizes around handling these problems suggests an important mechanism by which organizations keep in tune with their external environments. The strategic-contingencies model implies that subunits that contribute to the critical resources of the organization will gain influence in the organization. Their influence presumably is then used to bend the organization's activities to the contingencies that determine its resources. This idea may strike one as obvious. But its obviousness in no way diminishes its importance. Indeed, despite its obviousness, it escapes the notice of many organizational analysts and managers, who all too frequently think of the organization in terms of a descending pyramid, in which all the departments in one tier hold equal power and status. This presumption denies the reality that departments differ in the contributions they are believed to make to the overall organization's resources, as well as to the fact that some are more equal than others.

Because of the importance of this idea to organizational effectiveness, we decided to examine it carefully in a large midwestern university. A university offers an excellent site for studying power. It is composed of departments with nominally equal power and is administered by a central executive structure much like other bureaucracies. However, at the same time it is a situation in which the departments have clearly defined identities and face diverse external environments. Each department has its own bodies of knowledge, its own institutions, its own sources of prestige and resources. Because the departments operate in different external environments, they are likely to contribute differentially to the resources of the overall organization. Thus a physics department with close ties to NASA may contribute substantially to the funds of the university; and a history department with a renowned historian in residence may contribute to the intellectual credibility or prestige of the whole university. Such variations permit one to examine how these various contributions lead to obtaining power within the university.

We analyzed the influence of 29 university departments throughout an 18-month period in their history. Our chief interest was to determine whether departments that brought more critical resources to the university would be more powerful than departments that contributed fewer or less critical resources.

To identify the critical resources each department contributed, the heads of all departments were interviewed about the importance of seven different resources to the university's success. The seven included undergraduate students (the factor determining the size of the state allocations by the university), national prestige, administrative expertise, and so on. The most critical resource was found to be contract and grant monies received by a department's faculty for research or consulting services. At this university, contract and grants contributed somewhat less than 50 percent of the overall budget, with the remainder primarily coming from state appropriations. The importance attributed to contract and grant monies, and the rather minor importance of undergraduate students, was not surprising for this particular university. The university was a major center for graduate education; many of its departments ranked in the top ten of their respective fields. Grant and contract monies were the primary source of discretionary funding available for maintaining these programs of graduate education, and hence for maintaining the university's prestige. The prestige of the university itself was critical both in recruiting able students and attracting top-notch faculty.

From university records it was determined what relative contributions each of the 29 departments made to the various needs of the university (national prestige, outside grants, teaching). Thus, for instance, one department may have contributed to the university by teaching 7 percent of the instructional units, bringing in 2 percent of the outside contracts and grants, and having a national ranking of 20. Another department, on the other hand, may have taught one percent of the instructional units, contributed 12 percent to the grants, and be ranked the third best department in its field within the country.

The question was: Do these different contributions determine the relative power of the departments within the university? Power was measured in several ways; but regardless of how measured, the answer was "yes." Those three resources together accounted for about 70 percent of the variance in subunit power in the university.

But the most important predictor of departmental power was the department's contribution to the contracts and grants of the university. Sixty percent of the variance in power was due to this one factor, suggesting that the power of departments derived primarily from the dollars they provided for graduate education, the activity believed to be the most important for the organization.

THE IMPACT OF ORGANIZATIONAL POWER ON DECISION MAKING

While it is perhaps not absolutely valid, we can generally gauge the relative importance of a department of an organization by the size of the budget allocated to it relative to other departments. Clearly it is of importance to the administrators of those departments whether they get squeezed in a budget crunch or are given more funds to strike out after new opportunities. And it should also be clear that when those decisions are made and one department can go ahead and try new approaches while another must cut back on the old, then the deployment of the resources of the organization in meeting its problems is most directly affected.

Thus our study of the university led us to ask the following question: Does power lead to influence in the organization? To answer this question, we found it useful first to ask another one, namely: Why should department heads try to influence organizational decisions to favor their own departments to the exclusion of the other departments? While this second question may seem a bit naive to anyone who has witnessed the political realities of organizations, we posed it in a context of research on organizations that sees power as an illegitimate threat to the neater rational authority of modern bureaucracies. In this context, decisions are not believed to be made because of the dirty business of politics but because of the overall goals and purposes of the organization. In a university, one reasonable basis for decision making is the teaching workload of departments and the demands that follow from that workload. We would expect, therefore, that departments with heavy student demands for courses would be able to obtain funds for teaching. Another reasonable basis for decision making is quality. We would expect, for that reason, that departments with esteemed reputations would be able to obtain funds both because their quality suggests they might use such funds effectively and because such funds would allow them to maintain their quality. A rational model of bureaucracy intimates, then, that the organizational decisions taken would favor those who perform the stated purposes of the organization—teaching undergraduates and training professional and scientific talent—well.

The problem with rational models of decision making, however, is that what is rational to one person may strike another as irrational. For most departments, resources are a question of survival. . . . Thus goals rather than being clearly defined and universally agreed upon are blurred and contested throughout the organization. If such is the case, then the decisions taken on behalf of the organization as a whole are likely to reflect the goals of those who prevail in political contests, namely, those with power in the organization. . . .

We have examined three conditions that are likely to affect the use of power in organizations: scarcity, criticality, and uncertainty. The first suggests that subunits will try to exert influence when the resources of the organization are scarce. If there is an abundance of resources, then a particular department or a particular individual has little need to attempt influence. With little effort, he can get all he wants anyway.

The second condition, criticality, suggests that a subunit will attempt to influence decisions to obtain resources that are critical to its own survival and activities. Criticality implies that one would not waste effort, or risk being labeled obstinate, by fighting over trivial decisions affecting one's operations. . . .

The third condition that we believe affects the use of power is uncertainty: When individuals do not agree about what the organization should do or how to do it, power and other social processes will affect decisions. The reason for this is simply that, if there are no clear-cut criteria available for resolving conflicts of interest, then the only means for resolution is some form of social process, including power, status, social ties, or some arbitrary process like flipping a coin or drawing straws. Under conditions of uncertainty, the powerful manager can argue his case on any grounds and usually win it. Since there is no real consensus, other contestants are not likely to develop counter arguments or amass sufficient opposition. Moreover, because of his power and their need for access to the resources he controls, they are more likely to defer to his arguments.

Although the evidence is slight, we have found that power will influence the allocations of scarce and critical resources. In the analysis of power in the university, for instance, one of the most critical resources needed by departments is the general budget. First granted by the state legislature, the general budget is later allocated to individual departments by the university administration in response to requests from the department heads. Our analysis of the factors that contribute to a department getting more or less of this budget indicated that subunit power was the major predictor, overriding such factors as student demand for courses, national reputations of departments, or even the size of a department's faculty. Moreover, other research has shown that when the general budget has been cut back or held below previous uninflated levels, leading to monies becoming more scarce, budget allocations mirror departmental powers even more closely.

Student enrollment and faculty size, of course, do themselves relate to budget allocations, as we would expect since they determine a department's need for resources, or at least offer visible testimony of needs. But departments are not always able to get what they need by the mere fact of needing them. In one analysis it was found that high-power departments were able to obtain budget without regard to their teaching loads and, in some cases, actually in inverse relation to their teaching loads. In contrast, low-power departments could get increases in budget only when they could justify the increases by a recent growth in teaching load, and then only when it was far in excess of norms for other departments. . . .

When the four resources were arrayed from the most to the least critical and scarce, we found that departmental power best predicted the allocations of the most critical and scarce resources. In other words, the analysis of how power influences organizational allocations leads to this conclusion: Those subunits most likely to survive in times of strife are those that are more critical to the organization. Their importance to the organization gives them power to influence resource allocations that enhance their own survival.

HOW EXTERNAL ENVIRONMENT IMPACTS EXECUTIVE SELECTION

Power not only influences the survival of key groups in an organization, it also influences the selection of individuals to key leadership positions, and by such a process further aligns the organization with its environmental context. . . .

As with the selection of administrators, the context of organizations has also been found to affect the removal of executives. The environment, as a source of organizational problems, can make it more or less difficult for executives to demonstrate their value to the organization. In the hospitals we studied, long-term administrators came from hospitals with few problems. They enjoyed amicable and stable relations with their local business and social communities and suffered little competition for funding and staff. The small city hospital director who attended civic and Elks meetings while running the only hospital within a 100-mile radius, for example, had little difficulty holding on to his job. Turnover was highest in hospitals with the most problems, a phenomenon similar to that observed in a study of industrial organizations in which turnover was highest among executives in industries with competitive environments and unstable market conditions. The interesting thing is that instability characterized the industries rather than the individual firms in them. The troublesome conditions in the individual firms were attributed, or rather misattributed, to the executives themselves.

It takes more than problems, however, to terminate a manager's leadership. . . . For those hospitals dependent upon private donations, the length of an administrator's term depended not at all on the status of the operating budget but was fairly predictable from the hospital's relations with the business community.

On the other hand, in hospitals dependent on the operating budget for capital financing, the greater the deficit the shorter was the tenure of the hospital's principal administrators.

CHANGING CONTINGENCIES AND ERODING POWER BASES

The critical contingencies facing the organization may change. When they do, it is reasonable to expect that the power of individuals and subgroups will change in turn. . . .

One implication of the idea that power shifts with changes in organizational environments is that the dominant coalition will tend to be that group that is most appropriate for the organization's environment, as also will the leaders of an organization. . . .

THE NONADAPTIVE CONSEQUENCES OF ADAPTATION

From what we have said thus far about power aligning the organization with its own realities, an intelligent person might react with a resounding ho-hum, for it all seems too obvious: Those with the ability to get the job done are given the job to do.

However, there are two aspects of power that make it more useful for understanding organizations and their effectiveness. First, the "job" to be done has a way of expanding itself until it becomes less and less clear what the job is. Napoleon began by doing a job for France in the war with Austria and ended up Emperor, convincing many that only he could keep the peace. Hitler began by promising an end to Germany's troubling postwar depression and ended up convincing more people than is comfortable to remember that he was destined to be the savior of the world. In short, power is a capacity for influence that extends far beyond the original bases that created it. Second, power tends to take on institutionalized forms that enable it to endure well beyond its usefulness to an organization.

There is an important contradiction in what we have observed about organizational power. On the one hand we have said that power derives from the contingencies facing an organization and that when those contingencies change so do the bases for power. On the other hand we have asserted that subunits will tend to use their power to influence organizational decisions in their own favor, particularly when their own survival is threatened by the scarcity of critical resources. The first statement implies that an organization will tend to be aligned with its environment since power will tend to bring to key positions those with capabilities relevant to the context. The second implies that those in power will not give up their positions so easily; they will pursue policies that guarantee their continued domination. In short, change and stability operate through the same mechanism, and, as a result, the organization will never be completely in phase with its environment or its needs. . . .

MISTAKING CRITICAL CONTINGENCIES

One thing that allows subunits to retain their power is their ability to name their functions as critical to the organization when they may not be. Consider again our discussion of power in the university. One might wonder why the most critical tasks were defined as graduate education and scholarly research, the effect of which was to lend power to those who brought in grants and contracts. Why not something else? The reason is that the more powerful departments argued for those criteria and won their case, partly because they were more powerful.

In another analysis of this university, we found that all departments advocate self-serving criteria for budget allocation. Thus a department with large undergraduate enrollments argued that enrollments should determine budget allocations, a department with a strong national reputation saw prestige as the most reasonable basis for distributing funds, and so on. We further found that advocating such self-serving criteria actually benefited a department's budget allotments but, also, it paid off more for departments that were already powerful.

Organizational needs are consistent with a current distribution of power also because of a human tendency to categorize problems in familiar ways. An accountant sees problems with organizational performance as cost accountancy problems or inventory flow problems. A sales manager sees them as problems with markets, promotional strategies, or just unaggressive salespeople. But what is the truth? Since it does not automatically announce itself, it is likely that those with prior credibility, or those with power, will be favored as the enlightened. This bias, while not intentionally self-serving, further concentrates power among those who already possess it, independent of changes in the organization's context.

INSTITUTIONALIZING POWER

A third reason for expecting organizational contingencies to be defined in familiar ways is that the current holders of power can structure the organization in ways that institutionalize themselves. By institutionalization we mean the establishment of relatively permanent structures and policies that favor the influence of a particular subunit. While in power, a dominant coalition has the ability to institute constitutions, rules, procedures, and information systems that limit the potential power of others while continuing their own.

The key to institutionalizing power always is to create a device that legitimates one's own authority and diminishes the legitimacy of others. When the "Divine Right of Kings" was envisioned centuries ago, it was to provide an unquestionable foundation for the supremacy of royal authority. There is generally a need to root the exercise of authority in some higher power. Modern leaders are no less affected by this need. Richard Nixon, with the aid of John Dean, reified the concept of executive privilege, which meant in effect that what the President wished not to be discussed need not be discussed.

In its simpler form, institutionalization is achieved by designating positions or roles for organizational activities. The creation of a new post legitimizes a function and forces organization members to orient to it. By designating how this new post relates to older, more established posts, moreover, one can structure an organization to enhance the importance of a function in the organization. . . .

The structures created by dominant powers sooner or later become fixed and unquestioned features of the organization. Eventually, this can be devastating. It is said that the battle of Jena in 1806 was lost by Frederick the Great, who died in 1786. Though the great Prussian leader had no direct hand in the disaster, his imprint on the army was so thorough, so embedded in its skeletal underpinnings, that the organization was inappropriate for others to lead in different times.

Another important source of institutionalized power lies in the ability to structure information systems. Setting up committees to investigate particular organizational issues and having them report only to particular individuals or groups, facilitates their awareness of problems by the members of those groups while limiting the awareness of problems by the members of other groups. Obviously, those who have information are in a better position to interpret the problems of an organization, regardless of how realistically they may, in fact, do so.

Still another way to institutionalize power is to distribute rewards and resources. The dominant group may quiet competing interest groups with small favors and rewards. The credit for this artful form of cooperation belongs to Louis XIV. To avoid usurpation of his power, by the nobles of France and the Fronde that had so troubled his father's reign, he built the palace of Versailles to occupy them with hunting and gossip. Awed, the courtiers basked in the reflected glories of the "Sun King" and the overwhelming setting he had created for his court.

At this point, we have not systematically studied the institutionalization of power. But we suspect it is an important condition that mediates between the environment of the organization and the capabilities of the organization for dealing with that environment. The more institutionalized power is within an organization, the more likely an organization will be out of phase with the realities it faces. . . .

One of the more interesting implications of institutionalized power is that executive turnover among the executives who have structured the organization is likely to be a rare event that occurs only under the most pressing crisis. If a dominant coalition is able to structure the organization and interpret the meaning of ambiguous events like declining sales and profits or lawsuits, then the "real" problems to emerge will easily be incorporated into traditional molds of thinking and acting. If opposition is designed out of the organization, the interpretations will go unquestioned. Conditions will remain stable until a crisis develops, so overwhelming and visible that even the most adroit rhetorician would be silenced.

IMPLICATIONS FOR THE MANAGEMENT OF POWER IN ORGANIZATIONS

Instead of ending with homilies, we will end with a reversal of where we began. Power, rather than being the dirty business it is often made out to be, is probably one of the few mechanisms for reality testing in organizations. And the cleaner forms of power, the institutional forms, rather than having the virtues they are often credited with, can lead the organization to become out of touch. The real trick to managing power in organizations is to ensure somehow that leaders cannot be unaware of the realities of their environments and cannot avoid changing to deal with those realities. That, however, would be like designing the "self-liquidating organization," an unlikely event since anyone capable of designing such an instrument would be obviously in control of the liquidations. . . .

One conclusion you can, and probably should, derive from our discussion is that power—because of the way it develops and the way it is used—will always result in the organization suboptimizing its performance. However, to this grim absolute, we add a comforting caveat: If any criteria other than power were the basis for determining an organization's decisions, the results would be even worse.

36
Managing with Power

Jeffrey Pfeffer

It is one thing to understand power—how to diagnose it, what are its sources, what are the strategies and tactics for its use, how it is lost. It is quite another thing to use that knowledge in the world at large. And putting the knowledge of power and influence into action—managing with power—is essential for those who seek to get things accomplished:

> "There's a thing you learn at Data General, if you work here for any period of time," said West's lieutenant of hardware, Ed Rasala, "that nothing happens unless you push it."[1]

Computers don't get built, cities don't get rebuilt, and diseases don't get fought unless advocates for change learn how to develop and use power effectively. We saw that in the early 1980s the blood banks resisted testing for transfusion-transmitted AIDS, and even denied that a contaminated blood supply was a serious health risk. The 1980s saw an increase in the political skill of the AIDS lobby, and its tactics are now being borrowed by others:

> Women with breast cancer are taking a lesson from AIDS advocacy groups and using political action to urge the Federal and state governments to pay more attention to their disease. "They showed us how to get through to the government. . . . They took an archaic system and turned it around while we have been quietly dying."[2]

Women's health issues are sorely underfunded compared to the proportion of women in the population, a situation that is likely to change if, and only if, power and influence are brought to bear on, and more importantly, *in* those organizations that fund medical research and regulate the pharmaceutical and medical industries.

In corporations, public agencies, universities, and government, the problem is how to get things done, how to move forward, how to solve the many problems facing organizations of all sizes and types. Developing and exercising power require having both will and skill. It is the will that often seems to be missing. Power and influence have a negative connotation. We hound politicians from office, and try to bring down those institutions or individuals that seek to do things differently or better. . . .

WHAT DOES IT MEAN, TO MANAGE WITH POWER?

First, it means recognizing that in almost every organization, there are varying interests. This suggests that one of the first things we need to do is to diagnose the political landscape and figure out what the relevant interests are, and what

Source: Used by permission of the *Journal of Management*.

important political subdivisions characterize the organization. It is essential that we do not assume that everyone necessarily is going to be our friend, or agree with us, or even that preferences are uniformly distributed. There are clusters of interests within organizations, and we need to understand where these are and to whom they belong.

Next, it means figuring out what point of view these various individuals and subunits have on issues of concern to us. It also means understanding why they have the perspective that they do. It is all too easy to assume that those with a different perspective are somehow not as smart as we are, not as informed, not as perceptive. If that is our belief, we are likely to do several things, each of which is disastrous. First, we may act contemptuously toward those who disagree with us—after all, if they aren't as competent or as insightful as we are, why should we take them seriously? It is rarely difficult to get along with those who resemble us in character and opinions. The real secret of success in organizations is the ability to get those who differ from us, and whom we don't necessarily like, to do what we need to be done. Second, if we think people are misinformed, we are likely to "inform" them, or to try to convince them with facts and analysis. Sometimes this will work, but often it will not, for their disagreement may not be based on a lack of information; it may, instead, arise from a different perspective on what our information means. Diagnosing the point of view of interest groups as well as the basis for their positions will assist us in negotiating with them and in predicting their response to various initiatives.

Third, managing with power means understanding that to get things done, you need power—more power than those whose opposition you must overcome—and thus it is imperative to understand where power comes from and how these sources of power can be developed. We are sometimes reluctant to think very purposefully or strategically about acquiring and using power. We are prone to believe that if we do our best, work hard, be nice, and so forth, things will work out for the best. I don't mean to imply that one should not, in general, work hard, try to make good decisions, and be nice, but that these and similar platitudes are often not very useful in helping us get things accomplished in our organizations. We need to understand power and try to get it. We must be willing to do things to build our sources of power, or else we will be less effective than we might wish to be.

Fourth, managing with power means understanding the strategies and tactics through which power is developed and used in organizations, including the importance of timing, the use of structure, the social psychology of commitment and other forms of interpersonal influence. If nothing else, such an understanding will help us become astute observers of the behavior of others. The more we understand power and its manifestations, the better will be our clinical skills. More fundamentally, we need to understand strategies and tactics of using power so that we can consider the range of approaches available to us, and use what is likely to be effective. Again, as in the case of building sources of power, we often try not to think about these things, and we avoid being strategic or purposeful about employing our power. This is a mistake. Although we may have various qualms, there will be others who do not. Knowledge without power is of remarkably little use. And power without the skill to employ it effectively is likely to be wasted.

Managing with power means more than knowing the ideas discussed in this book. It means being . . . willing to do something with that knowledge. It requires political savvy to get things done, and the willingness to force the issue.

For years in the United States, there had been demonstrations and protests, court decisions and legislative proposals attempting to end the widespread discrimination against minority Americans in employment, housing, and public accommodations. The passage of civil rights legislation was a top priority for President Kennedy, but although he had charisma, he lacked the knowledge of political tactics, and possibly the will to use some of the more forceful ones, to get his legislation passed. In the hands of someone who knew power and influence inside out, in spite of the opposition of southern congressmen and senators, the legislation would be passed quickly.

In March 1965, the United States was wracked by violent reactions to civil rights marches in the South. People were killed and injured as segregationists attacked demonstrators, with little or no intervention by the local law enforcement agencies. There were demonstrators across from the White House holding a vigil as Lyndon Johnson left to address a joint session of Congress. This was the same Lyndon Johnson who, in 1948, had opposed federal antilynching legislation, arguing that it was a matter properly left to the states. This was the same Lyndon Johnson who, as a young congressional secretary and then congressman, had talked conservative to conservatives, liberal to liberals, and was said by many to have stood for nothing. This was the same Lyndon Johnson who in eight years in the House of Representatives had introduced not one piece of significant legislation and had done almost nothing to speak out on issues of national importance. This was the same Lyndon Johnson who, while in the House, had tried instead to enrich himself by influencing colleagues at the Federal Communications Commission to help him both obtain a radio station in Austin, Texas, and change the operating license to make the station immensely profitable and valuable. This was the same Lyndon Johnson who, in 1968, having misled the American people, would decide not to run for reelection because of both his association with the Vietnam War and a fundamental distrust of the presidency felt by many Americans. On that night Johnson was to make vigorous use of his power and his political skill to help the civil rights movement:

> With almost the first words of his speech, the audience . . . knew that Lyndon Johnson intended to take the cause of civil rights further than it had ever gone before. . . . He would submit a new civil rights bill . . . and it would be far stronger than the bills of the past. . . . "Their cause must be our cause, too," Lyndon Johnson said. "Because it is not just Negroes, but really it is all of us, who must overcome the crippling legacy of bigotry and injustice. . . . And we shall overcome."[3]

As he left the chamber after making his speech, Johnson sought out the 76-year-old chairman of the House Judiciary Committee, Emmanuel Celler:

> "Manny," he said, "I want you to start hearings tonight."
>
> "Mr. President," Celler protested, "I can't push that committee or it might get out of hand. I am scheduling hearings for next week."
>
> . . . Johnson's eyes narrowed, and his face turned harder. His right hand was still shaking Celler's, but the left hand was up, and a finger was out, pointing, jabbing.
>
> "Start them *this* week, Manny," he said. "And hold night sessions, too."[4]

Getting things done requires power. The problem is that we would prefer to see the world as a kind of grand morality play, with the good guys and the bad ones easily identified. Obtaining power is not always an attractive process, nor is its use. And it somehow disturbs our sense of symmetry that a man who was as sleazy, to use a term of my students, as Lyndon Johnson was in some respects, was also the individual who almost single-handedly passed more civil rights legislation in less time with greater effect than anyone else in U.S. history. We are troubled by the issue of means and ends. We are perplexed by the fact that "bad" people sometimes do great and wonderful things, and that "good" people sometimes do "bad" things, or often, nothing at all. Every day, managers in public and private organizations acquire and use power to get things done. Some of these things may be, in retrospect, mistakes, although often that depends heavily on your point of view. Any reader who always does the correct thing that pleases everyone should immediately contact me—we will get very wealthy together. Mistakes and opposition are inevitable. What is not inevitable is passivity, not trying, not seeking to accomplish things.

In many domains of activity we have become so obsessed with not upsetting anybody, and with not making mistakes, that we settle for doing nothing. Rather than rebuild San Francisco's highways, possibly in the wrong place, maybe even the wrong way, we do nothing, and the city erodes economically without adequate transportation. Rather than possibly being wrong about a new product, such as the personal computer, we study it and analyze it, and lose market opportunities. Analysis and forethought are, obviously, fine. What is not so fine is paralysis or inaction, which arise because we have little skill in overcoming the opposition that inevitably accompanies change, and little interest in doing so.

Theodore Roosevelt, making a speech at the Sorbonne in 1910, perhaps said it best:

> It is not the critic who counts; not the man who points out how the strong man stumbles, or where the doer of deeds could have done them better. The credit belongs to the man who is actually in the arena, whose face is marred by dust and sweat and blood; who strives valiantly; who errs, and comes short again and again; because there is not effort without error and shortcoming; but who does actually strive to do the deeds; who knows the great enthusiasms, the great devotions; who spends himself in a worthy cause, who at the best knows in the end the triumphs of high achievement and who at the worst, if he fails, at least fails while daring greatly, so that his place shall never be with those cold and timid souls who know neither victory nor defeat.[5]

It is easy and often comfortable to feel powerless—to say, "I don't know what to do, I don't have the power to get it done, and besides, I can't really stomach the struggle that may be involved." It is easy, and now quite common, to say, when confronted with some mistake in your organization, "It's not really my responsibility, I can't do anything about it anyway, and if the company wants to do that, well, that's why the senior executives get the big money—it's their responsibility." Such a response excuses us from trying to do things; in not trying to overcome opposition, we will make fewer enemies and are less likely to embarrass ourselves. It is, however, a prescription for both organizational and personal failure. This is why power and influence are not the organization's last dirty secret, but the secret of success for both individuals and their organizations. Innovation and change in almost any arena require the skill to develop power, and the willingness to employ it to get things accomplished. Or, in the words of a local radio newscaster, "If you don't like the news, go out and make some of your own."

REFERENCES

1. Tracy Kidder, *Soul of a New Machine* (Boston: Atlantic-Little, Brown, 1981), 111.
2. Jane Gross, "Turning Disease Into a Cause: Breast Cancer Follows AIDS," *New York Times* (January 7, 1991): A1.
3. Robert A. Caro, *Means of Ascent: The Years of Lyndon Johnson* (New York: Alfred A. Knopf, 1990), xix–xx.
4. Ibid., xxi.
5. Richard M. Nixon, *Leaders* (New York: Warner Books, 1982), 345.

CHAPTER VI

Organizational Change

For the audience, the orchestra experience during the last few performances has been "average at best." Many members of the orchestra would say the same. Attendance is above average, and everyone is just going along with the status quo. But in this community, there are many competing options for people interested in the arts. Within the leadership group, there is a sense that "change" is necessary. The board of trustees has been talking about funding, the future, and new strategic directions. There is a vague sense of unease, a sense that things may not remain stable for long.

As rumors about a new agenda for the orchestra emerge, rumbles of resistance arise from every corner. Many believe strongly that the orchestra should hold the course. No change is needed! Why fix something that isn't broken? The signs and signals come in gradually at first—lower attendance and fewer contributions. Orchestra members start to fuss and fume among themselves. There are meetings to discuss "who is to blame" and "what should be done." The conductor sees peers across the country and internationally doing new things and orchestras going in different directions. The momentum increases for change. But what direction to take? How do we know? Experts are gathered; studies are conducted. Market research is recommended, and consultants are employed and deployed. Politics intensify as competing interests emerge. Ethics are questioned. Finances are reviewed. Orchestra members gather and bond with a sense of impending disaster. The conductor updates her resume.

Leadership emerges within the board of trustees, and a common mission and purpose is defined. The conductor takes another job, and a new conductor is hired. Positive momentum takes hold; a new agenda is crafted. The new conductor is introduced to the community with a gala kick-off. Attendance swells; everyone senses that the orchestra is on the right track. Maybe leadership has learned a thing or two.

The board recognizes that it cannot "wait as long" next time around. When success is at a high point, board members should be planning for the next changes. The unpredictable and somewhat fickle marketplace requires constant attention. Change is the norm, not the exception. Paying attention and constantly learning is a requisite. Leadership matters: the more alert the leaders are, the better the organization functions. Intelligence, leadership, learning, change, and organizational excellence are all interrelated.

To confront organizational change in theory or in practice, one must tie together and use knowledge about human motivation, leadership, group and intergroup behavior, the relationship between people and their organizational contexts, and power and influence—all from the organizational behavior perspective. In examining the historical foundations and current practice of organizational change, we must become familiar with these pivotal ideas:

- The Hawthorne experiments, as described by Fritz Roethlisberger (included in Chapter II, *Motivation*)
- Transformative leadership, as explained in the 1984 article by Noel Tichy and David Ulrich (reprinted in Chapter I, *Leadership*)
- The sociotechnical systems-oriented group at the Tavistock Institute, as represented by Eric Trist and Kenneth Bamforth's article about the consequences of changing to the longwall method of coal mining, in Chapter IV
- Survey research and feedback techniques that draw extensively from work done by Kurt Lewin and his associates
- The development of sensitivity training (or T-groups), a phenomenon that incorporates theory, research, and practice on leadership, group development and behavior, intergroup behavior, motivation, power and influence, and individual-organizational context impacts

ORGANIZATIONAL CHANGE FROM THE ORGANIZATIONAL BEHAVIOR PERSPECTIVE

The subject of organizational change has received wide attention in the literature on organizational behavior and organizational theory. Like the Hugo Münsterberg (1913) and Henry Gantt (1908) work on behavior in organizations that preceded the development of the organizational behavior perspective, much of the new writing about change in organizations is not based on familiar humanistic-type assumptions. Change has perhaps been the most visible and heated battleground between proponents of the organizational behavior perspective (and its assumptions, values, and methods) and the advocates of change through manipulation of power and/or perceptions. (For more on this subject, see Shafritz & Ott, 2001.) So organizational change provides a fitting, integrative subject with which to close this collection of classic readings in organizational behavior.

For more than forty years (since about 1960), the organizational behavior perspective's interest in change has been riveted on *planned change*. The organizational behavior/planned change perspective assumptions have constituted the mainstream of organizational behavior literature and practice for so long that it sometimes is hard to think about any other. Thus, it is instructive to first take a brief glance at one of the more recent viewpoints on organizational change. A comparison between the 1960s-style "planned change" and "transformational change" makes it easy to understand and appreciate the uniqueness of the planned organizational change assumptions.

FOR COMPARISON: A DIFFERENT VIEW OF ORGANIZATIONAL CHANGE—TRANSFORMATION

The 1984 article by Noel Tichy and David Ulrich, "The Leadership Challenge—A Call for the Transformational Leader" (reprinted in Chapter I), provides an excellent example of the transformational view of organizational change. Tichy and Ulrich call for leaders who are able to manage *planned revolutionary organizational change* ("organizational transformations"). Transformational leaders (or as some authors call them, transformative leaders [Bennis, 1984; Bennis & Nanus, 1985]) are expected to accomplish different magnitudes of organizational change (qualitative and quantitative) using strategies and methods that are not compatible with the mores of human relations/planned change perspective. Transformative leaders use *transformative power* (Bennis, 1984) or *transforming leadership* (Adams, 1986) literally to transform organizations and their cultures—to alter organizational norms, realities, beliefs, values, and assumptions (Allaire & Firsirotu, 1985; Gemmill & Smith, 1985; Kilmann & Covin, 1988). In essence, transformative change is accomplished by violating organizational norms: by creating a new vision of the organization, often through conscious manipulation of symbols, and then "selling" the new vision to important stakeholders.

ASSUMPTIONS ABOUT CHANGE FROM THE ORGANIZATIONAL BEHAVIOR/PLANNED CHANGE PERSPECTIVE

Before transformational leadership and radical change started to attract attention, the literature and practice of people-oriented organizational change had been dominated by the assumptions, beliefs, and tactics of the organizational behavior perspective. These assumptions, which provided the technological and normative direction for two decades of change-oriented organizational behavior theory and practice, were articulated most clearly by Chris Argyris in the first chapter of his seminal 1970 book, *Intervention Theory and Methods*. Although Argyris's words are descriptive, his tone and his message are very prescriptive:

> Valid information, free choice, and internal commitment are considered integral parts of any intervention activity, no matter what the substantive objectives are (for a change). These three processes are called the primary intervention tasks. (p. 17)

As Argyris lists his three primary intervention tasks, his normative assumptions become unmistakably evident:

1. Without valid, usable information (including knowledge of the consequences of alternatives), there can be no free informed choice.
2. Without free informed choice, there can be no personal responsibility for decisions.
3. Without personal responsibility for decisions, there can be no internalized commitment to the success of a decision (no *psychological ownership*).

The organizational behavior perspective also embraces strong beliefs about what constitutes organizational effectiveness. These beliefs have further steered the pursuit of organizational improvement away from the manipulation of extrinsic variables such as systems of rewards and punishments. Under this line of reasoning, organizational effectiveness is not defined as *outcomes* but rather as *ongoing process states*. Warren Bennis uses the analogy of *health* or *healthy organization* to communicate his widely accepted concept of organizational process effectiveness. Bennis has four criteria for assessing organizational health, or effectiveness (as cited in Schein, 1980, p. 232):

1. *Adaptability:* The ability to solve problems and to react with flexibility to changing environmental demands.
2. A *sense of identity:* Knowledge and insight on the part of the organization of what it is, what its goals are, and what it is to do. . . .
3. *Capacity to test reality:* The ability to search out, accurately perceive, and correctly interpret the real properties of the environment, particularly those that have relevance for the functioning of the organization.
4. *Integration:* A fourth, often-cited criterion that in effect underlies the others is a state of "integration" among the subparts of the total organization, such that the parts are not working at cross-purposes.

In a philosophically consistent vein, Schein (1980) identifies the organizational coping processes that are necessary conditions for maintaining or increasing organizational effectiveness (health):

1. The ability to take in and communicate information reliably and validly.
2. . . . internal flexibility and creativity to make changes which are demanded by the information obtained.
3. . . . integration of and commitment to the multiple goals of the organization, from which comes the willingness to change when necessary.
4. . . . an internal climate of support and freedom from threat, since being threatened undermines good communications, reduces flexibility, and stimulates self-protection rather than concern for the total system.
5. . . . the ability to continuously redesign the organization's structure to be congruent with its goal and tasks. (p. 249)

By comparing Bennis's and Schein's necessary conditions for organizational health/effectiveness with those of Hugo Münsterberg (1913) or Frederick Winslow Taylor (1911) (they are summarized in the *Introduction*), the vastness of the differences between these organizational perspectives becomes very evident. The organizational behavior perspective defines organizational effectiveness as a process state—not as it has been defined traditionally in terms of organizational outcomes such as market penetration, profitability, or quantity and/or quality levels of output.

ORGANIZATION DEVELOPMENT

The most dynamic and energetic manifestation of organizational behavior–based change has been the subfield of *organization development* or simply OD. OD is a particular form of planned organizational changes (or development) that embodies the full set of premises, assumptions, values, and strategies of the organizational behavior perspective. Although authors' definitions of organization development may vary in emphasis, most are quite consistent in substance. For example:

> Organization development is an effort (1) *planned* (2) *organization-wide*, and (3) *managed* from the *top*, to (4) *increase organization effectiveness* and *health* through (5) *planned intervention* in the organization's "process," using *behavioral-science* knowledge. (Emphasis in original) (Beckhard, 1969)

and

> Organization development is a long-range effort to improve an organization's problem-solving and renewal processes, particularly through a more effective and collaborative management of organizational culture . . . with the assistance of a change agent, or catalyst, and the use of the theory and technology of applied behavioral science, including action research. (French & Bell, 1984)

Organization development is about planned organizational change as a process or strategy. OD is as concerned about *how* planned change is implemented as it is about specifically *where* change will lead an organization. Typically, the product or result of OD activities is an ongoing set of processes for organizational renewal that are *in-and-of-themselves defined as criteria of organizational effectiveness*. OD assumes that change is purposeful and dynamic, is accomplished through application of behavioral science knowledge, and is accomplished according to carefully prescribed ground rules derived from the assumptions of the organizational behavior perspective. Thus, for example, revolutionary and evolutionary change generally are not considered to be within the purview of OD.

OD is concerned with deep, long-lasting, organization-wide change or improvement—not in superficial changes in isolated organizational pockets. This concern for the broad based and long term led OD practitioners to an interest in the concept of organizational culture long before it became a fashionable management topic in the 1980s.

OD practitioners have developed numerous strategies and techniques for improving organizations. Most of them utilize interventions facilitated by outsiders (often called *change agents*). Some of the most common strategies include organizational diagnosis, process consultation, team building (in many forms), action research, data feedback, job enlargement, job enrichment, and conflict management. But each author has his or her own preferred tactics. For example, in one of the best known such lists, Schmuck and Miles (1971) include training and education, process consultation or coaching, confrontation meetings, data feedback, problem solving, goal setting, OD task force establishment, and technostructural activity.

Thus, organization development represents a very notable effort to apply to ongoing organizational improvement an impressive array of research-based social science knowledge within a prescriptive value framework.

The origins of organization development can be traced to several events and movements that started in the 1930s and 1940s:

1. The *Hawthorne studies*
2. The *sensitivity training* (or "T-group") *movement,* which originated in the late 1940s at the National Training Laboratories, under the leadership of such luminaries as Leland Bradford
3. *Developments in survey research and feedback techniques*, particularly through the work of Kurt Lewin (1952), which presaged creation of the basic *action research* model of organizational change
4. *The sociotechnical "school" of research and analysis*, pioneered at the Tavistock Institute by Eric Trist, Kenneth Bamforth, A. K. Rice, and Elliott Jaques

The *Hawthorne studies* and their importance to understanding organizational behavior-oriented change processes are discussed extensively in the *Introduction* and in Chapter I, *Leadership*. So, other than referring the reader to Fritz Roethlisberger's "The Hawthorne Experiments" (in Chapter II), we will move on to the remaining three historical trends and events that opened the way for organization development.

The *sensitivity training (or "T-group") movement* had its start in 1946 when Kurt Lewin, Leland Bradford, Ronald Lippitt, and Kenneth Benne collaboratively conducted a training workshop to help improve race relations and community leadership in New Britain, Connecticut (Bradford, Gibb, & Benne, 1964). During their evening staff meetings, they discussed the behavior of workshop participants and the dynamics of events. Several workshop participants asked to join the night discussions, and the results of the process eventually led to the initiation and institutionalization of *T-group technology*. Although the early T-groups focused primarily on individual growth and development, they quickly were adapted for organizational application. T-groups became the method by which organizational members learned how to communicate honestly and directly about facts and feelings (Argyris, 1962). (From the human relations perspective, *feelings are facts*.) Thus, T-groups became a keystone strategy for increasing organizational effectiveness by improving interpersonal communications (e.g., feedback), reducing defensiveness (and thus rigidity), and otherwise helping organizations achieve Bennis's criteria for organizational effectiveness—adaptability, sense of identity, capacity to test reality, and integration—through the development of coping processes that are necessary conditions for maintaining or increasing organizational effectiveness:

1. The ability to take in and communicate information reliably and validly
2. The internal flexibility and creativity to make changes demanded by the information obtained
3. The integration of and commitment to the multiple goals of the organization, from which comes the willingness to change when necessary
4. An internal climate of support and freedom from threat
5. The ability to continuously redesign the organization's structure to be congruent with its goal and tasks (Schein, 1980, p. 249)

Without sensitivity training groups (T-groups) there probably would never have been a subfield of organization development.

Survey research and feedback techniques particularly characterized the work initiated by Kurt Lewin and his associates at the Research Center for Group Dynamics first at M.I.T. and, after his death, at the University of Michigan. Survey research methodology, when combined with feedback/communication techniques, and applied to planned organizational change, resulted in the development of the *action research* model of organizational change—another mainstay of OD practitioners and theorists. The action research model is a prescribed process for identifying needs for organizational improvement and creating improvement strategies that utilizes external consultation but creates psychological ownership of problems and solutions by organizational members. Briefly, action research involves the following:

- Collecting organizational diagnostic-type data, usually either by questionnaire or through consultant interviews
- Systematically feeding back information to groups of people (organization members) who provided input
- Discussing what the information means to members and its implications for the organization in order to be certain the "diagnosis" is accurate and to generate psychological ownership of the need for improvement actions
- Jointly developing action-improvement plans, using the knowledge and skills of the consultant and the insider perspective of members, and generating psychological ownership of the improvement action plan

The action research model is diagrammed in Figure 1.

The *sociotechnical approach to research and analysis* made its appearance in the late 1940s and early 1950s through a group of organizational researchers at the Tavistock Institute in London who identified a tight link between human and technological factors in the workplace. They concluded that neither people nor work/technology takes precedence over the other. Once again, as was true with the Hawthorne studies, the sociotechnical group does not assume that the task is to increase productivity by fitting people to the work. Eric Trist and Kenneth Bamforth found that changing the coal-mining technology from small group production to a physically spaced *longwall*

FIGURE 1 • THE ORGANIZATION DEVELOPMENT ACTION RESEARCH MODEL

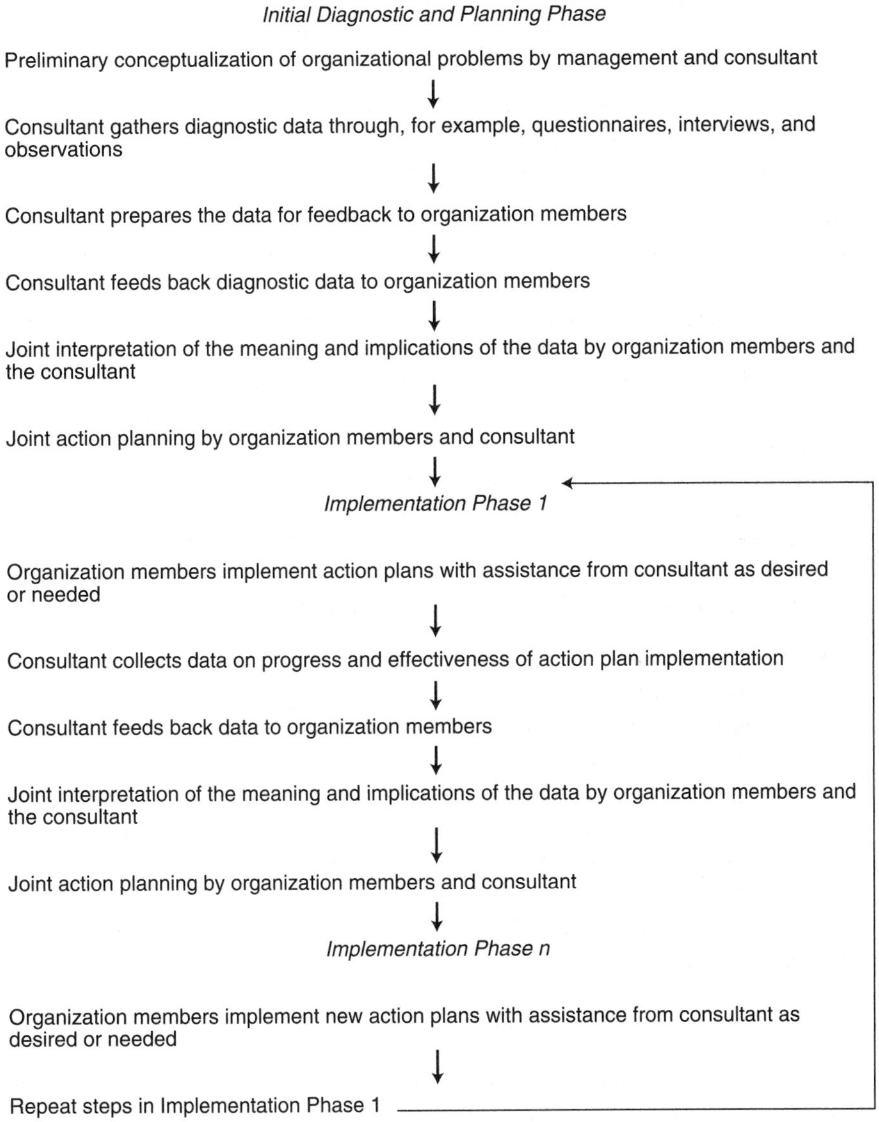

Initial Diagnostic and Planning Phase

Preliminary conceptualization of organizational problems by management and consultant

↓

Consultant gathers diagnostic data through, for example, questionnaires, interviews, and observations

↓

Consultant prepares the data for feedback to organization members

↓

Consultant feeds back diagnostic data to organization members

↓

Joint interpretation of the meaning and implications of the data by organization members and the consultant

↓

Joint action planning by organization members and consultant

↓

Implementation Phase 1

Organization members implement action plans with assistance from consultant as desired or needed

↓

Consultant collects data on progress and effectiveness of action plan implementation

↓

Consultant feeds back data to organization members

↓

Joint interpretation of the meaning and implications of the data by organization members and the consultant

↓

Joint action planning by organization members and consultant

↓

Implementation Phase n

Organization members implement new action plans with assistance from consultant as desired or needed

↓

Repeat steps in Implementation Phase 1 (→ returns to Implementation Phase 1)

method disrupts the social structure of the miners and in turn production. By modifying the work (technical) system to allow the social structure to reform, workers returned to helping each other, productivity and morale increased, and accidents and absenteeism decreased. (See "Some Social and Psychological Consequences of the Longwall Method of Coal-Getting," in Chapter IV.)

INTRODUCTION TO THE ARTICLES IN THIS CHAPTER

This chapter's first selection is one of the best known and most frequently quoted experiments on the introduction of organizational change, Lester Coch and John R. P. French's 1948 *Human Relations* article, "Overcoming Resistance to Change." Coch and French studied the relationship between worker participation in design decisions leading to the introduction of changes in work process, and their resistance to changes. The authors used a research design complete with experimental and control groups of pajama folders, pressers, and examiners at the Harwood Manufacturing Corporation in Marion, Virginia. Using Kurt Lewin's concepts of quasi-stationary equilibriums and change force fields, Coch and French conclude that group participation in planning reduces workers' resistance to changes, decreases turnover during and following changes, and accelerates worker relearning curves (the rapidity with which workers return to full-speed production following process changes).

Whenever organizational change is discussed, Kurt Lewin heads everyone's list of people who have made invaluable and lasting contributions to our understanding of change processes and dynamics. His 1952 article reprinted here, "Group Decision and Social Change," is a condensed restatement of ideas Lewin put forth in one of his best known works, "Frontiers in Group Dynamics: Concept, Method and Reality in Social Science; Social Equilibria and Social Change" (1947). Lewin describes social organizations as resting in a state of stable quasi-stationary equilibrium. To effect social change, one must begin with an "analysis of the conditions for 'no change,' that is, for the state of equilibrium." Quite obviously, the now-familiar technique of *force field analysis* evolved from this concept, in which there are but two basic approaches for accomplishing change: "Adding forces in the desired direction, or by diminishing opposing forces." Lewin argues that the latter approach is less preferable because it tends to be accompanied by a "high state of tension," which in turn causes anger, aggressiveness and a lower propensity to be constructive. In this piece, Lewin articulates his well-known assertion that social change must be viewed as a three-step process of unfreezing, change, and refreezing. If one focuses only on the change process per se, change will be short-lived at best.

Chris Argyris's 1980 book, *Intervention Theory and Methods*, is a comprehensive, widely cited, and enduring work on organizational consulting for change written from an organizational behavior/organization development perspective (a portion of the first chapter is reprinted here). The book has remained central to the field because Argyris unambiguously lays out the fundamental tenets that undergird the organizational behavior perspective of change. (Argyris calls the tenets "the three primary intervention tasks.") These tenets define such fundamentals as the nature of the change-agent/client relationship, the necessity for valid and usable information, and necessary preconditions for organization members to internalize change.

Whereas the article by Chris Argyris is about change processes in general, Herbert Kelman and Donald Warwick's (1978) "The Ethics of Social Intervention: Goals, Means, and Consequences" (which is reprinted here) analyzes one important organizational change issue: the ethics of intervening in ongoing social systems. The authors subsume Bennis's (1966) concepts of planned organizational change under the expanded topic of *social interventions*. Kelman and Warwick concentrate on four steps in any intervention in a social system that are likely to raise important ethical issues:

1. Choice of the change goal
2. Definition of the change target
3. Selection of intervention means
4. Assessment of the consequences of intervening in ongoing social systems

Ethical issues inevitably arise during these steps because each involves questions about which competing values will take priority over others.

For Peter Senge, change is learning, and learning is change—for people and organizations. Thus, organizations that can learn to change are possible because "deep down, we are all learners." In Chapter One from *The Fifth Discipline: The Art and Practice of the Learning Organization* (1990, reprinted here), Senge proposes that five new "component technologies" are gradually converging that will collectively permit the emergence of learning organizations. He labels these component technologies the "five disciplines": *systems thinking*—"systems" of the variety described by Margaret Wheatley (2000) in "Leadership and the New Science"; *personal mastery*—people approaching life and work "as an artist would approach a work of art"; *mental models*—deeply ingrained assumptions or mental images "that influence how we understand the world and how we take action"; *building shared vision*—"when there is a genuine vision . . . people excel and learn, not because they are told to, but because they want to"; and *team learning*—team members engaging in true dialogue with their assumptions suspended.

A learning organization employs the five disciplines in a never-ending quest to expand its capacity to create its future. As Senge explains, "systems thinking" is the fifth discipline—the integrative discipline that fuses the others into a coherent body of theory and practice. Learning organizations are organizations that are able to move past mere survival learning to engage in generative learning—"learning that enhances our capacity to create."

Warren Bennis is a classic writer and a long-time contributor to the evolving and exciting fields of leadership and organizational change. In the article from his book *Managing the Dream: Reflections on Leadership and Change* (2000) reprinted here, Bennis notes that "change is the metaphysics of our age." He discusses avenues of change, the nature of innovators and leaders, and how to avoid disaster during the change. Bennis's wisdom continues to enliven and enrich our concepts and practices in this important organizational arena.

In "Laws of the Jungle and the New Laws of Business" (reprinted here), Richard Pascale (2001) continues Senge's theme of organizational learning and change. Pascale points out that two imperatives govern survival and contribute to the excellence of organizations today: "agility in the face of high levels of strategic ambiguity" and "a shift in culture to a form that behaves like a living organism fostering entrepreneurial initiatives, consolidated learning, and moving rapidly to exploit a winning in the marketplace." Living with change, chaos, and ambiguity requires an atmosphere of ongoing learning and organizational modification—sometimes incremental and at other times transformational.

Our final selection on organizational change is by Lillas Brown and Barry Posner. In "Exploring the Relationship Between Learning and Leadership" (2001), Brown and Posner state that change involves both individual and organizational learning. Most organizational leaders describe themselves as living, growing, and competing in an environment that is rapidly evolving and changing. This requires agility, entrepreneurialism, consolidated learning, leadership and management of the ongoing change process, and exploitation of opportunities. Linking research, theories, models, and practices developed from the literatures in leadership and learning is a trend that will continue in the twenty-first century.

Organizational change involves the application of all of the topics that have been addressed in this book about organizational behavior. Change requires the application of knowledge about motivation, group and intergroup dynamics, leadership, teamwork, empowerment, effects of the work environment on individuals at work, power, and influence. Change brings it all together—it is where "the rubber meets the road" for organizational behavior.

REFERENCES

Adams, J. D. (Ed.). (1986). *Transforming leadership: From vision to results*. Alexandria, VA: Miles River Press.

Allaire, Y., & Firsirotu, M. (Spring, 1985). How to implement radical strategies in large organizations. *Sloan Management Review, 26*(3), 19–34.

Argyris, C. (1962). *Interpersonal competence and organizational effectiveness*. Homewood, IL: The Dorsey Press and Richard D. Irwin.

Argyris, C. (1970). *Intervention theory and methods*. Reading, MA: Addison-Wesley.

Argyris, C. (1993). *Knowledge for action: A guide to overcoming barriers to organizational change*. San Francisco: Jossey-Bass.

Beckhard, R. (1969). *Organization development: Strategies and models*. Reading, MA: Addison-Wesley.

Beckhard, R., & Harris, R. T. (1977). *Organizational transitions: Managing complex change*. Reading, MA: Addison-Wesley.

Beckhard, R., & Pritchard, W. (1992). *Changing the essence: The art of creating and leading fundamental change in organizations*. San Francisco: Jossey-Bass.

Bennis, W. G. (1966). Applying behavioral sciences to planned organizational change. In W. G. Bennis, *Changing organizations* (pp. 81–94). New York: McGraw-Hill.

Bennis, W. G. (1969). *Organization development: Its nature, origins and prospects*. Reading, MA: Addison-Wesley.

Bennis, W. G. (1984). Transformative power and leadership. In T. J. Sergiovanni & J. E. Corbally (Eds.), *Leadership and organizational culture* (pp. 64–71). Urbana, IL: University of Illinois Press.

Bennis, W. G. (2000). Change: The new metaphysics. In W. G. Bennis, *Managing the dream: Reflections on leadership and change* (pp. 31–38). Cambridge, MA: Perseus.

Bennis, W. G., Benne, K. D., & Chin, R. (1961). *The planning of change*. New York: Holt, Rinehart & Winston.

Bennis, W. G., & Nanus, B. (1985). *Leaders*. New York: Harper & Row.

Bradford, L., Gibb, J. R., & Benne, K. D. (Eds.). (1964). *T-group theory and laboratory method; innovation in re-education*. New York: Wiley.

Brown, L. M., & Posner, B. Z. (2001). Exploring the relationship between learning and leadership. *Leadership and Organization Development Journal*, 122(5–6), 274–280.

Coch, L., & French, J. R. P. Jr. (August, 1948). Overcoming resistance to change. *Human Relations*, 512–532.

French, W. L., & Bell, C. H. Jr. (1984). *Organization development* (3d ed.). Englewood Cliffs, NJ: Prentice-Hall.

French, W. L., Bell, C. H. Jr., & Zawacki, R. A. (Eds.). (1983). *Organization development: Theory, practice, and research* (rev. ed.). Plano, TX: Business Publications.

Gantt, H. L. (1908). Training workmen in habits of industry and cooperation. Paper presented to the American Society of Mechanical Engineers.

Gemmill, G., & Smith, C. (1985). A dissipative structure model of organization transformation. *Human Relations*, *38*, 751–766.

Gersick, C. (January, 1991). Revolutionary change theories: A multilevel exploration of the punctuated equilibrium paradigm. *Academy of Management Review*, 10–36.

Huber, G. P., & Glick, W. H. (1993). *Organizational change and redesign: Ideas and insights for improving performance*. New York: Oxford University Press.

Iacocca, L. (1984). *Iacocca, an autobiography*. Toronto: Bantam Books.

Jaques, E. (1951). *The changing culture of a factory*. London, UK: Tavistock Publications.

Kelman, H. C., & Warwick, D. (1978). The ethics of social intervention: Goals, means, and consequences. In H. C. Bermant, H. C. Kelman, & D. P. Warwick (Eds.), *The ethics of social intervention* (pp. 3–27). New York: Hemisphere.

Kilmann, R. H., & Colvin, T. J. (Eds.). (1988). *Corporate transformation*. San Francisco: Jossey-Bass.

Kozmetsky, G. (1985) *Transformational management*. Cambridge, MA: Ballinger.

Leavitt, H. J. (1965). Applied organizational change in industry: Structural, technological, and humanistic approaches. In J. G. March (Ed.), *Handbook of organizations* (pp. 1144–1170). Chicago: Rand McNally.

Lewin, K. (June, 1947). Frontiers in group dynamics: Concept, method and reality in social science; Social equilibria and social change. *Human Relations*, *1*(1).

Lewin, K. (1952a). Group decision and social change. In G. E. Swanson, T. N. Newcomb, & E. L. Hartley (Eds.), *Readings in social psychology* (rev. ed.). New York: Holt, Rinehart & Winston.

Lewin, K. (1952b). Quasi-stationary social equilibria and the problem of permanent change. In G. E. Swanson, T. N. Newcomb, & E. L. Hartley (Eds.), *Readings in social psychology* (rev. ed., pp. 207–211). New York: Holt, Rinehart & Winston.

McWhinney, W. (1992). *Paths of change: Strategic choices for organizations and society*. Newbury Park, CA: Sage.

Münsterberg, H. (1913). *Psychology and industrial efficiency*. Boston: Houghton Mifflin.

Ott, J. S. (1989). *The organizational culture perspective*. Belmont, CA: Wadsworth.

Pascale, R. T. (2001). Laws of the jungle and the new laws of business. *Leader to Leader, 20*, 21–35.

Rice, A. K. (1953). Productivity and social organization in an Indian weaving shed: An examination of some aspects of the socio-technical system of an experimental automatic loom shed. *Human Relations*, 6, 297–329.

Schein, E. H. (1980). *Organizational psychology* (3d ed.). Englewood Cliffs, NJ: Prentice-Hall.

Schein, E. H. (1988). *Process consultation: Its role in organization development* (2d ed.). Reading, MA: Addison-Wesley.

Schmuck, R. A., & Miles, M. B. (Eds.). (1971). *Organization development in schools*. Palo Alto, CA: National Press Books.

Senge, P. M. (1990). *The fifth discipline: The art and practice of the learning organization*. New York: Doubleday Currency.

Shafritz, J. M., & Ott, J. S. (2001). *Classics of organization theory* (4th ed.). Belmont, CA: Wadsworth.

Taylor, F. W. (1911). *The principles of scientific management*. New York: W. W. Norton.

Tichy, N. M., & Ulrich, D. O. (Fall, 1984). The leadership challenge—A call for the transformational leader. *Sloan Management Review, 26*(1), 59–68.

Trist, E., & Bamforth, K. W. (1951). Some social and psychological consequences of the longwall method of coal-getting. *Human Relations*, *4*, 3–38.

Wheatley, Margaret J. (2000). *Leadership and the new science*. San Francisco: Jossey-Bass.

37

Overcoming Resistance to Change[1]

Lester Coch and John R. P. French Jr.

INTRODUCTION

It has always been characteristic of American industry to change products and methods of doing jobs as often as competitive conditions or engineering progress dictates. This makes frequent changes in an individual's work necessary. In addition, the markedly greater turnover and absenteeism of recent years result in unbalanced production lines which again makes for frequent shifting of individuals from one job to another. One of the most serious production problems faced at the Harwood Manufacturing Corporation has been the resistance of production workers to the necessary changes in methods and jobs. This resistance expressed itself in several ways, such as grievances about the piece rates that went with the new methods, high turnover, very low efficiency, restriction of output, and marked aggression against management. Despite these undesirable effects, it was necessary that changes in methods and jobs continue. . . .

BACKGROUND

The main plant of the Harwood Manufacturing Corporation, where the present research was done, is located in the small town of Marion, Virginia. The plant produces pajamas and, like most sewing plants, employs mostly women. The plant's population is about 500 women and 100 men. The workers are recruited from the rural, mountainous areas surrounding the town, and are usually employed without previous industrial experience. The average age of the workers is 23; the average education is eight years of grammar school.

The policies of the company in regard to labor relations are liberal and progressive. A high value has been placed on fair and open dealing with the employees, and they are encouraged to take up any problems or grievances with the management at any time. Every effort is made to help foremen find effective solutions to their problems in human relations, using conferences and role-playing methods. Carefully planned orientation, designed to help overcome the discouragement and frustrations attending entrance upon the new and unfamiliar

[1] Grateful acknowledgements are made by the authors to Dr. Alfred J. Marrow, president of the Harwood Manufacturing Corporation, and to the entire Harwood staff for their valuable aid and suggestions in this study.

The authors have drawn repeatedly from the works and concepts of Kurt Lewin for both the action and theoretical phases of this study. Many of the leadership techniques used in the experimental group meetings were techniques developed at the first National Training Laboratory for Group Development held at Bethel, Maine, in the summer of 1947. Both authors attended this laboratory.

Source: From "Overcoming Resistance to Change" by Lester Coch and John R. P. French Jr., in *Human Relations* (1948), pp. 512–532. Reprinted by permission of Plenum Publishing Corporation.

situation, is used. Plant-wide votes are conducted where possible to resolve problems affecting the whole working population. The company has invested both time and money in employee services such as industrial music, health services, lunchroom, and recreation programs. In the same spirit, the management has been conscious of the importance of public relations in the local community; they have supported both financially and otherwise any activity which would build up good will for the company. As a result of these policies, the company has enjoyed good labor relations since the day it commenced operations.

Harwood employees work on an individual incentive system. Piece rates are set by time study and are expressed in terms of units. One unit is equal to one minute of the standard work: 60 units per hour equal the standard efficiency rating. Thus, if on a particular operation the piece rate for one dozen is 10 units, the operator would have to produce 6 dozen per hour to achieve the standard efficiency rating of 60 units per hour. The skill required to reach 60 units per hour is great. On some jobs, an average trainee may take 34 weeks to reach the skill level necessary to perform at 60 units per hour. Her first few weeks of work may be on an efficiency level of 5 to 20 units per hour. . . .

When it is necessary to change an operator from one type of work to another, a transfer bonus is given. This bonus is so designed that the changed operator who relearns at an average rate will suffer no loss in earnings after change. Despite this allowance, the general attitudes toward job changes in the factory are markedly negative. Such expressions as, "When you make your units (standard production), they change your job," are all too frequent. Many operators refuse to change, preferring to quit.

THE TRANSFER LEARNING CURVE

An analysis of the after-change relearning curve of several hundred experienced operators rating standard or better prior to change showed that 38 per cent of the changed operators recovered to the standard unit rating of 60 units per hour. The other 62 per cent either became chronically sub-standard operators or quit during the relearning period.

The average relearning curve for those who recover to standard production on the simplest type job in the plant (Figure I) is eight weeks long, and, when smoothed, provides the basis for the transfer bonus. The bonus is the percent difference between this expected efficiency rating and the standard of 60 units per hour. Progress is slow for the first two or three weeks, as the relearning curve shows, and then accelerates markedly to about 50 units per hour with an increase of 15 units in two weeks. . . .

It is interesting to note in Figure I that the relearning period for an experienced operator is longer than the learning period for a new operator. . . .

Figure II, which presents the relearning curves for 41 experienced operators who were changed to very difficult jobs, gives a comparison between the recovery rates for operators making standard or better prior to change, and those below standard prior to change. Both classes of operators dropped to a little below 30 units per hour and recovered at a very slow but similar rate. These curves show a general (though by no means universal) phenomenon: that the efficiency rating prior to change does not indicate a faster or slower recovery rate after change.

A PRELIMINARY THEORY OF RESISTANCE TO CHANGE

The fact that relearning after transfer to a new job is so often slower than initial

FIGURE I • A COMPARISON OF THE LEARNING CURVE FOR NEW, INEXPERIENCED EMPLOYEES WITH THE RELEARNING CURVE FOR ONLY THOSE TRANSFERS (38 PER CENT) WHO EVENTUALLY RECOVER TO STANDARD PRODUCTION

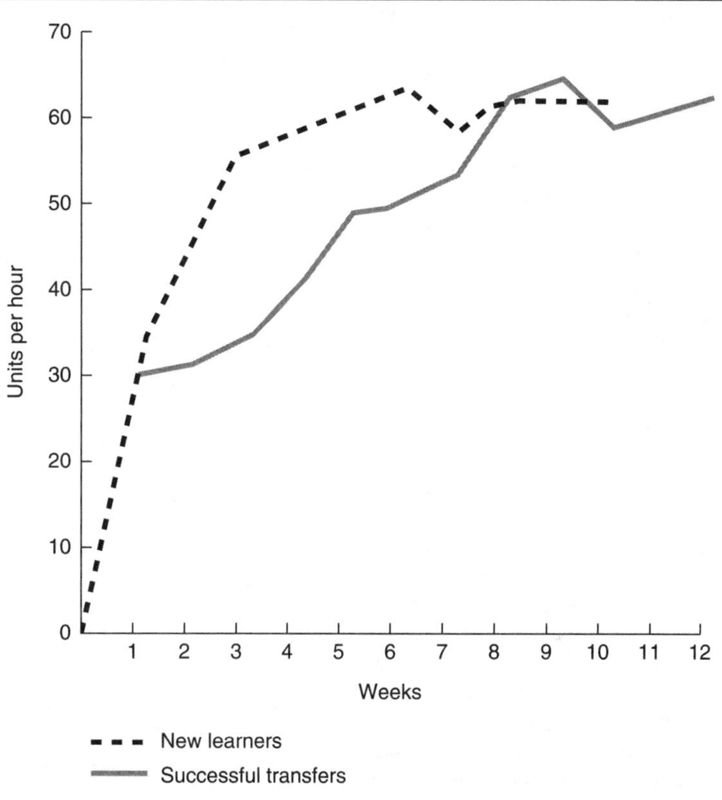

learning on first entering the factory would indicate, on the face of it, that the resistance to change and the slow relearning is primarily a motivational problem. The similar recovery rates of the skilled and unskilled operators shown in Figure II tend to confirm the hypothesis that skill is a minor factor and motivation is the major determinant of the rate of recovery. Earlier experiments at Harwood by Alex Bavelas demonstrated this point conclusively. He found that the use of group decision techniques on operators who had just been transferred resulted in very marked increases in the rate of relearning, even though no skill training was given and there were no other changes in working conditions **(1)**.

Interviews with operators who have been transferred to a new job reveal a common pattern of feelings and attitudes which are distinctly different from those of successful non-transfers. In addition to resentment against the management for transferring them, the employees typically show feelings of frustration, loss of hope of ever regaining their former level of production and status in the factory, feelings of failure, and a very low level of aspiration. In this respect these transferred operators are similar to the chronically slow workers studied previously.

FIGURE II • THE DROP IN PRODUCTION AND THE RATE OF RECOVERY AFTER TRANSFER FOR SKILLFUL AND FOR SUBSTANDARD OPERATORS

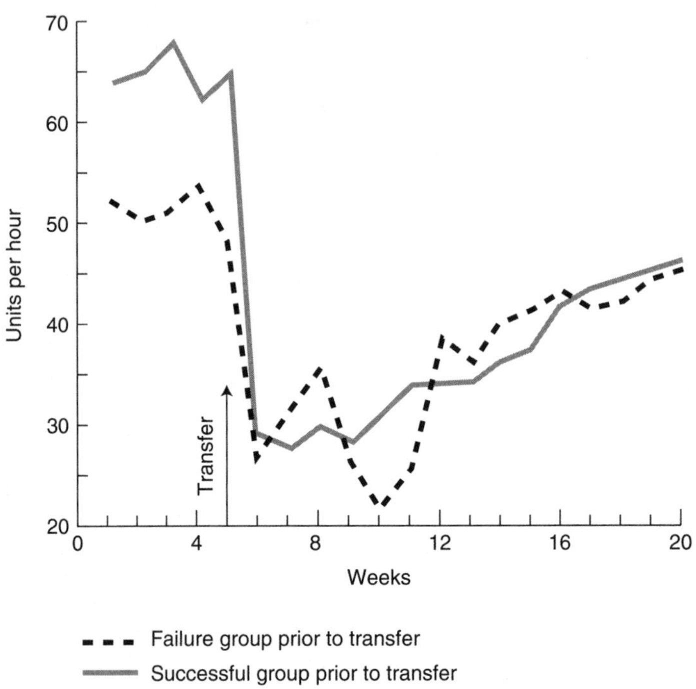

Earlier unpublished research at Harwood has shown that the non-transferred employees generally have an explicit goal of reaching and maintaining an efficiency rating of 60 units per hour. A questionnaire administered to several groups of operators indicated that a large majority of them accept as their goal the management's quota of 60 units per hour. This standard of production is the level of aspiration according to which the operators measure their success or failure; and those who fall below standard lose status in the eyes of their fellow employees. Relatively few operators set a goal appreciably above 60 units per hour.

The actual production records confirm the effectiveness of this goal of standard production. The distribution of the total population of operators in accordance with their production levels is by no means a normal curve. Instead, there is a very large number of operators who rate 60 to 63 units per hour and relatively few operators who rate just above or just below this range. Thus we may conclude that:

• Hypothesis (1): There is a force acting on the operator in the direction of achieving a production level of 60 units per hour or more. It is assumed that the strength of this driving force (acting on an operator below standard) increases as she gets nearer the goal—a typical goal gradient (see Figure I).

On the other hand, restraining forces operate to hinder or prevent her from reaching this goal. These restraining forces consist among other things of the

An analysis of turnover records for changed operators with high we-feeling showed a 4 per cent turnover rate per month at 30 to 34 units per hour, not significantly higher than in unchanged operators but significantly lower than in changed operators with little or no we-feeling. However, the acts of aggression are far more numerous among operators with high we-feeling than among operators with little we-feeling. Since both types of operators experience the same frustration as individuals but react to it so differently, it is assumed that the effect of the in-group feeling is to set up a restraining force against leaving the group and perhaps even to set up driving forces toward staying in the group. In these circumstances, one would expect some alternative reaction to frustration rather than escape from the field. This alternative is aggression. Strong we-feeling provides strength so that members dare to express aggression which would otherwise be suppressed.

One common result in a sub-group with strong we-feeling is the setting of a group standard concerning production. Where the attitudes toward management are antagonistic, this group standard may take the form of a definite restriction of production to a given level. This phenomenon of restriction is particularly likely to happen in a group that has been transferred to a job where a new piece rate has been set; for they have some hope that if production never approaches the standard, the management may change the piece rate in their favor.

A group standard can exert extremely strong forces on an individual member of a small sub-group. . . .

THE EXPERIMENT

On the basis of the preliminary theory that resistance to change is a combination of an individual reaction to frustration with strong group-induced forces it seemed that the most appropriate methods for overcoming the resistance to change would be group methods. Consequently an experiment was designed employing two variations of democratic procedure in handling groups to be transferred. The first variation involved participation through representation of the workers in designing the changes to be made in the jobs. The second variation consisted of total participation by all members of the group in designing the changes. A third control group was also used. Two experimental groups received the total participation treatment. The three experimental groups and the control group were roughly matched with respect to: (a) the efficiency ratings of the groups before transfer; (b) the degree of change involved in the transfer; (c) the amount of we-feeling observed in the groups. . . .

The control group of hand pressers went through the usual factory routine when they were changed. The production department modified the job, and a new piece rate was set. A group meeting was then held in which the control group was told that the change was necessary because of competitive conditions, and that a new piece rate had been set. The new piece rate was thoroughly explained by the time study man, questions were answered, and the meeting dismissed.

Experimental group 1 was changed in a different manner. Before any changes took place, a group meeting was held with all the operators to be changed. The need for the change was presented as dramatically as possible, showing two identical garments produced in the factory; one was produced in 1946 and had sold for 100 percent more than its fellow in 1947. The group was asked to identify the cheaper one and could not do it. This demonstration effectively shared with the group the entire problem of the necessity of cost reduction. A general agreement was reached that a savings could be effected by removing the "frills" and "fancy" work from the garment without affecting the folders' opportunity to achieve a high efficiency rating. Management then presented a plan to set a new job and piece rate:

1. Make a check study of the job as it was being done.
2. Eliminate all unnecessary work.
3. Train several operators in the correct methods.
4. Set the piece rate by time studies on these specially trained operators.
5. Explain the new job rate to all the operators.
6. Train all operators in the new method so they can reach a high rate of production within a short time.

The group approved this plan (though no formal group decision was reached), and chose the operators to be specially trained. A sub-meeting with the "special" operators was held immediately following the meeting with the entire group. They displayed a cooperative and interested attitude and immediately presented many good suggestions. This attitude carried over into the working out of the details of the new job; and when the new job and piece rates were set, the "special" operators referred to the resultants as "our job," "our rate," etc. The new job and piece rates were presented at a second group meeting to all the operators involved. The "special" operators served to train the other operators on the new job.

Experimental groups 2 and 3 went through much the same kind of change meetings. The groups were smaller than experimental group 1, and a more intimate atmosphere was established. The need for a change was once again made dramatically clear; the same general plan was presented by management. However, since the groups were small, all operators were chosen as "special" operators; that is, all operators were to participate directly in the designing of the new jobs, and all operators would be studied by the time study man. It is interesting to note that in the meetings with these two groups, suggestions were immediately made in such quantity that the stenographer had great difficulty in recording them. The group approved of the plans, but again no formal group decision was reached.

Results

. . . The control group improved little beyond their early efficiency ratings. Resistance developed almost immediately after the change occurred. Marked expressions of aggression against management occurred, such as conflict with the methods engineer, expression of hostility against the supervisor, deliberate restriction of production, and lack of cooperation with the supervisor. There were 17 per cent quits in the first forty days. Grievances were filed about the piece rate, but when the rate was checked, it was found to be a little "loose."

Experimental group 1 showed an unusually good relearning curve. At the end of fourteen days, the group averaged 61 units per hour. During the fourteen days, the attitude was co-operative and permissive. They worked well with the methods engineer, the training staff, and the supervisor. (The supervisor was the same person in the cases of the control group and experimental group 1.) There were no quits in this group in the first forty days. This group might have presented a better learning record if work had not been scarce during the first seven days. There was one act of aggression against the supervisor recorded in the first forty days. It is interesting to note that the three special representative operators in experimental group 1 recovered at about the same rate as the rest of their group.

Experimental groups 2 and 3 recovered faster than experimental group 1. After a slight drop on the first day of change, the efficiency ratings returned to a pre-change level and showed sustained progress thereafter to a level about 14 per cent higher than the pre-change level. No additional training was provided them after the second day. They worked well with their supervisors and no indications of aggression were observed from these groups. There were no quits in either of these groups in the first forty days.

A fourth experimental group, composed of only two sewing operators, was transferred by the total participation technique. Their new job was one of the most difficult jobs in the factory, in contrast to the easy jobs for the control group and the other three experimental groups. As expected, the total participation technique again resulted in an unusually fast recovery rate and a final level of production well above the level before transfer. Because of the difficulty of the new job, however, the rate of recovery was slower than for experimental groups 2 and 3, but faster than for experimental group 1.

In the first experiment, the control group made no progress after transfer for a period of 32 days. At the end of this period the group was broken up and the individuals were reassigned to new jobs scattered throughout the factory. Two and a half months after their dispersal, the thirteen remaining members of the original control group were again brought together as a group for a second experiment.

This second experiment consisted of transferring the control group to a new job, using the total participation technique in meetings which were similar to those held with the experimental groups 2 and 3. The new job was a pressing job of comparable difficulty to the new job in the first experiment. On the average it involved about the same degree of change. In the meetings no reference was made to the previous behavior of the group on being transferred.

The results of the second experiment were in sharp contrast to the first. With the total participation technique, the same control group now recovered rapidly to their previous efficiency rating, and, like the other groups under this treatment, continued on beyond it to a new high level of production. There was no aggression or turnover in the group for 19 days after change, a marked modification of their previous behavior after transfer. Some anxiety concerning their seniority status was expressed, but this was resolved in a meeting of their elected delegate, the union business agent, and a management representative. It should be noted that the pre-change level on the second experiment is just above 60 units per hour; thus the individual transfers had progressed to just above standard during the two and a half months between the two experiments.

INTERPRETATION

. . . The first experiment showed that the rate of recovery is directly proportional to the amount of participation, and that the rates of turnover and aggression are inversely proportional to the amount of participation. The second experiment demonstrated more conclusively that the results obtained depended on the experimental treatment rather than on personality factors like skill or aggressiveness, for identical individuals yielded markedly different results in the control treatment as contrasted with the total participation treatment.

Apparently total participation has the same type of effect as participation through representation, but the former has a stronger influence. In regard to recovery rates, this difference is not unequivocal because the experiment was unfortunately confounded. Right after transfer, experimental group number 1 had insufficient material to work on for a period of seven days. Hence their slower recovery during this period is at least in part due to insufficient work. In succeeding days, however, there was an adequate supply of work and the differential recovery rate still persisted. Therefore we are inclined to believe that participation through representation results in slower recovery than does total participation. . . .

Where we are dealing with a quasi-stationary equilibrium, the resultant forces upward and the forces downward are opposite in direction and equal in strength at the equilibrium level. Of course either resultant forces may fluctuate over a short period of time, so that the forces may not be equally balanced at a given moment. However, over a longer period of time and on the average the forces balance out. Fluctuations from the average occur but there is a tendency to return to the average level.

Just before being transferred, all of the groups in both experiments had reached a stable equilibrium level at just above the standard production of 60 units per hour. This level was equal to the average efficiency rating for the entire factory during the period of the experiments. Since this production level remained constant, neither increasing nor decreasing, we may be sure that the strength of the resultant force upward was equal to the strength of the resultant force downward. This equilibrium of forces was maintained over a period of time when production was stationary at this level. But the forces changed markedly after transfer, and these new constellations of forces were distinctly different for the control and the experimental groups.

For the control group the period after transfer is a quasi-stationary equilibrium at a lower level, and the forces do not change during the period of thirty days. The resultant force upward remains equal to the resultant force downward and the level of production remains constant. . . .

The situation for the experimental groups after transfer can be viewed as a quasi-stationary equilibrium of a different type. Figure IV gives a schematic diagram of the resultant forces for the experimental groups. At any given level of production, such as 50 units per hour or 60 units per hour, both the resultant forces upward and the resultant forces downward change over a period of thirty days. During this time the point of equilibrium, which starts at 50 units per hour, gradually rises until it reaches a level of over 70 units per hour after thirty days. Yet here again the equilibrium level has the character of a "central force field" where at any point in the total field the resultant of the upward and downward forces is in the direction of the equilibrium level. . . .

There are three main component forces influencing production in a downward direction: (1) the difficulty of the job; (2) a force corresponding to avoidance of strain; (3) a force corresponding to a group standard to restrict production to a given level. The resultant force upward in the direction of greater production is composed of three additional component forces: (4) the force corresponding to the goal of standard production; (5) a force corresponding to pressures induced by the management through supervision; (6) a force corresponding to a group standard of competition. Let us examine each of these six component forces.

1. *Job Difficulty*. For all operators the difficulty of the job is one of the forces downward on production. The difficulty of

FIGURE IV • SCHEMATIC DIAGRAM OF THE QUASI-STATIONARY EQUILIBRIUM FOR THE EXPERIMENTAL GROUPS AFTER TRANSFER

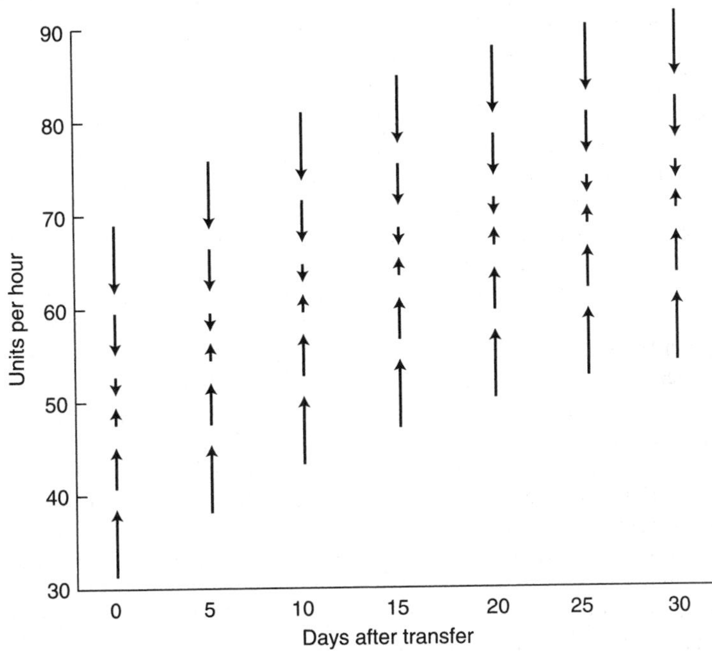

the job, of course, is relative to the skill of the operator. The given job may be very difficult for the unskilled operator but relatively easy for a highly skilled one. In the case of a transfer a new element of difficulty enters. For some time the new job is much more difficult, for the operator is unskilled at that particular job. In addition to the difficulty experienced by any learner, the transfer often encounters the added difficulty of proactive inhibition. Where the new job is similar to the old job there will be a period of interference between the two similar but different skills required. . . .

2. *Strain Avoidance.* The force toward lower production corresponding to the difficulty of the job (or the lack of skill of the person) has the character of a restraining force—that is, it acts to prevent locomotion rather than as a driving force causing locomotion. However, in all production there is a closely related driving force towards lower production, namely "strain avoidance." We assume that working too hard and working too fast is an unpleasant strain; and corresponding to this negative valence there is a driving force in the opposite direction, namely towards taking it easy or working slower. The higher the level of production the greater will be the strain and, other things being equal, the stronger will be the downward force of strain avoidance. Likewise, the greater the difficulty of the job the stronger will be the force corresponding to strain avoidance. But the greater the operator's skill the smaller will be the strain and the strength of the force of strain avoidance. Therefore:

• Hypothesis (4): The strength of the force of strain avoidance =

$$\frac{\textit{job difficulty} \times \textit{production level}}{\textit{skill of operator}}$$

The differential recovery rates of the control group in both experiments and the three experimental groups in Experiment I cannot be explained by strain avoidance because job difficulty, production level, and operator skill were matched at the time immediately following transfer. . . .

4. *The Goal of Standard Production.* In considering the negative attitudes toward transfer and the resistance to being transferred, there are several important aspects of the complex goal of reaching and maintaining a level of 60 units per hour. For an operator producing below standard, this goal is attractive because it means success, high status in the eyes of her fellow employees, better pay, and job security. On the other hand, there is a strong force against remaining below standard because this lower level means failure, low status, low pay, and the danger of being fired. Thus it is clear that the upward force corresponding to the goal of standard production will indeed be strong for the transfer who has dropped below standard.

It is equally clear why any operator, who accepts the stereotypes about transfer, shows such strong resistance to being changed. She sees herself as becoming a failure and losing status, pay, and perhaps the job itself. The result is a lowered level of aspiration and a weakened force toward the goal of standard production.

Just such a weakening of the force toward 60 units per hour seems to have occurred in the control group in Experiment I. The participation treatments, on the other hand, seem to have involved the operators in designing the new job and setting the new piece rates in such a way that they did not lose hope of regaining the goal of standard production. Thus the participation resulted in a stronger force toward higher production. However, this force alone can hardly account for the large differences in recovery rate between the control group and the experimental groups; certainly it does not explain why the latter increased to a level so high above standard.

5. *Management Pressure.* On all operators below standard the management exerts a pressure for higher production. This pressure is not harsh and autocratic treatment involving threats. Rather, it takes the form of persuasion and encouragement by the supervisors. They attempt to induce the low rating operator to improve her performance and to attain standard production. . . .

The reaction of a person to an effective induced force will vary depending, among other things, on the person's relation to the inducing agent. A force induced by a friend may be accepted in such a way that it acts more like an own force. An effective force induced by an enemy may be resisted and rejected so that the person complies unwillingly and shows signs of conflict and tension. Thus in addition to what might be called a "neutral" induced force, we also distinguish an *accepted* induced force and a *rejected* induced force. Naturally the acceptance and the rejection of an induced force can vary in degree from zero (i.e., a neutral induced force) to very strong acceptance or rejection. To account for the difference in character between the acceptance and the rejection of an induced force, we make the following assumptions:

- Hypothesis (5): The acceptance of an induced force sets up additional own forces in the same direction.
- Hypothesis (6): The rejection of an induced force sets up additional own forces in the opposite direction.

The grievances, aggression, and tension in the control group in Experiment I indicate that they rejected the force toward higher production induced by the management. The group accepted the stereotype that transfer is a calamity, but the control procedure did not convince them that the change was necessary and they viewed the new job and the new piece rates set by management as arbitrary and unreasonable.

The experimental groups, on the contrary, participated in designing the changes and setting the piece rates so that they spoke of the new job as "our job" and the new piece rates as "our rates." Thus they accepted the new situation and accepted the management induced force toward higher production. . . .

6. *Group Standards.* Probably the most important force affecting the recovery

under the control procedure was a group standard, set by the group, restricting the level of production to 50 units per hour. Evidently this explicit agreement to restrict production is related to the group's rejection of the change and of the new job as arbitrary and unreasonable. Perhaps they had faint hopes of demonstrating that standard production could not be attained and thereby obtain a more favorable rate. In any case there was a definite group phenomenon which affected all the members of the group. We have already noted the striking example of the presser whose production was restricted in the group situation to about half the level she attained as an individual. In the control group, too, we would expect the group to induce strong forces on the members. The more a member deviates above the standard the stronger would be the group-induced force to conform to the standard, for such deviations both negate any possibility of management's increasing the piece rate and at the same time expose the other members to increased pressure from management. Thus individual differences in levels of production should be sharply curtailed in the control group after transfer.

An analysis was made for all groups of the individual differences within the group in levels of production. In Experiment I the 40 days before change were compared with the 30 days after change; in Experiment II the 10 days before change were compared to the 17 days after change. As a measure of variability, the standard deviation was calculated each day for each group. The average daily standard deviations *before* and *after* change were as follows:

Group	Variability		
Experiment I	**Before Change**		**After Change**
Control group	9.8	. . .	1.9
Experimental 1	9.7	. . .	3.8
Experimental 2	10.3	. . .	2.7
Experimental 3	9.9	. . .	2.4
Experiment II			
Control group	12.7	. . .	2.9

There is indeed a marked decrease in individual differences within the control group after their first transfer. In fact the restriction of production resulted in a lower variability than in any other group. . . .

The table of variability also shows that the experimental treatments markedly reduced variability in the other four groups after transfer. In experimental group 1 (participation by representation) this smallest reduction of variability was produced by a group standard of individual competition. Competition among members of the group was reported by the supervisor soon after transfer. This competition was a force toward higher production which resulted in good recovery to standard and continued progress beyond standard.

Experimental groups 2 and 3 showed a greater reduction in variability following transfer. These two groups under total participation were transferred on the same day. Group competition developed between the two groups. This group competition, which evidently resulted in stronger forces on the members than did the individual competition, was an effective group standard. The standard gradually moved to higher and higher levels of production with the result that the groups not only reached but far exceeded their previous levels of production.

Turnover and Aggression

Returning now to our preliminary theory of frustration, we can see several revisions. The difficulty of the job and its relation to skill and strain avoidance has been clarified in hypothesis (4). It is now clear that the driving force toward 60 is a complex affair; it is partly a negative driving force corresponding to the negative valence of low pay, low status, failure, and job insecurity. Turnover results not only from the frustration produced by the conflict of these two forces, but also as a direct attempt to escape from the region of these negative valences. For the members of the control group, the group standard to restrict production prevented escape by increasing production, so that quitting their jobs was the only remaining escape. In the participation groups, on the contrary, both the group standards and the additional own forces resulting from the acceptance of management-induced forces combined to make increasing production the distinguished path of escape from this region of negative valence. . . .

The control procedure had the effect for the members of setting up management as a hostile power field. They rejected the forces induced by this hostile power field, and group standards to restrict production developed within the group in opposition to management. In this conflict between the power field of management and the power field of the group, the control group attempted to reduce the strength of the hostile power field relative to the strength of their own power field. This change was accomplished in three ways: (a) the group increased its own power by developing a more cohesive and well-disciplined group, (b) they secured "allies" by getting the backing of the union in filing a formal grievance about the new piece rate, (c) they attacked the hostile power field directly in the form of aggression against the supervisor, the time study engineer, and the higher management. Thus the aggression was derived not only from the individual frustration but also from the conflict between two groups. Furthermore, this situation of group conflict both helped to define management as the frustrating agent and gave the members strength to express any aggressive impulses produced by frustration.

CONCLUSIONS

It is possible for management to modify greatly or to remove completely group resistance to changes in methods of work and the ensuing piece rates. This change can be accomplished by the use of group meetings in which management effectively communicates the need for change and stimulates group participation in planning the changes.

For Harwood's management, and presumably for managements of other industries using an incentive system, this experiment has important implications in the field of labor relations. A majority of all grievances presented at Harwood have always stemmed from a change situation. By preventing or greatly modifying group resistance to change, this concomitant to change may well be greatly reduced. The reduction of such costly phenomena as turnover and slow relearning rates presents another distinct advantage.

REFERENCES

1. Lewin, Kurt. Frontiers in Group Dynamics, *Human Relations*, Vol. I, No. 1, 1947, pp. 5–41.

38
Group Decision and Social Change

Kurt Lewin

QUASI-STATIONARY SOCIAL EQUILIBRIA AND THE PROBLEM OF PERMANENT CHANGE

1. *The Objective of Change*. The objective of social change might concern the nutritional standard of consumption, the economic standard of living, the type of group relation, the output of a factory, the productivity of an educational team. It is important that a social standard to be changed does not have the nature of a "thing" but of a "process." A certain standard of consumption, for instance, means that a certain action—such as making certain decisions, buying, preparing, and canning certain food in a family—occurs with a certain frequency within a given period. Similarly, a certain type of group relations means that within a given period certain friendly and hostile actions and reactions of a certain degree of severity occur between the members of two groups. Changing group relations or changing consumption means changing the level at which these multitude of events proceed. In other words, the "level" of consumption, of friendliness, or of productivity is to be characterized as the aspect of an ongoing social process.

Any planned social change will have to consider a multitude of factors characteristic for the particular case. The change may require a more or less unique combination of educational and organizational measures; it may depend upon quite different treatments or ideology, expectation and organization. Still, certain general formal principles always have to be considered.

2. *The Conditions of a Stable Quasi-stationary Equilibrium*. The study of the conditions for change begins appropriately with an analysis of the conditions for "no change," that is, for the state of equilibrium.

From what has been just discussed, it is clear that by a state of "no social change" we do not refer to a stationary but to a quasi-stationary equilibrium; that is, to a state comparable to that of a river which flows with a given velocity in a given direction during a certain time interval. A social change is comparable to a change in the velocity or direction of that river.

A number of statements can be made in regard to the conditions of quasi-stationary equilibrium. (These conditions are treated more elaborately elsewhere.[1])

A. The strength of forces which tend to lower that standard of social life should be equal and opposite to the strength of forces which tend to raise its level. The resultant of forces on the line of equilibrium should therefore be zero.
B. Since we have to assume that the strength of social forces always shows variations, a quasi-stationary equilibrium presupposes that the forces

[1] K. Lewin, "Frontiers in Group Dynamics: Concept, Method and Reality in Social Science; Social Equilibria and Social Change," *Human Relations*, I, 1, June, 1947, pp. 5–42.

Source: "Group Decision and Social Change" by Kurt Lewin from *Readings in Social Psychology*, Revised Edition by Guy E. Swanson, Theodore M. Newcomb and Eugene L. Hartley, Copyright © 1952 and renewed 1980 by Holt, Rinehart and Winston, Inc.

FIGURE 1 • GRADIENTS OF RESULTANT FORCES (f*)

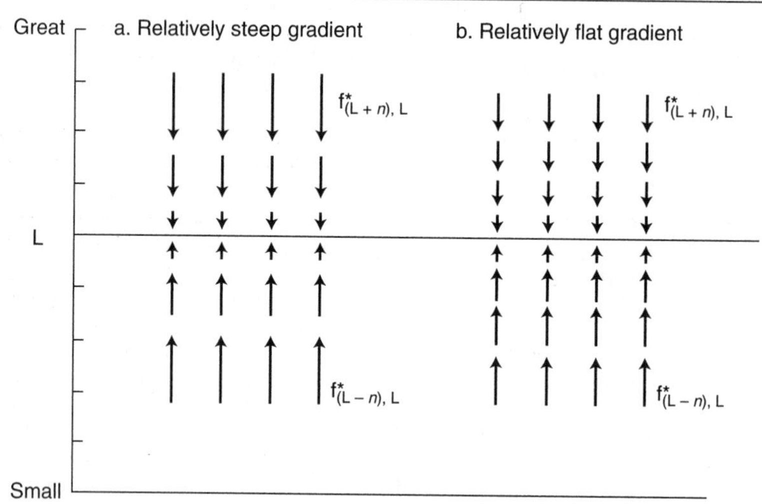

against raising the standard increase with the amount of raising and that the forces against lowering increase (or remain constant) with the amount of lowering. This type of gradient which is characteristic for a "positive central force field"[2] has to hold at least in the neighborhood of the present level (Fig. 1).

C. It is possible to change the strength of the opposing forces without changing the level of social conduct. In this case the tension (degree of conflict) increases.

3. *Two Basic Methods of Changing Levels of Conduct.* For any type of social management, it is of great practical importance that levels of quasi-stationary equilibria can be changed in either of two ways: by adding forces in the desired direction, or by diminishing opposing forces. If a change from the level L_1 to L_2 is brought about by increasing the forces toward L_2, the secondary effects should be different from the case where the same change of level is brought about by diminishing the opposing forces.

In both cases the equilibrium might change to the same new level. The secondary effect should, however, be quite different. In the first case, the process on the new level would be accompanied by a state of relatively high tension; in the second case, by a state of relatively low tension. Since increase of tension above a certain degree is likely to be paralleled by higher aggressiveness, higher emotionality, and lower constructiveness, it is clear that as a rule the second method will be preferable to the high pressure method.

The group decision procedure which is used here attempts to avoid high pressure methods and is sensitive to resistance to change. In the experiment by Bavelas on changing production in factory work (as noted below), for instance, no attempt was made to set the new production goal by majority vote because a majority vote forces some group members to produce more than they consider appropriate. These individuals are likely to have some inner resistance. Instead, a procedure was followed by which a goal was chosen on which everyone could agree fully.

It is possible that the success of group decision and particularly the permanency of the effect is, in part, due to the attempt

[2] *Ibid.*

to bring about a favorable decision by removing counterforces within the individuals rather than by applying outside pressure.

The surprising increase from the second to the fourth week in the number of mothers giving cod liver oil and orange juice to the baby can probably be explained by such a decrease of counterforces. Mothers are likely to handle their first baby during the first weeks of life somewhat cautiously and become more ready for action as the child grows stronger.

4. *Social Habits and Group Standards.* Viewing a social stationary process as the result of a quasi-stationary equilibrium, one may expect that any added force will change the level of the process. The idea of "social habit" seems to imply that, in spite of the application of a force, the level of the social process will not change because of some type of "inner resistance" to change. To overcome this inner resistance, an additional force seems to be required, a force sufficient to "break the habit," to "unfreeze" the custom.

Many social habits are anchored in the relation between the individuals and certain group standards. An individual P may differ in his personal level of conduct (L_P) from the level which represents group standards (L_{Gr}) by a certain amount. If the individual should try to diverge "too much" from group standards, he would find himself in increasing difficulties. He would be ridiculed, treated severely and finally ousted from the group. Most individuals, therefore, stay pretty close to the standard of the groups they belong to or wish to belong to. In other words, the group level itself acquires value. It becomes a positive valence corresponding to a central force field with the force $f_{P,L}$ keeping the individual in line with the standards of the group.

5. *Individual Procedures and Group Procedures of Changing Social Conduct.* If the resistance to change depends partly on the value which the group standard has for the individual, the resistance to change should diminish if one diminishes the strength of the value of the group standard or changes the level perceived by the individual as having social value.

This second point is one of the reasons for the effectiveness of "group carried" changes[3] resulting from procedures which approach the individuals as part of face-to-face groups. Perhaps one might expect single individuals to be more pliable than groups of like-minded individuals. However, experience in leadership training, in changing of food habits, work production, criminality, alcoholism, prejudices, all indicate that it is usually easier to change individuals formed into a group than to change any one of them separately.[4] As long as group standards are unchanged, the individual will resist changes more strongly the farther he is to depart from group standards. If the group standard itself is changed, the resistance which is due to the relation between individual and group standard is eliminated.

6. *Changing as a Three-Step Procedure: Unfreezing, Moving, and Freezing of a Level.* A change toward a higher level of group performance is frequently short lived: after a "shot in the arm," group life soon returns to the previous level. This indicates that it does not suffice to define the objective of a planned change in group performance as the reaching of a different level. Permanency of the new level, or permanency for a desired period, should be included in the objective. A successful change includes therefore three aspects: unfreezing (if necessary) the present level L_1, moving to the new level L_2, and freezing group life on the new level. Since any level is determined by a force field, permanency implies that the new force field is made relatively secure against change.

The "unfreezing" of the present level may involve quite different problems in different cases. Allport[5] has described the

[3] N. R. F. Maier, *Psychology in Industry* (Boston: Houghton Mifflin Co., 1946).

[4] K. Lewin and P. Grabbe (eds.), *op. cit.*

[5] G. W. Allport, "Catharsis and the Reduction of Prejudice" in K. Lewin and P. Grabbe (eds.), *op. cit.*, 3–10.

FIGURE 2 • EFFECT OF GROUP DECISION ON SEWING-MACHINE OPERATORS

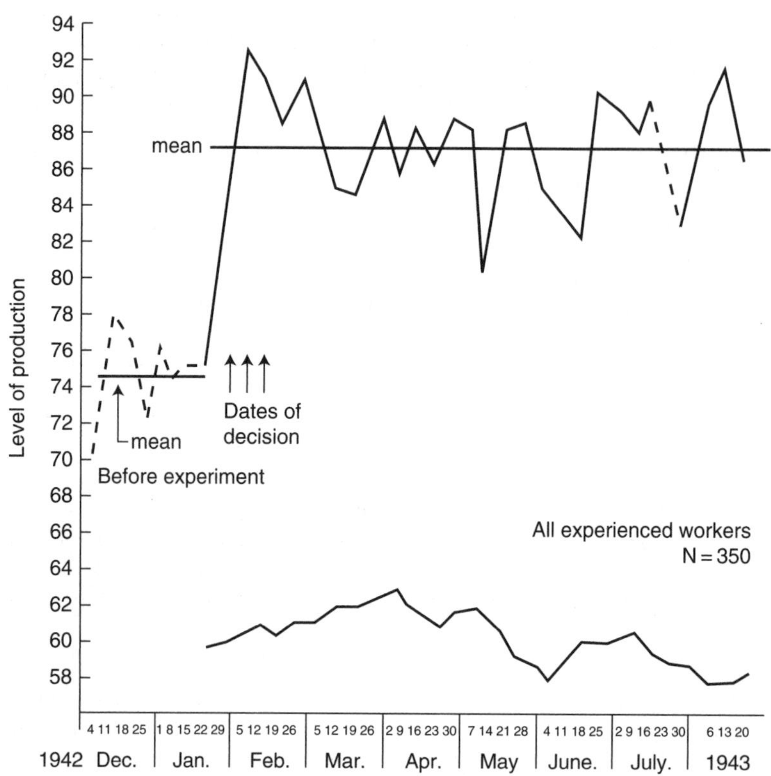

"catharsis" which seems to be necessary before prejudices can be removed. To break open the shell of complacency and self-righteousness, it is sometimes necessary to bring about deliberately an emotional stir-up.

Figure 2 presents an example of the effect of three group decisions of a team in a factory reported by Bavelas[6] which illustrates an unusually good case of permanency of change measured over nine months.

The experiments on group decision reported here cover but a few of the necessary variations. Although in some cases the procedure is relatively easily executed, in others it requires skill and presupposes certain general conditions. Managers rushing into a factory to raise production by group decisions are likely to encounter failure. In social management as in medicine there are no patent medicines and each case demands careful diagnosis.

One reason why group decision facilitates change is illustrated by Willerman.[7] Figure 3 shows the degree of eagerness to have the members of a students' eating cooperative change from the consumption of white bread to whole wheat. When the change was simply requested the degree of eagerness varied greatly with

[6] N. R. F. Maier, *op. cit.*

[7] K. Lewin, "Forces behind Food Habits . . . ," *op. cit.*

FIGURE 3 • RELATION BETWEEN OWN FOOD PREFERENCES AND EAGERNESS TO SUCCEED

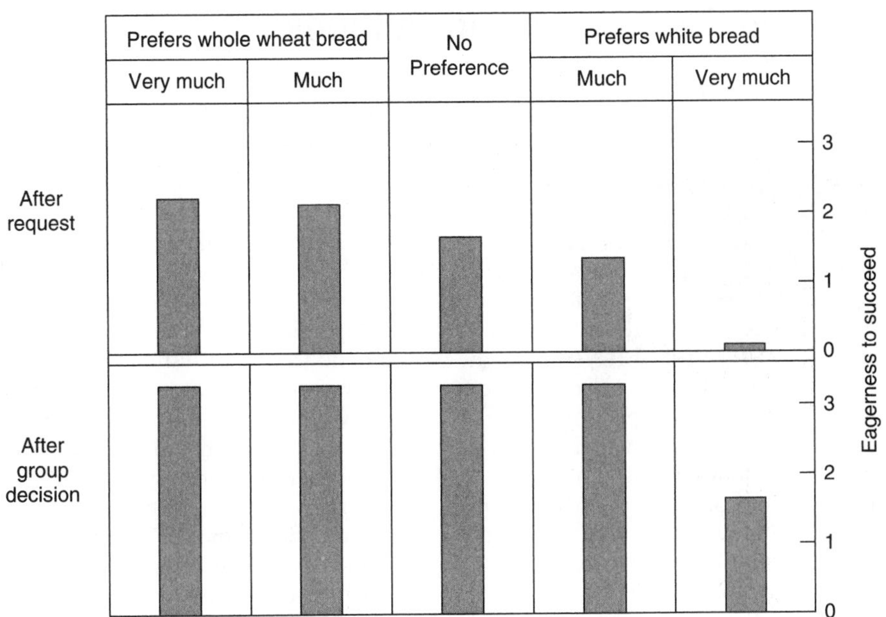

the degree of personal preference for whole wheat. In case of group decision the eagerness seems to be relatively independent of personal preference; the individual seems to act mainly as a "group member."

SUMMARY

Group decision is a process of social management or self management of groups. It is related to social channels, gates and gatekeepers; to the problem of social perception and planning; and to the relation between motivation and action, and between the individual and the group.

Experiments are reported in which certain methods of group decision prove to be superior to lecturing and individual treatment as means of changing social conduct.

The effect of group decision can probably be best understood by relating it to a theory of quasi-stationary social equilibria, to social habits and resistance to change, and to the various problems of unfreezing, changing and freezing social levels.

39

Intervention Theory and Methods

Chris Argyris

A DEFINITION OF INTERVENTION

To intervene is to enter into an ongoing system of relationship, to come between or among persons, groups, or objects for the purpose of helping them. There is an important implicit assumption in the definition that should be made explicit: the system exists independently of the intervenor. There are many reasons one might wish to intervene. These reasons may range from helping the clients make their own decisions about the kind of help they need to coercing the clients to do what the intervenor wishes them to do. Examples of the latter are modern black militants who intervene to demand that the city be changed in accordance with their wishes and choices (or white racists who prefer the same); executives who invite interventionists into their system to manipulate subordinates for them; trade union leaders who for years have resisted systematic research in their own bureaucratic functioning at the highest levels because they fear that valid information might lead to entrenched interests—especially at the top—being unfrozen.

The more one conceives of the intervenor in this sense, the more one implies that the client system should have little autonomy from the intervenor; that its boundaries are indistinguishable from those of the intervenor; that its health or effectiveness are best controlled by the intervenor.

In contrast, our view acknowledges interdependencies between the intervenor and the client system but focuses on how to maintain, or increase, the client system's autonomy; how to differentiate even more clearly the boundaries between the client system and the intervenor; and how to conceptualize and define the client system's health independently of the intervenor's. This view values the client system as an ongoing, self-responsible unity that has the obligation to be in control over its own destiny. An intervenor, in this view, assists a system to become more effective in problem solving, decision making, and decision implementation in such a way that the system can continue to be increasingly effective in these activities and have a decreasing need for the intervenor.

Another critical question the intervenor must ask is, who is he helping—management or employees, black militants or Negro moderates, white racists or white moderates? Several chapters of the book are concerned with this question. At this point, it is suggested that the intervenor must be concerned with

Source: Chris Argyris, *Intervention Theory and Methods: A Behavioral Science View* © 1980, Addison-Wesley Publishing Co., Inc., Reading, Massachusetts, pp. 15–20. Reprinted by permission of the author.

the system as a whole even though his initial contact may be made with only a few people. He therefore focuses on those intervention activities that eventually (not necessarily immediately) will provide *all* the members' opportunities to enhance their competence and effectiveness. If any individual or subsystem wishes help to prevent other individuals or subsystems from having these opportunities, then the intervenor may well have to question seriously his involvement in the project.[1]

BASIC REQUIREMENTS FOR INTERVENTION ACTIVITY

Are there any basic or necessary processes that must be fulfilled regardless of the substantive issues involved, if intervention activity is to be helpful with any level of client (individual, group, or organizational)? One condition that seems so basic as to be defined axiomatic is the generation of *valid information*. Without valid information, it would be difficult for the client to learn and for the interventionist to help.

A second condition almost as basic flows from our assumption that intervention activity, no matter what its substantive interests and objectives, should be so designed and executed that the client system maintains its discreteness and autonomy. Thus, *free, informed choice* is also a necessary process in effective intervention activity.

Finally, if the client system is assumed to be ongoing (that is, existing over time), the clients require strengthening to maintain their autonomy not only vis-à-vis the interventionist but also vis-à-vis other systems. This means that their commitment to learning and change has to be more than temporary. It has to be so strong that it can be transferred to relationships other than those with the interventionist and can do so (eventually) without the help of the interventionist. The third basic process for any intervention activity is therefore the client's *internal commitment* to the choices made.

In summary, valid information, free choice, and internal commitment are considered integral parts of any intervention activity, no matter what the substantive objectives are (for example, developing a management performance evaluation scheme, reducing intergroup rivalries, increasing the degree of trust among individuals, redesigning budgetary systems, or redesigning work). These three processes are called the primary intervention tasks.

PRIMARY TASKS OF AN INTERVENTIONIST

Why is it necessary to hypothesize that in order for an interventionist to behave effectively and in order that the integrity of the client system be maintained, the interventionist has to focus on three primary tasks, regardless of the substantive problems that the client system may be experiencing?

Valid and Useful Information

First, it has been accepted as axiomatic that valid and useful information is the foundation for effective intervention. Valid information is that which describes

[1] There is an important function within the scope of responsibility of the interventionist that will not be discussed systematically in this volume. It is the public health function. There are many individuals who do not ask for help because they do not know they need help or that help could be available to them. The societal strategy for developing effective intervention activity must therefore include a function by which potential clients are educated about organizational health and illness as well as the present state of the art in effecting change. The writer hopes that this volume plays a role in facilitating this function.

the factors, plus their interrelationships, that create the problem for the client system. There are several tests for checking the validity of the information. In increasing degrees of power they are public verifiability, valid prediction, and control over the phenomena. The first is having several independent diagnoses suggest the same picture. Second is generating predictions from the diagnosis that are subsequently confirmed (they occurred under the conditions that were specified). Third is altering the factors systematically and predicting the effects upon the system as a whole. All these tests, if they are to be valid, must be carried out in such a way that the participants cannot, at will, make them come true. This would be a self-fulfilling prophecy and not a confirmation of a prediction. The difficulty with a self-fulfilling prophecy is its indication of more about the degree of power an individual (or subset of individuals) can muster to alter the system than about the nature of the system when the participants are behaving without knowledge of the diagnosis. For example, if an executive learns that the interventionist predicts his subordinates will behave (a) if he behaves (b), he might alter (b) in order not to lead to (a). Such an alteration indicates the executive's power but does not test the validity of the diagnosis that if (a), then (b).

The tests for valid information have important implications for effective intervention activity. First, the interventionist's diagnosis must strive to represent the total client system and not the point of view of any subgroup or individual. Otherwise, the interventionist could not be seen only as being under the control of a particular individual or subgroup, but also his predictions would be based upon inaccurate information and thus might not be confirmed.

This does not mean that an interventionist may not begin with, or may not limit his relationship to, a subpart of the total system. It is totally possible, for example, for the interventionist to help management, blacks, trade union leaders, etc. With whatever subgroup he works he simply should not agree to limit his diagnosis to its wishes.

It is conceivable that a client system may be helped even though valid information is not generated. Sometimes changes occur in a positive direction without the interventionist having played any important role. These changes, although helpful in that specific instance, lack the attribute of helping the organization to learn and to gain control over its problem-solving capability.

The importance of information that the clients can use to control their destiny points up the requirement that the information must not only be valid, it must be useful. Valid information that cannot be used by the clients to alter their system is equivalent to valid information about cancer that cannot be used to cure cancer eventually. An interventionist's diagnosis should include variables that are manipulable by the clients and are complete enough so that if they are manipulated effective changes will follow.

Free Choice

In order to have free choice, the client has to have a cognitive map of what he wishes to do. The objectives of his action are known at the moment of decision. Free choice implies voluntary as opposed to automatic; proactive rather than reactive. The act of selection is rarely accomplished by maximizing or optimizing. Free and informed choice entails what Simon has called "satisficing," that is, selecting the alternative with the highest probability of succeeding, given some specified cost constraints. Free choice places the locus of decision making in the client system. Free choice makes it possible for the clients to remain responsible for their destiny. Through free choice the clients can maintain the autonomy of their system.

It may be possible that clients prefer to give up their responsibility and their autonomy, especially if they are feeling a sense of failure. They may prefer, as we shall see in several examples, to turn over their free choice to the interventionist. They may insist that he make recommendations and tell them what to do. The interventionist resists these pressures because if he does not, the clients will lose their free choice and he will lose his own free choice also. He will be controlled by the anxieties of the clients.

The requirement of free choice is especially important for those helping activities where the processes of help are as important as the actual help. For example, a medical doctor does not require that a patient with a bullet wound participate in the process by defining the kind of help he needs. However, the same doctor may have to pay much more attention to the processes he uses to help patients when he is attempting to diagnose blood pressure or cure a high cholesterol. If the doctor behaves in ways that upset the patient, the latter's blood pressure may well be distorted. Or the patient can develop a dependent relationship if the doctor cuts down his cholesterol—increasing habits only under constant pressure from the doctor—and the moment the relationship is broken off, the count goes up.

Effective intervention in the human and social spheres requires that the processes of help be congruent with the outcome desired. Free choice is important because there are so many unknowns, and the interventionist wants the client to have as much willingness and motivation as possible to work on the problem. With high client motivation and commitment, several different methods for change can succeed.

A choice is free to the extent the members can make their selection for a course of action with minimal internal defensiveness; can define the path (or paths) by which the intended consequence is to be achieved; can relate the choice to their central needs; and can build into their choices a realistic and challenging level of aspiration. Free choice therefore implies that the members are able to explore as many alternatives as they consider significant and select those that are central to their needs.

Why must the choice be related to the central needs and why must the level of aspiration be realistic and challenging? May people not choose freely unrealistic or unchallenging objectives? Yes, they may do so in the short run, but not for long if they still want to have free and informed choice. A freely chosen course of action means that the action must be based on an accurate analysis of the situation and not on the biases or defenses of the decision makers. We know, from the level of aspiration studies, that choices which are too high or too low, which are too difficult or not difficult enough will tend to lead to psychological failure. Psychological failure will lead to increased defensiveness, increased failure, and decreased self-acceptance on the part of the members experiencing the failure. These conditions, in turn, will tend to lead to distorted perceptions by the members making the choices. Moreover, the defensive members may unintentionally create a climate where the members of surrounding and interrelated systems will tend to provide carefully censored information. Choices made under these conditions are neither informed nor free.

Turning to the question of centrality of needs, a similar logic applies. The degree of commitment to the processes of generating valid information, scanning, and choosing may significantly vary according to the centrality of the choice to the needs of the clients. The more central the choice, the more the system will strive to do its best in developing valid information and making free and informed choices. If the research from perceptual psychology is valid, the very perception of the clients is altered by the needs involved. Individuals tend to scan more, ask for more information, and be more careful in the choices when they are making decisions that are central to them. High involvement may produce perceptual distortions, as does low involvement. The interventionist, however, may have a greater probability of helping the clients explore possible distortion when the choice they are making is a critical one.

INTERNAL COMMITMENT

Internal commitment means the course of action or choice that has been internalized by each member so that he experiences a high degree of ownership and has a feeling of responsibility about the choice and its implications. Internal commitment means that the individual has reached the point where he is acting on the choice because it fulfills his own needs and sense of responsibility, as well as those of the system.

The individual who is internally committed is acting primarily under the influence of his own forces and not induced forces. The individual (or any unity) feels a minimal degree of dependence upon others for the action. It implies that he has obtained and processed valid information and that he has made an informed and free choice. Under these conditions there is a high probability that the individual's commitment will remain strong over time (even with reduction of external rewards) or under stress, or when the course of action is challenged by others. It also implies that the individual is continually open to reexamination of his position because he believes in taking action based upon valid information.

40

The Ethics of Social Intervention: Goals, Means, and Consequences

Herbert C. Kelman and Donald P. Warwick

Social intervention is any act, planned or unplanned, that alters the characteristics of another individual or the pattern of relationships between individuals. The range of acts covered in this definition is intentionally broad. It includes such macro phenomena as national planning, military intervention in the affairs of other nations, population policy, and technical assistance. It also applies to psychotherapy, sensitivity training, neighborhood action programs, experiments done with human beings, and other micro changes. . . .

We prefer to subsume planned change efforts under a broader definition of social intervention that provides for the ethical evaluation of institutional structures and practices with critical social effects, as well as of situations with more readily identifiable change agents. We can thus explore the ethical implications of government policies or intellectual traditions, for example, even though these are not explicitly geared toward producing social change and are not associated with a single individual or agency. The major focus of this book, however, is on deliberate interventions. In this book, while keeping the broad definition in mind, we use social intervention more narrowly to refer to deliberate attempts by professionals to change the characteristics of individuals or groups, or to influence the pattern of relationships between individuals and/or groups. The last clause in this working definition is designed to cover such interventions as mediation, where the intent is not to change individuals and groups as such, but to shape the course of their relationships and interactions on a short-term or long-term basis.

VALUE PREFERENCES AND VALUE CONFLICTS

There are four aspects of any social intervention that are likely to raise major ethical issues: (1) the choice of goals to which the change effort is directed, (2) the definition of the target of the change, (3) the choice of means used to implement the intervention, and (4) the assessment of the consequences of the intervention. At each of these steps, the ethical issues that arise may involve conflicting values, that is, questions about what values are to be maximized at the expense of what other values. (We define *values* as individual or shared conceptions of the desirable—"goods" considered worth pursuing.)

Thus, values determine the choice of goals to which a change effort is directed. Clearly, an intervention is designed to

Source: Reprinted by permission of the Human Affairs Research Centers of the Battelle Memorial Institute from "The Ethics of Social Intervention: Goals, Means, and Consequences," by H. C. Kelman and D. P. Warwick from *The Ethics of Social Intervention*, 1978 (pp. 3–33).

maximize a particular set of values. But those setting the goals of the intervention are equally concerned with minimizing the loss of certain other values. These imperiled values thus serve as criteria of tolerable and intolerable costs in a given intervention. Under pressures of rapid demographic growth and limited resources, for example, a government might contemplate a set of coercive population control measures, such as involuntary sterilization. The benefit to be promoted by this program would be the common welfare or, in extreme cases, even the physical survival of the country. At the same time, the policy makers might be concerned about the effects of this program on two other values: freedom and justice. These values would be seen as social goods to be preserved—benefits that should not fall below some minimal threshold. Values may influence the choice of goals not only in such explicit, conscious ways, but also in a covert way. This may happen, as we shall see, when a change program departs from a value-based but unquestioned definition of a problem.

[Second,] the definition of the target of change is often based on just this kind of implicit, unexamined conception of where the problem lies. . . .

Third, values play a central role in an ethical evaluation of the means chosen to implement a given intervention. Questions about the morality of coercion, manipulation, deception, persuasion, and other methods of inducing change typically involve a conflict between the values of individual freedom and self-determination, on the one hand, and the values of social welfare, economic progress, or equal opportunity, on the other. For example, to what extent and under what conditions is a government justified in imposing limits on the freedom to reproduce for the sake of presumed long-run improvements in the quality of life?

Finally, conflicting values enter into assessment of the consequences of a social intervention. One of the consequences of industrialization, for example, may be a weakening of traditional authority structures or family bonds. The extent to which we are willing to risk these consequences depends on whether we are more committed to traditional values or to those values that industrialization is designed to enhance. In other words, our assessment of the consequences of an intervention depends on what values we are willing or unwilling to sacrifice in the interest of social change.

Analysis of the ethical problems that may arise at each of these four points in the change process, and of the value conflicts from which they derive, presupposes consideration of some more general procedural issues that must be faced in any effort at applied ethics. These refer to the procedures to be followed in deriving the values that apply in a social intervention, in determining whose values should be given what weight, and in adjudicating value conflicts.[1]

First, an analysis of the ethics of social intervention presumes some notion of what values should apply and how they are to be derived. The problem is simplified, of course, if the analyst simply accepts the values held by the initiators of the change. Thus, if a government agency says that it undertook a population control program in order to promote the general welfare and that it also considered the costs of the program

[1] These procedural issues are discussed in greater detail in Warwick and Kelman (1973). Much of the discussion in this chapter is derived from that earlier publication.

for individual freedom, an analyst might simply confine his or her attention to the values of freedom and welfare. Few students of ethics, however, would be content to let the individual or group initiating a change be the sole judge of the relevant values at stake. The human inclination toward selective perception and self-deception, not to mention the protection of vested political interests, is simply too great to justify this approach. In this example, the concerned observer might also wish to examine the effects of the population program on other values, such as justice, dignity, or the self-esteem of minority groups. To leave the definition of the ethical situation to the sponsor of a program would be to abdicate one's moral judgment. . . .

A second fundamental procedural question concerns the weights assigned to the different, and often competing, sets of values held by different groups. . . . Thus, at the national level, decisions about social intervention must weigh the claims and concerns of diverse groups within the society. The problem of "whose values" becomes even more complex in international programs of development or technical assistance. Such programs are often planned and carried out by individuals and agencies external to the society in which the changes are to be introduced. Therefore, there is a real possibility that the values of the change agents may deviate from those of the local population. The question of whose values determine the goals, targets, and means of change takes on special importance in such cases. The issue is not only whose interests are being served by the program, but whose conceptual framework generates the definition of the problem and the setting of goals. The issue persists even when representatives of the local society are fully involved in the planning and execution of the change program because these representatives, who are often trained abroad, may have adopted the conceptual framework of the external agency. Since the writings of social scientists often provide the conceptual frameworks for development programs, it is particularly important to scrutinize them in terms of whose values they reflect and to balance them by assuring that proper weight is given to competing points of view.

Third, deliberate attention to the content and derivation of values and to the different groups whose values are engaged by a given action often reveals value conflicts. Different values held within the same group and differences in value priorities set by different groups may present incompatible claims. For example, advocates of noninterventionist population policy typically stress the value of freedom, while those who favor strong measures of population control emphasize the values of welfare and survival of the human species. The critical question is not which of the two sets of values to pick, but what is the optimum balance between them. How much freedom, in other words, ought to be sacrificed in the interests of welfare and survival? Debates on national development often array advocates of cultural diversity, of the right of all peoples to determine their own destinies, and of the importance of traditional values as a matrix for the development of self-identity and self-esteem, against those who feel that traditional values are by definition obstacles to development and must, therefore, be changed as rapidly and efficiently as possible. Again the question concerns the most desirable trade-offs between conflicting values: How much traditional culture ought to be sacrificed for the sake of modernization?

Perhaps the most difficult challenge for ethical analysis is in providing some approximate guidelines for adjudicating such competing claims. Though no neat formulas or mechanistic answers are possible, one can try to establish a rough order of ethical priorities. . . .

With these procedural issues in mind, we now turn to some of the specific ethical questions raised by the four aspects of social intervention: the choice of goals, the definition of the target, the choice of means, and the assessment of consequences.

CHOICE OF GOALS

Social scientists and others writing about social change continually make explicit or implicit assumptions about the nature and the end-points of the changes that are necessary and desirable. These assumptions are influenced not only by the values that individual writers bring to their research but also by the interests and orientations that surround the general issue of social change in their societies. The choice of goals for social intervention thus depends on the particular intellectual and political perspectives from which the change agents and their advisors view the situation. Biased views cannot be avoided, but they can be counteracted insofar as they are made explicit and confronted with analyses based on alternative perspectives. . . .

The first and frequently neglected step, then, in an ethical analysis of social intervention is the recognition that the choice of goals for intervention is determined by the value perspective of the chooser, which is not necessarily shared by all interested parties. The goals to be pursued in social change are by no means self-evident. They depend very much on what we consider a desirable outcome and what costs in terms of other values we are prepared to bear for the achievement of this outcome—a complex judgment about which there may be considerable disagreement.

The role of cultural and ideological biases in the choice of goals is often ignored because the change effort may have a hierarchy of values built into its very definition. These values may simply be taken for granted without questioning their source and their possibly controversial nature. . . .

In recognizing the role of their own value preference, change agents (or social scientists who conceptualize the process of social change) do not abandon their values or attempt to neutralize them. It is neither possible nor desirable to do so. But being aware of their own value perspectives can allow change agents to bring other perspectives to bear on the choice of goals, which reduces the likelihood that they will impose their own values on the population in whose lives they are intervening. This process of relating our own values to those of others in the choice of goals for intervention—without either abandoning or imposing our own values—can often be aided by a distinction between general goals and specific institutional arrangements designed to give expression to these goals. It may be possible to identify certain broad, basic end-points that are widely shared across different cultures and ideological systems—at least among groups and individuals operating within a broadly humanistic framework. These groups or individuals may at the same time disagree about the specific political, social, and economic institutions that they regard as most conducive to the realization of these ends. Thus, one may be able to define the goals for intervention in more or less universal terms, while recognizing that these goals may be achieved through a variety of specific arrangements and that different cultures and ideologies may differ sharply in their preferences among these arrangements.

Ethical issues in the choice of goals for intervention revolve around the question of what values are to be served by the intervention and whether these are the right values for the target population. Since answers to these questions are likely to differ for different individuals—and to differ systematically for groups with different cultural backgrounds and positions in society—the question of *what* values inevitably brings up the question of *whose* values are to be served by the intervention.

Any society, community, or organization in which a change program is introduced contains different segments, with differing needs and interests that may be affected by the intervention. Thus, a key issue concerns the extent to which the values of these different population segments are reflected in the goals that govern the intervention and the extent to which they participate in the goal-setting process. The question of who decides on the goals often has implications for who ultimately benefits from the outcome of the intervention. Since the interests and values of different groups may, to varying degrees, be incompatible, the change program usually involves some compromise between competing preferences. Representation and participation in goal setting may thus have an important bearing on how the values of a given group are weighted in the final outcome.

The problem of competing interests and values in the goal-setting process is complicated by the fact that the change agents and those to whom the change effort is directed usually represent different segments of the population. . . . The change agents are in some sense outsiders to the target population in terms of social class, national affiliation, or both. Moreover, they are usually not disinterested outsiders: Social change programs may have important implications for the wealth, power, and status of their own groups. The problem is further exacerbated by the fact that the agents and the targets of change usually represent groups that differ along a power dimension. The change agents come from the more powerful classes and nations, the targets from the less powerful ones.

The change agents are in a strong position to influence the choice of goals for the intervention. Those who formulate and run the program clearly play a direct role in goal setting. Those who provide the conceptual frameworks may have a more subtle, yet highly pervasive, impact in that they establish the perspective from which the goal setting proceeds and thus the way in which the problem is defined and the range of choices seen as available. It is therefore quite possible that the change agents will view the problem from the perspective of their own group and set goals that will, often unintentionally, accrue to the benefit of their group at the expense of the target population. Given the power differential, their intervention may in fact strengthen the status quo and increase the impotence of those who are already disadvantaged. It is not surprising, therefore, that population control or educational programs sponsored by white middle-class agencies in black ghettoes, or by U.S. agencies in developing countries, are sometimes greeted with suspicion by the target populations. Whatever the merits of the specific case may be, there are sound structural bases for fearing that such programs may end up serving the purposes of the advantaged group at the expense of the disadvantaged.

The ethical problems created by the value and power differentials between change agents and target groups are not easily resolved. Clearly, the more the target group participates in the process of goal setting, the greater the likelihood that the change program will indeed reflect its values. But bringing in representatives of the target group or turning the program over to indigenous agents may not go very far in correcting power imbalances. . . .

Despite the ambiguities that often remain when an outside, more powerful change agent involves representatives of the less powerful target population in the change effort, such involvement constitutes the best protection against the imposition of foreign values. . . .

DEFINITION OF THE TARGET

Social intervention usually begins as an effort to solve a problem. A decision to undertake a program of organization development, for example, may spring from a concern about poor communication, intraorganizational conflicts, or underutilization of employee abilities. The adoption of population controls may be an effort to deal with the problem of scarce resources or an attempt to preserve the quality of life. In every case, identification of the problem represents, in large part, a value judgment. What we consider to be problematic—that is, what we see as falling short of some ideal state and requiring action—depends very much on our particular view of the ideal state. Moreover, identification of the problem depends on the perspective from which we make this evaluation. . . .

Identification of the problem has important ethical implications because it determines selection of the target to which change efforts are directed. Where we intervene depends on where we, with our personal value preferences and perspectives, perceive the problem to lie. Thus, those who see social unrest as a breakdown of social order are likely to define the protesters as the proper targets of change. . . .

Definition of the target of change has important consequences for the competing interests of different groups within a society.

Social scientists play a major role in identifying, or at least articulating, the problems to which change efforts are to be directed and thus in defining the targets for social intervention. . . .

Far from being ethically neutral, the models with which social scientists work may play a major role in determining the problems and targets for social intervention. In defining their research problems, choosing their models, and communicating their findings, therefore, social scientists have a responsibility to consider the consequences for the populations affected. More broadly, they have the responsibility to ensure that all segments of the population have the opportunity to participate in the research enterprise, which influences the definition of the problems for intervention, and have access to the research findings, which influence the setting of policy.

CHOICE OF MEANS

The most difficult ethical choices in deliberate social intervention usually concern the selection of means. Is it ever morally justified, for example, to force individuals to accept a program under the threat of death, physical harm, or other severe deprivation? What ethical problems are posed by manipulating the environment so that people are more likely to choose one alternative over others? Should a change program make full use of group pressures for conformity, or attempt to tamper with basic attitudes and motives? These are real questions in most change programs, and there are no easy answers.

It is possible, however, to clarify some of the issues at stake by relating the various means to the value of freedom. Warwick (1971) has defined freedom as the capacity, the opportunity, and the incentive to make reflective choices and to act on these choices. Individuals are thus free when:

1. The structure of the environment provides them with options for choice.
2. They are not coerced by others or forced by circumstances to elect only certain possibilities among those of which they are aware.
3. They are, in fact, aware of the options in the environment and possess knowledge about the characteristics and consequences of each. Though such knowledge may be less than complete, there must be enough to permit rational deliberation.
4. They are psychologically able to weigh the alternatives and their consequences. In practice this means not only possessing information but being able to use it in coming to a decision.
5. Having weighed the relative merits of the alternatives, they can choose among them. Rollo May (1969) has argued that one of the pathologies of modern existence is an inability to choose—a deficiency of will. A person who cannot pass from deliberation to choice must be considered less than free.
6. Having chosen an alternative, they are able to act on it. Among the conditions that may prevent them from doing so is a lack of knowledge about how to implement the choice, anxiety about acting at all, or a low level of confidence in their abilities, even when they have sufficient knowledge to act.

This discussion of freedom suggests a typology of means used in implementing social interventions. At the "least free" end is coercion, a situation in which people are forced to do something they do not want to do, or are prevented from doing something they do want to do. Next comes manipulation, then persuasion, and finally, at the "most free" end, facilitation.

Coercion

In simple terms, coercion takes place when one person or group uses the threat of severe deprivation to induce other people or groups either to carry out actions that they desire not to perform or normally would not perform, or to refrain from carrying out actions that they want to perform or, in the normal course of events, would perform. It is difficult to arrive at precise definitions of "threat" or "deprivation," but basically these refer to the loss of highly valued goods, such as one's life, means of livelihood, or the well-being of one's relatives. Coercion should be distinguished from compliance that occurs within the framework of legitimate authority. In a certain sense, tax laws may be coercive because they force people to do things that they would prefer not to do under the threat of penalties. However, insofar as people comply with the law out of a belief that it is right to do so, since they see the law as rooted in consensual processes, their behavior would not be coerced.

Coercion forms an integral part of many programs of social intervention. Some clear examples would be the nationalization of a foreign-owned petroleum refinery or the outright confiscation of land in agrarian reform programs. . . .

Is coercion ever ethically justified in social intervention and, if so, under what conditions? Two broad conditions are commonly invoked to defend coercive methods. The first is a grave threat to basic societal values. Thus, highly coercive population control programs are frequently recommended on the grounds that excessive fertility jeopardizes the continued survival of the human race or the material welfare of a nation's citizens. The second justification is the need for prompt and positive action to accomplish the goals of a change program, even when there is no threat to such values as physical survival. . . .

In the first case, an ethical justification of coercion requires the change agent to demonstrate, rather than assume, the threat to basic values. The population field is punctuated with dire predictions of disaster offered to the public with little supporting evidence. The legal concept of "clear and present danger" would seem to be an appropriate test of any proposal for coercion. Even then, however, coercion may not be justified. In the second case, the defense of coercion usually rests on personal evaluations of the system in question. In gross terms, those who favor a given regime will generally support its use of coercion to promote rapid change, while those who oppose it will reject its coercive methods.

Since the justification of coercive tactics often rests on the legitimacy of those who use them, determinations of legitimacy become an important part of ethical analysis. The legitimacy of a regime, in Western democratic tradition, is evidenced by the fact that its major officials have been duly elected, but there are other ways of establishing that a regime is representative of the population and governs with its consent. Even if the regime is seen as generally legitimate, some of its specific policies and programs may be considered illegitimate by various segments of the population because they exceed the regime's range of legitimate authority, because they are discriminatory, or because they violate certain basic values. . . .

Environmental Manipulation

Individual freedom has two core components: the availability of options in the environment, and the person's capacity to know, weigh, choose, and act on those options. Manipulation is a deliberate act of changing either the structure of the alternatives in the environment (environmental manipulation) or personal qualities affecting choice without the knowledge of the individuals involved (psychic manipulation). The cardinal feature of this process is that it maintains the semblance of freedom while modifying the framework within which choices are made. No physical compulsion or threats of deprivation are applied, and the individuals may be no more than dimly aware that they or the environment have been changed. Somewhat different ethical considerations are raised by environmental and psychic manipulation.

The term *environmental manipulation*, though it carries sinister overtones, applies to a broad range of activities generally regarded as necessary and desirable. These include city planning; governmental intervention in the economy through means such as taxation and control of interest rates; the construction of roads, dams, or railroads; and the addition of new consumer goods to the market. In each case a deliberate attempt is made to alter the structure of opportunities available, whether through addition, subtraction, or other modifications. . . .

Clearly, people make distinctions between justifiable and unjustifiable control of opportunities. But what are the limits of justifiable manipulation and what ethical calculus should be used to establish these limits? Is it morally justified, for example, to attempt to shape an entire cultural environment in the interest of promoting happiness and survival, as Skinner (1971) has proposed? Perhaps the key question raised by Skinner's proposals is who decides on the shape of the new environment and the controls to be instituted. . . .

Daniel Callahan (1971) has raised several questions about environmental manipulation, pointing to the ironic possibility that people can be manipulated by increasing their freedom.

Similar questions arise in any strategy for social change that relies on creating new realities that make it more necessary—or at least more possible—for people to change their behavior. In the field of race relations, for example, observers have noted that an effective way of changing individual attitudes and practices is to introduce a fait accompli: If an antidiscrimination law or policy is established without too much ado, people will be confronted with a new social reality that, for both practical and normative reasons, they are more likely to accept than to resist. . . .

In sum, if human freedom and dignity are taken as critical values, there is reason for concern about deliberate attempts to manipulate one person's environment to serve the needs of another. The value of freedom requires not only the availability of options for choice at a given point in time, but an awareness of major changes in the structure of these alternatives. . . . Assuming that this awareness will always be less than complete, who should have the right to tamper with the environment without our knowledge and what conditions should govern such intervention? Some thought has been given to criteria for an ethical evaluation of environmental manipulation. For example, manipulation would seem more acceptable to the extent that the people affected participate in the process, are free to enter and leave the program, and find their range of choices broadened rather than narrowed. Manipulation also seems more acceptable if the manipulators are not the primary beneficiaries of the manipulation, are reciprocally vulnerable in the situation, and are accountable to public agencies.

Psychic Manipulation

Even within a constant environment of choice, freedom can be affected through the manipulation of its psychological components: for example, knowledge of the alternatives and their consequences; motives; and the ability to reason, choose, and implement one's choices. Recent decades have seen dramatic developments in the techniques of psychic manipulation. These include insight therapies; the modification of brain functioning through surgery, chemicals, or electrical stimulation; hypnosis; sensitivity training; and programs of attitude change (cf. London, 1969). The emergence of behavior control technology raises fundamental questions about human nature and the baseline assumptions for ethical analysis.

The ethical questions raised by psychic manipulation are similar to those presented by environmental control, and the same criteria for ethical evaluation are applicable. In many interventions of this type, however, particular attention must be paid to moral problems of deception and incomplete knowledge of effects—conditions on which these programs often rely for their success. The use of deception in such programs is based on considerations similar to those used to justify deceptive methods in psychological experiments and other forms of social research. It is assumed that some of the phenomena that the investigator is trying to create or observe would be destroyed if people were aware of the precise nature of the experimental manipulation or of the behavior under study. The moral problems posed by the use of deception in social research have received increasing attention in recent years (cf. Kelman, 1968, 1972; Warwick, 1973, 1975). . . . Similar issues arise in all efforts at psychic manipulation.

In some situations, the ethical problem is not outright deception, but the participant's incomplete or distorted knowledge of the effects of an intervention. . . . The basic ethical question, however, concerns the right of the participant to be informed, not only of probable benefits, but also of potential dangers resulting from psychic manipulation. This question applies to other forms of psychic manipulation, such as brain stimulation or drug experimentation, as much as it does to group experiences.

Often change agents are unaware that they are engaged in manipulative efforts or that these efforts have ethical implications. They may be convinced that all they are doing is conveying information or providing a setting in which self-generated change processes are allowed to emerge. They may thus fail to recognize the situational and structural factors that enhance their power over their clients and the subtle ways in which they communicate their expectations of them. Even if they are aware of their manipulative efforts, they may be so convinced that what they are doing is good for the clients that they fail to recognize the ethical ambiguity of the control they exercise (cf. Kelman, 1968, Chapter 1). Such dangerous blindspots on the part of change agents, which preclude their even raising the ethical questions, are particularly likely to arise in the more subtle forms of psychic manipulation.

Persuasion

. . . At first blush, persuasion seems highly consistent with the value of freedom—almost its exemplification, in fact. The communication process appears to be carried out in the open, all parties appear to be free to consider the arguments, apparently have free choice whether to reject or accept them, and no coercion is consciously practiced. Quite clearly, when compared with outright coercion or the more gross forms of manipulation, persuasion emerges as a relatively free method of intervention. But at the same time, its seeming openness may sometimes mask covert and far-reaching efforts at personality change.

Insight therapies such as psychoanalysis would generally be regarded as persuasive means of attitude and behavior change. Through such therapy, individuals are led to a better understanding of the sources of their complaints—why they think, act, and feel as they do. The guiding assumption is that self-knowledge will take them a long way toward dealing with the problems. The techniques used to promote understanding are generally nondirective, and the client is urged to assume major responsibility for talking during the therapy sessions.

In principle, at least, insight therapy shows a high degree of respect for people's freedom. The patients do most of the talking, the therapist does not impose his or her personal values, and the process can be ended by the patient at any time. . . . The ethical problem posed by psychotherapy, however, is that the values guiding the influence process are hidden behind global notions such as mental health, self-actualization, and normality. The problem is mitigated to the extent that therapists recognize that they are bringing their own values into the relationship and label those values properly for their patients. "Among other things, such a recognition would allow the patient, to a limited extent, to 'talk back' to the therapist, to argue about the appropriateness of the values that the therapist is introducing" (Kelman, 1968, pp. 25–26).

When we move from persuasion in the one-to-one context to efforts at mass persuasion, the question of who has the opportunity and the capacity to mount a persuasion campaign takes on central importance. Since such opportunities and capacities are not equally distributed in any society, this question is fraught with ethical implications. . . . The question is, who should be responsible for deciding when and where persuasive campaigns are necessary? Should the interested parties from a community be involved in the decision about whether a campaign should be launched, as well as in the later stages of the intervention? Furthermore, how can illiterate villagers argue on an equal plane with sophisticated national planners armed with charts, statistics, debating skills, and prestige? Those in power are usually in a much better position to launch a persuasion campaign and to carry it out effectively. Thus, even though persuasion itself may be more consistent than other means of intervention with the principles of democratic dialogue and popular participation, it often occurs in a context where some are more equal than others.

Facilitation

Some strategies of intervention may simply be designed to make it easier for individuals to implement their own choices or satisfy their own desires. An underlying assumption in these strategies is that people have some sense of what they want to do and lack only the means to do it. Though facilitation, like persuasion, seems highly consistent with freedom, it too can move close to the borders of manipulation.

An example from the field of family planning can illustrate the different degrees of manipulativeness that a facilitation effort might involve. At the least manipulative extreme, a program providing a regular supply of contraceptive pills to a woman who is highly informed about the possibilities of contraception and strongly motivated to limit her family size, and who knows that she wants to use the pill but simply lacks the means to obtain it, would be a case of almost pure facilitation. At the other extreme would be the case of a woman who vaguely feels that she has too many children, but is not strongly motivated to limit her family size, and who possesses no information on contraception. . . .

The ethical problems of intervention increase as one moves from more or less pure facilitation to cases in which facilitation occurs as the last stage of a manipulative or persuasive strategy. But ethical questions can be raised even about seemingly pure facilitation. The most vexing problem is that the selective reinforcement of an individual's desires, even when these are sharply focused and based on adequate information, can be carried out for someone else's purposes. Here we face a critical question about the ethics of planned change: Is it right for party A to assist party B in attaining B's own desires when the reason for this assistance is that B's actions will serve A's interests? In other words, does any kind of facilitation also involve elements of environmental manipulation through the principle of selective reinforcement? . . .

Some have tried to handle the charge of manipulation through facilitation by being completely honest and open. Consider the case of a church-related action group that approaches a neighborhood organization with an offer of assistance. In such a relationship, open dialogue about why each party might be interested in the other, joint setting of goals, and complete liberty on both sides to terminate the relationship would certainly represent ethically laudable policies, but they would not remove the possibility of manipulation. The fact remains that the church group is making its resources available to one organization rather than another. It thereby facilitates the attainment of the goals associated with that organization and may weaken the influence and bargaining position of competing groups. In cases where there are numerous organizations claiming to represent essentially the same constituency, as among Puerto Ricans in the United States, the receipt of outside aid may give one contender for leadership considerable advantage over the others. Moreover, since the church group retains ultimate control of the resources provided, it can exercise great leverage in setting goals by the implicit threat of withdrawing its support. It is therefore essential to distinguish between honesty in the process by which an intervention is carried out and the underlying power relationships operating in the situation.

ASSESSMENT OF CONSEQUENCES

A final set of ethical concerns arises from the consequences of a change program—its products as well as its byproducts. Questions that might be raised about a specific case include: Who benefits from the change, in both the short and the long run? Who suffers? How does the change affect the distribution of power in the society, for example, between elites and masses, or between competing social groups? What is its impact on the physical environment? Which social values does it enhance and which does it weaken? Does the program create a lasting dependency on the change agent or on some other sponsor? What will its short-term and long-term effects be on the personalities of those involved? Many of these questions can be grouped under the heading of *direct* and *indirect consequences*.

As ethical analysis of the direct consequences, which flow immediately from the substance or contents of the intervention, would relate them to the set of basic values used as criteria for assessing the intervention. . . .

In addition to its direct consequences, almost any change program creates byproducts or side effects in areas of society and personality beyond its immediate intentions or scope of influence. These indirect effects must form part of any serious ethical evaluation. Such an evaluation requires a guiding theory of change, of how one part of a system affects another. Unfortunately, many efforts at social intervention completely ignore these systems effects, or discover them too late. Among the most common unanticipated effects are the destruction or weakening of integrative values in the society, change in the balance between aspirations and achievement, and strengthening the power of one group at the expense of another.

One of the latent consequences of many programs of modernization is to undercut or challenge existing values and norms, particularly in rural areas. The introduction of a new road, building of an industrial plant, teaching literacy, or even selling transistor radios may expose isolated villagers to a variety of new stimuli that challenge their traditional world view. Though the direct effects of such programs often serve the values of welfare, justice, and freedom, the indirect effects may generate abundant confusion and a search for new alternatives. . . .

Another common side-effect of change involves a shift in the balance between individual aspirations and the opportunities for achieving them. The delicate ethical question in this case concerns the degree to which a change agent is justified in tampering with aspirations. The dilemma is often severe. On the one hand, to do nothing implies an endorsement of the status quo. On the other hand, in raising aspirations to stir up motivation for change, a program may overshoot its mark. The unintended result may be a rise in frustration. Questions of this type could be raised about the innovative method of literacy instruction developed by Paulo Freire (1971), which attempts to develop not only an ability to read, but also a heightened consciousness of one's position in society and the forces shaping one's destiny. One can certainly argue that this experience enhances the person's freedom. But a change in critical consciousness and political aspirations without a corresponding modification of the social environment may also be a source of profound frustration. Where collective action to change the system is impossible, either because of strong political repression or other barriers to organization, the net effect may be short-term enthusiasm followed by long-term depression. In fact, the experience of having been stimulated and then frustrated may lead to a lower probability of future action than existed before the intervention. One must then ask if it is morally justifiable to raise political aspirations without ensuring that there are opportunities for implementing those aspirations. . . .

REFERENCES

Callahan, D. Population limitation and manipulation of familial roles. Unpublished manuscript. Hastings-on-Hudson, N.Y.: Institute of Society, Ethics, and the Life Sciences, 1971.

Freire, P. *Pedagogy of the oppressed.* New York: Herder and Herder, 1971.

Kelman, H. C. *A time to speak: On human values and social research.* San Francisco: Jossey-Bass, 1968.

Kelman, H. C. The rights of the subject in social research: An analysis in terms of relative power and legitimacy. *American Psychologist,* 1972, *27,* 989–1016.

London, P. *Behavior control.* New York: Harper & Row, 1969.

May, R. *Love and will.* New York: Norton, 1969.

Skinner, B. F. *Beyond freedom and dignity.* New York: Knopf, 1971.

Warwick, D. P. Freedom and population policy. In Population Task Force, *Ethics, population, and the American tradition.* Hastings-on-Hudson, N.Y.: Institute of Society, Ethics, and the Life Sciences, 1971.

Warwick, D. P. Tearoom trade: Means and ends in social research. *Hastings Center Studies,* 1973, *1*(1), 27–38.

Warwick, D. P. Social scientists ought to stop lying. *Psychology Today,* 1975, 8(9), 38–40, 105–106.

Warwick, D. P., & Kelman, H. C. Ethical issues in social intervention. In G. Zaltman (Ed.), *Processes and phenomena of social change.* New York: Wiley, 1973.

41

The Fifth Discipline: The Art and Practice of the Learning Organization

Peter M. Senge

From a very early age, we are taught to break apart problems, to fragment the world. This apparently makes complex tasks and subjects more manageable, but we pay a hidden, enormous price. We can no longer see the consequences of our actions; we lose our intrinsic sense of connection to a larger whole. When we then try to "see the big picture," we try to reassemble the fragments in our minds, to list and organize all the pieces. But, as physicist David Bohm says, the task is futile—similar to trying to reassemble the fragments of a broken mirror to see a true reflection. Thus, after a while we give up trying to see the whole altogether.

. . . When we give up this illusion—we can then build "learning organizations," organizations where people continually expand their capacity to create the results they truly desire, where new and expansive patterns of thinking are nurtured, where collective aspiration is set free, and where people are continually learning how to learn together.

As *Fortune* magazine recently said, "Forget your tired old ideas about leadership. The most successful corporation of the 1990s will be something called a learning organization." "The ability to learn faster than your competitors," said Arie De Geus, head of planning for Royal Dutch/Shell, "may be the only sustainable competitive advantage." As the world becomes more interconnected and business becomes more complex and dynamic, work must become more "learningful." It is no longer sufficient to have one person learning for the organization, a Ford or a Sloan or a Watson. It's just not possible any longer to "figure it out" from the top, and have everyone else following the orders of the "grand strategist." The organizations that will truly excel in the future will be the organizations that discover how to tap people's commitment and capacity to learn at *all* levels in an organization.

Learning organizations are possible because, deep down, we are all learners. No one has to teach an infant to learn. In fact, no one has to teach infants anything. They are intrinsically inquisitive, masterful learners who learn to walk, speak, and pretty much run their households all on their own. Learning organizations are possible because not only is it our nature to learn but we love to learn. Most of us at one time or another have been part of a great "team," a group of people who functioned together in an extraordinary way—who trusted one another, who complemented each others' strengths and compensated for each others' limitations, who had common goals that were larger than individual goals, and who produced extraordinary results. I have met many people who

Source: From *The Fifth Discipline* by Peter M. Senge. Copyright © 1990 by Peter M. Senge. Used by permission of Doubleday, a division of Random House, Inc.

have experienced this sort of profound teamwork—in sports, or in the performing arts, or in business. Many say that they have spent much of their life looking for that experience again. What they experienced was a learning organization. The team that became great didn't start off great—it *learned* how to produce extraordinary results. . . .

There is also another, in some ways deeper, movement toward learning organizations, part of the evolution of industrial society. Material affluence for the majority has gradually shifted people's orientation toward work—from what Daniel Yankelovich called an "instrumental" view of work, where work was a means to an end, to a more "sacred" view, where people seek the "intrinsic" benefits of work.[1] "Our grandfathers worked six days a week to earn what most of us now earn by Tuesday afternoon," says Bill O'Brien, CEO of Hanover Insurance. "The ferment in management will continue until we build organizations that are more consistent with man's higher aspirations beyond food, shelter and belonging."

Moreover, many who share these values are now in leadership positions. I find a growing number of organizational leaders who, while still a minority, feel they are part of a profound evolution in the nature of work as a social institution. "Why can't we do good works at work?" asked Edward Simon, president of Herman Miller, recently. "Business is the only institution that has a chance, as far as I can see, to fundamentally improve the injustice that exists in the world. But first, we will have to move through the barriers that are keeping us from being truly vision-led and capable of learning."

Perhaps the most salient reason for building learning organizations is that we are only now starting to understand the capabilities such organizations must possess. For a long time, efforts to build learning organizations were like groping in the dark until the skills, areas of knowledge, and paths for development of such organizations became known. What fundamentally will distinguish learning organizations from traditional authoritarian "controlling organizations" will be the mastery of certain basic disciplines. That is why the "disciplines of the learning organizations" are vital.

DISCIPLINES OF THE LEARNING ORGANIZATION

On a cold, clear morning in December 1903, at Kitty Hawk, North Carolina, the fragile aircraft of Wilbur and Orville Wright proved that powered flight was possible. Thus was the airplane invented; but it would take more than thirty years before commercial aviation could serve the general public.

Engineers say that a new idea has been "invented" when it is proven to work in the laboratory. The idea becomes an "innovation" only when it can be replicated reliably on a meaningful scale at practical costs. If the idea is sufficiently important, such as the telephone, the digital computer, or commercial aircraft, it is called a "basic innovation," and it creates a new industry or transforms an existing industry. In these terms, learning organizations have been invented, but they have not yet been innovated. . . .

Today, I believe, five new "component technologies" are gradually converging to innovate learning organizations. Though developed separately, each will, I believe, prove critical to the others' success, just as occurs with any ensemble. Each provides a vital dimension in building organizations that can truly "learn," that can continually enhance their capacity to realize their highest aspirations:

Systems Thinking

A cloud masses, the sky darkens, leaves twist upward, and we know that it will rain. We also know that after the storm, the runoff will feed into groundwater miles away, and the sky will grow clear by tomorrow. All these events are distant in time and space, and yet they are all connected within the same pattern. Each has an influence on the rest, an influence that is usually hidden from view. You can only understand the system of a rainstorm by contemplating the whole, not any individual part of the pattern.

Business and other human endeavors are also systems. They, too, are bound by invisible fabrics of interrelated actions, which often take years to fully play out their effects on each other. Since we are part of that lacework ourselves, it's doubly hard to see the whole pattern of change. Instead, we tend to focus on snapshots of isolated parts of the system, and wonder why our deepest problems never seem to get solved. Systems thinking is a conceptual framework, a body of knowledge and tools that has been developed over the past fifty years, to make the full patterns clearer, and to help us see how to change them effectively.

Though the tools are new, the underlying worldview is extremely intuitive; experiments with young children show that they learn systems thinking very quickly.

Personal Mastery

Mastery might suggest gaining dominance over people or things. But mastery can also mean a special level of proficiency. A master craftsman doesn't dominate pottery or weaving. People with a high level of personal mastery are able to consistently realize the results that matter most deeply to them—in effect, they approach their life as an artist would approach a work of art. They do that by becoming committed to their own lifelong learning.

Personal mastery is the discipline of continually clarifying and deepening our personal vision, of focusing our energies, or developing patience, and of seeing reality objectively. As such, it is an essential cornerstone of the learning organization—the learning organization's spiritual foundation. An organization's commitment to and capacity for learning can be no greater than that of its members. The roots of this discipline lie in both Eastern and Western spiritual traditions, and in secular traditions as well.

But surprisingly few organizations encourage the growth of their people in this manner. This results in vast untapped resources: "People enter business as bright, well-educated, high-energy people, full of energy and desire to make a difference," says Hanover's O'Brien. "By the time they are 30, a few are on the 'fast track' and the rest 'put in their time' to do what matters to them on the weekend. They lose the commitment, the sense of mission, and the excitement with which they started their careers. We get damn little of their energy and almost none of their spirit."

And surprisingly few adults work to rigorously develop their own personal mastery. When you ask most adults what they want from their lives, they often talk first about what they'd like to get rid of: "I'd like my mother-in-law to move out," they say, or "I'd like my back problems to clear up." The discipline of personal mastery, by contrast, starts with clarifying the things that really matter to us, of living our lives in the service of our highest aspirations.

Here, I am most interested in the connections between personal learning and organizational learning, in the reciprocal commitments between individual and organization, and in the special spirit of an enterprise made up of learners.

Mental Model

"Mental models" are deeply ingrained assumptions, generalizations, or even pictures or images that influence how we understand the world and how we take action. Very often, we are not consciously aware of our mental models or the effects they have on our behavior. For example, we may notice that a coworker dresses elegantly, and say to ourselves, "She's a country club person." About someone who dresses shabbily, we may feel, "He doesn't care about what others think." Mental models of what can or cannot be done in different management settings are no less deeply entrenched. Many insights into new markets or outmoded organizational practices fail to get put into practice because they conflict with powerful, tacit mental models.

Royal Dutch/Shell, one of the first large organizations to understand the advantages of accelerating organizational learning, came to this realization when they discovered how pervasive was the influence of hidden mental models, especially those that become widely shared. Shell's extraordinary success in managing through the dramatic changes and unpredictability of the world oil business in the 1970s and 1980s came in large measure from learning how to surface and challenge managers' mental models. (In the early 1970s Shell was the weakest of the big seven oil companies; by the late 1980s it was the strongest.) Arie de Geus, Shell's recently retired Coordinator of Group Planning, says that continuous adaptation and growth in a changing business environment depends on "institutional learning, which is the process whereby management teams change their shared mental models of the company, their markets, and their competitors. For this reason, we think of planning as learning and of corporate planning as institutional learning."[2]

The discipline of working with mental models starts with turning the mirror inward; learning to unearth our internal pictures of the world, to bring them to the surface and hold them rigorously to scrutiny. It also includes the ability to carry on "learningful" conversations that balance inquiry and advocacy, where people expose their own thinking effectively and make that thinking open to the influence of others.

Building Shared Vision

If any one idea about leadership has inspired organizations for thousands of years, it's the capacity to hold a shared picture of the future we seek to create. One is hard pressed to think of any organization that has sustained some measure of greatness in the absence of goals, values, and missions that become deeply shared throughout the organization. IBM had "service," Polaroid had instant photography, Ford had public transportation for the masses, and Apple had computing power for the masses. Though radically different in content and kind, all these organizations managed to bind people together around a common identity and sense of destiny.

When there is a genuine vision (as opposed to the all-too-familiar "vision statement"), people excel and learn, not because they are told to, but because they want to. But many leaders have personal visions that never get translated into shared visions that galvanize an organization. All too often, a company's shared vision has revolved around the charisma of a leader, or around a crisis that galvanizes everyone temporarily. But, given a choice, most people opt for pursuing a lofty goal, not only in times of crisis but at all times. What has been lacking is a discipline for translating individual vision into shared vision—not a "cookbook" but a set of principles and guiding practices.

The practice of shared vision involves the skills of unearthing shared "pictures of the future" that foster genuine commitment and enrollment rather than compliance. In mastering this discipline, leaders learn the counterproductiveness of trying to dictate a vision, no matter how heartfelt.

Team Learning

How can a team of committed managers with individual IQs above 120 have a collective IQ of 63? The discipline of team learning confronts this paradox. We know that teams can learn; in sports, in the performing arts, in science, and even, occasionally, in business, there are striking examples where the intelligence of the team exceeds the intelligence of the individuals in the team, and where teams develop extraordinary capacities for coordinated action. When teams are truly learning, not only are they producing extraordinary results but the individual members are growing more rapidly than could have occurred otherwise.

The discipline of team learning starts with "dialogue," the capacity of members of a team to suspend assumptions and enter into a genuine "thinking together." To the Greeks *dia-logos* meant a free-flowing of meaning through a group, allowing the group to discover insights not attainable individually. Interestingly, the practice of dialogue has been preserved in many "primitive" cultures, such as that of the American Indian, but it has been almost completely lost to modern society. Today, the principles and practices of dialogue are being rediscovered and put into a contemporary context. (Dialogue differs from the more common "discussion," which has its roots with "percussion" and "concussion," literally a heaving of ideas back and forth in a winner-takes-all competition.)

The discipline of dialogue also involves learning how to recognize the patterns of interaction in teams that undermine learning. The patterns of defensiveness are often deeply engrained in how a team operates. If unrecognized, they undermine learning. If recognized and surfaced creatively, they can actually accelerate learning.

Team learning is vital because teams, not individuals, are the fundamental learning unit in modern organizations. This is where "the rubber meets the road"; unless teams can learn, the organization cannot learn.

If a learning organization were an engineering innovation, such as the airplane or the personal computer, the components would be called "technologies." For an innovation in human behavior, the components need to be seen as *disciplines*. By "discipline," I do not mean an "enforced order" or "means of punishment," but a body of theory and technique that must be studied and mastered to be put into practice. A discipline is a developmental path for acquiring certain skills or competencies. As with any discipline, from playing the piano to electrical engineering, some people have an innate "gift," but anyone can develop proficiency through practice.

To practice a discipline is to be a lifelong learner. You "never arrive"; you spend your life mastering disciplines. You can never say, "We are a learning organization," any more than you can say, "I am an enlightened person." The more you learn, the more acutely aware you become of your ignorance. Thus, a corporation cannot be "excellent" in the sense of having arrived at a permanent excellence; it is always in the state of practicing the disciplines of learning, of becoming better or worse.

That organizations can benefit from disciplines is not a totally new idea. After all, management disciplines such as accounting have been around for a long time. But the five learning disciplines differ from more familiar management disciplines in that they are "personal" disciplines. Each has to do with how we think, what we truly want, and how we interact and learn with one another. In this sense, they are more like artistic disciplines than traditional management disciplines. Moreover, while accounting is good for "keeping score," we have never approached the subtler tasks of building organizations, of enhancing their capabilities for innovation and creativity, of crafting strategy and designing policy and structure through assimilating new disciplines. Perhaps this is why, all too often, great organizations are fleeting, enjoying their moment in the sun, then passing quietly back to the ranks of the mediocre.

Practicing a discipline is different from emulating "a model." All too often, new management innovations are described in terms of the "best practices" of so-called leading firms. While interesting, I believe such descriptions can often do more harm than good, leading to piecemeal copying and playing catch-up. I do not believe great organizations have ever been built by trying to emulate another, any more than individual greatness is achieved by trying to copy another "great person."

When the five component technologies converged to create the DC-3, the commercial airline industry began. But the DC-3 was not the end of the process. Rather, it was the precursor of a new industry. Similarly, as the five component learning disciplines converge they will not create *the* learning organization but rather a new wave of experimentation and advancement.

THE FIFTH DISCIPLINE

It is vital that the five disciplines develop as an ensemble. This is challenging because it is much harder to integrate new tools than simply apply them separately. But the payoffs are immense.

This is why systems thinking is the fifth discipline. It is the discipline that integrates the disciplines, fusing them into a coherent body of theory and practice. It keeps them from being separate gimmicks or the latest organization change fads. Without a systemic orientation, there is no motivation to look at how the disciplines interrelate. By enhancing each of the other disciplines, it continually reminds us that the whole can exceed the sum of its parts.

For example, vision without systems thinking ends up painting lovely pictures of the future with no deep understanding of the forces that must be mastered to move from here to there. This is one of the reasons why many firms that have jumped on the "vision bandwagon" in recent years have found that lofty vision alone fails to turn around a firm's fortunes. Without systems thinking, the seed of vision falls on harsh soil. If nonsystemic thinking predominates, the first condition for nurturing vision is not met: a genuine belief that we can make our vision real in the future. We may say "We can achieve our vision" (most American managers are conditioned to this belief), but our tacit view of current reality as a set of conditions created by somebody else betrays us.

But systems thinking also needs the disciplines of building shared vision, mental models, team learning, and personal mastery to realize its potential.

Building shared vision fosters a commitment to the long term. Mental models focus on the openness needed to unearth shortcomings in our present ways of seeing the world. Team learning develops the skills of groups of people to look for the larger picture that lies beyond individual perspectives. And personal mastery fosters the personal motivation to continually learn how our actions affect our world. Without personal mastery, people are so steeped in the reactive mindset ("someone/something else is creating my problems") that they are deeply threatened by the systems perspective.

Lastly, systems thinking makes understandable the subtlest aspect of the learning organization—the new way individuals perceive themselves and their world. At the heart of a learning organization is a shift of mind—from seeing ourselves as separate from the world to connected to the world, from seeing problems as caused by someone or something "out there" to seeing how our own actions create the problems we experience. A learning organization is a place where people are continually discovering how they create their reality. And how they can change it. As Archimedes has said, "Give me a lever long enough . . . and single-handed I can move the world."

METANOIA—A SHIFT OF MIND

When you ask people about what it is like being part of a great team, what is most striking is the meaningfulness of the experience. People talk about being part of something larger than themselves, of being connected, of being generative. It becomes quite clear that, for many, their experiences as part of truly great teams stand out as singular periods of life lived to the fullest. Some spend the rest of their lives looking for ways to recapture that spriit.

The most accurate word in Western culture to describe what happens in a learning organization is one that hasn't had much currency for the past several hundred years. It is a word we have used in our work with organizations for some ten years, but we always caution them, and ourselves, to use it sparingly in public. The word is "metanoia" and it means a shift of mind. The word has a rich history. For the Greeks, it meant a fundamental shift or change, or more literally transcendence ("*meta*"—above or beyond, as in "metaphysics") of mind ("noia," from the root "*nous*," of mind). In the early (Gnostic) Christian tradition, it took on a special meaning of awakening shared intuition and direct knowing of the highest, of God. "Metanoia" was probably the key term of such early Christians as John the Baptist. In the Catholic corpus the word metanoia was eventually translated as "repent."

To grasp the meaning of "metanoia" is to grasp the deeper meaning of "learning," for learning also involves a fundamental shift or movement of mind. The problem with talking about "learning organizations" is that the "learning" has lost its central meaning in contemporary usage. Most people's eyes glaze over if you talk to them about "learning" or "learning organizations." Little wonder—for, in everyday use, learning has come to be synonymous with "taking in information." "Yes, I learned all about that at the course yesterday." Yet, taking in information is only distantly related to real learning. It would be nonsensical to say, "I just read a great book about bicycle riding—I've now learned that."

Real learning gets to the heart of what it means to be human. Through learning we re-create ourselves. Through learning we become able to do something we never were able to do. Through learning we reperceive the world and our relationship to it. Through learning we extend our capacity to create, to be part of the generative process of life. There is within each of us a deep hunger for this type of learning. It is, as Bill O'Brien of Hanover Insurance says, "as fundamental to human beings as the sex drive."

This, then, is the basic meaning of a "learning organization"—an organization that is continually expanding its capacity to create its future. For such an organization, it is not enough merely to survive. "Survival learning" or what is more often termed "adaptive learning" is important—indeed it is necessary. But for a learning organization, "adaptive learning" must be joined by "generative learning," learning that enhances our capacity to create.

A few brave organizational pioneers are pointing the way, but the territory of building learning organizations is still largely unexplored. It is my fondest hope that this book can accelerate that exploration. . . .

NOTES

1. Daniel Yankelovich, *New Rules: Searching for Self-fulfillment in a World Turned Upside Down* (New York: Random House), 1981.
2. Arie de Geus, "Planning as Learning," *Harvard Business Review* (March/April 1988): 70–74.

42

Change: The New Metaphysics

Warren G. Bennis

Change is the metaphysics of our age. Everything is in motion. Everything mechanical has evolved, become better, more efficient, more sophisticated. In this century, automobiles have advanced from the Model T to the BMW, Mercedes, and Rolls Royce. Meanwhile, everything organic—from ourselves to tomatoes—has devolved. We have gone from such giants as Teddy Roosevelt, D. W. Griffith, Eugene Debs, Frank Lloyd Wright, Thomas Edison and Albert Michelson to Yuppies. Like the new tomatoes, we lack flavor and juice and taste. Manufactured goods are far more impressive than the people who make them. We are less good, less efficient, and less sophisticated with each passing decade.

People in charge have imposed change rather than inspiring it. We have had far more bosses than leaders, and so, finally, everyone has decided to be his or her own boss. This has led to the primitive, litigious, adversarial society we now live in. As the newscaster in the movie *Network* said, "I'm mad as hell, and I'm not going to take it anymore."

What's going on is a middle-class revolution. The poor in America have neither the time nor the energy to revolt. They're just trying to survive in an increasingly hostile world. By the same token, the rich literally reside above the fray—in New York penthouses, Concordes, and sublime ignorance of the world below. The middle class aspires to that same sublime ignorance.

A successful dentist once told me that people become dentists to make a lot of money fast and then go into the restaurant business or real estate, where they will really make money. Young writers and painters are not content to practice their craft and perfect it. Now they want to see and be seen, wheel and deal, and they are as obsessed with the bottom line as are IBM executives. The deal for the publication of a book is far more significant than the book itself, and the cover of *People* magazine is more coveted than a good review in the *New York Times*. The only unions making any noise now are middle-class unions. Professors who once professed an interest in teaching are now far more interested in deals—for the book, the TV appearance, the consulting job, the conference in Paris—leaving teaching to assistants.

When everyone is his or her own boss, no one is in charge, and chaos takes over. Leaders are needed to restore order, by which I mean not obedience but progress. It is time for us to control events rather than be controlled by them.

Source: From *Managing the Dream* by Warren Bennis. © 2000 by Warren Bennis. Reprinted by permission of Perseus Books Publishers, a member of Perseus Books, L.L.C.

AVENUES OF CHANGE

Change occurs in several ways.

• *Dissent and conflict*. We have tried dissent and conflict and have merely become combative. In corporations, change can be mandated by the powers that be. But this leads inevitably to the escalation of rancor. We are perpetually angry now, all walking around with chips on our shoulders.

• *Trust and truth*. Positive change requires trust, clarity and participation. Only people with virtue and vision can lead us out of this bog and back to the high ground, doing three things: (1) gaining our trust; (2) expressing their vision clearly so that we all not only understand but concur; and (3) persuading us to participate.

• *Cliques and cabals*. The cliques have the power, the money and the resources. The cabals, usually younger and always ambitious, have drive and energy. Unless the cliques can co-opt the cabals, revolution is inevitable. This avenue, too, is messy. It can lead to either a stalemate or an ultimate victory for the cabals, if for no other reason than they have staying power.

• *External events*. Forces of society can impose themselves on the organization. For example, the auto industry was forced to change its ways and its products, both by government regulation and by foreign competition. In the same way, student activists forced many universities to rewrite their curricula and add black studies and women's studies programs. Academicians are still debating both the sense and the efficacy of such programs, as they have altered not only what students learn but how they learn it.

• *Culture or paradigm shift*. The most important avenue of change is culture or paradigm. In *The Structure of Scientific Revolution*, Thomas Kuhn notes that the paradigm in science is akin to a zeitgeist or climate of opinion that governs choices. He defines it as "the constellation of values and beliefs shared by the members of a scientific community that determines the choice, problems which are regarded as significant, and the approaches to be adopted in attempting to solve them." The people who have revolutionized science have always been those who have changed the paradigm.

INNOVATORS AND LEADERS

People who change not merely the content of a particular discipline but its practice and focus are not only innovators but leaders. Ralph Nader, who refocused the legal profession to address consumer problems, was such a person. Betty Friedan, in truthfully defining how women lived, inspired them to live in different ways.

It's not the articulation of a profession's or organization's goals that creates new practices but rather the imagery that creates the understanding, the compelling moral necessity for the new way. The clarity of the metaphor and the energy and courage its maker brings to it are vital to its acceptance. For example, when Branch Rickey, general manager of the Brooklyn Dodgers, decided to bring black players into professional baseball, he chose Jackie Robinson, a paragon among players and among men.

How do we identify and develop such innovators? How do we spot new information in institutions, organizations and professions? Innovators, like all creative people, see things differently, think in fresh and original ways. They have useful contacts in other areas; they are seldom seen as good organization men or women and often viewed as mischievous troublemakers. The true leader not only is an innovator but makes every effort to locate and use other innovators in the organization. He or she creates a climate in which conventional wisdom can be challenged and one in which errors are embraced rather than shunned in favor of safe, low-risk goals.

In organizations, people have norms, values, shared beliefs and paradigms of what is right and what is wrong, what is legitimate and what is not, and how things are done. One gains status and power through agreement, concurrence, and conformity with these paradigms. Therefore, both dissent and innovation are discouraged. Every social system contains these forces for conservatism, for maintaining the status quo at any cost, but it must also contain means for movement, or it will eventually become paralyzed.

Basic changes take place slowly because those with power typically have no knowledge, and those with knowledge have no power. Anyone with real knowledge of history and the world as it is today could redesign society, develop a new paradigm in an afternoon, but turning theory into fact could take a lifetime.

Still, we have to try because too many of our organizations and citizens are locked into roles and practices that simply do not work. True leaders work to gain the trust of their constituents, communicate their vision lucidly, and thus involve everyone in the process of change. They then try to use the inevitable dissent and conflict creatively and positively, and out of all that, sometimes, a new paradigm emerges.

A Harris poll showed that over 90 percent of the people polled would change their lives dramatically if they could, and they ranked such intangibles as self-respect, affection and acceptance higher than status, money and power. They don't like the way they live now, but they don't know how to change. The poll is evidence of our need for real leaders and should serve as impetus and inspiration to potential leaders and innovators. If such people have the will to live up to their potential—and the rest of us have the gumption to follow them—we might finally find our way out of this bog we're in.

AVOIDING DISASTER DURING CHANGE

Constant as change has been and vital as it is now, it is still hard to effect, because the sociology of institutions is fundamentally antichange. Here, then, are 10 ways to avoid disaster during periods of change—any time, all the time—except in those organizations that are dying or dead.

1. *Recruit with scrupulous honesty*. Enthusiasm or plain need often inspires recruiters to transmogrify visible and real drawbacks and make them reappear as exhilarating challenges. Recruiting is, after all, a kind of courtship ritual. The suitor displays his or her assets and masks his or her defects. The recruit, flattered by the attention and the promises, does not examine the proposal thoughtfully. He or she looks forward to opportunities to be truly creative and imaginative and to support from the top.

Inadvertently, the recruiter has cooked up the classic recipe for revolution as suggested by Aaron Wildavsky: "Promise a lot; deliver a little. Teach people to believe they will be much better off, but let there be no dramatic improvement. Try a variety of small programs but marginal in impact and severely underfinanced. Avoid any attempted solution remotely comparable in size to the dimensions of the problem you're trying to solve."

2. *Guard against the crazies*. Innovation is seductive. It attracts interesting people. It also attracts people who will distort your ideas into something monstrous. You will then be identified with the monster and be forced to spend precious energy combating it. Change-oriented managers

should be sure that the people they recruit are change agents but not agitators. It is difficult sometimes to tell the difference between the innovators and the crazies. Eccentricities and idiosyncrasies in change agents are often useful and valuable. Neurosis isn't.

3. *Build support among like-minded people*, whether or not you recruited them. Change-oriented administrators are particularly prone to act as though the organization came into being the day they arrived. This is a delusion, a fantasy of omnipotence. There are no clean slates in established organizations. A new CEO can't play Noah and build the world anew with a handpicked crew of his or her own. Rhetoric about new starts is frightening to those who sense that this new beginning is the end of their careers. There can be no change without history and continuity. A clean sweep, then, is often a waste of resources.

4. *Plan for change from a solid conceptual base*. Have a clear understanding of how to change as well as what to change. Planning changes is always easier than implementing them. If change is to be permanent, it must be gradual. Incremental reform can be successful by drawing on a rotating nucleus of people who continually read the data provided by the organization and the society in which it operates for clues that it's time to adapt. Without such critical nuclei, organizations cannot be assured of continued self-renewal. Such people must not be faddists but must be hypersensitive to ideas whose hour has come. They also know when ideas are antithetical to the organization's purposes and values and when they will strengthen the organization.

5. *Don't settle for rhetorical change*. Significant change cannot be decreed. Any organization has two structures: one on paper and another that consists of a complex set of intramural relationships. A good administrator understands the relationships and creates a good fit between them and any planned alterations. One who gets caught up in his or her own rhetoric almost inevitably neglects the demanding task of maintaining established constituencies and building new ones.

6. *Don't allow those who are opposed to change to appropriate basic issues*. Successful change agents make sure that respectable people are not afraid of what is to come and that the old guard isn't frightened at the prospect of change. The moment such people get scared is the moment they begin to fight dirty. They not only have some built-in clout, they have tradition on their side.

7. *Know the territory*. Learn everything there is to know about the organization and about its locale, which often means mastering the politics of local chauvinism, along with an intelligent public relations program. In Southern California, big developers are constantly being blindsided by neighborhood groups because they have not bothered to acquaint the groups with their plans. Neighborhood groups often triumph, forcing big changes or cancellations. They know their rights and they know the law, and the developers haven't made the effort to know them.

8. *Appreciate environmental factors*. No matter how laudable or profitable or imaginative, a change that increases discomfort in the organization is probably doomed. Adding a sophisticated new computer system is probably a good thing, but it can instantly be seen as a bad thing if it results in overcrowded offices.

9. *Avoid future shock*. When an executive becomes too involved in planning, he or she frequently forgets the past and neglects the present. As a result, before the plan goes into effect, employees are probably already opposed to it. They, after all, have to function in the here and now, and if their boss's eye is always on tomorrow, he or she is not giving them the attention and support they need.

10. *Remember that change is most successful when those who are affected are involved in the planning*. This is a platitude of planning theory, but it is as true as it is trite. Nothing makes people resist new ideas or approaches more adamantly than their belief that change is being imposed on them.

The problems connected with innovation and change are common to every modern bureaucracy. University, government and corporation all respond similarly to challenge and to crisis, with much the same explicit or implicit codes, punctilios and mystiques.

Means must be found to stimulate the pursuit of truth—that is, the true nature of the organization's problems—in an open and democratic way. This calls for classic means: an examined life, a spirit of inquiry and genuine experimentation, a life based on discovering new realities, taking risks, suffering occasional defeats, and not fearing the surprises of the future. The model for truly innovative organizations in an era of constant change is the scientific model. As scientists seek and discover truths, so organizations must seek and discover their own truths—carefully, thoroughly, honestly, imaginatively, and courageously.

43

Laws of the Jungle and the New Laws of Business

Richard T. Pascale

Two imperatives govern survival in many industries today. The first requires agility in the face of high levels of strategic ambiguity. The second is a shift in culture and capability from slow, deliberate organizations to forms that behave like living organisms, fostering entrepreneurial initiatives, consolidating learning, and moving rapidly to exploit winning positions in the marketplace.

One of the best places to learn how to meet these challenges is by looking at life itself. Over many millions of years, nature has devised strategies for coping with prolonged periods of gradual change and occasional cataclysms in which only the most agile survive. This latter condition, in particular, teaches us much about how species deal with turmoil. Four principles, running counter to many current and conventional management beliefs, stand out as the primary lessons from life.

1. Equilibrium is a precursor to death. When a living system is in a state of equilibrium, it is less responsive to changes occurring around it. This places it at maximum risk.
2. In the face of threat, or when galvanized by a compelling opportunity, living things move toward the edge of chaos. This condition evokes higher levels of mutation and experimentation, making fresh new solutions more likely.
3. Once this excitation takes place, the components of living systems self-organize, and new forms and repertoires emerge from the turmoil. This property of life is called "self-organization and emergence."
4. Living systems cannot be directed along a linear path. Unforeseen consequences are inevitable. The challenge is to learn how to disturb them toward the desired outcome and then course-correct as the outcome unfolds.

Properly employed, these four principles allow enterprises to thrive and revitalize themselves. In contrast, the more familiar machine-age principles, while enduring, often prompt the stagnation and decline of traditional enterprises that face discontinuous change. The choice is that simple and that stark.

The assertion *equilibrium is death* derives from an obscure but important law of cybernetics, the Law of Requisite Variety, which states that the survival of any organism depends on its capacity to *cultivate* (not just tolerate) variety in its internal structure. Failure to do so leads to inability to cope successfully with variety when it is introduced from outside. For example, fish in a bowl can swim, breed, obtain food with minimal effort, safe from predators. But, as

Source: Reprinted by permission of the author.

aquarium owners know, such fish are excruciatingly sensitive to the slightest perturbations. Fish in the sea have to work much harder to sustain themselves and evade many threats. But because they cope with more variation, they are more robust when faced with change.

The lessons of Requisite Variety make us uneasy. Equilibrium is associated with balance—a good thing, surely. Disequilibrium is balance gone haywire. But consider the industrial landscape in this context. For a greater part of the last century, dazzling new technologies (electronics, engineered materials, computers and bioengineering . . .) opened vast frontiers of commerce in which traditional management models flourished. Add to that 55 years without destructive global conflict. One result was the emergence of industrial economies with vast wealth, spending power, and consumer appetites. A good part of the 20th century, excluding the Great Depression and the war years, may be regarded as an era of low-hanging fruit. Outdated approaches to management haven't changed because they didn't have to. True to Woody Allen's quip that 80 percent of success is just showing up, lumbering corporations thrived because they showed up; their lack of agility was not a significant drawback given their advantages of scale and the cornucopia of economic opportunity they had to feast upon. . . .

A qualification is warranted here. The extent to which balance or equilibrium is a precursor of disaster must be assessed in the context of scale and time. At small scales and in short time frames, equilibrium can be desirable. But over long intervals and on very large scales, it becomes hazardous. Why? Because the environment in which an organism (or organization) lives is always changing. At times, it is turbulent. Prolonged equilibrium dulls an organism's senses and saps its ability to arouse itself appropriately in the face of danger.

So why don't all living systems spiral into the thrall of equilibrium and die? Because two countervailing forces are at work. One is the *threat of death* (through the eternal Darwinian struggle for survival); the other is the *promise of sex* (that is, recombinations that introduce genetic diversity).

One of Darwin's most important contributions was his observation that species (by which we mean all members of a living system) do not evolve of their own accord. Rather, they change because of the forces, indeed threats, imposed on them from the environment. Life scientists call these "selection pressures." Selection pressures intensify during periods of radical upheaval. Most species, when challenged to adapt too far from their origins, are unable to do so and disappear. But nature is a fertile and indifferent mother, more dedicated to proliferating life in general than to the perpetuation of any particular species. From the vantage point of the larger system, selection pressures constantly enforce an ecological upgrade. The mutations that survive fit better in the new environment.

Reflecting on the competitive corporate landscape of the past decade or two, we can readily identify with Darwin's insights. New rivals are constantly converging on the same market opportunity and clamber relentlessly over one another toward a better position in the economic food chain. Whole sectors decline or disappear entirely. Office-supply stores are swept away by Staples, and the largest and best-established bookseller, Barnes & Noble, is badly shaken by Amazon.com. The examples speak to the ubiquity of selection pressures as they play out on the corporate landscape. There are no safe havens. From cell phones to cotton seeds, soap to software, it is a Darwinian jungle out there, and it isn't getting easier.

Sex is nature's second defense against stagnation. Organisms become more vulnerable as they become more homogeneous. To thwart homogeneity, nature relies on the rich structural recombinations triggered by sexual reproduction. Sex is decisively superior to evolution's other major alternative for species replication: fission.

Sexual reproduction maximizes diversity. Chromosome combinations are randomly matched in variant pairings, generating permutations and variety in offspring. Harmful diseases and parasites find it harder to breach the diverse defenses of a population generated by sexual reproduction. Microbes equipped to pick the locks of one generation of a particular species discover that the cellular tumblers have been changed in the next. When the bubonic plague swept through Europe in the 14th century, it killed 30 percent of the population. Subsequent waves of the deadly contagion claimed only a fraction of that number. Antibodies passed on to most of the progeny of the first wave's survivors made subsequent generations less susceptible when the bacteria returned for an encore.

Exchanges of DNA within social systems are unfortunately not nearly as reliable as those driven by the mechanics of reproductive biology. True, organizations can hire from outside, bring senior officers into frequent contact with iconoclasts from the ranks, or require engineers and designers to meet with disgruntled customers and listen to them. But the enemy of these mechanisms for exchanging metaphoric DNA is, of course, the existing social order. Like the body's immune defense system, the social order identifies foreign influences and seeks to neutralize them. . . .

Equilibrium enforcers—persistent social norms, corporate values, and orthodox beliefs about the business—often nullify the sought-after advantages of diversity. An executive team may recruit an outsider to gain diversity, then regress into behavior that nullifies the advantage by listening stereotypically. ("There goes the techie again!" "Ah—the feminist point of view.") The new token "genetic material" often finds itself frozen out of important informal discussions in which the real business gets done. Of course, humans have an important advantage. As self-knowing and intelligent entities, companies, at least in theory, are capable of recognizing danger (or opportunity) in advance and mobilizing to take appropriate action. They can wield the power of intention. To a greater extent than other species, humans and their constructs *can* lift themselves by their anticipatory bootstraps.

Nature is at its innovative best near the edge of chaos. The edge of chaos is a condition, not a location. It is a permeable, intermediate state through which order and disorder flow, not a finite line of demarcation. Moving to the edge of chaos creates upheaval but not dissolution. That's why the *edge* of chaos is so important. The edge is not the abyss. It's the sweet spot for productive change.

Innovations rarely emerge from systems high in order and stability: Systems in equilibrium lose diversity and give rise to the sorts of problems one encounters in incestuous communities and centrally planned economies. On the other hand, completely chaotic systems—riots, the stock market crash of 1929, or the Chinese Cultural Revolution of 1965–1976—are too hot to handle. Developments must wait until things settle down a bit.

When a complex adaptive system is moved toward the edge of chaos—when hurricanes and typhoons roil the deep seas, or fires rage through forests or prairies—the potential for generativity is maximized. Hurricanes recharge the oceans with oxygen and nutrients, and replenish carbon dioxide in the atmosphere. Fires cleanse a forest and make room for new life. In fact, fires have been found to be absolutely essential to the regeneration of the tall grass prairies of the Great Plains. The biodiversity inherent in prairies is stifled when fires are suppressed. . . .

But why *the edge*, many ask. Wouldn't it suffice to disturb equilibrium but give the edge of chaos a wide berth? Edges are important to life; in fact, people are drawn to them. When you are in the middle of things it is much harder to get your bearings, let alone experience the adrenaline rush of "pushing the envelope."

The visual cortex of the brain directs your eyes to look for edges, helping you distinguish figure from background and consequently to get your bearings. Living systems generally push up against the edge as a way of determining how much turbulence is enough. The yellow light of a traffic signal triggers motorists' response. They either apply the brakes or accelerate through the intersection. The yellow light is analogous to the edge. It stimulates heightened awareness and generates a burst of adrenaline and mental activity. Drivers strive to avoid ending up in cross traffic in the intersection—analogous to outright chaos.

Consider how most of us cope with deadlines. When deadlines are far in the future, we experience no urgency and may even feel complacent. And if the deadline is imminent and we know we cannot meet it, we experience unproductive stress and mental gridlock. Too much stress causes us to oversimplify, to jump to conclusions, become paralyzed, or default to old habits and prior success routines. We learn from experience how to make constructive use of an upcoming time limit; we know that an unmet deadline will evoke an optimal level of adrenaline, tension, and creativity. Many people experience their most productive moments near this temporal edge of chaos.

The trick, of course, is to navigate close to the edge of chaos without falling into it. There are three essential navigation devices:

> 1. *Attractors*, analogous to a compass, orient a living system in one direction and provide the impetus to migrate out of the comfort zone. . . .
>
> 2. *Amplifying and damping feedback* serve like the throttle and brake of a propulsion system. They cause a process to accelerate or to slow down. . . .
>
> 3. *Fitness landscape* is a term used by ecologists and other life scientists to map the relative competitive advantage of species. Such landscapes provide a useful device for visualizing today's competition—certainly superior to the traditional two-dimensional Strengths Weaknesses Opportunities Threats analysis one encounters in conventional strategic assessments. . . .

On fitness landscapes, higher degrees of fitness are depicted by linear height on the landscape. Loss of fitness is visualized as going downhill in this three-dimensional territory. Thus, when a threatened species, such as the North American coyote, is driven from its traditional habitat by human extermination programs, it descends the fitness landscape toward the edge of chaos. It must learn to cope with different terrain, climate, and rivals, and to find new sources of food. Coyotes have become urbanized in many sections of the country. Once established in a new territory, a coyote begins to master its new environment. This adaptation may, in fact, lead to overall prospects for survival that are better than those in the original habitat. In this context, the coyote's fitness has increased. It has carved out a niche on a superior fitness peak in the foothills above Malibu and Beverly Hills.

Biologists describe a species' or population's struggle to secure a niche as a long climb uphill, where "uphill" means better adaptation. When a species reaches a subsidiary peak (called a *local optimum*) on the fitness landscape, it may choose to remain there. Biologists call this perch on the fitness landscape a basin of attraction—a rest stop during the eternal competitive journey in which equilibrium is only temporarily restored.

Species become stranded on intermediate peaks or basins of attraction. Because there are no suspension bridges to get to the higher peaks on the horizon, the organism must "go down to go up." (This image is useful because most organisms don't do this voluntarily.) To do so, there must be sufficient internal unrest and instability; otherwise, an organism would not opt to leave its intermediate peak and suffer the indignities of the valley: low margins, undifferentiated products, customer defections, loss of competitive advantage—on the gamble of reaching a higher perch on the fitness landscape. And the apparent desirability of climbing a new peak can change radically if the environment changes. . . .

The third principle of nature, *self-organization and emergence*, captures two sides of the same coin of life. *Self-organization* is the tendency of certain (but not all) systems operating far from equilibrium to shift to a new state when their constituent elements generate unlikely combinations. When systems become sufficiently populated and properly interconnected, the interactions assemble themselves into a new order: proteins into cells, cells into organs, organs into organisms, organisms into societies. Simple parts networked together can undergo a metamorphosis. A single ant can't drive off a bee. A single brain cell is useless—but a few tens of millions of them can perform miracles. *Emergence* is the outcome of all this: a new state or condition. A colony of fire ants has emergent capabilities and constitutes an organism weighing 20 kilograms, with 20 million mouths and stings. A jazz ensemble creates an emergent sound that no one could imagine from listening to the individual instruments. Two hundred years ago, Adam Smith was on the scent of these insights. As one of the pioneers of the new discipline of economics, he called our attention to the "invisible hand" and its aggregate effects as a mercantile force. But Smith recognized that individual choice did not explain everything since individuals, as members of communities, generate fiduciary relationships and dependencies. All this, he noted, sums to a more complex *emergent* phenomenon: an economy.

The principle of self-organization and emergence resonates with a new consensus that is forming within the ranks of management: companies with talent and the instincts to mobilize distributed intelligence, innovate, and collaborate can commercialize ideas and seize the high ground before slower rivals even spot the new hill. By inspiring frontline personnel to improvise as quasi-independent agents and generate customer solutions without stultifying central controls, small breakthroughs can swell into formidable business enterprises and social movements. . . .

New destinations most often arise from unlikely combinations. Nature has demonstrated repeatedly that the most radical possibilities open up when intraspecies cooperation takes place. Within a species, innovation typically fosters new routes. Across species, new destinations often arise from improbable combinations. Some of the most radical innovations in biotechnology are taking place in unlikely crossovers between fish and mammals, fungi and insects, animals and plants. . . .

There are six guidelines for harnessing self-organization and emergence:

> 1. Decide whether self-organization and emergence are really needed. Do you face an adaptive challenge? Are new routes or new destinations sought? If nimbleness is required and discontinuous innovation is necessary, these dual properties can add value. Use the right tool for the right task.
>
> 2. Analyze the health of your network. Self-organization arises from networks that are fueled by nodes and connections. If you seek self-organization, enlarge the number of nodes and expect every organizational member to contribute. Enrich the quality of the connections with simple routines and protocols that cement strong relationships. . . .
>
> 3. Remember the Goldilocks principle: neither too many rules nor too few. The key to self-organization resides in the tension between discipline and freedom. Nature achieves this tension through selection pressures (which impose discipline) and by upending occurrences (such as chance mutations and environmental disruptions). In organizations, rules provide discipline. . . .
>
> 4. Harness the power of Requisite Variety. Juxtapose people from different fields and backgrounds and let their varied work histories enrich the potential of self-organizing networks. This mixing cannot be done with abandon. . . .
>
> 5. Look for the preconditions of emergence: the existence of "noise" or "heat" in the system; contradictions between words and actions; incongruencies between supply and demand; unexpressed needs. All hint at *emergent* possibilities and help identify when an issue is bubbling toward the surface. "An idea whose time has come" is the conventional way we talk about emergence.
>
> 6. Self-organization and emergence should not be thought of exclusively as episodic occurrences. True, self-organization can occur episodically . . . and emergence gives rise to periodic upwellings. . . . But these properties also have enduring power. When brought to the forefront of management consciousness, they can become sources of sustaining competitive advantage. They can exert a subtle influence—more akin to the way water wears away stone than to the way dynamite blasts through it.

. . .

In fitness landscape terms, it is impossible to get to a distant and higher fitness peak (discover radical breakthroughs) by climbing still higher on the peak one is already on (optimizing). Rather, one needs to descend into the unknown, disregard the proven cause-and-effect formulas, and defy the odds. One embarks on a journey of sequential disturbances and adjustments, not a lockstep march along a predetermined path. We may only be able to see as far as our headlights, but proceeding in this fashion can still bring us to our journey's destination.

Because discontinuous leaps, by their very nature, arise from unforeseen combinations, it is impossible to reverse engineer them. Extrapolation is possible when systems exhibit continuity over a wide range of conditions. In this circumstance, the relationship of the components is linear and the goal can be attained by progressing step by step. But if the system exhibits discontinuities, extrapolating "what's going to happen next" is unreliable. Something that does not lend itself to logical explanation after the fact does not respond predictably to direction beforehand. We must settle, instead, for a series of shrewd disruptions, proceeding with a reasonable degree of confidence that the outcome will tilt more in the desired direction than its opposite. When we overreach and attempt to hardwire a specific result, we almost always fail. Nobel Laureate Francis Crick, codiscoverer of the helical structure of DNA, once observed that "Evolution is more clever than you are." What trips us up is our inability to predict second- and third-order consequences that flow from seemingly straightforward intentions. Managers described as "street-smart" or "seasoned" have often garnered this wisdom about living systems the hard way. These veterans expect detailed plans to go awry. They know that the number of things that can go wrong is multiplied when a bold break with the past is attempted. . . .

At the core of all this unpredictability are two factors. One is the inherently *indeterministic* nature of Nature. Life is shaped by probabilities, not certainties. Parents discover the importance of indeterminism in the unfolding lives of living systems called "children." The second is *frozen accidents,* which occur occasionally and stem from an avalanche of consequences that are difficult to alter. As in a real avalanche, little actions trigger bigger ones that become irreversible. In business, frozen accidents do not obey the laws of scarcity (like diamonds); they follow the laws of plenitude (like language). The more accepted and available something becomes, the faster it accelerates ahead of its rivals and thrives. It becomes "frozen-in" as the de facto standard. . . .

Frozen accidents are coincidences that become locked in. *Indeterminism* deals the cards. Frozen accidents are what happen at the gaming table after the cards are dealt. Frozen accidents are the means by which a species acquires its destiny. Once a cell in an embryo embarks on a particular pathway, it leaves behind many other options. The number of cells it can change into from that point forward greatly diminishes. When a niche is wide open, one sees many prototypes. But as the niche is filled, extremes are weeded out. One sees this in e-commerce today.

So are there guidelines that can help us disturb things in the general direction we'd like them to go? Ancient masters of the Eastern martial arts had insight into how one co-opts the energy of a living system long before there were institutes in Santa Fe. *Jujitsu* means the gentle way. *Karate* means the empty hand. Both images seem counterintuitive when confronted with an opponent hell-bent on doing harm. Both rely on deflecting or harnessing an opposing force or energy toward desired goals. . . .

At the more concrete level of corporate application, there are three general guidelines:

- Design, don't engineer.
- Discover, don't dictate.
- Decipher, don't presuppose.

Consider airports in this context. The lounge areas surrounding each gate do not have signs or attendants who tell us not to talk too loudly, occupy more than one seat, or block the aisles. Yet, through the invisible hand of design, all these objectives are broadly accomplished. Seats are arranged so that conversation takes place with those in the immediate vicinity and not with those far away. Fixed armrests between seats prevent people from lying down and occupying seats that others may need. Seats are bolted together in rows, making movement of furniture difficult. Thus passengers are discouraged from rearranging the floor plan, blocking aisles, or inconveniencing the cleaning staff that comes late at night. The remarkable quality of design is that it seems to just happen; it works its magic without our awareness of how it does so. From the architect's perspective, what we are experiencing is an evolved discipline of disturbing, not directing, a living system at work.

In contrast, the rock that traditional management founders on is its obsession with directing the insurgent nature of social systems and their capacity, in turn, to subvert programmed change. A 1995 *Fortune* article, "Making Change Stick," addressed the difficulty and opened with a series of quotations resonating with the experience of many. In that article, MIT professor-turned-consultant Michael Hammer (coauthor of *Reengineering the Corporation*) explained the source of all the difficulty:

> Human beings' innate resistance to change is the most perplexing, annoying, distressing and confusing part of reengineering. [But] resistance to change is natural and inevitable. To think that resistance won't occur, to view those who exhibit its symptoms as difficult or intractable, is a fatal mistake. The real cause of reengineering failure is not the resistance itself, but management's failure to deal with it. Most dissenters won't stand and shout at you that they hate what you're doing to them and their comfortable old ways. Instead, they will nod, smile and agree with everything you say—and they behave as they always have. This is the kiss of "yes."

Not so fast. What we've been saying about living systems offers a different perspective. That these comments resonate with many people's change experience may suggest that we have been working against, rather than flowing with, the nature of things. The explanations offered may say more about the backlash directed at trying to hardwire behavior than about any valid evidence of innate human resistance to change.

A contrasting version of the earlier example of an airport lounge makes the point. In the former Soviet Union, some airports equipped their waiting areas with folding chairs. These were arranged in rows, and signs and announcements broadcast stern admonitions not to move the chairs, block aisles, and so forth. Security personnel occasionally enforced these policies, but passengers moved the chairs anyway to accommodate clusters of friends. The armless chairs were redeployed as beds or rearranged to make surfaces for dining or for playing cards. Children built ingenious play structures. And custodians complained of the extra work of restoring the rows before cleaning.

One way of thinking would identify all this as the predictable fall-out from trying to overcontrol living things. Passengers had to be controlled to compensate for design shortcomings. In contrast, the airport lounge in the earlier example achieves the desired behavior with no overt rules or commands. With the right design, people can be people without compromising the purposes of the space.

When change is driven from above and moves along a predetermined path, or when members of living systems are marched lockstep in frontal assaults on the fortress of discontinuous change, their efforts almost always fail. But if we *design* (and don't engineer), *discover* what's working and build on that (and don't dictate) and then *decipher* the second- and third-order consequences (rather than presuppose that it will all work as programmed) we are far more likely to succeed. When properly mobilized, the so-called resistant masses or "permafrost of middle management" simply cease to exist as such.

44

Exploring the Relationship Between Learning and Leadership

Lillas M. Brown and Barry Z. Posner

Learning and leadership represent two rich lines of research: one is about how people learn and the other is about how people lead. In this study we attempt to connect these two ideas together via the question: "What relationship does the way that people learn have with the manner in which they lead?"

How do people learn? This has been, and continues to be, the subject of voluminous research studies. Most consider learning from either a trait-based approach or as various information-processing strategies. Similarly, researchers investigate whether learning begins from an "inside out" or "outside in" perspective. In the last two decades, scholars have advanced a "transformational learning theory" that has received more attention than any other adult learning theory and continues to be of interest (Taylor, 1997). Transformational learning theory builds upon previous lines of inquiry into adult learning such as androgogy and self-directed learning. Mezirow (1994, p. 222) defines transformational learning as "the process of construing and appropriating a new or revised interpretation of meaning of one's experience as a guide to action." Essentially this approach to learning is about change—dramatic and fundamental change in the way we see ourselves and the world in which we live. Kegan (2000) describes transformational learning as an expansion of consciousness and observes that this kind of learning is more than merely adding to what we already know. "Transformational learning shapes people," asserts Clark (1993, p. 47): "they are different afterwards, in ways both they and others can recognize."

Rather than focusing on adult learner characteristics, as androgogy and self-directed learning theories tend to do, transformational learning centers squarely on the cognitive process of learning. The mental constructions of experience, inner meaning, and reflection are common components of this approach (Merriam and Caffarella, 1999). Key concepts in transformational learning are:

- experience—critical incidents or trigger events;
- critical reflection—content reflection, process reflection, and premise reflection (examine long held beliefs, values about the experience);
- affective learning—feelings play a primary role in triggering reflection;
- dialogue and relationships that are supportive and trusting; and
- individual development (Taylor, 2000).

Source: Reprinted by permission of the publisher from *Leadership and Organization Development Journal*, Vol. 22, No. 6, pp. 274–280 (2001).

Experience is envisioned as the starting point in this approach and becomes the content for reflection. Engaging the life experience in a critically reflective manner is a necessary condition for transformation. Indeed, the entire process of learning is a journey of change—change that is growth enhancing and developmental (Mezirow *et al.*, 2000).

The question of how people learn *to lead* is more narrowly focused than the broader topic of learning and, not surprisingly, reveals more widespread consensuses. For instance, in analyzing thousands of case studies, Kouzes and Posner (1995) found that people reported learning how to lead from three sources: trial and error, observation of others, and education. Honeywell undertook a six-year research program to determine how managers learn to manage. Findings from their study revealed these three categories: job experiences and assignments, relationships, and formal education/training (Zemke, 1985). The Center for Creative Leadership interviewed successful executives to find out what career events they considered to be important in their development and clustered the results into these sets: job assignments that the executives had experienced; other people with whom they had come into contact; hardships they had endured; and formal training (McCall *et al.*, 1988). More recently, research from the Center indicates that about 75 percent of the events that individuals report as critical to their careers comes from a combination of learning from the work itself and learning from others (Dalton *et al.*, 1999).

The case has been made about the importance of learning as a foundational element in effective leadership. Vaill (1999), for example, explains how the importance of learning is underscored by the exceedingly turbulent and unpredictable organizational environments within which corporate managers and executives are working. There is basically no limit, he says, to the kinds of learning a contemporary leader may have to engage: "All managerial leaders are feeling a dramatic quickening in the pace of change, an increasing complexity to their choices and a greater and greater cost of being wrong. There is a continual stream of things managers have to learn in order to thrive in this environment" (Vaill, 1999, p. 119). It may make more sense to say that in the present world, leadership is not learned but rather that it is learning. When we observe a leader at work, what we may really be observing is a learning process—and an exceedingly complex learning process at that.

How do people lead? This question is also the object of voluminous study, and reviews of this extensive literature can be found elsewhere (e.g., Bass, 1990; Conger, 1999; Yukl, 1994). Current behavioral approaches to leadership, however, are more consistent than inconsistent, and vary more in their emphasis and semantics. Bennis and Nanus (1997), for example, describe the four keys of effective leadership as: attention through vision, meaning through communication, trust through positioning, and the deployment of self through positive self-regard. Bass (1994) has described transformational leadership along the dimensions of charismatic leadership, inspirational leadership, intellectual stimulation, and individualized considerations. The five key practices of leaders, according to Kouzes and Posner's (1995) framework of what people are doing when they are leading, include: challenging the process, inspiring a shared vision, enabling others to act, modeling the way, and encouraging the heart. Moreover, it has been claimed that "effective leaders are constantly learning. They see all experiences as learning experiences" (Kouzes and Posner, 1995, p. 323).

Bennis and Nanus (1997) describe transformational leadership as achieving significant changes that reflects the community of interest of both leaders and their constituents, freeing up and pooling collective energies in pursuit of a common vision. They go on to make the following four generalizations about transformational leadership:

1. It is a collective, there is a symbiotic relationship between leaders and followers, and what makes it collective is the subtle interplay between the follower's needs and wants and the leader's capacity to understand, one way or another, these collective aspirations.
2. Leadership is causative, meaning that leadership can invent and create institutions that can empower employees to satisfy their needs.
3. Leadership is morally purposeful and elevating, which means, if nothing else, that leaders can, through deploying their talents, choose purposes and visions that are based on the key values of the workforce and create the social infrastructure that supports them.
4. Leaders can move constituents to heightened degrees of consciousness, such as liberty, justice, and self-actualization.

What this indicates is that leadership is closely connected with the concept of change, and change, in turn, as we have already indicated, is at the essence of the learning process. The wellspring of learning organizations is transformational leaders (Rolls, 1995). Indeed, it is precisely because leaders have successfully navigated deep personal change that they are able to create conditions in which employees can themselves be engaged in the practices of learning organizations.

This interest in connecting learning (and dealing with change) and actually providing leadership is relevant to the growing interest in the development of leaders. Today's turbulent economic marketplace requires people who thrive on the challenge of change, who can foster environments of innovation, who encourage trust and collaboration, and who are prepared to chart a course into uncharted territories. The Conference Boards of the USA and Canada have both recently affirmed that leadership is the number one competency that organizations seek to develop in their people (Hackett, 1997; McIntyre, 1997). Learning how to lead is both a personal and an organizational imperative.

McCall *et al.* (1988) point out that learning by managers is essential to their job performance and career success (and presumably, organizational effectiveness). As managers improve their ability to learn from experiences in the workplace (e.g., through challenging assignments, role models, hardships and the like), the better or more effective they will be as leaders. Lombardo *et al.* (1990) argue that people who use a variety of learning tactics will be best able to learn from their experiences and will consequently be more effective in the workplace.

A series of empirical studies from the Center for Creative Leadership has explored this relationship between learning and leadership (Dalton *et al.*, 1999). With a sample of army captains ($n = 279$) a modest relationship was found between learning tactics and self-reported effectiveness along these seven dimensions: acts with integrity, seeks broad business knowledge, brings out the best in people, adapts to cultural differences, insightfulness, commitment to making a difference, and has the courage to take risks. However, in a follow-up study involving a small civilian sample ($n = 36$), no significant relationships were found between participants' learning tactics and the ratings of their effectiveness by their supervisors. Potential managerial effectiveness was related to learning in a study involving individuals for a cross-section of organizations ($n = 188$). In this study, learning tactics were related to such abilities as turning around an organizational unit, starting something from scratch, having a significant role in an acquisition, negotiating a major contract, being promoted two or more levels, and the like. Most of these dimensions of effectiveness might be better thought of as essential aspects of managerial or leadership behavior that result in being effective.

In this study we were interested in extending the research on the relationship between learning and leadership. The guiding hypothesis was that individuals who are better learners are more engaged in leadership behaviors.

SAMPLE AND METHODOLOGY

Respondents for this study were drawn from three sources. The first were mid-level managers from a large high-technology company enrolled in a university-based management development course. The second were working professionals, across a variety of high-technology organizations, engaged in an evening MBA program. The third were a cross-section of managers enrolled in an Executive MBA program. The total sample consisted of 312 respondents. The demographic characteristics of the corporate managers and managers from the Executive MBA program were very consistent; the evening MBA participants were younger but all had both managerial and work experiences within similar corporate environments. There were 114 women (36 percent) in the sample. *Post-hoc* analysis revealed no statistically significant differences on any of the instruments or findings based upon respondent gender.

Respondents completed both the learning tactics inventory (LTI) and the leadership practices inventory (LPI). The LTI is a 32-item set of statements intended to assess how people report learning when faced with "the challenge of an unfamiliar task or experience." Each statement is measured on a five-point Likert scale, with 1 anchoring "I have almost never used this approach" to 5 indicating "I have almost always used this approach." The LTI yields four scales, each of which represents a different tactic for learning:

1. action (e.g., am proactive in my approach, preferring to learn by trial and error);
2. thinking (e.g., read articles or books or go online to gain knowledge and background);
3. feeling (e.g., confront myself on what I am worrying about); and
4. accessing other (e.g., bounce my hopes and fears off someone I trust).

Each of the learning tactics (scales) is measured by eight statements and Cronbach's alpha (internal reliability) for each has been reported at 0.70 or greater. In this study, Cronbach's alpha scores were slightly lower (ranging between 0.62 and 0.72). A variety index is computed by adding up how many tactics the respondent reports using, where the respondent's score was above the median for the sample. Scores can range from zero to four; thus a score of four means the respondent scored above the median on all four learning tactics and is a highly versatile learner. More information about the LTI is available in Dalton *et al.* (1999).

The leadership practices inventory reports on the frequency with which respondents engage in a specific set of leadership behaviors. Each of the 30 items on the LPI is assessed using a ten-point Likert scale, with 1 indicating "I almost never engage in this behavior" to 10 indicating that "I almost always engage in this behavior." The LPI yields five scales, each of which represents a separate set of leadership behaviors:

1. challenging the process (e.g., I seek out challenging opportunities that test my skills and abilities);
2. inspiring a shared vision (e.g., I describe a compelling image of what our future could be like);
3. enabling others to act (e.g., I develop cooperative relationships among the people I work with);
4. modeling the way (e.g., I set a personal example of what I expect from others); and
5. encouraging the heart (e.g., I praise people for a job well done).

Each of these five leadership practices (scales) is measured by six statements and Cronbach's alphas for each have been reported at 0.70 or greater. In this study, Cronbach's alpha scores were roughly equivalent (ranging between 0.66 and 0.84). A composite score is not typically computed for the LPI; however, in this study a composite score was calculated following the same procedure for constructing the variety index on the LTI. Hence a transformational leadership index was computed by adding up how many leadership practices the respondent reported using where the respondent's core was above the median for the sample. Scores could range from 0 to 5; thus a score of five means the respondent scored above the median on all five leadership practices and is a high transformational leader. More information about the LPI is available in Kouzes and Posner (1997).

We hypothesized, in general, that the various learning tactics and leadership practices would be positively correlated. Better learners, as defined by the LTI, are those with higher scores. More effective leaders, as defined by the LPI, are likewise those with higher scores. Variety, accordingly, was also hypothesized to be positively related with transformational leadership: people with the greatest ability to face unfamiliar and new situations with a repertoire of ways of learning would engage most frequently in behaviors associated with transformational leadership.

RESULTS

Table I presents correlations between respondents' learning tactics and their leadership practices. Cronbach's alphas for each scale are also reported. As these data illustrate, each of the learning tactics, as hypothesized, was significantly correlated with each of the leadership practices. The strongest correlations with leadership were with the learning tactic of thinking and the weakest correlations were with accessing others. Variety and transformational leadership were also significantly correlated.

Table II affords a more detailed view of the previous findings by looking at the relationship between respondents' frequent (high or above the median) use less frequent (low or below the median) use of each of the four learning tactics and how this manifested itself in their use of each of the five leadership practices. This analysis gives strong support to the argument that learning is subsequently related to leadership. Better learners, those with higher scores, regardless of learning mode, consistently engaged in leadership practices more frequently than did those in the low learning category. For example, those most comfortable with using the Action learning tactic reported being more frequently engaged in challenging the process. This same pattern was re-

TABLE I • CORRELATIONS BETWEEN LEARNING TACTICS AND LEADERSHIP PRACTICES

	Leader Practices					
Learning tactics	Challenge (0.78)	Inspire (0.84)	Enable (0.68)	Model (0.74)	Encourage (0.82)	Transformational leadership
Action (0.62)	0.35***	0.28***	0.15**	0.20***	0.18**	0.27***
Thinking (0.65)	0.39***	0.36***	0.31***	0.30***	0.23***	0.39***
Feeling (0.72)	0.30***	0.29***	0.18**	0.25***	0.25***	0.24***
Accessing others (0.62)	0.14*	0.15*	0.14*	0.13*	0.23**	0.18**
Variety	0.35***	0.33***	0.23***	0.24***	0.54***	0.33***

Notes: Numbers in parenthesis refer to Cronbach's alpha scores for internal reliability $*p < 0.02$; $**p < 0.01$; $***p < 0.001$

peated for the other three learning tactics and challenging. This same pattern was also found for Inspiring, with the better learners across all four tactics more frequently engaged in this leadership practice.

High action learners were generally engaged more frequently in four of the five leadership practices (challenging, inspiring, enabling, and modeling) than those in the low action learning mode. High thinking learners were more frequently engaged in all five of the leadership practices than their counterparts in the low thinking learners' category. High feeling learners engaged in the leadership practices of challenging, inspiring, modeling and encouraging more frequently than those in the low feeling group. Accessing others as a mode of learning differentiated between high and low learners on three leadership dimensions: challenging, inspiring and encouraging.

DISCUSSION

Managers differed in the extent to which they used various learning strategies when confronted with an unfamiliar task or experience. They also differed in the extent to which they engaged in a set of important leadership behaviors. Systematic relationships were found between these two experiences, such that a positive relationship was found between how people learned and how they acted as leaders. Respondents who reported using more frequently any one of the four learning tactics (action, thinking, feeling, and accessing others) also reported engaging more frequently in leadership behaviors like challenging, inspiring, enabling, modeling, and encouraging. Composite learning and leadership indices (variety and transformational leadership) were significantly correlated ($r = 0.33$, $p < 0.001$).

It might be argued that leaders from highly technical companies, such as those involved in this study, who are highly educated in a traditional sense, would have well-developed "thinking" learning tactics, and that they would be more self-reliant, independent and not particularly keen to "access other people" for help. In a challenging (new) environment, they may rely on what is known and what is comfortable as a way of learning. This cognitive preference, however, is likely to be quite limiting into the future. The techno-hip readers of *Fast Company* (1999) magazine give

TABLE II • MEAN SCORES OF LOW AND HIGH GROUPS ON LEARNING TACTICS AND LEADERSHIP PRACTICES (*t*-TESTS)

	Leadership Practices				
Learning tactics	Challenge	Inspire	Enable	Model	Encourage
Action					
Low (153)	41.4	37.0	47.9	45.7	43.8
High (159)	44.9***	40.0***	49.1*	47.7**	45.1
Thinking					
Low (148)	40.8	36.3	46.9	45.5	43.3
High (164)	45.2***	40.7***	49.9***	47.9***	45.5**
Feeling					
(Low (135)	41.6	36.2	47.9	45.4	42.9
High (177)	44.4***	40.4***	48.9	47.8***	45.7***
Accessing others					
Low (155)	42.0	36.8	47.9	45.9	42.9
High (157)	44.4***	40.3***	49.0	47.5	46.0***

Notes: Numbers in parentheses refer to sample sizes, which vary as a result of median splits. *$p < 0.02$; **$p < 0.01$; ***$p < 0.001$

credence to this view when they reported social skills as more important to future business success than Internet skills. This suggests that learning tactics, such as "feeling" and "accessing others" would best assist in developing these leadership abilities.

Consider the description Argyris (1991) provides of typical well-educated highly-committed professionals who occupy senior executive positions, who are almost always successful at what they do, and who rarely experience failure. As a result, it might be argued that they never learn how to learn from failure, never develop the tolerance for feelings of failure or the skills to deal with these feelings, and ultimately develop even some fear of failure. They typically screen out criticism, become defensive, and put the blame on external factors and others, all which blocks learning. Again "accessing others" and (acknowledging) "feelings" are tactics that break down defenses which, in turn, block learning.

Transformational learning concepts provide insights for leveraging the effective development of leadership competencies. Taylor (2000) describes the conditions conducive to fostering transformational learning as:

- creating a climate of openness, safety and trust, being learner centered and encouraging self-directed learning;
- providing learning activities that encourage the exploration of alternative personal perspectives via questioning, critical self reflection and self dialogue;
- facilitators who are trusting, empathetic, caring, authentic, with integrity, able to bring forth feelings to promote critical reflection;
- providing opportunities for assessment and feedback; and
- allowing and/or providing the time necessary for the personal exploration and the intensity of the experience.

These conditions underscore the evidence supporting comprehensive, longer-term leadership development programs with retreats and coaching as offering the best opportunities for leadership development. Professional development is an important component of transformative learning, especially when it includes practical and personal approaches that are self-directed, reflective and transformative (Cranton, 1996).

Closely related to transformational learning theory are the principles of adult learning. A key implication from these findings is the importance of following adult learning principles in designing and delivering leadership development programs (Zemke and Zemke, 1995). Using a tool like the LTI helps leaders become more self-aware of their preferred learning tactics, and more importantly the tactics to develop and use to be a more versatile learner.

A trademark competency of future leaders will be their ability to instill a learning mindset into their organizations (Conger and Benjamin, 1999). The upcoming generation of leaders will have to be a generation of learning evangelists. By accentuating the importance of learning and establishing a context where employees want to and are able to learn, leaders will be more capable of strengthening their organizations for future challenges and increasing competitive and innovative abilities. The effective development of future leaders will require leveraging adult learning principles as well as creating the conditions that foster transformational learning if such programs hope to accelerate and enhance strategic thinking and other equally critical and complex capabilities. The challenge, as suggested by the findings of this study, requires being able to translate learning principles into a meaningful leadership development experience that facilitates and, in fact, accelerates the learning process.

Before concluding, we should point out some of the limitations to this study. All of the data are self-reported and the sample fairly homogeneous in organizational backgrounds, and although the relationships are consistent across individuals they may be the simple result of self-report biases. Measures of learning tactics and more independent or third-party reports of leadership behaviors would help to substantiate these relationships. These quantitative findings would certainly be enriched through various qualitative methodologies, such as case studies and interviews with leaders.

Likewise, knowledge about the effectiveness of the respondents as leaders would go a long way toward increasing the validity of the relational findings. An implicit assumption in this study was that learning precedes leadership. A more complex investigation, and conceptual model, would examine how leadership, as an experience itself, affects people's subsequent learning inclinations. Insights from transformational learning theories also offer alternative approaches to understanding the development of transformational leadership development. Finally, greater concurrent validation would result from investigating these same relationships using different instruments of the same constructs. Questions about the generalizability of the sample for this study could be addressed by replicating the study across different (more heterogeneous) sample populations.

CONCLUSION

Leaders must establish direction in relation to the complex challenges and changes in their context, shape a culture that is conducive to that vision, and inspire their people, bringing forth their talents, uniqueness, and energies toward a worthy future. This calls for transformational leaders and results in a tremendous interest in leadership development. Leadership development is a learning process. Leadership development programs and approaches need to reach leaders at a personal and emotional level, triggering critical self-reflection, and providing support for meaning-making including creating learning and leadership mindsets, and for experimentation. Transformational learning theory can be used to assess, strengthen, and create leadership development programs that develop transformational leaders.

This study presents a starting point in exploring the relationship between learning versatility and transformational leadership. Applying adult learning principles and creating conditions that foster transformational learning are essential in the design and delivery of leadership development efforts. It will be important to conduct more in-depth investigations of transformational learning and transformational leadership in order to bring these two bodies of literature, as well as research and practice, together.

Research over these past two decades underscores that the majority of leadership skills are learned from naturally occurring experiences in the workplace. Being able to access and apply principles of adult learning and foster transformational learning would help aspiring leaders, those wanting to strengthen their leadership, and those concerned with the development of leadership, to accelerate and leverage leadership learning. Importantly, creating a culture of leadership and learning is the ultimate act of leadership development.

REFERENCES

Argyris, C. (1991), "Teaching smart people how to learn," *Harvard Business Review*, May–June.

Bass, B. M. (1990), *Bass and Stogdill's Handbook of Leadership*, 3rd ed., Free Press, New York, NY.

Bass, B. M. (1994), *Improving Organizational Effectiveness through Transformational Leadership*, Sage Publications, Thousand Oaks, CA.

Bennis, W. and Nanus, B. (1997), *Leaders: The Strategies for Taking Charge*, Harper and Row, New York, NY.

Clark, M. C. (1993), "Transformational learning," in Merriam, S. B. (Ed.), *An Update on Adult Learning Theory: New Directions for Adult and Continuing Education*, Jossey-Bass, San Francisco, CA.

Conger, J. A. (1999), "Charismatic and transformational leadership in organizations: An insider's perspective on these developing streams of research," *Leadership Quarterly*, Vol. 10 No. 2, pp. 145–79.

Conger, J. A. and Benjamin, B. (1999), *Building Leaders: How Successful Companies Develop the Next Generation*, Jossey-Bass, San Francisco, CA.

Cranton, P. (1996), *Professional Development as Transformative Learning*, Jossey-Bass, San Francisco, CA.

Dalton, M., Swigert, S., Van Velsor, E., Bunker, K., and Wachholz, J. (1999), *The Learning Tactics Inventory: Facilitator's Guide*, Jossey-Bass/Pfeiffer, San Francisco, CA.

Fast Company, (1999), "Where are we on the Web?", October, p. 306.

Hackett, B. (1997), *The Value of Training in an Era of Intellectual Capital*, The Conference Board of the USA, New York, NY.

Kegan, R. (2000), "What 'form' transforms? A constructive-developmental approach to transformative learning," in Mezirow, J. (Ed.), *Learning as Transformation: Critical Perspectives on a Theory in Progress*, Jossey-Bass, San Francisco, CA.

Kouzes, J. M. and Posner, B. Z. (1995), *The Leadership Challenge: How to Keep Getting Extraordinary Things Done in Organizations*, Jossey-Bass, San Francisco, CA.

Kouzes, J. M., and Posner, B. Z. (1997), *The Leadership Practices Inventory: Facilitator's Guide*, Jossey-Bass/Pfeiffer, San Francisco, CA.

Lombardo, M. M., Bunker, K. and Webb, A. (1990), "Learning how to learn," paper presented at the Fifth Annual Conference of the Society for Industrial and Organizational Psychology, Miami, FL.

McCall, M. W. Jr., Lombardo, M. M. and Morrison, A. M. (1988), *The Lessons of Experience:*

How Successful Executives Develop on the Job, Lexington Books, Lexington, MA.

McIntyre, D. (1997), *Learning at the Top: Evolution of Management and Executive Development in Canada*, Conference Board of Canada, Ottawa.

Merriam, S. B. and Caffarella, R. S. (1999), *Learning in Adulthood: A Comprehensive Guide*, Jossey-Bass, San Francisco, CA.

Mezirow, J. (1994), "Understanding transformative theory," *Adult Education Quarterly*, Vol. 44, pp. 222–3.

Mezirow, J. *et al* (2000), *Learning as Transformation: Critical Perspectives on a Theory in Progress*, Jossey-Bass, San Francisco, CA.

Rolls, J. (1995), "The transformational leader: The wellspring of the learning organization," in Chawla, S. and Renesch, J. (Eds.), *Learning Organizations: Developing Cultures for Tomorrow's Workplace*, Productivity Press, Portland, OR.

Taylor, E. (1997), "Building upon the theoretical debate: A critical review of the empirical studies of Mezirow's transformative learning theory," *Adult Education Quarterly*, Vol. 48, pp. 32–57.

Taylor, E. (2000), "Analyzing research on transformative learning theory," in Mezirow, J. and Associates (2000), *Learning as Transformation: Critical Perspectives on a Theory in Progress*, Jossey-Bass, San Francisco, CA.

Vaill, P. (1999), *Spirited Leading and Learning: Process Wisdom for a New Age*, Jossey-Bass, San Francisco, CA.

Yukl, G. A. (1994), *Leadership in Organizations*, Prentice-Hall, Englewood Cliffs, NJ.

Zemke, R. (1985), The Honeywell Studies: How managers learn to manage," *Training*, March, pp. 46–51.

Zemke, R. and Zemke, S. (1995), "Adult learning: What do we know for sure?", *Training*, March, pp. 27–33.